MIDRASH RABBAH

DEUTERONOMY

MIDRASH

TRANSLATED INTO ENGLISH

WITH NOTES, GLOSSARY AND INDICES

UNDER THE EDITORSHIP OF

RABBI DR. H. FREEDMAN, B.A., PH.D.

AND

MAURICE SIMON, M.A.

RABBAH

DEUTERONOMY

TRANSLATED BY

REV. DR. J. RABBINOWITZ, B.A., PH.D.

THE SONCINO PRESS
LONDON · NEW YORK

THIRD EDITION 1983

ISBN: 0-900689-38-2

MANUFACTURED IN THE UNITED STATES OF AMERICA
PRINTED BY NOBLE OFFSET PRINTERS, INC.

CONTENTS

INTRODUCTION

THE Midrash on the fifth book of the Pentateuch is known as אלה הדברים רבה or מדרש דברים רבה. Unlike the Midrashim on the other books of the Pentateuch it is not a running commentary on the text, but consists of twenty-seven independent sections, each commencing with a legal question, generally on a ritual subject, introduced by the term, '*Halachah*'; each homily as a rule being based on the commencing verse or verses of the section. The twenty-seven sections follow the division of the Sabbath scriptural readings (*Sidroth*) according to the triennial cycle in vogue in Palestine in ancient times.[1] In the ordinary printed editions of the text of the Midrash, Deuteronomy Rabbah consists of eleven chapters corresponding to the eleven Sabbath scriptural readings based on an annual cycle as in use in the synagogue at the present day. With a few exceptions the sections conclude with words of comfort and consolation and strike a Messianic note.

There is a close similarity between Deuteronomy and Midrash Tanḥuma in the fact that in the latter also the homilies commence with a legal question, introduced in this case, however, by the words *Yelamdenu rabbenu*. Ginzberg[2] considers that Deuteronomy Rabbah is but another recension of Midrash Tanḥuma. From the frequent use of Greek words in the Midrash, Weiss[3] argued that it must have been composed in a Greek-speaking country, probably somewhere in the Byzantine Empire. According to Zunz,[4] the probable date of its composition is the Geonic period, about the year 900 C.E. Of Halachic questions raised by the Midrash, twenty-one have their parallel in the Mishnah, five in the Tosefta, and six in the Jerusalem Talmud.

The Midrash is distinguished by the clarity and smoothness of its style and by the wealth of similes, parables

[1] Büchler, *Jewish Quarterly Review*, vol. v, pp. 420 ff.
[2] *Genizah Studies*, I, p. 495. [3] *Dor*, vol. III, p. 268.
[4] *Die Gottesdienstlichen Vorträge der Juden*, p. 264.

and stories it employs for illustrating the interpretation of the text of the Scriptures. The stories about R. Phinehas b. Yair (III, 3) and Abba Judan (IV, 8) furnish examples of the striking use made by the Midrash of such material. Quite a number of *Haggadoth* must be original to this Midrash, as they appear to have no parallels elsewhere in Rabbinical literature (II, 20, 24, 25; V, 13; VII, 7). The concluding section (XI, 6–9) of the Midrash which describes the death of Moses must have been taken from a special 'Midrash on the Death of Moses'.

J. RABBINOWITZ.

DEUTERONOMY

CHAPTER I

DEBARIM

1. THESE ARE THE WORDS. *Halachah*[1]*:* Is it permissible for a Jew to write a Scroll of the Law in any language, etc.? The Wise have learnt thus[2]: The difference between [sacred] books and phylacteries and *mezuzoth* is only that [sacred] books may be written in any language. R. Gamaliel says: With books too [the only other language] in which they permitted them to be written is Greek. And what is R. Gamaliel's reason for saying that a Scroll of the Law may be written in Greek? Our Rabbis have taught thus: Bar Kappara, interpreting the verse, *God enlarge Japheth, and he shall dwell in the tents of Shem* (Gen. IX, 27), said: This indicates that the words of Shem may be rendered in the languages of Japheth[3]; therefore have [the Rabbis] permitted [sacred books] to be written in Greek.

The Holy One, blessed be He, said: 'See how beloved is the language of the Torah; it is healing for the tongue.'[4] Whence do we know this? For so Scripture says: *A soothing* [lit. 'healing'] *tongue is a tree of life* (Prov. XV, 4); and '*tree of life*' is but another term for Torah, as it is written, *She is a tree of life to them that lay hold upon her* (Prov. III, 18).

That the language of the Torah lends fluency to the tongue you can learn from the fact that in the time to come God will bring from the Garden of Eden excellent trees. And wherein consists their excellence—In that they are soothing to the tongue. As it is said, *And by the river upon the bank thereof, on this side and on that side, shall grow*

[1] It is characteristic of this Midrash that every discourse in it begins with an halachic question introduced by the term *Halachah*: v. Introduction.
[2] M. Meg. I, 8; v. Rabbinowitz, *Mishnah Megillah*, p. 60.
[3] Shem is the ancestor of Israel and Japheth of the Greeks (Jawan). Cf. Gen. X, 2 and 21. Cf. Meg. 9*b*. [4] It gives it fluency even where one normally stammers, as the Midrash proceeds to explain.

every tree for food (Ezek. XLVII, 12). And whence do we know that this will soothe the tongue? For it is said, *And the fruit thereof shall be for food, and the leaf thereof for healing* (*ib.*). On the meaning of the word *'healing'* (lithrufah) R. Joḥanan and R. Joshua b. Levi join issue. One says: It means, For a laxative [to aid digestion]. And the other says: Whosoever is tongue-tied and eats greedily of it will have his tongue cured and will speak at once clearly in the words of the Torah, for our text [in Ezekiel] uses the words *'On this side and on that side'*, and this expression must surely refer to the Torah of which it is said, *Written on both their sides* (Ex. XXXII, 15).[1] R. Levi[2] said: Why learn this from an extraneous passage? Let us rather learn it from the context. For see, of Moses before he was privileged to receive the Torah Scripture writes, *I am not a man of words* (Ex. IV, 10); but after he had proved himself worthy of the Torah his tongue became cured and he began to speak words. Whence do we know this? From what we have read in the passage under comment, THESE ARE THE WORDS WHICH MOSES SPOKE.

2. Another explanation: THESE ARE THE WORDS. This bears out what Scripture said, *He that rebuketh a man shall in the end find more favour than he that flattereth with the tongue* (Prov. XXVIII, 23). R. Phinehas said in the name of R. Ḥama b. Ḥanina, *'He that rebuketh':* this applies to Moses; *'a man':* this refers to Israel, as it is said, *And ye My sheep, the sheep of My pasture, are men* (Ezek. XXXIV, 31). What is the force of the word *aḥarai?*[3] God said: '[Moses exhorted Israel] to talk after Me (*aḥarai*).' *'Shall find more favour':* this refers to Moses, of whom Scripture says, *And thou also hast found favour in My sight* (Ex. XXXIII, 12). *'Than he that flattereth':* this refers to Balaam, who spoke [to Israel] smooth words in his prophecy with

[1] Both read *lithrufah* as two words: *lehatter peh*, to open the mouth.
[2] So in Warsaw ed., where the name is written in full. But in Vilna ed. it is written abbreviated, ר"ל, which is more likely to stand for Resh Lakish. [3] The exposition is based on the various uses of the derivatives from אחר: (*a*) as a preposition, אחרי 'after me', (*b*) as an adverb, אחרי 'afterwards', 'in the end'.

the result that their heart grew haughty and they sinned at Shittim.[1]

Another explanation: '*He that flattereth a man in the end.*' R. Judah b. R. Simon said: What is the force of the word *aharai?* God said: 'Moses, if one may say so, admonished Me because of Israel and he also reproved Israel because of Me.' To Israel he said, *Ye have sinned a great sin*, etc. (*ib.* XXXII, 30); to God he said: '*Lord, why doth Thy wrath wax hot against Thy people*' (*ib.* 11)?

How could Moses ask, '*Why*, etc.?'[2] R. Isaac said: When Israel made the Golden Calf, the Holy One, blessed be He, desired to destroy them,[3] whereupon Moses said to Him: 'Master of the Universe! This Calf will be of great help to Thee.' God then asked him, 'How can it help Me?' Thereupon Moses replied: 'Thou causest rain to fall, the Calf will produce dew; Thou bringest out the winds, the Calf will bring out lightnings.' Said God to Moses: 'So you also are going astray after the Calf!' Whereupon Moses exclaimed before God: 'Then, "*Why doth Thy wrath wax hot against Thy people*" [seeing that the Calf is nought]?' To Israel, however, he said: '*Ye have sinned a great sin.*' R. Judah b. R. Simon said: This may be compared to a king who became angry with his wife and drove her out by force from his house. When the groomsmen heard of it they went to the king and said to him, 'Oh, Sire, is this the way to treat a wife? What has she done to you?' They then went to her and asked her, 'How long will you continue to provoke your husband? Is it your first offence? Is it your second offence?' Likewise when Moses approached God, he said to Him, '"*Why doth Thy wrath wax hot against Thy people*," etc.? Are they not Thy children?' But when he addressed Israel, he asked them, 'How long will you provoke Him? This is neither the first time nor the second time.' This is borne out by what Scripture says, IN THE WILDERNESS, IN THE ARABAH, OVER AGAINST SUPH.[4]

[1] Cf. Num. XXV, 1 *seq.* [2] Surely it was obvious!
[3] Lit. 'the enemies of Israel', a euphemism for Israel. Cf. Ex. XXXII, 7–10.
[4] At each of these places Israel sinned before God.

3. Another explanation: THESE ARE THE WORDS WHICH MOSES SPOKE. This bears out what Scripture says, *These things hast thou done, and should I have kept silence? Thou hadst thought that I was altogether such a one as thyself*, etc. (Ps. L, 21). What is the force of, '*These things hast thou done, and should I have kept silence*'? R. Samuel b. Naḥman said: The word '*These*' alludes to the exclamation, *These be thy Gods* (Ex. XXXII, 4) [applied by you to the Calf], which you made in the wilderness, and I kept silence. Why? Because Moses interceded with Me and said, *Pardon, I pray Thee*,[1] and I yielded unto him. '*Thou hadst thought that I was altogether such a one as thyself*': You have likened the image to its Creator, and the plant to Him who planted it.[2] '*But I will reprove thee and set* (we-e'erekah) *the cause before thine eyes.*' Two Amoraim join issue on the meaning of the word '*we-e'erekah*'.[3] One says: It means I will stir up all [your sins] against you. The other says: I will make an indictment of [your sins] against you. Moses said to Israel: 'I do not reprove you for any evil you may do in the future, but for what you have done in the past IN THE WILDERNESS, IN THE ARABAH, AND BEFORE SUPH.'

4. Another explanation: THESE ARE THE WORDS. R. Aḥa b. R. Ḥanina said: It would have been more fitting for the rebukes to have been uttered by Balaam and the blessings by Moses. But had Balaam uttered the rebukes, then Israel would say, 'It is an enemy who rebukes us'[4]; and had Moses uttered the blessings then the other nations of the world would say, 'It is their friend who blesses them.'[5] Therefore, the Holy One, blessed be He, commanded: 'Let their friend Moses reprove them, and their

[1] This is quoted from Num. XIV, 19, though the occasion was a different one.

[2] Cf. Gen. R. XXIV, 1. The meaning is, You attribute to God human weaknesses.

[3] The word *we-e'erekah* is derived by the one from the root '*ur*, to arouse, to stir up, and by the other, more correctly, from the root '*arak*, to arrange in order.

[4] And what he says is biased.

[5] And what he says is exaggerated.

foe Balaam bless them, so that the genuineness of the blessings and the rebukes of Israel may be clear beyond question.'

5. Another explanation: Had another rebuked them they might have said, 'Who is this one to rebuke us?' But Moses, of whom Scripture says, *I have not taken one ass from them* (Num. XVI, 15)—for him it was fitting to rebuke them.

Another comment[1]: Had another exclaimed, *Now I know that the Lord is greater than all the gods* (Ex. XVIII, 11), they might have said, 'Who is this one to declare, "*Now I know*"?' But Jethro who *did* know, for he had visited every idolatrous shrine in the world and found no reality in them and had only then become a proselyte—for him it was fitting to exclaim, '*Now I know.*'

Another comment: Had another said, *Vanity of vanities* (Eccl. I, 1), they might have said, 'How can one who has not even a *peruṭa*[2] for food declare, "*Vanity of vanities*"?' But Solomon of whom Scripture says, *And the king made silver to be in Jerusalem as stones* (I Kings X, 27)—for him it was fitting to say, '*Vanity of vanities.*'

Another comment: Had another said, *He hath made everything beautiful in its time* (Eccl. III, 11), they might have said, 'How can one who has not eaten a proper meal in his life declare, "*He hath made everything beautiful in its time*"?' But for Solomon, of whom Scripture says, *And those officers provided victual for king Solomon . . . they let nothing be lacking* (I Kings V, 7), which latter words R. Ḥama b. Ḥanina interpreted to mean that they supplied him with beet in the summer and with cucumbers in the winter, for him it was fitting to declare, '*He hath made everything beautiful in its time.*'

Another comment: Had another said, *And all the inhabitants of the earth are reputed as nothing* (Dan. IV, 32), they might have said, 'How can one who has not ruled even

[1] Not another explanation of the above, but a series of comments conceived in the same vein of thought. [2] The smallest coin.

over two flies in his life declare, "*And all the inhabitants of the earth are reputed as nothing*"?' But for Nebuchadnezzar, of whom Scripture says, *And wheresoever the children of men, the beast of the field and the fowls of the heaven dwell, hath He given them into thy hand, and hath made thee to rule over them all* (Dan. II, 38)—for him it was fitting to declare, '*And all the inhabitants of the earth are reputed as nothing.*'

Another comment: Had another said, *The Rock, His work is perfect* (Deut. XXXII, 4), they might have said, 'How can one who does not know the quality of [God's] Justice declare, "*The Rock, His work is perfect*"?' But Moses, of whom Scripture says, *He made known His ways unto Moses* (Ps. CIII, 7)—for him it was fitting to declare, '*The Rock, His work is perfect.*'

6. Another explanation: THESE ARE THE WORDS. R. Samuel b. Naḥman said: God said: 'My children have been guided through the world by the righteous and the prophets like a swarm of bees.'[1]

Another explanation: THESE ARE THE WORDS. Just as the honey of the bee is sweet and its sting sharp, so too are the words of the Torah; any one who transgresses them receives his punishment, as it is said, *Both the adulterer and the adulteress shall surely be put to death* (Lev. XX, 10); *Every one that profaneth it shall surely be put to death* (Ex. XXXI, 14). But any one who fulfils the Torah merits life, as it is said, *That thy days may be long* (*ib.* XX, 12).

Another explanation: THESE ARE THE WORDS. Just as the bee reserves honey for its owner and for the stranger its sting, so to Israel the words of the Torah are the elixir of life, but to the other nations the poison of death.[2]

R. Judah b. R. Simon said in the name of R. Levi: Just as everything the bee gathers, it gathers for its owner, so

[1] Following the queen bee. A play upon the words דבורים 'bees', and דברים 'words'. [2] Cf. *infra*, I, 21. The Rabbis resented the fulfilment of certain parts of the Torah by non-Jews; v. Sanh. (Sonc. ed.), p. 399, n. 10 and p. 400, n. 3.

too whatever merits and good deeds Israel accumulate, they accumulate for [the glory of] their Father in Heaven.

7. Another explanation: THESE ARE THE WORDS. R. Tanḥuma said: This may be compared to a man, who had some purple for sale and called out, 'Purple, purple.' The king looking out of the window heard his cry, so he called him and asked him, 'What have you for sale?' He replied, 'Nothing.' Thereupon the king exclaimed: 'I heard you calling out, "Purple, purple," and yet you say that you have nothing to sell!' He replied, 'Sire, true, it is purple, but to you it is as nothing.' Likewise it was with Moses. Before God who created the mouth and the power of speech he declared, *I am not a man of words* (Ex. IV, 10), but when he spoke with Israel, it is written of him, THESE ARE THE WORDS.[1]

8. Another explanation: R. Simon said: When the Holy One, blessed be He, bade Moses repeat the Torah he was unwilling to rebuke Israel for the evil they had previously done. R. Simon said: This may be compared to a disciple who walking with his master noticed a hot burning coal lying in the road, and thinking that it was a precious gem, picked it up and burnt himself. Some time later he was again walking with his master and noticed a precious gem lying in the road; thinking that it was a hot burning coal he feared to touch it. Thereupon his master said to him, 'Pick it up, for it is a sparkling jewel.' Similarly Moses argued: 'When I said to them [Israel] *Hear now, ye rebels* (Num. XX, 10), I was punished; how then can I now undertake to rebuke them?' Thereupon God said to Moses, 'Do not be uneasy.'

9. Another explanation: THESE ARE THE WORDS. The Rabbis say: God said to Moses: 'Seeing that Israel have meekly accepted your rebuke, you ought to bless them.' Thereupon he turned and blessed them. Whence

[1] He was a fluent speaker.

is this to be inferred? Because it is said, *The Lord your God hath multiplied you, and, behold, ye are this day as the stars of heaven for multitude* (Deut. I, 10). And whence do we know that any one who submits to rebuke merits blessing? From what Solomon clearly states, *But to them that rebuke*[1] *shall be delight, and a good blessing shall come upon them* (Prov. XXIV, 25).[2] God said to Israel: 'In this world you have been blessed by others, but in the World to Come I Myself will bless you,' as it is said, *God be gracious unto us, and bless us* (Ps. LXVII, 2).

10. THE LORD, THE GOD OF YOUR FATHERS. *Halachah:* May a Jew who has been appointed Rabbi or Judge of the community administer justice alone? Thus have our Rabbis learnt[3]: Do not judge alone, for there is only One[4] who judges alone, as it is said, *But He is at one with Himself, and who can turn Him* (Job XXIII, 13)? What is the meaning of, '*But He is at one with Himself*'? Resh Laḳish said: God both judges and seals the verdict alone. R. Reuben said: And what is God's seal? Truth (*emeth*). And why *emeth? Emeth* consists of the following three letters, *alef* the first of the letters of the Hebrew alphabet, *mem* the middle, and *taw* the last, indicating that, as Scripture says, *I am the first, and I am the last, and beside Me there is no God* (Isa. XLIV, 6).

The Rabbis say: Come and see. When Moses was appointed over Israel he said to them: 'I am not able alone to bear your burden; appoint therefore judges who shall judge you,' as it is said, *Get you wise men* (Deut. I, 13). R. Berekiah said in the name of R. Ḥanina: Judges must possess seven qualities and of these [three] are: They must be wise men, and understanding, and full of knowledge. And the other four are as enumerated elsewhere in Scripture, *Moreover thou shalt provide out of all the people able men, such as fear God, men of truth, hating unjust gain*

[1] E.V. '*decide justly*'.
[2] According to the Midrash the first half of the verse refers to those who administer the rebuke and the second half to those who accept it.
[3] M. Aboth, IV, 8; cf. Sanh. 5*a*. [4] God.

(Ex. XVIII, 21): this makes seven. And why are not all the seven stated together? To tell us that if men possessing all the seven qualities are not available then those possessing four are selected; and if such are not available, then those possessing three qualities are selected; and if even these are not available then those possessing one quality are selected, for so it is written, *A woman of valour who can find* (Prov. XXXI, 10)?[1]

AND I WILL MAKE THEM (WA-ASIMEM) HEADS OVER YOU (I, 13). The text reads, WA-ASIMEM [without the letter *yod*]. R. Joshua b. Levi said: Moses said to Israel: 'If you will not obey the judges, then sin[2] will be on your heads.' This may be illustrated as follows. The tail of the serpent said to the head, 'How much longer will you walk first? Let me go first.' The head replied, 'Go.' The tail went and coming to a ditch of water dragged the head into it; it encountered a fire and pulled [the head into it]; and coming to thorns dragged it amongst them. What was the cause of all this? Because the head followed the tail. So when the rank and file follow the guidance of the leaders, the latter entreat God and He answers their prayer; but when the leaders permit themselves to be led by the rank and file, they perforce must share in the visitation that follows.[3]

Another explanation: R. Hoshaiah said: This may be compared to a bride who, while standing under the bridal canopy, discovers that her hands are soiled. Should she wipe them on the wall, the wall will become dirty yet her hands will not be cleansed; if on the pavement, the pavement will become blackened and her hands will remain uncleansed; if, however, she wipes them on her hair, her hair improves in appearance and her hands are cleansed. So, too, when Israel obey their leaders and yet their leaders

[1] The *woman of valour* of Proverbs is parallel to the *able men* of Exodus (the same Hebrew word is employed in both verses). Apparently the idea is that this qualification alone may suffice.

[2] Without the letter *yod* the word ואשימם can be read ואשמם 'and their guilt'.

[3] Lit. 'they fall behind their faces,' an obscure phrase, the meaning of which seems to be fixed by the context.

do not attend to their wants, then the guilt is on the head of their leaders; but if not, then it is on their own heads. R. Isaac said: When Israel obey their leaders but the latter do not attend to their needs, then [of them the words of Scripture will be fulfilled], *The Lord will enter into judgment with the elders of His people, and the princes thereof* (Isa. III, 14). Why all this? Because the burden of the community is heavy and no one man alone is able to bear the burden. A proof of this is: Moses, the teacher of all the prophets, was not able to bear alone the burden of the community. Whence do we know this? [Scripture says], AND I SPOKE UNTO YOU AT THAT TIME SAYING: I AM NOT ABLE TO BEAR YOU MYSELF ALONE (I, 9). To what TIME does this refer? R. Johanan said: To the time of Jethro, for so it is written, *For the thing is too heavy for thee; thou art not able to perform it thyself alone* (Ex. XVIII, 18). R. Ḥiyya said: To the time when the people murmured [against God], as it is said, *I am not able to bear all this people myself alone, because it is too heavy for me* (Num. XI, 14); *Have I conceived all this people*, etc. (*ib.* 12)? R. Berekiah said in the name of R. Levi: Moses exclaimed before God, 'Master of the Universe, Thou hast referred [to Israel as those] *That are borne* [*by Me*] *from the birth* (Isa. XLVI, 3); for Thee it is fitting that Thou shouldst carry them.' To Israel Moses said: 'I swear that I can bear even ten times your number, but the reason why I am not able to bear you is because God has made you greater[1] than your judges.' Whence do we know this? From what we read in the same context, THE LORD YOUR GOD HATH MULTIPLIED YOU (I, 10).

11. Another explanation: THE LORD YOUR GOD HATH MULTIPLIED YOU. This bears out what the Scripture says, *I will bow down toward Thy holy temple in the fear of Thee* (Ps. V, 8). R. Ila'i b. R. Jose b. Zimra said: The Holy One, blessed be He, promised Abraham that

[1] Rendering הרבה (E.V. 'MULTIPLIED') in the sense of הגדיל, 'he hath made you greater.'—'E.J.: through the abundant benefits He has conferred upon you.

He would deliver his descendants with a word of two letters.[1] Whence do we know this? For so it is written, *And also that nation whom they shall serve, will I judge* (DaN), *and afterward shall they come out with great substance* (Gen. xv, 14). When, however, He came to redeem them, He redeemed by means of seventy-two letters. R. Judan said: Commencing with *To go and take Him a nation* to the end of the verse (Deut. iv, 34) there are seventy-two letters.[2] R. Abin said: He redeemed them by His Name which is made up of seventy-two letters.[3] Another explanation: R. Ila'i said in the name of R. Jose b. Zimra: Why did not God reveal to Abraham that He would give to his descendants the manna? R. Abba b. Kahana replied: This is the way of the righteous; they promise little and do much.

Another explanation: Why did He not reveal this to Israel? Had He revealed it to them they might have said: 'We have already long ago partaken of it at Pharaoh's table.' A proof of this is: The Egyptians did not give them even straw, yet the Israelites declared, *We remember the fish which we were wont to eat in Egypt* (Num. xi, 5). Therefore He did not reveal this unto them. Another explanation: R. Ila'i said in the name of R. Jose b. Zimra: At first God promised Abraham that He would make his children as numerous as the stars. Whence do we know this? For it is said, [*Look now toward heaven, and count the stars . . .*] *so shall thy seed be* (Gen. xv, 5). When, however, He came to bless them He blessed them with even greater numbers than He had promised them. What is the force of, FOR MULTITUDE[4]? It harks back to the promise contained in the words *In multiplying I will multiply thy seed* (Gen. xxii, 17). What is the meaning of

[1] The promise contained in the word דן (*I will judge*) forming two letters of the Divine Name, אדני.

[2] In the Hebrew, not counting the three letters of the two words, גוי (nation). Cf. Gen. R. xliv, 19. [3] What this name was is unknown. V. Ḳid. 71*a* and notes *ad loc.; J.E.* ix, 162[2] *seq.*

[4] Deut. i, 10, Heb. *larob;* the question is, why add this, seeing that the verse had already stated, *The Lord your God hath multiplied you,* the Hebrew having the same root (*hirbah*) as *larob.*

the verse, *Thou hast delivered* [lit. 'mayest Thou deliver'] *me from the contentions of the people; Thou hast made me the head of the nations* (Ps. XVIII, 44). This is what David meant: *Mayest thou deliver me from the contentions of my people* (II Sam. XXII, 44), so that I never have to bring a suit against them. '*Mayest Thou deliver me from the contentions of the people*' so that they may never have to bring a suit against me.[1] God said to David: 'Why do you sit here? Go to them!'[2] As you live! Already long ago have I appointed you king over them.' Whereupon he replied: 'Seeing that Thou hast appointed me over Thy children, put it into their hearts that they should obey me.' This is what [David] meant when he wrote, *As soon as they hear of me, they obey me* (Ps. XVIII, 45). David further said: '*Thou hast made me the head of the nations.*' R. Berekiah said: If you judge the nation [and err in judgment], then they will appeal against you to the Higher Power.[3] And who is He? The God of gods, who is all-seeing but is Himself invisible. Moses said to Israel: 'As you live! I am able to bear the burden of ten times your number and even a hundred times your number; the reason, however, why I AM NOT ABLE TO BEAR YOU MYSELF ALONE is because the Lord your God has raised you above your judges.'

12. THE LORD YOUR GOD HATH MULTIPLIED YOU, AND BEHOLD YE ARE THIS DAY AS THE STARS OF HEAVEN FOR MULTITUDE (I, 10). [Moses] said to them: 'To-day you are as the stars of heaven but in the time to come you will be like the Master; you will become like unto your Master.'[4] How so? Here [of God] it is written, *For the Lord thy God is a devouring fire* (Deut. IV,

[1] This is quoted here to show how difficult leadership is, that David has to thank God for enabling him to steer clear of lawsuits with the people.

[2] To receive the kingship. The Midrash holds that this psalm was composed after Saul's death (v. superscription) and before David's accession.

[3] Hence David's hesitancy in accepting kingship over Israel.

[4] *Larob*, being spelt defective (without *waw*), may be read *larab* 'like unto the Master', sc. God.

24); and of Israel in the time to come it is written, *And the light of Israel shall be for a fire,*[1] *and his Holy One for a flame* (Isa. x, 17). R. Levi b. Ḥama said: If one worships idols he becomes like unto them, as it is said, *They that make them shall be like unto them,* etc. (Ps. cxv, 8); should then not one who worships God all the more become like unto Him? And whence do we know that it is so? Because it is written, *Blessed is the man that trusteth in the Lord and whose trust the Lord is* (Jer. xvii, 7).[2] Another explanation: R. Abba said: In the time to come the enclosure occupied by the righteous will be inside of[3] that occupied by the ministering angels, and the latter will inquire of the former, 'What new *halachoth* has God propounded this day?'[4] R. Levi b. Ḥanina said: Do not wonder thereat; even in this world their enclosure is within the enclosure of the ministering angels, as it is said, *Lo, I see four men loose, walking in the midst of the fire, and they have no hurt; and the appearance of the fourth is like a son of the gods* (Dan. iii, 25). These men must have been within the enclosure of the angel[5] and he extinguished the fire in front of them.

13. THE LORD, THE GOD OF YOUR FATHERS, MAKE YOU A THOUSAND TIMES SO MANY MORE AS YE ARE. R. Eliezer b. Jacob said: If we look [well] into the blessings of Moses we shall find that they contain blessings from one end of the world to the other,[6] seeing that the text reads ELEF PE'AMIM; it is not written *elef pa'am* but ELEF PE'AMIM.[7]

Another explanation: MAKE YOU (KAKEM) SO MANY MORE. R. Aḥa said: Israel could have said to Moses,

[1] Referring this to Israel, not, as might appear, to God.
[2] Interpreting: and whose trust (i.e. confidence) arises from the fact that he is like the Lord ('E.J.).
[3] I.e., nearer to the centre, the Divine Throne. [4] Cf. Num. R. xx, 20.
[5] M.K. Since the angel is counted as the fourth, one may presume that we start counting from the inside, the angel following on after the three, like a disciple following his teachers. [6] I.e. blessings without end.
[7] Grammatically the sing. פעם would be more correct. The plural therefore indicates superabundance.

'Our Master, are we guilty of any one [of the sins] with which you charge us?[1] And yet we have accepted your rebuke.' But they kept silent,[2] therefore Moses made use of one word, KAKEM, meaning, [May God add to you] righteous men even as ye are [*kakem*], who accept rebuke in silence.

Another explanation: Why did God bless them with a word implying additional [blessing]?[3] Because God's addition to a blessing is greater than the original blessing.[4] In the ordinary way when a man buys a pound of meat he says [to the seller], 'Give me a little extra.' How much does the latter add? A trifle. But what God adds is more than the original. How? Isaac was Abraham's original family, but the children that God added unto him [later] were even more, as it is said, *And Abraham took another wife, and her name was Keturah. And she bore him Zimran, and Jokshan, and Medan, and Midian, and Ishbak, and Shuah* (Gen. XXV, 1 f). Joseph constituted the original family of his mother, Benjamin was her additional son, as it is said, *The Lord add to me another son* (Gen. XXX, 24). And of him it is written, *And the sons of Benjamin: Bela, and Becher and Ashbel*, etc. (Gen. XLVI, 21). Thus Benjamin had more children than Joseph. The original years of Hezekiah's reign were fourteen,[5] but the years that God added to him were more than those. Whence this? As it is said, *Behold, I will add unto thy days fifteen years* (Isa. XXXVIII, 5), because what God adds to a blessing is greater than the original blessing. Hence He blessed them with a word implying additional [blessing].

AND BLESS YOU. R. Levi said: This can be compared to a king who instructed the commander of his army to distribute a pound of gold to each of his legionaries. He went and gave them, some five golden pieces, and some

[1] They were the second generation descended from those that came out of Egypt.
[2] 'E.J. emends: instead of which *they* accepted his reproof and were silent.
[3] The text has the word, יוסף, 'may He *add*.' [4] Cf. Gen. R. LXI, 4.
[5] Since at the end of fourteen years he fell ill and was told that death was at hand (Isa. XXXVIII, 1; II Kings XX, 1).

ten.[1] Whereupon the soldiers said to him, 'The king commanded you to distribute a pound of gold to each of the legions but you have distributed instead five golden pieces to each of our legionaries. He replied: 'These are my own private gifts, but when the king will come he will give you of his own.' Similarly Israel said to Moses: 'Moses our Master, God has placed no limits to our blessings, whereas you have set a limit to them in saying "*a thousand times*".' Moses thereupon replied to them: 'The blessing that I gave you is mine own; when, however, the Lord will come, He will bless you *As He hath promised.*'[2]

14. Another explanation: THE LORD YOUR GOD HATH MULTIPLIED YOU, AND BEHOLD YE ARE THIS DAY AS THE STARS OF HEAVEN FOR MULTITUDE. Why did he bless them to be as the stars? Just as there are ranks above ranks amongst the stars [some being placed higher in the heavens than others], so too in Israel there are numerous gradations[3]; as the stars are unsearchable and innumerable, so too are Israel past finding out and without number; as the stars rule[4] from one end of the world to the other, so too are Israel [to be found from one end of the world to the other]. Moses asked God: 'Why didst Thou not liken Thy children to the sun and moon which are greater than the stars?' God answered him: 'By your life, the sun and moon are destined to be put to shame in the time to come.' Whence this? Because it is written, *Then the moon shall be confounded, and the sun shall be ashamed*, etc. (Isa. XXIV, 23). 'But the stars will never be subjected to shame.'[5] Whence this? For so it is written, *And ye shall know that I am in the midst of Israel, and that I am the Lord your God, and there is none else; and My people shall never be ashamed* (Joel II, 27).

[1] Which was less than the king had ordered.
[2] Thus the Midrash renders: *The Lord . . . make you a thousand times*—that was Moses' private blessing—*and may He bless you, as He hath promised you*—without any limit whatsoever.
[3] Various ranks.
[4] I.e. function (cf. Gen. I, 18: *And to rule over the day*, referring to the sun).
[5] And so too are Israel.

15. YE HAVE COMPASSED THIS MOUNTAIN LONG ENOUGH (II, 3). *Halachah:* What is the reward of a Jew who is zealous in his observance of the duty of honouring father and mother? The Rabbis have learnt thus[1]: These are the things the fruits of which a man enjoys in this world while the stock remains for the World to Come: the honouring of father and mother, etc. R. Abbahu said: R. Eliezer the Great was asked by his disciples: 'Can you give an example of [real] honouring of parents.' He replied: 'Go and see what Dama b. Nethina of Askelon did. His mother was mentally afflicted and she used to slap him in the presence of his colleagues, and all that he would say was, "Mother it is enough!"' Our Rabbis say: Once the Sages came to him to Askelon, where he lived, to buy from him a precious stone [to replace one] lost from the vestments of the [high] priest, and they fixed the price with him at a thousand golden pieces. He entered the house and found his father asleep with his leg stretched out on the chest wherein the stone was lying. He would not trouble him, and he came out empty-handed. As he did not produce the stone the Sages thought that he wanted a higher price, and they therefore raised their offer to ten thousand golden pieces. When his father awoke from his sleep Dama entered and brought out the stone. The Sages wished to give him ten thousand golden pieces, but he exclaimed: 'Heaven forfend! I will not make a profit out of honouring my parents; I will only take from you the first price, one thousand golden pieces, which I had fixed with you.' And what reward did the Holy One, blessed be He, give him? Our Rabbis report that in the very same year his cow gave birth to a red heifer[2] which he sold for more than ten thousand golden pieces. See from this, how great is the merit of honouring father and mother. R. Simeon b. Gamaliel said: No son has ever honoured his parents as I have done, and yet I find that Esau honoured his father even more than I. How? R. Simeon b. Gamaliel said: I usually waited on my father dressed in soiled clothes,

[1] Peah I, I. [2] Cf. Num. XIX.

but when I went out into the street I discarded these clothes and put on instead handsome clothes. Not so Esau; the clothes in which he was dressed when attending on his father were his best. The proof for this is this. When he went out hunting in order to bring venison to his father that he might bless him, what did Rebekah who loved Jacob do? She gave him dainties and said to him, 'Go to your father and receive the blessings before your brother receives them.' Whereupon Jacob said to her, 'Mother, do you not know that Esau my brother is *A hairy man, and I am a smooth man* (Gen. XXVII, 11): Perhaps my father will discover that I am not Esau and I will be put to shame before him.' Whence this? Because it is said, *Peradventure my father will feel me*, etc. (*ib.* 12). She replied to him: 'My son, your father's eyes are dim; I will dress you with the fine clothes which your brother wears when he attends on your father, and when you come to him and he takes hold of your hand he will think that you are Esau and he will bless you.' And whence this? Because it is said, *And Rebekah took the choicest garments of Esau*, etc. (*ib.* 15), that is to say those which he was wont to wear when attending on his father, as it is said, *And put them upon Jacob her younger son* (*ib.*). Hence when Jacob came to him, what did Isaac say? *The voice is the voice of Jacob, but the hands are the hands of Esau* (*ib.* 22).[1] Isaac blessed him and he went out. Then Esau arrived and entered into the presence of his father. Isaac asked him, 'Who are you addressing me in such a loud voice?'[2] He replied: '*I am thy son, thy firstborn, Esau*' (*ib.* 32). As soon as he heard his voice he knew that he was Esau. He said to him: 'My son, *Thy brother came with guile, and hath taken away thy blessing*' (*ib.* 35). Thereupon Esau began to cry and to complain: 'Come and see what this quiet man of whom it is written, *And Jacob was a quiet man, dwelling in tents* (Gen. XXV, 27), has done to me. Not enough that he mocked me

[1] He recognised that the garments were the best.
[2] Adopting the reading בקול גדול instead of בלב גדול. If the reading בלב גדול (lit. 'with a big heart') is retained, the meaning probably is: with sure confidence.

for selling him my birthright, *Behold, now he hath taken away my blessing'* (*ib.* XXVII, 36). Hence you learn that Esau was most scrupulous in honouring his parents. R. Judan said: When Israel came to wage war with him,[1] God showed to Moses the mountain[2] where the Patriarchs are buried. God said: 'Moses, say to Israel, you cannot successfully attack him! there is still owing to him the reward for the respect he paid to those who lie buried in this mountain.' Whence this? From what we read in the context, YE HAVE COMPASSED THIS MOUNTAIN LONG ENOUGH.[3]

16. Another explanation: YE HAVE COMPASSED THIS MOUNTAIN LONG ENOUGH. This bears out what Scripture says, *Who will bring me into the fortified city—*maẓor? (Ps. LX, 11). This refers to Rome.[4] And why does David call it '*maẓor*'? Because it is a city which oppresses (*meẓirah*) and diminishes (*mebaẓerah*) Israel.[5] Another explanation: *Maẓor.* The city which is well fortified on all sides, so that no man is able to capture it. Another explanation: '*Maẓor.*' The city which all strive to diminish [weaken].

R. Joḥanan said: David yearningly exclaimed, '"*Who will bring me into the fortified city*"? Would that I were able to exact vengeance from her?' God said to him: 'David, can you then prevail over her?' David replied: 'Master of the Universe, *Who will lead me unto Edom'* (*ib.*), i.e. He who long ago gave me sovereignty over Edom, will also give me dominion over this mighty people.[6] Whence

---

[1] This is learnt by inference from the words *Do not contend with them* (Deut. II, 5).   [2] Near Hebron, where the patriarchs and their wives are buried in the Cave of Machpelah.

[3] The inference is really from what follows: *Do not contend with them.*

[4] This exposition is influenced by the name, Edom, in the second half of the verse which the Midrash usually applies to Rome.

[5] Or 'confines Israel' (Levi). Both plays on the word *maẓor.* 'E.J. understands *mebaẓerah* in the sense of strengthens, fortifies: the very sufferings which Rome inflicts on Israel strengthen them for a glorious future.

[6] Apparently the meaning is that as God had given David dominion in the past, so would He do also in the future. The Rabbis, who read the hopes and aspirations of their own times into the Bible, thus expressed the longing for a time when the tables would be turned and the Jew no longer be under the heel of the Roman.

do we know that David had dominion over Edom? Because it says, *And he put garrisons* (neẓibim) *in Edom* (II Sam. VIII, 14). What are '*neẓibim*'? R. Simon said: Camps; the Rabbis said: Statues.[1] R. Judah b. Simon said: The Holy One, blessed be He, said: 'David, I know that your hands are quick and determined, and I desire to rule My world through them.' Another explanation: [God said]: 'David, I need [Rome] for future generations. Already long ago Moses, your teacher, desired to attack them and I said, ENOUGH FOR YOU (RAB LAKEM): Let the teacher (*rab*) charge his disciples, COMPASS THIS MOUNTAIN.'[2]

17. Another explanation: YE HAVE COMPASSED LONG ENOUGH. This bears out what Scripture says, *Resign thyself unto the Lord, and wait patiently for Him*, etc. (Ps. XXXVII, 7). What is meant by, '*Wait patiently* (hitḥolel) *for Him*'? Wait patiently for the Lord,[3] as the Scriptural text elsewhere says, *Why art thou cast down, O my soul? And why moanest thou within me? Hope thou in God: for I shall yet praise Him*, etc. (Ps. XLII, 12). Another explanation: '*And wait patiently for Him.*' R. Taḥlifa of Cæsarea said: What is implied by '*And wait patiently for Him*'? Should affliction befall you, accept it with rejoicings (*be-ḥelah*).[4]

Fret not thyself because of him who prospereth in his way (Ps. XXXVII, 7). This refers to Esau[5] of whom it says, *Wherefore doth the way of the wicked prosper?* (Jer. XII, 1). *Because of the man who bringeth wicked devices to pass.* This refers to Esau who conducts trials with guile. How? A judge of the [Roman] government tries a man for murder and asks him, 'Why did you murder?' The latter denies

[1] So Krauss, Lehnworter, and Levi (*Wörterbuch*), the meaning being that David erected statues as a symbol of victory. Jast. by emending the word renders 'garrisons', but this is identical with 'camps'.
[2] I.e. let Moses give this command to his successors. For that reason David's yearning could not be fulfilled.
[3] The Midrash adds nothing, but merely translates the Hebrew of the text (*hithḥolel*) by a word of more general use.
[4] The basic meaning of the root חול, of which התחולל is the *hithpael* form, is, 'to dance'; hence חילה means 'dance', 'rejoicing'. [5] Rome.

[the charge]. He then asks him, 'And wherewith did you murder the man; with a sword, or with a spear, or with a knife?'[1] Another explanation: '*Resign thyself unto the Lord, and wait patiently for Him.*' R. Joshua b. Levi said: When the enemies came to destroy Jerusalem,[2] there were sixty thousand myriads of evil spirits standing at the gate of the Temple ready to engage them in battle; but when they saw the *Shechinah* looking on in silence, as it is written, *He hath drawn back His right hand from before the enemy* (Lam. II, 3), they too gave way. R. Judah b. Simon said: [Moses said to Israel]: 'He sees the enemy destroying His house and He is silent and yet you wish to attack him; the reward for the honour he showed his parents is still owing to him.'[3] YE HAVE COMPASSED LONG ENOUGH THE MOUNTAIN. What is meant by COMPASSING THE MOUNTAIN (HAR)? R. Ḥanina said: Esau paid very great attention to his parent (*horo*),[4] namely his father whom he had the duty of supplying with meals. Whence this? [It is written], *Now Isaac loved Esau, because he did eat of his venison* (Gen. XXV, 28). R. Samuel b. R. Gedaliah said: God said: 'I will reward [Esau] for this.' When Jacob offered gifts to Esau, what did Esau answer him? '*I have* enough—*rab* (Gen. XXXIII, 9); do not trouble yourself.' God declared: 'With this very expression he paid respect to him [Jacob] and with this very same expression will I command him [Jacob's descendants] to keep away [from attacking] him'; YE HAVE COMPASSED LONG ENOUGH.

18. Another explanation: YE HAVE LONG ENOUGH. R. Aḥa said: If you touch him [Esau] you will really be attacking yourselves.' How? His father blessed him with but one blessing, *And by thy sword shalt thou live* (Gen. XXVII, 40), but Jacob he blessed with ten blessings. Whence do we know this? For so it is written, *So God give thee of*

[1] Thus seeking to trap him into a confession.
[2] At the siege of Jerusalem under Titus.
[3] Though this, of course, is an anachronism, the sense is clear: Moses foretold that even at a much later date Esau (Rome) would triumph.
[4] A play upon the word, הר 'mountain,' and הור 'parent.'

the dew of heaven, etc. (*ib*, 28 f); if his one blessing is nullified your ten blessings too shall be nullified. Hence, YE HAVE COMPASSED LONG ENOUGH.[1]

19. R. Berekiah said: When Esau entered his father's presence and discovered that Jacob had taken away the blessings he asked him, 'Have you not left even one blessing for me?' as it is said, *Hast thou not reserved a blessing for me* (*ib.* 36)? Isaac replied: 'Even if I bless you, the blessing will be his; for have I not said thus [to him]? *Be lord over thy brethren* (*ib.* 29); the servant and all that he has belong to the master.'[2]

What is the meaning of, TURN YOU NORTHWARD—ẒAFONAH (II, 3)? R. Ḥiyya interpreted: Moses said to Israel: 'If you see that he [Esau] seeks to make war on you, then do not stand up to him but hide (*haẓinu*) yourselves[3] from him, until his world [his day of sovereignty] has passed.' That is the force of the words, TURN YOU NORTHWARD. R. Judah b. Shallum said: Israel complained before God: 'Master of the Universe, his father blessed him with the words, "*By the sword shalt thou live*," and Thou didst approve of the blessing, and Thou sayest unto us, "Hide yourselves before him?" Whither shall we flee?' God replied: 'When you see that he would attack you, then flee to the Torah.' And ẒAFONAH (E.V. 'NORTHWARD') surely means the Torah, as it is said, *He layeth up* (yizpon)[4] *sound wisdom for the upright* (Prov. II, 7). Another explanation of ẒAFONAH: R. Isaac said: The Holy One, blessed be He, said [to Israel]: 'Wait, the King Messiah has yet to come to fulfil the words of the Scripture, *Oh, how abundant is Thy goodness which Thou hast laid up* (zafan-ta) *for them that fear Thee*' (Ps. XXXI, 20).

[1] Perhaps he interprets: let it be enough for you that he received only one blessing, and do not attempt to deprive him even of that.
[2] Mah.: He translates *rab*, master, and interprets: the privilege of being master is yours, Esau's blessing belonging to you. This is not very plausible, however, and 'E.J. holds that the text is in disorder.
[3] A play upon the meaning of the word צפן 'to hide', and 'north'.
[4] Connected by a play on words with *ẓafon*.

20. AND COMMAND THOU THE PEOPLE, SAYING (II, 4). God said to him [Moses]: 'Not you [Israel] alone do I command, but you also are to command your children.' God said to Moses: 'You charge also the leaders of the generations to come that they should treat him [Esau] with respect.' This is what is implied in the words, AND COMMAND THE PEOPLE, SAYING.[1] R. Samuel b. Naḥman said: When Esau and Jacob met, the former said, 'Jacob, my brother, let us two walk together in this world as one.' Jacob replied: '*Let my lord, I pray thee, pass over before his servant*' (Gen. XXXIII, 14). What is the meaning of '*Let . . . pass over*'? Do you enjoy your world first.[2] What is the meaning of, *And I will journey on gently, according to the pace of the cattle that are before me . . . and according to the pace of the* children (*ib.*). Jacob said to Esau: 'I have yet to raise up Hananiah, Mishael, and Azariah,' of whom Scripture says, Children *in whom was no blemish* (Dan. I, 4).

Another explanation: He said to him: 'I have yet to raise up the Messiah,' of whom it is written, *For a* child *is born to us* (Isa. IX, 5).

Until I come unto my Lord unto Seir (Gen. XXXIII, 14). R. Samuel b. Naḥman said: We have searched all the Scriptures and we have nowhere found [it stated] that Jacob ever came together with Esau at Seir. What then is the meaning of, '*Unto Seir*'? Jacob [meant] to say to him: 'I have yet to raise up judges and saviours to exact punishment from you.'[3] Whence this? For it is said, *And saviours shall come up on mount Zion to judge the mount of Esau* (Obad. I, 21). Israel asked God: 'Master of the Universe, how long shall we remain subjected to him?' He replied: 'Until the day comes of which it is written, *There shall step forth a star out of Jacob and a sceptre shall rise out of Israel* (Num. XXIV, 17); when a star shall step forth from Jacob and devour the stubble of Esau.' (Whence this? For it is said,

[1] The Heb. *lemor* literally means 'to say'; hence he renders: And command the people to say (the same thing to future generations).
[2] You receive your enjoyment in this world. Cf. Gen. R. LXXVIII, 14.
[3] Lit. 'From that man.'

And the house of Jacob shall be a fire, and the house of Joseph a flame, and the house of Esau for stubble, and they shall kindle in them and devour them; and there shall not be any remaining of the house of Esau (Obad. I, 18).) God said: 'At that time I will cause my kingdom to shine forth and I will reign over them,' as it is said, *And saviours shall come up on Mount Zion, to judge the mount of Esau; and the kingdom shall be the Lord's* (*ib.* 21).

21. AND THE LORD SAID UNTO ME: BEHOLD, I HAVE BEGUN TO DELIVER UP SIHON AND HIS LAND, etc. (II, 31). *Halachah:* If a Jew is journeying on the road on the eve of Sabbath [Friday] and is overtaken by nightfall and he has in his hand money or any other object, how shall he act?[1] The Rabbis have learnt as follows[2]: If nightfall overtakes a man on the road [on Friday] he hands over his purse to a non-Jew. And why is it permissible to hand over one's purse to a non-Jew? R. Levi said: When the children of Noah were charged [to observe certain laws], they were given seven Laws only,[3] the observance of the Sabbath not being among them; therefore have the Rabbis permitted a Jew to hand over objects to a non-Jew. R. Jose b. Ḥanina said: A non-Jew who observes the Sabbath whilst he is uncircumcised incurs liability for the punishment of death.[4] Why? Because [non-Jews] were not commanded concerning it. And what is your reason for saying that a non-Jew who observes the Sabbath becomes liable to the punishment of death? R. Ḥiyya b. Abba said in the name of R. Joḥanan: In mundane affairs, when a king and his consort are sitting and conversing together, should one come and interrupt them, does he not thereby make himself liable to punishment of death? So, too, the Sabbath is [a reunion] between Israel and God, as it is said, *It is a sign between Me and the children of Israel*

[1] As it is not permissible to carry on the Sabbath.
[2] Shab. 153*a*. [3] Cf. Sanh. 56*a* (Sonc. ed., pp. 381–2 and notes *ad loc.*); Gen. R. XVI, 6; *J.E.*, vol. VII, p. 648.
[4] This, of course, is not meant literally, but is merely an expression of strong resentment; v. Sanh. (Sonc. ed.), p. 399, n. 10.

(Ex. XXXI, 17); therefore any non-Jew who, being uncircumcised, thrusts himself between them incurs the penalty of death. The Rabbis say: Moses declared before God: 'Master of the Universe, just because the Gentiles have not been commanded to observe the Sabbath, wilt Thou show favour to them if they do observe it?' God replied to him: 'Do you really fear this? By your life, even if they fulfil all the commandments in the Torah, yet will I cause them to fall before you.' Whence this? Because the text says, BEHOLD, I HAVE BEGUN TO DELIVER UP BEFORE THEE.

22. Another explanation: BEHOLD, I HAVE BEGUN, etc. This bears out what Scripture says, *To bind their kings with chains* (Ps. CXLIX, 8). And what is meant by '*their kings*'? R. Tanḥuma said: Literally their kings. *And their nobles with fetters of iron* (*ib.*): these are their guardian angels [in heaven] above[1]; for God does not exact punishment of any nation before he first exacts punishment of its guardian angel. How? Before God drowned Pharaoh and all the Egyptians in the sea he first drowned their guardian angel.[2] How is this to be inferred from the Scripture? The Rabbis say: It is not written, 'horses and their riders,' but *The horse and his rider hath He thrown into the sea* (Ex. XV, 1); this refers to their guardian angel.[3] And when the Egyptians came out in pursuit of the Israelites the Israelites lifted up their eyes and saw the guardian angel of the Egyptians hovering in the air. Whence this? R. Isaac said: Because it is written, *Behold, Egypt was marching*[4] *after them* (Ex. XIV, 10); that is, their guardian angel. This is the force of the words, '*To bind their kings with chains*, etc.' The same, too, happened when Sihon and Og sought to attack Israel; God said to Moses: 'See, I have caused

[1] Every nation was thought to have a guardian angel ('prince') in heaven.
[2] Ex. R. XXI, 5.
[3] For otherwise the plural would have been used.
[4] The exposition is based on the fact that the M.T. has the sing. נוסע (*journeying*) and not the plural נוסעים, while the literal translation is 'Egypt', not '*The Egyptians*' as in E.V. Hence, the Midrash assumes that it was their guardian angel, his name being 'Egypt'. Cf. Ex. R. XXII, 2.

their guardian angel to fall,' as it is said, BEHOLD, I HAVE BEGUN TO DELIVER UP SIHON, etc.[1]

23. Another explanation: I HAVE BEGUN, etc. This bears out what Scripture says, *Hope deferred maketh the heart sick* (Prov. XIII, 12). R. 'Azariah said: This verse refers to the salvation yet to come. How? When the prophet says unto Israel, *Yet once, it is a little while, and I will shake the heavens and the earth* (Hag. II, 6), they reply, '*Hope deferred maketh the heart sick.*' But when the prophet said, *Behold, thy salvation cometh* (Isa. LXII, 11), they replied, *But desire fulfilled is a tree of life* (Prov. *loc. cit.*).

Another explanation: '*Hope deferred*'; this refers to Pharaoh, upon whom Moses continued to bring plagues, and after each plague Israel thought that they were going to be set free. '*But desire fulfilled is a tree of life*'; this refers to the wars of Sihon and Og, of whom God immediately said to Moses, BEHOLD, I HAVE BEGUN TO DELIVER UP.

Another explanation: What is the meaning of BEHOLD, I HAVE BEGUN? God said to Moses: 'Moses, see, I have cast down their guardian angel.'[1] R. Abba b. Kahana said: This is like unto a king who has his son's enemy bound in fetters before him, and says to him, 'Do unto him whatever you desire.'[2]

24. Another interpretation of BEHOLD, I HAVE BEGUN. R. Samuel b. Naḥman said: When Israel came out of Egypt and the Holy One, blessed be He, wrought for them all these miracles, dread of them fell upon all the nations of the world, as it is said, *Terror and dread falleth upon them* (Ex. XV, 16). And when Israel were about to make war on Sihon and Og, the Amorites inquired of

[1] Since in fact He had *not* yet begun to deliver Sihon, we assume that it means that He had already prepared Sihon's overthrow by destroying his guardian angel (M.K., 'E.J.).
[2] The previous passage stressed the words I HAVE BEGUN (v. preceding note), whereas this emphasises the word SEE, God showing him Sihon's guardian angel overthrown.

one another, 'By your life! Is this nation which seeks to make war on us strong or not? Of how many peoples is it made up?' And they answered, 'They are the children of three nations.'[1] Sihon and Og exclaimed: 'Seeing that the whole of this nation are children of three peoples, let us arm ourselves and attack them and we shall kill them.' Whence this? [Scripture says], THEN SIHON CAME OUT AGAINST US (II, 32). Moses and Israel came to the borders of Edrei. Moses said unto them [Israel]: 'Let us encamp here, and in the morning we will enter the city.' As they were about to enter, [it was so dark] that nothing could as yet be seen. Moses lifted up his eyes and beheld Og sitting upon the wall with his feet touching the ground; Moses said [to himself], 'I do not know what I see; these people must have built up an additional wall during the night.' Whereupon God said to Moses: 'Moses, what you see is Og.' R. Joḥanan said: The length of his feet was eighteen cubits. Thereupon Moses became frightened, but God said, 'Do not fear, because I will make him fall before you.' Whence this? Scripture says, AND THE LORD SAID UNTO ME: FEAR HIM NOT (III, 2). Og then uprooted a mountain[2] and threw it upon Israel, but Moses took a pebble and pronounced over it the Divine Name[3] and thus kept the mountain from falling. Israel exclaimed, 'Cursed be the hands which throw thus,' and the Emorites answered, 'Blessed be the hands which uphold thus.'

25. Another explanation: AND THE LORD SAID UNTO ME: FEAR HIM NOT: FOR I HAVE DELIVERED HIM INTO THY HAND. It is not written here, 'For I *will* deliver him into thy hand,' but, FOR I *HAVE* DELIVERED HIM INTO THY HAND! God said: 'Already in the days of Abraham did I decree his fate.' How? When Lot his nephew was taken captive, Og came and informed Abraham, as it is said, *And there came one that had escaped—*

[1] Of priests, Levites, and Israelites; or, the descendants of the three Patriarchs, Abraham, Isaac, and Jacob.
[2] Cf. Ber. 54*b*. [3] The Tetragrammaton.

hapalit (Gen. XIV, 13). R. Levi said in the name of Bar Ḳappara: His name was *Palit* and the reason why he was called Og is because when he came he found Abraham occupied in the preparation of unleavened bread and Passover cakes.[1] He did not, however, come for the sake of Heaven,[2] but on account of the beauty of Sarah. He said to himself: 'I will bring him the tidings and my troop will kill him and I will marry his wife Sarah.' God said to him, 'Wicked man, is that your intention! By your life, I will give you the reward for your journey, and will prolong your years. And as for your planning to kill Abraham and to marry Sarah, you will perish by the hand of her descendants.'

Another explanation: FOR I HAVE DELIVERED HIM INTO THY HAND. It is not written, 'For I *will* deliver him into thy hand,' but FOR I *HAVE* DELIVERED HIM INTO THY HAND. Already in the days of Isaac did I decree his fate. How? When Abraham circumcised Isaac he made a feast and invited all the kings of Canaan, as it is said, *And Abraham made a* great *feast*, etc. (Gen. XXI, 8). Why '*great*'? Because all the great men were there. Og too was there, and people on that occasion said to him, 'Did you not declare that Abraham was a barren mule and could not beget children?' When he looked at Isaac he exclaimed, 'What, this one! He is nought! I can kill him with my finger.' God said to him: 'You speak thus! You will yet live to see thousands and tens of thousands of descendants coming from him and by their hand shall you fall.'

Another explanation: FOR I HAVE DELIVERED HIM. It is not written, 'For I *will* deliver him into thy hand,' but, FOR I *HAVE* DELIVERED HIM INTO THY HAND. Already in the days of Jacob did I decree his fate. How? When Jacob entered before Pharaoh to bless him, as it is said, *And Jacob blessed Pharaoh* (Gen. XLVII, 10), Og was there present and on that occasion Pharaoh said to Og,

[1] A play upon the name Og and '*ugoth* ('cakes').
[2] On a mission of charity.

'Did you not say, "Abraham is a barren mule and will beget no children," and, behold, here is his grandson with his seventy descendants?' Whereupon Og began to cast an evil eye upon them[1]; whereupon God said to him: 'You wicked man, why do you cast your evil eye upon My children? May your eye run out; you are destined to fall by their hand.' This is what the text says, FOR I *HAVE* DELIVERED HIM INTO THY HAND. God said to Israel: 'Just as in this world the nations have heard your fame, and fear and dread you, so too will it be in the time to come,' as it is said, *And all the peoples of the earth shall see that the name of the Lord is called upon thee; and they shall be afraid of thee* (Deut. XXVIII, 10).

[1] To harm them.

Chapter II

VAETHCHANAN

1. And I besought the Lord (iii, 23). *Halachah:* Is it permissible for a Jew standing at prayer to pray loudly? The Sages have learnt thus: When one is standing at prayer, you might think that he may raise his voice; but Hannah has already long ago explicitly shown otherwise, [for of her Scripture says], *Now Hannah, she spake in her heart* (1 Sam. i, 13). You might perhaps think that a man may recite the three[1] services of the day all at once. The rule on this point has already been clearly shown in [the book of] Daniel where it is written, *And he kneeled upon his knees three times a day, and prayed, and gave thanks before his God* (Dan. vi, 11). You might perhaps think that a man may recite them at any time he desires; David has already long ago clearly stated, *Evening, and morning, and at noonday, will I complain, and moan; and He hath heard my voice* (Ps. lv, 18). You might perhaps think that a man may pray for his needs[2] and thereby discharge his obligation; Solomon has already long ago defined prayer as *To hearken unto the cry* (rinnah) *and to the prayer*—tefillah (1 Kings viii, 28). '*Rinnah*' means adoration of God, and '*tefillah*', praying for one's personal needs. Abba Saul said: A good omen for prayer is this: if a man directs his heart to his prayer he may be confident that his prayer will be answered, as it is said, *Thou wilt direct their heart, Thou wilt cause Thine ear to attend* (Ps. x, 17). R. Joḥanan said: Prayer is known by the following ten designations: *Shaw'ah, ẓe'aḳah, ne'aḳah, rinnah, pegi'ah, biẓur, ḳeri'ah, nippul, pillul, and taḥanunim. Shaw'ah* and *ẓe'aḳah*, as it is said, *And the children of Israel sighed by reason of the bondage, and they cried,*[3] *and their cry*[4]

[1] Morning, afternoon, and evening services.
[2] Without prefacing his prayer with hymns and psalms.
[3] ויזעקו (*wayyeze'aḳu* from *ze'aḳah*).
[4] שועתם (*shaw'atham* from *shaw'ah*).

came unto God by reason of the bondage (Ex. II, 23); *ne'aḳah*, as it is said, *And God heard their groaning* (*ib.* 24)[1]; *rinnah* and *pegi'ah*, as it is written, *Therefore pray not for this people, neither lift up cry*[2] *nor prayer for them, neither make intercession*[3] *to Me* (Jer. VII, 16); *biẓur and ḳeri'ah*, as it is written, *In my distress*[4] *I called*[5] *upon the Lord* (Ps. XVIII, 7); *nippul*, as it is written, *And I fell down*[6] *before the Lord* (Deut. IX, 18); *pillul*, as it is written, *Then stood up Phinehas, and wrought judgment* (Ps. CVI, 30)[7]; and *taḥanunim*, as it is written, AND I BESOUGHT[8] THE LORD. And of all these designations of prayer Moses made use only of *taḥanunim*. R. Joḥanan said: Hence you learn that no creature has any claim on his Creator, because Moses, the teacher of all the prophets, made use only of *taḥanunim*.[9] R. Levi said: The reason why Moses made use only of *taḥanunim* is because the proverb says: 'Take care that you are not taken at your own word.' How? The Holy One, blessed be He, spake to Moses thus: *And I will be gracious to whom I will be gracious* (Ex. XXXIII, 19). God said to Moses: 'To him who has any claim upon Me *I will show mercy* (*ib.*), that is, I will deal with him according to My Attribute of Mercy; and as for him who has no claim upon Me, to him "*I will be gracious*", that is, I will grant [his prayer] as an act of grace.' When Moses desired to enter the Land of Israel, God said to him: LET IT SUFFICE THEE (III, 26). Whereupon Moses exclaimed before Him: 'Master of the Universe, hast Thou not said to me, "Any one who has no claim of reward upon Me, to him '*I will be gracious*', that is, I will grant [his prayer] as an act of grace"? Now I do not claim that there is anything due to me from Thee, but grant Thou me [my prayer] as an act of grace.' Whence this? From what we

---

[1] נאקתם (*na'aḳatham* from *na'aḳah*).   [2] רנה (*rinnah*).
[3] תפגע (*tifgu'*, whence *pegi'ah*).
[4] בצר (*baẓẓer*)—The Midrash takes the preposition ב as part of the word (making a root בצר).   [5] אקרא (*eḳra*, whence *ḳeri'ah*).
[6] ואתנפל (*wa-ethnapal*).   [7] ויפלל (*wayyefallel*, whence *pillul*).
[8] ואתחנן (*wa-ethḥanan*, whence *taḥanunim*).
[9] *Taḥanunim* is connected with *ḥen*, grace, and thus implies that he prayed not as one who demands his right but as one who asks for grace.

have read in the text under comment, AND I BESOUGHT THE LORD.

2. Another explanation: AND I BESOUGHT THE LORD. This bears out what Scripture says, *With rebukes dost Thou chasten man for iniquity, and like a moth Thou makest his beauty to consume away: surely every man is vanity?* (Ps. XXXIX, 12). What is the meaning of, '*With rebukes dost Thou chasten man for iniquity*'? Because of the one sin which Moses committed in rebuking Thy children and saying unto them,[1] *Hear now, ye rebels* (Num. XX, 10), Thou hast chastened and reproved him. And '*man*' surely refers to Moses, as it is said, *Now the man Moses was very meek* (*ib.* XII, 3). What is the meaning of, '*And like a moth Thou makest his beauty* (ḥimudo) *to consume away*'? Every yearning (*ḥemdah*) that Moses had to enter the Land of Israel was made to vanish from him,[2] as the moth, when it gets into garments, rots them away. And '*his desire*' (ḥimudo) signifies nought else but the Land of Israel, as Scripture has it, *And give thee a pleasant* (ḥemdah) *land* (Jer. III, 19). If this fate befell Moses the righteous, how much more so will this be the case with other beings who are given over to vanity and are predestined for the Day of Judgment.[3] '*Surely every man is vanity.*' R. Aḥa said: He who was once made a god, as it is said, *See, I have set thee in God's stead to Pharaoh* (Ex. VII, 1), now supplicates and prostrates himself, [as it is written], AND I BESOUGHT THE LORD.

3. Another explanation: AND I BESOUGHT. This bears out what Scripture says, *And he changeth the times and the seasons* (Dan. II, 21). R. Abin said: This can be compared to a king who had a favourite, who had the power to appoint generals, governors, and commanders-in-chief.

[1] The Midrash inverts the order of the words and reads, על עון בתוכחות 'for the sin of rebuking'.

[2] Was completely disregarded, as though it did not exist.

[3] That is the comment on *Surely every man is vanity,* the end of the sentence.

Later, the people saw him entreating the gate-keeper to let him enter the palace, and he would not permit him. Everyone was amazed at this and said, 'Yesterday he was appointing generals, governors, and commanders-in-chief and now he in vain begs the gate-keeper to let him enter the palace.' The answer given to them was: '[His] hour is past.' So too with Moses. [Once] whatever he ordered God would fulfil, [as for example he said], *Rise up, O Lord* (Num. x, 35); *Return, O Lord* (*ib.* 36); *But if the Lord make a new thing* (Num. XVI, 30), that is to say, if an opening had been created for the earth during the six days of creation, it is well, and if not, let God create one[1]; and now he supplicates and prostrates himself to be permitted to enter the Land of Israel, and his prayers are not accepted. His hour is past [as is implied in the words], AND I BESOUGHT THE LORD *AT THAT TIME*.[2]

4. AND I BESOUGHT THE LORD. This bears out what Scripture says, *The poor useth entreaties; but the rich answereth harshly* (Prov. XVIII, 23). R. Tanḥuma said: '*The poor useth entreaties*'; this refers to Moses who approached his Creator with entreaties. '*But the rich answereth harshly*'; this refers to the richest Being in the world, God, who answered him harshly, as it is said, SPEAK NO MORE UNTO ME (III, 26). Another explanation: R. Joḥanan said: '*The poor useth entreaties*'; this refers to the prophets of Israel. '*But the rich answereth impudently*'[3]; this refers to the prophets of the other nations. R. Joḥanan said: There was no more righteous man amongst the nations of the world than Job, and yet he addressed God with reproaches, as it is said, *I would order my cause before Him, and fill my mouth with arguments* (Job XXIII, 4); there are no greater prophets than Moses and Isaiah, and yet both of them approached God with

[1] Num. R. XVIII, 20. [2] I.e. because he prayed AT THAT TIME; when his hour was gone, his prayer was not accepted.

[3] The Hebrew *'azuth* may mean both harshly and impudently, as E.V. '*Harshly*' is more suitable to the preceding interpretation, while here the E.V. can be retained.

supplications. Isaiah said, *O Lord, be gracious unto us; we have waited for Thee* (Isa. XXXIII, 2); and Moses said: AND I BESOUGHT THE LORD.

Another explanation: AND I BESOUGHT THE LORD. This can be compared to a noble lady who gave birth to a son; so long as he was alive she used to enter the palace by right; when, however, her son died she began to seek entry through supplications. Similarly, so long as Israel remained alive in the wilderness Moses used to address God peremptorily[1] [as for example], *Lord, why doth Thy wrath wax hot against Thy people* (Ex. XXXII, 11); *Pardon, I pray Thee, the iniquity of this people*, etc. (Num. XIV, 19). When, however, the Israelites had died out in the wilderness Moses began to entreat [God] with supplications to be permitted to enter the Land of Israel, [as it is said], AND I BESOUGHT, etc.

5. AT THAT TIME. At which time? At the time when Joshua was appointed leader, as it is said, *And I commanded Joshua at that time* (Deut. III, 21). R. Huna said: As soon as God said to Moses, 'Hand over your office to Joshua,' immediately Moses began to pray to be permitted to enter the land. He can be compared to a governor who so long as he retained his office could be sure that whatever orders he gave, the king would confirm; he redeemed whomsoever he desired and imprisoned whomsoever he desired. But as soon as he retired and another was appointed in his place, he had in vain to ask the gate-keeper to let him enter [the palace]. Similarly, so long as Moses remained in office he imprisoned whomsoever he desired, as it is said, *So they, and all that appertained to them, went down alive into the pit* (Num. XVI, 33); and he released whomsoever he desired, as it is said, *Let Reuben live, and not die* (Deut. XXXIII, 6). But when he was relieved of his office and Joshua was appointed in his stead, as it is said, *Take Joshua, the son of Nun* (Num. XXVII, 18), he began to supplicate to be permitted to enter the land. God replied: LET IT SUFFICE THEE (III, 26).

[1] Heb. בזרוע. Lit. 'with (a mighty) arm'.

6. Another explanation: AT THAT TIME, SAYING (LE'MOR). What is the force of the word LE'MOR? R. 'Azariah said: It is an intimation to the future generations to pray in time of trouble; for although to Moses it was said, *For thou shalt not go over this Jordan* (Deut. III, 27), yet he began to supplicate [God].

Another explanation: What is the force of the word LE'MOR? R. Akiba said: Moses said: 'Master of the Universe, give me an answer to my words, whether I am to enter the land or not.'[1]

Another explanation: What is the force of the word, LE'MOR? [Moses] said before God: 'Master of the Universe, let my [actual] sin be written down for future generations.'[2] R. Samuel said: This may be compared to a king[3] who issued a decree that whosoever should gather and eat from the [unripe] fruits of the Sabbatical year[4] should be made to walk around the public assembly grounds [in disgrace]. One woman went and gathered and ate of the fruits; and she was made to walk around the public assembly grounds. She said to the king: 'Your Majesty, I implore you, let these unripe fruits be suspended from my neck so that the people of the city shall not say that I am guilty of witchcraft or some act of immorality; and when they see the unripe fruits around my neck they will know that it is on their account that I am made to walk around the public assembly grounds.' So Moses said before God: 'Let my actual sin be written down for future generations that Israel may not say, "Moses falsified something in the Torah," or, "he spoke something which

[1] Interpreting: '*And I besought the Lord*' (beseeching Him) *to say* (whether I should enter the Promised Land).

[2] Now rendering: '*And I besought the Lord to say*' (what my real sin was). In this and the preceding passage the subject of LE'MOR is God, not Moses, as in E.V.

[3] Cf. Lev. R. XXXI, 4.

[4] Cf. Ex. XXIII, 10 f; Lev. XXV, 2-7; 'Unripe' is added in accordance with 'E.J., who substitutes פגי (unripe fruits) for פירות (fruits); it is likewise פגי in Yoma 86*b*. The word denotes presumably fruit which though not fully ripe is, nevertheless, capable of being eaten. Such fruit was forbidden in the Sabbatical year.

he had not been commanded"[1]; and they shall know that it was merely because of the water[2] [that I was punished].' This is the force of the words, AT THAT TIME, SAYING.

7. O LORD GOD, THOU HAST BEGUN (III, 24). What is the force of the words, O LORD GOD? R. Joshua b. Ḳarḥah said: On two occasions Moses compared himself to Abraham and it was of no avail to him. How? God called to Abraham, and he answered 'Here I am', as it is said, *And said unto him, Abraham; and he said: Here am I* (Gen. XXII, 1). What is the force of, '*Here am I*'? Here am I ready for priesthood, here am I ready for kingship. And he received both priesthood and kingship. Whence do we know that he received priesthood? For it is said, *The Lord hath sworn, and will not repent: Thou art a priest for ever after the manner of Melchizedek* (Ps. CX, 4). He also merited kingship, as it is said, *At the vale of Shaveh—the same is the king's vale* (Gen. XIV, 17).[3] Moses, too, desired to do the same, as it said, *And said: Moses, Moses. And he said: Here am I* (Ex. III, 4); here am I for priesthood, here am I for kingship. God, however, said to him: *Glorify not thyself in the presence of the king, and stand not in the place of great men* (Prov. XXV, 6). God said to him: '*Draw not nigh hither* (Ex. III, 5); you have no title to priesthood, as it is said, *And the common man that draweth nigh shall be put to death* (Num. I, 51); you have no title to kingship, as it is said, [*Who am I, O Lord God* . . .] *that thou hast brought me thus far?*' (II Sam. VII, 18).[4] Abraham said: *O Lord God, what wilt Thou give me* (Gen. XV, 2)? R. Levi said: Abraham said to God: 'Master of the Universe, if it is due to me that I should have children, then give them to me, and if not, give them to me for

[1] And for that he was punished by not being permitted to enter Eretz Israel. [2] Num. XX, 7 ff.

[3] Which according to the Rabbis was so called because Abraham was unanimously made king there; cf. Gen. R. XLII, 5.

[4] The first is based on the phrase 'drawing nigh' found in the first and second verses quoted; the second on the word *halom* (hither, thus far), which occurs in the first and third verses quoted.

mercy sake.' God answered him: 'I swear, that it is due to you,' [as it is written], *And behold, the word of the Lord came unto him, saying: This man shall not be thine heir* (*ib.* 4). Moses likewise said: 'O LORD GOD, THOU HAST BEGUN; if it is due to me that I should enter the Land of Israel, let me enter, and if not, let me enter for mercy sake.'[1] God, however, answered him: '"*Glorify not thyself in the presence of the king, etc.*" FOR THOU WILT NOT PASS OVER THIS JORDAN.' And when Moses saw how emphatic God's words were, he began to plead strenuously.[2]

8. O LORD GOD, THOU HAST BEGUN: [Moses] said to God: 'Master of the Universe, why may I not enter the land? Is it because I said [to Israel], "*Hear now, ye rebels*"? (Num. XX, 10). *Thou* hast made use of these words before I did, viz. *To be kept there for a token against the rebellious children*' (*ib.* XVII, 25).[3] Another explanation: THOU HAST BEGUN. R. Reuben said: Moses said to God: 'Why dost Thou act thus towards me? It was Thou who didst first approach me.' Whence this? For it is said, *And the angel of the Lord appeared unto him in a flame of fire out of the midst of a bush* (Ex. III, 2). Moses continued: 'Having made me great, wilt Thou now degrade me?' God replied: 'Behold I have sworn.' Said Moses: 'Master of the Universe, THOU HAST BEGUN (HAḤILOTHA). Didst Thou not break (*ḥillalta*) Thine own oath when Thou didst desire it? Didst Thou not swear to destroy Thy children because of the [Golden] Calf and yet Thou didst retract,' as it is said, *And the Lord repented* (Ex. XXXII, 14)?[4]

[1] This comment is based on the designation '*Lord God*'. According to the Rabbis 'Lord' (the Tetragrammaton) depicts Him under His Attribute of Mercy; 'God' (*Elohim*), under His Attribute of Justice; cf. Gen. R. XII, 15.

[2] The passage that follows is really a continuation of this, explaining what his harsh words were. It is erroneously made the commencement of a new section in the Wilna ed., but the Warsaw ed. runs the two together.

[3] Thus interpreting THOU HAST BEGUN, Thou wast the first to speak thus.

[4] The verse is now rendered: Thou didst break (Thine oath on a previous occasion), '*haḥilotha*' being now derived from *ḥallel*.

Another explanation: R. Levi said: Moses said to God: 'Master of the Universe, the bones of Joseph are entering the Land, and am I not to enter the Land?' The Holy One, blessed be He, answered him: 'He who acknowledged his native land is to be buried in that land but he who did not acknowledge his native land does not merit to be buried in his land.' Whence do we know that Joseph acknowledged his native land? His mistress exclaimed of him, *See, he hath brought in a Hebrew*, etc. (Gen. XXXIX, 14); and he did not deny it, but in addition said, *For indeed I was stolen away out of the land of the Hebrews* (Gen. XL, 15); he is to be buried in his native land. Whence do we know this? For it is said, *And the bones of Joseph, which the children of Israel brought up out of Egypt, buried they in Shechem* (Josh. XXIV, 32). 'But you who did not acknowledge your native land will not be buried in that land.' When was this? When the daughters of Jethro said, *An Egyptian delivered us out of the hand of the shepherds* (Ex. II, 19), and Moses heard and kept silence; therefore he is not to be buried in his land.

9. FOR THOU SHALT NOT GO OVER THIS JORDAN (III, 27). God said to Moses: 'If you are buried here, near those [who died in the wilderness], then they will enter the land for your sake [at the time of Resurrection].[1] R. Levi said: This may be compared to a man who dropped some coins[2] over the floor in a dark place; he thought to himself, 'If I call out, "Bring me a light so that I may pick up my coins," no one will take notice of me.' What did he do? He took a gold piece and threw it amongst his coins and began calling out, 'Bring me a light, I had a gold piece and I dropped it here,' and they brought him a light. What did he do? As soon as he picked up the gold piece he said to the people, 'I adjure you, wait for me until I have picked up my coins'; and he collected them. Because of the one golden piece all his smaller coins were collected. Similarly, God said to Moses: 'Should you be buried near those who

[1] Cf. Num. R. XIX, 13. [2] Of small denomination.

died in the wilderness, then they will enter the land for your sake, and you will be at their head,' as it is said, *And he chose a first part for himself, for there a portion of a ruler was reserved; and there came the heads of the people* (Deut. XXXIII, 21).[1]

10. FOR WHAT GREAT NATION IS THERE, THAT HATH GOD SO NIGH UNTO THEM (IV, 7). *Halachah:* Is it permissible for a Jew to make a pause after reading the *shema'*[2] before continuing with the *tefillah?*[3] Our Rabbis have learnt thus[4]: In three actions there must be an immediate sequence. The slaughtering of the sacrifice should follow immediately on the laying of the hands on the animal,[5] the grace [after meals] must follow immediately on the washing of the hands[6]; the *tefillah* must follow immediately on the benediction of redemption.[7] And what is the reward of him who acts thus? Rabbah b. Abbahu said: If one slaughters the sacrifice immediately after laying his hands on it, he may be confident that his sacrifice will be accepted; and if he recited the Grace [after meals] immediately after the washing of his hands he may rest assured that no mishap will mar his meal; and if immediately after reciting the *shema'* he continues with the *tefillah* he may be certain that his prayer will be answered.

R. Judah b. R. Simon said: You will find that idols are near and yet distant, and the Holy One, blessed be He, is distant and yet near. How are idols near? A heathen makes an idol and places it within his house, then that idol is near unto him. And whence do we know that [this very] idol is also distant? For it is said, *Yea, though one cry unto him, he cannot answer, nor save him*, etc. (Isa. XLVI, 7);

[1] Rendering: *And he* (Moses) *chose a first part for himself*—viz. a grave in the wilderness so that for his sake *There might come the heads of the people*—together with him, at the Resurrection. [2] Cf. P.B., p. 40 ff. [3] *Ib.*, pp. 44 ff. [4] Cf. Ber. 42*a*; J. Ber. I, 2*d*. See also Ginzberg, *Genizah Studies*, vol. I, p. 496, n. 6. [5] Cf. Lev. I, 4.
[6] I.e. the washing of the hands after meals, but from the Jerusalem Talmud (*loc. cit.*) it would appear to refer to the washing of the hands before meals. [7] Heb. *Ge'ulah*, the name given to the benediction coming immediately before the *tefillah*. Cf. P.B., p. 44.

thus the idol is distant. And God is distant and yet near. How? R. Judah b. Simon said: From here [the earth] unto heaven is a journey of five hundred years; hence He is distant. Whence do we know that He is also near? A man stands at prayer and meditates in his heart and God is near unto his prayer, as it is said, *O Thou that hearest prayer, unto Thee doth all flesh come* (Ps. LXV, 3). David said before God: 'Master of the Universe, when the nations of the world come to pray before Thee do not answer them, for they do not approach Thee with a perfect heart, but they first appeal to their idol, and when it does not answer them and they see their sore plight they approach Thee; then do Thou also not answer them,' as it says, *They cried, but there was none to save; even unto the Lord, but He answered them not* (Ps. XVIII, 42). What is the meaning of, '*They cried*'? [They cried] to their idol. And when they then approach Thee, '*Unto the Lord, but He answered them not.*' But when Israel call unto Thee, 'Hear Thou our prayer' immediately, as it is said, *Answer me when I call* (*ib.* IV, 2). God said to him [David]: 'You say, "*Answer me when I call*"; by your life, even before you call will I answer you,' as it is said, *Before they call, I will answer* (Isa. LXV, 24); for I have no other nation but you. Whence do you know this? From what we read in the same context, FOR WHAT GREAT NATION IS THERE THAT HATH GOD SO NEAR UNTO THEM, AS THE LORD OUR GOD IS WHENSOEVER WE CALL UPON HIM?

11. *The Lord answer thee in the day of trouble* (Ps. XX, 2). The Rabbis say: This may be compared to a son of a king who took to evil ways. He had three teachers, one of whom said: 'Let chains weighing one hundred pounds be made for him'; the second said, 'He cannot endure chains weighing one hundred pounds; let chains weighing twelve pounds be made for him'; the third came and said, 'How can he endure chains twelve pounds in weight? Let rather chains weighing one pound be made for him'. Likewise, Moses declared, 'Let chains weighing one hundred pounds be made for him [Israel],' as it is said,

And many evils and troubles shall come upon them (Deut. XXXI, 17); David said, 'Let chains weighing twelve pounds be made for him,' as it is said, '*The Lord answer thee in the day of trouble,*' just as the day consists of twelve hours; when, however, Jeremiah arose, he said to God, 'Master of the Universe, they have not the strength to endure even "*the day of evil*" of which David spoke, let then chains weighing one pound be made instead for them,' as it is said, *And it is a time*[1] *of trouble unto Jacob, but out of it shall he be saved* (Jer. XXX, 7).

Another explanation: '*The Lord answer thee in the day of trouble.*' What is the meaning of '*The day of trouble*'? Resh Laḳish said: Just as, when a women in labour is seated in the travailing chair, people say unto her, 'May He who answered your mother answer you,' so said David to Israel: 'He who answered Jacob, He will answer you.' What did Jacob pray? *And I will make there an altar unto God who answered me* in the day of my trouble (Gen. XXXV, 3); 'so as for you,' [said David to Israel], '"*The Lord answer thee* in the day of trouble"; *the name of the God of Jacob set thee up on high.*' Moses said before God: 'Master of the Universe, when Thou seest Thy children in distress, and they have no one to intercede on their behalf, answer Thou them immediately.' God replied: 'Moses, by your life, at any time that they call upon Me I will answer them,' as it is written, AS THE LORD IS WHENEVER WE CALL UPON HIM (IV, 7).

12. Another explanation: AS THE LORD OUR GOD. This bears out what Scripture says, *But as for me, let my prayer be unto Thee, in an acceptable time* (Ps. LXIX, 14). R. Ḥanina b. Papa asked R. Samuel b. Naḥman: 'What is the meaning of the verse, "*But as for me, let my prayer be unto Thee in an acceptable time*"?' He replied: 'The gates of prayer are sometimes open and sometimes closed, but the gates of repentance always remain open.' He then asked

[1] Understood as a short period, a single hour, and so corresponding to a chain one pound in weight.

him: 'Whence [do you know this]?' [R. Samuel replied]: 'Because it is written, *With wondrous works dost Thou answer us in righteousness, O God of our salvation; Thou the confidence of all the ends of the earth, and of the far distant seas* (*ib.* LXV, 6). Just as the ritual bath is sometimes open and sometimes closed, so too are the gates of prayer sometimes open and sometimes closed; but as the sea ever remains open, so is the hand of God ever open to receive the penitent.'[1] R. 'Anan said: The gates of prayer also are never closed, for it is written, AS THE LORD OUR GOD IS WHENEVER WE CALL UPON HIM; and CALLING is nothing else but praying, as Scripture in another context has it, '*And it shall come to pass that, before they call I will answer*' (Isa. LXV, 24). R. Ḥiyya the elder said: It is written, *Wait for the Lord; be strong, and let thy heart take courage; yea, wait thou for the Lord* (Ps. XXVII, 14); pray and pray again, and you may light upon the hour when your prayer will be answered.

Another explanation: '*But as for me, let my prayer*, etc.' David, because he prayed as an individual, said '*In an acceptable time*'[2]; but the prayer of a community never remains unanswered. This is the force of the expression AS THE LORD OUR GOD IS WHENEVER WE CALL UPON HIM.

13. FOR WHAT GREAT NATION IS THERE, THAT HATH GOD SO NIGH UNTO THEM. Some heretics[3] asked R. Simlai: 'How many Powers created the world?' He replied: 'You and I, let us together inquire into the record of creation.' Said they to him: 'Is it then written,

[1] The comparison is made because the sea too can serve as a ritual bath. Possibly he translates the end of the verse thus: *Thou art . . . a sea to those who are distant*—i.e. estranged—through sin.

[2] The prayer of an individual is not invariably answered. Therefore David expressed the hope that his prayer would be uttered at an '*acceptable time*' and so answered.

[3] מין, lit. 'kind, species'; used to denote a sectarian, heretic, or Christian Gnostic who doubted the authority of the Jewish Scriptures. See, Herford, *Christianity in Talmud and Midrash*, pp. 255 ff. Compare Gen. R. VIII, 9; San. 38*b*; J. Ber. IX, 12*d*, 13*a*.

In the beginning God created? It is written, *In the beginning Gods*[1] *created'* (Gen. I, 1). He replied: 'Is it then written, They created? it is written, "*He created.*" And [further] is it written, "And the gods said: Let there be a firmament; let the waters be gathered; let there be lights"? It is written, *And He said.*'[2] When they came to the account of the sixth day they triumphantly said to him: 'Behold it is written, *Let us make man in our image'* (*ib.* 26). He replied: 'It is not written here, "And they created man in their image," but, *And God created man in His own image'* (*ib.* 27). Said they to him: 'But is it written, "*For what great nation is there that hath gods so nigh*[3] *unto them*"?' He replied: 'Is it then written, "As the Lord our God is whenever we call upon them"? It is written, "*Whenever we call upon Him.*"'[4]

14. Another explanation: THAT HATH GOD SO NIGH UNTO THEM. R. Johanan said: When the ministering angels assemble before God and ask, 'When is the New Year and when is the Day of Atonement?'[5] God says to them: 'Why do you ask Me? You and I, let us all go to the Court[6] on earth [and inquire of them].' Whence [is this to be inferred]? For it is written, [FOR WHAT GREAT NATION IS THERE] THAT HATH GOD SO NIGH UNTO THEM. Scripture does not say here, 'That hath a people so nigh unto Him,' but, '*That hath a God so nigh unto them,*' that is to say, He and all his heavenly entourage.[7] R. Johanan said: God said to Israel: 'Before you became My people the festivals were *The appointed seasons* of the

[1] Translating the plural אלהים literally.
[2] The verbs are all in the singular.
[3] Here the participle, too, is in the plural.
[4] Hence the plural where it occurs is merely the *pluralis majestatis*.
[5] Cf. Ex. R. XV, 2.
[6] The Beth din.
[7] פמליא, Lat. *familia*. The point is that by describing God as near to Israel rather than the reverse the text indicates that God leans upon Israel, as it were, and depends on them, and the Midrash explains that this is the case in the fixing of the festivals, God accepting Israel's decision.—The addition of 'His heavenly entourage' is probably due to the plural form of '*nigh*' (*kerobim* instead of *karob*).

Lord (Lev. XXIII, 2), but henceforward they shall be the seasons *Which* ye *shall proclaim.*'[1]

15. Another explanation: THAT HATH GOD SO NIGH UNTO THEM. If a man has a rich relative he acknowledges him,[2] but if he is poor, he disowns him and disclaims any relationship with him; but the Holy One, blessed be He, if one may say so, when Israel found themselves in Egyptian bondage said: 'I am their relative.' Whence this? For it is said, *Even for the children of Israel, a people near unto Him* (Ps. CXLVIII, 14). Further, if a man has a poor relative he considers that he himself comes first and his relative is of secondary importance. What does he say? 'So-and-so claims relationship with me.' But God, if one may say so, gives Israel the first place. For Scripture does not say here, That hath a nation so nigh unto Him, but THAT HATH A GOD SO NIGH UNTO THEM.

Another explanation: FOR WHAT GREAT NATION. R. Ḥama b. Ḥanina said: What other nation is there whose God hath made her so powerful as God has made this people [Israel]? Usually when a nation desires to make war they do not know whether they will be victorious or not; but Israel are always confident of victory, as it is said, FOR WHAT GREAT NATION, etc.

16. Another explanation: R. Tanḥuma said: It happened that there was once a ship full of Gentiles and amongst them there was a Jew. When they came to an island the Gentiles said to the Jew: 'You, So-and-so, take money and go into the island and purchase something for us.' He replied: 'Am I not a stranger? Have I then any idea where to go?' Said they: 'Is then a Jew ever a stranger? Wherever you go, your God is with you.' This is the force of the words, THAT HATH GOD SO NIGH UNTO THEM.

[1] The authority to fix the exact times of these festivals is delegated to the religious leaders (the Beth din). Before the fixed Calendar was introduced by the Patriarch Hillel II, the new moon was fixed by observation and the incidence of the festivals depended upon the day fixed as new moon. [2] Cf. Ex. R. XXXI, 5.

17. What is the meaning of, WHENSOEVER WE CALL UPON HIM? The Rabbis said: A prayer can be answered after forty days, as can be learnt from Moses, as it is written, *And I fell down before the Lord . . . forty days*, etc. (Deut. IX, 18); it can be answered after twenty days, as can be learnt from Daniel, as it is written, *I ate no pleasant bread . . . till three whole weeks were fulfilled* (Dan. X, 3); and after this he prayed, *O Lord, hear, O Lord forgive* (*ib.* IX, 19); and it can be answered after three days, as can be learnt from Jonah, as it is written, *And Jonah was in the belly of the fish three days and three nights* (Jonah II, 1), and after that [Scripture says], *Then Jonah prayed unto the Lord his God out of the fish's belly* (*ib.* 2); it can be answered after one day, as can be learnt from Elijah, as it is written, *And it came to pass at the time of the offering of the evening sacrifice, that Elijah the prophet came near, and said*, etc. (I Kings XVIII, 36); and it can also be answered at its time of utterance,[1] as can be learnt from David, as it is written, '*But as for me, let my prayer be unto Thee, O Lord, in an acceptable time*' (Ps. LXIX, 14); while sometimes God answers a prayer even before it is uttered, as it is said, '*And it shall come to pass that, before they call, I will answer*' (Isa. LXV, 24).

18. WHEN THOU SHALT BEGET CHILDREN (IV, 25). *Halachah*[2]*:* Is it permissible for a Jew to round the corners of his head?[3] The Sages have learnt thus: These things are prohibited because they savour of heathen practices[4]; to trim the front of the hair[5] and to grow one's locks.[6] What is meant by, 'To trim the front of the hair'? It means to cut the front of one's hair so as to form 'a handle of

[1] I.e. in the same day or night. [2] Tosef. Shab. 6 (7); B.Ḳ. 83*a*.
[3] Cf. Lev. XIX, 27. [4] Lit. 'the ways of the Emorites'.
[5] קומי, Gk. *κόμη* hair. ספר קומי, to trim the front of the hair like a fringe on the forehead, and let the curls hang down on the temples.
[6] בלורית, etymology uncertain. According to Jast. it is derived from בלל = בלר, something twisted, hence plait, locks of hair. Krauss (*Wörterbuch*) takes it from the Latin, *galerus*, wig. Roman and Greek youths of the upper classes wore long locks of hair which they offered to the gods on arriving at puberty.

locks'.[1] What penalty does one incur [for so doing]? He receives forty lashes.[2] But he who grows his locks does so expressly as an act of idolatrous worship, and there is no severer penalty than that incurred for idolatry, for God Himself is jealous of it, as it is said, *Thou shalt have no other gods before Me*, etc. (Ex. xx, 3); and it is written, *For the Lord thy God is a devouring fire, a jealous God* (Deut. iv, 24). The Rabbis say: Seeing that there is no reality in idols, why does Scripture apply the term 'deity' to them? R. Phinehas b. Ḥama said: In order to assign a reward to anyone who turns away from idolatry. God said: 'Although there is no reality in it, yet as soon as a man turns away from it I account it unto him as if he were worshipping Him who really is, and as if he came to Me.'

R. Joshua b. Levi said: God said: 'Seeing that the penalty for idol worship is so severe I must forewarn them [Israel] against it, so that they should not later on say, "Had we been warned we would have kept away from it."' God said to Isaiah: 'Do not think that I have not warned Israel against idol worship, long ago. Already long before they came to Sinai to receive the Torah I warned them against idolatry.' Whence do we know this? For so it is written, *Therefore I have declared it to thee from of old; before thou camest*[3] *I announced it to thee* (Isa. xlviii, 5): 'Before you came to Sinai have I caused you to hear the Blessings and Curses.'[4] Why? Lest you should say: *Mine idol hath done them, and my graven image and my molten image hath commanded them* (*ib.*). Therefore have I forewarned them concerning it [idolatry], and it is through Moses, my servant, that I forewarned them.' Whence do we know this? From what is written in our context. WHEN THOU SHALT BEGET CHILDREN AND CHILDREN'S CHILDREN, etc.

[1] קורצין, corrected by Jast. into קווצות curls, locks; hence תפיסות קווצות 'a handle of locks'.

[2] Cf. Deut. xxv, 3. In practice only 39 lashes were administered.

[3] Regarding תבא as 2nd person masc.; E.V. '*Before it came to pass*', understanding it to be 3rd person fem.

[4] Lev. xxvi; Deut. xxviii.

19. Another explanation: This bears out what Scripture says, *The more they were increased* (ke-rubbam),[1] *the more they sinned against Me; I will change their glory into shame* (Hos. IV, 7). What is the meaning of, '*ke-rubbam*'? R. Samuel b. Naḥmani said: Whatever the leaders do, the masses[2] do. How? The *Nasi*[3] rules that a thing is permissible; the President of the Court then says[4]: The *Nasi* has ruled that the thing is permissible; shall I then forbid it? And the Judges say: The President of the Court has ruled that the thing is permissible; shall we then forbid it? And the masses say: The Judges ruled that the thing is permissible; shall we then forbid it? Who then caused the whole generation to sin? It is surely the *Nasi*, who was the first to sin. R. Simlai said: It is written, *For their mother hath played the harlot, she that conceived them hath done shamefully* (*ib.* II, 7). [The verse alludes to the leaders] who put their own words to shame before the ordinary people. How? The Sage expounds in public the prohibition against lending money on usury, and yet he himself lends his money on usury; he teaches, Thou shalt not rob, and yet he himself robs; *Thou shalt not steal*, and yet he himself steals. R. Berekiah said: Once it happened that a man had his cloak stolen and he went to complain to the judge and he found the cloak spread out on his bed. R. Berekiah further said: Once it happened that a man had his kettle stolen and he went to complain to the judge about it and he found it upon his oven. Hence [the force of] the words: '*Even as their teacher*,[1] so *they sinned against Me.*'

Another explanation: '*The more they were increased, the more they sinned against Me.*' R. Tanḥuma said: The more territory I gave them the more they sinned against me.[5] Whence this? For it is said, *Yea, their altars are as heaps in the furrows of the field* (*ib.* XII, 12).[6]

[1] The Midrash takes the word כרובם ('the more they were increased') in the sense of כרבם ('like their teacher').

[2] Lit. 'the generation'. [3] The Head of the Sanhedrin.

[4] Adopting the reading אומר instead of אוסר.

[5] כרובם is now interpreted literally.

[6] This is explained in the Proems to Lam. R. thus: They erected idolatrous altars on every furrow of the field.

Another explanation: The more riches I gave them, the more they sinned against Me. Whence this? For it is said, *Of their silver and their gold have they made them idols* (*ib.* VIII, 4).

Another explanation: The more kings I gave them, the more they sinned against Me. Whence this? For it is said, *All their kings are fallen, there is none among them that calleth unto Me* (*ib.* VII, 7).

Another explanation: The more children I gave them, the more they sinned against Me, as it is said, WHEN THOU SHALT BEGET CHILDREN.

20. Another explanation: WHEN THOU SHALT BEGET CHILDREN. This bears out what Scripture says, *The wages of the righteous is life; the increase of the wicked is sin* (Prov. X, 16). '*The wages of the righteous is life.*' R. Tanḥum says: This refers to Eliphaz, who grew up in the lap of Isaac.[1] '*The increase of the wicked is sin.*' This refers to Amalek, who grew up in the lap of Esau.

Another explanation: '*The wages of the righteous is life*': Whatever David and Solomon his son did was to give life to Israel. What is the meaning of, '*The increase of the wicked is sin*'? The one entry (*biah*)[2] that Manasseh made into the Temple was the cause of sin unto Israel, for he made a four-faced idol and brought it into the Holy of Holies. Whence this? For it is said, *And behold northward of the gate of the altar this image of jealousy*[3] *in the entry*—be-biah (Ezek. VIII, 5). R. Aḥa said: Oh, this great wrong (*bia*) in the world, that the stranger dislodges the owner![4]

[1] Eliphaz was Esau's son (v. Gen. XXXVI, 4). According to legend (quoted by Rashi in Gen. XXIX, 10) he was bidden by his father to pursue Jacob and slay him. Owing, however, to the influence of the teachings of Isaac, which he had imbibed, he forbore to do this, and as a compromise, in order not to disobey his father wholly, he deprived Jacob of all his possessions. To this legend the Midrash alludes.

[2] This is a play on words, *tebuath* ('the increase') being derived from *bo*, 'to come,' 'enter.'

[3] Cf. II Kings XXI, 7.

[4] I.e. the idols displace God. ביא״, Gk. *βία* 'violence': the verse is rendered: . . . *This image of jealousy* (whose presence there) was a great wrong.

And why did he make a four-faced idol? To correspond to the four *ḥayyoth* that bear God's throne.[1]

Another explanation: Why a four-faced idol? To correspond to the four cardinal points. He [Manasseh] said: Let every one who comes from the four cardinal points bow down to this idol. And what did God do unto him? He delivered him into the hand of his enemies. Whence do we know this? For it said, *Wherefore the Lord brought upon them the captains of the host of the king of Assyria, who took Manasseh with hooks, and bound him with fetters* (II Chron. XXXIII, 11). They made a copper mule and they put him into it and kindled a fire under it so that he was burnt within. Whereupon Manasseh called upon every idol to which he had [formerly] offered sacrifices and not one of them answered him, as it is said, *Yea, though one cry unto him, he cannot answer, nor save him out of his trouble* (Isa. XLVI, 7). When Manasseh saw that he was in a sore plight, and that not one of these idols answered him, he began to call upon God. He said: 'Master of the Universe, behold, I have called upon all the idols of the world and I have learnt that there is no reality in them; Thou Master of the Universe art a God above all gods, and if Thou wilt not answer me I will declare, heaven forfend, that all Beings are alike.' Thereupon God answered him: 'Ah, wicked man, by right, I should not answer you, because you have provoked Me to anger; but in order not to close the door before the penitent, that they should not say, "Lo, Manasseh sought to repent but he was not received," I will answer you.' Whence do we know this? For it is said, *And he prayed unto Him; and He was entreated* (wayye'ather) *of him* (II Chron. XXXIII, 13); read, *wayyeḥather*.[2] This teaches that the ministering angels had closed up the windows of the firmament to prevent his prayer reaching heaven, but what did God do? He broke through the firmament beneath His Throne of Glory and received his prayer, and He restored him to his kingdom in

[1] Cf. Ezek. I, 5.
[2] He allowed (the firmament) to be broken through.

Jerusalem.[1] R. Samuel b. Unya said in the name of R. Aḥa: He brought him back on the wind, as one says, 'Thou causest the wind to blow.' At that moment Manasseh knew that *the Lord, He is God.*[2] Another explanation: '*The wages of the righteous is life*': this refers to those righteous [Israelites], Moses' contemporaries, who entered the promised land[3]; '*The increase of the wicked is sin*': [this refers to the wicked of the same generation, as it is written], WHEN THOU SHALT BEGET CHILDREN AND CHILDREN'S CHILDREN, AND YE SHALL HAVE BEEN LONG IN THE LAND, AND SHALL DEAL CORRUPTLY . . . AND SHALL DO THAT WHICH IS EVIL IN THE SIGHT OF THE LORD THY GOD, TO PROVOKE HIM (IV, 25).

21. What is meant by TO PROVOKE HIM? R. Eleazar said: They sat and cudgelled their brains to find the gravest form of immorality, as it is said, *And each hath committed abomination with his neighbour's wife; and each hath lewdly defiled* (be-zimah) *his daughter-in-law* (Ezek. XXII, 11). What is meant by '*be-zimah*'? In their mind they argued[4]: The punishment for committing adultery with a married woman is strangulation; and for committing adultery with one's daughter-in-law is stoning; thus adultery with one's daughter-in-law is a grosser form of sin than adultery with a married woman.[5]

R. Ishmael taught: [Scripture says]: *And a man and his father go unto the same maid* (Amos II, 7): You might think that it was for the sake of lust, therefore the text adds, *To profane My holy name.* This is the force of the expression, TO PROVOKE HIM. R. Levi said: Israel was not exiled until seven generations[6] became wicked;

[1] The idea, of course, is that nothing can stand in the way of true repentance. [2] Quoted from I Kings XVIII, 39.

[3] Presumably this refers to the second generation after the Exodus.

[4] A play upon the double meaning of the word, זמה: (1) 'lewdness,' (2) 'thought,' 'calculation.'

[5] Since stoning is severer than strangulation.

[6] Or: seven royal dynasties, viz.: Jeroboam, Baasha, Ahab, Jehu, Pekah the son of Remalia, Menahem the son of Godi, and Hosea the son of Elah—each with his descendants ('E.J.).

BANIM[1] (CHILDREN) [signifies] two generations, BENE BANIM (CHILDREN'S CHILDREN) two generations, WENOSHANTEM (AND YE SHALL HAVE BEEN LONG) one; WEHISHḤATEM (AND SHALL CORRUPT YOURSELVES) one; WA'ASITHEM (AND MAKE) one; lo, these make seven.

22. The Rabbis say: May the name of God be blessed, who knows what has been, and what will in the future be, as it is written, *Declaring the end from the beginning*, etc. (Isa. XLVI, 10). How so? In this section Moses revealed to Israel how if they sinned they would be exiled, how they would repent, and how they would be redeemed. How they would sin, as it is written, AND SHALL DO THAT WHICH IS EVIL IN THE SIGHT OF THE LORD (IV, 25), and after this follows AND THE LORD SHALL SCATTER YOU AMONG THE PEOPLES (*ib.* 27), and after this, IN THY DISTRESS (BAẒAR LEKA) WHEN ALL THESE THINGS ARE COME UPON THEE (*ib.* 30). What is the force of BAẒAR LEKA? R. Joḥanan said in the name of R. Akiba: Any distress that is confined to an individual is a real distress, but any distress that is not confined to an individual [but is shared by the community] is not such a distress.[2]

Another explanation: BAẒAR LEKA. R. Joḥanan gave it as his own opinion: Any distress shared by Israel and the nations of the world is a real distress, but any distress confined to Israel is not such a distress.[3] R. Joḥanan elucidating his interpretation gave as an example the distress in Shushan, the capital, which was confined to Israel, as it is said, *There was great mourning among the Jews* (Est. IV, 3); God, however, immediately caused

[1] In Deut. IV, 25, which R. Levi makes a kind of *noṭariḳon*. Two is the least number expressed by plural.
[2] Hence the Jewish proverb, 'A distress shared by the community is in itself a half of consolation.' This is based on the use of the singular LEKA (THY) instead of *lakem* (your), whence we conclude: only when the trouble is thine alone may it really be called DISTRESS.
[3] Because God quickly hears their prayers ('E.J.). The Yalḳuṭ, however, reverses the reading, and this is preferable.

salvation to spring forth. Whence [do we know this? For Scripture says], *The Jews had light and gladness* (*ib.* VIII, 16).

23. Another explanation: R. Eleazar said: Israel were redeemed from Egypt only because of the following five reasons: (i) Distress, (ii) Repentance, (iii) The Merits of the Fathers, (iv) God's Mercy, (v) The Term [of their slavery, which had come to an end]. Because of Distress, as it is written, *And the children of Israel sighed* (Ex. II, 23). Repentance, as it is written, *And their cry came up* (*ib.*); because of the Merits of the Fathers, as it is written, *And God remembered His covenant* (*ib.* 24); because of God's Mercy, as it is written, *And God saw the children of Israel* (*ib.* 25); because of the Term, as it is written, *And God took cognizance of them* (*ib.*).[1] In the time to come also they will be redeemed only because of the same five reasons. Because of Distress, as it is written, IN THY DISTRESS: here we have THOU WILT RETURN TO THE LORD THY GOD (IV, 30); here we have Repentance; FOR THE LORD THY GOD IS A MERCIFUL GOD (*ib.* 31): here we have [God's] Mercy; NOR FORGET THE COVENANT OF THY FATHERS (*ib.*): here we have the Merits of the Fathers: WHEN ALL THESE THINGS ARE COME UPON THEE IN THE END OF DAYS (*ib.* 30): here we have the Term. David detailed them thus: *Nevertheless He looked upon their distress* (Ps. CVI, 44): this refers to Distress; *When he heard their cry* (*ib.*): this refers to Repentance; *And He remembered for them His covenant* (*ib.* 45): this refers to the Merits of the Fathers; *He made them also to be pitied* (*ib.* 46): this refers to God's Mercy; *Save us, O Lord our God, and gather us from among the nations* (*ib.* 47): this refers to the Term.

24. Another explanation: THOU WILT RETURN TO THE LORD THY GOD. There is nothing greater than Repentance. Once our Rabbis, R. Eliezer, R. Joshua, and R. Gamaliel, were in Rome when the Senate issued a

[1] Lit. 'And God knew'—that their term of slavery was at an end.

decree that within thirty days no Jew should be found in the [Roman] world. Now one of the Emperor's senators was a God-fearing man, and he came to R. Gamaliel and disclosed to him the decree. Our Rabbis were in great distress, but that God-fearing man said to them, 'Do not be distressed; within thirty days the God of the Jews will arise to help them.' At the end of twenty-five days he revealed the decree to his wife, and she said to him, 'Lo, twenty-five days have already gone.' He answered her, 'There are still five days remaining.' Now his wife was even more righteous than he and she said to him, 'Have you not a ring?[1] Suck it and die and the sitting of the Senate will be suspended[2] for thirty days and the decree will not come into force.'[3] He followed her advice and sucked his ring and died. When the Rabbis heard of it they came to his wife to express their sympathy. The Rabbis said to her: 'Alas for the ship that has sailed without paying her dues' (meaning thereby, that this righteous man [her husband] had not been circumcised).[4] Said his wife to them: 'I fully understand the meaning of what you say; by your life, before the ship sailed, she did pay her dues.' Immediately she entered the chamber and brought out thence unto them a box wherein was the foreskin with rags full of blood upon it. The Rabbis thereupon applied to him [her husband] the following Scriptural verse, *The princes of the peoples are gathered together, the people of the God of Abraham; for unto God belong the shields of the earth. He is greatly exalted* (Ps. XLVII, 10). What is the meaning of, '*The shields of the earth*'?—God said: 'To Abraham I became a strong shield.' Whence this? For it is said, *I am thy shield* (Gen. XV, 1); 'Whereas to this one [the senator] I shall become many shields.' How? God first said to Abraham, '*And I will make of thee a great nation, and I will bless thee . . . and make thy name great* (*ib.* XII, 2), and only after that assurance

[1] Containing poison. [2] The Hebrew phrase is נטל עליך.
[3] Cf. Ta'an. 29*a*. The Romans had a rule that if the Senate made a decree and before it was carried into effect one of the senators died, the decree was annulled.
[4] This is a marginal gloss that has been interpolated into the text ('E.J.).

did Abraham circumcise himself; but this one received no such assurance from Me [and yet he circumcised himself].'[1] What is the meaning of, '*He is greatly exalted*'? This one is exalted above Abraham.

Another explanation: THOU WILT RETURN TO THE LORD THY GOD. R. Samuel Pargrita[2] said in the name of R. Meir: This can be compared to the son of a king who took to evil ways. The king sent a tutor to him who appealed to him saying, 'Repent, my son.' The son, however, sent him back to his father [with the message], 'How can I have the effrontery to return? I am ashamed to come before you.' Thereupon his father sent back word, 'My son, is a son ever ashamed to return to his father? And is it not to your father that you will be returning?' Similarly, the Holy One, blessed be He, sent Jeremiah to Israel when they sinned, and said to him: 'Go, say to My children, "Return."' Whence this? For it is said, *Go and proclaim these words*, etc. (Jer. III, 12). Israel asked Jeremiah: 'How can we have the effrontery to return to God?' Whence do we know this? For it is said, *Let us lie down in our shame, and let our confusion cover us*, etc. (*ib.* 25). But God sent back word to them: 'My children, if you return, will you not be returning to your Father?' Whence this? [For it is said], *For I am become a father to Israel*, etc. (*ib.* XXXI, 9). R. 'Azariah said: God said to Jeremiah: 'Go, tell Israel, "I will not[3] prove false to you. At Sinai you declared, *My heart yearneth for Him* (S.S. V, 4); I too say the same to you."' Whence this? For it is said, *Is Ephraim a darling son unto Me . . . therefore My heart yearneth for him* (Jer. XXXI, 20).

25. THEN MOSES SEPARATED (IV, 41). *Halachah*: How many commandments were given to Adam? The

[1] He has thereby merited that I should become many shields—i.e. afford him even greater glory and protection.
[2] In the Pesikta de R. Kahana (ed. Buber, p. 164) his name is spelt פטרגריטא. See Buber's note *ad loc.* The Matnath Kehunah quoting the 'Aruch takes Pargrita to be the name of a place—possibly Phrygia.
[3] Adopting the reading איני for אני (Radal).

Sages have learnt thus[1]: Adam was given six commandments, viz., [To refrain from] idolatry and blasphemy, [to appoint] judges, [to refrain from] murder, immorality, and robbery by violence. Rabbi says: And all these are indicated in one verse of Scripture, as it is said, *And the Lord God commanded the man, saying: Of every tree of the garden thou mayest freely eat* (Gen. II, 16). '*And [He] commanded*': this indicates idolatry, as it is said, *Because he willingly walked after filth* (Hos. V, 11).[2] '*The Lord*': this indicates blasphemy, as it is said, *And he that blasphemeth the name of the Lord* (Lev. XXIV, 16). '*God*': this indicates [the appointment of] judges, as it is said, *The cause of both parties shall come before God* (Ex. XXII, 8). '*The man*': this indicates murder, as it is said, *Whoso sheddeth man's blood*, etc. (Gen. IX, 6). '*Saying*': this indicates immorality, as it is said, *Saying: If a man put away his wife* (Jer. III, 1). '*Of every tree of the garden thou mayest freely eat*': but not of that which has been robbed; thus [man] was commanded against robbery by violence.[3] And for all these there is forgiveness except for murder, as it is said, '*Whoso sheddeth man's blood, by man shall his blood be shed*' (Gen. IX, 6). R. Levi said: Lo, how many men are there who commit murder and yet die in their bed! The reply given to him was: The meaning of, '*By man shall his blood be shed,*' is that when man shall be brought [to judgment] in the Messianic era, then his blood will be shed.[4]

It is reported of two brothers, one of whom killed the other, that their mother took a cup and filled it with his blood and placed it in a turret, and day by day when she entered the turret and looked at it she found that [the blood] was boiling; once she entered and looked and found that [the blood] was still; she then knew that her other son was

[1] Ex. R. XXX, 9; Num. R. XIV, 12; Sanh. 56*a* (Sonc. ed., p. 381) speaks of seven commandments. These are known as the Noahide precepts.
[2] A play upon the words ויצו ('*commanded*') and צו ('*filth*'). '*Filth*' is understood as a synonym for idolatry.
[3] Cf. notes on the whole passage in Sanh. (Sonc. ed.) *loc. cit.*
[4] Cf. Gen. R. XXXIV, 14.

killed, in order that the words of Scripture might be fulfilled, '*Whoso sheddeth man's blood, by man shall his blood be shed.*'

26–27. THEN MOSES SEPARATED. This bears out what Scripture says, *He that loveth silver shall not be satisfied with silver* (Eccl. V, 9). Do we not know that a man can never be satisfied? What then is the force of the words, '*With silver*'? The Rabbis said: This verse refers to scholars who love the words of the Torah which is compared to silver, as it is said, *Yea, to get understanding is rather to be chosen than silver* (Prov. XVI, 16). R. Naḥman said: He who loves Torah can never have sufficient of Torah. And what is the meaning of, *Nor he that loveth abundance with increase* (Eccl. *loc. cit.*): If one is intensely eager to accumulate learning [Torah] yet *Without increase*, that is, he does not raise disciples, *This also is vanity*. R. Aḥa said: There is no greater vanity that a man who learns Torah and does not teach [it to others].

Another explanation: '*He who loveth silver.*' R. Isaac said: He that loveth the *mizwoth* can never have sufficient of them. How [can this be illustrated]? You find that the two Immortals, David and Moses, could never have enough of them. Although God said to David, *Nevertheless thou shalt not build the house* (II Chron. VI, 9), yet David said to himself, 'Just because the Holy One, blessed be He, said "*Thou shalt not build the house*", can I sit still?' What did he do? Before he died, he busied himself with the preparation of all the necessary materials for [the Temple], as it is said, *Now, behold, in my straits I have prepared for the house of the Lord* (I Chron. XXII, 14). And so it was too with Moses. Although God had said to him, *For thou shalt not go over this Jordan* (Deut. III, 27), yet Moses immediately exclaimed, 'Shall I then depart this world without setting aside Cities of Refuge [for Israel]?' Hence, THEN MOSES SEPARATED.

What is written just before? *Know this day, and lay it to thy heart* (Deut. IV, 39). What is the force of, '*And lay it to thy heart*'? R. Meir said: God said: 'Thou and thy heart know the deeds which thou hast done and that the chastisements which I have brought upon thee are not in proportion to thy deeds.'[1]

Another explanation: '*That the Lord, he is God*' (*ib.*). The Rabbis say: Jethro attributed reality to idols, as it is said, *Now I know that the Lord is greater than all gods* (Ex. XVIII, 11). Naaman partly acknowledged them, as it is said, *Behold, now, I know that there is no God in all the* earth, *but in Israel* (II Kings V, 15).[2] Rahab placed God in heaven and upon earth, as it is said, *For the Lord your God, He is God in heaven above, and on earth beneath* (Josh. II, 11). Moses placed Him also in the intervening space, as it is said, *That the Lord, He is God in heaven above and upon the earth beneath; there is none else* (Deut. IV, 39). What is the force of '*There is none else*'? Even in the intervening space. R. Hoshaiah said: God said: '*Give her of the fruit of her hands*' (Prov. XXXI, 31); [God said to Moses]: 'You have borne testimony in my favour by declaring, "*There is none else*," I too will bear testimony in your favour by saying, *And there hath not arisen a prophet since in Israel like unto Moses*' (Deut. XXXIV, 10).

It is written in Scripture, *That it may be well with thee, and that thou mayest prolong thy days* (*ib.* XXII, 7). Israel declared before God: 'Master of the Universe, is this an example of prolongation of days? A man kills another unwittingly and the avenger of blood[3] pursues him to kill him, and both die before their time?' God thereupon answered Moses: 'By your life, Israel speak rightly. Go and set aside for them Cities of Refuge,' as it is said, THEN MOSES SEPARATED, etc. What made Moses set his heart so much on Cities of Refuge? R. Levi said:

[1] The meaning is apparently that God claimed that the chastisement was less than the sins of Israel. This may be based on the usual Rabbinic interpretation of 'Lord' (the Tetragrammaton) and 'God' (Elohim) as His designations as a God of mercy and a God of strict justice respectively. Hence the rendering: Lay it to thy heart that the God of mercy is He who when necessary is a God of justice. The separation of Cities of Refuge then follows as an instance of His mercy.

[2] *In the earth* is emphasised, implying that there are other gods in heaven ('E.J.). [3] Num. XXXV, 19.

He who has eaten of the dish knows its taste. How does this apply here? After Moses had killed the Egyptian he went out on the second day and found Dathan and Abiram quarrelling with one another, as it is said, *And he went out the second day, and, behold, two men of the Hebrews were striving together* (Ex. II, 13). (R. Aibo said: This was Dathan.)[1] He began to abuse him saying, '*Thinkest thou to kill me*' (*ib.* 14)? When Pharaoh heard this he said: 'I have heard ever so many things [about Moses] and said nothing; now that he has gone so far as to commit murder, seize him.' How did he escape from Pharaoh, that it is written, *But Moses fled from the face of Pharaoh* (*ib.* 15)? R. Jannai said: When the executioner put the sword on his neck it slid off because his neck turned to marble. And it is he [whom] Solomon praises [in the words], *Thy neck is as a tower of ivory* (S.S. VII, 5). R. Abiathar said: And what is more, the sword slid off Moses's neck and turned on the executioner. Whence this? For it is said, *And delivered me from the sword of Pharaoh* (Ex. XVIII, 4). [By this] Moses implied, 'Me God saved but not the executioner.' Bar Ḳappara said: An angel in the guise of Moses came down and made him run away, and [the Egyptians] thought that the angel was Moses. R. Joshua said: See the miracles which God wrought for Moses: of all Pharaoh's attendants, some became dumb, others deaf, and others blind; and when Moses fled, no one saw him. A proof of this is: When God desired to send Moses on His mission Moses began to hesitate; God thereupon asked him, 'Do you remember what I did to the attendants of Pharaoh,' as it is said, *And the Lord said unto him: Who hath made man's mouth? or who maketh a man dumb, or deaf, or seeing, or blind* (*ib.* IV, 11)?[2] 'At that time I stood by you; shall I not stand by you now?' R. Isaac said: Come and see that God's way of doing things is not like man's way of doing things. A man will find a Patron [i.e. a protector] who is ever ready to protect him, and should

[1] V. Ex. R. I, 29.
[2] I.e. did I not smite Pharaoh's attendants with dumbness and blindness?

he be arrested on any charge,[1] people go and find his Patron and say to him, 'Your protégé has been arrested,' and he replies: 'I will protect him,' but if the man has been taken out to be executed, where is he and where is his Patron? Not so, however, is it with God. The ministering angels declared before God: 'Moses, Thy protégé, has been arrested,' whereupon God replied: 'I will protect him.' They said: 'Lo, he is standing before Pharaoh, his sentence is being pronounced,[2] he has gone forth to be executed.' He replied: 'I will protect him.' How do we know that when he went forth to be executed God delivered him? For it said, '*And He delivered me from the* sword *of Pharaoh*.'[3] Another comment: A man has a Patron and yet he is arrested for his crime and is cast into a den of wild beasts; where is he and where is his Patron? But though Daniel was cast into the den of lions, yet God delivered him. Whence [do we know this]? For it is said, *My God hath sent His angel, and hath shut the lions' mouths* (Dan. VI, 23).

Another comment: A man acquires for himself a Patron and he commits a crime, and the judges sentence him to be burned; where is he and where is his Patron? But with God it is not so. The ministering angels declared before God: 'Abraham, Thy protégé, has been arrested.' God replied: 'I will protect him.' They said to him: 'Lo, he is standing before Amraphel; lo, his sentence is being pronounced; lo, he is about to be burnt.' He replied: 'I will protect him.' When he was cast into the fiery furnace, God came down and delivered him. Whence this? For it is said, *I am the Lord that brought thee out of Ur of the Chaldees* (Gen. XV, 7).[4]

Another comment: A man acquires for himself a Patron,

[1] אנקליטון. Jast. corrects into אנקלימטין, Gk. ἐγκλήματα, 'written complaints,' 'charges.' Levi renders: If he is found guilty in the appeal court, etc.

[2] איפומניטא. Jast. reads איפיטמיא, Gk. ἐπιτίμια, 'the imposed penalty,' 'sentence.' Krauss (*Lehnwörter*) reads איפומנימא, Gk. ὑπόμνημα, 'charge,' 'indictment.'

[3] At the very moment when the sword was to come into action.

[4] Cf. Gen. R. XXXVIII, 13, XLIV, 13; Pes. 118*a*, where Nimrod is read instead of Amraphel.

and he is arrested for his crime, and the judge sentences him to be thrown into the sea; where is he and where is his Patron? But with God it is not so. Jonah was cast into the sea, and yet God saved him. Whence this? For it is said, *And the Lord spoke unto the fish, and it vomited out Jonah* (Jonah II, 11). Another explanation: THEN MOSES SEPARATED. R. Aibo said: When Moses fled he began to sing a song, as it is said, *And dwelt in the land of Midian; and he sat down by a well* (Ex. II, 15). Just as Israel sang a song by a well,[1] so too Moses sang a song by a well. R. Levi said: [He sang a song] because the section dealing with the homicide's [flight] to the Cities of Refuge was carried into effect through him.[2]

30.[3] THEN MOSES SEPARATED THREE CITIES BEYOND THE JORDAN TOWARD THE SUNRISING. What is the force of the words, TOWARD THE SUNRISING? R. Jose b. R. Ḥanina said: The Holy One, blessed be He, said to Moses: 'Cause the sun to shine for the homicide [who has killed a man unwittingly] and set aside for him an asylum whither he may be exiled, that he perish not for the sin of the murder, just as the sun gives light to the world.'

Another explanation: THAT THE MANSLAYER MIGHT FLEE THITHER (*ib.* 42). The Rabbis say: This can be compared to an artificer who was making a statue of the king, and whilst he was at work on it, it broke in his hand. The king said: 'Had he broken it intentionally he would have been executed; since he broke it unintentionally, let him be exiled to a place of banishment.'[4] Likewise, God decreed, '"*Whoso sheddeth man's blood, by man shall his blood be shed*" (Gen. IX, 6); but whoso kills a man unwittingly shall be exiled from his home,' as it is said, AND THAT FLEEING UNTO ONE OF THESE CITIES HE MIGHT LIVE (IV, 42). God said: 'In this world,

[1] Cf. Num. XXI, 17. [2] He had himself been in that position.
[3] The Wilna ed. has no sections numbered 28–9. This is presumably a mere misprint in numbering in the early edd.
[4] מטלון, Gk. μέταλλον, 'mine,' 'quarry.' Let him be sent to work as a prisoner in the mines, or quarries.

because the Evil Inclination is present, men kill one another and die, but in the time to come I will uproot the Evil Inclination from your midst and there will be no death in the world,' [as Scripture says], *He will swallow up death for ever* (Isa. XXV, 8).

31. HEAR, O ISRAEL: THE LORD OUR GOD, THE LORD IS ONE (VI, 4). *Halachah:* If a Jew recites the *shema'* and does not enunciate clearly its letters, has he fulfilled his duty? The Sages have learnt thus[1]: If one recited [the *shema'*] but did not clearly enunciate [its letters], R. Jose says: He has done his duty; R. Judah says: He has not done his duty. And what constitutes a clear enunciation of the letters? Our Rabbis taught us: [In reciting the words] *bekol lebabekem* (with all your heart, Deut. XI, 13), one should make a clear pause between the one [letter] *lamed* and the other *lamed;* in *wa'abadtem meherah* (and ye perish quickly, *ib.* 17), one should make a clear pause between the one *mem* and the other *mem.* R. Judah further said in the name of Rab[2]: And if one was reciting the *shema'* whilst walking [he should] stop, in order to accept the Kingdom of Heaven standing. And what part [of the *shema'*] is termed 'the Kingdom of Heaven'? [The words], *The Lord our God, the Lord is one.* Whence did Israel merit to recite the *shema'*? R. Phinehas b. Ḥama said: Israel merited to recite the *shema'* at the Revelation on Sinai. How [is this to be inferred]? You find that it was with this word [*shema'*] that God first began [to speak] at Sinai. He said to them: '*Hear, O Israel,*[3] *I am the Lord thy God,*' and they all answered and exclaimed: '*The Lord our God, the Lord is one.*' And Moses said, 'Blessed be the name of His glorious kingdom for ever and ever.'[4] The Rabbis say: God said to Israel: 'My children, all that I have created I have created in pairs; heaven and earth are a pair; sun and moon are a pair; Adam and Eve are

[1] Cf. M. Ber. II, 3; Ber. 15*a*. [2] Cf. Ber. 13*b*. [3] In Deuteronomy the Decalogue is introduced by the words *Hear, O Israel* (V, 1).
[4] In Pes. 56*a* it is stated that it was not Moses who said this but Jacob. Cf. Gen. R. XCVIII, 3.

a pair; this world and the world to come are a pair; but My Glory is One and unique in the world.' Whence this? From what we have read in our context, HEAR, O ISRAEL: THE LORD OUR GOD, THE LORD IS ONE.

32. Another explanation: HEAR, O ISRAEL. This bears out what Scripture says, *Whom have I in heaven but Thee? And beside Thee I desire none upon earth* (Ps. LXXIII, 25). Rab said: There are two firmaments, the heaven and the heavens of heavens. R. Eleazar said: There are seven firmaments[1]: Heaven (*shamayim*), the Heavens of Heavens (*sheme shamayim*), Firmament (*raḳi'ah*), Sky (*sheḥaḳim*), Habitation (*ma'on*), Residence (*zebul*), Thick Cloud (*'arafel*); and God opened them all unto Israel in order to show them that there is no God but He. The Assembly of Israel said before God: 'Master of the Universe, whom have I in heaven but Thy glory? As in heaven I have none but Thee, so too upon earth I desire no other; as I have not associated another God with Thee in heaven, so upon earth, too, I have not associated with Thee any other God; but daily I enter the synagogues and testify concerning Thee that there is no other God but Thou, and I exclaim, HEAR, O ISRAEL: THE LORD OUR GOD, THE LORD IS ONE.'

33. Another explanation: HEAR, O ISRAEL. This bears out what Scripture says, *My son, fear thou the Lord and the king, etc.* (Prov. XXIV, 21). What is the force of '*And the king*'? Abraham who feared Me[2]—did I not proclaim him as king in the world, as it is said, *At the vale of Shaveh—the same is the king's vale* (Gen. XIV, 17)[3]; Joseph who feared Me, of whom it is written, *For I fear God* (Gen. XLII, 18)—did I not proclaim him as king in the world, as it is written, *And Joseph was the governor over the land* (*ib.* 6)[4]?

[1] Cf. Lev. R. XXIX, 11. [2] Cf. Gen. XXII, 12. [3] V. § 7.
[4] Rendering: Fear thou the Lord, then thou wilt be a king. Perhaps the idea is that he who fears the Lord need fear none else, and is thus metaphorically a king.

Another interpretation: '*My son, fear thou the Lord and the king*,' and rule over your inclination. Once R. Simeon b. Eleazar came to a city in the South[1] and entering a synagogue he asked the teacher,[2] 'As you live, is there here any wine for sale?' The latter replied: 'Master, this is a city of Samaritans[3] and they do not prepare the wine with [the strict levitical] purity as my fathers were wont to do.' He [R. Simeon] then said: 'If you have any wine to spare give it to me and I will buy it from you.' The teacher replied: 'If you can master your desires you should not taste of it'; whereupon R. Simeon b. Eleazar exclaimed: 'As for me, I can master my desires.'[4] Hence the force of '*and king*', that is to say, Rule over thine inclination.[5]

Another explanation: '*My son, fear thou the Lord and the king*.' What is the force of, '*And the king*'? [It means], but [fear] not Molech, as [Scripture] in another context says, *And thou shalt not give any of thy seed to set them apart to Molech* (Lev. XVIII, 21).

Another explanation: What is the force of, '*And the king*'? Make [God] King over you. *And meddle not with them that are given to change* (Prov. *loc. cit.*): Do not meddle with those who declare that there is a second god.[6] R. Judah b. Simon said: [Scripture says], *And it shall come to pass, that in all the land, saith the Lord, two parts therein shall be cut off and die* (Zech. XIII, 8); the mouths that

[1] Heb. *darom*, the south of Palestine, south of Lydda. Cf. Neubauer, *Géographie*, pp. 63 f.

[2] Lit. 'the scribe'. The scribe was also the teacher of the community.

[3] Or Cutheans, v. Glos. Their religious status varied, until they were eventually declared to be non-Jews. But at the time of this story (R. Simeon b. Eleazar was a contemporary of R. Judah I and thus flourished about the second half of the second century C.E. and the early part of the third) they were still regarded as Jews, albeit lax in observance.

[4] And he did not drink the wine. 'E.J., by emending אמר (he said) to חמר (wine), renders thus: '. . . as my fathers were wont to do.' He (the teacher) continued: 'If you yield to your desires, give me money and I will buy you wine; but if you can master your desires, do not taste of it, etc.' This rendering is preferable. Cf. also Ḥul. 6*a*.

[5] Rendering: Fear thou the Lord, and be king—over your desires.

[6] The heretical followers of Persian dualism, v. Rabbinowitz, *Mishnah Megillah*, p. 130. A play upon the words שונים (given to change) and שנים (two).

declare that there are two Powers shall be cut off and die. And who will survive in the future? *But the third shall be left therein.* This refers to Israel who are termed 'thirds',[1] for they are divided into three groups, Priests, Levites, and Israelites; and are descended from the three Patriarchs, Abraham, Isaac, and Jacob. Another explanation: Because they praise God with the threefold expression of holiness, *Holy, holy, holy* (Isa. VI, 3). R. Aḥa said: God was angry with Solomon when he uttered the above verse. He said to him: 'Why do you express a thing that concerns the sanctification of My Name by an obscure allusion'[2] [in the words] '*And meddle not with them that are given to change*' (shonim)?[3] Thereupon immediately Solomon expressed it more clearly [in the words], *There is one that is alone, and he hath not a second; yea, he hath neither son nor brother* (Eccl. IV, 8); '*He hath neither son nor brother,*' but HEAR, O ISRAEL: THE LORD OUR GOD, THE LORD IS ONE.

34. R. Isaac opened [his discourse] with the text *The Lord is my portion, saith my soul; therefore will I hope in Him* (Lam. III, 24). R. Isaac said: This may be compared to a king who entered a province with his generals, rulers, and governors. Some of the citizens of the province chose a general as their Patron, others a ruler and others a governor. One of them who was cleverer than the rest said, 'I will choose the king.' Why? All others are liable to be changed, but the king is never changed. Likewise, when God came down on Sinai, there also came down with Him many companies of angels,[4] Michael and his company, Gabriel and his company. Some of the nations of the world chose for themselves [as their Patron] Michael, others Gabriel, but Israel chose for themselves God, exclaiming, '*The Lord is my portion, saith my soul*'; this is the force of, HEAR, O ISRAEL: THE LORD OUR GOD, THE LORD IS ONE.

[1] Or rather, threefold.
[2] This accepts Radal's emendation of שמא to שמי 'My Name'.
[3] Only by the assumption of this play on words could Solomon's meaning be understood.
[4] Cf. Num. R. II, 3.

35. Another explanation: HEAR, O ISRAEL: THE LORD OUR GOD, THE LORD IS ONE. Whence did Israel merit to recite the *shema'*? When Jacob was about to die he called together all the tribes and he said to them: '[I am anxious] lest you bow down to another God after I have departed this world.' Whence this? For so it is written, *Assemble yourselves, and hear, ye sons of Jacob* (Gen. XLIX, 2). What is the force of, *And hearken unto Israel your father* (*ib.*). Jacob said to them: 'The God of Israel,[1] He is your Father.' They replied: HEAR, O ISRAEL: THE LORD OUR GOD, THE LORD IS ONE. And he added softly, 'Blessed be the name of His glorious kingdom for ever and ever.' R. Levi said: And what do Israel imply when they now say, [HEAR, O ISRAEL]? HEAR our father ISRAEL,[2] what you have commanded us we still adhere to; THE LORD OUR GOD, THE LORD IS ONE.

36. Another explanation: HEAR, O ISRAEL. The Rabbis say: When Moses ascended to heaven he heard the ministering angels saying to God, 'Blessed be the name of His glorious kingdom for ever and ever.' This [declaration] Moses brought down to Israel. And why do not Israel make this declaration publicly [i.e. aloud]? R. Assi replied: This can be compared to a man who stole jewellery from the royal palace which he gave to his wife, telling her, 'Do not wear these in public, but only in the house.' But on the Day of Atonement when Israel are as pure as the ministering angels they do recite publicly, 'Blessed be the name of His glorious kingdom for ever and ever.'

37. AND THOU SHALT LOVE THE LORD THY GOD WITH ALL THY HEART, AND WITH ALL THY SOUL (VI, 5). What is the meaning of, WITH ALL THY HEART, AND WITH ALL THY SOUL? With every soul[3]

[1] A play upon the words אל ('unto') and אל ('God'). [2] I.e. Jacob.
[3] With every ounce of strength; or, with the five souls mentioned below.

that He has created within you. R. Meir said: For every single breath which a man breathes he should praise his Creator. Whence [can this be inferred]? For it is said, *For every breath praise thou the Lord* (Ps. CL, 6).[1] R. Simon said: The soul is called by the following five names: *ruaḥ*, *nefesh*, *neshamah*, *ḥayyah*, *yeḥidah*.[2] The Rabbis say: Come and see: God fills this world, and the soul fills the body; God bears His world and the soul bears the body; God is One in His world and the soul is one; before God there is no sleep and the soul too does not sleep; God is the Pure One in His world and the soul is the pure one in the body; God is all-seeing but invisible and the soul sees but cannot be seen; let then the soul which can see but is not seen come and praise God who is all-seeing but invisible. Israel said: 'Master of the Universe, how long will this soul that praises Thee lie in the dust, [as Scripture says], *For our soul is bowed down to the dust*' (Ps. XLIV, 26)? God replied to them: 'By your life, the end cometh and your souls shall rejoice.' Therefore Isaiah comforts [Israel] saying, *I will greatly rejoice in the Lord, my soul shall be joyful in God* (Isa. LXI, 10). R. Berekiah said: In the following ten places in Scripture God refers to Israel as a bride: *Come with Me from Lebanon, my bride* (S.S. IV, 8); *I am come into my garden, my sister, my bride* (*ib.* V, 1); *Thou hast ravished my heart, my sister, my bride* (*ib.* IV, 9); *How fair is thy love, my sister, my bride* (*ib.* 10); *Thy lips, O my bride, drop honey* (*ib.* 11)[3]; *And as the bridegroom rejoiceth over the bride* (Isa. LXII, 5); *The voice of the bridegroom and the voice of the bride* (Jer. VII, 34); *Thou shalt surely clothe thee with them all as with an ornament, and gird thyself with them, like a bride* (Isa. XLIX, 18); *And as a bride adorneth herself with her jewels* (*ib.* LXI, 10). And corresponding to these ten Israel adorn God with the following ten garments: *I put on righteousness, and it*

[1] E.V. '*Let everything that hath breath praise the Lord*'.
[2] This probably means that there are five souls, or that the soul is divided into five parts, each of which has a different function; v. Gen. R. XIV, 9.
[3] The whole of Song of Songs was interpreted as a dialogue between God and Israel.

clothed itself with me (Job XXIX, 14); this makes two; *And He put on righteousness as a coat of mail* (Isa. LIX, 17); *And He put on garments of vengeance for clothing* (*ib.*): this makes five; *His raiment was as white snow* (Dan. VII, 9); *Wherefore is thine apparel red* (Isa. LXIII, 2); *The Lord reigneth; He is clothed in majesty; the Lord is clothed, He hath girded Himself with strength* (Ps. XCIII, 1); *Thou art clothed with glory and majesty* (Ps. CIV, 1): this makes ten.

Another explanation: '*I will greatly rejoice in the Lord.*' This can be compared to a woman whose husband, son, and son-in-law went away to a far distant country, etc., as is interpreted in the Pesiḳta[1] on the section. '*I will greatly rejoice.*'

[1] Read with the Radal דשוש instead of עד שוש. Cf. Pesiḳta de R. Kahana (ed. Buber), p. 147.

Chapter III

EKEB

1. *Halachah:* Is it permissible for a Jew who possesses a candalabrum fitted together from separate parts to move it about on the Sabbath? The Sages have learnt thus[1]: One who puts together the parts of a candalabrum on the Sabbath renders himself liable for a sin-offering.[2] And under what counts is he liable? R. Abbahu said in the name of R. Joḥanan: He who puts together a candalabrum is like unto a man who builds on the Sabbath, and one who builds on the Sabbath is liable [for a sin-offering]. R. Jose b. Ḥanina said: Israel first observed the Sabbath in the proper manner when it was given to them at Alush.[3] Whence this? For it is said, *So the people rested on the seventh day* (Ex. XVI, 30). [Said God to Israel]: 'You might perhaps think that I have given you the Sabbath to your disadvantage[4]; I have surely given the Sabbath to you only for your own advantage.' How? R. Ḥiyya b. Abba said: [God said to Israel]: 'You sanctify the Sabbath with food and drink and clean clothes, deriving physical enjoyment therefrom, while I give you reward.'[5] Whence this? [Scripture says], *And call the Sabbath a delight*, etc. (Isa. LVIII, 13), and after this is written, *Then shalt thou delight thyself in the Lord* (*ib.* 14); that is to say, He will grant you the desires of your heart. Israel asked God: 'When wilt Thou grant us the reward of the *mizwoth* which we observe?' God replied: 'As for the *mizwoth* which you observe, you eat of their fruits now, but their full reward

[1] Tosef. Shab. 12 (13), 14; Shab. 47*a*.
[2] Because he desecrated the Sabbath by building, which is one of the 39 primary types of work forbidden on the Sabbath. (Cf. Shab. 73*a*.)
[3] A station of the Israelites in the wilderness. Cf. Num. XXXIII, 13 f; compare with this the statement of R. Judah in the name of Rab that Israel did not observe properly even the first Sabbath (Shab. 118*b*).
[4] Inasmuch as so many Sabbath restrictions are placed on Israel.
[5] Though you benefit materially by its observance.

I shall give you in the end'[1] [i.e. after death]. Whence [can this be inferred]? From what we read in our text, AND IT SHALL COME TO PASS, BECAUSE YE HEARKEN.

2. Another explanation: AND IT SHALL COME TO PASS BECAUSE. This bears out what Scripture says, *Gilead is mine, and Manasseh is mine* (Ps. LX, 9). What is meant by '*Gilead*, etc.'? Resh Laḳish said: . . . etc. (until the passage ending in the words, 'who are of the children of Judah').[2]

Another explanation: *Moab is my washpot* (*ib.* 10). R. Simeon b. Ḥalafta said: I set [over the fire] a cauldron of punishment for Moab.[3] What is the meaning of, *Upon Edom I cast my shoe* (*ib.*)? God said: 'When everything is ready [for Israel's] repentance, then I will tread with the heel of my foot[4] on the winepress of Edom.' When will this be? AND IT SHALL COME TO PASS, BECAUSE (EKEB)[5] YOU HEARKEN. God said to Israel: 'My children, do not think that I desire to treat you like a slave whose master desires to sell him at an auction[6] for what he may fetch, but I will go on bringing chastisement upon you until you direct your heart towards Me.' R. Aḥa said: God took an oath that He would never leave Israel.[7] Whence this? For it is said, *Therefore* (laken) *thus will I do unto thee, O Israel* (Amos IV, 12), and 'therefore (*laken*)' always implies an oath, as it is said, *And therefore* (we-laken) *I have sworn unto the house of Eli* (1 Sam. III, 14). And how long will I go on chastising you? To the end (*eḳeb*),[8] as

[1] A.Z. 3*a*. A play on עקב 'because' and עקב 'heel' interpreted homiletically to mean 'end', 'future world'. Correct שכרו into שכרן 'their reward'. [2] For the full passage, v. Num. R. XIV, 1.

[3] I.e. mete them out complete punishment. For the figure of speech 'cauldron of punishment', cf. Ezek. XXIV, 3.

[4] God is ready to punish Edom; all that He has to do is to throw off His shoe and tread them down with the heel of His foot. Cf. Num. R. XIV, 1.

[5] A play on עקב 'because' and עקב 'heel', the verse being rendered: 'And (My) heel will be (upon Edom) when ye hearken.'

[6] קירסין, Gk. κηρύσσων, 'at auction.' Levi: who desires to sell him when the time is opportune. [7] Without suffering, until they repented.

[8] Probably: till your complete repentance.

Scripture says, *Because I will do this unto thee* (Amos *loc. cit.*), that is to say, until you shall observe My commandments to the end.[1]

3. Another explanation: What is written before [the verse under comment]? *Know now therefore that the Lord thy God, He is God, the faithful God* (Deut. VII, 9). R. Ḥiyya b. Abba said: This can be compared to a king's friend who deposited with him an article of clothing for safe custody; when the friend died his son came and claimed from him the article, saying, 'Return unto me the article which my father deposited with you for safe custody'; whereupon the king asked, 'Have you then found a more trustworthy person than I? Have not I looked well after the article deposited with me, and have I not aired[2] it? Similarly when in the days of Jeremiah Israel sinned, God said to Jeremiah: 'Go, say to Israel, *What unrighteousness have your fathers found in Me* (Jer. II, 5)? Have I not fulfilled everything that I sware to your fathers? I swore unto them that I would bless their children, as it is said, *That in blessing I will bless thee* (Gen. XXII, 17), etc., have I not blessed you by the hand of Moses, as it is said, *The Lord your God hath multiplied you* (Deut. I, 10). I promised him [Abraham] that I would bring them out [from Egypt] with great substance, [as it is said], *And afterward shall they come out with great substance* (Gen. XV, 14), have I not done so, as it is said, *And he brought them forth with silver and gold; and there was none that stumbled among His tribes'* (Ps. CV, 37)? Therefore Moses said: '*From the fact that He kept the oath . . . and redeemed you out of the land of bondage* (Deut. VII, 8)[3] you know that "*He is God, the faithful*".'

Another explanation: '*That the Lord thy God, He is God.*' R. Levi said: This can be compared to a friend of a king, etc. . . . his son came to claim back the article deposited

[1] 'E.J.: until you fulfil even the comparatively unimportant precepts which people often disregard, as though they trod them under their heel (*aḳeb*). [2] Lit. 'folded it and unfolded it'
[3] E.V. '*Because He would keep the oath*', etc.

with him. The king said to him: 'Go and bring two commanders and twelve counsellors and through them I will return to you the article.' Likewise God said: 'When Israel came out of Egypt, your fathers deposited with Me an article.' Whence this? *I have surely taken you as a deposit* (Ex. III, 16).[1] He added: 'Let two commanders and twelve counsellors come': this refers to Moses and Aaron and the twelve heads of the tribes. Whence this? For it is said, *Ye shall number them by their hosts, thou and Aaron. And with you there shall be a man of every tribe* (Num. I, 3 f).[2] Another explanation: '*The faithful God.*' The Rabbis say: You can best learn the faithfulness of God from the faithfulness of man. It is related of R. Phinehas ben Jair[3] that when he was living in a city in the South some men came there to seek a livelihood. They had with them two *se'ahs* of barley which they deposited with him, but they forgot about it and went away. R. Phinehas b. Jair sowed the barley year by year and harvested it and stored it. After the lapse of seven years those men returned to that place to claim back their grain. As soon as R. Phinehas b. Jair recognised them he said to them: 'Come and take these your storehouses [full of grain].' Lo, from the faithfulness of man you can best learn the faithfulness of God. It is further related of R. Phinehas b. Jair that he once came to a city where the mice used to devour everything in the vicinity, and he was asked for some remedy against this. What did R. Phinehas do? He said to the people of the city: 'Why do you not separate the tithes in the proper way? Would you like me to be surety for you, that if you do separate your tithes in the proper way the mice shall not devour [the grain]?' They replied: 'Yes.' He gave them the guarantee and the mice departed and were not seen again.

Another explanation: There was once a man who used

[1] I.e. received you as a treasure in My charge. E.V. '*I have surely remembered you*'.

[2] Hence the twelve counsellors. Thus He is the faithful God, ready to restore what was deposited with Him. [3] For these and other stories about Phinehas b. Jair see J. Demai, I, 21*d* and 22*a*.

to dig cisterns for the benefit of the community, and his daughter went on a journey and when trying to cross a river was washed away. People came and said to R. Phinehas: 'This and this has happened to the daughter of So-and-so.' He replied: 'It is impossible! Seeing that that man did God's will [in providing] water, God would not destroy his daughter by water.' Immediately the cry went forth in the city: 'The daughter of So-and-so has returned.' Our Rabbis said: As soon as R. Phinehas b. Jair had spoken in this manner an angel came down and drew her out [of the water].

It is related of R. Simeon b. Sheṭaḥ that he once bought an ass from an Ishmaelite. His disciples came and found a precious stone suspended from its neck. They said to him: 'Master, *The blessing of the Lord, it maketh rich*' (Prov. x, 22). R. Simeon b. Sheṭaḥ replied: 'I have purchased an ass, but I have not purchased a precious stone.' He then went and returned it to the Ishmaelite, and the latter exclaimed of him, 'Blessed be the Lord God of Simeon b. Sheṭaḥ.' Thus from the faithfulness of man we learn the faithfulness of God, who is faithful to pay the reward of the precepts which [Israel] perform. Whence this? For it is said, *And ye shall observe the precepts* (Ex. XII, 17).[1] As regards the reward of the *miẓwoth* [when will they receive it? Scripture says], AND IT SHALL COME TO PASS, BECAUSE (EḲEB) YE HEARKEN, i.e. I will give it to you in the future.

4. Another explanation: THAT THE LORD THY GOD SHALL KEEP FOR THEE, etc. (VII, 12).[2] What is the force of, THAT [THE LORD] SHALL KEEP? R. Samuel b. Naḥmani said: All [the good] that Israel enjoys in this

[1] Reading מצות 'precepts' for the M.T. מצות 'unleavened bread'. This, however, is rather far-fetched, and 'E.J. substitutes *Thou shalt therefore keep the precept* (E.V. '*commandment*'), which occurs in the present passage (Deut. VII, 11) and immediately precedes the verse under discussion.

[2] This continues the verse, *And it shall come to pass, because ye hearken to these ordinances*, etc.—FOR (E.V. 'WITH') is the lit. translation, and preferable in view of the Midrashic interpretation of the verse.

world is a result of the blessings with which Balaam the wicked blessed them,[1] but the blessings with which the Patriarchs blessed them are reserved for the time to come, as it is said, THAT THE LORD THY GOD SHALL KEEP, etc.[2] Another explanation: R. Ḥelbo said: It is like the case of an orphan who was brought up in the house of a certain man, was fed and clothed by him, and was taught a trade by him. The orphan said: 'The man will deduct from my wages the cost of my food, of my drink, and of my clothing.' But the man answered him: 'By your life! your food and clothing are paid for by the service you rendered me in filling a cask of water and in chopping for me one log of wood; your full reward is stored up and reserved for you.' Likewise all that Israel enjoy in this world is a reward for the sufferings which befall them, but their full reward is stored up and reserved for them for the time to come, as it is said, THE LORD THY GOD WILL KEEP FOR THEE . . . [THE COVENANT AND THE MERCY].

What is meant by, THE COVENANT AND THE MERCY? R. Ḥiyya said: Israel are possessed of the following three fine characteristics: they are bashful, merciful, and benevolent. They are bashful: for it is said, *And that His fear may be before you* (Ex. XX, 17); merciful: for it is said, *And He shall give thee mercy*[3]; *and have compassion upon thee* (Deut. XIII, 18); benevolent: for it is said, [GOD] SHALL KEEP FOR THEE THE COVENANT AND THE MERCY.[4]

5. AND HE WILL LOVE THEE, AND BLESS THEE, AND MULTIPLY THEE; HE WILL ALSO BLESS THE FRUIT OF THY BODY AND THE FRUIT OF THY LAND (VII, 13). Why does Scripture compare the fruit of the body to the fruit of the ground? God said: 'As the fruit of your

[1] Cf. Num. XXII–XXIV. [2] I.e. He will keep them in store.
[3] The Midrash interprets: And He shall give thee the quality of mercy—towards others.
[4] Rendered: He shall keep for thee the reward for the mercy (or, rather, the benevolence) which you display.

ground will be of luxuriant growth, so too will the fruit of your body be.'[1]

Another explanation: As there can be no sin or iniquity in the fruit of your ground, so there will be neither sin nor iniquity in the fruit of your body.

Another explanation: As the fruit of your ground requires tithing, so too the fruit of the body requires tithing, namely circumcision.

Another explanation: R. Judah b. Simon said: Why does Scripture compare the fruit of the body to the fruit of the ground? [To teach you] that the fruit of the ground atones for the fruit of the body,[2] for so it is written, *And His land doth make expiation for His people* (Deut. XXXII, 43).[3]

6. THOU SHALT BE BLESSED ABOVE ALL PEOPLES (VII, 14). R. Ḥiyya b. Abba said: A noble lady feels herself flattered when she is praised, not by her relatives but by her rivals. THERE SHALL NOT BE MALE OR FEMALE BARREN AMONG YOU: neither eunuchs nor a woman incapable of conception. So far I know this only of human beings. Whence do we know that the same is true of animals? For it is written, OR AMONG YOUR CATTLE; here [you have] man and beast. Whence do we know that it holds good also of the ground? For it is written, *Nought shall miscarry, nor be barren, in thy land* (Ex. XXIII, 26)[4]: thus you have man, beast, and ground. Whence do we know that it is true likewise of trees? For it is written, *Neither shall your vine cast its fruit before the time in the field* (Mal. III, 11).

Another explanation: THERE SHALL NOT BE MALE OR FEMALE BARREN. R. Ḥanin b. Levi said: God said: 'Your prayer will never prove barren, but will ever

[1] This is the most likely meaning. Levi, however, renders: just as the fruit of your field contains refuse too, so the fruit of your body (e.g. Ishmael from Abraham, Esau from Isaac). Though the language warrants this rendering, the context makes it very unlikely.
[2] I.e. tithes atone for the sins of man.
[3] E.V. '*And doth make expiation for the land of His people*'.
[4] Which is rendered, 'Nought (E.V. '*none*') of thy land shall miscarry or be barren'—i.e. the land will always yield its produce.

continue to bring forth fruits.' Another explanation: R. Jonathan said: THERE SHALL NOT BE MALE OR FEMALE BARREN. This means that they will never be at a loss for an answer. Once R. Jonathan[1] was journeying towards Neapolis[2] of the Samaritans; he was riding on his ass and he was accompanied by the driver of the animal. On the road a Samaritan joined them and when they reached Mount Gerizim[3] he said to R. Jonathan: 'Rabbi, what does this mean,[4] for this mountain is holy?' R. Jonathan asked: 'Why is it holy?' The Samaritan replied: 'Because it was not affected by the waters of the Flood.' Thereupon R. Jonathan asked him: 'Whence do you know this?' He replied: 'Is it not written thus: *Son of man, say unto her: Thou art a land*[5] *that is not cleansed, nor rained upon in the day of indignation* (Ezek. XXII, 24)?' Said R. Jonathan: 'If that is so, God should have commanded Noah to ascend that [mountain] and not to build an ark.' The Samaritan replied: 'God only did this in order to try him.' R. Jonathan remained silent, whereupon the ass driver said to him: 'Give me permission to say a word to him.' He replied: 'Speak.' Then the ass driver said to the Samaritan: 'Is not this mountain beneath the heavens?' The Samaritan replied: 'Where then, beyond the heavens?' The ass driver then said to him, 'Is it not written, *Fifteen cubits upward did the waters prevail* (Gen. VII, 20); *And all the high mountains that were under the whole heaven were covered (ib.* 19)?'[6] Thereupon R. Jonathan dismounted from the ass and made the driver ride on it for four miles, and he applied to him the verse, *And every tongue that shall rise against thee in judgment thou shalt condemn* (Isa. LIV, 17). Thus it is that, THERE SHALL NOT BE MALE OR FEMALE BARREN AMONG YOU, OR AMONG

[1] Cf. Gen. R. XXXII, 10. Cf. J.'A.Z. IV, 44*d*, and Gen. R. LXXXI, 3, where a similar episode is related of R. Ishmael b. R. Jose.
[2] נימולין, Neapolis, on the site of the ancient Shechem.
[3] Where the Samaritans built their temple.
[4] What does our coming here betoken?
[5] Applied to Palestine. Cf. Zeb. 113*a*. The Samaritans, however, applied it to Mt. Gerizim.
[6] And therefore Mt. Gerizim would also have been under water.

YOUR CATTLE, that is to say among your [animal] drivers.[1]

7. Another explanation: THAT THE LORD THY GOD SHALL KEEP FOR THEE THE COVENANT AND THE MERCY. R. Simeon b. Ḥalafta said: This may be compared to a king who married a noble lady, who brought with her into the house two gems,[2] and the king too had two corresponding gems set for her. The lady lost her gems, whereupon the king took away his. After some time she arose and set herself right with him by bringing back the two gems. Thereupon the king too restored his. The king decreed that a crown should be made of both sets of gems and that it should be placed on the head of the noble lady. So you find that Abraham gave his children two gems [to guard], as it is said, *For I have known him, to the end that he may command his children and his household after him . . . to do righteousness and justice* (Gen. XVIII, 19). God too set up corresponding to them two gems, namely, lovingkindness and mercy, as it is said, GOD SHALL KEEP FOR THEE THE COVENANT AND THE MERCY: and it further says, *And He will give thee mercy,*[3] *and have compassion upon thee* (Deut. XIII, 18). Israel lost theirs, as it is said, *That ye have turned justice into gall, and the fruit of righteousness into wormwood* (Amos VI, 12). God thereupon took away His, as it is said, *For I have taken away My peace from this people, saith the Lord, even mercy and compassion* (Jer. XVI, 5). Israel then arose and set themselves right [with God] and restored the two gems. Whence do we know this? For so it is written, *Zion shall be redeemed with justice, and they that return of her with righteousness* (Isa. I, 27). God too restored His. Whence this? For so it is written, *For the mountains may depart, and the hills be removed, but My kindness shall not depart from thee, neither shall My covenant of peace be removed, saith the Lord that hath compassion on thee (ib.* LIV, 10). And after Israel have restored theirs and

[1] A play upon the word *behemah*, cattle and *bahamam*, cattle driver.
[2] אירים, Gk. ἶρις, name of a sparkling gem (Krauss and Levy). Jast. translates, an emblem set in a ring or chain. [3] V. p. 72, n. 3.

God has given back His, God will say, 'Let both pairs be made into a crown and be placed on the head of Israel,' as it is said, *And I will betroth thee unto Me for ever, yea, I will betroth thee unto Me in righteousness and in justice, and in lovingkindness, and in compassion. And I will betroth thee unto Me in faithfulness; and thou shalt know the Lord* (Hos. II, 21).

8. HEAR, O ISRAEL: THOU ART TO PASS OVER THE JORDAN THIS DAY (IX, 1). *Halachah*: A Jew who drinks water to sate his thirst recites the benediction, 'Blessed be He by whose word all things exist.' R. Ṭarfon says: He recites, 'He who createth many living beings with their wants.'[1] The Rabbis say: Come and see how all the miracles which God wrought for Israel He wrought only through water.[2] How? Whilst they were still in Egypt He wrought miracles for them through the river. R. Isaac said: The Egyptians and the Israelites went to drink[3] water from the river; the Egyptians drank blood, but the Israelites drank water. And when Israel came out of Egypt He wrought miracles for them only through water. Whence this? For it is said, *The sea saw it, and fled* (Ps. CXIV, 3). What did it see? R. Nehorai said: It saw the Tetragrammaton engraved upon [Moses'] staff and it parted. R. Nehemiah said: It saw, if one may say so, God's hand, and it parted, as it is said, *The waters saw Thee, they were in pain* (*ib.* LXXVII, 17). After they came out from the sea they arrived at Marah[4] where the waters were bitter, and He wrought for them miracles. Whence this? For it is said, *And the Lord showed him a tree*, etc. (Ex. XV, 25). At the Rock he wrought miracles for them through water. Whence this? For it is said, *And speak ye unto the rock*, etc. (Num. XX, 8). At the Well He wrought miracles for them and they sang a song, as it is said, *Then sang Israel* (Num. XXI, 17). Moses said to Israel: 'Know that all the miracles which God wrought for you, He wrought only through water,

[1] M. Ber. VI, 8; 'Er. 14*b* (where the words וחסרונן על כל מה שבראת are added). [2] The Rabbis therefore instituted a special grace for water. [3] Cf. Ex. R. IX, 10. [4] Cf. Ex. XV, 23.

and also when you pass over the Jordan to take possession of the land God will also work miracles for you through the waters of the Jordan.'[1]

9. Another interpretation: HEAR, O ISRAEL: THOU ART TO PASS OVER THE JORDAN. This bears out what Scripture says, *O God, we have heard with our ears, our fathers have told us; a work Thou didst in their days* (Ps. XLIV, 2). What is the force of, '*With our ears*'? R. Tanḥuma said: [Israel said]: 'We have heard what Thou didst say to Moses at the Bush.[2] To Moses at the Bush Thou didst say: "It is revealed and known before Me that they [Israel] will in the future provoke Me to anger, yet I will redeem them." And whence do we know that God did speak this to Moses? For it is written, *I have surely seen the affliction of My people that are in Egypt . . . for I know their pain* (Ex. III, 7). What is the force of "*For I know their pain*"? God said to Moses: "I know what pain they will cause [Me by declaring], *This is thy god, O Israel*" (*ib.* XXXII, 4), yet God said, *And I am come down to deliver them out of the hand of the Egyptians* (*ib.* III, 8). These are the conditions which Thou didst make with Moses, and with our ears have we heard the conditions which Thou didst make with him.' What is the force of '*Our fathers have told us*'? This refers to Moses who is the father of all the prophets. *Thou with Thy hand didst drive out the nations, and didst plant them in* (Ps. XLIV, 3): Moses said to Israel: 'You can learn from what God has done to the two kings of the Emorites, to Sihon[3] and Og[3] who were so mighty, what He will do to the thirty-one kings[4] when you cross the Jordan.' Hence the force of, HEAR, O ISRAEL: THOU ART TO PASS OVER THE JORDAN.

10. Another explanation: HEAR, O ISRAEL. What reason did Moses have for saying at this point, HEAR, O ISRAEL?[5] The Rabbis say: It is like the case of a king who betrothed unto himself a noble lady with two precious

[1] Cf. Joshua III. [2] Cf. Ex. III. [3] Deut. III, 1 ff.
[4] Cf. Josh. XII, 7–24. [5] More than elsewhere.

stones; when one of them was lost the king said to her: 'You have lost one, take [good] care of the other.' So God betrothed Israel unto Himself with the words, *We will do, and obey* (Ex. XXIV, 7). When they lost the '*We will do*' in making the Golden Calf, Moses said to them: 'You have lost the "*We will do*", observe then the "*We will obey*".' Hence the force of HEAR, O ISRAEL.

11. Another explanation: THOU ART TO PASS OVER THE JORDAN THIS DAY. Moses said to Israel: 'When you shall have passed the Jordan, a number of things will be different; do not think that it will be just like when you were in the wilderness where I prayed for you whenever you sinned.' He further said unto them: 'Did I not plead in your defence when you did that [unspeakable] act[1] and God desired to destroy you?' Whence this? For it is said, *And I prayed unto the Lord, and said: O Lord God, destroy not Thy people*, etc. (Deut. IX, 26). R. Ḥiyya b. Abba said: When God said to Moses in heaven: '*Arise, go down hastily from here*' (*ib.* 12), five[2] angels of destruction overheard this and they sought to harm him. These are they: *Af*, *Ḥemah*, *Ḳeẓef*, *Mashḥith*, and *Mekaleh*.[3] When, however, Moses made mention of the merits of the three Patriarchs, as it is written, *Remember Abraham, Isaac, and Israel Thy servants* (Ex. XXXII, 13), *Ḳeẓef*, *Mashḥith*, and *Mekaleh* fled and only the two fiercer ones, *Af* and *Ḥemah*, were left. Whereupon Moses exclaimed before God: 'Master of the universe, I made mention of the three [Patriarchs] and three [angels] have fled: rise up, Thou also, against *Af*.' Whence this? For it is said, *Arise, O Lord, against Thine* Af (Ps. VII, 7).[4] Hence the proof that God rose up against *Af*. And whence do we know that Moses rose up against *Ḥemah?* For it is said, *Had not Moses His chosen stood before Him in the breach, to turn back His wrath* (Ḥamatho)[5] *lest He should destroy them* (*ib.* CVI, 23). Moses

[1] The worship of the Golden Calf. [2] Cf. Ex. R. XLI, 7.
[3] Lit., 'Anger,' 'Fury,' 'Wrath,' 'Destroyer,' and 'Devourer'.
[4] E.V. '*Arise, O Lord, in Thine anger*'.
[5] *Ḥamatho* from *ḥemah* 'wrath'.

came down from heaven with the Tables in his hand, but he did not break them until he saw with his own eyes what they had done. Whence this? For it is said, *And it came to pass, as soon as he came nigh unto the camp, that he saw the Calf* (Ex. XXXII, 19). At that moment *Moses' anger waxed hot, and he cast the tables out of his hands* (*ib.*). The Holy One, blessed be He, thereupon said to Moses: 'You would not believe Me that they had made a Calf unto themselves,' as it is said, *They have turned aside quickly out of the way which I commanded them* (*ib.* 8). The Rabbis say: From this expression Moses seized a hint how to find some defence for Israel. He said before God: 'Master of the universe, *I* have received commands, have *I* then transgressed any one of them? They have received no commands and therefore they did not know.' God thereupon exclaimed: 'Moses, have they not been commanded?' He replied: 'No. What didst Thou declare at Sinai?[1] Thou didst not say, "I am the Lord *your* God," but *I am the Lord* Thy *God* (Ex. XX, 2). Thou didst not say, "*Ye* shall have no other gods," but Thou *shalt have no other gods*' (*ib.* 3). Hence, '*O Lord God, destroy not Thy people and Thine inheritance*' (Deut. IX, 26).

R. Ḥiyya b. Abba said: Moses left no corner in heaven upon which he did not prostrate himself in prayer.[2] And what did he say? What can the closed[3] mouth say?

Another explanation: '*O Lord God, destroy not Thy people and Thine inheritance.*' R. Ḥiyya b. Abba said: When the defender [Moses] had finished, the Holy Spirit pleaded[4] on their behalf and spoke thus to Israel: '*Be not a witness against thy companion* (E.V. "*neighbour*") *without cause, and deceive not with thy lips*' (Prov. XXIV, 28). '*Be not a witness against thy companion without cause*': this refers to Israel who are called 'Companions of God', as

[1] Cf. Ex. R. XLIII, 5; the singular form implies that the commands were spoken to Moses only.

[2] I.e. he used every conceivable argument ('E.J.).

[3] Read סכור 'closed' for סבור. Moses felt himself incapable of further prayer. The present reading may be retained rendering: What can a mouth even gifted with understanding say further?

[4] Lev. R. VI, 1.

it is said, *For my brethren and companions' sake*, etc. (Ps. CXXII, 8). *'And deceive not'*: [this refers also to Israel] of whom it is written, *But they deceived Him with their mouth* (*ib.* LXXVIII, 36). Although you declared at Sinai, *'We will do, and obey,'* yet you did not fulfil this. To God [the Holy Spirit] said: 'Say not: *I will do so to him as he hath done to me* (Prov. XXIV, 29), but *"O Lord God, destroy not Thy people and Thine inheritance"*.' Therefore, when they came to pass over the Jordan, Moses reminded them of every plea that he had made on their behalf, because he thought that they would pray on his behalf that he should enter the land with them. What is the force of THOU ART TO PASS OVER? R. Tanḥuma said: Moses prostrated himself before Israel and said to them: 'You are to pass over, but not I,' and he gave them the opportunity to pray for him, but they did not grasp it. This can be compared to a king who had many children by a noble lady. The lady was undutiful to him and he resolved to dismiss her. He said to her: 'Know that I am going to marry another wife.' She replied: 'Yes, but will you not tell me whom it is that you intend to marry.' He replied: 'So-and-so.' What did the noble lady do? She summoned her children and said to them: 'Know that your father intends to divorce me and to marry So-and-so; could you bear being subjected to her?'[1] They replied: 'Yes.' She then said to them: 'Know what she will do to you.' She thought that perhaps they would understand what she meant and would intercede with their father on her behalf, but they did not understand. As they did not understand, she said: 'I will command you only for your own sake, be mindful of the honour of your father.' So it was with Moses. When God said to him: *'Take thee Joshua the son of Nun*, etc. (Num. XXVII, 18); *For thou shalt not go over this Jordan'* (Deut. III, 27), Moses said to Israel, *'And it shall come to pass, when the Lord thy God shall bring thee into the land whither thou goest to possess it'* (*ib.* XI, 29); he stressed [the words] *THOU* ART TO PASS OVER

[1] Omitting שלא 'not' (Radal).

THIS DAY, *not* I, [He thought] that perhaps Israel would understand. As they did not understand, he said: 'I will command you only for your own sakes, be mindful of the honour of your Father in heaven.' Whence do we know this? For it is said, *That thou mightest fear the Lord thy God*, etc. (*ib.* VI, 2). God said: 'In this world all yearn for Eretz Israel, and because of your sin you have been exiled from it. But in the time to come, when you will be free from sin and iniquity, I will plant you therein to flourish as an undisturbed plant.' Whence this? For it is said, *And I will plant them upon their land, and they shall no more be plucked up out of their land* (Amos IX, 15).

12. AT THAT TIME THE LORD SAID UNTO ME: HEW THEE (X, 1). *Halachah:* When a Jew betroths a woman, who has to pay for the writing of the document of betrothal? Our Rabbis have learnt thus[1]: Documents of betrothal and marriage[2] are written only with the consent of the two parties, and the bridegroom pays the fee. And this we learn from God from His betrothal of Israel at Sinai, as it is written, *And the Lord said unto Moses: Go unto the people and betroth*[3] *them to-day and to-morrow* (Ex. XIX, 10). And who wrote this document? Moses. Whence do we know this? For it is said, *And Moses wrote this law* (Deut. XXXI, 9).[4] And what reward did God give him? A lustrous countenance, as it is written, *That Moses knew not that the skin of his face sent forth beams* (Ex. XXXIV, 29). To what time does *While He talked with him* (*ib.*) refer?[5] Resh Laḳish said: When Moses wrote the law

[1] M.B.B. x, 4; Keth. 102*b*; Ḳid. 9*b*.
[2] In former times marriage was divided into two stages: (1) *Erusin* or 'Betrothal'. This was a proper marriage, in so far as the woman would henceforth not be free to marry another unless she were divorced. Yet cohabitation was forbidden until (2) *Nesu'in* or 'Marriage', i.e. the home-taking of the bride. A considerable interval might elapse between the two. Nowadays they are combined.
[3] The Midrash takes the M.T. וקדשתם in the later, technical sense of writing the קידושין betrothal document. E.V. '*sanctify*'.
[4] Cf. Deut. XXXIII, 4, where תורה is parallel to מורשה (inheritance), which the Rabbis interpret homiletically to mean, מאורסה 'betrothed'. Cf. Ex. R. XXXIII, 7. [5] God spoke many times to Moses. What was the first time at which his face sent forth beams?

he acquired a lustrous appearance. How [did this come about]? Resh Laḳish said: The scroll that was given to Moses was made of a parchment of white fire,[1] and was written upon with black fire and sealed with fire and was swathed with bands of fire, and whilst he was writing it he dried his pen on his hair, and as a result he acquired a lustrous appearance.[2] R. Samuel b. Naḥman said: Moses acquired a lustrous appearance from the Tables; whilst the Tables were being passed to him from [God's] hands to his own hands he acquired a lustrous appearance. When Israel did that deed of shame [the Golden Calf] he took hold of the Tables and broke them. Whereupon God said to him: 'When you arranged [the Tables] for Israel I gave you as your reward a shining face, and now you have broken them.' R. Isaac said: Our Rabbis have learnt: When a cask is broken [before delivery to the buyer] it is the middleman who bears the loss.[3] God said to Moses: 'You were the intermediary[4] between Me and My children; you broke the Tables, and you must replace them.' Whence this? For so it is written, *And the Lord said unto Moses: Hew thee two tables of stone like unto the first; and I will write upon the tables the words that were on the first tables, which thou didst break. And be ready by the morning, and come up in the morning unto the Mount Sinai, and present thyself there to Me on the top of the mount. And no man shall come up with thee, neither let any man be seen throughout all the mount; neither let the flocks nor herds feed before that mount* (Ex. XXXIV, 1 ff).

13. Another explanation: HEW THEE. This bears out what Scripture says, *A time to cast away stones, and a time to gather stones together; a time to embrace, and a time to refrain from embracing* (Eccl. III, 5). R. Tanḥuma said: What is the meaning of, '*A time to cast away stones*'? There was a time for Hadrian, may his bones be turned to dust, to come up and break in pieces the stones of the

[1] J. Soṭ. VIII, 22; J. Sheḳ. VI, 49*d*. [2] Cf. Ex. R. XLVII, 6.
[3] B.B. 27*a*. [4] Lit. 'the middleman'.

Temple. '*And a time to gather stones together.*' [There will be] a time when God will rebuild it. Whence this? For it is said, *Therefore thus saith the Lord God: Behold, I lay in Zion for a foundation a stone, a tried stone, a costly cornerstone of sure foundation; he that believeth shall not make haste. And I will make justice the line, and righteousness the plummet; and the hail shall sweep away the refuge of lies, and the waters shall overflow the hiding-place* (Isa. XXVIII, 16 f).

Another explanation: '*A time to cast away stones.*' The Rabbis say: This refers to Moses. There was a time for Moses to cast away the Tables, as it is written, *And it came to pass, as soon as he came nigh unto the camp, that he saw the calf and the dancing; and Moses' anger waxed hot, and he cast the tables out of his hands, and broke them beneath the mount* (Ex. XXXII, 19). '*And a time to gather stones together.*' A time [came] for him to restore them [the Tables] to Israel, as it is said, HEW THEE TWO TABLES OF STONE.

14. Another explanation: HEW THEE. This bears out what Scripture says, *Be not hasty in thy spirit to be angry; for anger resteth in the bosom of fools* (Eccl. VII, 9). And who was it that was angry? It was Moses, as it is said, '*And Moses' anger waxed hot, and he cast the tables out of his hands.*' God said to him: 'Ah! Moses, you have vented your wrath on the Tables of the Covenant. Do you desire that I also should vent My wrath? You will see that the world could not endure even one hour.' Moses replied: 'And what can I do?' God replied: 'I will impose a fine on you; you have broken the Tables and you must replace them.' This is the meaning of that which is written, HEW THEE TWO TABLES OF STONE.

15. Another explanation of HEW THEE. R. Isaac said: It is written, *Then it shall be, if he hath sinned, and is guilty, that he shall restore that which he took by robbery, or the thing which he hath gotten by oppression, or the deposit which was deposited with him, or the lost thing which he*

found (Lev. v, 23). The Holy One, blessed be He, said to Moses: 'Were not the Tables deposited with you? You broke them, and you must replace them.' R. Isaac said: Moses reconciled God with Israel through the second Tables. What did Moses do? He went up to God angrily and said to Him: 'Thy children have sinned, and yet Thou hast put a fine on me.' He feigned anger on behalf of Israel. For it is said, *And Moses returned unto the Lord, and said: Oh, this people have sinned a great sin, and have made them a god of gold. Yet now, if Thou wilt forgive their sin—; and if not, blot me, I pray Thee, out of Thy book which Thou hast written* (Ex. XXXII, 31 f). When God saw this He said to him, 'Moses! Two beings are angry, you and I are angry with them!'[1] Immediately, *And the Lord spake unto Moses face to face, as a man speaketh unto his friend. And he would return into the camp; but his minister Joshua, the son of Nun, a young man, departed not out of the Tent* (Ex. XXXIII, 11). God said to him: 'Let not the two of us be angry,[2] but when you see Me pour hot [water],[3] you pour cold, and when you see Me pour cold, you pour hot.' Moses asked: 'Master of the Universe, how shall this come about?' God replied: 'Pray thou for mercy on their behalf.' What did he do? Immediately, *And Moses besought the Lord his God, and said: Lord why doth Thy wrath wax hot against Thy people, that Thou hast brought forth out of the land of Egypt with great power and with a mighty hand? Wherefore should the Egyptians speak, saying: For evil did He bring them forth, to slay them in the mountains, and to consume them from the face of the earth? Turn from Thy fierce wrath, and repent of this evil against Thy people* (*ib.* XXXII, 11 f). He said thus to God: 'Lo, they are Thy children; do Thou release them from this sin.'[4]

Another explanation: He said to God: 'Master of the

[1] Surely Israel cannot endure if we are both angry with them!
[2] This is the meaning assigned to *Face to face*; 'face' here being understood to refer to anger. Ex. R. XLV, 2. [3] Boiling with rage.
[4] 'E.J., accepting the reading in cur. edd. M.K. and others emend: Lo, Thy children are bitter (i.e. sinful); do Thou sweeten (i.e. forgive) them.

Universe, I know that Thou lovest Thy children and that Thou only seekest one who should plead on their behalf.' R. Simon said: It is as if a king[1] and his son were in an inner chamber and the son's tutor was in the vestibule, and the king kept on shouting out, 'Let me be while I kill my son,' but in reality he was seeking for someone to plead on his [son's] behalf.[2] Likewise, when God said to Moses: *Now therefore let Me alone, that My wrath may wax hot against them, and that I may consume them, and I will make of thee a great nation* (*ib.* 10), Moses said to himself: 'Am I then to hold back God's hands? If one may say so, He is surely looking for someone to plead on their behalf.' Whereupon, '*And Moses besought.*'

Another explanation: '*Now therefore let Me alone.*' Moses said: 'Lord of the Universe, dost Thou seek to destroy them? Uproot first all above and all below and then destroy them.' Whence this? For it is said, *Lift up your eyes to the heavens, and look upon the earth beneath; for the heavens shall vanish away like smoke, and the earth shall wax old like a garment, and they that dwell therein shall die in like manner; but My salvation shall be for ever, and My favour shall not be abolished* (Isa. LI, 6). First, '*The heavens shall vanish away like smoke,*' etc., and afterwards, '*And they that dwell therein shall die in like manner.*' Moses further said: 'Even if Thou wouldst destroy the heavens and the earth Thou canst not destroy Israel, because Thou didst swear to their fathers; and further, Thou didst not swear to them by the heavens nor by the earth, but by Thy great name.' Whence this? For it is said, *To whom Thou didst swear by Thine own self* (Ex. XXXII, 13).[3] 'Wouldst Thou then annul Thy name?' Moses further said to God: 'Account them as [the people of] Sodom. What didst Thou say to Abraham? *And the Lord said: If I find in Sodom fifty righteous within the city, then I will forgive all the place for their sake* (Gen. XVIII, 26); and Thou didst promise forgiveness even for ten [righteous].' Whence this? For it

[1] Ex. R. XLII, 9. [2] Otherwise he need not have shouted, since there was none to prevent him in any case.
[3] Hence as long as Thy name endureth, the oath is binding.

is said, *And he said: Oh, let not the Lord be angry, and I will speak yet but this once. Peradventure ten shall be found there. And he said: I will not destroy it for the ten's sake* (*ib.* XVIII, 32). But I can muster up before Thee from these [Israel] eighty righteous men.' God replied: 'Muster them up.' Said Moses to God: 'Master of the Universe, lo there are the seventy elders, as it is written, *And the Lord said unto Moses: Gather unto Me seventy men of the elders of Israel, whom thou knowest to be the elders of the people, and officers over them, and bring them unto the tent of meeting, that they may stand with thee: and I will come down and speak with thee and I will take of the spirit which is upon thee, and will put it upon them; and they shall bear the burden of the people with thee, that thou bear it not thyself alone* (Num. XI, 16 f). 'Add to them Aaron, Nadab, Abihu, Eleazar, Ithamar, Phinehas, and Caleb, lo these make seventy-seven.' God said to him: 'But, Moses, where are the three remaining righteous men?' Moses could not find them. He then exclaimed: 'Master of the Universe, if these [righteous] men though alive cannot stand for them [Israel] in the breach, let then the dead do so.' And continuing he said: 'Do it for the merit of the three Patriarchs[1] and lo, then there will be eighty,' [as Scripture says], *Remember Abraham, Isaac, and Israel, Thy servants* (Ex. XXXII, 13). As soon as Moses mentioned the merits of the Fathers immediately God replied: '*I have pardoned according to thy word*' (Num. XIV, 20).[2] When at a later date Solomon[3] arose and saw that though Moses had mentioned seventy-seven living righteous men it would have been of no avail had he not also mentioned the merits of the three dead Patriarchs, he began to remark: *Wherefore I praised the dead that are already dead more than the living that are yet alive; but better than they both is he that hath not yet been, who hath not seen the evil work that is done under the sun* (Eccl. IV, 2 f).

Another explanation: '*Remember Abraham, Isaac, and Jacob, Thy servants,*' *to whom Thou didst swear by Thine own*

[1] Cf. Ex. R. XLIV, 6.
[2] This occurs in the story of the spies: the Midrash quotes it here loosely to indicate God's answer. [3] Shab. 30*a*.

self, and saidst unto them: I will multiply your seed as the stars of heaven, and all this land that I have spoken of will I give unto your seed, and they shall inherit it for ever. And the Lord repented of the evil which He said He would do unto His people (Ex. XXXII, 13 f). R. Levi said: Moses said to God: 'Master of the Universe, will the dead live again?' God replied: 'Moses, are you also ignorant of the truth? Have I not said unto you, "I kill and I bring back to life"?' Whereupon Moses retorted: 'If the dead are to live again, account it as if the Patriarchs were now beseeching Thee on behalf of their children. If so, what wouldst Thou answer them?' As soon as Moses said this thing to God, immediately '*And the Lord repented of the evil*'.

16. Another explanation: HEW THEE TWO TABLES. Why two? The Rabbis say: The Holy One, blessed be He, said: 'These shall act as witnesses between Me and My children. They correspond to two witnesses [that must testify to a cause], to two groomsmen,[1] to bridegroom and bride, to heaven and earth, to this world and the World to Come.'

17. Another explanation: HEW THEE. R. Joḥanan b. Zakkai was asked: Why were the first Tables the work of God and the second two the work of man? He replied: It is like the case of a king who took a wife to himself and himself defrayed the cost of the paper [for the marriage document] and the [fee of] the scribe; he also adorned her at his own expense and brought her into his house. Seeing her behaving in a familiar manner with one of his servants he became angry with her and sent her away. Her groomsman came to the king and said to him, 'Sire, do you not know whence you took her? Was she not brought up among slaves? Since she was brought up amongst the servants she is familiar with them.' Said the king to him: 'And do you wish that I should become reconciled with her? Then bring at your expense the paper

[1] שושבין, bridegroom's friend or best man, and also bride's friend or agent.

and the scribe and I will append my signature to it. Similarly Moses spoke to God after Israel had done that deed.[1] He said to Him: 'Dost Thou not know whence Thou didst bring them out? Was it not from Egypt, from the house of idolatry?' Whereupon God answered, 'And do you desire that I should become reconciled with them? Then bring the Tables at your own expense and I will append My signature.' As it is said, *And I will write upon the tables*, etc. (*ib.* XXXIV, 1). He added: 'Moses, I swear to you, as you devoted your life to their service in this world, so too in the time to come when I bring Elijah, the prophet, unto them, the two of you shall come together.' Whence this? For so it is written, *The Lord is longsuffering and great in power, and will by no means clear the guilty; the Lord, in the whirlwind and in the storm is His way, and the clouds are the dust of His feet. He rebuketh the sea, and maketh it dry, and drieth up all the rivers; Bashan languisheth, and Carmel, and the flower of the Lebanon languisheth* (Nahum I, 3 f). '*In the whirlwind*' (be-Sufah)[2]: this refers to Moses, of whom it is written, *And when she could no longer hide him, she took for him an ark of bulrushes, and daubed it with slime and with pitch; and she put the child therein, and laid it in the flags* (ba-suf) *by the river's brink* (Ex. II, 3). '*And in the storm*': this refers to Elijah, of whom it is written, *And it came to pass, as they still went on, and talked, that, behold, there appeared a chariot of fire, and horses of fire, which parted them both asunder; and Elijah went up by a whirlwind into heaven. And Elisha saw it, and he cried: My father, my father, the chariot of Israel and the horsemen thereof. And he saw him no more; and he took hold of his own clothes and rent them in two pieces* (II Kings II, 11 f). At that time he will come and comfort you, as it is said, *Behold I will send you Elijah the prophet . . . And he shall turn the heart of the fathers to the children* (Mal. III, 23 f).

[1] The Golden Calf.
[2] Taking *sufah* 'whirlwind' as connected with *suf* 'flags'.

CHAPTER IV

RE'EH

1. *Halachah:* Is it permissible to divide up the public reading of the Curses[1] amongst several persons? Our Rabbis have learnt thus[2]: The Curses must be read without interruption, one person only reading them all. Our Rabbis have taught us: Why is it not permitted to interrupt the reading of the Curses? R. Ḥiyya b. Gamda said: Because it is written, *My son, despise not the chastening of the Lord, neither spurn* (taḳoẓ) *thou His correction* (Prov. III, 11). This means, Do not make the Rebukes appear as if cut in pieces (*ḳoẓin*),[3] but one person must read them all.

Another explanation: Why is it not permitted to break up the reading of the Curses? R. Joshua of Siknin[4] said in the name of R. Levi: The Holy One, blessed be He, says: 'I have written concerning Myself, *I will be with him in trouble* (Ps. XCI, 15): it would not be fair that my children should be cursed and I be blessed.' How [could this come about]? Should the reading of the Curses be frequently interrupted then every one called to the reading would have to recite two benedictions, one before it and one after it; therefore one only should read them all. The Rabbis say: God said: 'I did not give them [Israel] the Blessings[5] and the Curses for their hurt but only to show them the good way which they should choose in order to receive reward. Whence this? From what we have read in the context under comment, BEHOLD, I SET BEFORE YOU THIS DAY, etc. (XI, 26).

[1] Or, rather, Rebukes. Lev. XXVI, or Deut. XXVIII.
[2] Cf. Meg. III, 6. As the reading of the Law was accompanied by the recital of benedictions, it was felt to be inappropriate for one man to break off in the middle of the curses and for another to begin, because there was an established rule that no benediction should be recited over misfortune. Cf. Meg. 31*b*. V. Rabbinowitz, *Mishnah Megillah*, pp. 107–108. [3] A play upon the M.T. תקץ (*despise*) and the word קוץ, 'thorn,' i.e. piece, section.
[4] North of Jotapata in Galilee. V. Neubauer, *Géographie*, p. 204.
[5] In both Lev. and Deut. the Curses are preceded by Blessings.

2. This bears out what Scripture says, *Hear ye, and give ear, be not proud*, etc. (Jer. XIII, 15). What is the meaning of '*Hear ye, and give ear*, etc.'? R. Tanḥuma said: The Holy One, blessed be He, said: 'Hearken to the words of the Torah and speak not haughtily, *For the Lord hath spoken* [*it*]' (*ib.*). And where did He speak it? [In the words], *Every one that is proud in heart is an abomination* (Prov. XVI, 5).

Another explanation: '*Hear ye*' the words of the Torah, and do not make your ear too haughty to hearken to the words of the Torah, '*For the Lord hath spoken it.*' And where did He speak it? [In the words], *He that turneth away his ear from hearing the law, even his prayer is an abomination* (*ib.* XXVIII, 9).

Another explanation: '*Hear ye*' the words of the Torah; '*And give ear*' to the words of the Torah. What is the meaning of '*Be not proud*'? Do not prevent good from coming upon the world,[1] '*For the Lord hath spoken.*' And where did He speak it? [In the words], *If ye be willing and obedient, ye shall eat the good of the land; but if ye refuse and rebel, ye shall be devoured with the sword; for the mouth of the Lord hath spoken* (Isa. I, 19 f).

What is the meaning of '*If ye be willing and obedient*, etc.'? R. Eleazar said: The sword and the book[2] came down from heaven wrapped together.[3] God said to Israel: 'If you will do what is written in this book you will be saved from this sword; and if not, you will be slain by this sword.'

Another explanation: '*If ye be willing and obedient.*' R. Levi said: This can be compared to a servant to whom his master said: 'Here is a golden necklace, or otherwise, here are iron chains.' So God said to Israel: 'If you do My will, lo, here is the good and the blessing; and if not, lo, here is the curse. Lo, here are the two ways before you.' BEHOLD, I SET BEFORE YOU THIS DAY A BLESSING AND A CURSE.

[1] As a reward for your obedience *tigbahu* (E.V. '*be* [*not*] *proud*') lit. means 'to lift up'; here, by transference, it is rendered: do not remove (the good from this world). [2] Sc. the Torah.
[3] Lev. R. XXXV, 6; Sifré Deut. par. XL ed. Friedman, p. 78.

3. Another explanation: BEHOLD, I. R. Eleazar said: From the time when God uttered this on Sinia it has been laid down that *Out of the mouth of the Most High proceedeth not evil and good* (Lam. III, 38); but evil cometh on its account to those who do it, and good cometh to those who do good. R. Haggai said: [God said]: 'And what is more, not only have I set two paths before you, but I have not dealt with you according to the strict letter of the law,[1] and I said to you, THEREFORE CHOOSE LIFE (XXX, 19).

4. Another explanation: What is written in an earlier passage? *For if ye shall diligently keep [all this commandment,* etc.] (Deut. XI, 22). Which [is the precept referred to in] '*All this commandment'?* R. Levi said: The recitation of the *shema'*[2]; the Rabbis say: It is the Sabbath, which is equal to all the precepts of the Torah.

Another explanation: '*For if ye shall diligently keep.*' Bar Ḳappara said: The soul and the Torah are compared to a lamp. The soul, as it is written, *The soul of man is the lamp of the Lord* (Prov. XX, 27); and the law, as it is written, *For the commandment is a lamp, and the teaching is light* (*ib.* VI, 23).[3] God said to man: 'My light is in your hand, and your light is in My hand.' 'My light is in your hand': this refers to the Torah; 'and your light is in My hand': this refers to the soul. If you guard My light I will guard your light, but if you extinguish My light I will extinguish your light. Whence this? First it is written, *Only take heed to thyself*, and then *Keep thy soul diligently* (Deut. IV, 9). Hence the force of *For if ye shall diligently keep'*.[4]

Another explanation: R. Simeon said: This can be compared to two men, one of whom possessed a vineyard

[1] לפנים משורת הדין, lit. 'inside the line of justice', i.e. equity.
[2] The name given to the following three Biblical passages, Deut. VI, 4-9; XI, 13-21; Num. XV, 37-41. The term *shema'* is derived from the opening word שמע of the first section.
[3] Cf. Soṭ. 21*a* (Sonc. ed., p. 106).
[4] M.K. The second word is read *tishamerun* (passive) instead of *tishmerun* (active), as in M.T., and the phrase rendered: For if ye keep (My commandments), then ye shall be kept (i.e. your souls shall be guarded).

in Galilee and the other, etc.[1] Likewise, God said to man: 'My law is in your hand and your soul is in My hand; if you take care of what belongs to Me, I will take care of what belongs to you; if you destroy Mine I will destroy yours.' Hence, '*For if ye shall diligently keep*.'[2]

Another explanation: R. Judah b. Sima said: If you will keep the two hundred and forty-eight precepts,[3] etc., until the word 'broken'.

Another explanation: What is the meaning of '*For if ye shall diligently keep*'? God said [to Israel]: 'If you will keep the words of the law, I will guard you from the demons.' R. Abba b. Ze'ira said: There is not a *beth roba'*[4] in the universe where there are not to be found ever so many thousands of demons, every one of whom has a mask over his face to prevent him looking at man and injuring him. And when man's sins warrant it, he removes his mask and turns his gaze on him and injures him. Whence this? For it is said, *He hath redeemed my soul in peace so that none came nigh me*, etc. (Ps. LV, 19). When is this?—*For there were many that were with me* (*ib.*). And who are they? The angels who guard man. R. Joshua b. Levi said: A procession[5] [of angels] pass before man and the heralds proclaim before him saying: 'Make room for the image of God.'[6] See [says the Torah] how many watchmen guard you. When is this the case? When you observe the words of the Torah. Thus I have set two paths before you, blessing and

[1] The comparison is here incomplete. The full form, found in the Midrash Tanḥ. Lev., section Kedoshim (ed. Buber, p. 75), is as follows: R. Simeon b. Ḥalafta said: This may be compared to a man who lived in Galilee and owned a vineyard in Judah, while another lived in Judah and possessed a vineyard in Galilee. Each used to go to the other's vicinity to tend his vineyard. One day they met and one proposed to the other: 'Instead of your coming here, do you guard my vineyard in your neighbourhood, while I will guard yours in mine.' (Continue as in text.)

[2] M.K. The second word is read *tishamerun* (passive) instead of *tishmerun* (active), as in M.T., and the phrase rendered: For if ye keep (My commandments), then ye shall be kept i.e. your souls shall be guarded).

[3] See Tanḥ. *loc. cit.*; also Tanḥ. Deut. (ed. Buber, p. 33). The 248 positive precepts correspond to the 248 limbs of man. [4] The area in which can be sown a *roba'*, or quarter of a *ḳab*—a very minute quantity.

[5] אוקוניא, Gk. εἰκόνιον, 'an image'; hence a procession in which images are carried. [6] I.e. man created in the image of God.

curse, the blessing, if you will hearken to My words; and the curse, if you will not hearken to My words.

5. The Holy One, blessed be He, said: 'Hearken unto Me, for no man who hearkens unto Me loses thereby.' The Rabbis say: You find occasions when a man listened to his wife and lost thereby, and when a man listened to his wife and profited thereby. For example, Adam listened to his wife and lost thereby. Whence this? For it is said, *And unto Adam He said: Because thou hast hearkened unto the voice of thy wife*, etc. (Gen. III, 17). R. Isaac said: This can be compared to a king who said to his servant: 'Do not taste any food until I return from the bath'; but his wife said unto him: 'Taste the dish so that the king will not need to put in salt or sauce.' The king returned and found him smacking his lips, and he said to him: 'Did I not forbid you to eat, and yet you have eaten?' He replied: 'Sire, your maidservant gave it to me.' Whereupon the king exclaimed: 'And have you listened to my maidservant rather than to me?' So God commanded Adam, *But of the tree of the knowledge of good and evil, thou shalt not eat of it* (*ib.* II, 17). What did Eve do? She did give him to eat of it. R. Abin said: She merely had to weep and wail over him, whereupon he ate of it, for so it is written, '*Unto the* voice *of thy wife.*' Scripture does not say, 'Unto the *words* of thy wife,' but '*Unto the* voice *of thy wife*'. God said unto him: '*Hast thou eaten of the tree, whereof I commanded thee that thou shouldest not eat?*' (*ib.* III, 11). He replied: 'Sire, Thy maidservant gave it to me.' Whence this? For it is said, *And the man said: The woman whom Thou gavest to be with me, she gave me of the tree, and I did eat* (*ib.* 12). Whereupon [God] replied: 'And have you listened to Eve rather than to Me?' He was immediately driven out [of the Garden of Eden], as it is said, *So He drove out the man, and He placed at the east of the garden of Eden the Cherubim, and the flaming sword which turned every way, to keep the way to the tree of life* (*ib.* 24). Here, then, is an instance of a man listening to his wife and losing thereby.

And there have been occasions of a man listening to

his wife and profiting thereby; this is the case of Abraham. Whence this? For it is said, *And Sarai said unto Abram: Behold now, the Lord hath restrained me from bearing; go in, I pray thee, unto my handmaid; it may be that I shall be builded up through her. And Abram hearkened to the voice of Sarai* (*ib.* XVI, 2).

R. Samuel b. Naḥman said: This can be compared to a man to whom a son was born, on seeing whom an astrologer remarked: 'This lad will become the leader of robbers, it would be best for his father to cast him away.' When the father heard this he exclaimed: 'Shall I then cast away my son?' When the father of the astrologer heard this he said: 'Whatever my son has said hearken unto him.' So, Sarah saw Ishmael taking to evil ways, and she said to Abraham: '*Cast out this bondwoman and her son*' (*ib.* XXI, 10), and this grieved him. God thereupon appeared unto Abraham and said unto him: '*Let it not be grievous in thy sight because of the lad, and because of thy bondwoman; in all that Sarah saith unto thee, hearken unto her voice,*' etc. (*ib.* 12). He hearkened unto her voice and earned thereby that his line should descend through Isaac, as it is said, *For in Isaac shall seed be called to thee* (*ib.*). God said: 'If this is the reward of one who listens to his wife, how much greater will the reward be of one who hearkeneth unto Me.' And king Solomon came and stated this explicitly: *But whoso hearkeneth unto me shall dwell securely, and shall be quiet without fear of evil* (Prov. I, 33).

6. WHEN THE LORD THY GOD SHALL ENLARGE THY BORDER, etc. (XII, 20). *Halachah:* Is it permissible for a Jew to cover [with earth or ashes] the blood[1] of animals killed on the festival? The Sages have learnt thus[2]: If one kills beasts of the chase or birds on the festival, the School of Shammai say: He should dig up earth with a mattock and cover [with it the blood]; but the School of Hillel say: He may not kill [them on the festival] unless

[1] The blood of animals of the chase and of birds when slaughtered must be covered with earth or ashes (Lev. XVII, 13). Cf. M. Ḥul. VI, 1.
[2] M. Beẓ. I, 2.

he has earth prepared [from before the festival].[1] R. Ḥaggai said in the name of R. Aḥa: If one has no earth prepared one ought not to kill. Why? Because the only difference[2] between the festival and the Sabbath is the preparation of victuals. Therefore if one kills on a festival he must have earth prepared [wherewith] to cover [the blood]. R. Bisna said in the name of R. Aḥa: Come and see, God said: 'What I have forbidden you in the case of domestic animals I have permitted you in the case of beasts of the chase, etc. . . . until, all of them in the case of fish.'[3] The Rabbis say: God prohibited many things and He again made them permissible elsewhere [in Scripture]. A proof of this is the following: God forbade Israel to kill [an animal] and eat it unless it was first brought unto the door of the tent of meeting. Whence this? For it is said, *And bringeth it not unto the door of the tent of meeting, to sacrifice it unto the Lord, even that man shall be cut off from his people* (Lev. XVII, 9). What [else] is written there [in the same context]? *And hath not brought it unto the door of the tent of meeting to present it as an offering unto the Lord before the tabernacle of the Lord, blood shall be imputed unto that man; he hath shed blood; and that man shall be cut off from among his people* (*ib.* 4). And here [in our passage] God made it again permissible for them, as it is said, *Notwithstanding thou mayest kill and eat flesh within all thy gates, after all the desire of thy soul, according to the blessing of the Lord thy God which He hath given thee; the unclean*, etc. (Deut. XII, 15). Whence this? From what we have read in the context, WHEN THE LORD THY GOD SHALL ENLARGE THY BORDER.

7. Another explanation: WHEN THE LORD THY GOD SHALL ENLARGE. This bears out what Scripture says, *I will be glad and rejoice in Thy lovingkindness; for Thou hast seen mine affliction, Thou hast taken cognizance of the troubles of my soul, and Thou hast not given me over into the hand of the enemy; Thou hast set my feet in a broad*

[1] Because digging is forbidden on a festival even for the fulfilment of a precept. [2] M. Meg. I, 5. [3] Lev. R. XXII, 10.

place (Ps. XXXI, 8 f). The Rabbis say: This refers to Joseph. Joseph said: 'Master of the Universe, I will be glad and rejoice in Thy lovingkindness which Thou hast done with me; hadst Thou exacted punishment on my behalf from the wife of Potiphar[1] and not given me sovereign power I would still have had cause for gladness and joy; but now that I possess sovereign power, "*I will be glad and rejoice in Thy lovingkindness.*"' '*For Thou hast seen my affliction*': this refers to Joseph, of whom it is written, *His feet they hurt with fetters, his person was laid in iron* (*ib.* CV, 18).

'*And Thou hast not given me over into the hand of the enemy*': this refers to Potiphar. '*Thou hast set my feet in a broad place*': this alludes to the fact that God made him [Joseph] ruler over all the land of Egypt. Whence this? For it is said, *And Joseph was the governor over the land; he it was that sold to all the people of the land. And Joseph's brethren came, and bowed down to him with their faces to the earth. And Joseph saw his brethren, and he knew them, but made himself strange unto them, and spoke roughly with them: and he said unto them: Whence come ye? And they said: From the land of Canaan to buy food* (Gen. XLII, 6 f).

Another explanation: '*I will be glad and rejoice in Thy lovingkindness*': this refers to Israel. Israel said to God: 'Master of the Universe, "*I will be glad and rejoice in Thy lovingkindness*" which Thou hast done with us, for if Thou hadst exacted punishment from the Egyptians and not given us their riches we would still have cause to rejoice and be glad; our joy [is all the greater] now that Thou hast given us their riches.'[2]

'*For Thou hast seen mine affliction*': this refers to Israel, of whom it is written, *And the Egyptians dealt ill with us, and afflicted us, and laid upon us hard bondage. And we cried unto the Lord, the God of our fathers, and the Lord heard our voice, and saw our affliction*, etc. (Deut. XXVI, 6 f). '*Thou hast taken cognizance of the troubles of my soul*': this refers to Israel, of whom it is written, *And they made their lives*

[1] Cf. Gen. XXXIX. [2] Cf. Ex. XII, 36.

bitter (Ex. I, 14). '*And Thou hast not given me over into the hand of the enemy*': this refers to Pharaoh the wicked, of whom it is written, *The enemy said: I will pursue* (*ib.* XV, 9). '*Thou hast set my feet in a broad place*': this means, For Thou hast enlarged my border, as it is said, WHEN THE LORD THY GOD WILL ENLARGE.

8. WHEN THE LORD THY GOD WILL ENLARGE THY BORDER. This bears out what Scripture says, *A man's gift maketh room for him, and bringeth him before great men* (Prov. XVIII, 16). What is the meaning of '*A man's gift maketh room for him*'? Once R. Eliezer and R. Joshua[1] went out on a mission to gather funds for a charitable cause. They came to the valley of Antiochia,[2] where was a man, Abba Judan by name, who was in the habit of giving liberally to our Rabbis. This Abba Judan was now poor, and catching sight of R. Eliezer and R. Joshua who had come to collect funds he hid himself from them and went into his house and remained indoors for a day or two, and did not go out into the street. His wife asked him: 'Why have you not gone out for [the last] two days?' He replied: 'The Rabbis have come to gather funds for those who labour in the Torah and I am not in a position to give them anything, and I am therefore ashamed to go out into the street.' Now his wife, who loved pious deeds, said to him: 'We still have one field left, sell half of it and give it to them.' He went and did so; he sold a half of the field for five gold pieces and gave them to the Rabbis, saying to them: 'Pray for me.' They prayed for him and blessed him, 'May God fulfil your need,' and they went away to collect funds in another place. This same Abba Judan then ploughed the remaining half of the field, and he found there a great treasure and he became even richer than he was ever before. On their return journey the Rabbis again passed through that place and they said to a man: 'We adjure you: put us in touch with Abba

[1] Cf. Lev. R. v, 4.
[2] Capital of Syria. Antioch stood partly on a hill and partly in a plain. The Valley of Antioch probably denotes a district in the latter portion.

Judan.' The man replied: 'It is easier to approach the king than him.' The Rabbis said to the man: 'All that we wish is that he should not think that we passed through this place without sending greetings to him.' Meanwhile Abba Judan learnt of their arrival and he called on the Rabbis and gave them one thousand gold pieces. He said to them: 'Your prayer has borne fruit.' They replied: 'We too were aware of your good deeds and we placed your name at the head of the list of contributors.'[1] The Rabbis then applied to him the verse, '*A man's gift maketh room for him, and bringeth him before great men.*'

Another explanation: It happened once that R. Ḥiyya was collecting charity in the Great Synagogue in Tiberias,[2] and a man promised one pound of gold. R. Ḥiyya thereupon took him and placed him next to himself and applied to him the verse, '*A man's gift maketh room for him.*'

Another explanation: Resh Laḳish once went to Bozrah[3] and there was a man there who was called Abin Ramaah,[4] not because, heaven forfend! he was deceitful, but because he acted cunningly in matters of charity; after the congregation had announced their donations he would offer a sum equal to the donations of the whole congregation. Resh Laḳish made there a collection and he [Abin] gave as much as the whole congregation. Resh Laḳish thereupon took him and placed him next to himself and applied to him the verse, '*A man's gift maketh room for him, and bringeth him before great men.*' R. Abbahu said: We have no need to learn this from elsewhere, we can learn it from its own place [in our context], for it is written, *Take heed to thyself that thou forsake not the Levite* (Deut. XII, 19), and later [it is written], WHEN THE LORD THY GOD SHALL ENLARGE THY BORDER.[5]

9. AND THOU SHALT SAY: I WILL EAT FLESH, BECAUSE THY SOUL DESIRETH TO EAT FLESH; THOU

[1] Even when you gave a small sum.
[2] Situated on the Lake of Galilee in Palestine. [3] A town in Idumæa.
[4] רמאה from רמאי 'a deceiver'. [5] The reward for helping the Levite and the poor, etc., is the enlargement of borders, i.e. making Israel great.

MAYEST EAT FLESH, AFTER ALL THE DESIRE OF THY SOUL (XII, 20). This bears out what Scripture says, *Who executeth justice for the oppressed; who giveth bread to the hungry. The Lord looseth the prisoners* (Ps. CXLVI, 7). This refers to Israel. R. Phinehas b. Ḥama said: This teaches that in Egypt there were more than seventy peoples, and of them all only Israel were subjected to slavery. And who executed justice for them? He '*Who executeth justice for the oppressed*'. '*Who giveth bread to the hungry*': this refers to Israel. Whence this? For it is said, *And He afflicted thee, and suffered thee to hunger, and fed thee with manna, which thou knewest not, neither did thy fathers know; that He might make thee know that man doth not live by bread only, but by every thing that proceedeth out of the mouth of the Lord doth man live. Thy raiment waxed not old upon thee, neither did thy foot swell, these forty years. And thou shalt consider in thy heart, that, as a man chasteneth his son, so the Lord thy God chasteneth thee* (Deut. VIII, 3 ff). '*The Lord looseth the prisoners*': this refers to Israel. How? The Rabbis say: God forbade Israel eight things and made eight corresponding things permissible for them. God said: 'I prohibited you the fat,' etc. . . . until 'a linen cloak with woollen fringes'.[1] Hence the force of '*The Lord looseth the prisoners*'.[2] Likewise, whereas previously He prohibited the eating of meat for satisfying the appetite,[3] here He made it permissible for them. Whence this? THOU MAYEST EAT FLESH, AFTER ALL THE DESIRE OF THY SOUL.

10. Another explanation: What is written in the preceding passage? '*Take heed to thyself that thou forsake not the Levite,*' and later [it is written], WHEN THE LORD THY GOD SHALL ENLARGE THY BORDER: R. Levi said: This may be compared to a man who said to another: 'Lend me one gold piece.' The latter replied: 'I do not know what your credit is.' The man then said: 'Test me.'

[1] V. Lev. R. XXII, 10. [2] Translating: '*The Lord looseth* (i.e. giveth permission to) *those who are bound*' (by prohibitions).
[3] I.e. for an ordinary meal as opposed to a sacrificial meal.

He lent him the money and the man paid it back promptly. The lender then said to the man: 'If you want to borrow even up to twenty or thirty gold pieces, you can have them,' adding at the same time: 'The reason why you are able to get all the money that you need is because you have paid back [the last loan] promptly.' So likewise it is when a man is tested by paying his tithes in manner due; his border is enlarged. Hence you see, in proportion to your gift is your border enlarged.

11. Another explanation: WHEN THE LORD SHALL ENLARGE THY BORDER. Is it possible that God can enlarge Palestine? R. Isaac said: If one takes up a scroll, he would hardly suspect what its length is or its breadth, but when it is opened out its size becomes apparent. So it is with Palestine; the greater part of it consists of mountains and hills. Whence this? For it is said, *But the land, whither ye go over to possess it, is a land of hills and valleys, and drinketh water as the rain of heaven cometh down; a land which the Lord thy God careth for; the eyes of the Lord thy God are always upon it, from the beginning of the year even unto the end of the year* (Deut. XI, 11 f). When God will level it out, as it is said, *Every valley shall be lifted up, and every mountain and hill shall be made low; and the rugged shall be made level, and the rough places a plain* (Isa. XL, 4), then only will the full extent of Palestine become known.

Another explanation: WHEN THE LORD SHALL ENLARGE. The Rabbis say: this refers to Jerusalem. Only when God will enlarge it will the [full] prosperity of Jerusalem become known. R. Samuel b. Naḥman said: This can be compared to a country, etc. . . .[1] *Then shall the offering of Judah and Jerusalem be pleasant unto the Lord, as in the days of old, and as in ancient years* (Mal. III, 4). *Behold, I will send you Elijah the prophet before the coming of the great and terrible day of the Lord. And he shall turn*

[1] The source of this statement is unknown, and consequently the rest of the passage too is unknown.

the heart of the fathers to the children, and the heart of the children to their fathers: lest I come and smite the land with utter destruction (*ib.* 23 f). *Behold, I send My messenger and he shall clear the way before Me; and the Lord, whom you seek, will suddenly come to His temple; and the messenger of the covenant, whom ye delight in, behold, he cometh, saith the Lord of hosts* (*ib.* III, 1). *Therefore, thus saith the Lord: I return to Jerusalem with compassions; My house shall be built in it, saith the Lord of hosts, and a line shall be stretched forth over Jerusalem. Again, proclaim, saying: Thus saith the Lord of hosts: My cities shall again overflow with prosperity; and the Lord shall yet comfort Zion, and shall yet choose Jerusalem* (Zech. I, 16 f). *Rejoice greatly, O daughter of Zion, shout, O daughter of Jerusalem; behold, thy King cometh unto thee, He is triumphant and victorious, lowly, and riding upon an ass, even upon a colt the foal of an ass* (*ib.* IX, 9).[1]

[1] These verses are quoted in order to end the chapter on a note of comfort and hope (Mah.).

Chapter V

SHOFETIM

1. JUDGES AND OFFICERS SHALT THOU MAKE THEE IN ALL THY GATES, WHICH THE LORD THY GOD GIVETH THEE, TRIBE BY TRIBE; AND THEY SHALL JUDGE THE PEOPLE WITH RIGHTEOUS JUDGMENT (XVI, 18). *Halachah:* Is it permissible for a man's near relative to act as judge in his suit? The Sages have taught thus[1]: The following are regarded as [near] relatives: a man's father and his brother, and both his paternal and maternal uncles, etc. Why so?[2] Just as a relative is disqualified from giving evidence, so too is he disqualified from acting as judge. And what reason have you for saying so? R. Simeon b. Yoḥai said: It is written, *And the priests the sons of Levi shall come near—for them the Lord thy God hath chosen to minister unto Him, and to bless in the name of the Lord; and according to their word shall every controversy and every stroke be* (Deut. XXI, 5). Come and see. [Scripture] has compared controversies with strokes, and strokes with controversies, [in order to tell you] that just as strokes can only be adjudged by day,[3] so, too, suits can only be tried by day, and just as from controversies near relatives [adjudging] are excluded, so, too, are they excluded from strokes. R. Simeon b. Gamaliel said: Do not make mock of justice, for it is one of the three feet of the world. Why? For the Sages have taught[4]: On three things the world rests, on Justice, on Truth, and on Peace. Know then full well that if you wrest judgment, you shake the world, for it is one of its pillars. The Rabbis say: Great is the power of Justice, for it is one of the feet of the Throne of Glory. Whence this? [For it is said], *Righteousness and justice are the foundation of Thy throne; mercy and truth go before Thee* (Ps. LXXXIX, 15). God said: 'Since the punishment for [wresting] judgment is so severe, take [great] heed.' Whence

[1] Sanh. 27*b* (Sonc. ed.), p. 163. [2] I.e. why is he disqualified from acting as judge? Cf. Sanh. 34*b*. [3] Cf. Yeb. 104*a*. [4] Ab. I, 18.

this? From what we have read in the context, JUDGES AND OFFICERS, etc.

2. This bears out what Scripture says, *Go to the ant, thou sluggard; consider her ways, and be wise; which having no chief, overseer, or ruler, provideth her bread in the summer, and gathereth her food in the harvest* (Prov. VI, 6 ff). What led Solomon to draw a lesson for the sluggard from the ant? The Rabbis say: The ant has three storeys [in her house]; she does not store her food in the top storey on account of the drippings from the roof, nor in the bottom storey on account of the moisture of the soil, but only in the middle storey; and she lives only six months. Why? Because any creature which has no sinews and bones can live for six months only. Her food consists only of one and a half grains of wheat, and throughout the summer she goes about gathering all the wheat and the barley and lentils she can find. R. Tanḥuma asked: She subsists only on one and a half grains of wheat and yet she gathers all these, why does she do so? Because she says: 'Perhaps God will grant me [more] life and then I will have food in readiness.' R. Simeon b. Yoḥai said: Once in the hole of one of them were found three hundred *kor*[1] of wheat which she gathered in the summer for the winter. Therefore Solomon said, '*Go to the ant, thou sluggard; consider her ways, and be wise.*' So do you, too, [Israel] prepare for yourselves religious deeds in this world for the World to Come. And what is the meaning of, '*Consider her ways, and be wise*'? The Rabbis say: Consider her good conduct, how she keeps away from robbery.[2] R. Simeon b. Ḥalafta said: Once it happened that an ant dropped one grain of wheat and all the ants came and sniffed at it and yet not one of them took it, until the one to whom it belonged came and took it. Consider her wisdom and all her praiseworthiness inasmuch as she has not learnt [her ways] from any creature. She has no judge or officer over her, as it is said, '*Which having no chief, overseer, or ruler.*' Then you, for whom

[1] A dry measure equal to 39 *se'ah*. [2] Cf. 'Er. 100*b*.

I have appointed judges and officers—how much more should you hearken unto them. Hence, JUDGES AND OFFICERS SHALT THOU MAKE THEE IN ALL THY GATES.

3. This bears out what the Scripture says, *To do righteousness and justice is more acceptable to the Lord than sacrifice* (Prov. XXI, 3). Scripture does not say, As much as sacrifice, but 'More *than sacrifice*'. How? Sacrifices were operative only so long as the Temple stood, but righteousness and justice held good during the time when the Temple stood and also hold good now when the Temple is no longer.

Another explanation: Sacrifices atone only for sins committed unwittingly, but righteousness and justice atone for sins committed both unwittingly and presumptuously.

Another explanation: Sacrifices are practised only by those below [i.e. man], but righteousness and justice by those on high [angels] and by those below.[1]

Another explanation: Sacrifices are operative only in this world, but righteousness and justice are operative both in this world and in the World to Come.

R. Samuel b. Naḥmani said: When God said to Nathan: *Go and tell David My servant: Thus saith the Lord: Thou shalt not build Me a house to dwell in; for I have not dwelt in a house since the day that I brought up Israel, unto this day; but have* [*gone*] *from tent to tent, and from one tabernacle* [*to another*] (I Chron. XVII, 4 f); one who sought to curse David would say to him: 'It would be a good thing for the House to be built.'[2] A proof for this is what David says, *I rejoiced when they said unto me: Let us go unto the house of the Lord* (Ps. CXXII, 1). Thus they seek words against me, implying, 'You will not build it.'[3] Said the Holy One, blessed be He, to him, 'By your life, I will not shorten your life even by one hour.' Whence this? For it is said,

[1] Cf. Lev. R. XXXI, 1. [2] Since it was not to be built in David's lifetime, this was equivalent to wishing him dead.
[3] Even then I rejoiced, though it meant my death, so long as the Temple would be built. This proves that people did actually say this to him.

When thy days are fulfilled, *and thou shalt sleep with thy fathers, I will set up thy seed after thee, that shall proceed out of thy body, and I will establish his kingdom* (II Sam. VII, 12). God added: 'The righteousness and justice which you do are more beloved to me than the Temple.' Whence this? For it is said, *And David executed justice and righteousness unto all his people* (*ib.* VIII, 15).

What is the meaning of '*Justice and righteousness unto all his people*'? Rab Judah and R. Naḥman each has his own explanation of this. The one says: [David] executed justice, he acquitted the innocent and condemned the guilty; if, however, the guilty party had not the means to pay [the sum adjudged] he would pay it himself. This is the force of, '*Justice and righteousness.*'[1] Said R. Naḥman to him [Rab Judah]: If so, he would have encouraged Israel to practise deception. And what then is the meaning of, '*Justice and righteousness*'? He judged justly, acquitting the guiltless and condemning the guilty. This is the force of, '*Justice and righteousness,*' that he made him give up the thing he had robbed. God said: 'My children, seeing that justice is so beloved before Me, be mindful of it.'

4. Another explanation: JUDGES AND OFFICERS SHALT THOU MAKE THEE. This bears out what Scripture says, *If I whet my glittering sword, and My hand take hold on judgment; I will render vengeance to Mine adversaries and will recompense them that hate Me. I will make Mine arrows drunk with blood, and My sword shall devour flesh; with the blood of the slain and the captives, from the long-haired heads of the enemy* (Deut. XXXII, 41 f). What is the meaning of this verse? Rab Judah and R. Naḥman each has his own explanation of this. Rab Judah says: God said: 'If I whet My sword like lightning, I shall destroy My world. What then shall I do?' '*And My hand take hold on judgment.*' R. Naḥman said: God said: 'If I

[1] He acted charitably (*ẓedaḳah*) with the guilty party.—In Hebrew the same word *ẓedaḳah* means both charity and righteousness, the former being regarded as an aspect of the latter.

sharpen My administration of justice,[1] I will release one lightning flash and I will destroy My world. What then shall I do?' '*And My hand take hold on judgment.*' R. Isaac said: There are two things on the right hand of God, Righteousness and Torah. Righteousness, as it is written, *Thy right hand is full of righteousness* (Ps. XLVIII, 11); Torah, as it is written, *At His right hand was a fiery law unto them* (Deut. XXXIII, 2). Two things are in His hand, namely, the Soul and Justice. The Soul, as it is written, *In whose hand is the soul of every living thing* (Job XII, 10); and Justice, as it is written, '*And my hand take hold on judgment.*' God said: 'The Soul and Justice are in My power; do you respect Justice, and I will guard your souls.' Hence the force of JUDGES AND OFFICERS.

5. What is the force of JUDGES AND OFFICERS? The Rabbis say: [It implies that] the officer must be [as much beyond reproach] as the judge; that his own deeds should make him worthy of applying the staff and the lash to others; that the man administering punishment should never himself be meriting punishment.[2]

Another explanation: R. Eliezer says: In a place where there is judging there will be no further judging, but in a place where there is no judging there will be further judging. And what is meant by this? R. Eliezer explains: If justice is carried out [on earth] below there will be no further judging [in heaven] above, but if there is no justice below there will be judging above.[3]

6. Another explanation: JUDGES AND OFFICERS. R. Aḥa said: Come and see. Solomon's throne had six steps. Whence this? For it is said, *There were six steps to the throne* (I Kings X, 19).[4] And in our section there are six precepts in the form of negative commandments, and these are,

[1] I.e. do not temper justice with mercy. *Var. lec.:* If I change, etc., the meaning is the same.
[2] Cf. Pesiḳ. Rab. XXXIII (ed. Friedmann), pp. 149*b* and 150*a*.—By OFFICERS the Rabbis understood those who carried out the sentence of the judges. [3] Cf. Gen. R. XXVI, 6. [4] Cf. Num. R. XII, 17.

Thou shalt not wrest judgment; Thou shalt not respect persons; neither shalt thou take a gift (Deut. XVI, 19); *Thou shalt not plant thee an Asherah* (*ib.* 21); *Neither shalt thou set thee up a pillar* (*ib.* 22); *Thou shalt not sacrifice unto the Lord thy God an ox or a sheep* (*ib.* XVII, 1). [These are] six. A herald stood in front of Solomon's throne; as soon as he [Solomon] ascended the first step he called out, '*Thou shalt not wrest judgment*'; at the second, he called out, '*Thou shalt not respect persons*'; at the third step, he called out, '*Neither shalt thou take a gift*'; at the fourth, '*Thou shalt not plant thee an Asherah*'; at the fifth, '*Neither shalt thou set thee up a pillar*'; at the sixth, '*Thou shalt not sacrifice unto the Lord thy God.*' R. Ḥiyya b. Abba said: The procedure at a trial is as follows: the plaintiff states his claim, the defendant replies, and the judge gives his decision. R. Sima said: And the judge must recite their [respective] claims. From whom do you learn [this]? From Solomon, as it is said, *Then said the king: The one saith: This is my son that liveth, and thy son is dead; and the other saith: Nay; but thy son is dead, and my son is the living* (I Kings III, 23). R. Judah b. Ilai said: I have heard that if the judge wishes the litigants[1] to be seated,[2] he may have them seated; but what is not permissible? For the one to be seated and the other to remain standing. For R. Ishmael said: If before a judge two men appear for judgment, one rich and another poor, the judge should say [to the rich man], 'Either dress in the same manner as he is dressed, or clothe him as you are clothed.'

THOU SHALT NOT RESPECT PERSONS. R. Eleazar and R. Samuel b. Naḥman each has his own explanation of this. R. Eleazar said: If you know that one has the better case, do not be friendly towards him, that [his opponent] should not say that from the very commencement [the judge] desired to make the award in his favour. R. Samuel b. Naḥman said: If you know that one cannot win the case, be friendly towards him, that he should not say that from the very commencement [the judge] desired to declare

[1] אנטדיקון, Gk. ἀντίδικος, an opponent in a lawsuit. [2] Cf. Sheb. 30*a*.

him liable. R. Ḥanina said: One verse says, *And judge righteously* (Deut. I, 16),[1] and another verse says, *Then shalt thou inquire, and make search, and ask diligently* (*ib.* XIII, 15). How [are these verses] to be harmonised? If you see that the suit is a fraudulent one, go carefully into it, but if you see that the suit is a straight one, then give a direct verdict.[2]

7. JUDGES AND OFFICERS. R. Levi said: This can be compared to a king who had many sons, of whom he loved the youngest more than all of them. He also had a garden which he loved more than anything else he possessed. The king said: 'I will give the garden which I love more than anything I possess to my youngest son whom I love more than all my sons.' So God too said: 'Of all the nations whom I have created I love only Israel, as it is said, *When Israel was a child, then I loved him* (Hos. XI, 1); of all that I have created I love only justice, as it is said, *For I the Lord love justice*' (Isa. LXI, 8). Said the Holy One, blessed be He: 'I will give what I love to the people whom I love.' Hence the force of, JUDGES AND OFFICERS. God said to Israel: 'My children, by your life, as a result of your respecting justice, I am exalted.' Whence this? As it is said, *But the Lord of hosts is exalted through justice* (Isa. V, 16)[3]; 'and because you exalt Me through justice I too will act righteously and will cause My holiness to dwell amongst you.' Whence this? As it is said, *And God the Holy One is sanctified through righteousness* (*ib.*). 'And if you will respect both righteousness and justice I will immediately redeem you with a complete redemption.' Whence this? As it is said, *Thus*

[1] On the face of it the verse would mean that the judge should adjudicate according to the statement of the claim without going into the truth of the facts.

[2] If the pleas are obviously false, seek to penetrate to the truth. But if they appear true, accept them and give your ruling accordingly.

[3] The combination of the two statements removes any idea of vainglorious conceit that the former passage might appear to contain: Israel is beloved, but only when he cultivates justice, since thereby God is exalted.

saith the Lord: Keep ye justice, and do righteousness; for My salvation is near to come, and My favour to be revealed (*ib.* LVI, 1).

8. WHEN THOU ART COME UNTO THE LAND (XVII, 14). *Halachah:* Is it permissible for a king of Israel who has a suit to have it tried before the Court? Our Sages have taught thus[1]: A king may not judge nor may he be judged; he may not give evidence nor may evidence be given against him. Our Rabbis have taught us: Why may not a king be judged? R. Jeremiah said[2]: Because of King David it is written, *Let my judgment come forth from Thy presence* (Ps. XVII, 2). Hence no human being may judge the king, only God. The Rabbis say: God said to Israel: 'I planned that you should be free from kings' [lit. 'kingships']. Whence this? As it is said, *A wild ass used to the wilderness* (Jer. II, 24); 'just as the wild ass grows up in the wilderness and has no fear of man, so too I planned that you should have no fear of kings[3]; but you did not desire so, but, *That snuffeth up the wind in her desire* (*ib.*), and "*wind*" is nothing but kingship.' Whence this? As it is said, *And, behold, the four winds of the heaven broke forth upon the great sea* (Dan. VII, 2).[4] God said: 'Should you assert that I do not know that in the end you will forsake Me, already long ago have I forewarned [you] through Moses and said to him: "Seeing that in the end they will ask for a mortal king, let them appoint one of their own as a king, not a foreigner."' Whence this? From what we have read in the context, AND SHALT SAY: I WILL SET A KING OVER ME, etc. (XVII, 14).

This bears out what Scripture says, *That the godless man reign not, that there be none to ensnare the people* (Job XXXIV, 30). R. Joḥanan and Resh Laḳish each has his own explanation of this. R. Joḥanan said: If you see a godless and wicked man leader of the generation, it were better for that generation to fly away into the air and not to accept

[1] Sanh. 18*a* (Sonc. ed.), p. 92; Hor. 8*b* (Sonc. ed.), p. 58.
[2] Cf. J. Sanh. II, 20*a*. [3] I.e. you should not set a king over you.
[4] This verse is taken from the vision of the four world kingdoms.

him. And the expression *mi-moḳeshe 'am* ('there be none to ensnare the people') means, surely, to fly, as it is said, *Will a bird fall in a snare upon the earth, where there is no lure* (moḳesh)[1] *for it* (Amos III, 5)? *'That the godless man reign not';* the Rabbis say: When kings arose over Israel and began to enslave them, God exclaimed: 'Did you not forsake Me and seek kings for yourselves?' Hence the force of, I WILL SET A KING OVER ME.[2]

9.[3] This bears out what Scripture says, *Put not your trust in princes*, etc. (Ps. CXLVI, 3). R. Simon said in the name of R. Joshua b. Levi: Whosoever puts his trust in the Holy One, blessed be He, is privileged to become like unto Him.[4] Whence this? As it is said, *Blessed is the man that trusteth in the Lord, and whose trust the Lord is* (Jer. XVII, 7). But whosoever puts his trust in idols condemns himself to become like unto them. Whence this? As it is written, *They that make them shall be like unto them* (Ps. CXV, 8). The Rabbis say: Whosoever puts his trust in flesh and blood passes away and his patronage also passes away, as it is said, *Nor in the son of man, in whom there is no help* (*ib.* CXLVI, 3). What follows on this verse? *His breath goeth forth, he returneth to his dust* (*ib.* 4). God said: 'Although they know that man is nought, yet they forsake My glory and say: "Set a king over us." Why do you ask for a king? By your life, in the end you will learn to your cost what you will have to suffer from your king.' Whence this? As it is said, *All their kings are fallen, there is none among them that calleth unto Me* (Hos. VII, 7).

10. Another comment on, AND SHALT SAY: I WILL SET A KING OVER ME. R. Judah b. Ilai said:

[1] Thus the term *moḳesh* is applied to creatures that fly; hence the homiletical rendering of *mi-moḳeshe*, that the generation should fly away from their godless and wicked leaders.

[2] I.e. God reminded Israel of their own words. Resh Laḳish's explanation is here missing. V., however, Est. R. I, 9.

[3] This is not marked in Wilna ed., but is shown in the Warsaw ed.

[4] I.e. they are called 'men of God'. Also, God fulfils their decrees (i.e. petitions and prayers).—'E.J.

When Israel entered the promised land they were commanded three things,[1] namely, to blot out the memory of Amalek, to set a king over them, and to build a Temple unto themselves. They set a king over them, and they blotted out the memory of Amalek, but they did not build a Temple unto themselves, because there were informers amongst them.[2] A proof for this is the statement of R. Samuel b. Naḥman: The generation of Ahab were idolaters, and yet when they went out to war they were victorious. And why? Because there were no informers amongst them; therefore when they went out to war they were victorious. The proof is this: When Jezebel sought to kill all the prophets of God what did Obadiah do? He hid them in caves, as it is said, *How I hid a hundred men of the Lord's prophets by fifty in a cave* (I Kings XVIII, 13); and there was not a man to tell Ahab, Thus and thus did Obadiah do. But as for the generation of Saul, all of them were informers. The proof is this. When Saul was pursuing after David, all spoke evil concerning the latter to Saul, as it is said, *When Doeg the Edomite came and told Saul . . . David is come to the house of Ahimelech* (Ps. LII, 2); *When the Ziphites came and said to Saul: Doth not David hide himself with us* (*ib.* LIV, 2). Therefore they fell in battle.

Another explanation: R. Muna said: Any one who speaks slander causes the *Shechinah* to depart from earth to heaven. A proof for this is what David says, *My soul is among lions, I do lie down among them that are aflame; even the sons of men, whose teeth are spears and arrows, and their tongue a sharp sword* (*ib.* LVII, 5). What follows immediately on this? *Be thou exalted, O God, above the heavens*, etc. (*ib.* 6); David said: 'Master of the universe, what has the *Shechinah* to do on earth? Remove the *Shechinah* to heaven.'

Another explanation: R. Samuel b. Naḥman said: Why is the evil tongue named 'the threefold tongue'?[3] Because it slays three people, him who speaks evil, him who listens to it, and the victim of the slander. Whence

[1] Cf. Sanh. 20*b*. [2] 'E.J.: the presence of informers causes the *Shechinah* to depart; hence they were not worthy of a Temple for the *Shechinah* to dwell in. [3] Cf. 'Arak. 15*b*.

this? [From the case of] Doeg who spoke evil, Saul who listened to it, and of Nob, the city of priests slandered.

Another explanation: R. Samuel b. Naḥman said: The serpent was asked: 'Why are you to be found amongst the fences?' He replied: 'Because I broke the fence of the world.'[1] He was further asked: 'And why do you crawl about the ground with your tongue slavering on the ground?' He replied: 'The cause for this is my slandering my Creator.' And what was the slander? R. Joshua of Siknin said in the name of R. Levi: The first serpent possessed the power of speech like human beings; when Adam and Eve would not eat of that forbidden tree he began to slander his Creator, and he said to them: 'From this tree the Creator ate and created His world, and He therefore forbade you to eat thereof lest you create another world.' And what did God do unto him? He severed his feet and cut off his tongue, so that he should no [longer] be able to speak.

Another explanation: The serpent was asked: 'What benefit do you derive from biting?' He replied: 'Instead of asking me, ask those who engage in slander,' as it is said, *Surely the serpent will bite without enchantment, neither is there profit for the slanderer* (Eccl. x, 11),[2] which means: What benefit does the slanderer derive from his slander?[3]

Another explanation: The serpent was asked: 'How is it that though you bite only one limb, yet your poison spreads through all the limbs?' He replied: 'Instead of asking me, why not ask the slanderer, who though he be in Rome slays by his slander someone in Syria, and when in Syria, he slays [someone] in Rome.' See how great is the power of slander, for although Israel had been commanded to build a Temple, it was not built in their days, because it was a generation of slanderers.

[1] The serpent in tempting Eve to eat of the forbidden tree opened the way to lawlessness. [2] E.V. '*If the serpent bite without enchantment, then the charmer hath no advantage*'.
[3] He understands the second half to be the serpent's answer to the question, why he '*Will bite without enchantment*', i.e. without any apparent cause or motive.

11. Another comment on, I WILL SET A KING OVER ME. The Rabbis say: The Holy One, blessed be He, said: 'In this world you asked for kings, and kings arose in Israel and caused you to fall by the sword.' Saul caused them to fall on Mount Gilboa. Whence this? *And the men of Israel fled from before the Philistines* (I Sam. XXXI, 1). David brought about a plague, as it is said, *So the Lord sent a pestilence upon Israel* (II Sam. XXIV, 15). Ahab was the cause of the withholding of rain from them [Israel], as it is said, *There shall not be dew nor rain these years*, etc. (I Kings XVII, 1). Zedekiah was the cause of the destruction of the Temple. When Israel saw what befell them on account of their kings they all began to cry out: 'We do not desire a king, we desire our first king,' [as it is said], *For the Lord is our Judge, the Lord is our Lawgiver, the Lord is our King; He will save us* (Isa. XXXIII, 22). Whereupon God replied: 'By your life, I will do so.' Whence this? For it is said, *And the Lord shall be king over all the earth*, etc. (Zech. XIV, 9).

12. WHEN THOU DRAWEST NIGH UNTO A CITY (XX, 10). *Halachah:* Many regulations were made in the interests of peace. The Sages have taught thus[1]: The following rules were laid down in the interests of peace. The priest reads [the Law] first, and after him a Levite and after him an Israelite.[2] See how great is the power of peace. R. Joḥanan said: The sun never faces the concavity of the crescent moon.[3] Why? In the interests of peace, as it is said, *Dominion and fear are with Him; He maketh peace in His high places* (Job XXV, 2). R. Levi said: Not one of the constellations which travel in the firmament can see what is in front of him, but only what is behind him, like a man descending a ladder with his face backwards, in order that every single constellation should

[1] Cf. Giṭ. 59*a*, where the full list is given.

[2] This order was instituted so as to avoid quarrelling over precedence. In ancient times those who were called up to the Reading of the Law read each his own portion.

[3] Lest he should become discouraged through thinking that he too may become diminished like the moon. Cf. R.H. 23*b*.

exclaim: 'I am the first.' Thus, '*He maketh peace in His high places.*'

Another explanation: '*He maketh peace in His high places.*' R. Levi said: Michael is made up entirely of snow, and Gabriel of fire,[1] and though they stand near one another yet they do not injure each other. Bar Ḳappara said: If the heavenly beings who are free from envy and hatred and rivalry are in need of peace, how much more are the lower beings, who are subject to hatred, rivalry, and envy, in need of peace. The Rabbis say: The greatness of peace[2] can be gauged from the fact that even when dealing with war upon which one enters with swords and spears, God said: 'When you go to make war begin with proclaiming peace.' Whence this? From what we have read in the context, WHEN THOU DRAWEST NIGH UNTO A CITY TO FIGHT AGAINST IT, THEN PROCLAIM PEACE UNTO IT.

13. Another explanation: WHEN THOU DRAWEST NIGH UNTO A CITY, etc. This bears out what Scripture says, *Thou shalt also decree a thing, and it shall be established unto thee*, etc. (Job XXII, 28). The Rabbis say: This verse alludes to the time of the [Golden] Calf when God was wroth with Israel [and] He said to Moses, *I will smite them with pestilence* (ba-deber), *and destroy them* (Num. XIV, 12).[3] What is the meaning of, '*I will smite them with pestilence* (deber), *and destroy them*'? God said to him: 'They think that I need swords and spears with which to destroy them. As I created the world with a word (*be-dabar*), as it is said, *By the word* (bi-dbar)[4] *of the Lord were the heavens made; and all the host of them by the breath of His mouth* (Ps. XXXIII, 6), so will I do unto them; I will let a word go forth from My mouth and it will slay them.' This

[1] Cf. Num. R. XII, 8. 'E.J.: The idea is that it is Michael's function to cool God's anger, as it were, while Gabriel, on the other hand, seeks to inflame it. [2] Cf. Num. R. XI, 7. [3] The reference is to the spies and not to the Golden Calf, but the Rabbis quote it loosely, indicating that God spoke similarly on the latter occasion too.
[4] *Deber* (pestilence) is rendered as though it read *dabar*, a word.

is the meaning of, '*I will smite them with a word, and destroy them.*'

Another explanation: What is the force of, '*And destroy them*'? God said to him [Moses]: 'I will cause you to inherit them,[1] and cause others to be descended from you.' Whence this? For it is said, *And I will make of thee a great nation* (Ex. XXXII, 10; cf. Num. XIV, 12). When Moses heard this he began to pray on their behalf. And what did Moses say at this hour? [He said:] *Inasmuch as Thou Lord art seen face to face* (Num. XIV, 14). What is the meaning of, '*Face to face*'? R. Aḥa said in the name of R. Simeon b. Levi: Moses said: 'Lo, the Attribute of Justice lies on evenly balanced scales; Thou sayest, "*I will smite them with pestilence,*" but I say, *Pardon, I pray Thee*' (Num. XIV, 19). He [Moses] said further: 'The matter is evenly balanced; we will see, who will prevail, "*Thou O Lord*"[2] or I.' R. Berekya said: God said to him: 'By your life, you have nullified My [will] and yours prevails.' Whence this? For it is said, *And the Lord said: I have pardoned according to thy* word (*ib.* 20). Hence the force of, '*Thou shalt also decree a thing, and it shall be established unto thee.*'

Another explanation: '*Thou shalt also decree.*' R. Joshua of Siknin said in the name of R. Levi: God agreed to whatever Moses decided. How? God never commanded Moses to break the Tables. Moses, however, on his account went out and broke them. And whence do we know that God approved of [his action]? For it is written, *Which* (asher) *thou didst break* (Ex. XXXIV, 1)—as much as to say: A good thing that you have broken them.[3] God commanded him to make war on Sihon, as it is said, *And contend with him in battle* (Deut. II, 24), but he did not do so, but [as Scripture has it], *And I sent messengers*, etc. (*ib.* 26). God said to him: 'I have commanded you to make war with

[1] The Heb. *orishennu* is now interpreted as the literal causative (*hif'il*) of *yarash*, to inherit. [2] I.e. Moses or God. The words, '*Thou O Lord*' formed part of Moses' prayer; cf. Num. XIV, 14.

[3] A play upon the words אשר 'which', and ישר 'to be right', 'to be firm', whence the expression יישר כוחך or חילך 'may thy strength (or health) be firm', a phrase of approval and thanks. Cf. Shab. 87*a*.

him, but instead you began with peace; be your life, I will confirm your decision; every war upon which Israel enter, they shall begin with [a declaration of] peace,' as it is said, WHEN THOU DRAWEST NIGH UNTO A CITY TO FIGHT AGAINST IT, THEN PROCLAIM PEACE UNTO IT.

14. Who fulfilled [the command in] this section? Joshua the son of Nun. R. Samuel b. Naḥman said: What did Joshua do? He published an edict in every place he came to conquer wherein was written, Whosoever desires to go, let him go; and whosoever desires to make peace, let him make peace; and whosoever desires to make war, let him make war. What did the Girgashite do? He turned and went away from before them [Israel]. And God gave him another land, as beautiful as his own, namely, Africa: with the Gibeonites[1] who sought to make peace Joshua made peace; but the thirty-one kings who came to fight with him God caused to fall into his hands. Whence this? As it is said, *And they smote them, until they left them none remaining* (Josh XI, 8).

15. Another explanation: THEN PROCLAIM PEACE TO IT. Come and see how great is the power of peace. Come and see: If a man has an enemy he is ever seeking to do him some [injury]. What does he do? He goes and invites a man greater than himself to injure that enemy. But with God it is not so. All the nations of the world provoke Him to anger, yet when they fall asleep their souls go up to Him [for safe keeping]. Whence this? For it is said, *In whose hand is the soul of every living thing* (Job XII, 10). And yet in the morning He restores to every one his soul. Whence this? For it is said, *He that giveth breath unto the people upon it* (Isa. XLII, 5).

Another explanation: If a man injures his neighbour he never forgets it; but not so God. Israel were in Egypt and the Egyptians enslaved them with lime and bricks. After all the evil they had done unto Israel, God had pity upon

[1] Cf. Josh. IX, 3 ff.

them and decreed, *Thou shalt not abhor an Egyptian, because thou wast a stranger in his land* (Deut. XXIII, 8), but pursue after peace, as it is said, *Seek peace, and pursue it* (Ps. XXXIV, 15).

Another explanation: What is the meaning of, '*Seek peace, and pursue it*'? Once R. Meir was sitting and expounding, etc.,[1] that a woman went home, it being Sabbath evening, and found that her [Sabbath] light had gone out. Her husband asked her: 'Where have you been so late?' She replied: 'I have been listening to R. Meir's discourse.' Now that man, being a scoffer, said to her: 'You will not enter my house, whatever happens, until you have gone and spat in the face of R. Meir.' She left the house. Whereupon Elijah, of blessed memory, appeared to R. Meir and said to him: 'It is because of you that the woman has left her house.' Elijah, of blessed memory, then acquainted R. Meir of the episode. What did R. Meir do? He went and sat down in the Great Beth-Hamedrash. Now that woman came in to pray, and on seeing her R. Meir pretended to be blinking. He asked [aloud]: 'Who knows how to cure a sore eye by a charm?' Whereupon the woman replied: 'I have come to cure it by a charm'; and she spat into his face. Thereupon he said to her: 'Tell your husband: "Lo, I have spat into the face of R. Meir."' He further said to her: 'Go, and become reconciled with your husband. See how great is the power of peace.'

Another comment. R. Akiba said: I will prove to you how great is the power of peace. For God has commanded that when a man suspects his wife of adultery[2] the Holy Name written in holiness [upon the scroll] shall be blotted out in water in order to bring about peace between the woman suspected of adultery and her husband. Resh Laḳish said: Great is peace, for Scripture gave fictitious reasons[3] in order to make peace between Joseph and his brethren. When their father died, they feared lest he would avenge himself on them. And what did they say to him?

[1] V. Lev. R. IX, 9, for the story in full. [2] Cf. Num. V, 11 ff.
[3] I.e. recorded without disapproval the fictitious plea advanced by Jacob's sons.

Thy father did command before he died, saying: So shall ye say unto Joseph (Gen. L, 16 f). And yet nowhere do we find that Jacob our father had so commanded. Scripture, however, made use of fictitious reasons in the interests of peace.

Another comment: Beloved is peace, for God has given it to Zion, as it is said, *Pray for the peace of Jerusalem* (Ps. CXXII, 6).

Another comment: Beloved is peace, for God has placed it in heaven, as it is said, *He maketh peace in His high places* (Job XXV, 2).

Another comment: Beloved is peace, for God has given it both to those that are near and to those that are far off, as it is said, *Peace, peace, to him that is far off and to him that is near* (Isa. LVII, 19).

Another comment: Beloved is peace, for God has not given it to the wicked, as it is said, *There is no peace, saith the Lord, concerning the wicked* (*ib.* XLVIII, 22).

Another comment: Beloved is peace, for God gave it to Phinehas as his reward, as it is said, *Behold, I give unto him My covenant of peace* (Num. XXV, 12).

Another comment: Great is peace, for God announceth to Jerusalem that they [Israel] will be redeemed only through peace, as it is said, *That announceth peace*, etc. (Isa. LII, 7).

Another comment: R. Levi said: Beloved is peace, for all the blessings end with 'peace'.[1] The recitation of the *shema'* ends with 'peace', viz. 'He spreadeth the tabernacle of peace'[2]; the *tefillah*[3] ends with 'peace'; the priestly benediction ends with 'peace', viz. 'And give thee peace.'

Another comment: Beloved is peace, for God comforts Jerusalem only with [the promise of] peace. Whence this? For it is said, *Behold, I will extend peace to her like a river* (*ib.* LXVI, 12). David said: I sought to hear what God had to say concerning Israel, and I heard that He was busying Himself with their peace, as it is said, *I will hear what God*

[1] Cf. Lev. R. IX, 9. [2] A.P.B., p. 114.
[3] The prayer known as the Eighteen Benedictions, cf. A.P.B., p. 54.

the Lord will speak; for He will speak peace unto His people, and to His saints, etc. (Ps. LXXXV, 9). R. Simeon b. Ḥalafta said: See how beloved is peace; when God sought to bless Israel He found no other vessel which could comprehend all the blessings wherewith He would bless them, save peace. How do we know it? For it is said, *The Lord will give strength unto His people; the Lord will bless His people with peace* (*ib.* XXIX, 11).

Chapter VI

KI THETZE

1. WHEN THOU GOEST FORTH (XXI, 10). IF A BIRD'S NEST CHANCE BEFORE THEE (XXII, 6). *Halachah:* Is it obligatory[1] to circumcise an infant who has been born without a prepuce? The Sages have taught thus[2]: In the case of an infant born without a prepuce it is necessary to cause a few drops of the blood of the Covenant to flow from him, on account of the Covenant of Abraham. And whence do you learn this? From the Torah, as it is written, *He that is born in thy house, and he that is bought with thy money, must needs*[3] *be circumcised* (Gen. XVII, 13).

Another explanation: '*Must needs be circumcised.*' By the duplicate expression [*himmol yimmol*] two operations of circumcision are implied, namely, circumcision and uncovering.[4] R. Levi said: Scripture says, '*himmol yimmol*'; from this repetition of the word is to be inferred that he who performs the circumcision must himself be a circumcised person, for it is written, '*himmol yimmol.*'[5]

R. Judan b. Pazzi said: Of Zipporah, the wife of Moses, Scripture records, *Then she said: A bridegroom of blood in regard of the circumcision*—la-muloth (Ex. IV, 26). Scripture does not say, *la-milah*, but '*la-muloth*',[6] that is to say, two operations of circumcision, viz. circumcision and uncovering. And why is an infant circumcised on the eighth day? Because God had compassion upon him in delaying the circumcision until he should have gained strength. And just as God shows mercy to man, so too has He shown mercy to cattle. Whence this? For it is said,

[1] Correct with the Radal מותר 'permissible' into חייב 'obligatory' or 'in duty bound'. It is not a question of permissiveness here, but of duty. [2] Cf. Gen. R. XLVI, 12.

[3] This is deduced from the duplicate expression, *himmol yimmol* (lit., 'circumcising shall be circumcised'), which is interpreted thus: Even if the infant is born circumcised (*himmol*) it still has to undergo the circumcision ceremony (*yimmol*).

[4] *Milah*, cutting the foreskin; *peri'ah*, splitting the membrane and pulling it down. [5] Interpreting: He who is circumcised is to circumcise (others). [6] Plural.

But from the eighth day and thenceforth it [sc. the animal] *may be accepted for an offering*, etc. (Lev. XXII, 27). And what is more, God commands, *Ye shall not kill it and its young both in one day* (*ib.* 28). And in the same way that God had compassion upon the cattle, so too was God filled with mercy for the birds, as it is said, IF A BIRD'S NEST CHANCE BEFORE THEE . . . THOU SHALT NOT TAKE THE DAM WITH THE YOUNG.

2. This bears out what Scripture says, *Lest thou shouldst ponder* (tefalles) *the path of life, her ways wander, that thou canst not know them* (Prov. V, 6).[1] What is the meaning of, '*Lest thou shouldst ponder the path of life*'? R. Abba b. Kahana said: The Holy One, blessed be He, said: 'Do not spend time weighing up the precepts of the Torah, as Scripture hath it, *And weighed the mountains in scales*—ba-peles (Isa. XL, 12)[2]; and do not say, 'Seeing that this precept is a great one, I will perform it because its reward is great, and seeing that the other precept is a minor one, I will not perform it.' What did God do? He did not reveal to His creatures the reward for each separate precept, so that they may perform all the precepts without questioning. Whence this? For it is said, '*Her ways wander, that thou canst not know them.*' It is as if a king hired for himself labourers and brought them straight into his garden without disclosing what he intended to pay for the various kinds of work in the garden, lest they should neglect the work for which the pay was little for work for which the pay was high. In the evening he called each one in turn and asked him: 'At which tree have you worked?' He replied: 'At this one.' Thereupon the king said to him: 'This is a pepper tree and the pay for working at it is one golden piece.' He then called another and asked him: 'At which tree have you worked?' And he replied: 'Under this tree.' The king thereupon said: 'This is a white-blossom tree and the pay for working at it is a half a golden piece.' He then called yet another, and asked him: 'At which tree

[1] A.V. has been retained here in preference to the Jewish version.
[2] This is quoted to show that *te-falles* (fr. *feles*) means to weigh.

have you worked?' And he replied: 'At this one.' Whereupon the king exclaimed: 'This is an olive tree and the pay for working at it is two hundred *zuz*.' Said the labourers to the king: 'You should have informed us from the outset which tree had the greater pay attached to it, so that we might have worked at it.' Thereupon the king replied: 'Had I done this, how would the whole of my garden have been worked?' So God did not reveal the reward of the precepts, except of two, the weightiest and the least weighty. The honouring of parents is the very weightiest and its reward is long life, as it is said, *Honour thy father and thy mother, that thy days may be long* (Ex. XX, 12); and the sending away of the mother bird is the least weighty,[1] and what is its reward? Length of days, as it is said, THOU SHALT IN ANY WISE LET THE DAM GO . . . THAT THOU MAYEST PROLONG THY DAYS. Hence the force of, IF A BIRD'S NEST CHANCE TO BE.

3. This bears out what Scripture says, *For they shall be a chaplet of grace unto thy head* (Prov. I, 9). The Rabbis say: The words of the Torah are grace for your old age.[2] How? When a learned man grows old all flock around him and consult him on the words of the Torah.

Another explanation: What is the meaning of, '*For they shall be a chaplet of grace*'? R. Phinehas b. Ḥama said: Wherever you go, pious deeds will accompany you.

WHEN THOU BUILDEST A NEW HOUSE THEN THOU SHALT MAKE A PARAPET FOR THY ROOF (XXII, 8): If you have made for yourself a door, the precepts accompany you, as it is said, *And thou shalt write them upon the door-posts of thy house* (Deut. VI, 9); if you have put on a new garment the precepts accompany you, as it is said, *Thou shalt not wear a mingled stuff* (*ib.* XXII, 11); if you have gone to cut the hair of your head, the precepts accompany

[1] In the sense that it is the easiest to perform.
[2] A play upon the words ראש 'head' and רשיות 'poverty' (cf. Prov. VI, 11, ראשך). When a man becomes old he is no longer able to support himself, and then people look after him, and they respect him for his mature wisdom and great experience.

you, as it is said, *Ye shall not round the corners of your heads* (Lev. XIX, 27); if you have a field and you have gone to plough therein, the precepts accompany you, as it is said, *Thou shalt not plough with an ox and ass together* (Deut. XXII, 10); if you are about to sow it, the precepts accompany you, as it is said, *Thou shalt not sow thy vineyard with two kinds of seed* (*ib.* 9); and if you reap it, the precepts accompany you, as it is said, *When thou reapest thy harvest in thy field, and hast forgot a sheaf in the field* (*ib.* XXIV, 19). God said: 'Even if you are not engaged on any particular work but are merely journeying on the road, the precepts accompany you.' Whence this? For it is said, IF A BIRD'S NEST CHANCE TO BE BEFORE THEE IN THE WAY, etc.

4. Another comment: Ben 'Azzai said: Precept draws precept in its train, and transgression transgression. How [is this to be explained]? Above it is written, *When thou goest forth to battle . . . and seest among the captives*, etc. (Deut. XXI, 10 f); God said: 'Although I have permitted her [the captive woman] unto you, yet I commanded you, *And she shall shave her head and pare her nails* (*ib.* 12) that she may not find favour in your eyes and that you may send her away.' But if you will not do so, Scripture continues, *If a man have a stubborn and rebellious son* (*ib.* 18), and the result will be, *And if a man have committed a sin worthy of death* (*ib.* 22). Thus, transgression draws transgression in its train.

And whence do we know that precept draws precept in its train? First it is written, IF A BIRD'S NEST CHANCE TO BE BEFORE THEE, this leads to, '*When thou buildest a new house*,' and this further leads to, '*Thou shalt not sow thy vineyard with two kinds of seed*,' and this further leads to, '*Thou shalt not plough with an ox and ass together*,' and this further leads to, *Thou shalt make thee twisted cords* (Deut. XXII, 12). Thus, precept draws precept in its train.

5. Another comment: THOU SHALT IN ANY WISE LET THE DAM GO. R. Eleazar said: Scripture surely

ought not to be so concerned [about the dam]. But God said: 'As she busied herself with the honour and good order of the world[1] she is worthy of being spared [suffering].'

Another comment: R. Ḥiyya said: If a bird that has neither ancestral merit nor covenants[2] nor oaths[3] to rely upon, can be atoned for by her children,[4] how much more will the children of Abraham, Isaac, and Jacob who have ancestral merit to rely upon, if any of them sin, be atoned for by their children in the time to come.[5]

6. Another comment: THOU SHALT IN ANY WISE LET THE DAM GO. R. Berekiah said: There is a certain demon who shoots forth like an arrow and sweeps along like a bird. Whence this? For it is said, *Thou shalt not be afraid of the terror by night, nor of the arrow that flieth by day* (Ps. XCI, 5).[6] God said: 'If you fulfil the precept of sending away the dam I will save you from them.'

Another comment: The reward for some precepts is riches, and for others honour. And what is the reward of this precept? If you have no children, I will give you children. For it is said, THOU SHALT IN ANY WISE LET THE DAM GO. And your reward will be, BUT THE YOUNG THOU MAYEST TAKE UNTO THYSELF (*ib.*).[7]

7. Another comment: THOU SHALT IN ANY WISE LET THE DAM GO (SHALEAḤ TE-SHALLAḤ). The Rabbis say: Why is the word *shalaḥ* repeated? To tell you that if this precept comes your way a second time, do not

[1] I.e. with procreation.
[2] Such as God made with Abraham; cf. Gen. XV, 18.
[3] The oaths taken by God towards the tribes as envisaged by the prophet Habakkuk (III, 9), *The oaths to the tribes were a sure word* (R.V.).
[4] In accordance with the Biblical injunction she is spared because of her young. [5] So 'E.J. and Radal; cf. Eccl. R. IV, 1.
[6] Which is interpreted to refer to a demon.
[7] The Midrash homiletically interprets '*the young*' not to refer to the young of the mother bird, but to the children which will be the reward of the man who carries out the precept concerning the mother bird.

say, 'I have already done my duty,' but every time it comes your way you must fulfil it.

Another comment: THOU SHALT IN ANY WISE LET THE DAM GO. The Rabbis said: If you have fulfilled the precept of letting the dam go you will merit also to fulfil the precept of letting go free the Hebrew slave.[1] Whence this? For it is said, *And when thou lettest him go free from thee* (Deut. XV, 13).

Another explanation: What is the meaning of, THOU SHALT IN ANY WISE LET THE DAM GO? If you will fulfil this precept you will hasten thereby the coming of King Messiah, of whom Scripture uses the expression *shiluaḥ* ('sending free'), as it is said, *That send forth freely the feet of the ox and the ass* (Isa. XXXII, 20).[2]

Another comment: R. Tanḥuma said: If you fulfil this precept you will hasten the coming of Elijah the prophet, of blessed memory, of whom Scripture uses the expression, '*shiluaḥ*,' as it is said, *Behold, I will send* (sholeaḥ) *you Elijah the prophet* (Mal. III, 23); and he will come and comfort you. Whence this? For it is said, *And he shall turn the heart of the fathers to the children* (*ib.* 24).

8. REMEMBER WHAT THE LORD THY GOD DID UNTO MIRIAM (XXIV, 9). *Halachah:* If a man suffers from the plague of leprosy, is it permissible for a priest who is a near relative of his to examine him?[3] The Sages have taught thus[4]: A man may examine anybody's plague of leprosy except his own. R. Meir said: Except also the plagues of his near relatives. And why do plagues come? Because of the evil eye.[5] R. Isaac said: It often happens that when a man says to his friend: 'Lend me your axe to cleave this tree with,' the latter out of selfishness replies: 'I have none'; or if he even says to him: 'I implore you, lend me your sieve,' although the latter has one, he replies

[1] You will merit to have many slaves.
[2] Tanḥuma, par. וישלח, on Gen. XXXII, 6, refers this verse to the Messiah.
[3] To decide whether he is unclean or not. [4] Cf. Neg. II, 5.
[5] Cf. Lev. R. XVII, 3; Num. R. VII, 5. 'Evil eye' apparently means here, grudging selfishness, as in the examples that follow.

out of selfishness: 'I have none.' Immediately then the plague attacks his house first. Whence this? For it is said, *And he shall look on the plague, and, behold, if the plague be in the walls of the house* (Lev. XIV, 37). And what was done to the house? They removed everything he had in the house. Whence this? For it is said, *And the priest shall command that they empty the house* (*ib.* 36). When everything he had in the house was removed, his axes and his sieves, people exclaimed: 'See how selfish he is, he refused to lend anything he possessed!' What has he to thank for this clearance? His own selfishness.

Another explanation: R. Ḥanina said: Plagues [of leprosy] come on account of nought save slander. The Rabbis say: A proof that the plagues come on account of slander can be derived from the case of the pious Miriam. Because she uttered slander against her brother Moses, plagues attacked her. Whence this? For it is said, REMEMBER WHAT THE LORD THY GOD DID UNTO MIRIAM.

9. This bears out what Scripture says, *Thou sittest and speakest against thy brother; thou slanderest thine own mother's son* (Ps. L, 20). R. Joḥanan said: If you have accustomed your tongue to speak against your brother who is not of your own nation, in the end you will slander the son of your own nation. R. Judah b. Levi said: If you have accustomed your tongue to speak against your step-brother, who is of your father but not of your mother, in the end you will slander your own mother's son. For anyone who is so arrogant as to speak against one greater than himself causes the plagues to attack him. And if you do not believe this, lo, the pious Miriam is a warning to all slanderers. Hence the force of REMEMBER WHAT THE LORD THY GOD DID UNTO MIRIAM.

10. This bears out what Scripture says, *Suffer not thy mouth to bring thy flesh into guilt* (Eccl. V, 5). The Rabbis say: This verse refers to slanderers. How is this implied in the verse? '*Suffer not thy mouth*': when the mouth

speaks slander, it sins against the body and makes it liable to receive lashes. Hence the force of, '*To bring thy flesh into guilt*', for the mouth sins against the flesh. What is the force of, *Neither say thou before the messenger, that it was an error* (*ib.*). Do not say, 'I will go and speak slander and no one will know it'; for God has said: 'Know that I will send an angel [i.e. a messenger] who will stand by your side and will write down everything you say against your friend.' Whence this? For it is said, *Curse not the king, no, not in thy thought* (*ib.* x, 20). Why? *For a bird of the air shall carry the voice* (*ib.*). And what is meant by, *And that which hath wings shall reveal the matter* (*ib.*)? These are the angels of whom it says, *Each one had six wings* (Isa. VI, 2). [What is the meaning of] *Wherefore should God be angry at thy voice* (Eccl. v, 5)? At the voice [of the slander] which issues from your mouth. *And destroy the work of thy hands* (*ib.*): for you will be punished with plagues. And should you not believe me, lo, Miriam, because she slandered, was smitten [with leprosy]. Hence the force of, REMEMBER WHAT THE LORD THY GOD, etc., and because of this she was punished.

11. R. Isaac said: It was as if a snake was lying on the crossroads and biting everyone that passed by, when a keeper[1] came and sat down facing it. A snake-charmer came up and seeing the two of them, exclaimed: 'The habit of the snake is to bite, I am surprised at the keeper that he associates with it.' So Moses said: 'Miriam spoke slander against me, [that I can understand] since women as a rule are talkative. But did Aaron the righteous also need to speak against me?' Moses said, '*And Miriam spoke* (Num. XII, 1), but surely not Aaron!' When, however, he discovered that Aaron had also spoken he began to lament, *Yea, the man at peace with me,*[2] *in whom I trusted, who did eat of my bread, hath lifted up his heel against me* (Ps. XLI, 10). What is meant by, '*Yea, the man at peace with*

[1] So Levi. Jast. emends הדרבון into הדרקון 'dragon'.
[2] E.V. '*Mine own familiar friend*'.

me'? This refers to Aaron, whose function was to bless me with peace, as it is said, *And give thee peace* (Num. VI, 26). '*In whom I trusted'*: at the time when he stayed the Angel of Death. Whence this? For it is said, *And Aaron returned unto Moses unto the door of the tent of meeting, and the plague was stayed* (*ib.* XVII, 15). '*Who did eat of my bread'*: this refers to the twenty-four gifts of priesthood[1] which he received from Israel. And after all this praise, '[*He*] *hath lifted up his heel against me*,' [as it says], *And Miriam and Aaron spoke against Moses.*[2]

R. Levi said: Women possess the four following characteristics[3]: they are greedy, inquisitive,[4] envious, and indolent. Whence do we know that they are greedy? From what is written, *And when the woman saw that the tree was good for food*, etc. (Gen. III, 6). Whence do we know them to be inquisitive? For it is written, *And Sarah heard in the tent door* (*ib.* XVIII, 10), that is, she was eavesdropping on the angel. Whence do we know that they are envious? For it is said, *And Rachel envied her sister* (*ib.* XXX, 1). Whence do we know that they are indolent? For it is written, *Make ready quickly*[5] *three measures of fine meal* (*ib.* XVIII, 6). The Rabbis add two more characteristics; they are querulous and gossips. Whence do we know that they are querulous? [For it is written,] *And Sarai said unto Abram: My wrong be upon thee* (*ib.* XVI, 5). And whence that they are gossips? For it is written, '*And Miriam spoke.*'

Another explanation: '*And Miriam spoke.*' R. Joshua of Siknin said[6]: When God was about to create Eve from Adam, He was considering whence to create her, as it is said, *And the rib, which the Lord God had taken from the man, made He* (wayyiben) *woman*, etc. (Gen. II, 22).[7] God

[1] Twenty-four priestly prerogatives, enumerated in Tosef. Ḥallah, II, 7 ff.

[2] It seems better to regard this verse as fittingly rounding off the present paragraph, the next paragraph commencing with 'R. Levi said'. (This follows Warsaw ed., not the Wilna ed.)

[3] Cf. the parallel passage in Gen. R. XLV, 5, for additional characteristics.

[4] For צוותניות read צייתניות.

[5] Abraham had to hurry Sarah.

[6] Cf. Gen. R. XVIII, 2.

[7] By a play on words, *wayyiben* is connected with *bin*, 'to understand,' 'consider.'

said: 'I shall not create her from the eye, that her eye may not be haughty, nor from the ear, that she may not be an eavesdropper, nor from the mouth, that she may not be talkative, nor from the hand, that she may not be a thief, nor from the foot, that she may not be a gadabout; whence then shall I create her? From his most private limb, from the thigh.' And yet it was of no avail. And everything that God intended should not be in her is to be found even in the best of women. God said: 'I will not create her from the eye that her eye may not be haughty,' yet of Eve it is written, '*And when the woman saw*, etc.' (*ib.* III, 6); 'I will not create her from the ear that she may not be an eavesdropper,' [yet it is written,] '*And Sarah heard*' (*ib.* XVIII, 10); 'I will not create her from the hand that she may not be a thief,' [yet it is written], *And Rachel stole the teraphim* (*ib.* XXXI, 19); 'I will not create her from the foot that she may not be a gadabout,' yet of Leah it is written, *And Leah went out to meet him*, etc. (*ib.* XXX, 16); 'I will not create her from the mouth that she may not be talkative,' yet of Miriam the pious, it is written, '*And Miriam spoke.*' And see what befell her, REMEMBER WHAT THE LORD THY GOD DID UNTO MIRIAM.

12. Another comment: REMEMBER. The Rabbis say: This can be compared to a king who returned [in triumph] from war, and a noble lady sang his praises, and the king decreed that she should be called the Mother of the Senate.[1] Later, she began to cause disorder in the royal provisions.[2] Said the king thereupon: 'Is that what she does? Let her be sent away to the mines.'[3] So, when God waged war at the Red Sea, Miriam chanted a song, and she was named prophetess, as it is said, *And Miriam the prophetess . . . took* (Ex. XV, 20). When, however, she slandered her brother, God commanded that she should be sent to the mines, as it is said, *And Miriam was shut up* (Num. XII, 15).

[1] A title of honour. [2] Levi. Jast. emends the text and renders: royal headquarters. [3] Where malefactors were sent.

13. Another comment: REMEMBER. When Moses saw what befell his sister, he began to cry out and pray with all his heart and soul on her behalf, [as it is said], *Heal her now, O God, I beseech Thee* (*ib.* 13). The Rabbis say: Moses said: 'Master of the Universe, already long ago hast Thou granted me the power of healing, if Thou wilt heal her all is well; but if not, I will heal her.'

Another explanation: What is the meaning of, '*O God, I beseech Thee*'? R. Abba b. Kahana said: This can be compared to a doctor's assistant who was consulted by a woman suffering from nausea,[1] and he brought her to his teacher. Said the assistant to his master: 'Sir, you have already taught me the complete list of remedies; if you will heal her, all is well; but if not, I will cure her.' Similarly, Moses said: 'Master of the Universe, Thou hast long ago taught me the complete treatment for the plagues[2]; if Thou wilt heal her, all is well; but if not, I will heal her.'

Another explanation: *And Moses cried unto the Lord* (Num. XII, 13). Moses can be compared to a warrior who once had a chain [of punishment] around his neck of which he was later freed. Subsequently he observed the chain placed on the neck of another, and he began to cry. On being asked: 'Why do you cry?' he replied: 'You indeed do not know, but I know what suffering it causes lying there, for once the chain was on my neck and I know what pain it gave me.' So, when Moses was crying, God asked him: 'Why do you cry?' He answered: 'Master of the Universe, I know what pain [my sister] is suffering, for I remember the chain in which my hand was once placed.' Whence this? As it is said, *Behold, his hand was leprous, as white as snow* (Ex. IV, 6). After Moses had prayed on her behalf, God healed her. Whence this? For it is said, *And the people journeyed not till Miriam was brought in again* (Num. XII, 15). Therefore be mindful of what befell Miriam because of slander.

[1] מלכיא Gk. *μαλάκια*, 'nausea,' 'want of appetite.' Levi renders: who was consulted about a certain illness. [2] Lev. XIII–XV. Actually only the symptoms are stated there, but it is assumed that since he was taught their symptoms, he was also taught how to treat them.

14. Another explanation: R. Assi said: One does not speak slander until he denies God,[1] as it is said, *Who have said: Our tongue will make mighty; our lips are with us, who is lord over us?* (Ps. XII, 5). R. Simeon said: If this befell Miriam the pious who had no intention to slander [Moses], but only criticised him because of his neglect of his marital duty,[2] how much more so will the wicked, who deliberately slander their brethren in order to cut short their lives, have their own tongues cut off by God, as it is said, *May the Lord cut off all flattering lips*, etc. (*ib.* 4). God said: 'In this world, because there are amongst you slanderers, I have withdrawn My Divine Presence[3] from amongst you,' as it is said, *Be Thou exalted, O God, above the heavens* (Ps. LVII, 12). 'But in the time to come, when I will uproot the Evil Inclination from amongst you,' as it is said, *And I will take away the stony heart out of your flesh* (Ezek. XXXVI, 26), 'I will restore My Divine Presence amongst you.' Whence this? For it is said, *And it shall come to pass afterward, that I will pour out My spirit upon all flesh*, etc. (Joel III, 1); 'and because I will cause My Divine Presence to rest upon you, all of you will merit the Torah, and you will dwell in peace in the world,' as it is said, *And all thy children shall be taught of the Lord; and great shall be the peace of thy children* (Isa. LIV, 13).

[1] A strong expression, though perhaps hardly to be taken literally; cf. 'Ar. 15*b*.

[2] According to the Rabbis (Sifre on Num. par. 99), she criticised him for holding aloof from his wife.

[3] Cf. Deut. R. V, 6.

Chapter VII

KI THABO

1. *Halachah:* Is it permissible for one who acts as Reader to say 'Amen' after [the benediction of] the priests? Our Sages have taught thus[1]: One who acts as Reader should not answer 'Amen' after [the benediction of] the priests[2] for fear of becoming confused[3]; and our Rabbis have taught us[4]: If, however, he is able to answer 'Amen' without becoming confused, he should answer. For there is nothing greater before God than the 'Amen' which Israel answers. R. Judah b. Sima said: Amen contains three kinds of solemn declarations,[5] oath, consent, and confirmation. Whence oath? For it is said, *Then the priest shall cause the woman to swear . . . and the woman shall say: Amen, Amen* (Num. v, 21 f).[6] Whence consent? For it is said, *And all the people shall say: Amen* (Deut. XXVII, 26).[7] Whence confirmation? For it is said, *And Benaiah the son of Jehoiada answered the king, and said: Amen; so say the Lord* (I Kings I, 36).

Another comment: R. Judan said: Whosoever answers 'Amen' in this world will be privileged to answer 'Amen' in the time to come.

Another comment: R. Joshua b. Levi said: Whosoever enters synagogues and houses of study in this world will be privileged to enter synagogues and houses of study in the time to come. Whence this? For it is said, *Happy are they that dwell in Thy house, they will for ever praise Thee.*[8] *Selah* (Ps. LXXXIV, 5).

[1] Ber. v, 4; *ib.* 34*a*. [2] Num. VI, 24 ff. A.P.B., p. 53.
[3] He may forget the order of service—of course, there were no prayer-books in those days. [4] This is not explicitly stated in the Mishnah cited but inferred from the latter part of the Mishnah.
[5] אספליאות, pl. or אספליא, Gk. ἀσφάλεια, 'assurance' (from danger); hence, solemn declaration.
[6] By answering 'Amen', the woman accepts the oath.
[7] By answering 'Amen', the people formally accepted the blessings and curses. [8] I.e. in the future. (This rendering is more literal than E.V.)

Another comment: R. Judan said: Whosoever listens to the voice of the Torah in this world will be privileged to listen to the voice of which it is written, *The voice of mirth and the voice of gladness, the voice of the bridegroom and the voice of the bride*, etc. (Jer. XVI, 9). Moses said to Israel: 'Since whosoever listens to the words of the Torah is so exalted in both worlds, be diligent to listen to the words of the Torah.' Whence [can this be inferred]? From what is written in the context, AND IT SHALL COME TO PASS, IF THOU SHALT HEARKEN DILIGENTLY[1] UNTO THE VOICE OF THE LORD THY GOD (XXVIII, 1).

2. This bears out what Scripture says, *Happy is the man that hearkeneth to me* (Prov. VIII, 34). What is the meaning of, '*Happy is the man that hearkeneth to me*'? The Holy One, blessed be He, said: 'Happy is the man whose hearing is devoted to Me.'[2] What is the meaning of, *Watching daily at my gates* (*ib.*)? God said: 'When you come to the synagogue to pray, do not remain standing at the entrance and pray there, but see to it that you enter within the inner door,'[3] [for] Scripture does not say, 'watching at my *gate*,' but, '*At my gates*,' i.e. two gates. And why? Because God counts your steps and gives you reward [for each one]. And what is the meaning of, *Waiting at the* mezuzoth[4] *of my doors* (*ib.*)? R. Judah said: Is then a *mezuzah* required for a synagogue?[5] What it means is this: Just as the *mezuzah* is never removed from the door, so do you never be far away from synagogues and houses of study. God said: 'If you will do so, know that you will receive the

[1] The exposition is based on the repetition of the words שמע תשמע, the verse being rendered: If thou wilt listen (now), thou wilt listen (in the Hereafter). [2] Who seeks to hear such things only as will make him more fit to serve Me (M.K., 'E.J.).

[3] So as not to make it appear that you are eager to leave; the unspecified plural *gates* denotes two. Cf. Ber. 8*a*. [4] E.V. '*posts*', but the Midrash understands it in the usual meaning of *mezuzah*, q.v. Glos.

[5] From a literal interpretation of the words thy *house* (Deut. VI, 9), the Rabbis infer that a synagogue, which is God's house, needs no *mezuzah*. Cf. Yoma, 11*a* and *b*.

Divine Presence.' What follows immediately [on this verse]? *For whoso findeth Me findeth life* (*ib.* 35). God said: 'Has anyone ever come to the synagogue and not found My Glory therein?' R. Aibu said: And what is more, when you stand in the synagogue, God stands by your side. Whence this? For it is said, *God standeth in the congregation of God* (Ps. LXXXII, 1).[1] God said: 'Not merely do you receive the Divine Presence in the synagogue, but you also leave it laden with blessings.' Whence this? For it is said, '*For whoso findeth Me findeth life,*' *and obtaineth favour of the Lord* (Prov. VIII, 35). Hence the force of, AND IT SHALL COME TO PASS, IF THOU SHALT HEARKEN DILIGENTLY, etc.[2]

3. This bears out what Scripture says, *Thine ointments have a goodly fragrance* (S.S. I, 3). The Rabbis say[3]: The Torah is compared to five things, water, wine, honey, milk, and oil. Whence to water? [For it is written,] *Ho, everyone that thirsteth, come ye for water* (Isa. LV, 1). Whence to wine? For it is written, *And drink of the wine which I have mingled* (Prov. IX, 5). Whence to honey and milk? For it is said, *Honey and milk are under thy tongue* (S.S. IV, 11). Whence to oil? For it is said, *Thy name is as ointment* [oil] *poured forth* (*ib.* I, 3). Just as oil is at first bitter[4] but in the end sweet, so too are the words of the Torah; at first a man has to labour in them, but in the end he benefits by them, as it is said, *And though thy beginning was small, yet thy end should greatly increase* (Job VIII, 7).

Another explanation: Just as oil [gives] life[5] to the world, so too do the words of the Torah [give] life to the world. Just as oil gives light to the world, so too do the words of the Torah give light to the world.

Another explanation: Just as oil cannot mix with other

[1] Where ten people are assembled in prayer there the Divine Presence is to be found. Cf. Ber. 6*a*.

[2] The exposition is proved more forcibly from the verse that follows on this (Deut. XXVIII, 2), *And all these blessings shall come upon thee.*

[3] Cf. S.S. R. on ch. I, 2, *For thy love is better than wine*, § 3.

[4] The olive has a bitter taste but its oil when purified tastes sweet.

[5] Used for food and medicines and in industry.

liquids, so too Israel cannot intermingle with heathens. Whence this? For it is said, *And have set you apart from the peoples, that ye should be Mine* (Lev. xx, 26).

Another explanation: Just as oil even when mixed with ever so many liquids rises to the surface above them all, so too are Israel supreme above all the heathens, as it is written, THE LORD THY GOD WILL SET THEE ON HIGH ABOVE ALL THE NATIONS OF THE EARTH (XXVIII, 1).

Another explanation: AND IT SHALL COME TO PASS. R. Joshua of Siknin said in the name of R. Levi: God said: 'If you will hearken to My commandments, I, too, will hearken unto your prayer.'

Another explanation: R. Joshua said in the name of R. Naḥman: Whosoever comes into the synagogue and hearkens to the words of the Torah merits to sit amongst the Sages in the time to come, as it is said, *The ear that hearkeneth to the reproof of life will abide among the wise* (Prov. xv, 31).[1]

4. TO OBSERVE TO DO ALL HIS COMMANDMENTS (XXVIII, 1). R. Simeon b. Ḥalafta said[2]: If one learns the words of the Torah and does not fulfil them, his punishment is more severe than that of him who has not learnt at all. It is like the case of a king who had a garden which he let out to two tenants, one of whom planted trees and cut them down, while the other neither planted any [trees] nor cut any down. With whom is the king angry? Surely with him who planted [trees] and cut them down. Likewise, whosoever learns the words of the Torah and does not fulfil them, his punishment is more severe than that of him who has never learnt at all. Whence this? For it is said, *Let favour be shown to the wicked; he has not learnt*[3] *righteousness* (Isa. XXVI, 10). But if he has learnt and has not fulfilled, no favour will be shown to him. Hence the force of, TO OBSERVE TO DO ALL HIS COMMANDMENTS.

[1] For a similar idea, v. Baraitha of R. Meir (usually cited as Aboth VI), par. 9. [2] Cf. Ex. R. XL, 1. [3] E.V. '*Yet he will not learn*'.

5. BLESSED SHALT THOU BE IN THE CITY (XXVIII, 3). R. Isaac said: IN THE CITY means, as a reward for the precepts which you fulfil in the city, namely, *ḥallah*,[1] *ẓiẓith*,[2] *sukkah*,[3] and the kindling of the Sabbath light.[4]

AND BLESSED SHALT THOU BE IN THE FIELD (*ib.*) means, as a reward for the precepts you fulfil in the field—*leḳeṭ*,[5] *shikḥah*,[6] and *peah*.[7] The Rabbis interpret: You will feel blessed in the city because you have been blessed through the field, the earth having yielded its fruits.

BLESSED SHALT THOU BE WHEN THOU COMEST IN (*ib.* 6). R. Judah b. Simon said: This verse refers to Moses. WHEN THOU COMEST IN: this refers to Moses; when he came into the world he brought nearer to God those who were far away from Him, namely, Bathya[8] the daughter of Pharaoh. AND BLESSED SHALT THOU BE WHEN THOU GOEST OUT (*ib.*). This too refers to Moses; when he departed the world, he brought nearer those that were estranged, namely Reuben. Whence this? For it is said, *Let Reuben live and not die* (Deut. XXXIII, 6).[9]

Another explanation: BLESSED SHALT THOU BE WHEN THOU COMEST IN: in thy merchandise. AND BLESSED SHALT THOU BE WHEN THOU GOEST OUT: in thy merchandise. David states this explicitly: *The Lord shall guard thy going out and thy coming in* (Ps. CXXI, 8).[10]

[1] The portion of the first of the dough brought as an offering. Cf. Num. XV, 20 ff. [2] Cf. *ib.* 37 ff. [3] Cf. Lev. XXIII, 42.

[4] This is the duty of the Jewish woman; cf. M. Shab. II, 6. On the Sabbath Light, see Annotated edition of the A.P.B., p. cxviii.

[5] The gleanings in the field belonging to the poor. Cf. Lev. XIX, 9; and M. Peah IV, 10. [6] The forgotten sheaf in the field belonging to the poor; cf. Deut. XXIV, 19, and M. Peah VI.

[7] The corner of the field left unreaped for the poor; cf. XIX, 9, and M. Peah I, 2–3. [8] By saving Moses from drowning, she merited life in the World to Come; cf. Lev. R. I, 3.

[9] Reuben sinned grievously against his father (cf. Gen. XXXV, 22), and thereby became estranged from him (cf. *ib.* XLIX, 4), and forfeited his life in the World to Come. Moses, by blessing him with the words, *Let Reuben live*, regained for him that life, and thus reunited him with his father in that world; cf. Gen. R. XCVIII, 4.

[10] This is irrelevant to the present interpretation. The verse ends, *From this time forth and for ever*, and should be quoted after the next explanation, which makes coming and going refer to one's entry into and one's exit from the world ('E.J.).

Another explanation: BLESSED SHALT THOU BE WHEN THOU COMEST IN: in your first coming into the world; AND BLESSED SHALT THOU BE WHEN THOU GOEST OUT: in your departure from this world.[1] R. Berekiah said: It is written, *A time to be born, and a time to die* (Eccl. III, 2). Surely we know that there is a time when a man is born, and a time when a man dies? What it means is, Happy is the man the time of whose death is like unto the time of his birth; just as at the time of his birth he is free from sin, so too at the time of his death he is free from sin. In this way: BLESSED SHALT THOU BE WHEN THOU COMEST IN, AND BLESSED SHALT THOU BE WHEN THOU GOEST OUT.

6. THE LORD WILL OPEN UNTO THEE HIS GOOD TREASURE (XXVIII, 12). What is the force of WILL OPEN? R. Jonathan said: God holds three keys in His hands over which no creature, not even angel or Seraph, has any control. They are as follows: the key of resurrection, the key of the barren woman, and the key of rain. Whence the key of resurrection? For it is said, *And ye shall know that I am the Lord, when* I *have opened your graves* (Ezek. XXXVII, 13). Whence the key of the barren woman? For it is said, *And He opened her womb* (Gen. XXIX, 31). And the key of rain, as it is said, THE LORD WILL OPEN UNTO THEE HIS GOOD TREASURE.

Another explanation: THE LORD WILL OPEN. The Rabbis say: Great is the rainfall, for it is counted as equivalent to the Revival of the Dead. Whence this? For it says, *And he shall come unto us as the rain, as the latter rain that watereth the earth* (Hos. VI, 3). What does Scripture say immediately before this? *After two days will He revive us* (*ib.* 2). Therefore the Rabbis have inserted [the prayer for rain in the benediction of] the Revival of the Dead, because it is equal in importance to it.

Another explanation: THE LORD WILL OPEN

[1] You shall be as free from sin when you die as when you were born; cf. B.M. 107*a*.

UNTO THEE. R. Eliezer b. Jacob said: When rain falls even business is blessed thereby, as it is said, TO GIVE THE RAIN OF THY LAND IN ITS SEASON, AND BLESS ALL THE WORK OF THY HAND (XXVIII, 12). The Rabbis say: The fish also are blessed. Our Rabbis report: Once it happened that a fish was caught in Acco before the rain fell and it was estimated to weigh three hundred *litras*, but actually it weighed two hundred. Whereupon a certain old man exclaimed: 'Had the rain already fallen, the fish would have weighed more.' After the rain had fallen, another fish was caught, and it was estimated to weigh two hundred *litras*, but actually it weighed three hundred. This shows that the fish also are blessed.

Another explanation: THE LORD WILL OPEN UNTO THEE. See how great is rainfall. Whenever R. Judah b. Ezekiel saw the rain fall, he recited the prayer[1]: 'Let the name of Him at whose word the world came into being be glorified and magnified and blessed, who has countless myriads of angels over every single drop which comes down.' Why? From here [earth] to heaven is a journey of five hundred years, and yet when the rains fall, not one drop is intermingled with another.

Another explanation: Great is rainfall, for it is accounted equal to the Revival of the Dead. How [is this to be explained]? Scripture uses the term, '*opening*' of the one and the term '*opening*' of the other; of the one '*hand*' and of the other '*hand*'; of the one '*song*' and of the other '*song*'. Of the Revival of the Dead it is written, '*When I have* opened *your graves*' (Ezek. XXXVII, 13); and of the fall of rain, THE LORD WILL *OPEN* UNTO THEE; of the Revival of the Dead it is written, *The* hand *of the Lord was upon me* (*ib.* 1); and of the fall of rain, *Thou openest Thy* hand (Ps. CXLV, 16); of the Revival of the Dead it is written, *Let the inhabitants of Sela exult* (Isa. XLII, 11); and of the fall of rain, *They shout for joy, yea, they sing* (Ps. LXV, 14).

[1] Cf. Gen. R. XIII, 15; cf. Ber. 59*b*.

7. Another explanation: THE LORD WILL OPEN UNTO THEE. The Rabbis say: God said to Israel: 'All the benefits that come upon the world come on account of your merit. For example, The dew comes only on account of your merit.'[1] Whence this? For it is said, *So God give thee of the dew of heaven* (Gen. XXVII, 28). 'Rain falls on account of your merit.' Whence this? For it is said, THE LORD WILL OPEN UNTO THEE HIS GOOD TREASURE. 'Peace also comes only on account of your merit.' Whence this? For it is said, *And give thee peace* (Num. VI, 26), that is, on account of your merit.[2] It is related that once a Gentile put a question to R. Joḥanan b. Zakkai,[3] saying: 'We have festivals and you have festivals; we have the Calends,[4] Saturnalia,[5] and Kratesis,[6] and you have Passover, Pentecost, and Tabernacles; which is the day whereon we and you rejoice alike?' R. Joḥanan b. Zakkai replied: 'It is the day when rain falls.' For it is said, *The meadows are clothed with flocks; the valleys also are covered over with corn; 'they shout for joy, yea, they sing'* (Ps. LXV, 14). What follows immediately on this? *A Psalm. Shout unto God,* all *the earth* (*ib.* LXVI, 1).

8. AND MOSES CALLED UNTO ALL ISRAEL (XXIX, 1). *Halachah:* Is it permissible for a Jew who comes forward to read the law [in public] to read less than three verses? The Sages have taught thus[7]: He who reads the law should not read less than three verses. Our Rabbis have taught us: Why is it ordained that less than three verses should not be read? In order that [the number of the verses] should correspond to [the three Patriarchs] Abraham,

[1] Cf. Gen. R. LXVI, 2.
[2] In these three verses the Rabbis interpret לך not ('*to*) *thee*', but 'for thy sake', and render: The Lord will give (dew . . . rain . . . peace) to the whole world (not only 'to thee' but) for thy sake.
[3] Cf. Gen. R. XIII, 6, where the same story is related of R. Joshua b. Korḥah. [4] קלנדה, Lat. *Kalandae,* Calends, the first day of the month in the Roman calendar. [5] סטרנלים for סטרנלייא, Lat. *Saturnalia,* a Roman festival observed in December (beginning on the 17th).
[6] קרטיסים, Gk. *κράτησις*. A Roman festival commemorating the conquest of Eastern countries; cf. A.Z. 8*a* (Sonc. ed.), p. 36. [7] Cf. Meg. 23*b*.

Isaac, and Jacob. Another explanation: To correspond to Moses, Aaron, and Miriam, through whom the law was given.

R. Hoshaya said: The lowliest man in the days of Moses saw what was not vouchsafed to Ezekiel, the greatest of the prophets[1]; [the men in the days of Moses] were men with whom the Divine Presence spoke face to face, as it is said, *The Lord spoke with you face to face* (Deut. v, 4). R. Simeon b. Yoḥai said: Whence can you prove that if Israel had been short even of one man the Divine Presence would not have revealed itself to them? For it is written, *For the third day the Lord will come down in the sight of* all *the people upon mount Sinai* (Ex. XIX, 11). It is recorded of Rabbi, who was wont to hold discourses in the Great Synagogue, that when he was about to enter to give his discourse he would say: 'See if all the congregation are assembled.'[2] And whence do you learn that this [was the correct thing to do]? From the Revelation. Whence this? For it is said, *When the Lord said unto me: Assemble Me the people, and I will make them hear My words* (Deut. IV, 10).

Another comment: The Rabbis say: You find that when God gave the Torah to Moses, He gave it to him after 'calling'. Whence this? For it is said, *And the Lord called Moses to the top of the mount; and Moses went up* (Ex. XIX, 20). Also Moses our teacher, when he came to repeat the Torah to Israel, said to them: 'Just as I received the Torah with "calling", so too will I hand it over to [God's] children with "calling".' Whence this? From what is written in the context, AND MOSES CALLED UNTO ALL ISRAEL, AND SAID UNTO THEM.

9. This bears out what Scripture says, *My son, if thou wilt receive my words, and lay up my commandments with thee* (Prov. II, 1). What is the meaning of, '*If thou wilt*

[1] Cf. Lev. R. x, 2, where Isaiah is said to be the greatest of the prophets.
[2] Either Rabbi (i.e. R. Judah the Prince) was of a nervous temperament and so could not bear being disturbed by late comers, or he did not desire any of his hearers to miss part of his discourse.

receive my words'? R. Huna said in the name of R. Aḥa: The Holy One, blessed be He, said to Israel: 'My children, let not My Torah be unto you like a man's grown-up daughter whom he seeks to marry off to anyone whom he may find.' What is the meaning of, '*If thou wilt receive my words'?* 'If you will merit you will receive My Torah,[1] which the ministering angels coveted, but which I would not give unto them.' Whence this? For it is said, *Kings*[2] *of armies flee, they flee* (Ps. LXVIII, 13). And Scripture continues, *And the beauty of the home*[3] *Thou wilt divide as spoil* (*ib.*)? They said before God: 'Master of the Universe, wilt Thou divide amongst the earthly the beautiful thing which Thou hast in the high heavens?' Hence the force of, '*If thou wilt receive my words,*' that is to say, if you will have the merit.

And what is the meaning of, '*And lay up my commandments with thee*'? R. Abba b. Kahana said: God said: 'You lay up for Me Torah[4] and precepts in this world, and I will lay up for you a good reward for the World to Come,' as it is said, *Oh how abundant is Thy goodness, which Thou hast laid up for them that fear Thee* (Ps. XXXI, 20).

Another explanation: '*If thou wilt receive my words.*' R. Judah b. Shalom said: God said to Israel: 'When are you called My children? When you receive My words.' This can be compared to a king to whom his son said: 'Set some mark upon me in the land [that people should know] that I am your son.' Whereupon the king replied: 'If you wish that all should know that you are my son, then put on my purple cloak and place my crown on your head, and all will know that you are my son.' So God said to Israel: 'If you wish to be distinguished as My children, then occupy yourselves with the [study of the] Torah

[1] This explains the parable: do not think that the Torah is like an old spinster who can be had for the mere asking, for you will receive it (i.e. acquire it) only if you merit it. [2] The Midrash reads the word מלאכי (angels) instead of מלכי (kings), and renders: The angels of hosts speed on, they speed on (to receive the Torah).

[3] The Midrash takes נות בית in the sense of נאת בית, 'the beautiful thing in the house,' i.e. in heaven. E.V. '*And she that tarrieth at home divideth the spoil*'. [4] I.e. the study of the Torah.

and with the precepts, and all will see that you are My Children. So, when are you My children? When you receive My words.'

Rabbi said: When Israel were in the wilderness, a pillar of cloud journeyed in front of them, and the smoke of the altar and the smoke of the incense went up [towards heaven], and two sparks of fire issued from between the two staves of the Ark and devoured in front of them the serpents and scorpions; and when the nations of the world saw them they exclaimed: 'These are divine beings, for whatever they do is with fire.' Thereupon Moses said to Israel: 'All the distinction which [God caused to be] lavished upon you is only because you have accepted His Torah on Sinai.' Hence the force of, '*And Moses called unto all Israel, and said unto them*, etc.' (Deut. v, 1).[1] He said unto them: 'Know that all the miracles which God wrought for you, you have witnessed with your own eyes. In Egypt He wrought miracles for you and your eyes saw it.' Whence this? For it is said, *The great trials* (ha-massoth) *which thine eyes saw* (Deut. XXIX, 2). What is the force of '*ha-massoth*'? It implies that the plagues weakened (*me-massoth*) the bodies of the Egyptians. What is the meaning of '*the signs*' (*ib.*)? The Rabbis say: The plagues became engraven on their bodies. For example, the words *Dam* (Blood), *Ẓefardea'* (Frog), *Kinnim* (Vermin). What is the meaning of '*And the wonders*' (*ib.*)? The plagues deceived them.[2] How? The plagues came every thirty days[3] and lasted for seven days and then departed. The Egyptians had thus respite for twenty-three days between one plague and the next.[4] This proves that [the plagues] deceived them.

10. BUT THE LORD HATH NOT GIVEN YOU A HEART TO KNOW (XXIX, 3). What is the meaning of, BUT THE LORD HATH NOT GIVEN YOU A HEART TO KNOW? R. Isaac said: When Israel stood at Mount Sinai

[1] He proceeds to exhort them to keep God's laws.
[2] Connecting the word *mofethim* ('wonders') with the root *pathah* to deceive, and reading *ha-mefathim*. [3] Cf. Ex. R. IX, 12.
[4] Which made them think that no more would come.

and declared, *All that the Lord hath spoken will we do, and obey* (Ex. XXIV, 7),[1] God exclaimed: '*Who will grant that they had such a heart*' (Deut. V, 26). Israel heard this and kept silence. R. Judah b. Levi said: It was as if a charmer caught sight of a highly poisonous snake and exclaimed: 'Who is able to charm this one?' People asked him: 'Are you not the charmer? It depends entirely upon you.' So when God exclaimed, '*Who will grant that they had such a heart,*' Israel should have answered: 'Master of the Universe, do Thou grant it!' Therefore Moses said, BUT THE LORD DID NOT GIVE YOU A HEART TO KNOW.

Another explanation of '*Who will grant*'. R. Meir said: Who is [morally] superior, the thief or the man robbed? You must needs say, the man who is robbed, for although he has been robbed he keeps silence. Now it is written, *But they beguiled Him with their mouth, and lied unto Him with their tongue. For their heart was not steadfast with Him, neither were they faithful in His covenant* (Ps. LXXVIII, 36 f). God, if one may say so, exclaimed, '*Who will grant that they had such a heart.*'[2]

Another explanation: BUT THE LORD HATH NOT GIVEN YOU A HEART TO KNOW. R. Samuel b. Naḥmani said: Moses said this with reference to himself. How so? The Holy One, blessed be He, made two decrees, one affecting Israel, and one affecting Moses. The one affecting Israel was when they committed the unmentionable sin [Golden Calf]. Whence this? For it is said, *Let Me alone, that I may destroy them* (Deut. IX, 14). And the one affecting Moses? When Moses sought to go into Eretz Israel, God said to him, '*Thou shalt not go over this Jordan*' (*ib.* III, 27). Moses therefore entreated God to annul both decrees. He said to God: 'Master of the Universe, *Pardon, I pray Thee, the iniquity of this people according unto the*

[1] Cf. A.Z. 5*a* and *b* (Sonc. ed.), p. 21 f.

[2] R. Meir holds that at the very moment that they proclaimed their obedience, *Their heart was not steadfast with Him*, their promise being a sham. Hence God exclaimed, '*Who will grant that they had such a* heart', i.e. that what they now said they really meant in their hearts ('E.J.).

greatness of Thy lovingkindness' (Num. XIV, 19), and God's [decree] was annulled while his own [prayer] was fulfilled. Whence this? For it is said, *I have pardoned according to Thy word* (*ib.* 20). When he was about to enter the Land, Moses entreated: *Let me go over, I pray Thee, and see the good land* (Deut. III, 25). Whereupon God replied: 'Moses, on a former occasion you annulled My decree and I granted your prayer; I said: "*That I may destroy them,*" and you prayed: "*Pardon, I pray Thee,*" and your prayer was fulfilled; on this occasion I desire to carry out My decree and to refuse your prayer.' God added: 'Moses, you do not know how to act! You wish to hold the rope by both its ends.[1] If you insist on "*Let me go over, I pray Thee*" being granted, then you must withdraw the prayer, "*Pardon, I pray Thee*", and if you insist on "*Pardon, I pray Thee,*" then you must withdraw, "*Let me go over, I pray Thee.*"' R. Joshua b. Levi said: When Moses our teacher heard this, he exclaimed before God: 'Master of the Universe, let rather Moses and a hundred like him perish than that the finger-nail of even one of them [Israel] should be injured!' R. Samuel b. Isaac said: When Moses was nearing his end and Israel did not pray for him that he should enter the Land, he assembled them and began rebuking them with the words: One man saved sixty myriads at the time of the [Golden] Calf, and yet sixty myriads cannot save one man. This is the force of, BUT THE LORD HATH NOT GIVEN YOU A HEART TO KNOW. He asked [Israel]: 'Do you not remember how I led you in the wilderness,' as it is said, *I have led you forty years in the wilderness*, etc. (Deut. XXIX, 4)?

11. What is the meaning of, YOUR CLOTHES ARE NOT WAXEN OLD UPON YOU (*ib.*)? R. Jose b. Ḥanina said: The clothes they wore did not get old, but those they packed away in their trunks did get old.

Another explanation: YOUR CLOTHES ARE NOT WAXEN OLD. R. Eleazar, the son of R. Simeon b. Yoḥai,

[1] I.e. you wish to have it both ways.

asked R. Simeon b. Jose, his father-in-law: 'Did then the Israelites take with them leather garments into the wilderness?'[1] The latter replied: 'The clothes which they had on them were those wherewith the ministering angels had invested them at Sinai; therefore they were not waxen old.' He further asked him: 'Did the [Israelites] not grow so that the clothes became too small for them?' He replied: 'Do not wonder at this, when the snail grows, its shell grows with it.' He then asked him: 'Did not the clothes need washing?' He replied: 'The [pillar of] cloud rubbed against them and whitened them.' He asked him: 'Seeing that the cloud consisted of fire, were they not scorched?' He replied: 'Do not wonder at this, *amiant*[2] is cleansed only by fire.' So too, as their clothes were of heavenly make, the cloud rubbed against them without damaging them. He asked him: 'Did not vermin breed in them?' He replied: 'If in their death no worm could touch them, how much less in their lifetime!' He asked: 'Did they not emit an evil odour because of the perspiration?' He replied: 'They used to play[3] with the sweet-scented grass around the well, the fragrance of which permeated the world.' Whence this? For it is said, *And the smell of thy garments is like the smell of Lebanon* (S.S. IV, 11). And whence was all this excellency derived? From, *Thou art a fountain of gardens, a well of living waters* (*ib.* 15).

12. Another explanation: AND I HAVE LED YOU FORTY YEARS IN THE WILDERNESS. R. Judah said: Come and see the meekness of God. Among human beings, when a man has a young child he carries him on his shoulders, but if [the child] angers him he at once throws him down. But, if one may say so, with God it is not so; Israel were in the wilderness forty years and they provoked Him to anger and yet He bore them. Whence this? For it is said, *And in the wilderness, where thou hast seen how that the Lord thy God bore thee*, etc. (Deut. I, 31).

[1] That they never wore out. [2] For אמיטון Jast. and Krauss read אמיינטון, Gk. ἀμίαντος. *Amiant* is a kind of asbestos. [3] Cf. S.S.R. on IV, 11, and also Ps. XXIII, 2, *He maketh me to lie down in green pastures.*

Another explanation: Resh Laḳish said: What is the force of, '*That* [*the Lord thy God*] *bore thee*'? It means that God exalted them[1] and made them great; He made them like divine beings, as it is said, *I said: Ye are godlike beings* (Ps. LXXXII, 6).

Another explanation: R. Simeon b. Yoḥai said: Among human beings, when a man has a son he hands him over to a servant to nurse him, and if he has no servant to a [wet] nurse; and how long does she nurse him? Two or three years. With God, however, it is not so, *Even to old age I am the same, and even to hoar hairs will I carry you*, etc. (Isa. XLVI, 4). The Holy One, blessed be He, said: 'My children, by your life, in the same way as I have brought you up[2] in this world, so too will I bring you up and cherish you in the time to come.' Whence this? For it is said, *Is Ephraim a precious son unto Me*, etc. (Jer. XXXI, 20)?

[1] *Nasa*, E.V. '*bore*', also means to lift up, to exalt. Hence the verse is rendered: . . . the Lord thy God exalted thee.
[2] Or perhaps: magnified you.

Chapter VIII

NITZABIM

1. *Halachah:* If a Jew has not read the Morning Prayer, or the Additional Prayer, or the Afternoon Prayer—as it happens frequently that a man has not the time to pray, or was delayed because he had to attend to his natural needs, or was journeying on the road and forgot to pray—until what time may he pray and thereby perform his obligation? How should he act? The Sages have taught thus[1]: The Morning Prayer may be recited until midday, the Afternoon Prayer until the evening, while the Evening Service has no fixed limit of time[2]; the Additional Service, however, may be recited at any time during the day. R. Eleazar said[3]: If one forgot to recite the Additional Service and then came to read the Afternoon Service, he should first read the Afternoon Service, and after that the Additional Service. Why? Because every [prayer] should be recited[4] in its proper time. The Evening Service has no limit of time, it may be recited until the rise of dawn. Why? For so Scripture says, *I love them that love Me, and those that seek Me*[5] *earnestly shall find Me* (Prov. VIII, 17). And whosoever is conscientious in his praying may be assured that his prayer will be accepted, as it is written, *Lord, Thou hast heard the desire of the humble; Thou wilt direct their heart, Thou wilt cause Thine ear to attend* (Ps. X, 17).

Great is prayer in the sight of God. R. Eleazar said: If you wish to know the power of prayer, [know that] if it does not achieve the whole of its object, it achieves at least

[1] Ber. 26*a*. [2] It may be recited any time during the night.

[3] This statement of R. Eleazar is found nowhere else. The nearest parallel to it is in Ber. 28*a*.

[4] Correct מתבראת into מתברכת in accordance with the text of the first edition. V. Ginzberg, *Genizah Studies*, I, p. 500. 'E.J. defends the present reading, 'everything is *created*, etc.,' this being an echo of *He hath made everything beautiful in its time* (Eccl. III, 11).

[5] I.e. whenever they seek Me. The Midrash finds a connection between the word שחר 'dawn' and משחרי '*those that seek Me*', from root שחר.

half of it.[1] Cain rose up against Abel his brother and slew him, and the decree went forth, *A fugitive and a wanderer shalt thou be in the earth* (Gen. IV, 12); immediately he confessed before God, as it is said, *My punishment is greater than I can bear* (*ib.* 13); he said before Him: 'Master of the Universe, Thou bearest with the whole world, and yet with my sin Thou wilt not bear[2]; Thou hast written, [*Who is a God like unto Thee,*] *that pardoneth iniquity, and passeth by transgression* (Micah VII, 18); pardon my iniquity for it is great.' Immediately he found favour before God and He withheld from him [the curse of] 'fugitive'; that is half of the decree, for so it is written, *And dwelt in the land of Nod* (Gen. IV, 16).[3] Hence you learn that prayer is great in the sight of God. And likewise it was with Hezekiah.[4] When [God] said to him, '*Set thy house in order; for thou shalt die*' (Isa. XXXVIII, 1), immediately, *Then Hezekiah turned his face to the wall* (*ib.* 2). Whereupon God said to him, '*I have heard thy prayer . . . I will add unto thy days fifteen years*' (*ib.* 5). For so Scripture says, *He will fulfil the desire of them that fear Him; He also will hear their cry, and will save them* (Ps. CXLV, 19).

2. FOR THIS COMMANDMENT (XXX, 11). *Halachah:* What blessing should a Jew recite when about to read the law? The Sages have taught thus[5]: He who reads the law first and he who reads the law last should recite a blessing before it and after it. And whence is it to be inferred that the law requires a blessing before it and after it? For it is written, *Blessed art Thou, O Lord* (Ps. CXIX, 12), and then, *Teach me Thy statutes* (*ib.*). Hence the blessing before it.[6] And whence do we know that it requires a blessing after it? R. Samuel b. Naḥman said in the name of R. Jonathan: Because after the 'Song'[7] follows, *And this is the blessing*

[1] Cf. Lev. R. x, 5, and cf. Sanh. 37*b*. [2] Cf. Gen. R. XXII, 11.
[3] V. Lev. R. *ad loc.* [4] Cf. Ber. 10*a* and *b*. [5] Meg. 21*a*.
[6] This reason is not to be found amongst those given in the Jerusalem Talmud (Ber. VII, 11*a*, and Meg. IV, 74*d*). For an interesting liturgical suggestion, v. Ginzberg *loc. cit.*
[7] 'Song,' a name applied to Deut. XXXII. V. v. 44 of the chapter. The Midrash probably understands it to mean Deuteronomy as a whole.

(Deut. XXXIII, 1), which intimates that after Moses had repeated the law he recited a blessing. Hence the blessing after it.

Another explanation: God said: 'If you fulfil the duty of reciting a blessing for the law, I also will bless you,' as it is said, *In every place where I cause My name to be mentioned I will come unto thee and bless thee* (Ex. XX, 21). Another explanation: The Rabbis say: The Holy One, blessed be He, said: 'In blessing the law you are really blessing yourselves.' Whence this? For it is said, *For by Me thy days shall be multiplied*,[1] *and the years of thy life shall be increased* (Prov. IX, 11). 'And should you say that I have given you the law to your disadvantage, [know that] I have given it for your benefit, for the ministering angels eagerly desired it, but it was hidden from them,' as it is said, *Seeing it*[2] *is hid from the eyes of all living*—ḥay (Job XXVIII, 21); this refers to the *ḥayyoth*.[3] *And kept close from the flying beings of the air* (*ib.*); this refers to the angels, as it is written, *Then flew unto me one of the Seraphim* (Isa. VI, 6). God said to Israel: 'My children, the law is too abstruse for the ministering angels, but for you it is not too abstruse.' Whence this? From what we read in the context, FOR THIS COMMANDMENT WHICH I COMMAND THEE THIS DAY, IT IS NOT TOO HARD FOR THEE.

3. This bears out what Scripture says, *Wisdom is as unattainable to a fool as corals; he openeth not his mouth in the gate* (Prov. XXIV, 7). What is the meaning of, '*Wisdom is as unattainable to a fool as corals*'? R. Tanḥuma said: The fool enters a synagogue and sees people there engaged in discussing the law, and as he knows not what they are saying he feels ashamed, as it is said, '*He openeth not his mouth in the gate*,'[4] and by '*gate*', surely the Sanhedrin[5]

[1] This is apparently interpreted: For by attaching yourselves to Me (by means of the blessing recited before the Reading of the Law, which really proclaims the Israelite's allegiance to God), your days will be multiplied, etc. [2] I.e. wisdom, which is synonymous with Torah.
[3] Celestial creatures, cf. Ezek. I, 5. [4] '*Gate*' is of course the place of assembly. The synagogue is termed בית הכנסת, 'the House of Assembling'.
[5] The judges of the two highest Courts of Justice.

are meant, for it is written, *Then his brother's wife shall go up to the gate unto the elders* (Deut. xxv, 7).

Another explanation: The Rabbis say: The fool enters the synagogue, and seeing there people occupying themselves with the law he asks: 'How does a man begin to learn the law?' They answer him: 'First a man reads from a Scroll,[1] then the Book [of the law], and then the prophets, and then the Hagiographa; when he has completed the study of the Scriptures he learns the Talmud, and then the *Halachoth*, and then the *Haggadoth*.' After hearing all this [the fool] says to himself, 'When can I learn all this?' and he turns back from the gate. This is the force of, '*He openeth not his mouth in the gate*.' R. Jannai said: This can be compared to a loaf suspended in the air; the fool says, 'Who can bring it down?' But the wise man says, 'Did not someone suspend it?' And he takes a ladder or a stick and brings it down. So anyone who is a fool says: 'When will I succeed in reading the whole law?' But the man who is wise—what does he do? He learns one chapter every day until he completes the whole law. God said: 'IT IS NOT TOO HARD, but if [you find it] too hard, it is your own fault,[2] because you do not study it.' Hence the force of, FOR THIS COMMANDMENT, etc.

4. This bears out what Scripture says, *For they are life unto those that find them*, etc. (Prov. iv, 22). R. Ḥiyya said: The law is a salve for the eye, an emollient for a wound, a root-drink for the bowels. 'Salve for the eye,' as it is written, *The commandment of the Lord is pure, enlightening the eyes* (Ps. xix, 9); 'an emollient for a wound,' as it is written, *It shall be health to thy navel* (Prov. iii, 8); and 'a root-drink for the bowels', as it is written, *And marrow to thy bones* (*ib.*).

Another explanation: '*For they are life unto those that find them*,' that is to say, to him that speaks them out

[1] Portions from the Pentateuch were copied on to scrolls and used in the schools by children. Cf. Giṭ. 60*a*. V. Blau, *Studien zum althebraischen Buchwesen*, p. 67; Morris, *The Jewish School*, p. 38.
[2] Rendering ממך it is your own fault. Cf. Gen. R. i, 14.

aloud.[1] It is related of a disciple of R. Eliezer b. Jacob, that he used to run through the whole of his study in a single hour, and that once when he fell ill, he forgot all that he had learnt. What was the cause of this? Because he did not speak the words out aloud. When, however, R. Eliezer b. Jacob prayed for him, all his learning came back to him.

Another explanation: '*For they are life unto those that find them,*' that is, to the one who imparts them unto others.

Another explanation: '*For they are life unto those that find them*'; that is, unto him who carries them [the *mizwoth*] out completely.[2] Whence this? For Scripture says, *Kol ha-mizwah* (the whole commandment). What is the meaning of, '*Kol ha-mizwah'?* Until you completely carry out[3] all the precepts. *And health to all their flesh* (Prov. IV, 22); this refers to the two hundred and forty-eight limbs which a man has. Hence the force of, FOR THIS COMMANDMENT.

Another explanation: FOR THIS COMMANDMENT. R. Ḥiyya b. Abba said: If one begins a precept and does not complete it, the result will be that in the end he will bury his wife and children. And from whom do you learn this? From Judah, who began a precept and did not complete it. How so? When Joseph came to his brethren and they sought to slay him, as it is said, *Come now therefore, and let us slay him* (Gen. XXXVII, 20), Judah arose and would not let them. Whence this? For it is said, *What profit is it if we slay our brother?* (*ib.* 26), and they listened to him, for he was king over them. And had he said, 'Let us restore him to our father,' they would also have listened to him. And because he began a precept[4] and did not complete it he buried his wife and his two sons, as it is said, [*And in process of time*] *Shua's daughter, the wife of Judah, died* (*ib.*

[1] Cf. 'Er. 54*a*. A play upon the words מצא 'to find', and מוצאיהם from the root יצא 'to come out', hence in the *hiphil*, 'to bring forth.'
[2] A play upon the words ממציא from מצא 'to find', and מצה 'to drain out', hence 'to complete', 'to fulfil'. [3] Connecting the word כל with the root כלה 'to complete'. [4] The term is applied to any good deed.

XXXVIII, 12); and it is [further written], *But Er and Onan died in the land of Canaan* (*ib.* XLVI, 12).

Another explanation: FOR THIS COMMANDMENT. R. Levi said in the name of Ḥama b. Ḥanina: If one begins a precept and does not complete it, and another comes and completes it, it is attributed to him who has completed it. How [may this be illustrated]? Moses began a precept by taking the bones of Joseph with him. Whence this? For it is said, *And Moses took the bones of Joseph with him*, etc. (Ex. XIII, 19). But because he never brought them into Eretz Israel, the precept is attributed to Israel, who buried them, as it is said, *And the bones of Joseph, which* the children of Israel *brought up out of Egypt, buried they in Shechem* (Josh. XXIV, 32). Scripture does not say here, 'Which Moses brought up out of Egypt,' but '*Which* the children of Israel *brought up out of Egypt*'. Why did they bury them in Shechem? It is as if some thieves stole a cask of wine, and when the owner discovered them he said to them: 'May the wine taste sweet to you; but, by your life, after you have consumed the wine, return the cask to its proper place.' So when the brothers sold Joseph it was from Shechem that they sold him, as it is said, *And Israel said unto Joseph: Do not thy brethren feed the flock in Shechem?* (Gen. XXXVII, 13). God said to them: 'From Shechem you have sold him, to Shechem return his bones.' As they completed the precept, it is called by their name. Hence the force of, FOR THIS COMMANDMENT.[1]

5. Another explanation: The Holy One, blessed be He, said: 'If you read the Torah you do a good deed for the world, for were it not for the Torah the world would long ago have been reduced to its primeval state of waste and desolation.'[2]

[1] The passage ends: *But the word is very nigh unto thee, in thy mouth, and in thy heart, that thou mayest do it* (v. 14). '*Heart*' and '*mouth*' symbolise the beginning and the end of fulfilling a precept, and thus the passage is an exhortation to complete a good deed once it has been started ('E.J.).

[2] Without the moral law there is chaos. Cf. Gen. R. LXVI, 2.

Another explanation: FOR THIS COMMANDMENT. What is the force of THIS COMMANDMENT? The Rabbis say: [This is] a hard thing to say.[1] It is as if a king had a precious gem which he placed for safe custody with his friend, saying to him: 'I ask of you, take great care of this and guard it well; for if it is lost, you cannot find whence to pay me, nor have I another like it, and then you will have sinned against me and against yourself; therefore do your duty by both of us and guard it well.' Likewise Moses said to Israel: 'If you keep the Torah you will be acting charitably not only towards your own selves but also towards me.' Whence this? For it is said, *And it shall be righteousness towards us* (Deut. VI, 25), that is towards me and towards yourselves. When [will this come about]? *If we observe to do all this commandment* (*ib.*).

6. Another explanation: FOR THIS COMMANDMENT . . . IT IS NOT IN HEAVEN (XXX, 11 f). Moses said to Israel: 'Do not say: "Another Moses will arise and bring us another Torah from heaven"; I therefore warn you, IT IS NOT IN HEAVEN, that is to say, no part of it has remained in heaven.'[2]

Another explanation: R. Ḥanina said: The Torah has been given with all its characteristic teachings of meekness, righteousness, and uprightness, and also its reward.

Another explanation: What is the meaning of, IT IS NOT IN HEAVEN? Samuel said: The Torah is not to be found amongst astrologers whose work is to gaze at the heavens.[3] People said to Samuel: 'Lo, you are an astrologer, and yet you are also great in the Torah.' Whereupon he replied: 'I only engage in astrology when I am free from studying the Torah.' 'When is that?' 'When I am in the bath.'

Another explanation: IT IS NOT IN HEAVEN. Israel

[1] That God has only one Torah. Mah. explains: It is as though God Himself were pleading that Israel should not destroy His Torah (v. the illustration in the text), and this is indeed a hard thing to say.

[2] This probably is intended to have an anti-Christological bearing.

[3] Because they spend all their time in star-gazing.

said to Moses: 'Our teacher Moses, lo, you say to us, IT IS NOT IN HEAVEN, NEITHER IS IT BEYOND THE SEA, then where is it?' He answered them: 'It is in a very near place, IN THY MOUTH, AND IN THY HEART, THAT THOU MAYEST DO IT (*ib.* 14), it is not far from you, it is near unto you.'

Another explanation: IN THY MOUTH, AND IN THY HEART, THAT THOU MAYEST DO IT. The Rabbis say: Solomon said seven things of the sluggard, but what Moses said was greater than all of them. How so? People say to the sluggard: 'Your teacher is in the city, go and learn Torah from him.' To this the sluggard's answer is: 'I fear the lion in the road.' Whence this? For it is said, *The sluggard saith: There is a lion in the way* (Prov. XXVI, 13). People say to him: 'Lo, your teacher is in the province,[1] arise and go to him,' and he replies: 'I fear lest there be a lion in the streets,' as it is said, *Yea, a lion is in the streets* (*ib.*). They say to him: 'But he lives near your house,' and he replies: 'The lion is outside,' as it is said, *There is a lion without* (*ib.* XXII, 13). They say to him: 'He is in the very house.' He replies: 'If I go and find the door[2] locked I I will have to return.' They say to him: 'It is open.' Whence this? For it is said, *The door is turning upon its hinges, and the sluggard is still upon his bed* (*ib.* XXVI, 14). Finally, when he knows not what further answer to give, he says to them: 'Be the door open or closed, I desire to sleep a little longer,' as it is said, *How long wilt thou sleep, O sluggard*, etc.? (*ib.* VI, 9). When he arises from his sleep in the morning and food is placed before him, he is too lazy to put it into his mouth. Whence this? For it is said, *The sluggard burieth his hand in the dish, and will not so much as bring it back to his mouth* (*ib.* XIX, 24). And what is the seventh thing? *The sluggard will not plow when winter setteth in, therefore he shall beg in harvest and have nothing* (*ib.* XX, 4). What is the meaning of, '*The sluggard will not plow when the winter setteth in*'? R. Simeon b. Yoḥai said:

[1] The order should probably be reversed, 'province' coming first and then 'city' ('E.J.). [2] Of his room.

This refers to one who not having learnt Torah in his youth,[1] desires to learn it in his old age and is not able. And this is the meaning of, '*Therefore he shall beg in harvest*[2] *and have nothing.*' But what Moses said is the greatest of them all. How so? BUT THE WORD IS VERY NIGH UNTO THEE, IN THY MOUTH, AND IN THY HEART THAT THOU MAYEST DO IT. You need but utter the word with your mouth.[3]

7. Another explanation: BUT [THE WORD] IS VERY NIGH. R. Samuel b. Naḥman said: It is as if there was a king's daughter who was not acquainted with any man, and the king had a favourite who could visit him at any time, and the princess waited on him. Said the king to him: 'See how I love you; no one is acquainted with my daughter, yet on you she waits.' So the Holy One, blessed be He, said to Israel: 'See how beloved you are upon Me, for no being in My palace is acquainted with the Torah, yet to you have I entrusted it,' as it is said, *Seeing it is hid from the eyes of all living* (Job. XXVIII, 21). But as for you, IT IS NOT TOO HARD FOR THEE . . . BUT THE WORD IS VERY NIGH UNTO THEE. God said to them: 'My children, if the words of the Torah will be near unto you, I too will call you "near ones".' For so Scripture says, *Even for the children of Israel, a people near unto Him. Hallelujah* (Ps. CXLVIII, 14).

[1] Taking חרף as implying youth. Cf. Job XXIX, 4, בימי חרפי.
[2] קציר '*harvest*', a symbol of old age.
[3] You need not even go into another room for it, as it were.

Chapter IX

VAYELECH

1. And the Lord said unto Moses: Behold, thy days approach (xxxi, 14). *Halachah:* Is it permissible for a Jew whose dead relative lies unburied before him to pray? The Sages have taught thus[1]: One whose dead [relative] lies unburied before him is exempt from the duty of reciting the *shema'* and the *tefillah*. And why did our Rabbis teach thus? Because when a man sees his loss before him his mind is distraught; but after the burial throughout the whole of the seven days of mourning it is incumbent on him to carry out all religious duties. And whence do you know that mourning [continues] for seven days?[2] R. Abba b. Abina said: For so we find in the case of Joseph, *And he made a mourning for his father seven days* (Gen. l, 10); and Sabbath is included in the number. R. Jose b. Zebida said in the name of Resh Laḳish: You can learn this from elsewhere. Whence? For it is said, *And I will turn your feasts into mourning* (Amos viii, 10). As the Feast [of Tabernacles] lasts for seven days,[3] so too the days of mourning are seven. Our Rabbis said[4]: Once R. Simeon b. Ḥalafta went to a circumcision ceremony. The father of the child made a feast and gave those present wine seven years old to drink, he also said: 'Of this wine, I will store away a portion for my son's wedding feast.' The feast continued until midnight. R. Simeon b. Ḥalafta, who trusted in his own [moral] strength, left at midnight to return to his city. On the road, the Angel of Death met him and R. Simeon noticed he was looking strange. He asked him: 'Who are you?' And the latter answered: 'I am God's messenger.' He asked him: 'Why are you looking strange?' He replied: 'On account of the talk of human

[1] The parallel passages also specify תפילין (phylacteries). Cf. Ber. 17*b*; M.Ḳ. 23*b*. [2] Cf. Gen. R. c., 7. [3] 'Feast' is generally applied to Tabernacles.—The eighth day (v. Lev. xxiii, 39; Num. xxix, 35) counted as a separate festival. [4] Cf. Eccl. R. on iii, 2.

beings who say: "This and that we will do," and yet not one of them knows when he will be summoned to die. The man in whose feast you have shared, and who said to you: "Of this wine I will store away a portion for my son's wedding feast," lo, his [child's] time has come, he is to be snatched away after thirty days.' R. Simeon said to him: 'Show me my end.' He replied: 'Neither over you nor over the likes of you have I any dominion; often God finds delight in your good deeds and grants you additional life,' as it is said, *The fear of the Lord prolongeth days* (Prov. x, 27). The Rabbis say: God finds it hard to decree death upon the righteous. Whence this? For it is said, *Precious in the sight of the Lord is the death of His saints* (Ps. CXVI, 15). And this is the proof. God should have spoken to Moses thus: 'Behold you are about to die.' He, however, did not speak in this way, but He spared him, and He attached 'death' to the days. Whence this? From what we read in the context, BEHOLD, THY DAYS[1] APPROACH THAT THOU MUST DIE.

2. This bears out what Scripture says, *I returned, and saw under the sun, that the race is not to the swift*, etc. (Eccl. IX, 11). What is the meaning of, '*That the race is not to the swift*'? R. Tanḥuma said: The verse refers to Moses. How so? Yesterday he went up[2] to heaven like an eagle and now he seeks to pass over the Jordan and he is not able, as it is written, *For thou shalt not go over this Jordan* (Deut. III, 27). *Nor the battle to the strong* (Eccl. *loc. cit.*); yesterday the angels were trembling before him,[3] and now he declares, *For I was in dread of the anger and hot displeasure* (Deut. IX, 19). *Neither yet bread*[4] *to the wise* (Eccl. *loc. cit.*); yesterday [to him could be applied the words,] *A wise man scaleth the city of the mighty, and bringeth down the stronghold wherein it trusteth* (Prov. XXI, 22), that is, from heaven, and now [wisdom] has been taken away from him and given to

[1] The days approach their end. [2] Cf. Eccl. R. on IX, 11.
[3] Cf. Ex. R. XXVIII, 1.
[4] *Bread* symbolising Torah or wisdom. Cf. Prov. IX, 5.

Joshua,[1] the son of Nun. *Nor yet riches to men of understanding* (Eccl. *loc. cit.*); yesterday he was speaking haughtily to God, like a rich man, *Turn from Thy fierce wrath* (Ex. XXXII, 12); *Pardon, I pray Thee, the iniquity of this people* (Num. XIV, 19); but now he speaks [humbly] like a poor man,[2] *And I besought* (wa'ethḥanan), that is, Grant it to me out of Thy charity (*ḥinam*).[3] *Nor yet favour to men of skill* (Eccl. IX, 11); yesterday he knew how to appease his Creator, *Rise up, O Lord* (Num. X, 35), *Return, O Lord* (*ib.* 36), but now after he had entreated Him for seven days[4] God finally said to him: BEHOLD, THY DAYS APPROACH.

3. This bears out what Scripture says, *There is no man that hath power over the spirit* (ruaḥ) *to retain the spirit* (Eccl. VIII, 8). R. Judah and R. Nehemiah each has his own explanation of this. R. Judah says: No man has power over the Angel of Death[5] to keep him from himself; and '*ruaḥ*' is none other than angel, as it is said, *Who makest spirits* [E.V. '*winds*'] *Thy messengers* (Ps. CIV, 4). R. Nehemiah said: No man has power over foreign governments to destroy them from the world, and '*ruaḥ*' is none other than foreign governments, as it is said, *And, behold, the four winds* (ruḥe) *of the heaven*, etc. (Dan. VII, 2).[6]

Another explanation: R. Eliezer b. Jacob said: No man has power over his own soul to destroy it.[7] Why? Because God has caused it to permeate the whole body. Had God concentrated it into one limb,[8] then if a man found himself in trouble he would cut off that limb and die. Therefore is it spread throughout the whole body, that he should not be able to destroy it. This is the force of, '*There is no man that hath power over the spirit.*' What is the meaning of, *And there is no sending* (mish-laḥath) *in war* (Eccl. *loc. cit.*)?

[1] V. Soṭ. 13*b*, where it is stated that Moses was deprived of his wisdom.
[2] Cf. Prov. XVIII, 23. [3] Lit. 'for nothing'.
[4] The first seven days of Adar. Moses according to Jewish tradition died on the seventh of Adar. [5] Cf. Eccl. R. on VIII, 8.
[6] The whole chapter (*q.v.*) was applied to the four kingdoms or states that have held Israel in subjection.
[7] A man cannot expel his soul from within him. [8] Cf. Gen. R. XIV, 4.

No man when about to die can say, 'I will send my slave in my stead.' R. Simeon b. Ḥalafta says: No man can make weapons which will save him from the Angel of Death, such as are referred to in Scripture, *And made weapons* (shelaḥ) *and shields in abundance* (II Chron. XXXII, 5). What is the meaning of, *Neither hath he power over the day of death* (Eccl. *loc. cit.*)? No man has the power to say [to the Angel of Death]: 'Wait for me until I have made up my accounts,' or 'until I have set my house in order, and then I will come'.

Another explanation: What is the meaning of, '*Neither hath he power*'? The Angel of Death does not say, 'Seeing that this man is king we will grant him one or two days more.' On that day there is no respecting of persons. The proof is this. Throughout his life David is referred to as king, as it is said, *Now King David was old and stricken in years* (I Kings I, 1). When, however, he was approaching death, Scripture no longer mentions his kingship. Whence this? For it is said, *Now the days of David drew nigh that he should die* (I Kings II, 1).[1] *Neither shall wickedness deliver him that is given to it* (Eccl. *loc. cit.*); no one can appeal against him [the Angel of Death], nor can one lodge a protest against him. Lo, after all the greatness which Moses had enjoyed, when the day of his death came, he could not hold it back. Forthwith God said to him: BEHOLD, THY DAYS APPROACH THAT THOU MUST DIE.

4. Another explanation: Moses said to God: 'Master of the Universe, must I die after my eyes have witnessed all that glory and that power?'[2] Whereupon God replied: 'Moses, *What mighty man*[3] *is he that liveth and shall not see death*' (Ps. LXXXIX, 49). What is the meaning of, '*What mighty man is he that liveth*'? R. Tanḥuma said: What mighty man is there like Abraham who went down into the fiery furnace and was saved,[4] and yet afterwards Scripture says of him, *And Abraham expired, and died*

[1] Cf. Gen. R. XCVI, 3. [2] Which I have enjoyed and wielded.
[3] Heb. *geber*, which the Midrash now identifies with *gibbor* 'a mighty man', and not simply '*man*' as in E.V. [4] V. Gen. R. XXXVIII, 13.

(Gen. XXV, 8)? What mighty man is there like Isaac[1] who stretched out his neck on the altar, and yet afterwards Scripture says of him, *Behold now, I am old, I know not the day of my death* (*ib.* XXVII, 2)? What mighty man is there like Jacob who wrestled with an angel, and yet afterwards Scripture says of him, *And the time drew near that Israel must die* (*ib.* XLVII, 29)? What mighty man is there like Moses who spoke with his Creator face to face, and yet afterwards [God said to him]: BEHOLD, THY DAYS APPROACH THAT THOU MUST DIE?

5. Another explanation: All creatures go down to the grave with their eyes dimmed, but as for you [Moses], your eye is not dim. All mortals are disposed of at burial in vestments made by man, namely, coffin, bier, and shrouds, but you are disposed of in shrouds made in heaven, a coffin made in heaven, and a bier made in heaven.

Another explanation: When all mortals die, their relatives and their neighbours attend to their burial, but as for you [Moses], I and My Court[2] [will] attend to your burial. Whence this? For it is said, *And* He *buried him in the valley* (Deut. XXXIV, 6).

6. Another explanation: BEHOLD (HEN), THY DAYS APPROACH. Why was death decreed upon Moses with the expression, '*hen*' ('behold')? The Rabbis say: It is as if a man, to pay honour to the king, brought to him as a gift a sharp sword, and the king exclaimed: 'Behead him with it,' whereupon the man asked: 'My lord king, will you behead me with the very object with which I honoured you?' So Moses said: 'Master of the Universe, with the expression "*hen*" I praised Thee, for so Scripture says, *Behold* (hen), *unto the Lord thy God belongeth the heaven, and the heaven of heavens*, etc. (Deut. X, 14); and wilt Thou decree death upon me with the same expression, "*hen*"?'[3] Whereupon God replied: 'A bad neighbour

[1] Spiritually mighty, in that he could bring himself to such a sacrifice.
[2] The angelic hosts of heaven. [3] Cf. *infra*, XI, 9.

observes his neighbour's earnings but not his expenditure.'[1] God continued: 'Do you not remember that when I sent you to deliver them [Israel] from Egypt, you said to me: *But, behold* (hen), *they will not believe me'* (Ex. IV, 1)? Hence He said: BEHOLD, THY DAYS APPROACH.

7. Another explanation: R. Abin said: What is the force of HEN? It is as though a noble lady made for the king an exceptionally beautiful [purple] garment, which the king took and put away, and when the days of the lady approached their end the king said: 'Let her take the garment with which she honoured me.' So God said to Moses: 'You praised Me with "*hen*", and with "*hen*" I will decree death upon you.'

8. Another explanation: R. Levi said: It is like the case of a pregnant woman who was thrown into prison and gave birth to a son there. When the child grew up the king once passed by the prison, whereupon the lad began to cry out: 'My lord king, why am I kept in prison?' and the king replied: 'You are kept here for the sin of your mother.' So Moses pleaded: 'Master of the Universe, there are thirty-six transgressions[2] punishable by extinction enumerated in the Torah, for the commission of any one of which a man is liable to be put to death. Have I then transgressed any one of them? Why dost Thou decree death upon me?' God replied: 'You are to die because of the sin of the first man who brought death into the world.' [Thus Scripture says], BEHOLD (HEN)! What is the force of HEN? For the sin of him of whom the expression '*hen*' is used [in Scripture], *Behold* (hen), *the man is become as one of us* (Gen. III, 22).

9. Another explanation: What is the force of HEN? R. Sima said: The day cried out before God saying:

[1] Moses recalls that he used the word '*hen*' in praise of God, but he forgets that he also used it in a derogatory sense against Israel, when he doubted whether they would obey the divine call, as the verse cited shows.
[2] Ker. I, 1.

'Master of the Universe, am I not to move nor to set while Moses shall live!'[1]

Another explanation: The Rabbis say: When Moses learnt that he was to die on that day, what did he do? R. Jannai said: He wrote thirteen scrolls of the law, twelve for the twelve tribes, and one which he placed in the ark, so that if a man should seek to forge anything therein, they would refer to the scroll in the ark. Moses said: 'Through my busying myself with the Torah, the whole of which is life, the day will set and the decree will become nullified.' What did God do? He signed to the sun and it refused to obey him, saying: 'I will not set and leave Moses alive in the world.' Therefore Job says explicitly, *Did I not weep at the refusal of the day* (Job XXX, 25),[2] thus intimating that the day refused to obey Him. HEN. What is the meaning of, BEHOLD (HEN) THY DAYS APPROACH? It was like a man saying to his friend: 'So-and-so has complained against you to the king.'[3]

CALL JOSHUA (XXXI, 14). Moses said to God: 'Master of the Universe, let Joshua take over my office and I will continue to live.' Whereupon God replied: 'Treat him as he treats you.' Immediately Moses arose early and went to Joshua's house, and Joshua became frightened. Moses said to Joshua: 'My teacher, come to me,' and they set out to go, Moses walking on the left of Joshua.[4] When they entered the tent of meeting the pillar of cloud came down and separated them. When the pillar of cloud departed Moses approached Joshua and asked him: 'What was revealed to you?' Joshua replied: 'When the word was revealed to you did I know what God spoke with you?' At that moment Moses bitterly exclaimed: 'Better it is to die a hundred times than to experience envy, even once.' Solomon has expressed this clearly: *For love is strong as*

[1] For the time has come for Joshua to begin his rule—is another day then never to dawn, and Moses' last day to continue indefinitely? The verse is understood: Behold, thy day approaches to plead that thou must die (M.K.). [2] E.V. '*If I have not wept for him that was in trouble*'.
[3] 'To approach' sometimes means to approach the judges for a lawsuit; cf. Ex. XXII, 7. It may also have the sense of to approach in battle.
[4] The disciple walks on the left of his teacher.

death, jealousy is cruel as the grave (S.S. VIII, 6). This refers to the love wherewith Moses loved Joshua, and the jealousy of Moses towards Joshua. When Moses resigned himself to death, God began to appease him. He said to him: 'By your life, in this world you have led My children, in the time to come also, I will have you lead them.' Whence this? For it is said, *Then His people will remember*[1] *the days of old, the days of Moses* (Isa. LXIII, 11).

[1] The Midrash evidently understands this as a *future* tense, referring to the Messianic era. E.V. '*remembered*'.

CHAPTER X

HA'AZINU

1. *Halachah:* Is it permissible for a Jew suffering from earache to heal it on the Sabbath? The Sages have taught thus[1]: Where there is the least question of danger to life, the Sabbath laws are suspended. And therefore in the case of earache, if it is dangerous it may be healed[2] on the Sabbath. The Rabbis say: If you desire not to suffer earache or pain in one of your limbs, then incline your ears to the Torah, and you will inherit life. Whence this? For it is said, *Incline your ear, and come unto Me; hear, and your soul shall live* (Isa. LV, 3). R. Ḥanina b. Papa said: Whosoever turns away his ear from the Torah, his prayer is rejected, as it is said, *He that turneth away his ear from hearing the law, even his prayer is an abomination* (Prov. XXVIII, 9).[3]

R. Levi said: The ear is to the body what the fumigating vessel[4] is to garments; for many garments may be placed upon it and if spices are put under it, all are fumigated, and so too a man has two hundred and forty-eight limbs, and they all function on account of the ear [i.e. by listening to the word of God]. Whence this? For it is said, '*Hear, and your soul shall live.*' The Holy One, blessed be He, said: 'If you incline your ear to the Torah, then when you come to begin [speaking] the Words of the Torah all will remain silent before you and listen to you, in the same way as you have inclined your ear to listen to the words of the Torah.' And whence do you learn this? From Moses our teacher. Because he inclined his ear to the Torah, when he came to begin [speaking] the words of the Torah, both the heavenly[5] and the earthly beings remained silent and hearkened unto his words. Whence this? From what we read in our text, GIVE EAR, YE HEAVENS, AND I WILL SPEAK (XXXII, 1).

[1] Cf. Yoma 83*a*. [2] On remedies for earache, v. A.Z. 28*b* (Sonc. ed.), pp. 140 f. [3] Cf. Shab. 10*a*; *supra*, IV, 2.
[4] קינקל, Gk. κιγκλίς 'perforated vessel'. [5] Cf. Gen. R. V, 5; Deut. XI, 5.

2. This bears out what Scripture says, *I know that whatsoever God doeth, it shall be for ever, nothing can be added to it*, etc. (Eccl. III, 14). R. Joseph b. Zimra said: What is the meaning of, '*Nothing can be added to it*'? God said thus from the beginning of the Creation of the world, *Let the waters under the heaven be gathered together unto one place*, etc. (Gen. I, 9).[1] Why then does Scripture say, *That calleth for the waters of the sea, and poureth them out upon the face of the earth*[2]*; the Lord is His name* (Amos V, 8)? That they may fear Him, that the creatures may fear Him. This can be compared to a city which rebelled against the king. What did the king do? He brought a mighty legion and invested it so that the citizens might see it and fear him.

Another comment: The Holy One, blessed be He, created the world in such a manner that the day should be day, and the night night. Jacob came and turned the day into night, since for his sake, God caused the sun to set before its proper time, as it is said, *And he lighted upon the place, and tarried there all night, because the sun was set* (Gen. XXVIII, 11).[3] Joshua came and turned the night into day, as it is said, *Sun, stand thou still upon Gibeon* (Josh. X, 12). Thus the righteous both take away and add to the words of God, so that the creatures may fear Him.

Another comment: God created [the world] so that the sea should be sea, and the dry land dry land. Moses came and turned the sea into dry land, as it is said, *But the children of Israel walked upon dry land in the midst of the sea* (Ex. XIV, 29). Elisha came and turned the dry land into sea, as it is said, *Thus saith the Lord: Make this valley full of trenches . . . yet that valley shall be filled with water* (II Kings III, 16 f). Similarly God so created the winter that it should be winter and the summer summer. Elijah came and turned the winter into summer, for so Scripture says, *As the Lord, the God of Israel, liveth . . . there shall not be dew nor rain these years, but according to my word* (I Kings XVII, 1).[4]

[1] Cf. Gen. R. V, 6.—The bounds of the world were set and they cannot be exceeded. [2] And therefore in more places than one, which would contradict the previous statement. [3] V. Gen. R. LXVIII, 10.
[4] Thus the winter, normally a rainy season, would be as the summer.

Samuel came and turned summer into winter, for so Scripture says, *Is it not wheat harvest to-day? I will call unto the Lord, that He may send thunder and rain* (I Sam. XII, 17).[1]

Another comment: God so created the world that the upper realms should be for the upper beings, and the lower realms for the lower, for so Scripture says, *The heavens are the heavens of the Lord, but the earth hath He given to the children of men* (Ps. CXV, 16). Moses came and changed the earthly into heavenly,[2] and the heavenly into earthly, for so Scripture says, *And Moses went up unto God* (Ex. XIX, 3), *And the Lord came down upon Mount Sinai* (*ib.* 20).

Another comment: God so created heaven and earth that they should praise Him. Whence this? For it is said, *The heavens declare the glory of God* (Ps. XIX, 2). When Moses came he silenced them. Whence this? For it is said, GIVE EAR, YE HEAVENS.

3. This bears out what Scripture says, *The God of Israel said, The Rock of Israel spoke to me: Ruler over men shall be the righteous, even he that ruleth in the fear of God* (II Sam. XXIII, 3). And what means, '*The righteous, even he that ruleth in the fear of God*'? The righteous have power over the same things as God, if one may say so. In which way? Everything that God does, the righteous do.[3] How [is this illustrated]? God remembers barren women; Elisha, too, remembered the Shunammite woman. Whence this? For it is said, *At this season, when the time cometh round, thou shalt embrace a son* (II Kings IV, 16). God quickens the dead; and Elisha, too, brought back to life the son of the Shunammite woman. God parts the seas, Elijah and Elisha, too, parted seas. Whence this? For it is said, *And smote the waters, and they were divided hither and thither* (II Kings II, 8). God heals without emollients, and Elisha healed Naaman without emollients. God sweetens the bitter waters, and Elisha sweetened the bitter waters, for so

[1] V. preceding note; it is the reverse here.
[2] Cf. Ex. R. XII, 3. [3] Gen. R. LXXVII, 1.

Scripture says, *And he said: Bring me a new cruse*, etc. (*ib.* 20), and it is [further] written, *So the waters were healed* (*ib.* 22). God withholds the rain, and Elijah withheld the rain, as it is said, '*As the Lord, the God of Israel, liveth, before whom I stand, there shall not be dew nor rain these years*, etc.' (I Kings XVII, 1). God causes rain to fall, and Samuel caused rain to fall, as it is said, '*Is it not wheat harvest to-day? I will call unto the Lord*, etc.' (I Sam. XII, 17). God sends down fire, and Elijah brought down fire [from heaven], as it is said, *Then the fire of the Lord fell, and consumed the burnt-offering* (I Kings XVIII, 38).[1]

4. Another explanation: GIVE EAR, YE HEAVENS. R. Joshua of Siknin said: From here you learn that the heavens have mouth, heart, and ear. 'Mouth,' whence? For it is written, '*The heavens declare the glory of God*' (Ps. XIX, 2). And 'heart', whence? For it is written, *And the mountain burned with fire unto the heart of heaven* (Deut. IV, 11). And 'ear', whence? For it is written, GIVE EAR.

Another explanation: Why [did Moses call upon] the heavens and the earth? R. Samuel b. Naḥman said: He can be compared to a general who held office in two provinces, one a Roman province, the other a colony,[2] and who, being about to make a feast, said [to himself]: 'If I invite this set, the other will be offended with me, and if I invite that set, this will be offended with me.' So what did he do? He invited both the one and the other. So it was with Moses. He himself was born on earth, but he became great in heaven. Whence this? For it is said, *And he was there with the Lord forty days and forty nights*, etc. (Ex. XXXIV, 28). He said: 'If I call upon the heavens the earth will rage, and if I call upon the earth the heavens will

[1] It is not stated what bearing all this has on our text. The passage is probably unfinished, having originally ended something like this: God commands heaven and earth, and Moses commanded heaven and earth, as it says, GIVE EAR, YE HEAVENS . . . AND LET THE EARTH HEAR, etc. (Mah.).

[2] Reading with Jast. רומי וקלאונה for פרס וק׳. Levi, retaining the present text, renders quite differently: '. . . to a general who governed two cities, one being liable to taxation while the other was exempt.'

rage.' He [therefore] said: 'I will call upon both of them, the heavens and the earth,' as it is said, GIVE EAR, YE HEAVENS etc.

Another explanation: Why upon the heavens and the earth? R. Tanḥuma said: Because God will redeem Israel only through the agency of them both, for so it is written, *Sing, O ye* heavens, *for the Lord hath done it; shout, ye lowest parts of the* earth (Isa. XLIV, 23).

Another explanation: Why upon the heavens and earth? For the Torah was given only through the agency of them both, as it is said, *Out of* heaven *He made thee to hear His voice, that He might instruct thee; and upon* earth *He made thee to see His great fire* (Deut. IV, 36).

Another explanation: Because the manna and the quails were given through the agency of them both, as it is said, *Behold, I will cause to rain bread from heaven for you* (Ex. XVI, 4); and quails from the earth, as it is written, *That the quails came up* (*ib.* 13).

Another explanation: Because God compared Israel unto the stars of heaven and the dust of the earth. Unto the stars of heaven, whence? For it is written, *Look now toward* heaven, *and count the stars*, etc. (Gen. XV, 5); and unto the dust of the earth, whence? For it is said, *And thy seed shall be as the dust of the* earth (*ib.* XXVIII, 14).

Another explanation: Why unto the heavens and the earth? Because they are the witnesses of Israel, for it is written, *I call heaven and earth to witness against you this day* (Deut. IV, 26). This can be compared to the son of a king over whom his father appointed two guardians. Whenever his father adorned him with any crown, he did so only through the agency of both of them, so on the day of his marriage he appointed them as witnesses between himself and his father. Similarly, all the miracles which God wrought for Israel, He performed through the agency of heaven and earth; so when Israel were about to enter Palestine, they sang a song through the agency of them both, because they serve as witnesses between Him and them. Whence this? For it is said, *Hear, O* heavens, *and give ear, O* earth, *for the Lord hath spoken* (Isa. I, 2).

What follows immediately on this? *Children I have reared, and brought up* (*ib.*). This is the force of, GIVE EAR, YE HEAVENS.

Another explanation: Why unto heaven and earth? R. Ḥanina said: This can be compared to a man who deposited an article with his friend for safe custody; the man who had deposited the article died, whereupon his son arose and paid special honour to the man and his wife, with whom the article had been deposited. On being asked why he was paying such honour to the two of them, he answered: 'An article belonging to me is in the possession of the two of them, and I am not certain with which of them it is deposited, with the man or with his wife. Be my article where it may, let it be well guarded.' Similarly, when Moses was asked: 'Why do you call upon the heavens and the earth?' he replied: 'I am about to die, and I do not know whither my soul will go, to heaven or to earth.' Whence this? For it is said, *Who knoweth the spirit of man whether it goeth upward*, etc. (Eccl. III, 21), 'therefore I charge the two of them; wherever my soul finds rest may it be well guarded.' Thereupon God answered him: 'By your life, no created thing shall have power over your soul.' And where will it find rest? Under the Throne of Glory[1] in heaven, for so Abigail says, *Yet the soul of my lord shall be bound in the bundle of life with the Lord thy God* (I Sam. XXV, 29).

Another explanation: Why unto heaven and earth? Because through them God testified against Israel, and through them they sinned, and through them they were punished, and through them will they be comforted. Through them God testified [against Israel]: for it is written, '*I call heaven and earth to witness against you this day*'; and through them they sinned: as it is written, *To make cakes to the queen of heaven* (Jer. VII, 18); and through them they were punished: whence? For it is written, *And the heavens, and they had no light* (*ib.* IV, 23). Whence [do we know that they were punished through the earth]?

[1] Cf. Shab. 152*b*.

For it is written, *The earth* (*ib.*). And against the earth they sinned; for it is written, *Yea, their altars shall be as heaps in the furrows of the field* (Hos. XII, 12). And through the earth they were punished: for it is written, *I beheld the earth, and, lo, it was waste and void* (Jer. IV, 23). And through heaven and earth they will be comforted: for it is written, *For as the new heavens and the new earth which I will make, shall remain before Me, saith the Lord, so shall your seed and your name remain* (Isa. LXVI, 22).[1]

[1] Heaven and earth were called to testify against them, so that they might reform; they sinned through heaven and earth, by ascribing divine powers to them and giving them divine honours; they were punished through them, in that their natural productivity was curtailed, and they will be comforted through them, when their natural productivity will be greatly increased, thereby bringing a blessing upon them ('E.J.).

Chapter XI

VE'ZOT HA'BRACHAH

1. *Halachah:* If a Jew acting as Reader[1] makes a mistake in the Service, how shall he proceed? The Sages have taught thus[2]: If a man acting as Reader makes a mistake, another takes his place. Our Rabbis have taught us[3]: R. Jose b. Ḥanina said: If he makes a mistake in any of the first three [benedictions of the *tefillah*], he goes back to the beginning of 'Shield'.[4] R. Huna said: If he makes a mistake in any one of the middle [benedictions],[5] he goes back to 'The Holy God'.[6] Rab said: If he makes a mistake in any one of the last three [benedictions], he goes back to the beginning of 'We give thanks'.[7]

Another view: If a man acting as Reader makes a mistake, another takes his place. And where does he begin? From the commencement of the benediction wherein the previous Reader had made his mistake. And whence have [the Rabbis] learnt this? From the ancient Patriarchs. How so? For each of them began [his prayer] at the place where his predecessor had left off. How? Abraham blessed Isaac. Whence? For it is written, *And Abraham gave all that he had unto Isaac* (Gen. xxv, 5). And what did he give him?[8] R. Judah and R. Nehemiah gave different answers: R. Judah said: He gave him the birthright, as Scripture in another context says, *And he sold his birthright unto Jacob*

[1] The expression עבר לפני התבה (lit. 'to pass before the Ark') is a technical term denoting the Reader who recites in public the *tefillah* (i.e. the Eighteen benedictions). [2] Cf. Ber. 34*a*. [3] J. Ber. v, 9*c*.
[4] I.e. the first benediction ending in the words 'Shield of Abraham'. Cf. A.P.B., p. 44.
[5] I.e. 4–15 (or 16 if the prayer against the slanderers is included).
[6] The conclusion of the third benediction. Cf. A.P.B., p. 45.
[7] A.P.B., p. 51. He begins from the words 'Accept, O Lord' (p. 50), which is the commencement of the sixteenth benediction.
[8] Cf. Gen. R. LXI, 6.

(*ib.* 33).[1] R. Nehemiah said: He gave him a blessing, as Scripture in another context says, *So God give thee of the dew of heaven*, etc. (*ib.* XXVII, 28).[2] When Isaac was about to bless Jacob[3] he said: I will begin from the place where my father left off—my father left off at [the word] '*Give*', I will begin with '*Give*'. Whence this? For it is said, '*So God give thee*,' etc. And with what did Isaac conclude? With '*calling*'; as it is said, *And Isaac* called *Jacob, and blessed him* (*ib.* XXVIII, 1). When Jacob was about to bless the tribes he said: I [too] will begin with '*calling*', as it is said, *And Jacob* called *his sons* (*ib.* XLIX, 1). And with what did he conclude: With, '*And this is*,' as it says, *And this is it that their father spoke unto them* (Gen. XLIX, 28). When Moses was about to bless Israel he said, I therefore will begin with '*And this is*'. Whence this? From what we read in the context, AND THIS IS THE BLESSING (XXXIII, 1).

2. Another explanation: AND THIS IS THE BLESSING. This bears out what Scripture says, *Who shall ascend into the mountain of the Lord?* (Ps. XXIV, 3). The Rabbis say: This refers to Moses. '*Who shall ascend into the mountain of the Lord?*' refers to Moses, as it is said, *And Moses went up to God*, etc. (Ex. XIX, 3). *And who shall stand in His holy place?* (Ps. *loc. cit.*); this refers to Moses, for it is said, *For the place whereon thou standest is holy ground* (Ex. III, 5). *He that hath clean hands* (Ps. *loc. cit.*); this refers to Moses, as it is said, *I have not taken one ass from them*, etc. (Num. XVI, 15). *And a pure heart* (Ps. XXIV, 4); this refers to Moses. R. Isaac said: Even for an ordinary man to speak to his friend in such a manner would be unseemly, yet Moses said, *Lord, why doth Thy wrath wax hot against Thy people?* (Ex. XXXII, 11).[4] It was only because his motive was perfectly unselfish, in that he was not pleading

[1] This verse really has no direct bearing upon the statement that Abraham gave the birthright to Isaac. But the point is this: just as Jacob, though not the natural firstborn, could acquire the birthright through purchase, so could Abraham give the birthright to Isaac, though Ishmael was his firstborn (Mah.). [2] V. preceding note. The reasoning is the same here too. [3] Cf. Gen. R. C, 12.
[4] How could Moses ask this after Israel's apostasy!

for his own needs, but for the needs of Israel. *Who hath not taken a soul*[1] *in vain* (Ps. *loc. cit.*); this refers to the life of the Egyptian which he took not without cause, but acting with good justice. *And hath not sworn deceitfully* (*ib.*)*;* this refers to Moses, as it is said, *And Moses swore*[2] *to dwell with the man* (Ex. II, 21). *He shall receive a blessing from the Lord* (Ps. XXIV, 5); this refers to Moses. R. Tanḥuma said: Do not read *yiso* ['he shall receive'] but *yasi* ['he will transmit'] blessing to others.[3]

3. AND THIS IS THE BLESSING: This bears out what Scripture says, *Many daughters have done valiantly, but thou excellest them all* (Prov. XXXI, 29). What is the meaning of, '*But thou excellest them all'?* This refers to Moses who was far superior to all. How? Adam said to Moses: 'I am greater than you because I have been created in the image of God.' Whence this? For it is said, *And God created man in His own image* (Gen. I, 27). Moses replied to him: 'I am far superior to you, for the honour which was given to you has been taken away from you, as it is said, *But man* (Adam) *abideth not in honour* (Ps. XLIX, 13)[4]; but as for me, the radiant countenance which God gave me still remains with me.' Whence? For it is said, *His eye was not dim, nor his natural force abated* (Deut. XXXIV, 7).

Another explanation: Noah said to Moses: 'I am greater than you because I was delivered from the generation of the Flood.' Whereupon Moses replied: 'I am far superior to you; you saved yourself, but you had no strength to deliver your generation; but I saved both myself and my generation when they were condemned to destruction at the time of the Golden Calf.' Whence this? For it is said, *And the Lord repented of the evil which He said He would do unto His people* (Ex. XXXII, 14). It is as if there were two ships in danger on the high seas, on board of which were

[1] Lit. translation. E.V. '*My name*'.
[2] So translated in Ex. R. I, 33; cf. Ex. R. IV, 1. E.V. '*was content*'.
[3] The point is obvious, though not stated here: 'He will transmit a blessing,' as it says, AND THIS IS THE BLESSING WHEREWITH MOSES . . . BLESSED THE CHILDREN OF ISRAEL.
[4] Cf. Gen. R. XI, 2.

two pilots; one saved himself but not his ship, and the other saved both himself and his ship. Who received the praise? Surely the one who saved both himself and his ship. Similarly, Noah saved himself only, whereas Moses saved himself and his generation. Hence, '*And thou excellest them all.*'

Another explanation: Abraham said to Moses: 'I am greater than you, because I used to give hospitality to all passers-by.'[1] Whereupon Moses replied: 'I am far superior to you; you fed uncircumcised men, but I fed circumcised ones.[2] And further you gave hospitality in an inhabited land, but I fed them in the wilderness.'

Isaac said to Moses: 'I am greater than you, because I stretched out my neck upon the altar and beheld the Divine Presence.' Whereupon Moses replied to him: 'I am far superior to you; for your eyes became dim after beholding the Divine Presence.'[3] Whence this? For it is written, *And it came to pass, that when Isaac was old, and his eyes were dim from seeing* (Gen. XXVII, 1). What is meant by, '*from seeing*'? Because he had beheld the Divine Presence. 'But I spoke with the Divine Presence face to face, and yet my eyes did not become dim. And what is more,[4] the skin of my face shone,' as it is said, *That Moses knew not that the skin of his face sent forth beams* (Ex. XXXIV, 29).

Jacob said to Moses: 'I am greater than you, for I wrestled with the angel and prevailed over him.' Whereupon Moses replied: 'You wrestled with the angel in your own territory[5] [on earth], but I went up to them [the angels] into their territory, and they were afraid of me.'[6] Whence this? For it is said, *The angels of hosts*[7] *flee, they flee* (Ps. LXVIII, 13). Therefore Solomon said: '*Many daughters have done valiantly*, etc.' God said: 'Seeing that

[1] Cf. Gen. R. LIV, 6. [2] Israelites.

[3] Cf. Gen. R. LXV, 10. The word מראות is to be translated not in a negative sense, '*So that he could not see,*' as E.V., but the מ is to be treated as a preposition, 'from seeing.'

[4] The text is here out of order. The translation follows the emendation of Radal. [5] פירבורין emended by Jast. to פריכורין, Gk. *περίχωρα* 'territory'.

[6] Cf. *supra*, IX, 2. [7] So translated by the Midrash, reading מלאכי for מלכי.

he is far superior to them all, *he* shall bless Israel': AND THIS IS THE BLESSING.

4. Another explanation: AND THIS IS THE BLESSING. R. Samuel b. Naḥman said: When Moses was about to bless Israel, the Torah and God [also] came to bless Israel. Thus: AND *THIS* IS THE BLESSING: this indicates the Torah of which it is said, *And* this *is the law which Moses set before the children of Israel* (Deut. IV, 44). WHEREWITH MOSES BLESSED (XXXIII, 1): this indicates Moses. THE MAN OF GOD: this indicates God, of whom it is said, *The Lord is a man of war* (Ex. XV, 3).[1] And why all this? In order that the Scriptural verse may be fulfilled, *And a threefold cord is not quickly broken* (Eccl. IV, 12).

Another explanation: AND THIS IS THE BLESSING. R. Tanḥuma said: If [Moses] is referred to as 'God', why [is he also termed] 'man', and if 'man', why also 'God'?[2] The reason is this. When he was cast into the river of Egypt [the Nile] he was a man; but when the river was turned into blood [by Moses] he was as God.

Another explanation: When he fled from before Pharaoh he was a man, but when he drowned [Pharaoh in the sea] he was as God.

Another explanation: When he went up to heaven he was a man. And in which respect was he a man? Compared with the angels who are made entirely of fire. But when he came down from heaven he was as God. Whence this? For Scripture says, *And they were afraid to come nigh him* (Ex. XXXIV, 30).

Another explanation: When he went up to heaven he was as God. Just as the angels neither eat nor drink, so too he neither ate nor drank. Whence this? For it is said, *And he was there with the Lord . . . he did neither eat bread, nor drink water* (*ib.* 28).

[1] Rendering: And this, sc. the Torah, *and* Moses, and the Man of God, sc. God, blessed the Children of Israel.

[2] He regards 'man' and 'God' as being in apposition, rendering: And this is the blessing wherewith Moses, a man, God, blessed, etc. Hence the question.

Another explanation: What is the meaning of THE MAN, GOD? R. Abin said: His lower half was 'man', but his upper half was as God.[1]

5. What is the meaning of, BEFORE HIS DEATH? The Rabbis say: What did Moses do? He seized the Angel of Death and cast him down in front of him and blessed the tribes, each according to his blessing.[2] R. Meir said: The Angel of Death came to Moses and said to him: 'God has sent me to you, for you are to depart this life to-day.' Moses replied: 'Go away hence, for I desire to praise God.' Whence this? For Scripture says, *I shall not die, but live, and declare the works of the Lord* (Ps. CXVIII, 17). Thereon the Angel of Death said to him: 'Moses, why do you give yourself airs? There are sufficient things in creation to praise Him; heaven and earth praise Him at all times,' as it is said, *The heavens declare the glory of God* (Ps. XIX, 2). Whereupon Moses replied: 'But I shall silence them and praise Him,' as it is said, *'Give ear, ye heavens, and I will speak,'* etc. He then came to him a second time. What did Moses do? He pronounced over him the Ineffable Name and he fled.[3] Whence this? For it is said, *For I will proclaim the name of the Lord* (Deut. XXXII, 3). When he came to him a third time Moses said: 'Seeing that this is from God, I must now resign myself to God's will,' as it is said, *The Rock, His work is perfect* (*ib.* 4).

R. Isaac said: The soul of Moses struggled to go forth, and Moses conversed with her saying: 'My soul, perhaps you think that the Angel of Death is seeking to gain dominion over you?' Whereupon she replied: 'God will

[1] Only the lower half of his body, the seat of the sexual and secretory organs, belonged to the earthly within him, but his head and heart, given over entirely to holiness, were as divine. For an interesting parallel to this, v. the statement made by a Magian to Amemar, Sanh. 39*a* (Sonc. ed.), p. 249.

[2] He either renders: . . . '*Wherewith Moses blessed the Children of Israel*' in front of his (angel of) death, who thus lay before him; or literally, 'Before his death,' i.e. though the moment of death had come, he gathered sufficient strength to defy it (metaphorically, he cast down the Angel of Death) until he had blessed the Children of Israel ('E.J.).

[3] I.e. the Angel of Death.

[surely] not permit it,' [as it is said], *For thou hast delivered my soul from death* (Ps. CXVI, 8). [Said Moses to her]: 'Perhaps you have seen Israel weeping and you have wept with them?' Whereupon she replied: '*Mine eyes from tears*' (*ib.*). Said Moses to her: 'Do you think then that they have sought to thrust you into the nether world?' Whereupon she replied: '*And my feet from stumbling*' (*ib.*). Said Moses to her: 'And whither are you destined to go?' She replied: '*I shall walk before the Lord in the lands of the living*' (*ib.* 9). When Moses heard this he gave her permission [to leave], saying to her: '*Return, O my soul, unto thy rest,*' etc. (*ib.* 7). R. Abin said: When Moses departed this world, the earthly beings praised him saying, *Moses commanded us a law, an inheritance of the congregation of Jacob* (Deut. XXXIII, 4), and the heavenly beings praised him saying, *He executed the righteousness of the Lord* (*ib.* 21), and God praised him [saying], *And there hath not arisen a prophet since in Israel like unto Moses* (*ib.* XXXIV, 10).

6. AND THIS IS THE BLESSING. *Halachah:* When a Jew goes up to read the Law, he is not permitted to commence reading it before he has recited the blessings. First he must recite the blessings and then he reads.[1] And thus Moses, when he had the privilege of receiving the Torah, first recited[2] a blessing, and then he read it. R. Eleazar asked: What was the blessing which Moses recited before reading it? [It was], Blessed art Thou, O Lord, King of the Universe, who hast chosen this law and sanctified it and hast found pleasure in them who fulfil it. He did not say, 'in them that labour at it,'[3] nor, 'in them who meditate in it,' but, 'in them that fulfil it,' that is to say, in them who carry out the words of the Torah.

'In them that fulfil it.' A man may say, 'I have acquired wisdom, but I have not learnt Torah; what shall I do under such circumstances?' God said to Israel: 'By your life, the whole of wisdom and the whole of the Torah are comprised in one trifling thing; whosoever fears Me and

[1] Cf. Meg. IV, 1. [2] Cf. *supra*, VIII, 2.
[3] In its study. Cf. Lev. R. XXV, 1.

fulfils the Torah holds all wisdom and all the Torah in his heart.' Whence this? For it is written, *The fear of the Lord is the beginning of wisdom, a good understanding have all they that do thereafter* (Ps. CXI, 10); *The fear of the Lord is clean, enduring for ever* (*ib.* XIX, 10); *Behold, the fear of the Lord, that is wisdom* (Job XXVIII, 28).

7. And why did Moses merit that God should busy Himself with his burial? Because when God went down to Egypt and the time for the redemption of Israel had come, all Israel were occupied with gathering silver and gold, but Moses was going round the city, and for three days and three nights was labouring to find Joseph's coffin, for the Israelites could not leave Egypt without Joseph. Why? Because he so bound them by oath before his death, as it is said, *And Joseph took an oath of the children of Israel saying*, etc. (Gen. L, 25). After Moses had tired himself out, a certain Segulah[1] met him and observing that he was weary from his efforts she said to him: 'My lord Moses, why are you tired?' He replied: 'For three days and three nights I have been going round the city to find Joseph's coffin and I cannot find it.' Said she to him: 'Come with me and I will show you where it is.' She took him to the river and said to him: 'In this place have the magicians and astrologers made for him a coffin of five hundred talents in weight and cast it into the river, and thus have they spoken to Pharaoh: "If it is your wish that this people should never leave this place, then as long as they will not find the bones of Joseph, so long will they be unable to leave."' Immediately Moses placed himself by the bank of the river and called out: 'Joseph, Joseph, you know how you have adjured Israel [with the words], *God will surely remember you* (*ib.*); give honour to the God of Israel and do not hold up the redemption of Israel; you have good deeds to your credit, intercede then with your Creator and come up from the depths.' Whereupon

[1] She is elsewhere referred to as Serah the daughter of Asher. Cf. Ex. R. XX, 19.

immediately Joseph's coffin began to break through the waters and to rise from the depths like a stick. Moses took it and placed it upon his shoulder and carried it, and all Israel followed him. And whilst Israel carried the silver and gold which they had taken away from Egypt, Moses was carrying Joseph's coffin. God said to him: 'Moses, you say that you have done a small thing; by your life, this act of kindness is a great thing; since as you ignored silver and gold, I too will do unto you this kindness in that I will busy Myself with your burial.'

8. When Moses was about to depart this world, God said to him: '*Behold, thy days approach.*' Whereupon Moses replied: 'Master of the Universe, after all my labour, Thou sayest unto me, "*Behold, thy days approach*"; *I shall not die, but live, and declare the works of the Lord*' (Ps. CXVIII, 17). Thereupon God said: 'You cannot prevail [in this matter], *For this is* [the destiny of] *all men*' (Eccl. XII, 13).[1] Moses then said: 'Master of the Universe, I ask of Thee one favour before I die, that I may enter,[2] and that all the gates of heaven and the deep be opened and people shall see that there is none beside Thee.' Whence this? For it is said, *Know this day, and lay it to thy heart, that the Lord, He is God . . . there is none else* (Deut. IV, 39). Whereupon God replied: 'You declare: "*There is none else* ('od)"; I too say, *And there hath not arisen a prophet since* ('od) *in Israel like unto Moses*, etc. (*ib.* XXXIV, 10); *In all the signs and the wonders*, etc. (*ib.* 11); *And in all the great terror, which Moses wrought in the sight of all Israel*' (*ib.* 12).

9. BEHOLD, THY DAYS APPROACH THAT THOU MUST DIE. R. Aibu said: Moses said: 'Master of the Universe, with the word [behold][3] with which I have praised Thee in the midst of the sixty myriads who hallowed

[1] E.V. '*For this is the whole of man*'.
[2] It is not clear to what this refers. Radal and 'E.J. explain: that I may enter Eretz Israel. It is more likely, however, that he is referring to death: that I may enter the future life. [3] Cf. *supra*, IX, 9.

Thy name, hast Thou decreed death upon me, as it is said, BEHOLD, THY DAYS APPROACH THAT THOU MUST DIE. In all Thy acts [one sees] measure for measure; [then why dost Thou repay me] a bad measure for a good measure, a short measure for a full measure, a grudging measure for an ample measure?' Whereupon the Holy One, blessed be He, answered: 'Moses, My use of the expression "behold" is also a good measure, as it is said, Behold, *I send an angel before thee* (Ex. XXIII, 20); Behold, *the righteous shall be requited in the earth* (Prov. XI, 31); Behold, *I will send you Elijah the prophet* (Mal. III, 23). And just as you have exalted Me before sixty myriads of people, so too will I exalt you in the time to come in the midst of fifty-five myriads of altogether righteous men,' as it is said, *hen* (behold), the numerical value of *hen* being as follows, [the letter] *hé*, five and *nun*, fifty.

10. R. Joḥanan said: Scripture refers ten times to the death of Moses, as follows: *Behold, thy days approach that thou must die* (Deut. XXXI, 14); *And die in the mount* (*ib.* XXXII, 50); *But I must die* (*ib.* IV, 22); *For I know that after my death* (*ib.* XXXI, 29); *And how much more after my death* (*ib.* XXXI, 27); *Before his death* (*ib.* XXXIII, 1); *A hundred and twenty years old when he died* (*ib.* XXXIV, 7); *So Moses the servant of the Lord died there* (*ib.* 5); *Now it came to pass after the death of Moses* (Josh. I, 1); *Moses My servant is dead* (*ib.* 2). This teaches that ten times was it decreed that Moses should not enter Eretz Israel, but the harsh decree was not finally sealed until the High Court[1] revealed itself to him and declared: 'It is my decree that you should not pass over,' [as it is said,] *For thou shalt not go over this Jordan* (Deut. III, 27). Moses, however, made light of this, saying: 'Israel have many times committed great sins, and whenever I prayed for them, God immediately answered my prayer, as it is said, *Let Me alone, that I may destroy them* (*ib.* IX, 14); yet what is written there? *And the Lord repented of the evil* (Ex. XXXII, 14); *I will smite them*

[1] I.e. God as Head of the Court on High.

with the pestilence, and destroy them (Num. XIV, 12); What is written there? *And the Lord said: I have pardoned*, etc. (*ib.* 20). Seeing then that I have not sinned from my youth, does it not stand to reason that when I pray on my own behalf God should answer my prayer?' And when God saw that Moses made light of the matter and that he was not engaging in prayer, He seized the opportunity to swear by His great Name that Moses should not enter Eretz Israel, as it is said, *Therefore* (laken) *ye shall not bring this assembly* (*ib.* XX, 12), and '*laken*' always implies an oath, as it is said, *And therefore* (laken) *I have sworn unto the house of Eli* (I Sam. III, 14). When, however, Moses saw that the decree against him had been sealed, he took a resolve to fast, and drew a small circle[1] and stood therein, and exclaimed: 'I will not move from here until Thou annullest that decree.' What else did Moses do then? He donned sackcloth and wrapped himself with sackcloth and rolled himself in the dust and stood in prayer and supplications before God, until the heavens and the order of nature were shaken. Said they: 'Perhaps it is the desire of God to create His world anew.' Whereupon a heavenly voice was heard proclaiming: 'It is not yet God's desire to renew His world . . . but, *In whose hand is the soul of every living thing, and the breath of all mankind*—ish' (Job XII, 10), and 'man' must surely refer to Moses, as it is said, *Now the man Moses was very meek, above all men that were upon the face of the earth* (Num. XII, 3). What did God do? At that hour He had it proclaimed in every gate of each of the heavens,[2] and in every Court, that they should not receive Moses' prayer, nor bring it before Him, because the decree against him had been sealed. Now at that hour God hastily summoned the Angel in charge of Proclamations, Achzeriel by name, and He commanded the ministering angels: 'Descend quickly, bolt all the gates of every heaven, because the voice of the prayer threatens to force its way to heaven.' And the angels sought to ascend to heaven because of the

[1] This is reminiscent of the exploits of Ḥoni the Circle Drawer, cf. Ta'an. 23*a*. [2] There are seven heavens.

sound of Moses' prayer, for his prayer was like a sword which tears and cuts its way through everything, and spares nothing, seeing that his prayer was of the nature of the Ineffable Name which he had learnt from Zagzagel the Master Scribe of the children of heaven. It is to that hour that [the prophet] alludes when he says, *And I heard behind me the voice of a great rushing: Blessed be the glory of the Lord from His place* (Ezek. III, 12); and '*rushing*' surely means trembling, and '*great*' surely refers to Moses, as it is said, *Moreover the man Moses was very great in the land of Egypt, in the sight of Pharaoh's servants, and in the sight of the people* (Ex. XI, 3). What is the meaning of, '*Blessed be the glory of the Lord from His place*'? When the wheels of the Chariot and the fiery Seraphim saw that God commanded that Moses' prayer should not be accepted and that He did not respect [Moses'] person, nor grant him more life, nor bring him into Eretz Israel, they exclaimed: '*Blessed be the glory of the Lord from His place,*' for before Him there is no respecting of persons, great or small. And whence do we know that Moses prayed at this juncture five hundred and fifteen times? For it is said, *And I besought* (wa-ethḥanan) *the Lord at that time, saying* (Deut. III, 23), the numerical value of '*wa-ethḥanan*' is this number. Moses said to God: 'Master of the Universe, the labour and the pains which I have devoted to making Israel believe in Thy name are manifest and known to Thee, to what trouble have I gone with them in connection with the precepts in order to fix for them Torah and precepts. I thought, just as I witnessed the woe, so too will I behold their weal; but now that the weal of Israel has come, Thou sayest to me, "*Thou shalt not go over this Jordan*" (Deut. XXXI, 2); lo, Thou makest of Thy Torah a fraud. Therein it is written, *In the same day thou shalt give him his hire, neither shall the sun go down upon it, for he is poor, and setteth his heart upon it; lest he cry against thee unto the Lord, and it be sin in thee* (*ib.* XXIV, 15). Is this the reward for the forty years' labour that I went through in order that [Israel] should become a holy and faithful people, as it is said, *But Judah yet ruleth with God, and is faithful with the saints'* (Hos. XII, 1)?[1] Sammael the wicked angel, the chief of all the accusing angels, was awaiting the death of Moses every hour, saying, 'When will the time or the moment arrive for Moses to die, so that I may descend and take away his soul from him.' And it is of him that David said, *The wicked watcheth the righteous, and seeketh to slay him* (Ps. XXXVII, 32). There is no one among the accusing angels so wicked as Sammael and there is none so righteous among the prophets as Moses, as it is said, *And there hath not arisen a prophet since in Israel like unto Moses, whom the Lord knew face to face* (Deut. XXXIV, 10). He was like a man who has been invited to a wedding feast, and looks forward to it, saying: 'When will their rejoicing come that I may share therein.' So, Sammael the wicked was waiting for Moses' soul saying, 'When will Michael[2] be weeping and I be filling my mouth with laughter?' Whereupon Michael replied: 'What, you wicked one, I shall cry, and you laugh!' as it is said, *Rejoice not against me, O mine enemy; though I am fallen, I shall arise; though I sit in darkness, the Lord is a light unto me* (Micah VII, 8). '*Though I am fallen,*' because of the demise of Moses, yet, '*I shall arise,*' on account of the leadership displayed by Joshua when he shall have defeated the thirty-one kings.[3] '*Though I sit in darkness,*' because of the destruction of the first and the second Temples, yet, '*The Lord is a light unto me,* in the days of Messiah. Meanwhile there remained unto Moses only one hour. Whereupon Moses said to God: 'Master of the Universe, if Thou wilt not bring me into Eretz Israel, leave me in this world so that I may live and not die.' God thereupon said to Moses: 'If I will not slay you in this world, how can I bring you back to life in the World to Come? And what is more, you make of My Torah a fraud, for in My Torah it is written by your hand, *And there is none that can deliver out of My hand*' (Deut. XXXII, 39). Said Moses to God: 'Master of the Universe, if Thou wilt not bring me into Eretz

[1] The A.V. has been retained here, as the Midrash obviously understands it in that sense. [2] Michael is one of the angels who save people. Cf. Ex. R. XVIII, 5. [3] Cf. Josh. XII.

Israel, let me become like the beasts of the field that eat grass and drink water and live and enjoy the world; likewise let my soul be as one of them.' Whereupon God replied: '*Let it suffice thee*' (*ib.* III, 26). Moses then prayed: 'Master of the Universe, if not, let me become in this world like the bird that flies about in every direction, and gathers its food daily, and returns to its nest towards evening; let my soul likewise become like one of them.' Whereupon God answered: '*Let it suffice thee.*' What is the meaning of '*Let it suffice thee*'? God said to him: 'You have spoken sufficiently.' When Moses saw that no creature could save him from the path of death, he thereupon exclaimed, '*The Rock, His work is perfect; for all His ways are justice; a God of faithfulness and without iniquity, just and righteous is He*' (*ib.* XXXII, 4). What did Moses do? He took a scroll and wrote down upon it the Ineffable Name, nor had the Book of Song[1] been completely written down when the moment of Moses' death arrived. At that hour God said to Gabriel: 'Gabriel, go forth and bring Moses' soul.' He, however, replied: 'Master of the Universe, how can I witness the death of him who is equal to sixty myriads, and how can I behave harshly to one who possesses such qualities?' Then [God] said to Michael: 'Go forth and bring Moses' soul.' He, however, replied: 'Master of the Universe, I was his teacher, and he my pupil, and I cannot therefore witness his death.' [God] then said to Sammael the wicked: 'Go forth and bring Moses' soul.' Immediately he clothed himself with anger and girded on his sword and wrapped himself with ruthlessness and went forth to meet Moses. When Sammael saw Moses sitting and writing down the Ineffable Name, and how the radiance of his appearance was like unto the sun and he was like unto an angel of the Lord of hosts, he became afraid of Moses and declared: 'Of a surety, angels cannot take away Moses' soul.' Now before Sammael showed himself to Moses, Moses knew of his coming, and when Sammael caught sight of Moses trembling, fear took hold of him, as of a

[1] Name applied to Deut. XXXII

woman in travail, and he had not the effrontery to speak to Moses, until Moses said to Sammael, '*There is no peace, saith God, concerning the wicked* (Isa. LVII, 21). What are you doing here?' He replied: 'I have come to take away your soul.' Moses asked him: 'Who sent you?' He replied: 'He who created all the creatures.' Moses then said to him: 'You shall not take away my soul.' Whereupon he replied: 'The souls of all who come into this world are delivered into my hands.' Whereupon Moses said: 'I have greater strength than all who come into this world.' He then asked: 'And wherein lies your strength?' Moses replied: 'I am the son of Amram,[1] and came out from my mother's womb without prepuce, and had no need to be circumcised; and on the very day on which I was born I found myself able to speak and was able to walk and to converse with my father and mother, and I did not even take suck of [my mother's] milk; and when I was three months old I prophesied and declared that I was destined to receive the law from the midst of flames of fire; and [once] when I was walking in the street I entered the palace of the king and removed the crown from his head; and when I was eighty years old I wrought signs and wonders in Egypt and brought forth sixty myriads before the eyes of all Egypt; and I divided the sea into twelve divisions, and I made the bitter waters sweet; and I ascended heaven and trod out a path there, and engaged in battle with the angels, and received the law of fire, and sojourned under [God's] Throne of fire, and took shelter under the pillar of fire, and spoke with God face to face; and I prevailed over the heavenly *Familia*,[2] and revealed unto the sons of man their secrets,[3] and received the Law from the right hand of God, and taught it to Israel; and I made war on Sihon and Og,[4] the two giants of the heathens to whose ankles the waters of the flood did not reach because of their [great] stature; I caused sun and moon to stand still on high, and I smote them[5] with the staff in my hand and killed them[6]; is there

[1] Cf. Soṭ. 12*a*. [2] Cf. Ex. R. XXVIII, 1. [3] Cf. Shab. 89*a*.
[4] Cf. Deut. II, 17–III, 11. [5] I.e. Sihon and Og.
[6] Cf. Sifre on Deut. par. 101.

any one amongst mankind who is able to do likewise? Away, wicked one, from here, you must not speak thus, go, flee before me, I will not surrender my soul to you.' Immediately Sammael went back and reported to God. Whereupon God commanded Sammael, 'Go, and bring Moses' soul.' Straightway he drew his sword from the sheath and placed himself at the side of Moses. Immediately Moses became wroth, and taking hold of the staff on which was engraven the Ineffable Name he fell upon Sammael with all his strength until he fled from before him, and he pursued him with the Ineffable Name and removed the beam of glory [halo] from between his eyes and blinded him. Thus much did Moses achieve. At the end of a moment, a heavenly voice was heard, declaring: 'The end, the time of your death has come.' Said Moses to God: 'Master of the Universe, remember the day when Thou didst reveal Thyself unto me in the bush and didst say to me, *Come now therefore, and I will send thee unto Pharaoh, that thou mayest bring forth My people the children of Israel from Egypt* (Ex. III, 10); remember the time when I abode on Mount Sinai for forty days and forty nights, I implore Thee, do not hand me over into the hand of the Angel of Death.' Thereupon a heavenly voice was heard saying to him: 'Fear not, I myself will attend to you and your burial.' At that hour, Moses arose and sanctified himself like the Seraphim, and God came down from the highest heavens to take away the soul of Moses, and with Him were three ministering angels, Michael, Gabriel, and Zagzagel. Michael laid out his bier, Gabriel spread out a fine linen cloth at his bolster, Zagzagel one at his feet; Michael stood at one side and Gabriel at the other side. God said: 'Moses, fold your eyelids over your eyes,' and he did so. He then said: 'Place your hands upon your breast,' and he did so. He then said: 'Put your feet next to one another,' and he did so. Forthwith the Holy One, blessed be He, summoned the soul from the midst of the body, saying to her: 'My daughter, I have fixed the period of thy stay in the body of Moses at a hundred and twenty years; now thy end has come, depart, delay not.' Whereupon she replied: 'Master of the Universe, I know that Thou art the God of all spirits and all souls, the souls of the dead and the living are in Thy keeping, and Thou hast created and formed me and placed me within the body of Moses for a hundred and twenty years. And now, is there a body in the world purer than the body of Moses in which there has never been an offensive smell, nor worm nor maggot, nor any kind of vermin; therefore I love him and I do not desire to leave him.' Whereupon God exclaimed: 'Soul, go forth, do not delay, and I will raise thee to the highest heavens and will place thee under the Throne of Glory next to the Cherubim, Seraphim, and other troops of angels.' Thereupon the soul replied: 'Master of the Universe, two angels, Uzah and Azael, came down from near Thy divine Presence and coveted the daughters of the earth and they corrupted their way upon the earth until Thou didst suspend them between earth and heaven. But the son of Amram from the day Thou didst reveal Thyself unto him at the Bush has had no marital relations with his wife,' as it is said, *And Miriam and Aaron spoke against Moses because of the Cushite woman whom he had married; for he had married a Cushite woman* (Num. XII, 1).[1] 'I implore Thee let me remain in the body of Moses.' Thereupon God kissed Moses and took away his soul with a kiss of the mouth, and God, if one might say so, wept [as it is said], *Who will rise up for me against the evil-doers? Who will stand up for me against the workers of iniquity?* (Ps. XCIV, 16). And the Holy Spirit said, *And there hath not arisen a prophet since in Israel like unto Moses* (Deut. XXXIV, 10). The heavens wept and said, *The godly man is perished out of the earth* (Micah VII, 2). The earth wept and said, *And the upright among men is no more* (*ib.*). And when Joshua was looking for his master and did not find him, he also wept and said, *Help, Lord; for the godly man ceaseth, for the faithful fail from among the children of men* (Ps. XII, 2). And the ministering angels said, *He executed the righteousness of the Lord* (Deut. XXXIII, 21). And Israel said, *And His ordinances with Israel* (*ib.*). These

[1] V. Shab. 87*a*; Yeb. 62*a*; Ex. R. XIX, 3.

and those said, *He entereth into peace, they rest in their beds, each one that walketh in his uprightness* (Isa. LVII, 2); *The memory of the righteous shall be for a blessing* (Prov. X, 7), and his soul for the life of the World to Come. Amen. May this be His will. Blessed be the Lord for ever. Amen and amen.

MIDRASH RABBAH

LAMENTATIONS

MIDRASH

TRANSLATED INTO ENGLISH

WITH NOTES, GLOSSARY AND INDICES

UNDER THE EDITORSHIP OF

RABBI DR. H. FREEDMAN, B.A., PH.D.

AND

MAURICE SIMON, M.A.

RABBAH

LAMENTATIONS

TRANSLATED BY

REV. DR. A. COHEN, M.A., PH.D.

THE SONCINO PRESS
LONDON • NEW YORK

THIRD EDITION 1983

ISBN: 0-900689-38-2

MANUFACTURED IN THE UNITED STATES OF AMERICA
PRINTED BY NOBLE OFFSET PRINTERS, INC.

CONTENTS

INTRODUCTION

The recital of the Book of Lamentations forms part of the ritual of the Synagogue on the ninth of Ab (the fifth month of the year), the anniversary of the destruction of the first and second Temple. The dirge of Jeremiah was the obvious selection of a Biblical book appropriate for such an observance.

The overwhelming catastrophe which resulted in the downfall of Temple and State made a profound impression which lingered in the hearts of Jews throughout the succeeding generations. They saw in it the cause of the hardships they had to endure in the lands of dispersion. So devastating a calamity, it was felt, must have been the consequence of the sins of the people, which not only withdrew the Divine protection from their forefathers in the hour of crisis but also weakened their power of resistance against the enemy and brought about their defeat.

A deep-rooted conviction of this kind gave the Rabbis the opportunity of expatiating during the fast of Ab upon the evils which had in the past sapped Israel's vitality in times of national danger, and of drawing parallels between their present and the past. They, accordingly, had a practical end in view in the framing of their discourses, and the Midrash to Lamentations should be read from that standpoint.

The work falls into two distinct divisions: first a series of Proems or Introductions, and secondly comments on the verses of the Biblical text. The editor of the critical edition, S. Buber, holds that the two parts are of different authorship and that the Proems are a later addition. On the other hand, Theodor is of the opinion that their collection was 'certainly made by the author of the Midrash' (*J.E.*, v, p. 85). The arguments which Buber adduces in support of his view are certainly weighty. He points out, e.g., that several times a Proem is duplicated in the body of the Midrash from which it is a quotation (cf. Proem XVII with the Midrash to III, 14; XVIII with III, 15; XXX with IV, 12). Furthermore the first three, and sections of other

Proems are taken from the Pesikta d'Rab Kahana which is subsequent to Midrash Ekah; and generally speaking, much of the material in these Introductions is drawn from sources which are comparatively late. A difference in style and language may also be detected.

Our Midrash is one of the earliest in the 'Rabbah' series. It is now usual to place it in order of time after Genesis, which is the oldest of them all. Buber assigns it to the fourth century, and that date is now accepted. On the strength of the allusion to 'Ishmael' in I, 14, i.e., to Arab hegemony over the Jews, Zunz[1] maintained that the composition could not be earlier than the second half of the seventh century, since the reference was to the Mohammedans. This interpretation has been rejected by modern scholars, and Weiss[2] is correct in explaining the word as denoting the pre-Islamic Arabs.

On the question of the land of its origin opinions are divided. Weiss suggests that the author was a Babylonian, while Buber and Theodor declare him to have been a Palestinian. The latter view is the more probable, and is confirmed by such a passage as, 'There were no cedars in Babylon, and when Nebuchadnezzar came here (i.e., to Palestine)' (I, 4); and in I, 7 the Palestinian teachers are called 'the Rabbis of here' and the Babylonian 'the Rabbis of there'. Consequently the geographical standpoint of the writer is Palestine. The large number of Greek words which occur in the text, as well as the constant use of the Palestinian Talmud as a source, provide an additional argument in favour of this opinion.

While the prevailing tone of the comments is naturally sombre and many of the stories narrated in connection with the destruction of the Temple and the Hadrianic persecution give harrowing details, the dark colour is relieved by the inclusion of a series of anecdotes in a lighter vein (v. on I, I).

A. Cohen.

[1] *Die Gottesdienstlichen Vorträge der Juden*, 2nd ed., p. 191.
[2] *Dor*, 4th ed., III, p. 232, n. 17.

LAMENTATIONS

THE PROEMS OF THE SAGES

I

R. Abba b. Kahana opened his discourse with the text, *Cry thou with a shrill voice, O daughter of Gallim* (Isa. x, 30). Isaiah said to Israel, Rather than you should utter songs and praises before idols, cry with a shrill voice in words of Torah,[1] cry with a shrill voice in the Synagogues. '*O daughter of Gallim*': as the waves (*gallim*) are conspicuous in the sea, so are the patriarchs in the world. Another interpretation of '*O daughter of Gallim*' is to read the text as *bath Golim*, i.e. 'O daughter of wanderers'—daughter of[2] Abraham, of whom it is written, *And there was a famine in the land; and Abram went down into Egypt* (Gen. XII, 10); daughter of Isaac, of whom it is written, *And Isaac went unto Abimelech, king of the Philistines unto Gerar* (*ib.* XXVI, 1); daughter of Jacob, of whom it is written, *And he went to Paddan-aram* (*ib.* XXVIII, 5).

'*Hearken*' (Isa. x, 30): hearken to My commandments, hearken to words of Torah, hearken to words of prophecy, hearken to the dictates of righteousness and benevolence. '*O Laish*': otherwise *layeshah*, i.e. a lion, will come up against you, alluding to the wicked Nebuchadnezzar, of whom it is written, *A lion is gone up from his thicket* (Jer. IV, 7). '*O thou poor*': poor in righteous men, poor in words of prophecy, poor in performance of the Divine precepts and in good deeds. '*Anathoth*': otherwise, *Anathoth*, i.e. the man of Anathoth, will come and prophesy against you; as it is written, *The words of Jeremiah the son of Hilkiah, of the priests that were in Anathoth* (*ib.* I, 1). Since retribution came upon Israel, he lamented over them, *Ekah*.[3]

[1] The meaning is: use your voice for study and prayer.
[2] Descendant of, the feminine being used of the nation.
[3] 'How'—*How doth the city sit solitary* (Lam. I, 1).—*Ekah* is the usual way of commencing a dirge or lamentation.

II

R. Abba b. Kahana opened his discourse with the text, *Who is the wise man, that he may understand this?* (Jer. IX, 11). R. Simeon b. Yoḥai taught: If you behold cities uprooted from their site in the land of Israel, know that the inhabitants failed to pay the fees of the instructors in Bible and Mishnah; as it is said, *Wherefore is the land perished? . . . And the Lord saith: Because they have forsaken My law* (*ib.* 11 f.).

Rabbi[1] sent R. Assi and R. Ammi on a mission to organise [religious education in] the cities of the land of Israel. They came to a city and said to the people, 'Bring us the guardians of the city.' They fetched the captain of the guard and the magistrate. The Rabbis exclaimed, 'These the guardians of the city! They are its destroyers!'[2] The people inquired, 'Who, then, are its guardians?' and they answered, 'The instructors in Bible and Mishnah, who meditate upon, teach and preserve the Torah day and night.' This is in accordance with what is said, *Thou shalt meditate therein day and night* (Josh. I, 8); and it is similarly stated, *Except the Lord build the house,*[3] *they labour in vain that build it* (Ps. CXXVII, 1).

R. Huna and R. Jeremiah said in the name of R. Samuel b. R. Isaac: We find that the Holy One, blessed be He, may overlook idolatry, immorality, or bloodshed, but He does not overlook rejection of the Torah; as it is said, '*Wherefore is the land perished?*' It is not written here 'because of idolatry, immorality, or bloodshed', but '*because they have forsaken My law*'.

R. Huna and R. Jeremiah said in the name of R. Ḥiyya b. Abba: It is written, *They have forsaken Me and have not kept My law* (Jer. XVI, 11)—i.e. would that they had forsaken Me but kept My law, since by occupying themselves

[1] R. Judah the Prince, grandson of the R. Judah who edited the Mishnah. He lived in the 3rd cent.

[2] Mah.; if you rely solely upon these the city will certainly be destroyed.

[3] I.e. unless it is built upon the basis of education in and observance of the Divine precepts.

therewith, the light which it contains would have led them back to the right path.

R. Huna said: Study Torah even if it be not for its own sake,[1] since even if not for its own sake at first it will eventually be for its own sake. R. Joshua b. Levi said: Every day a *Bath Ḳol* issues from Mount Horeb, declaring, 'Woe to mankind for slighting Torah!'

Samuel[2] taught in the name of R. Samuel b. Ammi: When can the Government enact an oppressive measure and render it effective? At the time that Israel casts words of Torah to the ground[3]; and so it is written, *And the host was given over to it together with the continual burnt-offering through transgression* (Dan. VIII, 12). '*Host*' signifies nothing else than the [non-Jewish] Governments; as it is said, *The Lord will punish the host of the high heaven*[4] *on high* (Isa. XXIV, 21). '*The continual burnt-offering*'[5] is Israel; as it is written, '*Thou shalt meditate therein day and night.*' '*Through transgression*' means through neglect of Torah. Whenever Israel casts words of Torah to the ground, the Government enacts an oppressive measure which proves effective, as it is said, *And it cast down truth to the ground* (Dan. *ib.*). '*Truth*' signifies nothing else than Torah; as it is said, *Buy the truth, and sell it not* (Prov. XXIII, 23). If you have cast words of Torah to the ground, the Government is immediately successful [in its oppressive measures]; and so it is written, *And it wrought, and prospered* (Dan. *ib.*).

R. Judah b. Pazzi said: *Israel hath cast off that which is good* (Hos. VIII, 3). '*Good*' signifies nothing else than Torah; as it is said, *For I give you good doctrine* (Prov. IV, 2).

R. Abba b. Kahana said: There arose not among the heathen peoples philosophers like Balaam the son of Beor and Oeonamos of Gadara.[6] They were once asked, 'Can we

[1] With the hope of deriving advantage therefrom.
[2] A third cent. Rabbi. [3] Despises and neglects them.
[4] Lit. 'the host of the height', interpreted as the men in the high places, the ruling powers. [5] Lit. 'that which is continuous', and it is Israel's duty to be continuously engrossed in Torah.
[6] The former is alluded to in Num. XXII ff. The latter was a pagan philosopher of the early second cent. v. *J.E.* IX, 386. The anecdote occurs in Gen. R. LXV, 20.

overcome this people [of Israel]? They replied, 'Go round to their Synagogues; if there is a hum of children's voices [there studying the Torah], you cannot prevail over them, otherwise you can. For thus their patriarch assured them, saying, "*The voice is the voice of Jacob, but the hands are the hands of Esau*" (Gen. XXVII, 22)—i.e., so long as the voice of Jacob persists in the Synagogues and Houses of Study, the hands are not Esau's hands[1]; but whenever there is no hum of voices in the Synagogues and Houses of Study, the hands are Esau's hands.' Similarly it declares, *Therefore as stubble devoureth the tongue of fire*[2] (Isa. V, 24). Can stubble devour fire? Is it not the nature of fire to devour stubble, and yet you say '*As stubble devoureth the tongue of fire*'! In fact, '*stubble*' denotes the house of Esau; as it is said, *And the house of Jacob shall be a fire, and the house of Joseph a flame, and the house of Esau for stubble* (Obad. 18). '*The tongue of fire*' denotes the house of Jacob. '*And as the chaff is consumed in the flame*' (Isa. *ib.*) denotes the house of Joseph. '*So their root shall be as rottenness*' (*ib.*) denotes the patriarchs who are the roots of Israel.[3] '*And their blossom shall go up as dust*' denotes the tribes who are the blossoms of Israel. Why [will this fate befall them]? '*Because they have rejected the law of the Lord of hosts*' (*ib.*). R. Judan said: '*Because they have rejected the law of the Lord of hosts*' denotes the written Torah; '*and contemned the word of the Holy One of Israel*' (*ib.*) denotes the oral Torah.[4] Since they cast the words of Torah to the ground, Jeremiah began to lament over them, *Ekah*.

Thus saith the Lord of hosts: Consider ye, and call for the mourning women (Jer. IX, 16). R. Joḥanan, R. Simeon b. Laḳish, and the Rabbis [comment as follows]. R. Joḥanan said: God may be likened to a king who had two sons. He became enraged against the first of them, took a stick,

[1] They cannot overcome Israel.

[2] That is the order of the words in the Hebrew. E.V. '*Therefore as the tongue of fire devoureth the stubble*'.

[3] When Israel rejects the Torah, even the merit of the patriarchs cannot sustain them.

[4] '*Word*' denotes what is transmitted orally, i.e. the traditional explanations of the ordinances contained in the text of the Pentateuch.

thrashed him, drove him into banishment, and exclaimed, 'Woe to him! From what comfort has he been banished!' He later became enraged against the second son, took a stick, thrashed him, drove him into banishment, and exclaimed, 'The fault is with me, since I must have brought them up badly.' Similarly the ten tribes were exiled, and the Holy One, blessed be He, began to proclaim this verse over them, '*Woe unto them, for they have strayed from Me*' (Hos. VII, 13). But when Judah and Benjamin were exiled, the Holy One, blessed be He—if it is possible to say so[1]—declared, '*Woe is me for My hurt*'[2] (Jer. X, 19).

R. Simeon b. Laḳish said: God may be likened to a king who had two sons. He became enraged against the first of them, took a stick, and thrashed him so that he writhed in agony and died; and the father then began to lament over him. He later became enraged against the second son, took a stick, and thrashed him so that he writhed in agony and died; and the father then exclaimed, 'No longer have I the strength to lament over them, so call for the mourning women[3] and let them lament over them.' Similarly the ten tribes were exiled, and He began to lament over them, '*Hear ye this word which I take up for a lamentation over you, O house of Israel*' (Amos V, 1). But when Judah and Benjamin were exiled, the Holy One, blessed be He—if it is possible to say so—declared, 'No longer have I the strength to lament over them.' Hence it is written, *Call for the mourning women . . . and let them make haste, and take up a wailing for Us* (Jer. IX, 16 f.). It is not written here 'for them', but '*for Us*', i.e. for Me and them. '*That Our eyes may run down with tears*'—it is not written here 'that *their* eyes may run down with tears', but '*Our eyes*', i.e. Mine and theirs. It is not written here, 'And *their* eyelids gush out with water', but '*Our eyelids*', i.e. Mine and theirs.

The Rabbis say: God may be likened to a king who had twelve sons of whom two died. He began to console himself

[1] An expression inserted when a rather bold statement is being made with reference to God. [2] The word for '*hurt*' is identified with a similar word in Aramaic, and interpreted 'Woe is Me for My upbringing of Israel'. [3] Professional mourners hired in the East at funerals.

with the ten. Two more died and he began to console himself with the eight. Two more died and he began to console himself with the six. Two more died and he began to console himself with the four. Two more died and he began to console himself with the two. But when they had all died, he began to lament over them, '*How sitteth solitary*' (Lam. I, I).

III

R. Abba b. Kahana opened his discourse with the text, *I sat not in the assembly of them that make merry, nor rejoiced* (Jer. XV, 17). The Community of Israel spake before the Holy One, blessed be He: 'Sovereign of the Universe, never did I enter the theatres and circuses[1] of the heathen peoples and make merry and rejoice.' *I sat alone because of Thy hand* (*ib.*): Pharaoh's hand attacked me, but I sat not alone.[2] Sennacherib's hand attacked me, but I sat not alone. Since, however, Thy hand attacked me, I sat alone. '*How sitteth solitary.*'[3]

IV

R. Abbahu opened his discourse with the text, *But they like men*[4] *have transgressed the covenant* (Hos. VI, 7). This alludes to the first man, of whom the Holy One, blessed be He, said, 'I brought him into the Garden of Eden and imposed a command upon him, but he transgressed it; so I punished him by driving him out and sending him forth,[5] and lamented over him, *Ekah*.' 'I brought him into the Garden of Eden,' as it is said, *And the Lord God took the man, and put him into the Garden of Eden* (Gen. II, 15). 'I imposed a command upon him,' as it is said, *And the Lord God commanded the man, saying* (*ib.* 16). 'But he transgressed My command,' as it is said, *Hast thou eaten of the*

[1] The objection of the Rabbis to circuses was due to the fact that the athletes appeared there naked, and to the grossness and cruelty which characterised the sports held there. [2] God's help was with Israel. [3] I.e. only when God forsook me could my enemies make me desolate. [4] Lit. 'like a man (*'adam*)'. [5] M.K. 'driving out' connotes expulsion from a particular place; 'sending forth' connotes to a further distance.

tree, whereof I commanded thee that thou shouldest not eat? (*ib.* III, 11). 'So I punished him by driving him out,' as it is said, *So He drove out the man* (*ib.* 24), and 'by sending him forth', as it is said, *Therefore the Lord God sent him forth* (*ib.* 23), and 'lamented over him, *Ekah*', as it is said, *Where art thou?*—ayyekah (*ib.* 9), this being written *ekah*.[1]

Similarly with his descendants. I brought them into the land of Israel, as it is said, *And I brought you into a land of fruitful fields* (Jer. II, 7). I gave them commandments, as it is said, *Command the children of Israel* (Lev. XXIV, 2). They transgressed My ordinances, as it is said, *Yea, all Israel have transgressed Thy law* (Dan. IX, 11). So I punished them by driving them out, as it is said, *I will drive them out of My house* (Hos. IX, 15), and by sending them forth, as it is said, *Cast them out of My sight and let them go forth* (Jer. XV, 1); and I lamented over them, '*How sitteth solitary.*'

V

R. Abbahu, in the name of R. Jose b. Ḥanina, opened his discourse with the text, *Wherefore thus saith the Lord God; Woe to the bloody city* (Ezek. XXIV, 6): alas for the city in the midst of which they shed blood.[2] '*To the pot whose filth is therein*': in which the dregs[3] remain. '*And whose filth is not gone out of it*': whose dregs have not departed from it. '*Bring it out piece by piece*': they went into exile in sections.

In what order were they exiled? R. Eleazar says: The tribes of Reuben and Gad went into exile first. R. Samuel b. Naḥman says: The tribes of Zebulun and Naphtali went into exile first; and so it is written, *As at the first time He made light the land of Zebulun and the land of Naphtali*[4]

[1] 'Where art thou' is normally written איך; here it is written איכה which with a different punctuation renders איכה (*Ekah*)—M.K.
[2] Each part of the verse is followed by an Aramaic paraphrase.
[3] A figurative expression for the wicked elements in the population.
[4] 'He made light'—i.e. He depopulated the country, thus making it light, as it were (Mah.). E.V. '*Now the former hath lightly afflicted the land*', etc.

(Isa. VIII, 23). How, then, does R. Eleazar interpret the verse quoted by R. Samuel b. Naḥman? As[1] the tribes of Reuben and Gad went into exile, so did the tribes of Zebulun and Naphtali go into exile. '*But the latter hath dealt a more serious blow* (hikbid)': R. Abba b. Kahana said: [The meaning is,] He swept them as with a broom (*makbid*): and so it is written, *I will sweep it with the besom of destruction*(*ib.* XIV, 23). *No lot is fallen upon it* (Ezek. XXIV, 6): R. Naḥman said in the name of R. Aḥa: What means '*no lot is fallen upon it*'? The Holy One, blessed be He, said, 'At the time when I caused lots to be cast for the heathen nations of the world to be exiled,[2] they did not go into captivity; so why were *you* exiled? *Because her blood*[3] *is in the midst of her* (*ib.* 7).' To what purpose is all this? *That it might cause fury to come up* (*ib.* 8).[4]

R. Judan asked R. Aḥa, 'Where did the Israelites slay Zechariah,[5] in the Court of Israel or the Court of Women?'[6] He replied, 'In neither of these, but it was in the Court of the Priests. Nor did they treat his blood as was done with the blood of a ram or hind; for in connection with the blood of these animals it is written, *He shall pour out the blood thereof and cover it with dust* (Lev. XVII, 13), but of this incident it is written, *For her blood is in the midst of her, she set it upon the bare rock; she poured it not upon the ground, to cover it with dust* (Ezek. XXIV, 7).'

Another interpretation of '*Wherefore thus saith the Lord God, Woe to the bloody city*' (*ib.* 9): alas for the city in the midst of which they shed blood.[7] '*I also will make the pile great*' (*ib.* 9): I will multiply punishments. '*Heaping on the wood*' (*ib.* 10): these are the enemy's legions.[8] '*Kindling*

[1] Buber reads כשם for כעת, i.e. the verse means that the tribes of Zebulun and Naphtali had the same experience as had already befallen Reuben and Gad. [2] V. Proem XXIII, p. 31.

[3] The blood of Zechariah, as the next paragraph explains.

[4] They deliberately left the blood uncovered for the purpose of provoking God's anger.

[5] A priest in the reign of Joash. For his murder v. II Chron. XXIV, 20 f.

[6] Two sections of the Temple precincts.

[7] 'Another . . . blood' is absent in the Yalkut and should be deleted here too, because the Midrash expounds v. 9 and not v. 6 of Ezek. XXIV.

[8] The heathen army was the fuel which was to destroy Judea.

the fire': these are the kings.[1] *'That the flesh be consumed'*: this refers to the Community.[2] *'And preparing the mixture'*: R. Joshua and R. Nehemiah in the name of R. Aḥa said: Inasmuch as all Israel kept saying, 'Nebuchadnezzar has gathered to himself all the wealth of the world, will he need ours?' the Holy One, blessed be He, retorted: 'By your lives, I will make your wealth as desirable to him as the spices which are used at a banquet.' *'That the bones also may be burned'*: you find that at the time when the Israelites went into exile, their bodies steamed[3] like a spiced dish. *'Then will I set it empty upon the coals thereof'* (*ib.* 11): R. Eleazar said: Had the text said 'broken', there would never have been a remedy for them; but since it says *'empty'* [there is hope of a remedy, because] an empty vessel may eventually be filled. To what purpose is all this? *'That it may be hot, and the bottom thereof may burn, and that the impurity of it may be molten in it, that the filth of it may be consumed.'* Since they sinned, they were exiled; and since they were exiled, Jeremiah began to lament over them, *'How sitteth solitary.'*

VI

R. Abbahu, in the name of R. Jose b. Ḥanina, opened his discourse with the text, *Ephraim shall be desolate* (Hos. v, 9). When? *'In the day of rebuke* (tokeḥah),' i.e. the day on which the Holy One, blessed be He, will argue (*hithwakkaḥ*) with them in judgment.[4] You find that when the ten tribes were exiled, Judah and Benjamin were not exiled; and the ten tribes kept asking, 'Why did He exile us and not them? Is it because they reside in His Palace?[5] Is there perhaps some favouritism here?' God forbid! There is no favouritism here; but the reason is that they had not yet sinned. When they did sin, He exiled them. Then the tribes exclaimed: 'O our God, O our God, O mighty One,

[1] As fire draws upwards, so the kings are above the people (Mah.). M.K. and יפה ענף: the reference is to the Jewish kings who corrupted the people by their wickedness. [2] V. the Midrash on Lam. III, 4.
[3] Were heated with grief. [4] To prove His impartiality.
[5] Jerusalem, which included the Temple, was their capital.

O mighty One, O truthful One, O truthful One! Even towards the children of His house He displays no partiality.' Since they sinned, they were exiled; and since they were exiled, Jeremiah began to lament over them, '*How sitteth solitary.*'

VII

R. Abbahu, in the name of R. Jose b. Ḥanina, opened his discourse with the text, *And her gates shall lament and mourn* (Isa. III, 26): lamenting is internal and mourning is external.[1] '*Her gates*': i.e. the destruction of the first and second Temples.[2] '*And utterly bereft*': she shall be bereft of words of Torah, bereft of words of prophecy, bereft of righteous men, bereft of Divine precepts and good deeds. On that account '*she shall sit upon the ground*' [which corresponds to] *They sit upon the ground, and keep silence, the elders of the daughter of Zion* (Lam. II, 10).

VIII

R. Isaac opened his discourse with the text, *For a voice of wailing is heard out of Zion, How are we undone!* (Jer. IX, 18). Can, then, wood and stone weep that you declare, '*For a voice of wailing is heard out of Zion.*'[3] In truth the wailing is from Him Who causes His *Shechinah* to dwell in Zion. '*How are we undone*'[4]: i.e. how has this happened to us? Through despoilers. '*We are greatly confounded, because we have forsaken the land*': the land of Israel, of which it is written, *A land which the Lord thy God careth for* (Deut. XI, 12). '*Because our dwellings have cast us out*': these are the Synagogues and Houses of Study.

Another interpretation of '*We are greatly confounded, because we have forsaken the land*': this refers to the words of the Torah, of which it says, *The measure thereof*[5] *is longer*

[1] The first term denotes grief in the heart, the second outward manifestations of mourning. [2] The plural '*gates*' alludes to the two Temples.
[3] Since the text does not state 'from the dwellers in Zion'. Mah.: it cannot refer to the inhabitants, since it goes on to say, '*we have* forsaken *the land*.'
[4] The Midrash takes it as a question, E.V. as an exclamation.
[5] The context refers to the knowledge of God.

than the earth (Job XI, 9). '*Because our dwellings have cast us out*': these are the Synagogues and Houses of Study.

Still another interpretation of '*We are greatly confounded, because we have forsaken the land*': this refers to the Temple, of which it says, *And from the bottom of the ground*[1] *to the lower settle* (Ezek. XLIII, 14). '*Because our dwellings have cast us out*': this alludes to the destruction of the first and second Temples.[2] Since they sinned, they were exiled; and since they were exiled, Jeremiah began to lament over them, *Ekah*.

IX

R. Isaac opened his discourse with the text, *We are ashamed, because we have heard reproach, confusion hath covered our faces; for strangers are come into the sanctuaries of the Lord's house* (Jer. LI, 51). You find that at the time when enemies entered Jerusalem, Ammonites and Moabites entered together with them; as it is said, *The adversary hath spread out his hand upon all her treasures; for she hath seen that the heathen are entered into her sanctuary, concerning whom Thou didst command that they should not enter into Thy congregation* (Lam. I, 10).[3] They penetrated the Holy of Holies and found there the two cherubim, which they seized, placed in a chest, and carried around the streets of Jerusalem,[4] exclaiming, 'Did you not declare that this people were not idolaters? See what we found belonging to them and what they were worshipping; behold, all faces are alike!'[5] Hence it is written, *Because that Moab and Seir do say, Behold, the house of Jacob is like unto all the nations* (Ezek. XXV, 8). At that time the Holy One, blessed be He, swore that He would utterly exterminate them, as it is said, *Therefore as I live, saith the Lord of hosts, the God of Israel, surely Moab shall be as Sodom, and the children of Ammon as Gomorrah* (Zeph. II, 9). Since Israel sinned, they were

[1] Viz. the site of the Temple.
[2] The plural '*dwellings*' points to the two Temples.
[3] This prohibition is mentioned in connection with Ammon and Moab (Deut. XXIII, 4). [4] To display them to the heathens who were in the city.
[5] I.e. all peoples follow a similar mode of worship.

exiled; and since they were exiled, Jeremiah began to lament over them, *Ekah*.

Another interpretation of '*We are ashamed, because we have heard reproach*': it refers to the seventeenth of Tammuz.[1] '*Confusion hath covered our faces*' refers to the ninth of Ab.[2] '*For strangers are come into the sanctuaries*[3] *of the Lord's house*' alludes to the destruction of the First and Second Temples. Since they sinned, they were exiled, and since they were exiled, Jeremiah began to lament over them, *Ekah*.

X

R. Isaac opened his discourse with the text, *Yet thou hast not called upon Me, O Jacob, because*[4] *thou hast been weary of Me, O Israel* (Isa. XLIII, 22). R. Joḥanan derived the same teaching from the following verse: *The burden of Damascus. Behold, Damascus is taken away from being a city, and it shall be a ruinous heap. The cities of Aroer are forsaken* (*ib*. XVII, 1 f.). The prophet holds forth in Damascus and mentions Aroer; but is not Aroer in the territory of Moab?[5] The fact is that there were three hundred and sixty-five idolatrous temples in Damascus, and each idol was worshipped in turn one day in the year, but on one special day all were worshipped. Israel, however, constituted them all a single deity and worshipped it every day; for it is written, *And the children of Israel again did that which was evil in the sight of the Lord, and served the Baalim, and the Ashtaroth, and the gods of Aram,*[6] *and the gods of Zidon, and the gods of Moab, and the gods of the children of Ammon, and the gods of the Philistines; and they forsook the Lord, and served Him not* (Judg. X, 6)—not even in conjunction with these idols.

R. Abba b. Kahana said: Should not a priest's wife be at least the equal of a female inn-keeper![7] R. Jose b. R.

[1] Which heralded the coming downfall of Jerusalem, since on that day a breach was made in the wall of the city.
[2] The anniversary of the destruction of the Temple.
[3] The plural indicates both Temples. [4] E.V. '*but*'.
[5] V. Jer. XLVIII, 19 f. [6] The country in which Damascus was situated.
[7] A proverb. Here the application is: shall not God be revered as much as idols?

Ḥanina said: [God declared,] 'Would that My children treated Me like the dessert which is served at the end of the meal!'[1] R. Judan said: They were like a king's servant who prepared a banquet, and invited all his colleagues but not his master. The king exclaimed, 'Would that my servant treated me as the equal of his colleagues!' Similarly spake the Holy One, blessed be He, 'Would that they treated Me like the dessert which is served at the end of the meal!—But [it is not even so], *thou hast not called upon Me, O Jacob*. A man will stand transacting business the whole day and not grow weary, but to pray to Me thou art weary. A man will stand transacting business the whole day and not grow weary; but if his friend says to him, "Come and pray," he replies that he cannot do so.[2] In connection with Baal what is written? *They called on the name of Baal from morning even until noon, saying, O Baal, answer us. But there was no voice, nor any that answered. And they danced in halting wise about the altar which was made* (I Kings XVIII, 26).[3] But, alas, "*thou hast not called upon Me, O Jacob*." Would that I had never given thee recognition, O Jacob. Why? "*Because thou hast been weary of Me*" '.

'*Thou hast not brought Me the small cattle of thy burnt-offerings*' (Isa. XLIII, 23): viz. the two continual offerings which were to be brought daily; as it is said, *The one lamb shalt thou offer in the morning, and the other lamb shalt thou offer at dusk* (Num. XXVIII, 4). '*Neither hast thou honoured Me with thy sacrifices*': these are the most holy offerings. '*I have not burdened thee with a meal-offering*': this refers to the handful of flour brought of the meal-offering.[4] '*Nor wearied thee with frankincense*': this refers to the handful of frankincense which was offered. '*Thou hast bought Me no sweet cane with money*' (Isa. XLIII, 24): R. Huna said in the name of R. Joseph: Cinnamon used to grow in the land of Israel, and the goats and hinds ate it.[5] '*Neither*

[1] The dessert was only an addition to the meal. Similarly God deplored the fact that the worship of Himself was not even additional to the people's idolatry. [2] I am too tired.
[3] Thus Baal's devotees never became tired, yet Israel did. [4] Cf. Lev. II, 2.
[5] It was so plentiful and cheap, and yet the Israelites withheld it from the Temple.

hast thou satisfied Me with the fat of thy sacrifices': these are the limbs of the sacrifices holy in a minor degree. '*But thou hast burdened Me with thy sins, thou hast wearied Me with thine iniquities'*: behold what your iniquities caused Me to do—to burn My temple, destroy My city, exile My children among the nations of the world, and that I should sit solitary. '*How sitteth solitary.*'

XI

R. Isaac opened his discourse with the text, *Because thou didst not serve the Lord thy God with joyfulness, and with gladness of heart, by reason of the abundance of all things, therefore shalt thou serve thy enemy* (Deut. XXVIII, 47 f.). Had you been worthy you would have read in the Torah, *Thou* bringest *them in, and plantest them in the mountain of Thine inheritance* (Ex. XV, 17); but now that you are unworthy you read, *Let all their wickedness* come *before Thee* (Lam. I, 22). Had you been worthy you would have read in the Torah, *The peoples have* heard, *they tremble* (Ex. XV, 14); but now that you are unworthy you read, *They have* heard *that I sigh* (Lam. I, 21). Had you been worthy you would have read in the Torah, *I have surely* seen *the affliction of My people that are in Egypt* (Ex. III, 7); but now that you are unworthy you read, See, *O Lord, for I am in distress, mine inwards burn* (Lam. I, 20). Had you been worthy you would have read in the Torah, *And ye shall* make proclamation *on the selfsame day* (Lev. XXIII, 21); but now that you are unworthy you read, *I* called *for my lovers but they deceived me* (Lam. I, 19). Had you been worthy you would have read in the Torah, Justice, justice *shalt thou follow* (Deut. XVI, 20); but now that you are unworthy you read, *The Lord is* righteous, *for I have rebelled against His word* (Lam. I, 18). Had you been worthy you would have read in the Torah, *Thou shalt surely open thy* hand *unto thy brother* (Deut. XV, 11); but now that you are unworthy you read, *Zion spreadeth forth her* hands (Lam. I, 17). Had you been worthy you would have read in the Torah, These *are the appointed seasons of the Lord* (Lev. XXIII, 4); but now that you are unworthy you read, *For* these *things I weep* (Lam. I, 16). Had you been worthy you would have read in the Torah, *We will go up by the highway*—mesillah (Num. xx, 19); but now that you are unworthy you read, *The Lord hath set at nought* (sillah) *all my mighty men* (Lam. I, 15). Had you been worthy you would have read in the Torah, *And I have broken the bars of your* yoke (Lev. XXVI, 13); but now that you are unworthy you read, *The* yoke *of my transgressions is impressed by His hand* (Lam. I, 14). Had you been worthy you would have read in the Torah, Fire *shall be kept burning upon the altar continually* (Lev. VI, 6); but now that you are unworthy you read, *From on high hath He sent* fire *into my bones* (Lam. I, 13). Had you been worthy you would have read in the Torah, *In all the* way *that ye went* (Deut. I, 31); but now that you are unworthy you read, *Let it not come unto you, all ye that pass in the* way (Lam. I, 12). Had you been worthy you would have read in the Torah, *And ye shall eat your* bread *until ye have enough* (Lev. XXVI, 5); but now that you are unworthy you read, *All her people sigh, they seek* bread (Lam. I, 11). Had you been worthy you would have read in the Torah, *Neither shall any man* covet *thy land* (Ex. XXXIV, 24); but now that you are unworthy you read, *The adversary hath spread out his hand upon all her* coveted *treasures* (Lam. I, 10). Had you been worthy you would have read in the Torah, *For on this day shall atonement be made for you to cleanse you* (Lev. XVI, 30); but now that you are unworthy you read, *Her filthiness was in her skirts* (Lam. I, 9). Had you been worthy you would have read in the Torah, *From all your* sins *shall ye be clean before the Lord* (Lev. *ib.*); but now that you are unworthy you read, *Jerusalem hath grievously* sinned (Lam. I, 8). Had you been worthy you would have read in the Torah, *And ye shall be* remembered *before the Lord your God* (Num. X, 9); but now that you are unworthy you read, *Jerusalem* remembereth *in the days of her affliction* (Lam. I, 7). Had you been worthy you would have read in the Torah, *And I will* walk *among you* (Lev. XXVI, 12); but now that you are unworthy you read, *And* gone *is from the daughter of Zion all her splendour* (Lam. I,

6). Had you been worthy you would have read in the Torah, *And the Lord will make thee the* head (Deut. XXVIII, 13); but now that you are unworthy you read, *Her adversaries are become the* head, *her enemies are at ease* (Lam. I, 5). Had you been worthy you would have read in the Torah, *Three times a year shall all thy males appear before the Lord* (Deut. XVI, 16); but now that you are unworthy you read, *The ways of Zion do mourn* (Lam. I, 4). Had you been worthy you would have read in the Torah, *And ye shall dwell in your land safely* (Lev. XXVI, 5); but now that you are unworthy you read, *Judah is gone into exile because of affliction* (Lam. I, 3). Had you been worthy you would have read in the Torah, *It was a* night *of watching unto the Lord* (Ex. XII, 42); but now that you are unworthy you read, *She weepeth sore in the* night (Lam. I, 2). Had you been worthy you would have read in the Torah, How *can I myself bear*? (Deut. I, 12); but now that you are unworthy you read, How *sitteth solitary* (Lam. I, 1).[1]

XII

R. Ḥanina b. Papa opened his discourse with the text, *As one that taketh off a garment in cold weather, and as vinegar upon nitre, so is he that singeth songs to a heavy heart* (Prov. XXV, 20). R. Ḥanina and R. Jonathan both say: What did the ten tribes and the tribes of Judah and Benjamin resemble? Two men who were both wrapped in the same new cloak on a winter's day; one pulled one way and one pulled the other way until they ripped it. Similarly the ten tribes ceased not worshipping idols in Samaria and the tribes of Judah and Benjamin worshipping them in Jerusalem, until they caused Jerusalem to be destroyed.

Another interpretation of '*As one that taketh off a garment in cold weather*' is given by R. Ḥanina b. Papa and R. Simeon. R. Ḥanina b. Papa said: At the time that Nebuchadnezzar waged war with Israel, he divested them of two sets of garments, viz. the priestly vestments and the

[1] The point in most of these contrasting verses is that the same word (in Hebrew) originally used to describe Israel's state of happiness and glory now describes her misery and degradation.

royal robes.[1] '*In cold weather* (ḳarah)': because they called (*ḳar'u*) the calf *This is thy god, O Israel* (Ex. XXXII, 4).[2] '*As vinegar upon nitre*': R. Joshua said: It is as if a man had a store of wine, and examined the first cask and found it sour, the second and found it sour, and the third and found it sour, whereupon he exclaimed, 'This is enough to prove that they have all gone bad.'[3] '*So he is that singeth songs to a heavy heart*': R. Berekiah said: Whatever tune the singer may sing, it does not enter the ear of the dancer; whatever tune the singer may sing, the foolish son pays no attention.[4]

Another interpretation of '*As one that taketh off a garment in cold weather*' is given by R. Simon who said: At the time that Nebuchadnezzar waged war with Israel, he divested them of two sets of garments, viz. the priestly vestments and the royal robes. '*In cold weather*': and so it is written, *And it came to pass that, as He called* (ḳara), *and they would not hear* (Zech. VII, 13).[2] '*As vinegar upon nitre*': R. Joshua b. Nehemiah said: They were like a man who places vinegar upon nitre and dissolves it; so did they contradict[5] words of Torah, as it is written, *But they mocked the messengers of God* (II Chron. XXXVI, 16). R. Abba b. Kahana said: [They moved their mouths derisively] like a cow which licks up [fodder] with its mouth.

'*So is he that singeth songs to a heavy heart*': R. Ḥaggai said in the name of R. Isaac: Because the scoffers of that generation kept mumbling with their mouths, winking with their eyes, pointing with their fingers, and saying, *The vision that he seeth is for many days to come, and he prophesieth of times that are far off* (Ezek. XII, 27), the Holy One, blessed be He, said to them, 'By your lives, *For in your days, O rebellious house, will I speak the word and will perform it* (*ib.* 25).' Immediately, *He brought upon them the*

[1] He suspended the priesthood and monarchy.
[2] Translating: in the day of calling.
[3] By a play on words, *nether* (E.V. '*nitre*') is read as *nothar* (the remainder), and he translates: As the rest too is vinegar. Similarly God exiled Israel because He regarded them as all sinful and without hope of reformation.
[4] Absorbed in dancing he ignores the melody; and in like manner a foolish son, intent upon going his own way, ignores advice.
[5] The Hebrew word means both 'dissolve' and 'contradict'.

king of the Chaldeans, who slew their young men with the sword (II Chron. XXXVI, 17); and it is written, *And he burnt the house of the Lord* (II Kings XXV, 9)—i.e. the Temple; *and the king's house*, i.e. Zedekiah's palace; *and all the houses of Jerusalem*: R. Phinehas said in the name of R. Hoshaia: There were four hundred and eighty Synagogues in Jerusalem, apart from the Temple. Whence is this derived? From the word *'full'* [in *she that was full of justice* (Isa. I, 21)], the numerical value of its letters being that total.[1] In each there was an elementary school for Scripture and an advanced school for Mishnah, and Vespasian[2] went up and destroyed all of them. *Even every great man's house* (II Kings XXV, 9): i.e. the academy of Rabban Joḥanan b. Zakkai. Why does he call it 'great house'? Because there he taught the praise of the Holy One, blessed be He.[3] Since they sinned, they were exiled; and since they were exiled, Jeremiah began to lament over them, '*How sitteth solitary*.'

XIII

R. Ḥanina b. Papa opened his discourse with the text, *As a scatterer and a sword and a sharp arrow, so is a man that beareth false witness against his neighbour* (Prov. XXV, 18): '*a scatterer*,' because of *the Lord shall scatter thee among all peoples* (Deut. XXVIII, 64); '*a sword*,' because of *and I will draw out the sword after you* (Lev. XXVI, 33); and '*a sharp arrow*', because of *when I shall send upon them the evil arrows of famine* (Ezek. V, 16). To whom are all these likened? To '*a man that beareth false witness against his neighbour*'. This is an allusion to Israel who responded with the declaration, *This is thy God, O Israel* (Ex. XXXII, 4).

Confidence in an unfaithful man in time of trouble is like a broken tooth and a foot out of joint (Prov. XXV, 19): Israel spake before the Holy One, blessed be He: 'Sovereign of

[1] The total is 481, i.e. 480 Synagogues and the Temple.

[2] The Commander of the Roman Army. There is, of course, an anachronism here, the verses quoted referring to the first Temple, whereas Vespasian and R. Joḥanan b. Zakkai lived at the destruction of the second Temple. Nevertheless the translation from the one to the other is quite intelligible.

[3] '*Great house*' is understood as 'the house of Him Who is great'.

the Universe, when Thou camest to feed us, our tooth devoured and broke others in pieces; why, then, does an evil tooth devour us and the foot stamp upon us?'[1] Because of our placing trust in idolatry. ['*In an unfaithful man*':] because we were unfaithful to our Rock '*As one that taketh off a garment in cold weather*' (*ib.* 20): As it is written, *And it came to pass that, as He called, and they would not hear* (Zech. VII, 13).[2]

Another interpretation of '*a broken tooth and a foot out of joint*': a loose tooth and tottering foot.[3] The Holy One, blessed be He, spake, 'I exhorted Israel to reject idolatry and trust in Me,[4] but they acted otherwise, and rejected Me and trusted in idols.' And so it is written, *Who say to a stock, Thou art my father* (Jer. II, 27). Since they sinned, they were exiled; and since they were exiled, Jeremiah began to lament over them, *Ekah.*

XIV

R. Ḥanina b. Papa opened his discourse with the text, *If a wise man is judged with*[5] *a foolish man, whether he be angry or laugh, there will be no rest* (Prov. XXIX, 9). R. Simon said: Whoever judges a fool is himself judged; and so it is written '*is judged with*'—'judgeth' is not written here, but '*is judged with*'.

Another interpretation of '*a wise man is judged*': '*wise*' alludes to the Holy One, blessed be He, as it is said, *He is wise in heart and mighty in strength* (Job IX, 4). '*With a foolish man*': this is Israel, as it is said, *For My people is foolish* (Jer. IV, 22). '*Whether he be angry or laugh*': I was angry [says God] and had no rest, and I laughed and had no rest. I was angry with you in the days of Pekah the son of Remaliah, as it is said, *For Pekah the*

[1] Cf. Dan. VII, 19.
[2] In the original this sentence occurs in the preceding Proem and has been inserted here in error.
[3] As such defective organs are useless to the body, so it is, as the verse declares, useless to place confidence in a treacherous man.
[4] This is the meaning read into the two words in Prov. XXV, 19, '*confidence*, and '*unfaithful*'.
[5] So the text literally. E.V. '*contendeth with*'.

son of Remaliah slew, etc. (II Chron. XXVIII, 6). I smiled upon you in the days of Amaziah,[1] as it is said, *And Amaziah took courage, and led forth his people and went to the Valley of Salt* (*ib.* XXV, 11). What means '*Valley of Salt*'? [He led them] beneath banks of salt; [or, according to another explanation: he led them] beneath boulders into battle.[2] *And other ten thousand did the children of Judah carry away alive, and brought them unto the top of the Rock, and cast them down* (*ib.* 12). At that time the Holy One, blessed be He, said: 'I decreed death upon the descendants of Noah only by the sword[3] but these *brought them unto the top of the Rock, and cast them down from the top of the Rock, that they all were broken in pieces.*' '*There will be no rest*': at that time the Holy One, blessed be He, said, 'Since they acted thus, they shall go into exile.' Since they sinned, they were exiled; and since they were exiled, Jeremiah began to lament over them, *Ekah.*

XV

R. Ḥanina b. Papa opened his discourse with the text, *He that correcteth a scorner getteth to himself shame* (Prov. IX, 7). R. Isaac said: Whoever raises up a wicked disciple will in the end earn disgrace through him, as it is said, '*He that correcteth a scorner getteth to himself shame.*' That is the opinion of R. Isaac, for R. Isaac said: If one raises up a wicked disciple in the land of Israel it is as though he trains a robber, and outside the land of Israel as though he trains a slave.[4]

R. Simeon b. Laḳish said: It is written, *It is an honour for a man to keep aloof from strife* (*ib.* XX, 3). The Holy One, blessed be He, said: 'It would have been to My honour if I had had no dealings with this people.' You find that when Israel was exiled among the nations of the world, the Holy One, blessed be He, went round to the doors

[1] By granting Israel a decisive victory.
[2] Text and meaning here are uncertain.
[3] And not by so barbaric a method as throwing them from a high rock.
[4] Some commentators suggest the reading 'an idolater', which is preferable.

of these peoples to hear what they were saying. And what were they saying? 'The God of this people punished Pharaoh, Sisera, Sennacherib, and others like them.'[1] They went on to say, 'And shall He always be young?'[2] If it is possible so to express oneself, their words made Him out to be old[3]; and so it is written, *And when He came*[4] *unto the nations whither they came, they profaned My holy name* (Ezek. XXXVI, 20). The text should have read 'they came', but it reads '*and He came*'. The meaning, if one may so express oneself, is He Himself; hence it is written, '*And when He came unto the nations.*' And what were they saying? 'If *these are the people of the Lord*, why *are they gone forth out of His land*?'[5]

Another interpretation of the text is: '*He that correcteth*' refers to Jeremiah; '*a scorner*' refers to his contemporaries who were scorners; '*getteth to himself shame,*' because they cursed him, as it is written, *I have not lent, neither have men lent me; yet every one of them doth curse me* (Jer. XV, 10). *And he that reproveth a wicked man, it becometh unto him a blot* (Prov. IX, 7): he reproved Israel and uttered over them *Ekah.*

XVI

R. Abbahu opened his discourse with the text, *Thy way and thy doings have procured these things unto thee* (Jer. IV, 18). Where can a king provide for his legions in a more praiseworthy [i.e. satisfactory] manner, in a wilderness or an inhabited place? Surely in an inhabited place! Yet with reference to the wilderness it is written, *Behold, I will cause to rain bread from heaven for you* (Ex. XVI, 4), but here [in an inhabited place] it is written, *The young children ask bread* (Lam. IV, 4). With reference to the wilderness

[1] The inference is that He will also punish us (Mah.). M.K.: why then has He permitted us to harm His people?
[2] I.e. strong—of course not, and that is the reason He has not dealt with us, but had to permit us to harm His people.
[3] All His mighty acts were performed in the past; now He is aged and powerless. [4] So literally; E.V. '*they came*'.
[5] Hence God said that He would have been more honoured and not accused of weakness had He never had dealings with Israel.

it is written, *Behold, He smote the rock, that waters gushed out* (Ps. LXXVIII, 20), but here it is written, *The tongue of the sucking child cleaveth to the roof of his mouth for thirst* (Lam. IV, 4). With reference to the wilderness it is written, *He spread a cloud for a screen* (Ps. CV, 39), but here it is written, *Their skin is shrivelled upon their bones* (Lam. IV, 8). What caused this to happen to you? '*Thy ways and thy doings,*' i.e. your evil ways and rebellious acts.

'*This is thy wickedness; yea, it is bitter, yea, it reacheth unto thy heart*' (Jer. IV, 18): this alludes to the Great Sanhedrin[1] who are called 'the heart' of Israel; for it is written, *My heart is towards the governors of Israel* (Judg. V, 9). But since they provoked Me, My heart is not towards the governors of Israel.[2] The Holy One, blessed be He, said,[3] '*Yea, it reacheth unto thy heart,*' i.e. the Temple, as it is declared, *Mine eyes and My heart shall be there perpetually* (II Chron. VII, 16). Another interpretation of '*Yea, it reacheth unto thy heart*' is that it alludes to the Holy One, blessed be He. R. Ḥiyya said: Whence do we gather that the Holy One, blessed be He, is described as 'the heart' of Israel? From the following verse, *God is the rock of my heart and my portion for ever* (Ps. LXXIII, 26).

XVII

R. Abbahu opened his discourse with the text, *They that sit in the gate talk of me* (Ps. LXIX, 13). This refers to the nations of the world who sit in theatres and circuses. '*And I am the song of the drunkards*': after they have sat eating and drinking and become intoxicated, they sit and talk of me, scoffing at me and saying, 'We have no need to eat carobs[4] like the Jews'! They ask one another, 'How long do you wish to live?' To which they reply, 'As long as the shirt of a Jew which is worn on the Sabbath'![5] They then take a camel into their theatres,

[1] The supreme governing body in Israel.
[2] The Sanhedrin has been disbanded.
[3] Instead of 'The Holy One, blessed be He, said', a variant reads, 'Another interpretation of', and this is to be preferred.
[4] The food of the poorest.
[5] Since he reserves the shirt for wear on the Sabbath, it lasts a long while

put their shirts upon it, and ask one another, 'Why is it in mourning?' To which they reply, 'The Jews observe the law of the Sabbatical year[1] and they have no vegetables, so they eat this camel's thorns, and that is why it is in mourning'! Next they bring a corpse[2] with shaven head into the theatre and ask one another, 'Why is his head shaven?' To which they reply, 'The Jews observe the Sabbath, and whatever they earn during the week they eat on the Sabbath. Since they have no wood to cook with, they break their bedsteads and use them as fuel; consequently they sleep on the ground and get covered with dust, and anoint themselves with oil which is very expensive for that reason!'[3]

Another interpretation of '*They that sit in the gate talk of me*' is that it alludes to the Israelites who sit in the Synagogues and Houses of Study. '*And I am the song of the drunkards*': after they have sat eating and drinking and become intoxicated[4] at the feast which is preparatory to [the fast] of the ninth of Ab, they sit reading dirges and lamentations and *Ekah*.

XVIII

R. Abin opened his discourse with the text, *He hath filled me with bitterness* (Lam. III, 15): on the first nights of the Passover Festival.[5] *He hath sated me with wormwood*: on the ninth of Ab. What He filled me with on the first nights of Passover, therewith He sated me on the nights of the ninth of Ab, viz. wormwood. The night of the week on which the first day of Passover occurs is always the same as that on which the ninth

[1] The seventh year when the land lies fallow and its produce is not gathered. [2] *Var. lec.* clown, which is preferable.

[3] Therefore, after a time they cannot afford it at all, and so shave their heads so as not to need it.

[4] According to Jewish law, wine may not be included in the last meal before the fast, so the reference must be to a meal eaten before noon (Radal). Mah., however, explains that 'intoxicated' means 'with their sorrows'.

[5] At the institution of the Passover, the command was given that the paschal lamb must be eaten '*with bitter herbs*' (Ex. XII, 8), and this remains a feature of the celebration of the Festival.

of Ab falls. On that account Jeremiah lamented, '*How sitteth solitary.*'

XIX

R. Abin opened his discourse with the text, *And He changeth the times and the seasons* (Dan. II, 21). Jeremiah said to Israel, 'Had you been worthy, you would be dwelling in Jerusalem and drinking the waters of Shiloah[1] whose waters are pure and sweet; but now that you are unworthy, you are exiled to Babylon and drink the waters of the Euphrates whose waters are impure and evil-smelling. Hence it is written, *And now what hast thou to do in the way to Egypt, to drink the waters of Shihor? Or what hast thou to do in the way to Assyria, to drink the waters of the River?*[2] (Jer. II, 18). Had you been worthy, you would be dwelling in Jerusalem uttering songs and praises to the Holy One, blessed be He; but now that you are unworthy, you are exiled to Babylon where you utter lamentations.' Alas! *By the rivers of Babylon* (Ps. CXXXVII, 1), *Ekah.*

XX

R. Alexandri opened his discourse with the text, *I watch, and am become like a sparrow that is alone upon the housetop* (Ps. CII, 8). The Holy One, blessed be He, said, 'I watched[3] to bring My children into the land of Israel[4]; immediately "*I am become like a sparrow that is alone upon the housetop*".' As a sparrow is driven from roof to roof, from fence to fence, from tree to tree, and from bush to bush.[5] When Israel left Egypt they journeyed in disunion and encamped in disunion, [as it is said,] *and they*[6] *journeyed . . . and they encamped* (Num. XXXIII, 3); but when they came to Mount Sinai they all became united, for it is not written in this

[1] V. Isa. VIII, 6. [2] Viz. the Euphrates. [3] I.e. I was eager.
[4] The text is defective, and some such words as 'as soon as they left Egypt, but when they sinned in the matter of the spies' have fallen out.
[5] Add here: 'so had I to wander with Israel from place to place for forty years'. Before the next sentence insert: 'I was eager to give the Torah to Israel immediately on their departure from Egypt, but.'
[6] The plural indicates that there were divisions in the ranks of Israel.

connection, 'and they encamped' but *there Israel encamped*[1] (Ex. XIX, 2). On that occasion the Holy One, blessed be He, said, 'Now is the time for Me to give the Torah to My children.'

Another interpretation of '*I watch and am become like a sparrow*': the Holy One, blessed be He, said, 'I watched carefully to cause My *Shechinah* to abide in the Temple for ever.' '*And am become like a sparrow*': just as when you take away its young a sparrow is left solitary, so spake the Holy One, blessed be He, 'I burnt My house, destroyed My city, exiled My children among the nations of the world, and I sit solitary.' *Ekah!*

XXI

R. Alexandri opened his discourse with the text, *And the leper in whom the plague is* (Lev. XIII, 45): '*the leper*' is like the Temple; '*in whom the plague is*,' i.e. idolatry which defiles like a plague, as it is said, And they profaned My sanctuary and defiled it.[2] '*His clothes shall be rent*,' i.e. the priestly vestments; '*the hair of his head shall go loose*': and so it is said, *And the covering of Judah was laid bare* (Isa. XXII, 8)—that which should have been covered He disclosed.[3] '*And he shall cover his upper lip*': when Israel was exiled among the nations of the world, not one of them was able to bring a word of Torah out of his mouth. '*And shall cry, Unclean, unclean*': i.e. the destruction of the first and second Temples.[4]

R. Jose b. Ḥalafta said: Whoever knows how many years Israel worshipped idols also knows when the son of David[5] will come; and we have three verses to support this statement. The first is, *And I will visit upon her the days of the Baalim, wherein she offered unto them* (Hos. II, 15),

[1] The verb is here in the singular, showing that they were then a unanimous people.

[2] There is no such verse in Scripture. Perhaps what is intended is, *Thou hast defiled My sanctuary with all thy detestable things* (Ezek. V, 11).

[3] Another possible translation is: He uncovered (i.e. disgraced) its (the Temple's) chiefs.

[4] The repetition of '*unclean*' points to two defilements, viz. of the two Temples.

[5] The Messiah.

i.e. according to the number of the days of the [worship of the] Baalim shall the visitation endure. The second is, *And it came to pass that, as*[1] *He called, and they would not hear, so shall they call and I will not hear* (Zech. VII, 13). The third is, *And it shall come to pass that ye shall say, Wherefore hath the Lord our God done*, etc., *like* (i.e. as long as) *ye have forsaken me . . . so shall ye serve strangers in a land that is not yours* (Jer. V, 19).

R. Joḥanan and R. Simeon b. Laḳish both made a statement on this point. R. Joḥanan said: [This lesson may be derived from] *Because, even because* (Lev. XXVI, 43),[2] indicating measure for measure. R. Simeon b. Laḳish said: [It may be derived from] *Your land, strangers devour it in your presence* (Isa. I, 7): i.e. as against what you have done,[3] strangers devour it. R. Alexandri derived it from this verse, *All the days wherein the plague*[4] *is in him he shall be unclean* (Lev. XIII, 46). *Ekah!*

XXII

R. Joshua of Siknin,[5] in the name of R. Levi, opened his discourse with the text, *Woe unto them that join house to house* (Isa. V, 8). R. Joḥanan and R. Simeon b. Laḳish [make a comment]. R. Joḥanan said: '*Woe unto them that join house to house*': [woe to them] who make a loan on a man's house and field to take them from him. The Holy One, blessed be He, said, 'What do you think, that you will inherit the land and *Ye shall be made to dwell alone in the midst of the land* (*ib.*)?' '*In mine ears said the Lord of hosts: Of a truth many houses shall be desolate, even great and fair, without inhabitant*' (*ib.* 9): R. Simeon

[1] I.e. as long as.
[2] The twofold expression indicates that the duration of the punishment will equal the duration of the sin.
[3] The Hebrew for '*in your presence*' is lit. 'as against you', i.e. the strangers will devour the land for a period of time equal to that in which you provoked God.
[4] Viz. idolatry, as explained at the beginning of the Proem; and '*unclean*' denotes that the people are under God's displeasure.
[5] A town in Galilee.

b. Laḳish said[1]: Like one who cries into the ears of his fellow not once but twice, so [is the cry of the dispossessed] in the ears of the Lord of hosts.

R. Simeon b. Laḳish said: '*Woe unto them that join house to house*': ye have joined the destruction of the first Temple to that of the second Temple. As with the first Temple *Zion shall be ploughed like a field* (Jer. XXVI, 18), so with the second Temple '*Zion shall be ploughed like a field*'. '*Till there be no place*'[2]: what caused the '*place*' to be destroyed? Because they left no place where idolatry was not practised by them. At first they used to worship idols in secret places, as it is stated, *Then said He to them, hast thou seen what the elders of the house of Israel do in the dark?* (Ezek. VIII, 12). Because they were not restrained [by the authorities] from doing this, they next practised it behind the door, as it is said, *And behind the door and the posts hast thou set up thy symbol* (Isa. LVII, 8). Because they were not restrained from doing this, they next practised it upon the roofs, as it is said, *And them that worship the host of heaven upon the housetops* (Zeph. I, 5). Because they were not restrained from doing this, they next practised it in gardens, as it is said, *That sacrifice in gardens* (Isa. LXV, 3). Because they were not restrained from doing this, they next practised it upon mountain-tops, as it is said, *They sacrifice upon the tops of the mountains, and offer upon the hills* (Hos. IV, 13). Because they were not restrained from doing this, they next practised it in the fields, as it is said, *Yea, their altars shall be as heaps in the furrows of the field* (*ib.* XII, 12).

R. Judan, R. Aibu, and R. Ṭabi said in the name of R. Joshaia: [This passage indicates that] they set up an idolatrous image upon every mound. R. Phinehas and R. Ḥilkiah said in the name of R. Hoshaia: Each of them used to plough his field crosswise and set up an image in the centre, so that the tops of the ridges should display it.

[1] A MS. omits 'R. Simeon b. Laḳish said'. What follows is then part of R. Joḥanan's comment.
[2] E.V. '*room*'. Here explained as the Temple.

Because they were not restrained from doing this, they next practised it at the cross-roads, as it is said, *Thou hast built thy lofty place at every head of the way* (Ezek. XVI, 25). Because they were not restrained from doing this, they next practised it in the public squares, as it is said, *Thou hast built unto thee an eminent place, and hast made thee a lofty place in every street* (*ib.* 24). Because they were not restrained from doing this, they next practised it in the cities, as it is said, *According to the number of thy cities are thy gods, O Judah* (Jer. XI, 13). Because they were not restrained from doing this, they next practised it in the streets, as it is said, *And according to the number of the streets of Jerusalem have ye set up altars to the shameful thing* (*ib.*).

To what extreme did this go? Until they introduced it into the Holy of Holies, as it is said, *This image of jealousy in the entry*—babi'ah (Ezek. VIII, 5). What means '*babi'ah*'? R. Aḥa said: Woe, woe[1] to the lodger because of the Owner of the house. R. Berekiah said: *For the bed is too short for a man to stretch himself*—mehistarea' (Isa. XXVIII, 20). What means '*mehistarea'*'? A woman and two lovers,[2] i.e. [the bed is too short] to hold a woman, her husband, and her paramour. '*And the covering* (massekah) *too narrow when he gathereth himself up*' (*ib.*)—i.e. ye made a molten image (*massekah*) as a rival to Him of Whom it is written, *He gathereth the waters of the sea together as a heap* (Ps. XXXIII, 7). Since they sinned, they were exiled; and since they were exiled, Jeremiah began to lament over them, *Ekah*.

XXIII

R. Joshua of Siknin, in the name of R. Levi, opened his discourse with the text, *Remember then thy Creator in the days of thy youth* (Eccl. XII, 1). Solomon said to Israel, '*Remember then thy Creator*': remember Who

[1] The word is read as the Latin *vae, vae*.

[2] This is the reading proposed by Luzzatto who takes השתרע as divisible into אשה ותרי ריעי 'a woman and two lovers'. Israel is the wife, God the husband, and idols the paramour.

created you while His selection[1] of you still endures; while the covenant of priesthood still endures, as it is said, *And I did choose him out of all the tribes of Israel to be My priest* (I Sam. II, 28); while the covenant of the Levites still endures, as it is said, *The city which I have chosen* (I Kings XI, 32); while the covenant with the Sanctuary still endures, as it is said, *For the Lord thy God hath chosen him out of all thy tribes* (Deut. XVIII, 5); while the covenant with the kingship of the house of David still endures, as it is said, *He chose David also His servant* (Ps. LXXVIII, 70); while the covenant with Jerusalem still endures, as it is said, *For now have I chosen and hallowed this house* (II Chron. VII, 16); while you still endure, as it is said, *The Lord thy God hath chosen thee* (Deut. VII, 6).

'*Before the evil days come*' (Eccl. XII, 2): these are the days of the exile. '*And the years draw nigh when thou shalt say, I have no pleasure in them*': neither prosperity nor calamity.[2] '*Before the sun is darkened*'—for the kingship of the house of David of which it is written, *And his throne as the sun before Me* (Ps. LXXXIX, 37). '*The light*' (Eccl. *ib.*): this is the light of the Torah, in which is written, *For the commandment is a lamp and the Torah is light* (Prov. VI, 23). '*The moon*' (*ib.*): this refers to the Sanhedrin, of which it is taught: The seating of the Sanhedrin was in the shape of a semi-circular threshing floor.[3] '*The stars*' (*ib.*): these are the Rabbis, of whom it is written, *They that turn the many to righteousness are as the stars for ever and ever* (Dan. XII, 3). '*And the clouds return after the rain*': you find that all the hard and calamitous prophecies which Jeremiah prophesied against Israel only befel them after the destruction of the Temple.

'*In the day when the keepers of the house shall tremble*' (Eccl. XII, 3): this refers to the watches of the priests and Levites.[4] '*And the strong men shall bow themselves*': these are the priests. R. Abba b. Kahana said: Aaron

[1] In the Hebrew this resembles the word for '*youth*'.
[2] The text is doubtful. The Midrash to Eccl., a.l. reads: These are the days of the Messiah in which there is neither merit nor guilt.
[3] I.e. shaped like the crescent moon. V.M. Sanh. IV, 3 (Sonc. ed.), p. 230.
[4] Kept in the Temple. V. Ber. 3*b*.

consecrated twenty-two thousand Levites on one day,'[1] as it is said, *And Aaron offered them for a sacred gift before the Lord* (Num. VIII, 21).[1] R. Ḥanina said: The bird's crop is a light thing,[2] yet the priest used to throw it backwards upon the step of the altar, a distance of thirty-two cubits. '*And the grinders cease*': these are the great collections of Mishnah, as, e.g., the Mishnah of R. Akiba, the Mishnah of R. Oshaia, and the Mishnah of Bar Ḳappara.[3] '*Because they are few*': this is the Talmud[4] which is included in them. '*And those that look out shall be darkened*': you find that when Israel was exiled among the nations of the world, not one was able to remember his studies.

'*And the doors shall be shut in the street*' (Eccl. XII, 4): these are the doors of Neḥushta son[5] of Elnathan which were open wide. '*When the sound of the grinding is low*': because they did not occupy themselves with words of Torah.[6] R. Samuel b. Naḥman said: Israel is compared to millstones; as millstones are never kept idle, so Israel is idle in Torah neither by day nor night, as it is said, *Thou shalt meditate therein day and night* (Josh. I, 8). '*And one shall start up at the voice of a bird*': this refers to the wicked Nebuchadnezzar.[7] Rabbi[8] said: For eighteen years a *Bath Ḳol* used to go forth in the palace of Nebuchadnezzar and proclaim, 'Wicked servant, go and destroy thy Master's house, because His children disobey Him.' '*And all the daughters of music shall be brought low*': thus Nebuchadnezzar went up and stopped all singing in the house of feasting, and so it is written, *They drink not wine with a song* (Isa. XXIV, 9).

[1] Cited to illustrate the extraordinary strength of the priests.
[2] Literally, 'raised' or 'made a wave-offering'. [3] Difficult to make travel far. [4] These Rabbis each compiled a Mishnah, but their work was superseded by that of R. Judah the Prince.
[5] 'Talmud' in this instance denotes the manner in which the *halachah* stated in the Mishnah is exegetically derived from the Biblical text.
[6] Read '*daughter*', v. II Kings XXIV, 8. She was the mother of king Jehoiachin. There was a tradition that the doors of her house were kept always open to offer hospitality, but in the national disaster they were closed. [7] '*Grinding*' is explained as Torah-study in the same manner that '*grinders*' was defined as Mishnah collection.
[8] V. Lev. R. XXXIII end. [9] Emend to 'R. Levi' as Buber found in a MS.

'Also when they shall be afraid of that which is high' (Eccl. XII, 5): i.e. Nebuchadnezzar was afraid of Him Who is supreme in the Universe and was not willing to do His bidding. He said, 'He wishes to entrap me in order to do to me what He did to my ancestor.'[1] *'And terrors shall be in the way'*: R. Abba b. Kahana and R. Levi [explain differently]. R. Abba b. Kahana said: The terror of the journey fell upon him. R. Levi said: He began to consult charmers[2] on the way. *For the king of Babylon standeth at the parting of the way* (Ezek. XXI, 26): i.e. at the point where the roads branch off. *'At the head of the two ways'*: which was midway between two roads, one leading to the wilderness and the other leading to Jerusalem. *'To use divination'*: he began to practise divination. *'He shaketh the arrows to and fro'*: he began to shake arrows in the name of Rome but without success, in the name of Alexandria but without success, then in the name of Jerusalem and it succeeded. He sowed seeds and planted plants in the name of Rome but without success, in the name of Alexandria but without success, then in the name of Jerusalem and it succeeded and they sprouted. He tried to kindle torches and lanterns in the name of Rome but they would not light, in the name of Alexandria and they would not light, and then in the name of Jerusalem and they lit up.[3] *'He inquireth of the teraphim'*: i.e. of the idolatrous kind which he had; and so it is stated, *And stubbornness is as idolatry and teraphim*[4] (I Sam. XV, 23).

'He looketh at the liver' (Ezek. XXI, 26): R. Levi[5] said: Just like a certain Arab who slew a lamb and inspected the liver.[6]

'In his right hand is the lot of Jerusalem' (Ezek. XXI, 27):

[1] Viz. Sennacherib.
[2] Adopting the emendation of Jast. מחבר חברים. The continuation describes the various methods of divination which were employed.
[3] These divinations showed him that campaigns against Rome and Alexandria (Egypt) would be unsuccessful. Rome is an anachronism here, but is probably meant to symbolise the great Powers of his days.
[4] This proves that there were idolatrous *teraphim*.
[5] Buber reads 'R. Levi' from a MS.
[6] For omens. This was a common form of divination.

the lot against Jerusalem appeared in his right hand.[1] '*To set battering-rams*': [i.e. he appointed] generals. '*To open the mouth for the slaughter*': this refers to executioners. '*To lift up the voice with shouting*': this alludes to trumpets. '*To set battering-rams against the gates*': [this is taken to mean] observation-posts. '*To cast up mounds*': i.e. catapults. '*To build forts*': i.e. scaling-ladders. '*And it shall be unto them as a false divination in their sight who have weeks upon weeks*' (*ib.* 28): Ezekiel said to Israel, 'Had you been worthy you would have read in the Torah which is capable of exposition in seven times seven ways,[2] but now that you are unworthy, behold Nebuchadnezzar comes and practises divinations against you seven times seven; and so it is stated, "*who have weeks upon weeks.*"'

'*But it bringeth iniquity to remembrance, that they may be taken*' (*ib.*): this is the sin of Zechariah, of whom it is stated, *And the spirit of God clothed Zechariah the son of Jehoiada the priest, and he stood above the people* (II Chron. XXIV, 20). Was he, then, over the heads of the people that you say '*above the people*'? What it means is that he imagined himself high above all the people. He was son-in-law of the king, high priest, a prophet, and a judge, so he began to speak arrogantly; hence it is stated, *And he said unto them, Thus saith God, Why transgress ye the commandments of the Lord, that ye cannot prosper? Because ye have forsaken the Lord, He hath also forsaken you. And they conspired against him, and stoned him with stones* (*ib.* et seq.).[3] Nor did they treat his blood like the blood of the hind or ram concerning which it is written, *He shall pour out the blood thereof, and cover it with dust* (Lev. XVII, 13). But in this instance *her blood is in the midst of her* (Ezek. XXIV, 7). And for what purpose was all this? *That it might cause fury to come up, that vengeance might be taken* (*ib.* 8).

[1] The lot which came up in the right hand was the decisive one.
[2] The expert in Torah, it was said, is able to adduce 49 reasons for and against in any disputed point of law. [3] It is not clear why this is called arrogance. יפה ענף maintains that he was arrogant in saying '*He hath also forsaken you*', by which he intimated that all hope was lost.

R. Judan asked R. Aḥa, 'Where did Israel slay Zechariah, in the Court of Women or in the Court of Israel?' He replied, 'In neither of these, but it was in the Court of the Priests. Nor did they treat his blood as was done with the blood of the hind or ram of which it is written, "*He shall pour out the blood thereof, and cover it with dust.*" But in this instance, they set it *upon the bare rock* (*ib.* 7). And for what purpose was all this? "*That it might cause fury to come up, that vengeance might be taken, I have set her blood upon the bare rock, that it should not be covered.*"'[1]

Seven transgressions were committed by Israel on that day: they killed a priest, a prophet, and a judge, they shed innocent blood, they profaned the Divine Name, they defiled the Temple Court, and all this was done on the Sabbath which was also the Day of Atonement.[2] When Nebuzaradan[3] came up against Israel, the blood began to seethe; so he asked them, 'What kind of blood is this?' They replied, 'The blood of bulls, rams, and lambs which we slay.' He immediately sent and had some blood of sacrificial animals brought to him, but it did not behave similarly. He said to them, 'If you tell me, well and good; otherwise I will comb your flesh with iron combs.' They replied, 'What shall we say to you? He was a prophet who reproved us, so we rose against him and killed him, and for several years now his blood has not stopped seething.' He answered, 'I will appease it.' They brought before him the men of the Great Sanhedrin and Minor Sanhedrin[4] and slew them until their blood mingled with the blood of Zechariah, to fulfil that which was said, *They break all bounds, and blood toucheth blood* (Hos. IV, 2). The blood, however, continued to seethe; so they brought youths and maidens and he slew them by it, and still it did not stop. They brought school-children and slew them by it, and still it did not stop. Then they brought eighty

[1] Cf. Proem V. [2] Either the last (Sabbath and the Day of Atonement) is counted as a single transgression, or 'they profaned the Divine Name' must be omitted, as in Jer. a.l. (M.K.). [3] V. II Kings XXV 8. [4] The former consisted of 71 members; the latter of 23. For their respective functions v. Sanh. 2*a*.

thousand priestly novitiates and he slew them until their blood mingled with that of Zechariah, and still it continued to seethe. He exclaimed, 'Zechariah, Zechariah! All the choicest of them have I destroyed. Is it your pleasure that I exterminate them all?' As soon as he spoke thus, it stopped. Thereupon he debated with himself whether to repent, saying, 'If such vengeance is exacted for one life, how much more will happen to me for having taken so many lives'! He fled, sent a parting gift to his household, and became a convert to Judaism.

'And the almond-tree shall blossom' (Eccl. XII, 5): this alludes to the prophecy of Jeremiah, as it is stated, *Moreover the word of the Lord came unto me, saying, Jeremiah, what seest thou? And I said, I see a rod of an almond-tree* (Jer. I, 11). R. Eleazar said: What is the symbolic meaning of the almond-tree? From the time it begins to blossom until the time it finishes is twenty-one days; similarly from the seventeenth of Tammuz until the ninth of Ab[1] is twenty-one days.

'And the grasshopper shall drag itself along' (Eccl. XII, 5): this alludes to the image made by Nebuchadnezzar[2] of which it is written, *Nebuchadnezzar the king made an image of gold whose height was threescore cubits, and the breadth thereof six cubits* (Dan. III, 1). R. Joḥanan said: Can anything whose height is sixty cubits and breadth six cubits stand upright? Unless its breadth is a third of its height it cannot stand upright,[3] and yet it is stated, *he set it up in the plain of Dura* (*ib.*)! R. Levi said: They set it up like a stick and it fell; they set it up again and it fell. How long did they continue doing this? R. Haggai answered in the name of R. Isaac: Until they brought all the silver and gold which they had taken from Jerusalem and poured it out as a base around its feet; to fulfil that which was said, *They shall cast their silver in the streets, and their gold shall be as an unclean thing* (Ezek. VII, 19).

[1] V. p. 12, n. 1 f.
[2] The image, despite its height, is contemptuously called '*grasshopper*'.
[3] Possibly this was assumed from the measurements of the Ark; cf. Gen. R. XXXI, 10.

'And the caperberry (abiyonah) *shall fail'* (Eccl. XII, 5): this refers to ancestral (*aboth*) merit. *'Because man goeth to his long home'*: from Babylon they came[1] and there shall they return. *'And the mourners go about the streets'*: this refers to the exile of Jeconiah.[2] You find that when Nebuchadnezzar went down to Babylon after capturing Jerusalem and the exiles of Zedekiah with him, the exiles of Jeconiah came out to meet him, wearing black underneath but white outside, and hailed him as 'conqueror of barbarians'![3] The exiles of Jeconiah asked those of Zedekiah, 'What happened to my father? What happened to my brother? What happened to my children?' They replied, *'Such as are for death to death, and such as are for the sword to the sword'* (Jer. XV, 2). They thus praised Nebuchadnezzar with one breath and mourned with the other,[4] to fulfil that which was said, *Your tires shall be upon your heads, and your shoes upon your feet; ye shall not make lamentation nor weep* (Ezek. XXIV, 23).

'Before the silver cord is snapped asunder' (Eccl. XII, 6): this refers to the genealogical chain.[5] *'And the golden bowl is shattered'*: these are words of Torah which are *more to be desired than gold, yea, than much fine gold* (Ps. XIX, 11). *'And the pitcher is broken at the fountain'*: two *Amoraim* [explain the phrase differently]. One says that it means the pitcher of Baruch [was broken] upon the fountain of Jeremiah, whereas the other says that the pitcher of Jeremiah [was broken] upon the fountain of Baruch[6]; and so it is stated, *He pronounced all these words unto me with his mouth* (Jer. XXXVI, 18). *'And the wheel falleth*

[1] Abraham was born in that region. [2] Jer. XXVII, 20. He is identical with Jehoiachin, and his captivity occurred eleven years earlier.
[3] To curry favour with Nebuchadnezzar they described their fellow-Jews as 'barbarians'.
[4] Lit. 'other hand'. Overwhelmed by the bad news, they mingled their praises with signs of grief by beating their breasts.
[5] Gaps were caused in family trees by the slaughter.
[6] *'Fountain'* is the teacher, *'pitcher'* the pupil. According to the first view, Baruch was deprived of Jeremiah's teaching; according to the second, Jeremiah had been dependent upon Baruch who acted as his scribe and wrote down his words in a book which was burnt by Jehoiachin (Jer. XXXVI).

shattered into the pit': this refers to Babylon which is the depository of the world.[1]

R. Johanan said: *That saith to the deep* (ẓulah), *Be dry* (Isa. XLIV, 27): this alludes to Babylon; and why is it called '*ẓulah*'? Because [those who perished in] the waters of the Flood sank (*ẓalelu*) there; for it is written, *As Babylon hath caused the slain of Israel to fall, so at Babylon shall fall the slain of all the land* (Jer. LI, 49). R. Simeon b. Laḳish said: It is written, *They found a plain in the land of Shinar, and they dwelt there* (Gen. XI, 2). Why is it called '*shinar*'? Because the generation of the Flood were emptied out there (*shenin'ar*). Another explanation of '*shinar*' is: [The exiled Israelites] were emptied (*shehem menu'arim*) of all the commandments,[2] the commandment of *terumoth* and tithes. Another explanation of '*shinar*' is that [the inhabitants] die of suffocation[3] without a lamp burning and without the body being washed. Another explanation of '*shinar*' is that [the inhabitants] die young (*ne'arim*). Another explanation of '*shinar*' is, a city whose princes (*sar*) are youths (*ne'arim*) who trample upon the Torah. Another explanation of '*shinar*' is, it raised up a hater (*son'eh*) and enemy (*'ar*) of the Holy One, blessed be He, viz. Nebuchadnezzar.

'*And the dust returneth to the earth as it was*' (Eccl. XII, 7): from Babylon they came, and there they returned. '*And the spirit returneth unto God Who gave It*': this refers to the Holy Spirit. Since the Holy Spirit departed from Israel they were exiled; and since they were exiled Jeremiah lamented over them, '*How sitteth solitary.*'

XXIV

R. Johanan opened his discourse with the text, *The burden concerning the Valley of Vision* (Isa. XXII, 1); i.e.

[1] Its treasures came to Babylon as spoil. V. p. 9.

[2] I.e. commandments which could only be performed in the holy land, such as those relating to tithes and to *terumoth*, the portions of offerings and the harvest due to the priests (Num. XVIII, 8 ff.).

[3] In Ex. XIV, 27, the verb *vayena'er* ('He overthrew') is rendered in the Aramaic version by 'He suffocated' and that meaning is read into '*shinar*'.

a valley concerning which all the seers prophesied, a valley from which all the seers originated. For R. Joḥanan said: Any prophet whose place of origin is not specified was born in Jerusalem. '*The Valley of Vision*': [it is so called] because they cast the words of the seers to the ground.

'*What aileth thee now, that thou art wholly gone up to the housetops?*' (*ib.*). Had they, then, gone up to the roofs? R. Levi said: It refers to those who were haughty in spirit. '*Thou that art full of uproar*' (*ib.* 2): R. Eleazar b. Jacob said: The word [rendered '*uproar*'] is used in three senses, viz. troubles, disorders, and darkness. 'Troubles,' as it is said, *Neither heareth he the troubles caused by the taskmaster*[1] (Job XXXIX, 7). 'Disorders,' as it is said, '*Thou that art full of uproar.*' 'Darkness,' as it is said, *The gloom of wasteness and desolation* (*ib.* XXX, 3).

'*A tumultuous city*' (Isa. XXII, 2): that means a city thrown into confusion. '*A joyous town*': that means a city indulging in revelry. '*Thy slain are not slain with the sword, nor dead in battle*': what, then, are they? [Dead by] *the wasting of hunger, and the devouring of the fiery bolt* (Deut. XXXII, 24). '*All thy rulers are fled together, without the bow* (ḳesheth) *they are bound* (Isa. XXII, 3): because of their stubbornness (*ḳashyutham*) were they delivered over to foreign dominion. Another interpretation of '*all thy rulers are fled together, without the bow they are bound*': they loosened the strings of their bows and bound them therewith. '*All that are found of thee are bound together, they are fled afar off*' (*ib.*): they placed themselves at a distance so as not to hear words of Torah, as it is stated, *From afar*[2] *the Lord appeared unto me* (Jer. XXXI, 3).

'*Therefore said I: Look away from Me,*[3] *I will weep bitterly*' (Isa. XXII, 4). R. Simeon b. Laḳish said: On three occasions the Ministering Angels wished to utter song before the Holy One, blessed be He, but He would not let them, viz. [at the destruction of] the generation of the Flood, [at the overthrow of the Egyptians in] the

[1] E.V. '*the shoutings of the driver*'.
[2] I.e. when Israel was far away from Him. [3] Taken as referring to God.

Red Sea, and at the destruction of the Temple.[1] In connection with the generation of the Flood, what is written? *And the Lord said: My spirit shall not abide in man for ever* (Gen. VI, 3).[2] At the Red Sea it is written, *And the one came not near the other all the night* (Ex. XIV, 20).[3] At the destruction of the Temple it is written, '*Therefore said I, Look away from Me,*[4] *I will weep bitterly, strain not to comfort Me*' (Isa. XXII, 4). It is not written here 'do not gather together', but '*strain*[5] *not*', [which indicates that] the Holy One, blessed be He, said to the Ministering Angels, 'The words of comfort which you offer to Me are insults to Me.' For what reason? '*For it is a day of trouble, and of trampling, and of perplexity for*[6] *the Lord, the God of hosts*' (Isa. XXII, 5): it is a day of confusion, a day of plundering, a day of weeping. '*In the Valley of Vision*': a valley concerning which all the seers prophesied. '*Kir shouting*, (meḳarḳer) *and Shoa at the mount*': i.e. they demolished (*ḳirḳer*) the walls (*ḳir*) of their houses, made them into barricades, and set them upon their strongholds (*shoa*).

'*And Elam bore the quiver*' (*ib.* 6): Rab said: [The word means] a receptacle for arrows. '*With troops of men, even horsemen; and Kir uncovered the shield*': this indicates that they demolished the walls of their houses and made them into barricades. '*And it came to pass, when thy choicest valleys* ('amaḳaik) *were full of chariots*' (*ib.* 7): Rab said: They were filled to the same extent as the depth (*'amḳo*) of the ocean. '*And the horsemen set themselves in array* (shot shatu) *at the gate*': troops watering (*mashtaye*) their horses went and troops watering their horses came, so that they appeared to be very numerous.

'*And the covering of Judah was laid bare*' (*ib.* 8): that

[1] In the case of the last this must mean that God forbade the angels to utter their daily hymns (cf. Ḥul. 91*b*) on that occasion.
[2] *Yadon* ('abide') is read as *yaron* ('sing') and the word '*spirit*' is applied to God's messengers as in Ps. CIV, 4.
[3] Explained by the Rabbis as referring to the bands of angels who join in praise of God. [4] Supposedly addressed to the angels.
[5] The root is אוץ which is identified with נאץ 'to insult'; hence 'do not insult Me'. [6] E.V. '*from the Lord*'.

which should have been covered He disclosed.[1] '*That thou didst look in that day to the armour in the house of the forest*': R. Simeon b. Yoḥai taught: At Sinai Israel possessed weapons upon which the Tetragrammaton was inscribed, but when they sinned He removed the inscription from them; and so it is written, *And the children of Israel were stripped of their ornament*[2] *from Mount Horeb onward* (Ex. XXXIII, 6). How did He remove it from them? R. Aibu and the Rabbis [differ in their answer]. R. Aibu said that it erased itself, whereas the Rabbis maintain that an angel descended and erased it.

'*And ye saw the breaches of the city of David, that they were many . . . and ye numbered the houses of Jerusalem, and ye broke down the houses to fortify the wall*' (Isa. XXII, 9 f.): this teaches that they demolished their houses and extended the city wall. Did not Hezekiah do this previously; for is it not written, *And he took courage, and built up all the wall that was broken down* (II Chron. XXXII, 5)? Hezekiah, however, trusted in the God of Israel, whereas you had no such trust; and so it is stated, *But ye looked not unto Him that had done this, neither had ye respect unto Him that fashioned it long ago* (Isa. XXII, 11).

'*And in that day did the Lord, the God of hosts, call to weeping, and to lamentation*' (*ib.* 12): [the Ministering Angels] said before Him, 'Sovereign of the Universe, it is written *Honour and majesty are before Him* (I Chron. XVI, 27), and Thou speakest thus'![3] He replied to them, 'I will teach you: It is stated, *Strip you, and make you bare, and gird sackcloth upon your loins* (Isa. XXXII, 11); so will you lament. "*Smiting for*[4] *the breasts*" (*ib.* 12), i.e. over the destruction of the first and second Temples. "*For the pleasant fields*": i.e. for My desirable house which I made like a field; and so it is stated, *Zion shall be ploughed as*

[1] See p. 25, n. 3. [2] Viz. the Divine Name on their weapons. E.V. '*they stripped themselves of their ornaments by the mount*'.
[3] We do not know how to lament, our daily task being to sing of Your majesty.
[4] I.e. 'For the destruction of', E.V. '*upon*'. The Temple is compared to a breast as a source of spiritual nourishment, and the plural indicates the two Temples.

a field (Micah III, 12). "*For the fruitful vine*": this is Israel, as it is said, *Thou didst pluck up a vine out of Egypt* (Ps. LXXX, 9).'

Another interpretation of '*And in that day did the Lord, the God of hosts, call*, etc.': that is what Scripture declares by the Holy Spirit through the sons of Korah, *These things I remember and pour out my soul within me* (Ps. XLII, 5). With reference to whom did the sons of Korah utter this verse? They uttered it with reference to none other than the Community of Israel. For the Community of Israel spake before the Holy One, blessed be He, 'Sovereign of the Universe, I recall the safety, contentment, and prosperity in which I formerly dwelt, but they are now far removed from me; and I weep and sigh and say, "Would that it were like the former years when the Sanctuary was standing, in which Thou didst descend from the high heavens and cause Thy *Shechinah* to alight upon me; and the nations of the world used to praise me; and when I begged mercy for my sins Thou didst answer me. Now, however, I am in shame and contempt."' Further did it speak before Him, 'Sovereign of the Universe, my soul is appalled[1] within me when I pass by Thy house which is in ruins, and therein is a small voice proclaiming, "In the place where the seed of Abraham used to offer the sacrifices before Thee, and the priests stood on the dais, and the Levites sang hymns of praise to the accompaniment of lyres, do foxes now run about." And so it is written, *For the mountain of Zion, which is desolate, the foxes walk upon it* (Lam. V, 18). But what can I do, seeing that my iniquities have caused this to happen, and the false prophets who were in my midst seduced me from the path of life to the path of death?' On that account it is said, '*These things I remember and pour out my soul within me*.'

Another interpretation of '*And in that day did the Lord, the God of hosts, call to weeping and to lamentation*': at

[1] Radal reads 'cast down', the reference being to the continuation of the psalm: *Why art thou cast down, O my soul?* (*ib.* 5).

the time when the Holy One, blessed be He, sought to destroy the Temple, He said, 'So long as I am in its midst, the nations of the world will not touch it; but I will close My eyes so as not to see it, and swear that I will not attach Myself to it until the time of the end[1] arrives.' Then came the enemy and destroyed it. Forthwith the Holy One, blessed be He, swore by His right hand and placed it behind Him. So it is written, *He hath drawn back His right hand from before the enemy* (*ib.* II, 3). At that time the enemy entered the Temple and burnt it. When it was burnt, the Holy One, blessed be He, said, 'I no longer have a dwelling-place in this land; I will withdraw My *Shechinah* from it and ascend to My former habitation; so it is written, *I will go and return to My place, till they acknowledge their guilt, and seek My face*' (Hos. V, 15). At that time the Holy One, blessed be He, wept and said, 'Woe is Me! What have I done? I caused My *Shechinah* to dwell below on earth for the sake of Israel; but now that they have sinned, I have returned to My former habitation. Heaven forfend that I become a laughter to the nations and a byword to human beings!' At that time Metatron[2] came, fell upon his face, and spake before the Holy One, blessed be He: 'Sovereign of the Universe, let me weep, but do Thou not weep.' He replied to him, 'If thou lettest Me not weep now, I will repair to a place which thou hast not permission to enter, and will weep there,' as it is said, *But if ye will not hear it, My soul shall weep in secret for pride* (Jer. XIII, 17).

The Holy One, blessed be He, said to the Ministering Angels, 'Come, let us go together and see what the enemy has done in My house.' Forthwith the Holy One, blessed be He, and the Ministering Angels went, Jeremiah leading the way. When the Holy One, blessed be He, saw the Temple, He said, 'Certainly this is My house and this is My resting-place into which enemies have come, and they have done with it whatever they wished.' At that

[1] The Messianic era.
[2] Name of an angel who defended the interests of Israel.

time the Holy One, blessed be He, wept and said, 'Woe is Me for My house! My children, where are you? My priests, where are you? My lovers, where are you? What shall I do with you, seeing that I warned you but you did not repent?' The Holy One, blessed be He, said to Jeremiah, 'I am now like a man who had an only son, for whom he prepared a marriage-canopy, but he died under it. Feelest thou no anguish for Me and My children? Go, summon Abraham, Isaac and Jacob, and Moses from their sepulchres, for they know how to weep.' He spake before Him: 'Sovereign of the Universe, I know not where Moses is buried.' The Holy One, blessed be He, replied to him: 'Go, stand by the bank of the Jordan, and raise thy voice and call out, "Son of Amram, son of Amram, arise and behold thy flock which enemies have devoured."'

There and then Jeremiah went to the cave of Machpelah and said to the patriarchs of the world[1]: 'Arise, for the time has come when your presence is required before the Holy One, blessed be He.' They said to him, 'For what purpose?' He answered, 'I know not,' because he was afraid lest they say, 'In thy lifetime has such a thing happened to our children!' Jeremiah left them, and stood by the bank of the Jordan and called out, 'Son of Amram, son of Amram, arise, the time has come when thy presence is required before the Holy One, blessed be He.' He said to him, 'How is this day different from other days that my presence is required before the Holy One, blessed be He?' Jeremiah replied, 'I know not.' Moses left him and proceeded to the Ministering Angels whom he recognised from the time of the giving of the Torah.[2] He said to them, 'O celestial ministers, know ye why my presence is required before the Holy One, blessed be He?' They replied, 'Son of Amram, knowest thou not that the Temple is destroyed and Israel gone into exile?' He cried aloud and wept until he reached the patriarchs. They immediately

[1] Cf. Gen. XVII, 4, *Thou* (sc. Abraham) *shalt be the father of a multitude of nations*. [2] According to the legend, when Moses ascended Mount Sinai he had to contend with the angels who wished God to withhold the Torah (Shab. 88*b*).

also rent their garments, placed their hands upon their heads, and cried out and wept until they arrived at the gates of the Temple. When the Holy One, blessed be He, saw them, immediately '*In that day did the Lord, the God of hosts, call to weeping, and to lamentation, and to baldness, and to girding with sackcloth*' (Isa. XXII, 12). Were it not explicitly stated in Scripture, it would be impossible to say such a thing, but they went weeping from one gate to another like a man whose dead is lying before him, and the Holy One, blessed be He, lamented saying, 'Woe to the King Who succeeded in His youth but failed in His old age!'

R. Samuel b. Naḥman said: When the Temple was destroyed, Abraham came weeping before the Holy One, blessed be He, plucking his beard, tearing his hair, striking his face, rending his garments, with ashes upon his head, and walked about the Temple, lamenting and crying. He spake before the Holy One, blessed be He, 'Why have I been treated differently from every other people, that I have come to this shame and contempt!' When the Ministering Angels saw him, they also composed lamentations arranging themselves in rows [like mourners] and saying, '*The highways lie waste, the wayfaring man ceaseth*, etc.' (Isa. XXXIII, 8). What means '*the highways lie waste*'? The Ministering Angels spake before the Holy One, blessed be He: 'How have the ways become a desolation which Thou didst plan for Jerusalem so that travellers[1] should not cease therefrom!' '*The wayfaring man ceaseth*': the Ministering Angels spake before the Holy One, blessed be He: 'How have the ways become deserted in which Israel used to pass to and fro on the pilgrimage Festivals!' '*He hath broken the covenant*': the Ministering Angels spake before the Holy One, blessed be He: 'Sovereign of the Universe, broken is the covenant made with their patriarch Abraham through which the world is peopled and through which men acknowledge Thee in the world that Thou art God, Most High, Maker of heaven and earth.'[2] '*He hath*

[1] Going to the Temple.
[2] It was said that until Abraham came, God was only known as God of heaven; he proclaimed Him as God of the earth. V. Gen. R. LIX, 8.

despised the cities': the Ministering Angels spake before the Holy One, blessed be He, 'Thou hast despised Jerusalem and Zion after Thou hast chosen them'; and so it is stated, *Hast Thou utterly rejected Judah? Hath Thy soul loathed Zion?* (Jer. XIV, 19). '*He regardeth not man*' (Enosh): the Ministering Angels spake before the Holy One, blessed be He: 'Thou hast not regarded Israel even so much as the generation of Enosh[1] who were the foremost idolaters.'

Thereupon the Holy One, blessed be He, turned upon the Ministering Angels, saying to them, 'Why do you string dirges together over this incident, standing rows upon rows?' They answered before Him: 'Sovereign of the Universe, because of Abraham Thy friend who came to Thy house, and lamented and wept; why didst Thou disregard him?' He said to them, 'From the day My friend departed from before Me to his eternal home, he came not to My house; but now, *What hath My beloved to do in My house?* (Jer. XI, 15).' Abraham spake before the Holy One, blessed be He, 'Sovereign of the Universe, why hast Thou exiled My children and delivered them over to heathen nations who have put them to all kinds of unnatural death, and destroyed the Temple, the place where I offered my son Isaac as a burnt-offering before Thee?' The Holy One, blessed be He, replied to Abraham, 'Thy children sinned and transgressed the whole of the Torah and the twenty-two letters[2] in which it is composed'; and so it is stated, *Yea, all Israel have transgressed Thy law* (Dan. IX, 11). Abraham spake before the Holy One, blessed be He: 'Sovereign of the Universe, who testifies against Israel that they transgressed Thy law?' He replied to him, 'Let the Torah come and testify against Israel.' Forthwith the Torah came to testify against them. Abraham said to the Torah, 'My daughter, art thou come to testify against Israel that they transgressed thy commandments and hast no shame before me! Remember the day when the Holy One, blessed be He, handed thee about to every nation but

[1] Gen. IV, 26, *then began men to call upon the name of the Lord*, is interpreted by the Rabbis as: *then began men* to profane *the name of the Lord*. V. Gen. R. XXIII, 7. [2] The number of letters in the Hebrew alphabet.

they refused to accept thee until my children came to Mount Sinai, accepted thee and honoured thee[1]; and now thou comest to testify against them in the day of their trouble!' When the Torah heard this, she stood aside and gave no testimony against them.

The Holy One, blessed be He, said to Abraham, 'Let the twenty-two letters come and testify against Israel.' Forthwith the twenty-two letters appeared. The *aleph* came to testify that Israel had transgressed the Torah. Abraham said to it, 'Thou, *aleph*, art the first of all the letters, and thou comest to testify against Israel in the day of their trouble! Remember the day when the Holy One, blessed be He, revealed Himself upon Mount Sinai and opened with thee, *I*[2] *am the Lord thy God* (Ex. XX, 2), and no nation accepted thee but my children, and thou comest to testify against my children!' The *aleph* immediately stood aside and gave no testimony against them. The *beth* came to testify against Israel, and Abraham said to it, 'My daughter, thou comest to testify against my children who were zealous about the Pentateuch[3] of which thou art the first letter, as it is written, *In the beginning*[4] *God created* (Gen. I, 1).' The *beth* immediately stood aside and gave no testimony against them. The *gimel* came to testify against Israel, and Abraham said to it, '*Gimel*, thou art come to testify against my children that they transgressed the Torah! Is there a nation which observes the commandment of fringes,[5] of which thou art the first letter, except my children; as it is written, *Thou shalt make thee twisted cords*[6] (Deut. XXII, 12)!' The *gimel* immediately stood aside and gave no testimony against them.

When the remainder of the letters saw that Abraham silenced these, they felt ashamed and stood apart and did not testify against Israel. Abraham thereupon began to speak before the Holy One, blessed be He, saying,

[1] V. Mekilta to Ex. XX, 2, ed. Friedmann 67*a*.
[2] 'I' in Hebrew is *anoki* (אנכי), the initial letter being *aleph*.
[3] Mah.: to study it, though they had neglected practical observance.
[4] *Bereshith*, the first letter being *beth*.
[5] V. Num. XV, 38.
[6] *Gedilim*, the first letter being *gimel*.

'Sovereign of the Universe, when I was a hundred years old Thou gavest me a son, and when he reached years of discretion and was a young man of thirty-seven,[1] Thou didst order me, "Offer him as a sacrifice before Me." I steeled my heart against him and I had no compassion on him; but I myself bound him. Wilt Thou not remember this on my behalf and have mercy on My children?' Isaac began, saying, 'Sovereign of the Universe, when my father said to me, "*God will provide Himself the lamb for a burnt-offering, my son*" (Gen. XXII, 8),[2] I raised no objection to the carrying out of Thy words, and I willingly let myself be bound on the top of the altar and stretched out my neck beneath the knife. Wilt Thou not remember this on my behalf and have mercy on my children?' Jacob began, saying, 'Sovereign of the Universe, did I not stay twenty years in Laban's house? And when I left his house, the wicked Esau met me and sought to kill my children, and I risked my life on their behalf.[3] Now they are delivered into the hands of their enemies like sheep to the slaughter, after I reared them like chickens and endured for their sakes the pain of child-rearing. For throughout most of my days I experienced great trouble on their account. Now, wilt Thou not remember this on my behalf to have mercy on my children?' Moses began, saying, 'Sovereign of the Universe, was I not a faithful shepherd to Israel for forty years, running before them like a horse in the desert? When the time arrived for them to enter the promised land, Thou didst decree against me that my bones should fall in the wilderness. Now that they are exiled, Thou hast sent for me to lament and weep over them. This bears out

[1] Israel was born when Sarah was aged 90 (cf. Gen. XVII, 17 and XXI, 5). She died at the age of 127 (*ib.* XXIII, 1); according to tradition her death was caused by hearing of Isaac's sacrifice before the news reached her that he had been spared.

[2] The Rabbis translated this: *God will provide Himself the lamb for a burnt-offering*, but if not, *then my son* will be the offering (Gen. R. LVI, 4). Thus Isaac knew that he was to be sacrificed.

[3] This probably means that he risked his own life for their sake, the reference presumably being to Gen. XXXIII, 2 f., his passing in front of them being to defend them.

the popular proverb, "I derive no benefit from my master's good fortune, but suffer from his bad fortune."'

Thereupon Moses said to Jeremiah, 'Walk before me, so that I may go and bring them in and see who dares to touch them.' Jeremiah replied, 'It is impossible for me to walk along the road because of the slain.' He said to him, 'Nevertheless let us go.' Forthwith Moses went, Jeremiah leading the way, until they arrived at the rivers of Babylon. When the exiles beheld Moses, they said one to another, 'The son of Amram has come from his grave to redeem us from the hand of our adversaries.' A *Bath Ḳol* issued forth and announced, 'This is a decree from Me.'[1] Moses at once said to them, 'My children, it is not possible to take you back [now] since it is so decreed, but the All-present will soon cause you to return'; and then he left them. Thereupon they lifted their voices in loud weeping, until the sound of it ascended above. So it is written, *By the rivers of Babylon, there we sat down, yea, we wept* (Ps. CXXXVII, 1). When Moses came to the patriarchs of the world, they asked him, 'What did the enemy do to our children?' He replied, 'Some of them they killed; the hands of others they bound behind their backs; others were fettered with iron chains; others were stripped naked; others died by the way and their carcasses were food for the birds of the heaven and the beasts of earth; and others were exposed to the sun, hungry and thirsty.' Forthwith they all began to weep and utter lamentations: 'Woe for what has befallen our children! How have you become like orphans without a father! How you had to sleep at noon during summer without clothing and covering![2] How you walked over rocks and pebbles stripped of shoes and without sandals! How were you laden with heavy bundles of sand! How were your hands bound behind your backs! How were you unable to swallow the spittle in your mouths!'

Moses lifted up his voice, saying, 'Cursed be thou sun! Why didst thou not become dark when the enemy entered the Temple!' The sun replied, 'By thy life, O Moses,

[1] That they remain in captivity. [2] To protect you from the burning sun.

faithful shepherd, how could I become dark when they did not permit me and did not leave me alone? But they beat me with sixty whips of fire and said to me, "Go, pour forth thy light."'[1] Moses again lifted up his voice, saying, 'Woe to thy brilliance, O Temple, how has it become obscured! Woe that its time has come to be destroyed, for the edifice to be reduced to ruins, for school children to be massacred, and their parents to go into exile and captivity and perish by the sword!' Moses again lifted up his voice, saying, 'O captors, I charge you, if you kill, do not kill with a cruel death; do not make a complete extermination; do not slay a son in the presence of his father nor a daughter in the presence of her mother; because a time will come when the Lord of heaven will exact a reckoning of you.' But the wicked Chaldeans refused to comply with his request, and they brought a son into the presence of his mother, and said to his father, 'Arise, slay him!' His mother wept, and her tears fell upon him, and his father hung his head.

He further spake before Him: 'Sovereign of the Universe, Thou hast written in Thy Torah, *Whether it be a cow or ewe, ye shall not kill it and its young both in one day* (Lev. XXII, 28); but have they not killed many, many mothers and sons, and Thou art silent!' At that moment, the matriarch Rachel broke forth into speech before the Holy One, blessed be He, and said, 'Sovereign of the Universe, it is revealed before Thee that Thy servant Jacob loved me exceedingly and toiled for my father on my behalf seven years. When those seven years were completed and the time arrived for my marriage with my husband, my father planned to substitute another for me to wed my husband for the sake of my sister. It was very hard for me, because the plot was known to me and I disclosed it to my husband; and I gave him a sign whereby he could distinguish between me and my sister, so that my father should not be able to make the substitution. After that I relented, suppressed my desire, and had pity upon my sister that she should not be

[1] Cf. Ned. 39*b*.

exposed to shame. In the evening they substituted my sister for me with my husband, and I delivered over to my sister all the signs which I had arranged with my husband so that he should think that she was Rachel. More than that, I went beneath the bed upon which he lay with my sister; and when he spoke to her she remained silent and I made all the replies in order that he should not recognise my sister's voice.[1] I did her a kindness, was not jealous of her, and did not expose her to shame. And if I, a creature of flesh and blood, formed of dust and ashes, was not envious of my rival and did not expose her to shame and contempt, why shouldest Thou, a King Who liveth eternally and art merciful, be jealous of idolatry in which there is no reality, and exile my children and let them be slain by the sword, and their enemies have done with them as they wished!'

Forthwith the mercy of the Holy One, blessed be He, was stirred, and He said, 'For thy sake, Rachel, I will restore Israel to their place.' And so it is written, *Thus saith the Lord: A voice is heard in Ramah, lamentation and bitter weeping, Rachel weeping for her children; she refuseth to be comforted for her children, because they are not* (Jer. XXXI, 15). This is followed by, *Thus saith the Lord: Refrain thy voice from weeping, and thine eyes from tears; for thy work shall be rewarded . . . and there is hope for thy future, saith the Lord; and thy children shall return to their own border* (*ib.* 16 f.).

XXV

R. Joḥanan opened his discourse with the text, *Give glory to the Lord your God, before it grow dark*, etc. (Jer. XIII, 16). When was this verse fulfilled upon them? On the death of Hezekiah; for so it is written, *And Hezekiah slept with his fathers, and they buried him in the ascent of the sepulchres of the sons of David; and all Judah and the inhabitants of Jerusalem did him honour at his death* (II Chron. XXXII, 33). What honour did they do him? R. Judah b. Simon, R. Ḥanin, and the Rabbis [suggest answers]. R. Judah b. Simon

[1] A different story is told in Gen. R. LXX, 19.

said: They built a meeting-place [for study] above Hezekiah's grave, and when they went there they used to say to him, 'Teach us.' R. Ḥanin said: They placed a Torah-scroll over Hezekiah's grave and said, 'He who lies in this coffin fulfilled what is written herein.' The Rabbis said: They laid carpets for him from the door of their houses to the sepulchres of the sons of David. For what purpose? So that their feet should not be exposed to cold; but for all that their feet were exposed to cold. Jeremiah said to them, 'If your feet are exposed to cold when you lay carpets from the door of your houses to the sepulchres of the sons of David, how much more when *your feet will stumble upon the mountains of twilight* (Jer. *ib.*).'

Ten journeys were made by the *Shechinah*: from cherub to cherub, from the cherub to the threshold of the house, from the threshold of the house to the cherubim, from the cherubim to the east gate, from the east gate to the Court, from the Court to the roof, from the roof to the altar, from the altar to the wall, from the wall to the city [of Jerusalem], and from the city to the Mount of Olives. From cherub to cherub; for it is written, *And the glory of the Lord mounted up from the cherub* (Ezek. x, 4). From the cherub to the threshold of the house; for it is written, *And the glory of the God of Israel was gone up from the cherub, whereupon it was, to the threshold of the house* (*ib.* IX, 3). From the threshold of the house to the cherubim; for it is written, *And the glory of the Lord went forth from off the threshold of the house, and stood over the cherubim* (*ib.* x, 18). (The text should not have said '*went forth*' but 'came'[1]; but it says '*went forth*', so what means '*went forth*'? R. Aḥa said: The *Shechinah* may be likened to a king who left his palace in anger. After going out, he came back and embraced and kissed the walls of the palace and its pillars, weeping and exclaiming, 'O the peace of my palace, O the peace of my royal residence, O the peace of my beloved house! O peace, from now onward let there be peace!' Similarly when the *Shechinah* went forth from the Temple, it returned and embraced

[1] Since the *Shechinah* proceeded *into* the Temple.

and kissed its walls and pillars, and wept and said, 'O the peace of the Temple, O the peace of My royal residence, O the peace of My beloved house! O peace, from now onward let there be peace!')

From the cherubim to the east gate; for it is written, *And the cherubim lifted up their wings . . . and they stood at the door of the east gate* (*ib.* 19). From the east gate to the Court; for it is written, *And the court was full of the brightness of the Lord's glory* (*ib.* 4). From the Court to the roof; for it is written, *It is better to dwell in a corner of the housetop* (Prov. XXI, 9). From the roof to the altar; for it is written, *I saw the Lord standing beside the altar* (Amos IX, 1). From the altar to the wall; for it is written, *Behold, the Lord stood beside a wall made by a plumbline* (*ib.* VII, 7). (Another interpretation is: what means 'anak ('*plumbline*')? It alludes to the Sanhedrin of seventy-one members. Whence is this derived? From the numerical value of the letters of *'anak*.[1] *Then said the Lord, Behold I will set a plumbline* (*ib.* 8): R. Judah b. R. Simon said, etc.[2]) From the wall to the city; for it is written, *Hark! the Lord crieth unto the city* (Micah VI, 9). From the city to the Mount of Olives; for it is written, *And the glory of the Lord went up from the midst of the city, and stood upon the mountain which is on the east side of the city* (Ezek. XI, 23).

R. Jonathan said: Three and a half years[3] the *Shechinah* abode upon the Mount of Olives hoping that Israel would repent, but they did not; while a *Bath Kol* issued announcing, '*Return, O backsliding children* (Jer. III, 14), *Return unto Me, and I will return unto you* (Mal. III, 7).' When they did not repent, it said, '*I will go and return to My place* (Hos. V, 15).' Concerning that time it is said, '*Give glory to the Lord your God, before it grow dark*' (Jer. XIII, 16): before it becomes dark to you for lack of words of Torah, before it becomes dark to you for lack of words of prophecy, '*and before your feet stumble upon the mountains of twilight.*' '*And while ye look for light,*' in Babylon, '*He turn it into the*

[1] אנך = א (1), and נ (50), and כ (20) = 71.
[2] His comment is not quoted here; v. Lev. R. XXXIII, 2.
[3] Cf. Proem XXX, p. 56, n. 4.

shadow of death,' in Media, *'and make it gross darkness'* in Greece. *'But if ye will not hear it'* (*ib.* 17) in Edom,[1] *'My soul shall weep in secret for your pride.'* Why is it stated *'for your pride'*? It alludes to the idols on which they pride themselves, saying, *Where are their gods, the rock in whom they trusted* (Deut. XXXII, 37). Another interpretation of *'for your pride'*: on account of the Ministering Angels who are proud of themselves and say, *'What is man, that Thou art mindful of him,* etc.?' (Ps. VIII, 5).[2]

'And mine eye shall weep sore, and run down with tears, because the Lord's flock is carried away captive' (Jer. XIII, 17). You find that before Israel was exiled, they were divided into sections—the section of the priesthood being separate, the section of the Levites separate, and the section of the lay-Israelites separate. But when they were exiled, they were formed into one party. *'Because the Lord's flock is carried away captive'*: '[flocks] are carried away captive' is not written here, but *'because the Lord's* flock *is carried away captive'*.

XXVI

R. Naḥman opened his discourse with the text, *Ah, Ariel, Ariel* (Isa. XXIX, 1): i.e. mighty lion[3]; *'the city where David encamped'*: i.e. the city in which David set up his camp, a city in which only David encamped,[4] the city which David made for his army. *'Add ye year to year, let the feasts come round'*: year came and year departed but the Israelites did not go up to Jerusalem for the pilgrimage Festivals, and the roads grew shrubs (*hegim*). That is the meaning of *'let the feasts* (ḥaggim) *come round'*.[5] *'Then will I distress Ariel'* (*ib.* 2): R. Nissa of Cæsarea said: From this it is

[1] I.e. Rome.
[2] According to the Midrash (Gen. R. VIII, 6) that means that they were opposed to the creation of man, as he would be unworthy. Thus God wept that the forecast of the angels, the proud ones, was now apparently justified. (*'Your'* in *'for* your *pride'* must be omitted on this interpretation, and is indeed absent in the original Hebrew.)
[3] The word is divided into *'ari* ('lion') and *'el* ('mighty').
[4] Luzzatto emends חניא to הניא, i.e. 'the city from which David derived advantage'. The phrase is entirely omitted in the Yalkuṭ.
[5] Translated: Shrubs overrun (the roads).

to be deduced that Israel had enjoyed being there.[1] '*And there shall be mourning and moaning*': i.e., the most intense afflictions. '*And she shall be unto Me as a hearth of God*': like the destruction of the first Temple will be the destruction of the second Temple.[2] Since they sinned, they were exiled; and since they were exiled, Jeremiah began to lament over them, *Ekah*.

XXVII

R. Phinehas opened his discourse with the text, *And if ye will not yet for these things hearken unto Me*, etc. (Lev. XXVI, 18). R. Eliezer and R. Joshua [make comments]. R. Eliezer says: The Holy One, blessed be He, does not bring punishments upon Israel without first warning them. That is the meaning of what is written, '*And if ye will not yet* ('ad)[3] *for these things*.' R. Joshua says: So that Israel shall not declare, 'The afflictions are exhausted; He has no others to bring upon us,' therefore Scripture states, '*And if ye will not yet* ('ad) *for these things*' [which may be read as] 'if further ('*od*) these things', i.e. He has other and similar afflictions to bring.

'*Then I will chastise you seven times more for your sins.*' You committed seven transgressions before Me,[4] come and receive seven punishments upon yourselves. 'You committed seven transgressions before Me'; therefore Jeremiah came to utter over you *Lamentations* consisting of verses the initial letters of which form a sevenfold alphabet. *Ekah*.

XXVIII

R. Ḥama b. Ḥanina opened his discourse with the text, *Then took Jeremiah another roll*, etc. (Jer. XXXVI, 32).

[1] Before the destruction. This thought is derived from the future '*then will I distress*'.

[2] After the mourning over the first Temple, Jerusalem will again undergo the same experience as the '*hearth of God*' had previously endured.

[3] '*Ad* ('yet') is read as '*ed* ('witness').

[4] They are enumerated by Rashi on Lev. XXVI, 15, viz. not studying the commandments, not practising them, scorning those who do perform them, hating teachers, preventing others from carrying out the commandments, denying their Divine origin, and denying God's existence.

R. Ḥama b. Ḥanina[1] and the Rabbis [joined issue]. R. Ḥama said: *And there added besides unto them:* this refers to [the second chapter of Lamentations beginning with] *How hath the Lord covered with a cloud.*[2] '*Words*': this refers to [the fourth chapter beginning with] *How is the gold become dim.* '*Many*': this refers to [the third chapter beginning with] *I am the man.* '*Like*': this refers to [the fifth chapter beginning with] *Remember, O Lord.* The Rabbis, on the other hand, say: '*And there added besides unto them*': this refers to [the second chapter beginning with] '*How hath the Lord covered with a cloud*'. '*Words*': this refers to [the fourth chapter beginning with] '*How is the gold become dim*'. '*Many*': this refers to [the fifth chapter beginning with] '*Remember, O Lord*'. '*Like*': this refers to [the third chapter beginning with] '*I am the man*', which is in alphabetical order with three verses to each letter of the alphabet.

XXIX

Zabdi b. Levi opened his discourse with the text, *God maketh the solitary to dwell in a house* (Ps. LXVIII, 7). You find that before the Israelites were delivered from Egypt they lived apart by themselves, and the *Shechinah* was by itself; but when they were delivered, they were amalgamated. When, however, they were exiled, the *Shechinah* again resumed its separate existence and the Israelites theirs. That is the meaning of what is written, *The rebellious dwell but in a parched land*[3] (*ib.*); hence '*How sitteth solitary*'.

XXX

Zabdi b. Levi opened his discourse with the text, *The kings of the earth believed not*, etc. (Lam. IV, 12). There arose four kings each of whom made a different request, viz., David, Asa, Jehoshaphat, and Hezekiah. David said, *Let*

[1] Buber's MS. reads: R. Ḥanina b. Papa, which is preferable, since R. Ḥama enumerates the divergent opinions of Rabbis other than himself.
[2] They all agree that the original scroll contained only Lam. I, but they differ about the order in which the other chapters were added.
[3] '*Parched land*' indicates that it was deprived of the presence of the *Shechinah*.

me pursue[1] *mine enemies, and overtake them* (Ps. XVIII, 38). The Holy One, blessed be He, said to him, 'I will do so.' So it is written, *And David smote them from the twilight even unto the evening of the next day* (I Sam. XXX, 17). What means '*the next day*'? R. Joshua b. Levi said: [It indicates that he smote them] for two nights and one day. The Holy One, blessed be He, illumined the nights with meteors and lightning-flashes, as we have learnt in the Mishnah, 'For meteors, earthquakes, and lightnings.'[2] Hence it is written, *For Thou dost light my lamp* (Ps. XVIII, 29).

Asa stood up and said, 'I have not the strength to slay them, but I will pursue them and do Thou perform [the slaying].' He replied to him, 'I will do so'; as it is said, *And Asa . . . pursued them* (II Chron. XIV, 12), and it is not written here, *and they were shattered* before Asa, but *before the Lord and before His host.*

Jehoshaphat stood up and said, 'I have the strength neither to slay nor to pursue, but I will utter a song and do Thou perform [the slaying and pursuing].' The Holy One, blessed be He, replied, 'I will do so'; as it is said, *And when they began to sing and to praise, the Lord set liers-in-wait* (*ib.* XX, 22).

Hezekiah stood up and said, 'I have the strength neither to slay nor to pursue nor to utter a song, but I will sleep upon my bed and do Thou perform [all these things].' The Holy One, blessed be He, replied, 'I will do so'; as it is said, *And it came to pass that night, that the angel of the Lord went forth, and smote in the camp of the Assyrians* (II Kings XIX, 35).[3] How many of them survived? Rab said: Ten, as it is stated, *And the remnant . . . shall be few, that a child may write them down* (Isa. X, 19), and it is the way of a child to write the letter *yod*.[4] R. Eleazar said: Six survived,

[1] E.V. '*I have pursued*'.

[2] Ber. IX, 2. The Mishnah formulates the benediction to be recited on beholding these phenomena.

[3] Since it happened at night, it is assumed that Hezekiah was then in bed.

[4] Because it is a small letter and easy to write. As a numeral it denotes ten.

because it is the way of a child to make just a stroke.[1] R. Joshua b. Levi said: Five survived, as it is said, *Two* [and][2] *three berries in the top of the uppermost bough* (*ib.* XVII, 6). R. Judah and R. Simon said: Nine survived; and so it is written, *Four* [and] *five in the branches of the fruitful tree* (*ib.*). R. Tanḥum b. Ḥanilai said: Fourteen survived; and so it is written, '*Two* [and] *three berries in the top of the uppermost bough, four* [and] *five in the branches of the fruitful tree.*' According to all opinions Nebuchadnezzar was one of the survivors; but when the Holy One, blessed be He, said to him, 'Go up and destroy the Temple,' he said, 'He only wants to entrap me in order to do to me as He did to my ancestor.' So what did he do? He went and resided at Daphne in Antioch,[3] and sent Nebuzaradan, the captain of the guard, to destroy Jerusalem. He was occupied with the task for three years and a half.[4] He daily encompassed Jerusalem but was unable to subdue it. He wished to return, but the Holy One, blessed be He, placed an idea in his mind, and he began to measure the wall, which thereupon sank daily two and a half handbreadths until the whole of it was sunk in the ground. When it was wholly sunk, the enemy entered Jerusalem. With reference to that time it states, *The kings of the earth believed not, neither all the inhabitants of the world, that the adversary and the enemy would enter into the gates of Jerusalem* (Lam. IV, 12). Since they sinned they were exiled; and since they were exiled, Jeremiah began to lament over them, *Ekah.*

XXXI

R. Simeon b. Yoḥai opened his discourse with the text, *It is bad, it is bad, saith the buyer; but when he is gone his way, then he boasteth* (Prov. XX, 14). You find that before the

[1] A vertical stroke represents the letter *vav* which is the numeral six.
[2] E.V. '*or*'. The Hebrew is lit. 'two three berries . . . four five'.
[3] Daphne was a suburb.
[4] From the Biblical dates it is deduced that the campaign lasted a year and a half (cf. II Kings XXV, 1, 8). The figure three and a half years is copied erroneously from the duration of Vespasian's campaign against Jerusalem (v. p. 101).

Israelites were exiled, the Holy One, blessed be He, used to call them '*bad*'; and so it is written, *Even this evil people, that refuse to hear My words* (Jer. XIII, 10). But when they were exiled, He began to praise them, as it is said, '*But when he is gone his way, then He boasteth*' (Prov. *ib.*). Since they sinned they were exiled; and since they were exiled, Jeremiah began to lament over them, *Ekah.*

Woe to her that is filthy (mor'ah) *and polluted* (nig'alah), *to the oppressing city!* (Zeph. III, 1). What means, '*Woe* mor'ah'? Woe because of the dread when I impose the fear of Me upon all the nations.[1] When?—*When Israel shall be delivered.*[2] You find that when Israel was delivered from Egypt, the dread of them fell upon all the peoples; as it is written, *The peoples have heard, they tremble . . . then were the chiefs of Edom affrighted* (Ex. XV, 14 f.).

'*The oppressing* (yonah) *city*': a people whom I distinguished with Divine precepts and meritorious deeds like a dove (*yonah*).[3] Despite all this praise, *she hearkened not to the voice, she received not correction; she trusted not in the Lord, she drew not near to her God* (Zeph. III, 2). If a bride does not obey [her husband], is she not a fool? R. Reuben said: The word is Greek, because they call a foolish woman '*morah*'.[4] '*Woe* mor'ah' therefore means: woe on account of the foolish woman [Zion]! '*And polluted*': because they removed themselves from hearing words of Torah, she hath been polluted in the priesthood. '*Oppressing* (yonah) *city*': ought she not have learnt from the city of Jonah, viz. Nineveh?[5] One prophet I sent to Nineveh and she turned in penitence; but to Israel in Jerusalem I sent many prophets; and so it is written, *Yet the Lord forewarned Israel, and Judah, by the hand of every prophet, and of every seer, saying: Turn ye from your evil ways, and*

[1] Radal reads: Woe because of the nation (sc. Israel) whose fear I have set upon all peoples. This agrees better with what follows.
[2] *Mor'ah* can mean 'dread' and *nig'alah* 'she was redeemed'. Hence the Midrash interprets: Woe when the fear of Me is upon the nations, then shall Israel be redeemed. Or possibly: When [was the fear of Israel upon all nations]?—when they were redeemed [from Egypt].
[3] Translating: the dove-like city.
[4] The Greek word μωρός.
[5] Translating: the city of Jonah.

keep My commandments and My statutes, etc. (II Kings XVII, 13); and it is written, *And though I have sent unto you all My servants the prophets, sending them daily betimes and often* (Jer. VII, 25)—rising up early to send them in the morning, and rising up early to send them in the evening.[1] *Yet they hearkened not* (*ib.* 26), and since they hearkened not they were exiled, and since they were exiled Jeremiah began to lament over them, '*How sitteth solitary.*'

XXXII

R. Ḥanina opened his discourse with the text, *Though I would take comfort* (mabligithi) *against sorrow, my heart is faint within me* (Jer. VIII, 18). What means '*mabligithi*'? Because there are none (*mibli*) who meditate (*hogim*) in the Torah to perform Divine precepts and meritorious acts, I have made My house into My wine-press (*gitti*). For all that, '*My heart is faint within Me,*' over the destroyed Temple. So it is written, *For this our heart is faint*, etc. (Lam. V, 17); for it is written, *Behold the voice of the cry* (shaw'ah) *of the daughter of My people from a land far off* (Jer. VIII, 19). R. Joḥanan said: The term *shaw'ah* has three meanings, viz. *ẓa'aḳah* 'crying', *shaw'ah* 'calling for help', and *na'aḳah* 'groaning'. 'Crying,' for it is written, *And the children of Israel sighed by reason of the bondage, and they cried* (vayiẓ'aḳu), *and their cry* (shaw'atham) *came up* (Ex. II, 23). 'Calling for help,' for it is written, '*The voice of the cry of* (shaw'ath) *the daughter of my people.*' 'Groaning,' for it is written, *And God heard their groaning*—na'aḳah (*ib.* 24). R. Huna the Elder of Sepphoris says: It means writhing in death-agony; for it is written, *And he shall groan before him with the groaning of a deadly wounded man* (Ezek. XXX, 24), and it is written, *And the soul of the wounded crieth out*—shaw'eah (Job XXIV, 12).[2]

'*Is not the Lord in Zion? Is not her King in her?*' (Jer. VIII, 19). If He had been in her, they would not have

[1] V. *infra*, II, 13, § 7.
[2] Both passages refer to the wounded. The first uses *na'aḳ* and the second *shaw'ah*, thus proving that they have the same meaning.

gone into exile.[1] But since they sinned, they were exiled; and since they were exiled, Jeremiah began to lament over them, '*How sitteth solitary.*'

XXXIII

R. Zera opened his discourse with the text, *Therefore is my harp turned to mourning, and my pipe into the voice of them that weep* (Job XXX, 31). Elsewhere we have learnt[2]: R. Simeon b. Gamaliel said: The Israelites had no greater holidays than the fifteenth of Ab and the Day of Atonement, on which occasions the maidens of Israel used to go out in white garments, borrowed for the event in order not to put to shame them who possessed none of their own. All these garments required to be dipped[3]; and in them the maidens of Israel used to go out to dance in the vineyards. It was taught: The unmarried man would repair there, and what used the maidens to say? 'Young man, lift up your eyes and see whom you will select. Pay no regard to beauty but to family descent.' Similarly it states,[4] *Go forth, O ye daughters of Zion, and gaze upon king Solomon, even upon the crown wherewith his mother hath crowned him in the day of his espousals, and in the day of the gladness of his heart* (S.S. III, 11). '*In the day of his espousals*' alludes to the giving of the Torah; '*and in the day of the gladness of his heart*' alludes to the building of the Temple, may it be rebuilt speedily in our days!

It is quite right that the Day of Atonement [should be an occasion for dancing] since it was a day of forgiveness and expiation for Israel, and the day upon which the second Tables were given.[5] But what is the reason of the fifteenth of Ab? R. Jacob b. Aḥa said in the name of R. Assi: On that day begins the favourable season for

[1] Their sins had driven Him out, as it were.
[2] Ta'an, 30*b*. [3] In a ritual bath to purify them.
[4] In the Mishnah the reading is: 'And the young man replied.' The comment on '*the day of his espousals*', etc., is unconnected with the statement of R. Simeon, but was added to the Mishnah so that the Tractate should end with a note of consolation.
[5] Ex. XXXIV. The Rabbis calculated that this happened on the tenth of the seventh month, which is the date of the Day of Atonement.

cutting down trees [for the fuel required in the Temple], because all timber cut down then does not become grub-eaten, while it has been taught[1]: Any wood in which a worm or grub is found is unfit for use upon the altar. R. Abba b. Kahana and R. Assi said in the name of 'Ulla who derived it from Rabbi [Judah the Prince]: On that day Hosea the son of Elah abolished the guards whom Jeroboam the son of Nebat had set upon the roads.[2]

R. Kahana asked Rab: Is it possible that [Hosea] can have accomplished so much good, and yet it is reported of him, *Against him came up Shalmaneser king of Assyria*, etc. (II Kings XVII, 3)? But this happened to him because he removed the chain from off his own neck and set it round the necks of the masses,[3] and he did not say, 'Let all the people go up and pray,' but 'Let whoever wants to go up do so'.

R. Samuel b. Naḥmani (others state this in the name of R. Samuel b. Isaac): It was the day on which the tribes were permitted to intermarry,[4] for it is said, *And every daughter, that possesseth an inheritance in the tribes of the children of Israel*, etc. (Num. XXXVI, 8), and it is written, *So shall no inheritance remove from one tribe to another tribe*, etc. (*ib.* 9).[5] Is it then possible for a daughter to inherit land belonging to two tribes?[6] Deduce from this statement that her father was of one tribe and her mother of another.[7]

The Rabbis say: It was the day when the tribe of Benjamin was allowed to re-enter the Community; for

[1] Mid. II, 5.
[2] To prevent the people from going to Jerusalem on the Festivals.
[3] He left it optional with the people whether they should make the pilgrimage instead of making it obligatory.
[4] Therefore it was particularly appropriate that men should choose their brides on that day (Mah.).
[5] I.e., in view of this injunction, how can the preceding verse speak of a daughter possessing an inheritance in the tribes of Israel?
[6] Lit. 'whence it appears that a daughter might inherit from two tribes'. (The E.V. '*in any tribe*' is not literal.)
[7] I.e., in v. 8, Scripture envisages the injunction against the intermarrying of tribes as abrogated (v. B.B. 121*a*, where this is deduced from the text).

it is written, *Cursed be he that giveth a wife to Benjamin* (Judg. XXI, 18). R. Joḥanan said: They cited a text in virtue of which they brought the tribe near, and they cited a text in virtue of which they repelled it. They cited a text in virtue of which they brought it near, viz. *A nation and a company of nations shall be of thee* (Gen. XXXV, 11)[1]; and they cited a text in virtue of which they repelled it, viz. *Ephraim and Manasseh, even as Reuben and Simeon, shall be mine* (*ib.* XLVIII, 5),[2] showing that the Benjamites were not to be reckoned with their brethren. R. Judah said in the name of Samuel: It was the day when permission was given to the tribes to intermarry. R. Mathna said: It was the day when they allowed the slain of Bethar[3] to be buried.

R. Eliezer the Great said: It is quite right [to cut the wood for the altar] on the fifteenth of Ab[4]; but from then onward the power of the sun declines and they do not cut wood for the altar. R. Menasia remarked: The day was called 'the day of breaking the axe'.[5] From the day onward, whoever increases[6] increases [his years], and whoever does not increase study decreases [the duration of his life].

R. Abin and R. Joḥanan said: It was the day when the grave-digging ceased for those who died in the wilderness.[7] R. Levi said: On every eve of the ninth of Ab Moses used to send a herald throughout the camp and announce, 'Go out to dig graves'; and they used to go

[1] According to Rabbinic interpretation, this was a promise to Jacob of further issue to be born to him. Therefore '*nation*' is explained as Benjamin who was then unborn, and '*a company of nations*' as Ephraim and Manasseh who became Jacob's children by adoption. The deduction drawn is that Benjamin must be included among the tribes despite the sin committed.

[2] In the preceding verse Jacob recalled that God had said to him '*I will make of thee a company of nations*', not as in Gen. XXXV, 11, '*a nation and* a company of nations.' '*A nation,*' referring to Benjamin, is omitted to indicate that this tribe would one day have to be excluded.

[3] Where Bar Kokeba was defeated by the Romans.

[4] M.K. translates: they rested . . . Ab, for from then, etc.

[5] Since no more use was required of it for the time being.

[6] Study of Torah, continuing it at night, now that the evenings begin to lengthen.

[7] The penalty of Num. XIV, 23 was completed.

out and dig graves in which they slept. On the morrow he sent out a herald to announce, 'Arise and separate the dead from the living.' They would then stand up and find themselves in round figures 15,000 short of 600,000.[1] In the last of the forty years, they acted similarly and found themselves in undiminished numerical strength.[2] They said, 'It appears that we erred in our calculation'[3]; so they acted similarly on the nights of the 10th, 11th, 12th, 13th, and 14th. When the moon was full[4] they said, 'It seems that the Holy One, blessed be He, has annulled that decree from us all'; so they proceeded to make [the fifteenth] a holiday. Their sins subsequently caused it to become a day of mourning in this world, in the twofold destruction of the Temple. That is what is written, '*Therefore is my harp turned to mourning, and my pipe into the voice of them that weep.*' Hence *and the people wept that night*[5] (Num. XIV, 1). Since they sinned they were exiled; and since they were exiled, Jeremiah began to lament over them, '*How sitteth solitary.*'

XXXIV

For the mountains will I take up a weeping and wailing, etc. (Jer. IX, 9). R. Aḥa said: Nebuchadnezzar gave Nebuzaradan three orders concerning Jeremiah, viz. *Take him, and look well to him* (*ib.* XXXIX, 12)—to him, but not to his people; '*and do him no harm*'—do it not to him, but with his people act as cruelly as you wish; '*but do unto him even as he shall say unto thee*'—this applies to him, but not to his people. Jeremiah, however, beheld a band of young men set in neck-chains; so he put his head among them, but Nebuzaradan came and removed him from them. He then beheld a band of old men fastened with fetters; so he put his head among them, but Nebuzaradan came and removed him from them.

[1] I.e. one-fortieth of the adults died each year.
[2] No death had occurred that night.
[3] Of the new moon and it had not been the night of the ninth of Ab.
[4] So that it was certain that the ninth of the month had passed.
[5] Because of sin, the ninth of Ab became a night of weeping.

Nebuzaradan said to Jeremiah, 'I see one of three possibilities in you: either you are a false prophet, or you are impervious to pain, or you are a shedder of blood. Either you are a false prophet, because all these years you prophesied against this city that it would be destroyed, yet since it has been destroyed you are deeply distressed. Or you have a contempt for pain, because I have no desire to do you harm but you wish to do yourself harm, as though to say, "I take no notice of pain." Or you are a shedder of blood, because the king gave me strict orders concerning you not to harm you, but you wish harm to be done to yourself so that the king may hear of it and put me to death.' Finally he said to him, 'If it is pleasing in your sight, come and I will look well after you'; but he refused, as it is mentioned in the end of the chapter, until it was told him by the mouth of the Almighty. That is what is written, *The word which came to Jeremiah from the Lord* (Jer. XL, 1). What was that word? God said to Jeremiah, 'If thou remainest here, I will go with them into captivity, and if thou goest with them, I will remain here.' He spake before Him, 'Sovereign of the Universe, if I go with them, what good can I do for them? So let their King, their Creator, go with them, for He can do them much good.' Hence it is written, *After that Nebuzaradan the captain of the guard had let him go (ib.)*. '*Being bound in chains*' (*ib.*): R. Aḥa said: If it is possible to say so, both He and Jeremiah were bound in chains. As a parallel it is written, *I*[1] *was among the captives* (Ezek. I, 1).

To where does the prophecy of Jeremiah extend?[2] R. Jacob and R. Abba (another version is: R. Eleazar and R. Joḥanan) [gave varying answers]. One said: Down to *He that scattered Israel doth gather him* (Jer. XXXI, 10). The other said: Down to *and there is hope for thy future, saith the Lord; and thy children shall return to their own border* (*ib.* 17).

[1] Viz. God. Yalkut Jer. 327 reads preferably: *I was among the captives* means I (Ezekiel) and He.

[2] This reading is difficult to explain. A preferable variant is: 'What was that word?' i.e. what message did God deliver to him then?

Upon Jeremiah's return, he found fingers cut off and cast upon the mountains. He collected them, embraced, fondled, and kissed them, placed them in his cloak, and said to them, 'My children, did I not warn and tell you, *Give glory to the Lord your God, before it grow dark, and before your feet stumble upon the mountains of twilight* (*ib.* XIII, 16)?' With reference to that time it is said, *For the mountains will I take up a weeping and wailing, and for the pastures of the wilderness a lamentation* (*ib.* IX, 9), i.e. for those beautiful and praiseworthy mountains[1] will I take up a weeping and wailing, for the excellent men of Jacob who have been turned into a subject for lamentation. '*And they hear not the voice of the cattle* (miḳneh),' i.e. because they did not listen to the voice of words of Torah or to the voice of the words of prophecy, but [they only listened to] '*miḳneh*', that means to the voice of the seducer (*meḳanne*'), and provoked Him with idolatry, concerning which it is stated, *They roused Him to jealousy with strange gods* (Deut. XXXII, 16). '*Therefore both the fowl of the heavens and the beast are fled and gone.*' R. Jose b. Ḥalafta said: For fifty-two years no bird was seen flying in the land of Israel. What is the proof? '*Both the fowl of the heaven and the beast are fled and gone.*' The word for beast (*behemah*) has the numerical value of fifty-two.[2]

R. Ḥanina said: Forty years before [the exile occurred], palm-trees were planted in Babylon, to indicate that sweet species of fruit accustom the tongue to the Torah. R. Ḥanina b. Abbahu said: There are seven hundred species of clean fish, eight hundred of clean grasshoppers, and birds beyond number; and they all went into exile with Israel to Babylon; and when the people went back, they returned with them excepting one species of fish called 'mullet'. But how did the fish go into exile? R. Huna said in the name of R. Jose: They went into exile by the way of the deep and returned the same way.

R. Zera said: Come and see how irrepressible is the

[1] Symbolical of the flower of Israel.
[2] בהמה = ב (2) and ה (5) and מ (40) and ה (5) = 52.

land of Israel,[1] since it still produces fruits. And why does it produce them? R. Ḥanina and R. Joshua b. Levi [give varying answers]. One said: Because they manure it. The other said: Because they turn over its soil.[2]

R. Judan said: For seven years there was fulfilled against them, *The whole land thereof is brimstone, and salt* (Deut. XXIX, 22). Why that length of time? Because of *He shall make a firm covenant with many for one week*[3] (Dan. IX, 27). How did the Cutheans in the land manage? They sowed it in strips; as they sowed here it was burned up and as they sowed there it was burned up. It happened that a man was standing and ploughing in the valley of Beth Arba.[4] His hand grasped the ploughshare when a piece of burning earth jumped up and burned his arm, to fulfil that which is written, '*The whole land thereof is brimstone and salt and a burning.*'

Rabbah b. Kahana said: They[5] are not from the hollows of the earth nor from the deserts of the earth but depend upon Him, to fulfil that which was said, *And the fear of you and the dread of you shall be upon every beast of the earth* (Gen. IX, 2). But in the hereafter all will return; as it is written, *And the land that was desolate shall be tilled, whereas it was a desolation in the sight of all that passed by* (Ezek. XXXVI, 34).

[1] Although it is in the possession of idolaters since Israel was driven out.
[2] The soil cannot display ingratitude! (Mah.).
[3] '*Week*' represents a period of seven years.
[4] Emend to 'Beth Arbel', i.e. Arbela, north of Tiberias.
[5] The text is uncertain. This passage apparently is a continuation of what is related above about the fishes, grasshoppers, and birds accompanying Israel into and from captivity. The Midrash declares that the revival of the land of Israel will not be brought about by such means, but simply by the Divine will.

Chapter I

1. How (ekah) doth the city sit solitary! (I, 1). Three uttered prophecies using the word *ekah*, viz. Moses, Isaiah, and Jeremiah. Moses said, *How can I myself alone bear your cumbrance!* (Deut. I, 12). Isaiah said, *How is the faithful city become a harlot!* (Isa. I, 21). Jeremiah said, How doth the city sit solitary!

R. Levi said: It may be likened to a matron who had had three groomsmen: one beheld her in her happiness, a second beheld her in her infidelity, and the third beheld her in her disgrace. Similarly, Moses beheld Israel in their glory and happiness and exclaimed, '*How can I myself alone bear your cumbrance!*' Isaiah beheld them in their infidelity and exclaimed, '*How is the faithful city become a harlot!*' Jeremiah beheld them in their disgrace and exclaimed, How doth the city sit solitary!

[The disciples] requested Ben 'Azzai saying, 'Master, expound to us something connected with the Book of Lamentations.' He said to them: 'Israel did not go into exile until they had repudiated the Divine Unity, circumcision which had been given to the twentieth generation,[1] the Decalogue, and the Pentateuch. Whence have we this? From the letters constituting the word *ekah*.'[2]

R. Levi said: Israel did not go into exile until they had repudiated the thirty-six ordinances in the Torah for which the penalty is excision,[3] and also the Decalogue. Whence have we this? From the numerical value of the letters constituting the words *Ekah* and *badad* ('solitary').[4]

R. Berekiah said in the name of R. Abdimi of Ḥaifa: It may be likened to a king who had a son. So long as he obeyed the will of his father he clothed him in garments of fine wool, but when he disregarded his will he clothed him

[1] Abraham, who first received the commandment of circumcision, belonged to the twentieth generation from Adam.
[2] The *aleph* indicates one (the Divine Unity), the *yod* ten (the Decalogue), the *kaph* twenty (circumcision), and *he* five (the Pentateuch).
[3] I.e. where the text states *That soul shall be cut off from its people*.
[4] The numerical value of the first is thirty-six and of the second ten.

in exiles' garments. Similarly with Israel. So long as they obeyed the will of the Holy One, blessed be He, it is written, *I clothed thee also with richly woven work* (Ezek. XVI, 10). (R. Sima said: The word means 'in purple garments', and Onkelos[1] renders by 'embroidered garments'.) But when they disregarded the will of the Holy One, blessed be He, He clothed them in exiles' (*bedadin*) garments, as it is written, HOW DOTH THE CITY SIT SOLITARY—BADAD!

R. Naḥman reported that Samuel said in the name of R. Joshua b. Levi: The Holy One, blessed be He, summoned the ministering angels and said to them: 'If a human king had a son who died and mourns for him, what is it customary for him to do?' They replied, 'He hangs sackcloth over his door.' He said to them, 'I will do likewise.' That is what is written, *I clothe the heavens with blackness, and I make sackcloth their covering* (Isa. L, 3). [He again asked them,] 'What does a human king do [when mourning]?' They replied, 'He extinguishes the lamps.' He said to them, 'I will do likewise'; as it is said, *The sun and the moon are become black, and the stars withdraw their shining* (Joel IV, 15). 'What does a human king do?' They replied, 'He overturns his couch.'[2] He said to them, 'I will do likewise'; as it is stated, *Till thrones were cast down,*[3] *and One that was ancient of days did sit* (Dan. VII, 9)—if it is possible to say so, they were overturned.[4] 'What does a human king do?' They replied, 'He walks barefoot.' He said to them, 'I will do likewise'; as it is stated, *The Lord, in the whirlwind and in the storm is His way, and clouds are the dust of His feet* (Nahum I, 3).[5] 'What does a human king do?' They replied, 'He

[1] So the text. The Biblical translation of Onkelos is, however, in Aramaic, whereas the rendering here given consists of two Greek words; the reference must therefore be to Akylas, who produced a Greek translation.
[2] This was an ancient custom; cf. Tal. B. M.Ḳ. 15*a*. It was subsequently discontinued owing to the fact that a differently constructed couch came into use which made it impracticable.
[3] This is A.V., which agrees better with the Midrash's interpretation than E.V.
[4] As a sign of mourning.
[5] If the feet are covered with dust they must be without covering.

rends his purple robes.' He said to them, 'I will do likewise'; as it is written, *The Lord hath done that which He devised* (bizza' emrato) *He hath performed His word* (Lam. II, 17). (R. Jacob of Kefar-Ḥanan explained: What means '*bizza' emrato*'? He rent His purple.)[1] 'What does a human king do?' They replied, 'He sits in silence.' He said to them, 'I will do likewise'; as it is stated, *He sitteth alone and keepeth silence* (*ib.* III, 28). 'What does a human king do when mourning?' They replied, 'He sits and weeps.' He said to them, 'I will do likewise'; as it is written, *And in that day did the Lord, the God of hosts, call to weeping, and to lamentation, and to baldness* (Isa. XXII, 12).[2]

Another interpretation of HOW DOTH THE CITY SIT SOLITARY!: Jeremiah said to Israel: What do you see in an idol that you so yearn for it? If it possessed a mouth so as to be able to argue, we would have spoken thus and thus.[3] Since, however, [it is incapable of speech,] let us state its position and let us state His.[4] Let us state its position: *Thus saith the Lord: Learn not the way of the nations, and be not dismayed at the signs of heaven; for the nations are dismayed at them* (Jer. X, 2). And let us state His: *Thus shall ye say unto them: The gods that have not made the heavens and the earth, these shall perish* (*ib.* 11). But *Not like these is the portion of Jacob; for He is the former of all things, and Israel is the tribe of His inheritance; the Lord of hosts is His name* (*ib.* 16).

R. Judah and R. Nehemiah comment. R. Judah says: The word '*ekah*' implies nothing else than reproof; as it is stated, *How* (ekah) *do ye say: We are wise, and the Law*

[1] The verb is connected with *bizza'* 'to tear' and the noun is read as *imrato* 'His state robe'. Here it alludes to the curtain before the Holy of Holies which He allowed Titus to rend.

[2] *Var. lec.* adds: 'What does a mortal king do? He sits solitary. So will I do likewise. Hence it is written, HOW SITTETH SOLITARY.' This reading is preferable, since without it the whole passage is irrelevant in its present position ('E.J.).

[3] Presenting the case against idolatry, and the idols would have to admit the justice of our words.

[4] Let us show how powerless the idol is and how powerful is God; cf. Ex. R. XVI, 2. This comment is based on the reading of איכה as two words: אי כה, 'how (could ye speak) thus,' or, 'if (you had a tongue we would speak) thus.'

of the Lord is with us? (*ib.* VIII, 8). R. Nehemiah says: The word '*ekah*' implies nothing else than lament; as it is stated, *And the Lord God called unto the man, and said unto him: Where art thou*—ayyekah? (Gen. III, 9),[1] meaning, 'woe unto thee' (*oi lekah*).

When was the Book of Lamentations composed? R. Judah says: In the days of Jehoiakim.[2] R. Nehemiah said to him, 'Do we, then, weep over a dead person before he dies! When was the Book composed? After the destruction of the Temple; and behold proof is to be found in the words, HOW DOTH THE CITY SIT SOLITARY!'[3]

2. THE CITY THAT WAS FULL OF PEOPLE. R. Samuel taught: There were twenty-four thoroughfares in Jerusalem. Each thoroughfare had twenty-four side-turnings; each side-turning had twenty-four roads; each road had twenty-four streets; each street had twenty-four courts; each court had twenty-four houses; and each court residents double the number of those who came out of Egypt. Know that it was really so, because R. Eleazar related: It once happened that a merchant was journeying to Jerusalem with two hundred camels laden with pepper. He passed by the city of Tyre and met a tailor who was sitting at the city gate. The latter said to him, 'What are you carrying?' He replied, 'Pepper.' He asked him, 'Will you not let me have a small quantity?' He answered, 'No.'[4] He said to him, 'Then you can only sell it in another town.' When he arrived in Jerusalem, he met a tailor who was sitting at the entrance of the gate. The latter asked him, 'What are you carrying?' He answered, 'Go on with your cutting.' Another tailor met him and asked what he was carrying. He replied, 'Go on with your sewing.' The tailor said to him, 'Tell me; if I am able to buy it, well and good, and if not, I will bring you somebody who will purchase the whole stock. So what is it you are carrying?' He replied,

[1] V. p. 1, n. 7. [2] Before the destruction actually occurred—in that case it was composed as a warning (Y.A.). [3] Lit. 'how hath sat'. At all events it implies that the calamity had taken place.
[4] He would only sell the whole of his stock to one purchaser

'Pepper.' The tailor conducted him to a dwelling-place, showed him a heap of *dinars*, and said to him, 'Look at this coin. If it has currency in your country, take of them [for your pepper].' On the morrow the merchant went to walk in the street and met a friend who asked him what he was carrying [as wares]. He answered, 'Pepper.' The friend said to him, 'Will you sell me some for a hundred *dinars*, as I am giving a party to-day?' He replied, 'I have already disposed of it to a certain person.' He went to this man and inquired, 'Have you the pepper which you bought? Let me have a little of it because I am giving a party.' He answered, 'What can I say to you? I have already sold it to a certain tailor, but I will speak to him and he will let you have it.' He went and found the house [full of buyers], so that those who were in the first room secured an ounce each, and those in the second room half an ounce each, while those in the third received no attention at all. This is to fulfil what was said, THE CITY THAT WAS FULL OF PEOPLE.

If you wish to know how many multitudes there were in Jerusalem, you can ascertain it from the priests. R. Joshua b. Levi said: It may be likened to a heap which stood in the market-place, and everybody tried to estimate its quantity, but they could form no idea. There was a wise man who said to them, 'You want to estimate its quantity? You can arrive at it from the amount of *terumah*[1] which is taken from it.' Similarly if you wish to know how many multitudes there were in Jerusalem, you can ascertain it from the priests. That is what is written, *And Solomon offered for the sacrifice of peace-offerings, which he offered unto the Lord, two and twenty thousand oxen, and a hundred and twenty thousand sheep* (I Kings VIII, 63). We have learnt that a bull was offered by twenty-four priests, and a ram by eleven.[2] This refers to the first Temple; but with regard to the second Temple, [we may learn from this]. King Agrippa once wished to know how many multitudes there were in Jerusalem. He said to the priests, 'Set aside

[1] V. p. 36, n. 2. [2] Yoma 26*b*.

for me one kidney from each paschal offering.' They set aside for him 600,000 pairs of kidneys, double the number of those who went out of Egypt, and there was not a single paschal offering in which less than ten persons participated. R. Ḥiyya taught: It might be even forty or fifty persons, and this was besides those who were unclean and those who were on a journey afar off. On one occasion [the crowds] entered the Temple Mount, but it could not accommodate them; and there was an old man who was crushed to death. They consequently called that Passover 'the Passover of the crushed', because the old man was crushed to death.[1]

How used the Israelites to multiply? A man married his son at the age of twelve to a wife who was capable of bearing children. Then he married the grandson at the age of twelve, so that he himself did not attain the age of twenty-six without seeing grandchildren. This is to fulfil what was said, *And see thy children's children. Peace be upon Israel* (Ps. CXXVIII, 6).

3. HOW IS SHE BECOME AS A WIDOW! R. Abba b. Kahana said: They [the Israelites] did not go to the extreme of rebellion against justice, and it [justice] did not go to the extreme in punishing them. They did not go to the extreme of rebellion against justice, as it is said, *And the people were as murmurers* (Num. XI, 1)—'murmurers' is not written here but '*as murmurers*'. *The princes of Judah are like them that remove the landmark* (Hos. V, 10)—'remove' is not written here but '*like them that remove*'. *For Israel is like a stubborn heifer* (*ib.* IV, 16)—'is a stubborn heifer' is not written here but '*is like a stubborn heifer*'. It [justice] did not go to the extreme in punishing them. It is not written here 'she is become a widow' but AS A WIDOW—she is like a woman whose husband went to a distant country but with the intention of returning to her. *He hath bent His bow like an enemy* (Lam. II, 4)—'an enemy' is not written here but '*like an enemy*'. *The Lord*

[1] Quoted from Pes. 64*b*; v. notes *ad loc.* in the Sonc. ed. of the Talmud.

is become as an enemy (*ib.* 5)—'an enemy' is not written here but '*as an enemy*'.

Another interpretation of HOW IS SHE BECOME AS A WIDOW!: R. Ḥama b. Uḳba and the Rabbis offer explanations. R. Ḥama b. Uḳba said: It may be likened to a widow who demanded her alimony but not her marriage settlement.[1] The Rabbis said: It may be likened to a king who was angry with his consort and wrote out her *geṭ*, but got up and snatched it from her. Whenever she wished to remarry, he said to her, 'Where is your *geṭ?*' and whenever she demanded her alimony, he said to her, 'But have I not divorced you?' Similarly, whenever Israel wished to practise idolatry, the Holy One, blessed be He, said to them, '*Where is the bill of your mother's divorcement?*' (Isa. L, 1); and whenever they wished that He should perform miracles for them as formerly, the Holy One, blessed be He, said to them, 'Have I not already divorced you?' That is what is written, *I had put her away and given her a bill of divorcement* (Jer. III, 8).

Another interpretation of HOW IS SHE BECOME AS A WIDOW!: R. Akiba and the Rabbis offer explanations. R. Akiba says: She *is* a widow, and you state AS A WIDOW. The meaning, however, is: she is a widow bereft of the ten tribes[2] but not of the tribes of Judah and Benjamin. The Rabbis said: she was widowed of both,[3] but not of the Holy One, blessed be He, as it says, *For Israel is not widowed, nor Judah, of his God* (*ib.* LI, 5).

4. SHE THAT WAS GREAT AMONG THE NATIONS. But has it not just been mentioned 'that was full of

[1] At the marriage an agreement had been made that so long as she remained in her husband's house, she was entitled to maintenance, but not to the sum of money stipulated in the settlement which was due to her if she left. She forfeited this money to stay in her husband's house. In like manner Israel refused to be parted from the Temple.

[2] Which constituted Northern Israel. These were taken into captivity by Shalmaneser, king of Assyria, and finally lost to Jewry; v. II Kings XXV.

[3] Both the ten northern tribes and the two southern tribes, in that the latter, too, were sent into exile and Jerusalem was bereft of them. But she was never deserted by God.

people'?[1] Why, then, is it stated SHE THAT WAS GREAT AMONG THE NATIONS? The meaning is that she was great in intellect.[2] R. Huna said in the name of R. Jose: Wherever a Jerusalemite went in the provinces, they arranged a seat of honour for him to sit upon in order to listen to his wisdom.

A Jerusalemite went to a province, and the time arrived for him to die. He summoned the owner of the house and entrusted him with his property, saying, 'If my son comes from Jerusalem and performs for you three clever things give it to him; otherwise do not give it to him.' (Now the inhabitants of this place had arranged among themselves that no one of them should disclose the address of his neighbour to a stranger who inquired for it.) The man then died and departed to his eternal rest. After a while his son arrived, and when he reached the gate-entrance of that town he saw a man carrying a load of twigs. He asked, 'Will you sell that load of twigs?' The man answered that he was willing. 'Then take the money for it and carry it to So-and-so.'[3] He took the money and carried the twigs to the person named. As he went the son followed him until he arrived at the person's house. The man said to the house-owner, 'Heigh you! come and take this load of twigs!' He exclaimed, 'Did I ask you to bring me a load of twigs?' The man said to him, 'True, you did not tell me to do so, but it belongs to the person who is following me.' He immediately opened his house to the son who entered and they greeted one another. This was the first [clever act performed by him].

The house-owner asked him, 'Who are you?' He replied, 'I am the son of the man who died in your house.' He took him in and prepared a meal for him. Now this man had two sons and two daughters. When the hour of the repast came, he set before him at the meal five chickens as a course. When they were ready to eat, the host said to him, 'Take

[1] The Heb. could be translated 'that was great as a people', and so the words '*she that was great among the nations*' are superfluous.
[2] The inhabitants of Jerusalem were exceptionally clever.
[3] Naming the owner of the house where his father had died.

it and serve.' He answered, 'This is not mine [that I should serve it].' The man said to him, 'I wish you to take it and serve.' He thereupon apportioned one chicken between the man and his wife, a second between the two sons, a third between the two daughters, and set two before himself. They ate without making any comment. That was the second [clever act performed by him].

In the evening the host brought in a fat capon at the meal and asked him to serve it. He replied, 'This is not mine.' He said to him, 'Serve it at my request.' He thereupon apportioned the head to the host, the entrails to the wife, the two thighs to the two sons, the two wings to the two daughters, and set the whole body before himself. That was the third clever act [performed by him].

The host inquired, 'Is that how they serve in your place? You served on the first occasion and I said nothing; but now you act in this manner!' He replied, 'Did I not tell you that it was not mine? Nevertheless, what I have served I apportioned properly. On the first occasion you brought five chickens at the meal. You, your wife, and one chicken total three; your two sons and one chicken total three; your two daughters and one chicken total three; and I and two chickens total three. So have I taken any of your portion? On the present occasion you brought a hen. I took the head and gave it to you, because you are the head of the house. I took the entrails and set it before your wife, because children issue from the womb. I took the two thighs and gave them to your two sons, because they are the pillars of the house. I took the two wings and gave them to your two daughters, because in the future they will fly away from your house and go to their husbands. I took the [body which is shaped like a] boat, because I came in a boat and will leave in a boat. Now come and give me my property which my father entrusted to you and I will leave forthwith.' He handed him his property and he departed in peace. This is to fulfil what is said, SHE THAT WAS GREAT AMONG THE NATIONS, i.e. great in intellect.

Four Jerusalemites came to Athens and were given

hospitality by a certain man. In the evening he made a repast for them; and after they had eaten and drunk, he prepared four beds for them, one of them being damaged and supported by the next. When they got up to retire he said to himself, 'I have heard that the men of Jerusalem are very clever. I will listen to their conversation.' So he went to sleep in a room which was adjacent to their bedroom. In the night the man who was sleeping in the damaged bed got up and said to his companions, 'Do you think I am sleeping in a bed? I am sleeping on nothing else than the floor and I am suspended in mid-air.' Another of them remarked, 'Also the meat which we ate in the evening had the flavour of dog's flesh.' Another of them remarked, 'Also the wine which we drank in the evening had the flavour of a grave.' The fourth man exclaimed, 'Are you surprised at this? Why, our host is not even his father's son!' When the man heard what they said, he declared, 'One spoke the truth,[1] but three uttered lies.'

The next morning he went to the butcher and said, 'Give me some of the meat with which you supplied me last night.' He answered, 'I have no more of it.' He inquired, 'What was there special about it [that it had a peculiar flavour]?' He replied, 'I had one lamb which was sucking but its dam died. I also had a bitch and the lamb sucked from her. In the evening I was short of meat and you came to buy some; but I had no other and gave you some of it.' He said to himself, 'Two spoke the truth and two uttered lies.' He went to the wine-dealer and said to him, 'Give me some of the wine with which you supplied me last night.' He answered, 'I have no more of it.' He inquired, 'What was there special about it?' He replied, 'I had one vine which was planted over my father's grave. I pressed its grapes and poured the wine into casks. I was short of wine when you came to buy some; but I had no other and gave you some of it.' He said to himself, 'Three spoke the truth and one uttered a lie.' He then went to his mother and asked her, 'Whose child am I?' She answered,

[1] The one who remarked that he was sleeping on the floor.

'My son, you are your father's child.' He said to her, 'Tell me the truth, whose child am I? Otherwise I will cut your head off.' She then said to him, 'My son, your father was incapable of having a child. I was afraid that his relatives would deprive me of my property [if he died childless]. Did I do wrong by going and misconducting myself and thereby securing for you all this wealth and property?' He said to her, 'What do we see here? The Jerusalemites will come and make us all illegitimate. Come, let us agree not to give any of them hospitality.'[1]

5. A Jerusalemite went to see a merchant in Athens. On his arrival there he put up at an inn where he found several persons sitting and drinking wine. After he had eaten and drunk he wished to sleep there. They said to him, 'We have agreed among ourselves not to accept a guest until he has made three jumps.' He replied to them, 'I do not know how you jump. You do it before me and I will copy you.' One of them stood up and jumped, and found himself in the middle of the inn; a second jumped[2] and found himself by the door at the entrance of the inn; the third jumped and found himself outside. He got up and bolted the door in their faces and said to them, 'By your lives, what you intended to do to me I have done to you.'[3]

6. An Athenian came to Jerusalem where he met a child to whom he gave some money, saying, 'Go bring us[4] figs and grapes.' The child replied, 'Thank you, you with your money and I with my legs.' When he returned the man said to him, 'Take and share it.' The child placed the inferior fruit before himself and set the good before him. The man exclaimed, 'Rightly do they say that the people of Jerusalem are very clever. Since this child was aware that he had laid out no money of his own, he took the inferior for himself and gave me the good.' [The child thereupon said,] 'Come, now, let us cast lots; if I throw

[1] Cf. Sanh (Sonc. ed.), p. 709, n 4. [2] From where the first man finished. [3] Presumably the first two, after jumping, had followed the third to see how far he would get. [4] He used 'us' instead of 'me'.

and win, then I take your share, but if you win you take my share.'[1] They both agreed, and the child took the man's portion.

7. An Athenian came to Jerusalem where he met a child to whom he gave money, saying, 'Go and bring me something of which I can eat my fill and have something left over to take on my journey.' He went and brought him salt. The man said to him, 'Did I tell you to bring me salt!' He answered, 'But did you not tell me to go and bring you something of which you can eat your fill and leave some over to take on your journey? By your life, in this you have something of which you can eat your fill and leave something over to take on your journey!'

8. An Athenian came to Jerusalem; he found a mortar which had been thrown away [because it was cracked]. He picked it up and took it to a tailor, saying, 'Sew this broken mortar for me.' He produced a handful of sand and said, 'Twist this into threads for me and I will sew it.'

9. An Athenian came to Jerusalem where he met a child to whom he gave some money, saying, 'Bring me eggs and cheese.' On his return the man said to him, 'Show me which cheese is from a white goat and which from a black goat.' He replied, 'You are a grown-up man, so show me which egg is from a white hen and which from a black!'

10. An Athenian came to Jerusalem where he met a priest and said to him, 'How much of that load of wood will become smoke?' He replied, 'When moist it all becomes smoke; but when dry, a third becomes smoke, a third becomes ash, and a third fire.'[2] Where had he learnt this? From the wood on the altar.

11. An Athenian came to Jerusalem and entered a school where he found the children sitting, but their teacher was

[1] The child's proposal was on the principle of heads I win, tails you lose. [2] Reversed in Warsaw ed.: When *dry* it all becomes smoke, etc.

not present with them. He put questions to them which they answered. Then they said to him, 'Come, let us make up that if one of us asks a question which the other cannot answer, the latter's garments shall be taken from him.' He accepted the proposal and said, 'Since you belong to this place, you answer first.' They replied, 'You answer first, seeing that you are an old man.' [Whereupon they asked him,] 'What are the following: nine go out but eight come in, two pour out but one drinks, and twenty-four serve?' He was unable to answer them and they took his garments from him. He went to R. Joḥanan, their teacher, and said to him, 'Oh Rabbi, what great mischief there is among you; when a stranger comes among you, you deprive him of his garments!' He answered, 'I suppose they put a question to you to which you were unable to give a reply and they took your garments from you?' 'Yes,' he said. 'What was the question they asked you?' He related it to him, and the teacher told him, 'The nine which go in are the nine months of gestation, and the eight which come out are the eight days of circumcision; the two which pour out are the two breasts that both supply milk, and the one which drinks is the child that has been born; and the twenty-four which serve are the twenty-four months of nursing.'[1] He forthwith went and gave them the answer and regained his garments; and they quoted against him, *If ye had not plowed with my heifer, ye had not found out my riddle* (Judg. XIV, 18).

12. An Athenian came to Jerusalem where he studied for three and a half years to learn philosophy,[2] but could not master it. After the three and a half years had passed he bought a slave who was blind [in one eye]. He exclaimed [in disgust at his folly], 'After three and a half years [of studying] I have bought a slave who is [half] blind!' The seller said to him, 'By your life, he is very wise and can see at a distance.' When they came out of the gate, the

[1] In the East a child is not usually weaned until he is two years old.
[2] Lit. 'the language of wisdom.' The translation is approximate, and possibly it should simply be 'wisdom'.

slave said to him, 'Hasten that we may overtake the caravan.' 'Is there, then, a caravan in front of us?' he asked. 'Yes, and there is a she-camel in front of us which is blind in one eye. It has twins in its womb, and is carrying two skin-bottles, one containing wine and the other vinegar. It is four miles away and the camel-driver is a gentile.' He said to the slave, 'Oh you who belong to a stiff-necked people! With one eye, how do you know the camel is blind in one eye?' He answered, 'I notice that one side of the path has been grazed [by the camel] but not the other.' 'And how do you know that there are twins in its womb?' He replied, 'It lay down, and I noticed the trace of two of them.' 'And how do you know that it is carrying two skin-bottles, one containing wine and the other vinegar?' He answered, 'From the drippings; those of wine are absorbed in the ground but those of vinegar ferment.' And how do you know that the camel-driver is a gentile?' He replied, 'Because he urinated in the middle of the road; a Jew would not do that but retire to a corner.' 'And how do you know that it is four miles away?' He said to him, 'Up to four miles the mark of the camel's hoof is perceptible but not beyond that distance.'

13. An Athenian went to Jerusalem and made great fun of the inhabitants of that city They said, 'Who will go and bring him to us?' One said, 'I will go and bring him with his head shaven.' The Jerusalemite went to Athens and was given hospitality by that man. In the morning the two of them went out to walk in the market-place. One of his [the Jerusalemite's] sandals broke, and he said to a workman, 'Take this *tremis*[1] and repair this sandal.' He did it for him. The next day the two of them went out to walk in the market-place, and the other sandal broke. He said to the Athenian, 'Take this *tremis* and go and get the workman to repair my sandal.' He asked, 'Are, then, sandals so expensive with you?' 'Yes.' 'How many

[1] A Roman coin, a third of an *aureus* which was a gold piece. He paid him an absurdly high price.

dinars?' he inquired. 'Nine or ten,' he replied, 'and when they are cheap seven or eight *dinars*.' He said to him, 'If I were to come to you with a stock of sandals, could you sell them for me?' 'Certainly,' he answered, 'only you must not enter the city without first informing me.'

When the Athenian had finished his work, he bought a stock of sandals, set forth for Jerusalem, and sat at the gate-entrance of the city. He sent for the Jerusalemite, who came to him. When he arrived he said to him, 'We have agreed among ourselves that nobody may enter to sell his wares unless his head is shaven and his face blackened.' He replied, 'What do I care if my head is shaven so long as I sell my goods!' After shaving his head, he took him and seated him in the middle of the market-place. When a person came to buy sandals of him and asked him how much a pair cost he answered, 'There are some at ten *dinars* and some at nine; but I will not take less than eight.' On hearing this the would-be purchaser struck him on the head with a sandal and went away without buying. The Athenian said to the Jerusalemite, 'Did I treat you so badly when you were in my place?'[1] He replied, 'Henceforward do not jeer at the men of Jerusalem.'

14. A Samaritan set himself up as an interpreter of dreams. R. Ishmael b. R. Jose heard of this and said, 'Shall I not go and see this fool of a Samaritan who tricks his fellows?' He went and sat by him. A person came and said, 'In my dream I saw an olive tree feeding oil.' The Samaritan told him, 'The olive denotes light and oil denotes light; you will see much light.' R. Ishmael said to the interpreter, 'A curse upon you! The dream signifies that he had committed incest with his mother.'[2] Another person came and said, 'I dreamt that one of my eyes swallowed the other.' He told him, 'You will see much light.' R. Ishmael b. R. Jose said to the interpreter, 'A curse upon you! That man has two children and one of

[1] He understood now that a trick had been played on him.
[2] Cf. Ber. 56*b*

them committed incest with the other.' Another came to him and said, 'I dreamt that I swallowed a star.' He told him, 'You will see much light. The star denotes light and you are light, so it is light added to light.' R. Ishmael said to the interpreter, 'A curse upon you! That person has killed a Jew.' (Whence did R. Ishmael know this? From the verse, *Look now toward heaven and count the stars* (Gen. xv, 5).)[1] Another came to him and said, 'I dreamt that I had three eyes.' He told him, 'You will see much light.' R. Ishmael said to the interpreter, 'A curse upon you! He is a baker; two eyes were his own and the third represents the glowing oven.' Another came to him and said, 'I dreamt that I had four ears, and all the people were listening to my words.' He told him, 'You will be very famous.' R. Ishmael said to the interpreter, 'A curse upon you! He is a gatherer of thorns, and when he carries them everybody flees before him.' Another came and said to him, 'I dreamt that I was carrying a book containing twenty-four pages which were written on one side and erased on the other and then vice versa.' He told him, 'You will achieve greatness, and your business affairs will be numerous so that you will keep on writing and erasing.' R. Ishmael said to the interpreter, 'A curse upon you! He has a garment made up of twenty-four patches, and he sews in one place and it becomes torn in another place.' Another came and said, 'I dreamt that I was carrying a pole[2] to which was tied a bundle of lettuce.' He told him, 'You will achieve greatness.' R. Ishmael said to the interpreter, 'A curse upon you! He has a large store of wine which will all turn sour, and everybody will come and take some of it in their bottles, formed of gourds,[3] to pickle lettuce in.' Another came and said, 'I dreamt that everybody pointed the finger at me.' He told him, 'You will achieve greatness and all will point at you.' R. Ishmael said to the man, 'Give me a fee and I will interpret it for

[1] Referring to Abraham's descendants. [2] Radal substitutes *ḳanḳanya* (a vessel) for *ḳanya* (a cane, pole). The grounds of his interpretation are not clear. Perhaps he regarded the pole as symbolising the mace or sceptre of office. [3] Some delete this phrase.

you'; but he replied, 'It is already interpreted.' The same man came again and said to the interpreter, 'I dreamt that all the people were puffing at me with their cheeks and praising me with their fingers.' He told him, 'You will achieve greatness, and everybody will praise you with his cheeks.' R. Ishmael said to the interpreter, 'A curse upon you! He has a store of wheat; and when he dreamt that people pointed the finger at him, it denotes that the drippings of the rain had fallen upon it; and when he dreamt that people were puffing at him with their cheeks, it denotes that the wheat had become swollen [because of the moisture]; and when he dreamt that people praised him with their fingers, it denotes that the wheat had sprouted so that he would derive no profit therefrom.'

15. A Samaritan said, 'I will go and see a certain old Jew who jeers at everybody.'[1] He went and sat by him. He said to him, 'I dreamt of four cedars, four sycamores, a hide stuffed with straw, and an ox riding upon them.' R. Ishmael said to him, 'A curse upon you! The four cedars denote the four bedposts, the four sycamores represent the four legs of the bed, the hide stuffed with straw indicates its cords, and the ox riding upon them is the leather mattress upon which you sleep. You will climb into the bed but not descend from it.' And so it happened to him. Another came and said to him, 'I dreamt of an olive-tree at the time of planting.' He told him, 'You will see much light.' Another came and said to him, 'I dreamt of olives at the time of beating.' He told him, 'You must prepare your loins for blows.' He said to him, 'Rabbi, you gave the other man a favourable interpretation and me a bad one!' He replied, 'A curse upon you! He saw the olive at the time of planting, you at the beating!'

16. A disciple of R. Joḥanan sat before him listening to his instruction but unable to take it in. He asked him, 'Why are you unable to grasp what I say?' He replied,

[1] Meaning R. Ishmael. In Buber's text the reading is: 'I will go and have a laugh out of that old Jew.'

'I dreamt of three unpleasant things in the night and I do not know what they mean.' 'Tell me about them,' he said. 'I dreamt that I was told that I would die in the month of Adar, that I would not behold the month of Nisan, and that I would sow but not reap.' He told him, 'All three are good omens. You will die in Adar; that means you will die[1] in the glory (*hiddur*) of the Torah. You will not behold Nisan; that means you will not experience trials (*nisyonim*). You will sow but not reap; that means you will not bury the children born to you.'[2] Another said to him, 'I dreamt that I wore no breeches on my legs.' He told him, 'By your life, that is not a bad omen but a good one. When the Festival arrives you will have nothing.'[3] Whence did R. Johanan derive this? From the fact that the word for 'leg' (*regel*) also means 'festival'.

17. A man came to R. Jose b. Halafta and said, 'I dreamt that people told me to go to Cappadocia and receive my father's property.' He asked him, 'Had your father ever been to Cappadocia?' 'No,' was the reply. 'Go, then, and count the twentieth beam in your house.' He answered, 'There are not twenty.' 'Go, then, and count from top to bottom and from the bottom to the top, and where the number twenty ends, there you will find [your father's money].' He proceeded to do so, and found the property and became rich. Whence did R. Jose know this? In Greek *kappa* means 'twenty' and *dokoi* means 'beams'.[4]

18. A woman came to R. Eleazar and said, 'I dreamt that the beam of the house was split.' He told her, 'You will bear a son.' She departed and it happened so. On another occasion she came to inquire of him and said, 'I dreamt that the beam of the house was split.' He told

[1] Others translate: You will wax strong. Possibly he connected the word for death (*meth*) with the same word meaning people (cf. Deut. XXVI, 5: *bi-methe me'at*, lit. 'with few souls'), hence: You will be a man in the glory of the Torah (Mah.). [2] Reaping symbolising death.

[3] It is difficult to interpret this in a favourable sense. Buber's text reads: 'When the Festival arrives you will have fat meat,' indicated by the exposed leg. [4] Cf. Gen. R. LXVIII, 12 and cf. Ber. 56*b*.

her, 'You will bear a son.' She departed and it happened so. A third time she came to him and found the disciples assembled in the school, but their teacher was not present. She asked them, 'Where is your teacher?' They said, 'What do you want of him?' She said to them, 'Perhaps you are as wise as your teacher to interpret a dream which I saw.' They said to her, 'Tell us what you require and we will interpret it for you.' She told them, 'I dreamt that the beam of the house was split.' They replied, 'You will bury your husband.' When she left them she began to cry. R. Eleazar heard this and asked them, 'Why is this woman crying?' They answered, 'She came to inquire of you but did not find you.' He said to his disciples, 'What did she come to ask?' 'To interpret a dream,' they said. 'And what did you tell her?' They informed him; and he thereupon said to them, 'You have killed a man; for is it not written, *And it came to pass, as he interpreted it to us, so it was* (Gen. XLI, 13)? And did not R. Joḥanan say, "A dream follows its interpretation,[1] except when it is of wine; some dream they are drinking it and it is a good omen, while others dream they are drinking it and it is a bad omen"?'[2] R. Abbahu said: Dreams are of no consequence either for good or for ill.[3]

19. R. Joshua[4] was once walking along a path when a man met him who was also walking along it. He said to him, 'What are you doing?' He answered, 'I am walking along a path.' He retorted, 'You have well said that you are walking along a path, because robbers like you have trodden it.' He proceeded further and met a child sitting by the crossroad. He asked, 'Which is the nearest way to

[1] It has no absolute significance, save that of the interpretation given to it. The story is also found in Gen. R. LXXXIX, 8.

[2] In Ber. 55*b* R. Eleazar is reported as saying, 'A dream follows its interpretation,' and in 57*a* a teacher taught in the presence of R. Joḥanan: 'With the exception of wine,' etc.

[3] Sanh. 30*a* (Sonc. ed., p. 183). Lit. 'neither raise nor lower'.

[4] In 'Er. 53*b* the story is told in connection with R. Joshua b. Ḥananyah, that as he was walking along a path in a field a little girl rebuked him for being on private property; and when he claimed that it was a trodden path, she retorted, 'Robbers like you have trodden it.'

the city?' He replied, 'This way is near and far, and that way is far and near.' R. Joshua went along the road which was near and far; but as he approached the city he found gardens and orchards surrounding the wall [and he could not get through]. So he returned to the child and asked, 'My son, is that the nearest way to the city?' He replied, 'You are a sage in Israel! Did I not tell you that this way is near and far and that way far and near?' Thereupon R. Joshua exclaimed, 'Happy are ye, oh Israel, for you are all wise, from the oldest among you to the youngest.' He went on from there and met a child holding a covered dish. He asked, 'What have you got covered in that dish?' He answered, 'If my mother wanted you to know what I had, she would not have told me to cover it.' He proceeded on his way and met a child, whom he asked, 'What is the water of the city like?' He replied, 'Why worry? Garlic and onions are plentiful.'[1] When he entered the city, he met a little girl standing and filling her pitcher from the well. He said to her, 'Give me some water to drink.' She replied, 'Both for you and your ass.' When he had drunk and was turning to go away, he said to her, 'My daughter, you have acted like Rebekah.' She retorted, 'I acted like Rebekah but you have not acted like Eliezer!'[2]

It has been taught: We should leave over *pe'ah* of a dish prepared in *ḳederah*, but not of a dish prepared in an *ilpes*.[3] Now it is related that R. Joshua was once the guest of a

[1] They sweeten the water when it is not good.

[2] Who rewarded Rebekah's kindness with gifts (Gen. XXIV).

[3] Derek Ereẓ VI. In 'Er. 53*b* the reading is different: 'You do not leave *pe'ah* in the *ilpes* (a tightly covered stew pot) but you leave *pe'ah* in the plate.' It is possible that these are two complementary statements, and following Rashi *ad loc.* are to be explained thus: When food is poured from the pot into the plates, none is left over in the pot for the servants, but each diner must leave over some in his plate for them. This, however, holds good only of a dish prepared in a *ḳederah* (a boiling pot), but not of a dish prepared in an *ilpes* (a tightly covered stew pot); this is the reading in the Midrash, but is reversed in Derek Ereẓ. There seems no adequate reason for this distinction. Tosaf. in 'Er. suggests that in the case of the one it savours of greed not to leave anything over, but not in the case of the other. Perhaps the residue of food prepared in a *ḳederah* (or in an *ilpes*, in the reversed reading) would be fit for servants, but not of that prepared in an *ilpes*, which possibly was more handled.

widow. On the first day she brought him a dish of food which he ate leaving none for her as *pe'ah*. On the second day she brought him a dish which he again ate without leaving any for her as *pe'ah*. On the third day she over-salted for him a dish of pounded grain. When R. Joshua tasted it he pushed it aside. She asked, 'Rabbi, why have you pushed aside this dish of pounded grain?' He answered, 'I have already had a meal during the day.' She said, 'If you already had a meal during the day, why did you not decline the bread as you declined this pounded grain? Perhaps you have left it over as *pe'ah!* Why did you not leave it from the two dishes you ate as you have left it from this pounded grain?' Thereupon R. Joshua exclaimed, 'Never has anyone got the better of me except this widow, the little girl and those children, to fulfil that which is said, SHE THAT WAS GREAT AMONG THE NATIONS, i.e. great in intellect.'

20. AND PRINCESS AMONG THE PROVINCES, HOW IS SHE BECOME TRIBUTARY (LAMAS)! R. Joḥanan said: Because Israel transgressed the condition which they accepted at Sinai, for that reason they have become tributary. 'Sinai' and the word for TRIBUTARY (LAMAS) have the same numerical value.[1] R. Ishmael b. Naḥman said: Because Israel worshipped idols, for that reason they have become tributary. The word for 'tributary' and the word for 'idolatrous image' (*semel*) have the same letters. R. Berekiah said: The *semel* inverted it to become tributary[2]; while the Rabbis said: LAMAS means for the melting (*lemassa*) of the heart [because of tribulation].[3]

R. Uḳba said: On the night of the ninth of Ab[4] our father Abraham entered the Holy of Holies. The Holy One, blessed be He, seized him by the hand and walked with him in all directions. The Holy One, blessed be He, asked

[1] סיני (Sinai): ס (60) + י (10) + נ (50) + י (10) = 130; למס (TRIBUTARY): ל (30) + מ (40) + ס (60) = 130. [2] Just as למס is the inverted form of סמל.
[3] She who was mistress of provinces has now become craven-hearted.
[4] The anniversary of the destruction of the Temple.

him, '*What hath My beloved to do in My house?*' (Jer. XI, 15). He answered, 'My Lord, where are my children?' He said to him, 'They have sinned, and I have exiled them among the nations.' Abraham asked, 'Were there no righteous among them?' He replied, '*She* [Israel] *hath wrought lewdness* (*ib.*). Abraham said, 'Thou shouldest have considered the good among them.' He replied, 'The mass of them bad, were for it is written, "*She hath wrought lewdness, yea, even the multitudes.*"'[1] Abraham said, 'Thou shouldest have had regard to the covenant of circumcision in their flesh.' He replied, 'By thy life, they have repudiated it,[2] as it is stated, *And the hallowed flesh is passed from thee* (*ib.*). Not only that, but they rejoiced in each other's downfall'; as it is written, *When thou doest evil, then thou rejoicest* (*ib.*); and it is written, *And he that is glad at calamity shall not be unpunished* (Prov. XVII, 5).

Why is the Book of Lamentations composed as an alphabetical acrostic? R. Judah, R. Nehemiah, and the Rabbis suggest answers. R. Judah said: Because it is written, *Yea, all Israel have transgressed Thy law* (Dan. IX, 11), which is written [with all the letters] from *alef* to *taw;* therefore is this Book composed as an alphabetical acrostic, one corresponding to the other.[3]

21. R. Nehemiah said: Although Jeremiah cursed them with the alphabetical acrostic of Lamentations, Isaiah anticipated him and pronounced a healing for them verse by verse down to *Let all their wickedness come before Thee* (Lam. I, 22).[4]

22. SHE WEEPETH SORE (I, 2). It is written, *My tears have been my food day and night* (Ps. XLII, 4). R. Aḥa and

[1] Midrashic translation. E.V. '. . . *lewdness with many*'.
[2] This may be an anachronistic allusion to the Hellenistic Jews and the Judeo-Christians who underwent an operation to obliterate the evidence of circumcision; v. Sanh (Sonc. ed.), p. 672, n. 5. Or it may simply mean that they had slackened in the performance of this precept.
[3] Lamentation corresponding to sin. Buber's text reads: 'R. Judah said: Because they transgressed the Torah from *alef* to *taw*, therefore it is composed as an alphabetical acrostic. R. Nehemiah said: Because they transgressed the Torah, since it is written, *Yea*, etc., therefore it is composed, etc. The Rabbis said: Because they transgressed from *alef* to *taw*.' The first and last letters of the Hebrew alphabet.
[4] V. *infra*, § 23.

the Rabbis comment. R. Aḥa said: As food is constant so are my tears constant. The Rabbis said: Whoever weeps does not eat, as it is said, *Therefore she wept, and would not eat* (I Sam. I, 7). And thus[1] spake the Holy One, blessed be He, to Ezekiel, *Therefore, thou son of man, prepare thee stuff for exile* (Ezek. XII, 3). What means '*stuff for exile*'? R. Ḥiyya b. Abba and R. Simeon b. Ḥalafta suggest answers. R. Ḥiyya b. Abba said: A skin bottle, a mat, and a dish, and each of them serves two purposes. He puts flour into the bottle[2] and uses it as a pillow; he uses the dish as a vessel both for eating and drinking; and the mat is to sit on and also to sleep on. R. Simeon b. Ḥalafta said: It means a basket with four handles which can hold everything. Therefore the Holy One, blessed be He, said to Israel, *Thus shall Ezekiel be unto you a sign; according to all he hath done shall ye do* (*ib*. XXIV, 24). They, however, did not do so; but when they were exiled, one wanted to knead his dough but did not know in what. So he dug in the ground and made a pit in which he kneaded; and gravel adhered to the dough, and when he placed it in his mouth his teeth were blunted on it, to fulfil what was said, *He hath also broken my teeth with gravel stones* (Lam. III, 16). All this I did not take to heart; but when did I take it to heart? *While they say unto me all the day: Where is thy God?* (Ps. XLII, 4).

23. *In the night I will call to remembrance my song, I will commune with mine own heart; and my spirit maketh diligent search* (*ib*. LXXVII, 7). R. Judah b. R. Simon, R. Aibu, and the Rabbis say: Because they sinned from *alef* to *taw*, they are comforted from *alef* to *taw*. And so you find that all the severe prophecies which Jeremiah prophesied against Israel Isaiah anticipated and healed. Jeremiah said, *How doth the city sit solitary!* (Lam. I, 1); Isaiah said, *Then shalt thou say in thy heart: Who hath begotten me these?*

[1] 'And thus' is omitted in older MSS. ('E.J.) and should probably be deleted, as there is not such a close connection between the passage that follows and the preceding. [2] Yalḳuṭ reads: 'he puts water into the bottle.' This is more in keeping with its normal usage.

(XLIX, 21). Jeremiah said, *She weepeth sore in the night* (Lam. I, 2); Isaiah said, *Thou shalt weep no more; He will surely be gracious unto thee* (XXX, 19). Jeremiah said, *Judah is gone into exile because of affliction* (Lam. I, 3); Isaiah said, *He will assemble the dispersed of Israel* (XI, 12). Jeremiah said, *The ways of Zion do mourn* (Lam. I, 4); Isaiah said, *Hark! one calleth: Clear ye in the wilderness the way of the Lord* (XL, 3). Jeremiah said: *Her adversaries are become the head* (Lam. I, 5); Isaiah said, *And the sons of them that afflicted thee shall come bending unto thee* (LX, 14). Jeremiah said, *And gone is from the daughter of Zion all her splendour* (Lam. I, 6); Isaiah said, *And a redeemer will come to Zion* (LIX, 20). Jeremiah said, *Jerusalem remembereth the days of her affliction* (Lam. I, 7); Isaiah said, *For, behold, I create new heavens and a new earth; and the former things shall not be remembered, nor come into mind* (LXV, 17). Jeremiah said, *Jerusalem hath grievously sinned* (Lam. I, 8); Isaiah said, *I have blotted out, as a thick cloud, thy transgressions* (XLIV, 22). Jeremiah said, *Her filthiness was in her skirts* (Lam. I, 9); Isaiah said, *When the Lord shall have washed away the filth of the daughters of Zion* (IV, 4). Jeremiah said, *The adversary hath spread out his hand* (Lam. I, 10); Isaiah said, *The Lord will set His hand again the second time* (XI, 11). Jeremiah said, *All her people sigh, they seek bread* (Lam. I, 11); Isaiah said, *They shall not hunger nor thirst* (XLIX, 10). Jeremiah said, *Let it not come unto you, all ye that pass by* (Lam. I, 12); Isaiah said, *Until the spirit be poured upon us from on high* (XXXII, 15). Jeremiah said, *From on high hath He sent fire into my bones* (Lam. I, 13); Isaiah said, *I dwell in the high and holy place, with him also that is of a contrite and humble spirit* (LVII, 15).[1] Jeremiah

[1] The parallelism of the last two pairs of verses is not really apparent, though it can be made so by a forced interpretation. Mah. transposes them on the authority of Pesiḳ. R., thus: Jeremiah said, *Let it not come unto you, all ye that pass by! Behold, and see if there be any pain like unto my pain . . . wherewith the Lord hath afflicted me;* Isaiah said, *I dwell in the high and holy place to revive the spirit of the humble*—thus the Lord's affliction is set off by His reviving their spirits. Again, Jeremiah said, From on high *hath He sent fire into my bones;* Isaiah said, *Until the spirit be poured upon us* from on high. This gives the correct parallelism.

said, *The yoke of my transgressions is impressed by His hand* (Lam. I, 14); Isaiah said, *Loose thyself from the bands of thy neck* (LII, 2). Jeremiah said, *The Lord hath trampled down* [E.V. '*set at nought*'] *all my mighty men in the midst of me* (Lam. I, 15); Isaiah said, *Cast up, cast up the highway*,[1] *gather out the stones* (LXII, 10). Jeremiah said, *For these things I weep, mine eye, mine eye runneth down with water* (Lam. I, 16); Isaiah said, *For they shall see, eye to eye, the Lord returning to Zion* (LII, 8). Jeremiah said, *Zion spreadeth forth her hands; there is none to comfort her* (Lam. I, 17); Isaiah said, *I, even I, am He that comforteth you* (LI, 12). Jeremiah said, *The Lord is righteous* (Lam. I, 18); Isaiah said, *Thy people also shall be all righteous* (LX, 21). Jeremiah said, *I called for my lovers* [*for help*] (Lam. I, 19); Isaiah said, *Thou shalt call thy walls Salvation* (LX, 18). Jeremiah said, *See, O Lord, for I am in distress* (Lam. I, 20); Isaiah said, *And when ye see this, your heart shall rejoice* (LXVI, 14). Jeremiah said, *They have heard that I sigh* (Lam. I, 21); Isaiah said, *Comfort ye, comfort ye, My people* (XL, 1). Jeremiah said, *Let all their wickedness come before Thee* (Lam. I, 22); Isaiah said, *Even them will I bring to My holy mountain* (LVI, 7).[2]

Another interpretation of '*In the night I will call to remembrance my song*': R. Aibu and R. Judah b. Simon comment. R. Aibu says: The Community of Israel spake before the Holy One, blessed be He, 'I remember the breach wherewith I was shattered before Thee in the nights of [persecution by] the heathen kingdoms,' in accordance with what is stated, *Blessed be God the Most High, Who hath delivered*[3] *thine enemies into thy hands*

[1] I.e. make a highway by trampling the earth down.

[2] The contrast may lie in the fact that whereas Jeremiah spoke of their *wickedness* coming before God, Isaiah spoke of their being brought before God's holy mountain, which would naturally mean in their righteousness. Or it may lie in the ends of the verses: Jeremiah: . . . *for my sighs are many, and my heart is faint*; Isaiah: . . . *and make them joyful in My house of prayer*.

[3] '*My song*' (neginathi) is connected with '*delivered*' (miggen), but the Biblical text suggests the opposite of what it is quoted to prove, viz. victories instead of defeats. Therefore the version in Ex. R. XVIII, 5, is perhaps to be preferred: 'The Community of Israel spake, "I

(Gen. XIV, 20). R. Judah said: [The Community of Israel spake before Him,] 'I remember the songs which I sang before Thee in the nights,' in accordance with what is stated, *Therefore we will sing songs to the stringed instruments all the days of our life* (Isa. XXXVIII, 20). '*In the night,*' i.e. the night of Pharaoh, of which it is written, *And it came to pass at midnight* (Ex. XII, 29); and the night of Gideon on which he smote the camp of Midian and Amalek, as it is written, *And it came to pass the same night* (Judg. VII, 9); and the night of Sennacherib, of which it is written, *And it came to pass that night, that the angel of the Lord went forth*, etc. (II Kings XIX, 35). *I will commune with mine own heart*, i.e. I will speak with my heart. *And my spirit maketh diligent search*, i.e. I scrutinise my actions and exclaim, *Will the Lord cast off forever, and will He appease no more?* (Ps. LXXVII, 8). Heaven forfend! He has not abandoned nor will He abandon me, for it is written, *For the Lord will not cast off for ever* (Lam. III, 31). *And will He appease no more* (Ps. *loc. cit.*) nor allow Himself to be appeased?[1] In the past He caused others to be appeased. Moses was angry and it is stated, *And he would return* (weshab) *into the camp* (Ex. XXXIII, 11)—read here *weshub* ('and return').[2] Elijah was angry and it is stated, *And the Lord said unto him: Go, return on thy way to the wilderness of Damascus* (I Kings XIX, 15). And now will He neither appease others nor allow Himself to be appeased? *Is His mercy clean gone for ever?*

remember the breaches wherewith Thou didst shatter the enemies on my behalf in the night."' It is possible, however, that the verse '*who hath delivered* (miggen)', etc., is quoted merely to prove that *neginathi* means 'my disaster, destruction', the second verse being translated, 'who hath *destroyed* thine enemies,' as it is rendered in Ex. R. *loc. cit.*, but there is no actual parallelism in the *context*. Thus in Ex. R., which deals with the deliverance from Egypt, the verse is made to refer to the *enemies'* disasters; here, however, where *Israel's* disasters are being discussed, it is naturally interpreted in that vein.

[1] As the Midrash proceeds to explain: Will God no more appease others, as He made Moses and Elijah to be appeased, and will He no longer allow Himself, etc. Both meanings can be read into the Heb. לרצות by punctuating it לרצות (to appease—others) and לרצות (to be appeased) respectively.

[2] Read the verb as imperative. God commanded Moses to become reconciled with the people.

(Ps. LXXVII, 9)—what means *ha'efes* ('is clean gone')? R. Reuben said: It is a Greek word,[1] as it is stated, *And he shall say: No*—efes (Amos VI, 10).[2] R. Ḥanina b. Papa and R. Simon comment on the verse. R. Ḥanina said: Has the word which the Holy One, blessed be He, spake to Moses, viz. *And I will be gracious to whom I will be gracious* (Ex. XXXIII, 19), spent itself?[3] R. Simon said: Was it made final and confirmed by Jeremiah who said, *I have taken away My peace from this people* (Jer. XVI, 5)?[4]

Hath God forgotten to be gracious—ḥanoth? (Ps. LXXVII, 10), i.e. hath God forgotten His encamping (*ḥanotho*), [as it is said,] *According to the commandment of the Lord they remained encamped* (Num. IX, 20)? Has He forgotten *God, merciful and gracious* (Ex. XXXIV, 6)?[5] *Hath He in anger shut up His compassions? Selah.* (Ps. *loc. cit.*)—although He is angry His mercy is near.[6] But Zion declared, 'The Lord hath forsaken me and the Lord hath forgotten me,'[7] as it is written, *But Zion said: The Lord hath forsaken me* (Isa. XLIX, 14).

And I say: This is my weakness (ḥallothi), *that the right hand of the Most High could change* (Ps. LXXVII, 11). R. Alexandri said: The meaning is, because we did not entreat (*ḥillinu*) Thy presence in penitence, Thy right hand has changed. R. Samuel b. Naḥmani said: The meaning is, the oath which Thou didst make with us at Horeb has been desecrated (*nithḥallelah*), and therefore Thy right hand

[1] ἄφες 'let go'.

[2] Apparently understood: everything is gone.

[3] Is that promise of grace and mercy exhausted, so that '*His mercy is clean gone for ever*'?

[4] M.K. and 'E.J. render: Has that which was said by Jeremiah, viz. *I have . . . people*, been made final and confirmed, so that '*His mercy is clean gone for ever*'? Both comments are interpretations of this latter verse.

[5] The two words, *ḥanoth* (to be gracious) and *el* (God), are now interpreted: has He forgotten His encamping; and has He forgotten that He is an 'el (*God*), *merciful and gracious*'?

[6] Translating the אם in the Heb. 'even though': Even though He has shut Himself away from us in His anger, yet His compassions are everlasting—near.

[7] This is apparently irrelevant. Perhaps it should be rendered: Although He is angry, His mercy is near, and yet Zion declares . . . forgotten one! Surely Zion should not say thus! The Yalḳuṭ, however, omits it altogether

has changed. R. Simon said: Did you ever hear of the orb of the sun being sick so that it was unable to rise and function? Then seeing that [it is inconceivable that] His servants[1] should be afflicted with indisposition, can He be thus afflicted?[2] R. Isaac said: It may be likened to a warrior who had a great reputation in a province and all its inhabitants relied upon him, saying, 'Enemy troops will not enter here.' If enemy troops came to his city, as soon as he went out and confronted them they fled. But once troops came and he exclaimed, 'My right hand pains me.' With the Holy One, blessed be He, however, it is not so; but *Behold, the Lord's hand is not shortened, that it cannot save* (Isa. LIX, 1). '*That the right hand of the Most High could change*'—R. Simeon b. Laḳish said: If it is due to illness there is hope, because whoever is ill may in the end become well again; but if there is a change in His right hand there is no hope. That is the view of R. Joshua b. Levi, who said: *Thou canst not have utterly rejected us, and be exceedingly wroth against us* (Lam. V, 22)—if there is rejection there is no hope, but if there is anger there is hope, because whoever is angry may in the end be appeased.[3]

R. Simeon b. Yoḥai said: The Holy One, blessed be He, spake to Israel: 'You are weeping [now] with a frivolous weeping, but in the end you will weep with a real weeping.' Where did Israel weep with a frivolous weeping? *And Moses heard the people weeping, family by family* (Num. XI, 10), *And all the congregation lifted up their voice, and cried* (*ib.* XIV, 1). And where did they weep with a real weeping? R. Aibu and R. Judah b. R. Simon give answers. R. Aibu said: Once in Ramah and once in Babylon. In Ramah, for it is written, *A voice is heard in Ramah, lamentation, and bitter weeping* (Jer. XXXI, 15); in Babylon, for it is written, *By the rivers of Babylon, there we sat down, yea, we wept* (Ps. CXXXVII, 1). R. Judah b. R. Simon said: Once in the province of Judah and once in Babylon. In the province of

[1] The heavenly bodies.
[2] This stresses the possessive 'my' in the text: *This is* my *infirmity*, but not His, that has caused His right hand to change.
[3] In the Midrash to this verse, the saying is quoted in the name of R. Simeon b. Laḳish.

Judah [it is said], SHE WEEPETH SORE IN THE NIGHT (I, 2); in Babylon [it is said], '*By the rivers of Babylon*,' etc. R. Aibu said: The Holy One, blessed be He, spake to Israel: 'As a reward for weeping I will restore your captivity'; for is it not written, *Thus saith the Lord: Refrain thy voice from weeping . . . and there is hope for thy future, saith the Lord* (Jer. XXXI, 16 f.)?

SHE WEEPETH SORE[1] IN THE NIGHT—WEEPING on account of one calf, SHE WEEPETH on account of the two calves.[2] Another interpretation: [WEEPING] on account of Judah, [SHE WEEPETH] on account of Zion and Jerusalem. Another interpretation: WEEPING on account of the exile of the ten tribes, SHE WEEPETH on account of the exile of the tribes of Judah and Benjamin. Another interpretation: she weeps and makes others to weep with her. Thus: she weeps and makes the Holy One, blessed be He, to weep with her, for it is written, *And in that day did the Lord, the God of hosts, call to weeping, and to lamentation* (Isa. XXII, 12)[3]; she weeps and makes the Ministering Angels to weep with her, for it is written, *Behold, their valiant ones*[4] *cry without*—ḥuẓah (*ib*. XXXIII, 7). (R. Ze'ira said: It is written *ḥiẓah*,[5] i.e. it is unnatural (*ḥiẓah*) for him [Abraham] to slay him [Isaac]. R. Berekiah said: Its meaning is as in the verse, *And He brought him forth abroad*—ḥuẓah (Gen. XV, 5).[6]) [Again,] she weeps and makes heaven and earth to weep with her, for is it not written, *The sun and the moon are become black* (Joel II, 10)? She weeps and makes mountains and hills to weep with her, as it is written, *I beheld the mountains, and,*

[1] Lit. 'weeping she weepeth'. [2] I.e. the golden calf and the two calves set up by Jeroboam (I Kings XII, 28).

[3] Interpreting the verse as a summons by God *to Himself* to weep.

[4] Understood to mean the angels. [5] The word for '*without*' is written without a *waw* and may be read as *ḥiẓah*. V. Gen. R. LVI, 5.

[6] The point of R. Berekiah's quotation is not clear. Mah. maintains that he holds that '*Behold, their valiant ones cry* ḥuẓah' (E.V. '*without*'), is meant literally 'without', i.e. in heaven, and to prove this he quotes '*And he brought him forth* ha-ḥuẓah' (E.V. '*abroad*'), which is likewise translated 'in heaven' in Gen. R. XLIV, 12. According to R. Ze'ira, the first verse is rendered: Behold, their valiant ones (the angels) cry, 'It is unnatural!' The whole passage is a digression.

lo, they trembled (Jer. IV, 24). She weeps and makes the seventy nations to weep with her. R. Phinehas[1] said: The seventy bulls which Israel used to offer on the Feast of Tabernacles corresponded to the seventy nations, so that the world should not be depopulated through[2] them. [Further,] she weeps and makes the Community of Israel to weep with her, for is it not written, '*And all the congregation lifted up* (watissa) *their voice, and cried*' (Num. XIV, 1)? R. Ḥunia taught in the name of R. Nehemiah: The word is written *watishsha* ('lend'), i.e. an evil loan was lent to the generations,[3] as, e.g., the word is used in *When thou dost lend* (tashsheh) *thy neighbour* (Deut. XXIV, 10).

24. IN THE NIGHT. Why in the night? Because sound only travels in the night; therefore it is stated IN THE NIGHT. R. Aibu said: Night draws lamentation along with it.[4] A woman in the neighbourhood of R. Gamaliel had a grown-up son who died and she used to weep for him at night. R. Gamaliel, hearing her voice, was reminded of the destruction of the Temple, and wept with her until his eyelashes fell out. When his disciples noticed this, they removed her from his neighbourhood.[5]

25. AND HER TEARS ARE ON HER CHEEKS. That means, on account of her priests,[6] as it is stated, *They shall give unto the priest the shoulder, and the two cheeks, and the maw* (Deut. XVIII, 3). Another interpretation: on account of her mighty men, as it is stated, *And he* [Samson] *found a new jawbone of an ass* (Judg. XV, 15). Another interpretation: on account of her judges, as it is stated, *They smite the judge of Israel with a rod upon the cheek* (Micah IV, 14).

[1] Suk. 55*b* has R. Eleazar. The bulls were offered in atonement for the sins of the heathen peoples to save the world from being destroyed because of their evil. Hence the heathens may well weep with her, because there is none now to atone for them. [2] Or perhaps 'of'.
[3] Because that weeping had its sequel in the weeping of the ninth of Ab.
[4] More sympathy is aroused when weeping is heard in the night.
[5] Cf. Sanh. 104*b* (Sonc. ed., p. 710).
[6] Who suffered by the destruction of the Temple in being deprived of the portions of the offerings which were their perquisite.

Another interpretation: on account of her young men. You find that when the enemy entered the Temple, they seized the young men and bound their hands behind their backs. They wept and the tears ran down their cheeks. They were unable to wipe them, and the tears ate themselves[1] into their cheeks like the scar of a boil.

26. SHE HATH NONE TO COMFORT HER. R. Levi said: Wherever it says '*hath none*', it indicates that there would be in the future.[2] [For instance], *And Sarai was barren; she had no child* (Gen. XI, 30); but she did have one later, as it is said, *And the Lord remembered Sarah* (*ib.* XXI, 1). Similarly, *But Hannah had no children* (I Sam. I, 2); she did have them later, as it is said, *So the Lord remembered Hannah* (*ib.* II, 21). Similarly, *She is Zion, there is none that careth for her* (Jer. XXX, 17); but she will have one later, as it is said, *And a redeemer will come to Zion* (Isa. LIX, 20). In like manner you say, SHE HATH NONE TO COMFORT HER; but she will have later, as it is said, *I, even I, am He that comforteth you* (*ib.* LI, 12).

27. ALL HER FRIENDS HAVE DEALT TREACHEROUSLY WITH HER, THEY ARE BECOME HER ENEMIES. R. Jacob of Kefar-Ḥanan said: This alludes to Michael and Gabriel.[3]

28. JUDAH IS GONE INTO EXILE (I, 3). Do not heathen nations go into exile? The fact is, however, that though they go into exile, it is not really exile. The heathen nations who eat of their bread and drink of their wine do not experience real exile[4]; but Israel who do not eat of their bread or drink of their wine do experience real exile. The heathen nations who travel in their litters[5] do not experience

[1] Reading נושבות. The text has 'they fall upon'. Radal conjectures נשארות 'remained'. [2] Cf. Gen. R. XXXVIII, 14.
[3] Yalḳuṭ *ad loc.* represents a discussion taking place between God and these archangels wherein they admitted that the Temple was dearer to them than Israel, and they were commanded to set the Sanctuary afire in consequence.
[4] They do not experience privation because of adherence to dietary laws as do Israel. [5] So Jast. and Krauss. M.K. explains it as foot-covering.

real exile; but Israel who walk barefooted do experience exile. Therefore is it said, JUDAH IS GONE INTO EXILE. Here it states, JUDAH IS GONE INTO EXILE,[1] and elsewhere it is stated, *So Judah was carried away captive out of his land* (Jer. LII, 27). The reason is that when they were exiled their strength became weak like a woman's and therefore it is stated, JUDAH IS GONE INTO EXILE.

BECAUSE OF AFFLICTION. Because they ate leaven on Passover, contrary to what is stated, *Thou shalt eat no leavened bread with it; seven days shalt thou eat unleavened bread therewith, even the bread of affliction* (Deut. XVI, 3). Another interpretation of BECAUSE OF AFFLICTION ('ONI): because they seized the pledge of the poor within their houses, contrary to what is stated, *And if he be a poor man, thou shalt not sleep with his pledge* (*ib.* XXIV, 12).[2] Another interpretation of BECAUSE OF AFFLICTION: because they dealt oppressively in the matter of the wages of a hired servant, contrary to what is stated, *Thou shalt not oppress a hired servant that is poor* ('oni) *and needy* (*ib.* 14). Another interpretation of BECAUSE OF AFFLICTION: because they robbed the poor of what was due to them, contrary to what is stated, *Thou shalt leave them for the poor and for the stranger* (Lev. XIX, 10). Another interpretation of BECAUSE OF AFFLICTION: because they ate the tithe which belonged to the poor. R. Bibi and R. Huna said in the name of Rab: He who eats tithable produce from which the poor-tithe has not been separated is liable to the death penalty. Another interpretation of BECAUSE OF AFFLICTION ['ONI]: because they worshipped idols, according to what is stated, *But the noise of them that sing* ('anoth) *do I hear* (Ex. XXXII, 18). R. Aḥa said: [the meaning of this is,] the sound of the praise of idolatry do I hear. R. Judah says in the name of R. Jose: There is not a single generation which does not receive some punishment for the sin of the golden calf.[3]

[1] The verb is feminine whereas in Jer. it is masculine.
[2] Reading *'oni* as *'ani*, poor, and rendering: Because of the poor.
[3] When it is punished for its own sins. Cf. Sanh. 102*a* (Sonc. ed., p. 694).

29. AND BECAUSE OF GREAT SERVITUDE. R. Aḥa said: Because they kept in servitude the Hebrew slave, contrary to what is stated, *At the end of seven years ye shall let go every man his brother that is a Hebrew* (Jer. XXXIV, 14).

SHE DWELLETH AMONG THE NATIONS, SHE FINDETH NO REST. R. Judan b. R. Nehemiah said in the name of R. Simeon b. Lakish: If she had found rest, she would not have returned [to Eretz Israel]. Similarly we read, *But the dove found no rest for the sole of her foot, and she returned unto him to the ark* (Gen. VIII, 9); and similarly, *And among these nations shalt thou have no repose, and there shall be no rest for the sole of thy foot* (Deut. XXVIII, 65).

ALL HER PURSUERS OVERTOOK HER WITHIN THE STRAITS. As we have learnt in the Mishnah: These are the words of Ben Nannus; within its marks and boundaries.[1] Another interpretation of ALL HER PURSUERS OVERTOOK HER WITHIN THE STRAITS: within the days of distress from the seventeenth of Tammuz to the ninth of Ab,[2] during which *Keṭeb meriri*[3] is prevalent, as it is stated, *Of the pestilence* (keṭeb) *that walketh in darkness* (Ps. XCI, 6). R. Abba b. Kahana and R. Levi make observations. R. Abba b. Kahana said: It [the demon *Keṭeb*] stalks through the greater part of the midday period, from the beginning of the sixth hour until the end of the ninth.[4] R. Levi said: It spoils the course of the day from the end of the fourth hour until the beginning of the ninth[5]; and it does not walk in the sun or shade but in the shadow near the sun. R. Joḥanan and R. Simeon b. Lakish make observations.

[1] The word '*straits*' is explained as equal to the technical term 'boundaries' in the Mishnah cited from B.B. 105*a*, 106*a* (Sonc. ed., pp. 436, 439).—I.e. her pursuers overtook her on her borders.

[2] The first breach in the walls of Jerusalem was made on the former date, while the Temple was destroyed on the latter date, exactly three weeks later.

[3] The demon of pestilence who is most destructive during the period mentioned, which is the hottest season of the year.

[4] Levi. Jast. translates differently. The day is reckoned as beginning at 6 a.m., so the sixth hour is midday.

[5] I.e. makes this an uncomfortable period.

R. Joḥanan said: It is all over full of eyes, scales, and hair. R. Simeon b. Laḳish said: It has one eye set over its heart and whoever looks at it falls down dead. Once a pious man looked at it and fell dead upon his face, and some say that it was R. Judah b. Rabbi. Samuel saw it but did not fall; for he said, 'It is the snake of the house.'[1]

R. Abbahu was sitting and teaching in the Synagogue in a place in Cæsarea. He noticed a man carrying a stick and about to strike his neighbour. He also saw a demon standing behind him with an iron rod; so he stood up and restrained him, crying, 'Do you want to kill your neighbour?' The man said to him, 'Can anyone kill with such a stick as this?' He answered, 'Behold, there is a demon standing behind you with an iron rod; you will strike the man with this stick, but he will strike him with the other and the man will die!' R. Joḥanan enjoined elementary and Mishnah teachers not to use a strap on the children during these days.[2] R. Samuel b. Naḥmani enjoined the elementary and Mishnah teachers to dismiss the young children during those four hours.[3]

30. THE WAYS OF ZION DO MOURN (I, 4). R. Huna said: All creatures seek their mates. It is related that a wild bitch climbed to the top of a cliff to mate with a dog. R. Ammi said: Even the cedars seek their mate, for take note that there were no cedars in Babylon,[4] and when Nebuchadnezzar came here [to Palestine], he uprooted cedars from here and planted them in Babylon. When he died, the trees rejoiced over his downfall; that is what is written, *Yea, the cypresses rejoice at thee, and the cedars of Lebanon* (Isa. XIV, 8). R. Abdimi of Ḥaifa said: Even the roads seek their mate; that is what is written, THE

[1] Hence he was not afraid of it — which indicates that death would normally ensue through fright. But the parallel passage in Num. R. XII, 3, reads: it was said that nevertheless he died.
[2] Between the 17th of Tammuz and the 9th of Ab, because the blow might prove fatal.
[3] The teachers would be irascible and liable to chastise the pupils.
[4] Because cedars do not grow in soil where water abounds, as it does in Babylon. V. Sanh. 106*a* (Sonc. ed., p. 721).

WAYS OF ZION DO MOURN, BECAUSE NONE COME TO THE SOLEMN ASSEMBLY.[1] It is not written here [that the ways mourn] because there are not cottagers or counsellors,[2] but BECAUSE NONE COME TO THE SOLEMN ASSEMBLY.

ALL HER GATES ARE DESOLATE. Because none enter or leave through them.

HER PRIESTS SIGH. Because there are none to give them the priestly dues, according to what is stated, *And they shall give unto the priest the shoulder, and the two cheeks, and the maw* (Deut. XVIII, 3).

HER VIRGINS ARE AFFLICTED. R. Isaac b. R. Simon said: These are the disciples of the Sages who were beautiful as virgins but have become like wax.[3] R. Samuel said in the name of R. Isaac: These are the councillors who were beautiful as virgins and have been made like women that are afflicted. Another interpretation of HER VIRGINS ARE AFFLICTED: one after another outraged her until they exposed her wound.

AND SHE HERSELF IS IN BITTERNESS. It is bitter to her on account of her [exposed] nakedness.

31. HER ADVERSARIES ARE BECOME THE HEAD (I, 5). R. Hillel b. Berekiah said: Whoever undertakes to vex Israel becomes a chief.[4] What is the ground [of R. Hillel's statement]? HER ADVERSARIES ARE BECOME THE HEAD. You find that before Jerusalem was destroyed no province was held in any esteem; but after Jerusalem was destroyed Cæsarea became a metropolis.[5] Another interpretation of HER ADVERSARIES ARE BECOME THE HEAD: this refers to Nebuchadnezzar; HER ENEMIES ARE AT EASE, this refers to Nebuzaradan. Another interpretation of HER ADVERSARIES ARE BECOME THE

[1] The roads longed for the pilgrims who used to go up to Jerusalem.

[2] Levi. [3] *Nugoth* ('afflicted') is connected with *donag* ('wax').

[4] The status of Israel is so high that they can only be overcome by a general of great eminence.

[5] The word ותנופילין is due to dittography of מטריפולין. Buber's text reads: 'Cæsarea became a metropolis, Antipatris a province, and Neapolis a Roman colony.'

HEAD: this refers to Vespasian; HER ENEMIES ARE AT EASE, this refers to Titus.[1]

For three and a half years Vespasian surrounded Jerusalem, having four generals with him: the general of Arabia, of Africa, of Alexandria, and of Palestine. With regard to the general of Arabia two teachers differ as to his name, one declaring that it was Ḳillus and the other Pangar. In Jerusalem there were four councillors, viz. Ben Ẓiẓit, Ben Gorion, Ben Naḳdimon, and Ben Ḳalba-Shabua'.[2] Each of them was capable of supplying food for the city for ten years.[3] There was also there Ben Baṭṭiaḥ,[4] the nephew of R. Joḥanan b. Zakkai, who was appointed in charge of the stores, all of which he burnt.[5] When R. Joḥanan b. Zakkai heard of this he exclaimed, 'Woe!' It was reported to Ben Baṭṭiaḥ, 'Your uncle exclaimed "woe!"' He sent and had him brought before him and asked, 'Why did you exclaim "woe!"?' He replied, 'I did not exclaim "woe!" but "wah!"'[6] He said to him, 'You exclaimed "wah!"? Why did you make that exclamation?' He answered, 'Because you burnt all the stores, and I thought that so long as the stores were intact the people would not expose themselves to the dangers of battle.' Through the difference between 'woe' and 'wah' R. Joḥanan b. Zakkai escaped death[7]; and the verse was applied to him, *The excellency of knowledge is, that wisdom preserveth the life of him that hath it* (Eccl. VII, 12).

Three days later R. Joḥanan b. Zakkai went out to walk in the market-place and saw how people seethed straw and drank its water[8]; and he said [to himself], 'Can men

[1] Radal emends the name to Trajan, since both Vespasian and Titus were involved in the destruction of the Temple. The emendation, however, is hardly necessary, since Nebuchadnezzar and Nebuzaradan, too, were both involved in the destruction of the first Temple.

[2] In Giṭ. 56*a* the number is three, two names being read as one, viz. Naḳdimon ben Gorion.

[3] They were extremely wealthy.

[4] He was a leader of the Zealot party.

[5] To induce the men to go out to fight and obtain food.

[6] An exclamation denoting approval.

[7] The Zealot would have had his uncle put to death if he had expressed disapproval.

[8] They were reduced to such straits to escape starvation.

who seethe straw and drink its water withstand the armies of Vespasian?' He added, 'I have come to the conclusion that I must get out of here.'[1] He sent a message to Ben Baṭṭiaḥ, 'Get me out of here.' He replied, 'We have made an agreement among ourselves that nobody shall leave the city except the dead.' He said, 'Carry me out in the guise of a corpse.' R. Eliezer carried him by the head, R. Joshua by the feet, and Ben Baṭṭiaḥ walked in front. When they reached [the city gates, the guards] wanted to stab him.[2] Ben Baṭṭiaḥ said to them, 'Do you wish people to say that when our teacher died his body was stabbed!' On his speaking to them in this manner, they allowed him to pass. After going through the gates, they carried him to a cemetery and left him there and returned to the city. R. Joḥanan b. Zakkai came out and went among the soldiers of Vespasian. He said to them, 'Where is the king?' They went and told Vespasian, 'A Jew is asking for you.' He said to them, 'Let him come.' On his arrival he exclaimed, '*Vive domine Imperator!*'[3] Vespasian remarked, 'You give me a royal greeting but I am not king; and should the king hear of it he will put me to death.' He said to him, 'If you are not the king you will be eventually, because the Temple will only be destroyed by a king's hand'; as it is said, *And Lebanon shall fall by a mighty one* (Isa. x, 34). They took and placed him in the innermost of seven chambers[4] and asked him what hour of the night it was and he told them. They subsequently asked him what hour of the day it was and he told them. How did R. Joḥanan b. Zakkai know it? From his study.[5]

Three days later Vespasian went to take a bath at Gophna.[6] After he had bathed and put on one of his shoes,

[1] To carry out his plan for establishing a school at Jabneh which should become a religious centre after Jerusalem was destroyed.
[2] To assure themselves that he was really dead.
[3] 'Live, O lord Emperor.' The reading in the 'Ar. has the actual Latin he used. [4] From which all light was excluded.
[5] He was accustomed to rehearse his studies and knew how long they took. When placed in the chamber, he spent the time in this way and so was able to fix the hour.
[6] The modern Jifna, about 15 miles N.W. of Jerusalem.

a message arrived and it was announced to him that Nero had died and the Romans had proclaimed him king. He wished to put on the other shoe but it would not go on his foot. He sent for R. Joḥanan and asked, 'Will you not explain to me why all these days I wore two shoes which fitted me, but now one fits and the other does not?' He answered, 'You have been informed of good news,' because it is written, *A good report maketh the bones fat* (Prov. xv, 30). He inquired, 'What must I do to get it on?' He replied, 'Is there anybody whom you hate or who has done you wrong? Let him pass in front of you and your flesh will shrink,' because it is written, *A broken spirit drieth the bones (ib.* xvii, 22).

Then they began to speak to him in parables.[1] 'If a snake nested in a cask, what is to be done with it?'[2] He answered, 'Bring a charmer and charm the snake, and leave the cask intact.' Pangar said, 'Kill the snake and break the cask.' [Then they asked,] 'If a snake nested in a tower, what is to be done with it?' He answered, 'Bring a charmer and charm the snake, and leave the tower intact.' Pangar said, 'Kill the snake and burn the tower.' R. Joḥanan said to Pangar, 'All neighbours who do harm, do it to *their* neighbours[3]; instead of putting in a plea for the defence you argue for the prosecution against us!' He replied, 'I seek your welfare; so long as the Temple exists, the heathen kingdoms will attack you, but if it is destroyed they will not attack you. R. Joḥanan said to him, 'The heart knows whether it is for *'aḳḳel* or *'aḳalḳaloth.'*[4]

Vespasian said to R. Joḥanan b. Zakkai, 'Make a request of me and I will grant it.' He answered, 'I beg that you

---

[1] For the purpose of trapping him.
[2] The 'snake' is Israel who had rebelled against Rome, the 'cask' is Jerusalem, and in the next question the 'tower' is the Temple. The Rabbi's answer was a plea for lenient treatment so that the Jews might be won over.
[3] The Arabs were neighbours of Israel; and if, as their general suggested, a harsh policy was followed by Vespasian, his own people would in due course meet with a like fate.
[4] V. Sanh. 26a (Sonc. ed., p. 151). It is a proverbial expression. The root of both words is 'bend' or 'twist', i.e. either woven or crooked. The meaning is: your heart knows what your real intention is.

abandon this city of Jerusalem and depart.' He said to him, 'Did the Romans proclaim me king that I should abandon this city? Make another request of me and I will grant it.' He answered, 'I beg that you leave the western gate which leads to Lydda,[1] and everyone who departs up to the fourth hour shall be spared.' After Vespasian had conquered the city he asked him, 'Have you any friend or relative there? Send and bring him out before the troops enter.' He sent R. Eliezer and R. Joshua to bring out R. Ẓadoḳ.[2] They went and found him in the city gate. When he arrived R. Joḥanan stood up before him. Vespasian asked, 'You stand up before this emaciated old man?' He answered, 'By your life, if there had been [in Jerusalem] one more like him, though you had double your army, you would have been unable to conquer it.' He asked, 'What is his power?' He replied, 'He eats one fig and on the strength of it teaches at one hundred sessions in the academy.' 'Why is he so lean?' he inquired. He answered, 'On account of his numerous abstinences and fasts.' Vespasian sent and brought physicians who fed him on small portions of food and doses of liquid until his physical powers returned to him. His son Eleazar said to him, 'Father, give them their reward in this world so that they should have no merit with respect to you in the world to come.'[3] He gave them calculation by fingers[4] and scales for weighing.

When Vespasian had subdued the city, he assigned the destruction of the four ramparts to the four generals, and the western gate was allotted to Pangar. Now it had been decreed by Heaven that this should never be destroyed because the *Shechinah* abode in the west.[5] The others demolished their sections but he did not demolish his. Vespasian sent for him and asked, 'Why did you not destroy your section?' He replied, 'By your life, I acted so for the honour of the kingdom; for if I had demolished

[1] A town to the S.E. of Jaffa.
[2] A Rabbi renowned for his piety and ascetic life. It was said that he had fasted for forty years to avert the destruction of Jerusalem.
[3] The remark was inspired by bitter feeling because of the way the Romans had dealt with Jerusalem. [4] A kind of game (Levi).
[5] V.S.S.R. II, 9, § 4. The western or wailing wall still exists.

it, nobody would [in time to come] know what it was you destroyed[1]; but when people look [at the western wall], they will exclaim, "Perceive the might of Vespasian from what he destroyed!"' He said to him, 'Enough,[2] you have spoken well, but since you disobeyed my command, you shall ascend to the roof and throw yourself down. If you live, you will live; and if you die, you will die.' He ascended, threw himself down and died. Thus the curse of R. Joḥanan b. Zakkai alighted upon him.[3]

32. FOR THE LORD HATH AFFLICTED HER FOR THE MULTITUDE OF HER TRANSGRESSIONS. Perhaps He acted so without reason; therefore it is stated, FOR THE MULTITUDE OF HER TRANSGRESSIONS.

HER YOUNG CHILDREN ARE GONE INTO CAPTIVITY BEFORE THE ADVERSARY. R. Judah said: Come and see how beloved are children by the Holy One, blessed be He. The Sanhedrin was exiled, but the *Shechinah* did not go into exile with him. The priestly watches were exiled, but the *Shechinah* did not go into exile with them. When, however, the children were exiled, the *Shechinah* went into exile with them. That is what is written, HER YOUNG CHILDREN ARE GONE INTO CAPTIVITY BEFORE THE ENEMY. This is immediately followed by [AND GONE IS FROM THE DAUGHTER OF ZION HER SPLENDOUR].[4]

33. AND GONE IS FROM THE DAUGHTER OF ZION ALL HER SPLENDOUR (I, 6). The Scriptural text reads *min bath*.[5] R. Aḥa said: We possess one excellent portion, viz. the Holy One, blessed be He, of whom it is written, *O Lord, the portion of* (menath) *mine inheritance and of my*

[1] There would be no relic to show how strong the walls had been.
[2] Buber's text reads חייך 'by your life' for דייך 'enough'.
[3] His fate proved that his intentions against Israel were hostile.
[4] The '*splendour*' of Jerusalem being the *Shechinah*.
[5] The preposition 'from' is in Heb. either the word *min* or *mi* prefixed to a word. In this verse the written text has *min bath* whereas the traditional reading is *mi-bath*. *Min* is therefore expounded as the equivalent of *manah* 'a portion'.

cup (Ps. XVI, 5). ALL HER SPLENDOUR: this alludes to the Holy One, blessed be He; as it is said, *Thou art clothed with glory and splendour* (Ps. CIV, 1). Another interpretation of ALL HER SPLENDOUR: this alludes to the Sanhedrin; as it is written, *Strength and splendour are her clothing* (Prov. XXXI, 25). Another interpretation of ALL HER SPLENDOUR: this alludes to the disciples of the sages; as it is written, *Thou shalt rise up before the hoary head, and honour the face of the old man* (Lev. XIX, 32).[1] Another interpretation of ALL HER SPLENDOUR: this alludes to the priestly watches[2]; as it is written, *And praise in the splendour of holiness* (II Chron. XX, 21). Another interpretation of ALL HER SPLENDOUR: this alludes to the children. R. Judah said: Come and see how beloved are children by the Holy One, blessed be He. The Sanhedrin were exiled but the *Shechinah* did not go into exile with them. The priestly watches were exiled but the *Shechinah* did not go into exile with them. When, however, the children were exiled, the *Shechinah* went into exile with them. For is it not written, HER YOUNG CHILDREN ARE GONE INTO CAPTIVITY BEFORE THE ADVERSARY, which is immediately followed by AND GONE IS FROM THE DAUGHTER OF ZION ALL HER SPLENDOUR?

HER PRINCES ARE BECOME LIKE HARTS[3] THAT FIND NO PASTURE. R. Judah said: When they are tender-hearted they are likened to lambs; as it is said, *Then shall the lambs feed as in their pasture* (Isa. V, 17); but when they are hard-hearted they are likened to harts, as it is said HER PRINCES ARE BECOME LIKE HARTS. R. Simon said in the name of R. Simeon b. Abba and R. Simeon b. Laḳish said in the name of R. Joshua: As harts turn their faces one beneath the other in the time of intense heat, so the eminent men of Israel would see a transgression

[1] *Old man* is defined by the Rabbis as 'the learned man'. The verb *honour* is of the same root as the Heb. for '*splendour*'.
[2] Radal conjectures *ha-meshorarim* 'the temple-singers' for *ha-mishmeroth* 'the priestly watches', and they are mentioned in the verse which is quoted. [3] The word has the meaning of 'hardness'.

committed but turn their faces away from it. The Holy One, blessed be He, said, 'A time will come when I will do the same to you.'[1]

AND THEY ARE GONE WITHOUT STRENGTH BEFORE THE PURSUER. R. 'Azariah said in the name of R. Judah b. R. Simon: When Israel perform the will of the Omnipresent they add strength to the heavenly power; as it is said, *To God we render strength* (Ps. LX, 14).[2] When, however, Israel does not perform the will of the Omnipresent, they weaken, if it is possible to say so, the great power of Him Who is above; as it is written, *Thou didst weaken the Rock that begot thee* (Deut. XXXII, 18).[3] R. Judah b. R. Simon said in the name of R. Levi b. R. Ṭarfon: When Israel perform the will of the Omnipresent they add strength to the heavenly power; as it is stated, *And now, I pray thee, let the power of the Lord be great* (Num. XIV, 17).[4] When, however, Israel do not perform the will of the Omnipresent they weaken, if it is possible to say so, the great power of Him Who is above, and they too ARE GONE WITHOUT STRENGTH BEFORE THE PURSUER.[5]

R. Huna, R. Aḥa, and R. Simon said in the name of R. Simeon b. Laḳish, and the Rabbis said it in the name of R. Ḥanina: A man would say to his fellow in Jerusalem, 'Teach me a page of Scripture,' but he would reply, 'I have not the strength.'[6] [He would say] 'Teach me a chapter of Mishnah,' but he would reply, 'I have not the

[1] They went into captivity like harts which are pastureless, but He turned His face from them.

[2] The verse ending (as the Midrash interprets it) And then (i.e. through this added strength) He will tread down our adversaries. The translation follows Y.'A. E.V. '*Through God we shall do valiantly; for He it is that will tread,*' etc.

[3] E.V. '*Of the Rock that begot thee thou wast unmindful*'.

[4] This is rather difficult, as Moses prayed in these terms when Israel had *not* performed God's will. The Midrash probably means that Moses prayed that God should overlook Israel's lack of faith and regard them as though they had performed His will, whereby His strength would be great (Mah.).

[5] Their weakness in exile, as it were, caused a corresponding weakness in God.

[6] It was only a pretext to avoid his duty to impart knowledge.

strength.' The Holy One, blessed be He, said to them, 'A time will come when I will act so with you.'[1] AND THEY ARE GONE WITHOUT STRENGTH BEFORE THE PURSUER: R. Aḥa said: Just as Israel was sent into exile by a 'pursuer' written *plene*,[2] so will they be rescued by a 'redeemer' written *plene*, as it says, *And a redeemer will come to Zion* (Isa. LIX, 20), where the word is written *plene*.[3]

34. JERUSALEM REMEMBERETH IN THE DAYS OF HER AFFLICTION AND HER ANGUISH—MERUDEHAH (I, 7). In the days of her affliction she remembered the revolts (*meradin*) in which she rebelled against the Holy One, blessed be He. ALL HER TREASURES THAT SHE HAD: these are the words of the Torah, as it is stated, *More to be desired are they than gold, yea, than much fine gold* (Ps. XIX, 11).

NOW THAT HER PEOPLE FALL BY THE HAND OF THE ADVERSARY. The Babylonian Rabbis say: When the ox falls many are the slaughterers; while the Palestinian Rabbis[4] say: When the ox falls men sharpen their knives.

AND NONE DOTH HELP HER. The Babylonian Rabbis say: When the bride is ill-treated,[5] she recalls the seven days of her marriage feast; while the Palestinian Rabbis say: When the son goes barefoot[6] he recalls the comfort of his father's house.

THE ADVERSARIES HAVE SEEN HER, THEY HAVE MOCKED AT HER DESOLATIONS (MISHBATTEHAH): i.e. at her sabbaths, as it is stated, *Remember the sabbath day, to keep it holy* (Ex. XX, 8). Another interpretation of MISHBATTEHAH: at her sabbatical years, as it is stated,

[1] God will say 'I have no strength', when they plead with Him in exile.
[2] With the *waw* added, רודף and not רדף.
[3] גואל and not גאל. The fuller spelling in both cases symbolises completeness. The pursuer was a complete pursuer, stern and inexorable; but the Redeemer shall likewise bring full and complete redemption, never again to be followed by servitude ('E.J.).
[4] Lit. 'the Rabbis of there . . . the Rabbis of here'; v. Introduction Mah. and M.K. reverse it. What follow are local proverbs.
[5] Levi. Jast., reading מספין, translates: when they give the bride (coarse food) to eat. The nuptial celebrations usually lasted a week.
[6] Wandering homeless and footsore.

But in the seventh year shall be a sabbath of solemn rest for the land (Lev. XXV, 4).[1] Another interpretation of MISHBATTEHAH: this alludes to R. Joḥanan b. Zakkai who ceased to be in Jerusalem.[2]

35. JERUSALEM HATH GRIEVOUSLY SINNED (I, 8). Do the heathen nations, then, not sin? But although they sin, it has no sequel in punishment.[3] Israel, however, sinned and were punished. THEREFORE SHE IS BECOME AS ONE UNCLEAN (LE-NIDAH): i.e. she was doomed to vagabondage.[4]

ALL THAT HONOURED HER DESPISE HER, BECAUSE THEY HAVE SEEN HER NAKEDNESS· SHE HERSELF ALSO SIGHETH, AND TURNETH BACKWARD; BACKWARD from the priesthood, BACKWARD from kingship.

36. HER FILTHINESS WAS IN HER SKIRTS (I, 9). R. Berekiah said in the name of R. Abba b. Kahana: All the priests who officiated in the days of Zedekiah were uncircumcised.[5] That is what is stated, *In that ye have brought in aliens, uncircumcised in heart and uncircumcised*

[1] Rashi on Lam. *ad loc.* explains: the Jews observed the sabbaths and sabbatical years in exile, though they had not done so in their own country, whereat their captors derided them, saying, 'Fools that you are! You did not keep these in your own country, yet keep them in a strange land.' 'E.J. explains differently.

[2] Cf. § 31; his departure left the city desolate. The general idea is that the enemy mocks (or is happy, as the verb may mean 'laughed with joy') when Israel's great men and teachers are forced to leave her.

[3] This can hardly be meant literally, but rather that their punishment is not so severe because since they did not accept the Torah and since they were not redeemed from Egypt their obligations are not so great (Mah.). Incidentally, this throws an important light on the doctrine of the Selection of Israel: the Rabbis did not claim greater privileges on that account, but on the contrary recognised that it entailed greater responsibilities. M.K. explains that this means that even when the heathens are exiled for sin, their exile is not so severely felt; cf. *supra*, § 28.

[4] *Niddah* 'unclean' is explained as *nadah* 'a wanderer'.

[5] SKIRTS is explained as the sacerdotal garments and the FILTHINESS was the lack of circumcision. Zedekiah was the king in whose reign the first Temple was destroyed and the Jews exiled to Babylon. Her skirts are thus interpreted as an allusion to the low-lying Topheth, while FILTHINESS is the idolatrous worship, particularly the burning of children for Moloch, which took place there.

in flesh, to be in My sanctuary (Ezek. XLIV, 7). Another interpretation of HER FILTHINESS WAS IN HER SKIRTS: in her nether limbs,[1] as it is stated, *Upon the skirts of the robe* (Ex. XXVIII, 34). Another interpretation of HER FILTHINESS WAS IN HER SKIRTS: As we have learnt: There was a place below Jerusalem with the name Topheth.[2] R. Judah said: [It was so called] because of the seduction (*tophteh*) to idolatry which was there. R. Jose said: [The Targum translates it] 'the valley of Bar Hinnon'.[3] A hollow image was set up there within the innermost of seven chambers, holding a copper plate in its hand upon which a fire-pan was placed. When a person brought an offering of flour one chamber was opened for him; when he brought one of doves and pigeons, two chambers were opened for him; of a lamb, three were opened for him; of a ram, four were opened for him; of a calf, five were opened for him; of an ox, six were opened for him; but when a person brought an offering of his child the seven were opened for him. They placed the child on the copper plate, kindled the fire-pan beneath him, and sang before the image, 'May the sacrifice be pleasant and sweet to thee!' Why did they do this? So that the parents should not hear the groans of their children and retract.

A heathen priest went to a certain man and said to him, '[I have come to you] because the image has declared to me that of all the children you have you are unwilling to sacrifice one.' He replied, 'Are they, then, under my control? One works with gold, another with silver, a third with sheep, and a fourth with the herds.[4] But wait! You have seen that I have a young child at school. When he arrives home I will give him to you.' The Holy One, blessed be He, said to him, 'Wretch! Of all the sons you have there is none you are willing to sacrifice for idol-worship except this child who is consecrated to My name!'[5] R. Judan b. R. Simon said in the name of R. Levi b.

[1] This seems to be the same explanation as the former in different words.
[2] V. Jer. VII, 31.
[3] Known as Gehinnom or Gehenna.
[4] He probably meant that they were therefore independent of him and would not submit.
[5] By the fact of his attendance at school.

Parṭa: It may be likened to a lady whose lover said to her, 'Prepare some hot food for me.' So she took the king's portrait[1] and used it as fuel to prepare hot food for him. The king said to her, 'Of all the wood that is in this house you could not use any to prepare hot food for your lover except my image!' In like manner the Holy One, blessed be He, said to the wicked man: 'Of all the sons you have there is none you are willing to sacrifice for idol-worship except the child who is consecrated to My name!' That is what is stated, *Moreover thou hast taken thy sons and thy daughters whom thou hast borne unto Me, and these hast thou sacrificed unto them to be devoured* (Ezek. XVI, 20).[2] Nevertheless, THEREFORE IS SHE COME DOWN WONDERFULLY: she is come down into sore trials.[3]

37. When R. Jose of Milḥaya[4] died, R. Joḥanan and R. Simeon b. Laḳish went up to pay their last respects to him,[5] and R. Isaac Pesaḳa went up with them. In the town there was an old man who wished to go in and deliver [a funeral address] over him, but he was not permitted to do so. R. Isaac Pesaḳa said to him, 'Before these eminent scholars[6] you would presume to open your mouth!' R. Joḥanan said to the people, 'Let him speak since he is an old man. Let him enter and obtain renown for himself in his own place.'[7] He entered and opened his discourse as follows: 'We find that the demise of the righteous is more grievous before the Holy One, blessed be He, than the ninety-eight curses mentioned in Deuteronomy and the destruction of the Temple. In connection with the curses it is written, *Then the Lord will make thy plagues wonderful*

[1] Levi translates 'bathing-tub'.
[2] He probably emphasises '*whom thou hast borne unto Me*'—i.e. the only children specifically dedicated to My service.
[3] In spite of these enormities, sufferings were inflicted upon Israel not in a spirit of vindictiveness, but as trials to make Israel reform (M.K. and 'E.J.). [4] A town in Upper Galilee.
[5] Attend his funeral. The original is lit. 'perform a benevolent act'—everything that is done for the dead being so termed, since the dead cannot make any return. [6] Lit. 'lions of the Torah'.
[7] Since he was a fellow-townsman of the deceased he might be allowed the privilege.

(Deut. XXVIII, 59); and in connection with the destruction of the Temple it is written, THEREFORE IS SHE COME DOWN WONDERFULLY. But in connection with the demise of the righteous it is written, *Therefore, behold, I will again do a marvellous work among this people, even a marvellous work and a wonder* (Isa. XXIX, 14).[1] To what purpose? *And the wisdom of their wise men shall perish, and the prudence of their prudent men shall be hid (ib.)*.[2] R. Isaac Pesaḳa exclaimed, 'May the mouth of this man be blessed!'[3] R. Joḥanan said to them, 'If you had not allowed him to speak, whence should we have heard this pearl [of wisdom]?'

The Holy Spirit cried,[4] BEHOLD, O LORD, MY AFFLICTION, FOR THE ENEMY HATH MAGNIFIED HIMSELF (I, 9). [It is written,] *The proud have digged pits for me, which is not according to Thy law* (Ps. CXIX, 85). R. Abba b. Kahana said: In two matters [the enemy transgressed the Torah]. It is written, *Thou shalt not take the dam with the young* (Deut. XXII, 6), but here [it is recorded], *The mother was dashed in pieces with her children* (Hos. X, 14), which was contrary to Thy Torah. R. Abba b. Kahana said: The other instance is where it is written, *To cut off the children from the street* (Jer. IX, 20)—but not from the Synagogues, *and the young men from the broad places*—but not from the Houses of Study, whereas here [it is recorded], *When the anger of God went up against them, and slew of the lustiest among them, and smote down the young men of Israel* (Ps. LXXVIII, 31),[5] which was contrary to Thy Torah. R. Judah b. R. Simon said: In two matters [the enemy transgressed the Torah]. It is written, *Whether it be cow or ewe, ye shall not kill it and its young both in one day* (Lev. XXII, 28); but here child was slain together with

[1] The word '*wonder*' occurs three times in this connection but only once in the other two instances.
[2] I.e. the loss of their wise men shall be triply wondrous—in the present sense, triply grievous. [3] He was so impressed by the remark.
[4] This is to be connected with the statement above, 'she is come down into sore trials'—hence the passage is introduced by the conjunctive *waw*. [5] The *lustiest* and the *young men* were those who frequented the synagogues and schools.

its mother on one day, as it is said, *The mother was dashed in pieces with her children*, which was contrary to Thy Torah. R. Judah b. R. Simon said: The other instance is where it is written, *And whatsoever man there be of the children of Israel, or of the strangers that sojourn among them, that taketh in hunting any beast or fowl that may be eaten, he shall pour out the blood thereof, and cover it with dust* (*ib.* XVII, 13); but here [it is recorded], *They have shed their blood like water round about Jerusalem, with none to bury them* (Ps. LXXIX, 3), which was contrary to Thy Torah.[1]

R. Berekiah said: The Community of Israel spake before the Holy One, blessed be He: 'Lord of the Universe, to asses Thou gavest burial but to Thy children Thou gavest no burial!' 'To asses Thou gavest burial'—by this the Egyptians are meant, as it is written, *Whose flesh is as the flesh of asses* (Ezek. XXIII, 20),[2] and R. Berekiah further remarked: Since the sea kept casting them back to the land and the land back to the sea, the sea saying, 'Receive your hordes,' and the land saying to the sea, 'Receive your hordes,' the land exclaimed, 'If at the time that I only received the blood of Abel it was pronounced against me, *Cursed is the ground* (Gen. III, 17), how can I receive the blood of this multitude?' until the Holy One, blessed be He, swore to it that He would not hold it to account. For is it not written, *Thou stretched out Thy right hand, the earth swallowed them* (Ex. XV, 12)? '*Right hand*' signifies nothing else than an oath, as it is said, *The Lord hath sworn by His right hand* (Isa. LXII, 8).[3] 'But to Thy people Thou gavest no burial'; hence [the cry] '*Which is not according to Thy law*'.[4]

[1] These comments by R. Abba b. Kahana and R. Judah b. R. Simon explain how it is that the Holy Spirit cried, BEHOLD . . . MAGNIFIED HIMSELF—i.e. the enemy has magnified himself *against the Torah* (which is probably what is connoted here by the 'Holy Spirit') by trampling upon its laws.

[2] The context refers to the Egyptians, and the Midrash alludes to their drowning in the Red Sea.

[3] Hence translating: 'Thou swearest (by stretching out Thy right hand), and (only then) the earth swallowed them'—i.e. they were granted burial. Thus the asses (sc. the Egyptians) were given burial. [4] It is obligatory to bury the dead (cf. p. 111, n. 5); v. Glos. s.v. *Meth Mizwah*.

38. THE ADVERSARY HATH SPREAD OUT HIS HAND UPON ALL HER TREASURES (I, 10). You find that when the enemies entered the Temple, Ammonites and Moabites entered among them[1]; and while all the others ran to plunder the silver and gold, the Ammonites and Moabites ran to plunder the Torah for the purpose of expunging, *An Ammonite or a Moabite shall not enter into the assembly of the Lord* (Deut. XXIII, 4). R. Judah b. R. Simon said in the name of R. Levi b. Parṭa: It may be likened to a lighted torch which fell within a king's palace and everybody ran to plunder the silver and gold, whereas a slave ran to plunder his title-deed.[2] Similarly when the enemies entered the Temple, Ammonites and Moabites entered among them; and while all the others ran to plunder the silver and gold, the Ammonites and Moabites ran to plunder the Torah for the purpose of expunging, '*An Ammonite or a Moabite shall not enter into the assembly of the Lord.*'[3]

Four benefits did Abraham bestow upon Lot.[4] Is it not written, *So Abram went, as the Lord had spoken unto him; and Lot went with him* (Gen. XII, 4)?[5] And it is stated, *And Lot also, who went with Abram, had flocks, and herds and tents* (*ib.* XIII, 5)[6]; and it is also stated, *And he brought back all the goods, and also brought back his brother Lot, and his goods* (*ib.* XIV, 16); and it is further stated, *And it came to pass, when God destroyed the cities of the Plain, that God remembered Abraham, and sent Lot out of the midst of the overthrow* (*ib.* XIX, 29). They [Lot's descendants][7] should therefore have repaid kindness to the Israelites, but instead

[1] V. Proem IX.
[2] Wherewith he had been sold as a slave.
[3] The passage is based on the end of the verse: . . . THE HEATHEN . . . CONCERNING WHOM THOU DIDST COMMAND THAT THEY SHOULD NOT ENTER INTO THY CONGREGATION. The Midrash interprets: it was that enemy who had been debarred from entering into the congregation, sc. the Ammonite and Moabite, who now spread out his hand upon all her treasures, viz. the *Torah* ('E.J.).
[4] V. Gen. R. XLI, 3.
[5] He bestowed a privilege on Lot in taking him with him.
[6] He benefited because of his association with the patriarch.
[7] The Moabites and Ammonites were descendants of Lot (Gen. XIX, 37 f.).

they did harm; for is it not written, *And he sent messengers unto Balaam . . . Come now, therefore, I pray thee, curse me this people . . . and the elders of Moab and the elders of Midian departed* (Num. XXII, 5 ff.)? [And it is further written,] *And he gathered unto him the children of Ammon and Amalek; and he went and smote Israel* (Judg. III, 13); and also, *It came to pass after this, that the children of Moab, and the children of Ammon, and with them some of the Ammonites, came against Jehoshaphat to battle* (II Chron. XX, 1); and there is likewise the present instance of THE ADVERSARY HATH SPREAD OUT HIS HAND.[1] Correspondingly their sins are recorded in four places, viz. *An Ammonite or a Moabite shall not enter into the assembly of the Lord . . . because they met you not with bread and with water in the way* (Deut. XXIII, 4 f.); *O My people, remember now what Balak king of Moab devised* (Micah VI, 5); *Because they met not the children of Israel with bread and with water, but hired Balaam against them, to curse them* (Neh. XIII, 2); *And he sent and called Balaam the son of Beor to curse you* (Josh. XXIV, 9). Correspondingly four prophets stood up and sealed their doom upon them, viz. Isaiah, Jeremiah, Ezekiel, and Zephaniah. Isaiah said, *The burden of Moab. For in the night that Ar of Moab is laid waste, he is brought to ruin! for in the night that Kir of Moab is laid waste, he is brought to ruin* (XV, 1). Jeremiah said, *Therefore, behold, the days come, saith the Lord, that I will cause an alarm of war to be heard against Rabbah of the children of Ammon; and it shall be burned with fire; then shall Israel dispossess them that did possess him, saith the Lord* (XLIX, 2). Ezekiel said, *Together with the children of Ammon, unto the children of the east, and I will give them for a possession, that the children of Ammon may not be remembered among the nations* (XXV, 11); and it is further written, *And I will execute judgments upon Moab; and they shall know that I am the Lord* (*ib.*). Zephaniah said,[2] *Therefore as I live saith the Lord of hosts, the God of Israel:*

[1] In which these peoples were concerned, as explained above. Four references to their attack upon Israel are quoted in contrast to the four benefits Lot had received from Abraham. [2] Zeph. II, 9.

Surely Moab shall be as Sodom, and the children of Ammon as Gomorrah, even the breeding-place of nettles, and saltpits, and a desolation for ever; the residue of My people shall spoil them, and the remnant of My nation shall inherit them.

39. ALL HER PEOPLE SIGH, THEY SEEK BREAD (I, 11). It is written, *In the fourth month, in the ninth day of the month, the famine was sore in the city, so that there was no bread for the people of the land* (Jer. LII, 6)—there was no bread '*for the people of the land*', but there was bread for the sons of Judah.[1] This happened at the destruction of the first Temple; but at the destruction of the second Temple ALL HER PEOPLE SIGH, THEY SEEK BREAD. At first [during the siege] they used to let down a golden basket in exchange for which the enemy gave them [an ordinary] basket filled with wheat. Later, when they let down a golden basket, they were given a basket filled with barley. Subsequently when they let down a golden basket, they were given a basket filled with straw. What did they do? They seethed it and drank its water.[2] Finally, when they let down a golden basket, they received nothing in return. R. Judah b. Signa said in the name of R. Aḥa: If in connection with one who is to give though he has not received anything in return it is stated, *Thou shalt surely give him* (Deut. XV, 10),[3] how much more so must it be in connection with one who receives and does not give![4]

TO REFRESH THE SOUL. With what minimum quantity of food is the soul refreshed? Rabbi [Judah] says: About the size of a date; R. Ḥananiah said: About the size of a berry.

SEE, O LORD, AND BEHOLD, HOW ABJECT I AM BECOME. R. Phinehas said: It happened that two harlots of Ashkelon were quarrelling. In the course of the quarrel

[1] I.e. for the members of the ruling tribe. V. Jer. XLI, 8.
[2] V. *infra*, p. 101.
[3] For if not, it is *Sin in thee* (v. 9)—though you have received nothing.
[4] Radal emends: if of one who neither received nor gave Scripture says, *And he cry unto the Lord against thee, and it be sin in thee*, how much more so, etc. The text of cur. edd. means the same (v. preceding note), but does not express it so clearly.

one said to the other, 'You should not go out because you look like a Jewess.' They subsequently became reconciled, and the one said, 'I forgive you everything you said except the remark that I look like a Jewess.' Therefore it is stated, SEE, O LORD, AND BEHOLD, HOW ABJECT I AM BECOME.[1]

40. LET IT NOT COME UNTO YOU (I, 12). The Community of Israel says to the nations of the world: 'May there not come upon you what has come upon me! May there not occur to you what has occurred to me!'

ALL YE THAT PASS BY. This means, all ye that pass by [transgress] the way of the Torah.

BEHOLD AND SEE. We have learnt in the Mishnah: The judgment of the generation of the Flood lasted twelve months;[2] the judgment of the Egyptians lasted twelve months[3]; the judgment of Job lasted twelve months[4]; the judgment of Magog[5] will last twelve months[6]; the judgment of the wicked in Gehenna lasts twelve months.[7] [The judgment of] Nebuchadnezzar will last for three years and a half, and of Vespasian for a like period.[8]

BEHOLD AND SEE IF THERE BE ANY PAIN LIKE UNTO MY PAIN, WHICH IS DONE ('OLAL) UNTO ME. For He has been strict with me and cut off my gleanings

[1] That to say that one was like a Jew was an unforgivable insult!

[2] Cf. Gen. VII, 11, with VIII, 14. [3] Ex. IV, 12, is said to have occurred in the month of Iyyar, while the Exodus took place twelve months later in Nisan. [4] *Months of vanity*, Job VII, 3, is interpreted to imply a full twelve months. [5] Cf. Ezek. XXXVIII, 2 ff.

[6] Ezek. XXXIX, 4, 17, is combined with Isa. XVIII, 6, implying that the birds and beasts of prey will feast on the bodies of Gog and Magog a whole summer and a whole winter, i.e. twelve months.

[7] V. Isa. LXVI, 23 f. The Midrash understands *from one new moon to another* as meaning to the *same* new moon the following year, viz. twelve months, and for that period will the punishment mentioned in v. 24 endure. This is a quotation from 'Ed. II, 10 (Sonc. ed., p. 14 f.).

[8] Because that is the length of time they besieged Jerusalem. V. p. 56, n. 4. The whole passage is quoted as an illustration of the text, BEHOLD, AND SEE IF THERE BE ANY PAIN LIKE UNTO MY PAIN: though the wicked are normally punished in Gehenna for twelve months only, yet the destroyers of the Temple were punished for a much longer period, which shows what extraordinary sufferings they inflicted upon Israel.

(*'olalti*),[1] *'olal* bearing the same meaning as in the verse, *When thou gatherest the grapes of thy vineyard, thou shalt not glean it* (te-'olel) *after thee* (Deut. XXIV, 21).

WHEREWITH THE LORD HATH AFFLICTED ME IN THE DAY OF HIS FIERCE ANGER. R. Aḥa said: One day did the anger of the Holy One, blessed be He, burn fiercely, and if Israel had repented they would have cooled it.[2]

41. FROM ON HIGH HE SENT FIRE INTO MY BONES (I, 13). R. Ammi asked R. Samuel b. Naḥmani: Inasmuch as I have heard about you that you are a master of *Haggadah*, what is the meaning of the text, *Thy righteousness also, O God, which reacheth unto high heaven* (Ps. LXXI, 19)? He replied: In the same manner that the creatures of the terrestrial world need to practise righteousness one towards the other, so is it necessary for the beings of the celestial world to practise righteousness one towards the other.

R. Joḥanan said in the name of R. Simeon b. Yoḥai[3]: Wherever '*He said*' occurs twice in a passage, the purpose is to convey some inner meaning. For instance, *And He said unto the man clothed in linen, and He said: Go in between the wheelwork, even under the cherub, and fill both thy hands with coals of fire* (Ezek. X, 2). Why is '*He said*' repeated? It signifies that the Holy One, blessed be He, spoke to the angel and the angel said to the cherub, 'Although the Holy One, blessed be He, decreed that I should take the coals of fire, I am unable to enter within your domain; so perform an act of righteousness with me, and give me two burning coals of yours in order that I may not be scorched.' Hence it is stated, *And* [*the cherub*] *took thereof, and put it into the hands of him that was clothed in linen, who took it and went out* (*ib.* 7). What means '*And*

[1] WHICH IS DONE TO ME ('OLAL) is explained as 'gleaning' (*'olelah*). In His punishment God spared none, unlike the Torah which commands that in vintaging the gleanings must be left over.

[2] Since it states '*In the* day *of His fierce anger*'. Though the siege and the final catastrophe with all the suffering it entailed lasted much longer, yet repentance on the single day of God's anger would have averted it all ('E.J.).

[3] What follows occurs in Lev. R. XXVI, 8. Cf. notes *in loc.*

took thereof and put it'?[1] R. Isaac said: The cherub cooled them and placed them in his hand. R. Joshua of Siknin said in the name of R. Levi: For six years the coals were kept dimly glowing in the hands of Gabriel, who thought that Israel would repent. When they failed to repent he wanted to cast them upon the people in his wrath. The Holy One, blessed be He, called to him, saying, 'Gabriel, Gabriel! Be not so hasty, for there are many among them who practise righteousness one towards the other!' It is therefore stated, *And there appeared in the cherubim the form of a man's hand under their wings* (*ib.* 8).[2] R. Abba b. Kahana said in the name of R. Levi: What[3] enables all beings above and below to endure? The righteousness which Israel perform with the hand; hence it is stated, '*Thy righteousness also, O God, which reacheth unto high heaven.*'

Another instance [of '*he said*' being repeated is], *And a man of God came near and he said unto the king of Israel, and he said: Thus saith the Lord* (I Kings XX, 28). Why is '*he said*' repeated? With the first announcement he told him, 'If Benhadad comes into your power, have no pity on him.' With the second announcement he told him, 'How many traps I set, how many nets[4] I laid, how many conquests I planned before I subdued him beneath your hand, and now you have allowed him to depart in peace. *Therefore thy life shall go for his life, and thy people for his people*' (*ib.* 42).

Another instance [of the twofold '*he said*'] is, *Then said the king Ahasuerus and said unto Esther the queen* (Est. VII, 5). Why is '*said*' repeated? Rab said in the name of R. Eleazar[5]: Before the king detected that she was a Jewess,

[1] '*And put it*' alone would have sufficed (M.K.).
[2] M.K. *a man's hand* symbolises the practising of righteousness, as it is written, *Thou shalt surely open thy hand unto thy poor and needy brother* (Deut. XV, 11)—righteousness and charity are expressed by the same word in Hebrew, being regarded as synonymous.
[3] So Buber's text. The edd. have 'who'.
[4] The text has רמיזות 'hints'. Levi conjectures רשתות 'nets'.
[5] Without further specification this is R. Eleazar b. Pedath who was a disciple of Rab and would not therefore be quoted by the latter. The name should therefore probably be R. Eleazar b. Simeon.

he used to speak with her in public; but when he became aware of it, he spoke to an intermediary and the latter spoke to Queen Esther.[1]

Still another occurrence is, *And the Lord said unto Moses: Say unto the priests the sons of Aaron, and say unto them* (Lev. XXI, 1). Why is '*say*' repeated? With the first announcement he told them, *There shall none defile himself for the dead among his people* (*ib.*). While with the second announcement he told them, 'If a *meth mizwah* should chance to you, defile yourself for his sake. Since you defile yourselves for a *meth mizwah* in this world, in the hereafter you will not contract defilement by the dead at all, because there will be no death in the hereafter'; as it is said, *He will swallow up death for ever* (Isa. XXV, 8).

Another interpretation of '*Thy righteousness also, O God, which reacheth unto high heaven*': it alludes to the two luminaries.[2] *O God, who is like unto Thee?* (Ps. LXXI, 19): since Thou subduest the Attribute of Justice.[3] At the time[4] [when the enemy conquered Jerusalem] the accuser sprang before the Throne of Glory and exclaimed, 'Lord of the universe, shall this wicked person boast, saying, "I destroyed the house of God, I burnt His Temple!" Let fire descend from above and let it burn [the Temple].' What is immediately written? FROM ON HIGH HE SENT FIRE INTO MY BONES.

R. Joshua said: [This verse explains] the rebuke which the prophet addressed to [the *daughter of the Chaldeans*], viz. *Take the millstones, and grind meal* (Isa. XLVII, 2). Everybody grinds *wheat and yet* it says '*Grind* meal'![5]

[1] In Lev. R. XXVI, 8, and Meg. 16*a* the text is reversed, viz. At first he spoke to her through an intermediary (because he was unaware that she was of royal lineage), but when he discovered that fact he spoke with her direct.

[2] The sun and the moon which God placed in the heavens, created by Him in His Attribute of Mercy.

[3] In favour of the Attribute of Mercy in His dealings with His creatures.

[4] Y.'A. points out that there is a lacuna in the text here and the following must be added: Another interpretation of '*Thy righteousness*', etc.: He executes justice in the heights, and when it was decreed that the Temple was to be destroyed, the accuser, etc.

[5] Surely when it is already *meal* it requires no grinding!

The meaning, however, is: Jerusalem said to the daughter of Babylon, 'Had they not fought against me on high, would you have been able to fight me? Had they not sent fire against me from on high, could you have conquered me? Only a slain lion have you killed, ground meal you have ground, a burnt city did you set ablaze!' Therefore is it stated, FROM ON HIGH HE SENT FIRE INTO MY BONES AND IT PREVAILETH AGAINST THEM. What means '*wayyirdennah*' (E.V. 'it prevaileth against them')? He removed [i.e. banished] them, as the word is used in that sense in, *And he scraped it out* (wayyirdehu) *into his hands* (Judg. XIV, 9). Another interpretation of '*wayyirdennah*': He conquered them, as the word is used in, *May he have dominion* (weyerd) *also from sea to sea* (Ps. LXXII, 8). Another interpretation of '*wayyirdennah*': he bore sway over them, as the word is used in, *For he had dominion* (rodeh) *over all the region of this side the River* (I Kings V, 4). Another interpretation of '*wayyirdennah*': he ploughed it,[1] as it has been taught: Tineius Rufus ploughed the Temple.[2] R. Bebai of Sergunieh[3] said: '*wayyirdennah*' indicates, 'He saw that the Attribute of Justice overtook her.'[4]

HE HATH SPREAD A NET FOR MY FEET. R. Abba b. Kahana said: If you see benches filled with Babylonians set up in the land of Israel look for the feet of the Messiah. What is the reason? HE HATH SPREAD A NET FOR MY FEET.[5] R. Simeon b. Yoḥai taught: If you see a Persian horse tethered[6] in Eretz Israel look for the

[1] The root has that meaning in Aramaic, and for that reason a Rabbinical passage is quoted. [2] A statement in P. Ta'an. IV, 5 (69*b*). T.R. was a Roman Governor of Judea.

[3] A town near Tiberias. The name is corrupt in the text.

[4] Sc. Jerusalem and the Jewish nation. The word is explained as a compound, viz. He saw (*ra'ah*) justice (*din*).

[5] This is repeated in S.S.R. VIII, 9, § 3, but in both places the point is rather obscure. M.K. and E.J. explain that פרש ('*he hath spread*') is read פרס, 'a Persian' (equivalent to Babylonian), and the text is rendered: When the Persian (Babylonian) is like a net, i.e. so numerous that he occupies all places, then watch for the feet—of the Messiah. This explanation is as plausible as any.

[6] In S.S.R., *loc. cit.*, the reading is: tethered to graves in Eretz Israel.

feet of the Messiah. What is the reason? *And this shall be peace: when the Assyrian shall come into our land* (Micah v, 4).

HE HATH TURNED ME BACK: back from the priesthood and from the kingdom.

HE HATH MADE ME DESOLATE: i.e. [doomed] to devastation.

AND FAINT ALL THE DAY: i.e. [doomed] to the axe.[1]

42. THE YOKE OF MY TRANSGRESSIONS IS IMPRESSED (NISḲAD) BY HIS HAND (I, 14). I was mistaken (*seḳudah*) with regard to my iniquities.[2] I thought that He would forgive me them all, when I heard that my indictment had been read[3] on high. Another interpretation of NISḲAD is to read the word as *nishḳad:* The Holy One, blessed be He, carefully considered (*shaḳad*) how to bring the calamity upon me.[4] He said, 'If I exile them at the winter solstice, they will be afflicted by the cold and perish. I will therefore banish them at the summer solstice, so that even if they sleep on the roads and in the open places, not one of them will come to harm.' Another interpretation of NISḲAD: He carefully considered how to bring the calamity upon me. He said, 'If I exile them at the winter solstice, there will be no grapes on the vine and no figs on the fig-trees. I will therefore banish them at the summer solstice, when there are grapes on the vine and figs on the fig-trees, and even the leaves are not withered.'[5] Another interpretation of NISḲAD: He carefully considered how to bring the calamity upon me. He said, 'If I exile them by the way of the desert, they will perish from hunger. I will therefore banish them by the way of Armenia where there are town and cities, so that food and drink will be available for them.'

Another interpretation of NISḲAD: I was mistaken with regard to my iniquities. I thought that He would

[1] For execution. [2] Jast. Levi translates: I was chained to my sins—i.e. I had to bear their consequences. [3] Emended text (Radal and Levi). [4] To punish severely but without destroying the people. [5] Cf. Jer. VIII, 13.

forgive me them all, but THEY ARE KNIT TOGETHER, i.e. He made them alternate in their behaviour to me.[1] He brought them upon me in pairs, viz. Babylon and the Chaldeans, Media and Persia, Greece and Macedon, Edom (Rome) and Ishmael. He made them alternate in their treatment, so that Babylon was severe but Media lenient, Greece severe but Edom lenient, the Chaldeans severe but Persia lenient, Macedon severe but Ishmael lenient.[2] Thus it is written, *So part of the kingdom shall be strong, and part thereof broken* (Dan. II, 42).[3] Through it all I did not repudiate my God, but THEY ARE COME[4] UPON MY NECK, and twice daily I proclaimed His unity, saying, *Hear, O Israel, the Lord our God, the Lord is one* (Deut. VI, 4).

43. HE HATH MADE MY STRENGTH TO FAIL. R. Tanḥum b. R. Jeremiah said: Four things weaken a man's strength, viz. fasting, a journey, sin, and the kingdom of Babylon.[5] 'Fasting,' as it is written, *My knees totter through fasting* (Ps. CIX, 24). 'A journey,' as it is written, *He weakened my strength in the way* (*ib.* CII, 24). 'Sin,' as it is written, *My strength faileth because of mine iniquity* (*ib.* XXXI, 11). 'The kingdom,' as it is written, *And Judah said: The strength of the bearers of burdens is decayed,*[6] *and there is much rubbish; so that we are not able to build the wall* (Neh. IV, 4).

THE LORD HATH DELIVERED ME INTO THEIR HANDS, AGAINST WHOM I AM NOT ABLE TO STAND.

[1] This is apparently the meaning, as is explained in the text. Jast. renders: in broken lines,—i.e. at intervals.

[2] Radal would emend the text as follows, as being more accurate historically: the Chaldeans were severe but Babylon lenient, Persia severe but Media lenient, Greece severe but Macedon lenient, Edom severe but Ishmael lenient.

[3] *Kingdom* is the conqueror, *strong* means severe and *broken* lenient.

[4] '*They are come*' ('alu) is read as '*ulo*, 'His yoke.' The declaration of the *shema*' ('Hear, O Israel') is called by the Rabbis 'acceptance of the yoke of the Kingdom of Heaven', and is included in the morning and evening prayers.

[5] 'Kingdom of Babylon' is typical of an oppressive government. In Giṭ. 70*a* the reading is: Three things weaken a man's strength, viz. fear, a journey, and fasting.

[6] Through interference of the Samaritans.

Our Rabbis declared: This applies to a bad wife whose marriage settlement is large.[1] R. Huna said: *And man became a living soul* (Gen. II, 7) means, He made him a slave indentured to himself, so that if he does not work he does not eat. That is the opinion of R. Ḥanina; because R. Ḥanina said: THE LORD HATH DELIVERED ME INTO THEIR HANDS, AGAINST WHOM I AM NOT ABLE TO STAND: INTO THEIR HANDS, AGAINST WHOM I AM NOT ABLE TO STAND, i.e. if I do not work by day I am not able to stand by night.[2]

44. THE LORD HATH SET AT NOUGHT (SILLAH) ALL MY MIGHTY MEN (I, 15). He hath made me like refuse before them. R. Abba b. Kahana said: In Bar Gamza[3] they call refuse '*sallutha*'.[4] R. Levi said: In Arabia they call a comb '*mesalselah*'.[5]

HE HATH CALLED A SOLEMN ASSEMBLY AGAINST ME TO CRUSH MY YOUNG MEN. We find that the death of youths is considered as grievous as the destruction of the Temple; for it is written, THE LORD HATH TRODDEN AS IN A WINEPRESS THE VIRGIN DAUGHTER OF JUDAH,[6] and in the same way, HE HATH CALLED A SOLEMN ASSEMBLY AGAINST ME TO CRUSH MY YOUNG MEN.[7]

45. FOR THESE THINGS I WEEP (I, 16). Vespasian filled three ships with eminent men of Jerusalem to place them in Roman brothels.[8] They stood up and said, 'Is it not enough that we have provoked Him to anger in His

[1] Yeb. 63*b*. The husband would like to divorce her but is deterred by the heavy payment he must make to her.
[2] The interpretation seems to be based upon the reading *beyadai* 'into my hands' instead of *bidey* 'into their hands', i.e. man is enslaved to his needs. If he does not work by day to supply his wants, he cannot endure by night, cf. Gen. R. XIV, 10. [3] S.E. of Lydda.
[4] The text reads סרקין, but a word is required sounding like *sillah*.
[5] He would therefore translate: 'The Lord hath combed the flesh of all my mighty men.' Combing the flesh was a common form of torture.
[6] Cf. Proem XXXII where '*wine-press*' is explained as the Temple.
[7] Since both are related in the same verse, they are equal tragedies.
[8] Pederasty was rife in Rome; v. Weiss, *Dor* II, 23.

Sanctuary, that we shall do so also outside the Holy Land [by consenting to immoral practices]!' They said to the women [of Jerusalem who were in the ships], 'Do you desire such a fate?' They replied, 'We do not.' They then said, 'If women who are formed by nature for coition refuse, how much more must we [refuse to be used for an unnatural purpose]! Think you, if we throw ourselves into the sea, will we enter into the life of the world to come?' Immediately the Holy One, blessed be He, enlightened their eyes with this verse, *The Lord said: I will bring them back from Bashan, I will bring them back from the depths of the sea* (Ps. LXVIII, 23). '*I will bring them back from Bashan*,' i.e. I will bring them back from between the teeth of (*ben shinne*) lions; '*I will bring them back from the depths of the sea*' is to be understood literally.[1]

The first company [in the first ship] stood up and said, '*Surely we had not forgotten*[2] *the name of our God, or spread forth our hands to a strange god*' (*ib.* XLIV, 21), and they threw themselves into the sea. The second company stood up and said, '*Nay, but for Thy sake are we killed all the day*' (*ib.* 23), and they threw themselves into the sea. The third company stood up and said, '*Would not God search this out? For He knoweth the secrets of the heart*' (*ib.* 22), and they threw themselves into the sea. Then the Holy Spirit cried out, FOR THESE THINGS I WEEP.

Hadrian the accursed[3] set up three garrisons, one in Emmaus, a second in Kefar Leḳaṭia, and the third in Bethel of Judea.[4] He said, 'Whoever attempts to escape from one of them will be captured in another and vice versa.' He also sent out heralds to announce, 'Wherever there is a Jew, let him come forth, because the king wishes to give him an assurance [of safety].' The heralds proclaimed this

[1] I.e. even those who have been devoured by lions or drowned in the sea will be brought back to life at the Resurrection—an affirmative answer to their query. [2] I.e. we have not forgotten our God, although we are contemplating suicide to avoid disgrace.

[3] Lit. 'his bones be pulverised!'—an imprecation which generally followed his name because of the carnage he wrought in the Hadrianic wars (132 C.E.–135 C.E.). The story relates how he rounded up the fugitives.

[4] Strategical points in preventing the Jews from escaping from the country.

to them and so captured the Jews. That is what is written, *And Ephraim is become like a silly dove, without understanding* (Hos. VII, 11). [The heralds taunted the captured Jews with these words,] 'Instead of trying to restore the dead to life, pray that those still living shall not be seized.'[1] Those who understood [the ruse] did not come out [from their hiding places], but those who did not understand it all gathered in the valley of Beth Rimmon.[2] [Hadrian] said to the captain of his army, 'By the time I eat this slice of cake and the leg of this fowl, I must be able to look for a single person of all these [alive] without finding him.' He immediately surrounded them with his legions and slaughtered them, so that their blood streamed [to the coast and stained the sea] as far as Cyprus.[3] Then the Holy Spirit cried out, FOR THESE THINGS I WEEP.

Those Jews who were hidden [in the caves] devoured the flesh of their slain brethren.[4] Every day one of them ventured forth and brought the corpses to them which they ate. One day they said, 'Let one of us go, and if he finds anything let him bring it and we shall have to eat.' On going out he found the slain body of his father which he took and buried and marked the spot. He returned and reported that he had found nothing. They said, 'Let somebody else go, and if he find anything let him bring it and we shall have to eat.' When he went out he followed the scent; and on making a search, he discovered the body [of the man who had been buried]. He brought it to them and they ate it. After they had eaten it, they asked him, 'From where did you bring this corpse?' He replied, 'From a certain corner.' They then asked, 'What distinguishing mark was over it?' He told them what it was, and the son exclaimed, 'Woe to me! I have eaten the flesh of my father!' This is to fulfil what was said, *Therefore the fathers*

[1] The text is uncertain. With Y.'A. we must read מתין for איתי.

[2] Cf. II Kings V, 18. The valley where the Temple to the idol Rimmon was located.

[3] The text has 'the river of Cyprus'. What is related here is historically true. Cf. Graetz, *History* (Amer. ed.), II, p. 398.

[4] Since they were reduced to starvation.

shall eat the sons in the midst of thee, and the sons shall eat their fathers (Ezek. v, 10).

The wife of Trajan the accursed[1] gave birth to a child do the night of the ninth of Ab while all the Israelites were mourning [the destruction of the Temple]. The child nied on Ḥanukkah.[2] The Israelites said, 'Shall we kindle the lights or not?' They decided to light them and risk the consequences. They lit the candles, and persons slandered them to Trajan's wife, saying, 'When your child was born the Jews mourned, and when it died they kindled lights!' She sent a letter to her husband, 'Instead of subduing the barbarians, come and subdue the Jews who have revolted against you.' He boarded a ship and planned to do the voyage in ten days, but the winds brought him in five. On his arrival he found the Jews occupied with this verse, *The Lord will bring a nation against thee from far, from the end of the earth, as the vulture swoopeth down* (Deut. xxviii, 49). He said to them, 'I am the vulture who planned to come in ten days, but the wind brought me in five.' He surrounded them with his legions and slaughtered them. He said to the women, 'Yield yourselves to my troops, or I will do to you what I did to the men.' They replied to him, 'Do to the inferiors what you did to the superiors.' He forthwith surrounded them with his legions and slaughtered them, so that their blood mingled with that of the men, and streamed [to the coast and stained the sea] as far as Cyprus. Then the Holy Spirit cried out, FOR THESE THINGS I WEEP.

46. It is related that the two children of Zadok the priest,[3] one a boy and the other a girl, were taken captive, each falling to the lot of a different officer. One officer resorted to a harlot and gave her the boy [as a slave]. The other went to a store-keeper and gave him the girl for

[1] Cf. p. 125, n. 3. The following story shows why the same imprecation was applied to Trajan, Hadrian's predecessor. [2] The Feast of Dedication which marks the victory of Judas Maccabeus over Antiochus Epiphanes. It is observed by lighting candles for eight nights.
[3] In Buber's text he is called 'High Priest'. In Giṭ. 58*a* a similar story is related of the children of the High Priest Ishmael b. Elisha.

wine; to fulfil the text which is written, *And they have given a boy for a harlot, and sold a girl for wine* (Joel IV, 3). After a while the harlot brought the boy to the shopkeeper and said to him, 'Since I have a boy who is suitable for that girl, will you agree that they should marry and the issue will be divided by us?' He accepted the offer. They immediately took the two of them and placed them in a room. The girl began to weep, and the boy asked her why she was crying. She answered, 'Should I not weep when the daughter of a High Priest is given in marriage to a slave?' He inquired of her whose daughter she was and she replied, 'I am the daughter of Zadok the [High] Priest.' He then asked her where she used to live and she answered, 'In the upper market-place.' He next inquired what was the sign above the house and she told him. He said, 'Have you a brother or sister?' She answered, 'I had a brother and there was a mole upon his shoulder; and whenever he came home from school I used to uncover and kiss it.' He asked, 'If you were to see it, would you know it?' She answered that she would. He bared his shoulder[1] and they recognised one another. They embraced and kissed until they expired. Then the Holy Spirit cried out, FOR THESE THINGS I WEEP.

47. It is related of Miriam, the daughter of Boethus, that Joshua b. Gamla[2] married her, and the king appointed him to be High Priest. She once went to see him and said, 'I will go and see him reading[3] on the Day of Atonement in the Temple.' They laid carpets for her from the door of her house to the entrance of the Temple so that her feet might not be exposed, nevertheless they were exposed.[4] When her husband, Joshua, died, the Rabbis allowed her two *se'ah* of wine daily. But it has been taught: We do not allow wine to a woman,[5] and R. Ḥiyya b. Abba said:

[1] This is Buber's reading. The edd. have 'he bared himself'.
[2] Famous as the pioneer of the educational system in Palestine (B.B. 21*a*).
[3] From the Scriptures. The procedure is described in Yoma VII, 1.
[4] I.e. that she should not feel the damp, yet she did feel it, showing how delicate she was.
[5] When arranging her alimony. Keth. 65*a*.

It was a precaution against dissoluteness, as it is stated, *Harlotry, wine, and new wine take away the heart* (Hos. IV, 11). R. Hezekiah and R. Abbahu said in the name of R. Joḥanan: [They made the allowance] for cooking purposes [but not to drink]. It has further been taught: But if she was nursing a child they impose less work on her and increase her alimony; and R. Joshua b. Levi commented: What do they add? Wine, because it makes the milk abundant.[1] R. Eleazar b. R. Zadok remarked: May I not live to behold[2] the consolation [of Zion] if I did not see the Romans bind her hair to the tails of the horses of Arabs and make her run from Jerusalem to Lydda; and I quoted this verse in connection with her, *The tender and delicate woman among you, who would not adventure to set the sole of her foot upon the ground for delicateness and tenderness* (Deut. XXVIII, 56).

48. It is related of Miriam, the daughter of Naḳdimon,[3] that the Rabbis allowed her five hundred gold *dinars* daily to be spent on her store of perfumes. Nevertheless, she stood up and cursed them, saying, 'Make such a [paltry] allowance for your own daughters!' R. Aḥa said: We responded with Amen! R. Eleazar said: May I not live to behold the consolation [of Zion] if I did not see her gathering barley from beneath horses' hoofs in Acco; and I quoted this verse in connection with her, *If thou know not, O thou fairest among women, go thy way forth by the footsteps of the flock and feed thy kids* (S.S. I, 8)—read not '*gediyothayik*' ('thy kids') but *gewiyothayik* ('thy bodies').[4]

49. It is related of Miriam, the daughter of Tanḥum,[5] that she was taken captive and was ransomed at Acco. The people bought her a shift, and when she went to wash it in

[1] Keth. 65*b*. [2] Lit. 'May I behold', etc., a euphemistic expression.
[3] He is enumerated on p. 101 among the wealthy men of Jerusalem.
[4] The verse is interpreted: If you know not how to observe the Torah, then the time will come when you will have to go out among the footsteps of the flocks to seek grain to feed your bodies. [5] This is the correct form of the name. The text has: 'daughter of Boethus Naḥtum'.

the sea, a wave came and carried it away. They bought her another, and when she went to wash it in the sea a wave came and carried it away. They wished to buy her still another, but she said to them, 'Leave the Collector to collect His debt.' When she justified the heavenly decree against herself,[1] the Holy One, blessed be He, gave a hint to the sea which restored her garments to her.

50. It is related of Miriam, the daughter of Tanḥum,[2] that she was taken captive with her seven sons. The emperor took and placed them in the innermost of seven rooms. He had the eldest brought and said to him, 'Prostrate yourself before the image.' He answered, 'God forbid! I will not prostrate myself before an image.' 'Why?' asked the king. 'Because it is thus written in our Torah, *I am the Lord thy God'* (Exod. XX, 2). He immediately had him taken out and slain. He had the second brought and said to him, 'Prostrate yourself before the image.' He answered, 'God forbid! My brother did not prostrate himself and I will not.' 'Why?' the king asked. He replied, 'Because it is thus written in our Torah, *Thou shalt have no other gods before Me'* (*ib.* 3). He immediately ordered him to be slain. He had the third brought and said to him, 'Prostrate yourself before the image.' He answered, 'I will not prostrate myself.' 'Why?' the king asked. 'Because it is written in the Torah, *For thou shalt bow down to no other god'* (*ib.* XXXIV, 14). He immediately ordered him to be slain. He had the fourth brought who quoted, *He that sacrificeth unto the gods, save unto the Lord only, shall be utterly destroyed* (*ib.* XXII, 19), and he was ordered to be slain. He had the fifth brought, who also quoted, *Hear, O Israel, the Lord our God, the Lord is one* (Deut. VI, 4), and he was immediately ordered to be slain. He had the sixth brought who likewise quoted, *For the Lord thy God is in the midst of thee, a God*

[1] She admitted she must have done something wrong to be punished in this way. [2] Not 'Naḥtum' as in the text. In Giṭ. 57*b* the name of the woman is not given. A similar story is related of a woman named Hannah in connection with the persecution of Antiochus Epiphanes.

great and awful (*ib.* VII, 21), and he was ordered to be slain. He had the seventh brought, who was the youngest of them all, and the king said, 'My son, prostrate yourself before the image.' He answered, 'God forbid!' 'Why?' asked the king. 'Because it is thus written in our Torah, *Know this day, and lay it to thy heart, that the Lord, He is God in heaven above and upon the earth beneath; there is none else* (*ib.* IV, 39). Not only that, but we have sworn to our God that we will not exchange Him for any other god; as it is said, *Thou hast avouched the Lord this day to be thy God* (*ib.* XXVI, 17). And as we swore to Him, so He swore to us not to exchange us for another people; as it is said, *And the Lord hath avouched thee this day to be His own treasure*' (*ib.* 18). The emperor said to him, 'Your brothers had had their fill of years and of life and had experienced happiness; but you are young, you have had no fill of years and life and have not yet experienced happiness. Prostrate yourself before the image and I will bestow favours upon you.' He replied, 'It is written in our Torah, *The Lord shall reign for ever and ever* (Ex. XV, 18), and it is said, *The Lord is King for ever; the nations are perished out of His land* (Ps. X, 16). You are of no account and so are His enemies. A human being lives to-day and is dead to-morrow, rich to-day and poor to-morrow; but the Holy One, blessed be He, lives and endures for all eternity.' The emperor said to him, 'See, your brothers are slain before you. Behold, I will throw my ring to the ground in front of the image; pick it up so that all may know that you have obeyed my command.' He answered, 'Woe unto you, O emperor! If you are afraid of human beings who are the same as yourself, shall I not fear the supreme King of kings, the Holy One, blessed be He, the God of the universe!' He asked him, 'Has, then, the universe a God?' He replied, 'Shame on you, O emperor! Do you, then, behold a world without a Master!' He asked, 'Has your God a mouth?' He answered, 'In connection with your gods it is written, *They have mouths, but they speak not* (*ib.* CXV, 5); in connection with our God it is written, *By the word of the Lord were the heavens made*' (*ib.* XXXIII, 6). 'Has your God eyes?'

He answered, 'In connection with your gods it is written, *Eyes have they, but they see not* (*ib.* CXV, 5); in connection with our God it is written, *The eyes of the Lord, that run to and fro through the whole earth*' (Zech. IV, 10). 'Has your God ears?' He answered, 'In connection with your gods it is written, *They have ears, but they hear not* (Ps. CXV, 6); in connection with our God it is written, *And the Lord hearkened, and heard*' (Mal. III, 16). 'Has your God a nose?' He answered, 'In connection with your gods it is written, *Noses have they, but they smell not* (Ps. *loc. cit.*); in connection with our God it is written, *And the Lord smelled the sweet savour*' (Gen. VIII, 21). 'Has your God hands?' He answered, 'In connection with your gods it is written, *They have hands, but they handle not* (Ps. CXV, 7); in connection with our God it is written, *Yea, My hand hath laid the foundation of the earth*' (Isa. XLVIII, 13). 'Has your God feet?' He answered, 'In connection with your gods it is written, *Feet have they, but they walk not* (Ps. *loc. cit.*); in connection with our God it is written, *And His feet shall stand in that day upon the Mount of Olives*' (Zech. XIV, 4). 'Has your God a throat?' He answered, 'In connection with your gods it is written, *Neither speak they with their throat* (Ps. *loc. cit.*); in connection with our God it is written, *And sound goeth out of His mouth*' (Job XXXVII, 2). The king asked, 'If there are all these attributes in your God, why does He not deliver you out of my hand in the same manner that He rescued Hananiah, Mishael, and Azariah from the hands of Nebuchadnezzar?' He answered, 'Hananiah, Mishael, and Azariah were worthy men, and king Nebuchadnezzar was deserving that a miracle should be performed through him. You, however, are undeserving; and as for ourselves, our lives are forfeit to heaven. If you do not slay us, the Omnipresent has numerous executioners. There are many bears, wolves, serpents, leopards, and scorpions to attack and kill us; but in the end the Holy One, blessed be He, will avenge our blood on you.' The king immediately ordered him to be put to death.

The child's mother said to him, 'By the life of your head,

O emperor, give me my son that I may embrace and kiss him.' They gave him to her, and she bared her breasts and suckled him. She said to the king, 'By the life of your head, O emperor, put me to death first and then slay him.' He answered her, 'I cannot agree to that because it is written in your Torah, *And whether it be cow or ewe, ye shall not kill it and its young both in one day*' (Lev. XXII, 28). She retorted, 'You unutterable fool! Have you already fulfilled all the commandments save only this one!' He immediately ordered him to be slain. The mother threw herself upon her child and embraced and kissed him. She said to him, 'My son, go to the patriarch Abraham and tell him, "Thus said my mother, 'Do not preen yourself [on your righteousness], saying I built an altar and offered up my son, Isaac.' Behold, our mother built seven altars and offered up seven sons in one day. Yours was only a test, but mine was in earnest."' While she was embracing and kissing him, the king gave an order and they killed him in her arms. When he had been slain, the Sages calculated the age of that child and found that he was two years, six months, and six and a half hours old.[1] At that time all the peoples of the world cried out, 'What does their God do for them that they are all the time slain for His sake!' And concerning them it is written, *Nay, but for Thy sake are we killed all the day* (Ps. XLIV, 23). After a few days the woman became demented and fell from a roof and died, to fulfil what is said, *She that hath borne seven languisheth* (Jer. XV, 9). A *Bath Ḳol* issued forth and proclaimed, '*A joyful mother of children*' (Ps. CXIII, 9); and the Holy Spirit cried out, FOR THESE THINGS I WEEP.

51. It is related that Doeg b. Joseph died and left a young son to his mother,[2] who used to measure him by handbreadths and give his weight in gold to the Temple[3] every year. When, however, the besieging army surrounded

[1] Buber's reading is: Six years and a half and two hours.
[2] In Yoma 38*b* the child's name is given as Doeg b. Joseph, and his mother is said to have donated his weight in gold every day.
[3] Lit. 'to heaven'.

Jerusalem, his mother slaughtered him and ate him; and Jeremiah lamented before the Omnipresent, saying, '*See, O Lord, and consider, to whom Thou hast done thus! Shall the women eat their fruit, the children that are dandled in the hands?*' (Lam. II, 20).[1] But the Holy Spirit retorted, '*Shall the priest and the prophet be slain in the sanctuary of the Lord?*' (*ib.*) referring to Zechariah the son of Jehoiada.[2]

Another interpretation of FOR THESE THINGS I WEEP: R. Judah and R. Nehemiah offer explanations. R. Judah says: [The weeping was] over the loss of sense and the departure of the *Shechinah*. Was it possible that Zedekiah should see others piercing his eyes[3] without having the sense to dash his head against the wall until he expired? But instead he caused his sons to be slain in his presence[4]; and concerning that time it was said, *The heart of the king shall fail,*[5] *and the heart of the princes* (Jer. IV, 9). R. Nehemiah said: [The weeping was] over the cessation of the priesthood and kingship. That is what is written, *These are the two anointed ones, that stand by the Lord of the whole earth* (Zech. IV, 14), alluding to Aaron and David. Aaron puts in a claim on behalf of his priesthood and David on behalf of his kingship. R. Joshua b. Levi said: [The weeping was] over the cessation of Torah,[6] as it is stated, These *are the statutes and the ordinances* (Deut. XII, 1).[7] R. Samuel b. Naḥmani said: [The weeping was] over idolatry. That is what is stated, This[8] *is thy God, O Israel* (Ex. XXXII, 4). Zabdi b. Levi said: [The weeping was] over the cessation of the sacrifices. That is what is stated, *These ye shall offer unto the Lord in your appointed seasons* (Num. XXIX, 39).

[1] *Ṭippuḥim* ('dandled in the hands') is read as *ṭefuḥim* 'measured by handbreadths', as a mark of intense love.
[2] V. p. 8. We have here cause and effect, the sin and its punishment.
[3] Cf. II Kings XXV, 7.
[4] By not committing suicide. The Rabbis maintain that he did not actually become blind until his sons were killed (M.K. and 'E.J.).
[5] Lit. 'shall be lost', which is a Hebrew idiom for loss of understanding and common sense.
[6] Which led to the exile—similarly the following statements.
[7] And for *these* (statutes and ordinances) I weep—similarly the following.
[8] Heb. *èleh,* lit. 'these'.

The Rabbis say: [The weeping was] over the cessation of the levitical watches. What advantage, then, had the world from these watches? On Monday they fasted for the safety of those who were travelling by sea. On Tuesday they fasted for the safety of wayfarers. On Wednesday they fasted for the children that they should not be afflicted with croup and die. On Thursday they fasted for pregnant women that they should not miscarry and for nursing mothers that their children should not die.[1] But is it not a fact that we may not fast for two objects at the same time[2]; as it is written, *So we fasted and besought our God* for this (Ezra VIII, 23),[3] and a verse in Daniel declares, *That they might ask mercy of the God of heaven concerning* this secret (II, 18)—i.e. not for two secrets? The fact, however, is as R. Ḥiyya b. Abba said: For both the withholding of rain and the exile[4] we may fast at one and the same time, but we may not fast on Friday or the Sabbath because of the honour of the Sabbath.

MINE EYE, MINE EYE RUNNETH DOWN WITH WATER. R. Levi said: It may be likened to a physician one of whose eyes was weak [and watered] and he said, 'My eye weeps for my other eye.' Similarly Israel is called 'the eye of the Holy One, blessed be He', as it is said, *For the Lord's is the eye of man and all the tribes of Israel* (Zech. IX, 1). If it is possible to say so, the Holy One, blessed be He, said, 'Mine eye weeps for My other eye' [i.e. Israel].[5]

BECAUSE THE COMFORTER IS FAR FROM ME, EVEN HE THAT SHOULD REFRESH MY SOUL. What is the name of King Messiah? R. Abba b. Kahana said: His name

[1] Ta'an. 27*b*. [2] *Ib*. 8*b*. [3] The phrase *for this* denotes one thing.
[4] In the version in P. Ta'an. 68*b* the reference is to the withholding of rain and *locusts*, the two things being similar as a danger to the food-supply. On the present reading 'E.J. explains that drought and exile are likewise regarded as the same thing, because through the famine caused by drought people must wander away from their homes to seek sustenance. So here, too, fasting for expectant mothers and nursing-mothers is for a similar object.
[5] This is the Midrashic explanation of the repetition, MINE EYE, MINE EYE.

is 'the Lord'; as it is stated, *And this is the name whereby he shall be called, The Lord is our righteousness* (Jer. XXIII, 6).[1] For R. Levi said: It is good for a province when its name is identical with that of its king, and the name of its king identical with that of its God. 'It is good for a province when its name is identical with that of its king,' as it is written, *And the name of the city from that day shall be the Lord is there* (Ezek. XLVIII, 35).[2] 'And the name of its king identical with that of its God,' as it is stated, '*And this is the name whereby he shall be called, The Lord is our righteousness.*' R. Joshua b. Levi said: His name is 'Shoot'; as it is stated, *Behold, a man whose name is Shoot, and who shall shoot up out of his place, and build the temple of the Lord* (Zech. VI, 12). R. Judan said in the name of R. Aibu: His name is 'Comforter'; as it is said, THE COMFORTER IS FAR FROM ME. R. Ḥanina said: They do not really differ, because the numerical value of the names is the same, so that 'Comforter' is identical with 'Shoot'.

The following story supports what R. Judan said in the name of R. Aibu: It happened that a man was ploughing, when one of his oxen lowed. An Arab passed by and asked, 'What are you?' He answered, 'I am a Jew.' He said to him, 'Unharness your ox and untie your plough' [as a mark of mourning]. 'Why?' he asked. 'Because the Temple of the Jews is destroyed.' He inquired, 'From where do you know this?' He answered, 'I know it from the lowing of your ox.' While he was conversing with him, the ox lowed again. The Arab said to him, 'Harness your ox and tie up your plough, because the deliverer of the Jews is born.' 'What is his name?' he asked; and he answered, 'His name is "Comforter".' 'What is his father's name?' He answered, 'Hezekiah.' 'Where do they live?' He answered, 'In Birath 'Arba[3] in Bethlehem of Judah.'

The man sold his oxen and plough and bought felt garments for children. He journeyed from one city to

[1] Cf. B.B. 75*b* (Sonc. ed., p. 303).
[2] The Talmud (*loc. cit.*) adds: 'Do not read *shamah* "there" but *shemah* "its name",' i.e. 'the Lord shall be its name'.
[3] In J. Ber. 5*a* the reading is: 'in the royal capital of Bethlehem.'

another and from one province to another until he reached that place. All the villagers came to buy garments from him, but the mother of that child made no purchase of him. He asked her, 'Why do you not buy children's felt garments?' She answered, 'Because a hard fate is in store for my child.'[1] 'Why?' he asked; and she answered, 'Because close on his coming the Temple was destroyed.' He said to her, 'We trust in the Lord of the Universe that as close on his coming it was destroyed so close on his coming it will be rebuilt.' He continued, 'Take some of these felt garments for your child and after some days I will come to your house to collect the money.' She took some and departed. After some days the man said, 'I will go and see how the child is getting on.' He came to the woman and asked, 'How is the child?' She answered, 'Did I not tell you that a hard fate is in store for him? Misfortune has dogged him.[2] From the time [you left] there have been strong winds and a whirlwind came and carried him off.' He said to her, 'Did I not tell you at his coming [the Temple] was destroyed and at his coming it will be rebuilt?'[3] R. Abun said: Why should I learn this from an Arab when there is an explicit text wherein it is stated, *And Lebanon*[4] *shall fall by a mighty one* (Isa. X, 34), which is followed by, *And there shall come forth a shoot out of the stock of Jesse, and a twig shall grow forth out of his roots* (*ib.* XI, 1)?[5]

The school of R. Shila said: The Messiah's name is 'Shiloh', as it is stated, *Until Shiloh come* (Gen. XLIX, 10), where the word is spelt *Shlh.*[6] The School of R. Ḥanina

[1] So Jastrow. The text is doubtful, and the Pal. Talmud has a different version. The tradition was that the Messiah would be born on the day that the Temple was destroyed. [2] The text is uncertain.

[3] The fact that the storm carried him away was evidence that the child was to be used for a supernatural purpose. [4] The Temple, v. p. 102.

[5] Which teaches that on the same day that the Lebanon (sc. the Temple) shall fall, there shall come forth a shoot, etc., sc. the Messiah.

[6] The point is not clear. The received text is actually שילה, not שלה as the Midrash states. Following M.K. and 'E.J. the passage is to be explained thus: The School of R. Shila said: The Messiah's name is 'Shilah' (not 'Shiloh'), as it is stated, *Until Shiloh come*, where the word is written Shilah (שילה as emended), i.e. without a *waw* at the end, and so it may read, 'Shilah'.

said: His name is 'Ḥaninah', as it is stated, *I will not give you* Ḥaninah (Jer. XVI, 13).[1] The School of R. Jannai said: His name is 'Yinnon'; for it is written, *E'er the sun was, his name is* Yinnon (Ps. LXXII, 17).[2] R. Biba of Sergunieh[3] said: His name is 'Nehirah', as it is stated, *And the light* (nehorah) *dwelleth with Him* (Dan. II, 22), where the word is spelt *nehirah.*

R. Judah b. R. Simon said in the name of R. Samuel b. R. Isaac: King Messiah, whether he be of those still living or of those who are dead, bears the name of David. R. Tanḥuma said: I will give his reason, viz. *Great salvation giveth He to His king; and showeth mercy to His Messiah* (Ps. XVIII, 51), and the text continues, not 'and to David' but *to David and to his seed, for evermore.*[4]

MY CHILDREN ARE DESOLATE, BECAUSE THE ENEMY HATH PREVAILED. R. Aibu said: It is like the tuber of a cabbage; as the latter grows the former diminishes in size.[5] R. Judah b. R. Simon said: It is like a sow which grows smaller as her litter grows bigger.[6]

52. ZION SPREADETH FORTH HER HANDS (I, 17).[7] It is written, *Oh that My head were waters, and Mine eyes a fountain of tears* (Jer. VIII, 23). Who spoke this verse? If you answer that it was Jeremiah, is it possible that he should exist without food and sleep?[8] Who, then, spoke it? He Who indulges neither in eating nor sleeping; as it is written, *Behold, He that keepeth Israel doth neither slumber nor sleep* (Ps. CXXI, 4).

[1] E.V. *'I will show you no favour'.*
[2] E.V. *'May his name be continued as long as the sun'.* Each school discovered a name similar to that of their teacher. This passage is quoted from Sanh. 98*b* (Sonc. ed., p. 667). [3] Near Tiberias.
[4] This is interpreted: to David His Messiah or to one of his seed who will be named David. [5] Similarly, the more powerful the enemy grows the weaker Israel becomes. [6] M.K. quoting the reading in an old MS. states that this refers to when the sow is suckling its young.
[7] Radal suggests that what follows belongs to the preceding verse, FOR THESE THINGS I WEEP, and not to ZION SPREADETH FORTH HER HANDS. It is omitted in Buber's ed.
[8] The verse continues, *That I might weep day and night,* i.e. without stopping to eat or sleep.

R. Abba b. Kahana said in the name of R. Levi: It is written, *And God said: Let the waters under the heavens be gathered together unto one place* (Gen. I, 9). The Holy One, blessed be He, said, 'Let the waters gather themselves unto Me for the purpose for which I will utilise them.'[1] R. Ḥaggai said in the name of R. Isaac: It may be likened to a king who built a palace for himself in which he placed dumb residents; and every day they arose in the morning and greeted the king and praised him with gestures and pointing. The king said, 'If these persons who are dumb praise me thus, how much more so if they could speak!' What did he do? He placed in the palace residents possessed of the power of speech. They arose and seized the king's palace, saying, 'This palace belongs to nobody but us!' Then said the king, 'Let the palace return to its former condition.' Similarly, at the beginning of the world's creation His praise ascended only from the waters; as it is written, *From the voices of many waters, the mighty breakers of the sea* (Ps. XCIII, 4). And what did they say? *The Lord on high is mighty* (*ib.*). At that time the Holy One, blessed be He, said, 'If these waters which possess no mouth, tongue, utterance or speech praise Me thus, how much more [shall I be praised] when I create human beings!' When, however, He created human beings, the generation of Enosh[2] and the generation of the Flood rebelled against Him. Then said the Holy One, blessed be He, 'Let the world return to its former condition'; as it is stated, *And the rain was upon the earth* (Gen. VII, 12).[3]

R. Judah b. R. Simon said: It may be likened to a man who possessed nothing but a staff and a basket. By dint of saving he procured himself some sheep; but wolves entered and tore them to pieces. Whereupon the shepherd said, 'I will return to my staff and my basket.' Like this shepherd is the Holy One, blessed be He; as it is said, *Give ear, O Shepherd of Israel, Thou that leadest Israel like*

[1] To weep for the destruction of the Temple ('E.J.).
[2] V. Gen. IV, 26. They 'profaned' (not *called upon*) the name of the Lord, according to Rabbinic interpretation. [3] Quoted from Gen. R. V, 1.

a flock; Thou that art enthroned upon the cherubim, shine forth (Ps. LXXX, 2). The sheep are Israel; as it is said, *And ye are My sheep, the sheep of My pasture* (Ezek. XXXIV, 31). Wolves penetrated among His flock and tore them to pieces; this refers to the enemies who entered the Temple. At that time the Holy One, blessed be He, said, 'Oh that My head were waters.'

It is written, *These things I remember, and pour out my soul within me* (Ps. XLII, 5). The Community of Israel spake before the Holy One, blessed be He: 'In the past I used to go up to Jerusalem along well-kept roads, but now through thorny hedges'; as it is said, *Therefore, behold, I will hedge up thy way with thorns* (Hos. II, 8). Another interpretation of '*These things I remember*': In the past I used to go up and the trees formed a covering above my head, but now I am exposed[1] to the sun. '*These things I remember*': In the past I used to go up in the shade of the Holy One, blessed be He, but now in the shadow of [oppressive] governments.

'*These things I remember*': The emperor Vespasian placed watchmen eighteen miles from Emmaus[2] who used to question the pilgrims and ask them, 'To whom do you belong?' They would answer, 'We are the men of Vespasian, or Trajan, or Hadrian.'[3] R. Berekiah said: The Community of Israel spake before the Holy One, blessed be He: 'In the past I used to go up with baskets of first-fruits on my head.' Early in the morning [the pilgrims] used to exclaim, '*Arise ye, and let us go up to Zion*' (Jer. XXXI, 6). While on the road they used to exclaim, '*Our feet are standing within thy gates, O Jerusalem*' (Ps. CXXII, 2).[4] When they were on the Temple Mount

[1] Reading גלויה with Radal. The text has תלויה 'dependent'.

[2] The text has פומעים; commentaries assume this to be another reading of פמיים, Pameas (Cæsarea Philippi) in the north of Palestine. But it is preferable to adopt the reading עימום, Emmaus, which was 22 miles from Jerusalem.

[3] This explains the phrase 'but now in the shadow of [oppressive] governments'; because if they had not acknowledged allegiance to the emperor they would have been killed.

[4] This is cited from P. Bik. III, 2 (65*c*), but Maimonides states while on the road they used to exclaim, '*I rejoiced when they said unto me: Let us go into the house of the Lord*' (Ps. CXXII, 1), and when they arrived at the gates of Jerusalem they exclaimed, '*Our feet,*' etc.

what used they to say? '*Hallelujah. Praise God in His sanctuary*' (*ib.* CL, 1). And what used they to say when in the Temple Court? '*Let everything that hath breath praise the Lord*' (*ib.* 6). But now, *I will silence them* (*ib.* XLII, 5)[1]: in silence I go up and in silence I come down. '*These things I remember*': In the past I used to go up with songs and psalms before the Holy One, blessed be He, as it is stated, *With the voice of joy and praise* (*ib.*). Now I go up with weeping and come down with weeping. '*These things I remember*': In the past I used to go up in crowds of holiday-makers, as it is stated, *A multitude keeping holy-day* (*ib.*). R. Levi said: They were like a cataract which stops neither by day nor night. But now I go up in silence and come down in silence: '*These things I remember, and pour out my soul within me.*'

Another interpretation of[2] ZION SPREADETH FORTH HER HANDS: R. Joshua of Siknin said in the name of R. Levi: It may be likened to a king who had a son whom he struck, and the latter said, 'I have sinned.' He struck him again and he said, 'I have sinned and acted foolishly.' He kept on striking him until he spread out his ten fingers before his father.[3] Similarly the Holy One, blessed be He, kept chastening Jerusalem, and it exclaimed, 'I have sinned' until ZION SPREADETH FORTH HER HANDS.

THERE IS NONE TO COMFORT HER. R Levi said: Wherever it is stated '*there is none*' it indicates that there would be in the future. For example, *And Sarai was barren; she had no child* (Gen. XI, 30). But she did later have one, as it is said, *And the Lord remembered Sarah* (*ib.* XXI, 1). Similarly, *But Hannah had no children* (1 Sam. I, 2), but she did later have them, as it is said, *So the Lord remembered Hannah* (*ib.* II, 21). Similarly, *She is Zion, there is none that careth for her* (Jer. XXX, 17); but she will later have one, as it is said, *And a redeemer will come to Zion*

[1] E.V. '*and led them*'.
[2] These words should perhaps be omitted, because the exposition of '*Zion spreadeth*' really begins here; v. p. 138, n. 7.
[3] In agony or supplication.

(Isa. LIX, 20). And so here THERE IS NONE TO COMFORT HER, but she will have later, as it is said, *I, even I, am He that comforteth you* (*ib.* LI, 12).[1]

THE LORD HATH COMMANDED CONCERNING JACOB, THAT THEY THAT ARE ROUND ABOUT HIM SHOULD BE HIS ADVERSARIES: like Ḥallamish to Naveh, Castra to Ḥaifa, Susitha to Tiberias, Jericho to Naaran, Lydda to Ono.[2]

JERUSALEM IS AMONG THEM AS ONE UNCLEAN: she has become an abomination.

53. THE LORD IS RIGHTEOUS; FOR I HAVE REBELLED AGAINST HIS WORD (I, 18). Who uttered this: It was said by Josiah; as it is stated, *After all this, when Josiah had prepared the temple, Neco king of Egypt went up to fight against Carcemish by the Euphrates* (i.e. Circesium which is by the Euphrates) . . . *But he sent ambassadors to him, saying: What have I to do with thee, thou king of Judah? I come not against thee this day, but against the house wherewith I have war; and God hath given command to speed me* (II Chron. XXXV, 20 f.). [Neco said,] 'By command of the Holy One, blessed be He, do I come up.' [He continued,] *Forbear thee from meddling with the god who is with me* (*ib.*)—this is the language of idolatry.[3] *Nevertheless Josiah would not turn his face from him . . . and hearkened not unto the words of Neco, from the mouth of God* (*ib.* 22)—this alludes to Jeremiah who said to Josiah, 'I have this tradition from my teacher, Isaiah,[4] *And I will spur Egypt against Egypt*' (Isa. XIX, 2)[5]; but he would not

[1] Repeated from § 26. [2] V. Lev. R. XXIII, 5 and S.S. R. II, 2, § 5.

[3] In the E.V. the reference is to God, but the Midrash regards the word as denoting a heathen deity. Hence according to the Midrash he first referred to a command of the true God, and then added that his own heathen deities were assisting him.

[4] Jeremiah, of course, could not have had a tradition directly from Isaiah, as far too great an interval separated them. But he meant that Isaiah, being an earlier prophet, could in general be regarded as his teacher.

[5] The continuation is *I will give over the Egyptians into the hand of a cruel lord* (*ib.* 4), and the tradition which Jeremiah received was that the conqueror of Egypt would be Nebuchadnezzar and not Josiah (Mah.). Or perhaps it simply means that Egypt's defeat would come about through internal dissension, without Josiah's intervention.

listen to him. Josiah replied to him, 'Has not your teacher's teacher, Moses, declared, *Neither shall the sword go through your land* (Lev. XXVI, 6)? Then shall the sword of this wicked person pass through my land and borders!' He was, however, unaware that all the people of his generation were idolaters.[1] Josiah had sent two disciples [of the Sages] to eradicate idolatry from the people's houses. When they entered the houses they found nothing.[2] As they went out they were told to shut the doors; and when they shut the doors the people inside could see the idol. They said concerning these disciples, 'What they rectified[3] on entering they spoilt on departing.' On that account, *The archers shot at King Josiah* (II Chron. XXXV, 23). R. Manni said: They shot three hundred arrows into him until his body became like a sieve, and Jeremiah placed his ear behind [the dying king] to know what he was saying. And what did he say? '*The Lord is righteous; for I have rebelled against His word*'—against His word and the word of His agent.

54. I CALLED FOR MY LOVERS, BUT THEY DECEIVED ME (I, 19). The Rabbis interpret the verse as an allusion to the false prophets who made me to love their idol-worship. THEY DECEIVED ME—yes, they deceived me and ceased not uttering false prophecy concerning me until they caused me to go into exile from my place; as it is said, *Thy prophets have seen visions for thee of vanity and delusion* (Lam. II, 14), the word for '*delusion*', viz. *madduḥim*, being read as *maddiḥim*,[4] 'they seduce' [me into exile]. R. Simeon b. Yoḥai interpreted the verse as an allusion to the true prophets who made me beloved by the

[1] And therefore the promise, made to Israel if loyal to God, did not hold good in his time.
[2] M.K. explains: the idol was affixed to the door on the inside which was formed in two leaves, so that when the door was opened one half covered the other and the idol was hidden.
[3] From their point of view, viz. they divided up the idol when they opened the door, but made it whole again when they shut the door.
[4] This variant is not found in our text of the Hebrew Bible. Y.'A., however, apparently reads: this is written, 'through their casting me away,' i.e. they are responsible for my exile. The Biblical text can be made to mean this by a change in vocalisation.

Holy One, blessed be He. THEY DECEIVED ME—they deceived me by saying, 'Separate the priestly due and the tithes.' But does the law concerning the priestly due and the tithes apply in Babylon? They said this, however, to make me beloved by the Holy One, blessed be He. That is what Jeremiah says, *Set thee up waymarks*—ẓiyyunim (Jer. XXXI, 21), i.e. distinguish thyself with the precepts wherewith Israel is distinguished (*meẓuyyanim*). '*Make thee guide-posts*' (*ib.*)[1]: this alludes to the destruction of the Temple; and thus it states, *If I forget thee, O Jerusalem, let my right hand forget her cunning* (Ps. CXXXVII, 5). *Set thy heart toward the highway, even the way by which thou wentest* (Jer. *loc. cit.*). R. Ḥiyya said: The consonantal text reads 'I went'.[2] You find that when the Israelites were exiled to Babylon, what is written? *For your sake I have sent*[3] *to Babylon* (Isa. XLIII, 14). When they were exiled to Elam, the *Shechinah* was with them, as it is written, *And I will set My throne in Elam* (Jer. XLIX, 38). When they were exiled to Greece the *Shechinah* was with them, for it is written, *And I will stir up thy sons, O Zion, against thy sons, O Javan* (Zech. IX, 13),[4] and this is followed by, *And the Lord shall be seen over them* (*ib.* 14). Therefore it is written, '*Even the way by which I* (God) *went.*'

Another interpretation of '*Set thy heart toward the highway, even the way by which thou wentest*': Jeremiah said to them, 'Look to the ways in which you walked and repent,' as it is written, *Return, O virgin of Israel* (Jer. XXXI, 21), 'and you shall immediately be restored to your cities,' as it is written, *Return to these thy cities* (*ib.*).

55. BEHOLD, O LORD, FOR I AM IN DISTRESS, MINE INWARDS BURN—ḤOMARMARU (I, 20). R. Ḥiyya b. Ḥanina said: He made them like ruined piles (*ḥamoroth*). R. Samuel b. Naḥmani said: Like clods of earth.

[1] M.K. explains *guide-posts* as something to be a constant reminder of the destruction of the Temple. [2] God went with them into captivity. [3] The Rabbis read שלחתי 'I was sent', instead of שלחתי 'I sent' and thus deduced that the *Shechinah* accompanied them in exile; cf. Ex. R. XV, 16. [4] The Rabbis understood Javan to mean Greece, v. *J.E.* art. Javan.

MY HEART IS TURNED WITHIN ME. Why? FOR I HAVE GRIEVOUSLY REBELLED.

ABROAD THE SWORD BEREAVETH, AT HOME THERE IS THE LIKE OF DEATH. That is what Moses said, *Without shall the sword bereave, and in the chambers terror* (Deut. XXXII, 25).

56. THEY HAVE HEARD THAT I SIGH (I, 21). R. Joshua interpreted the verse as referring to Aaron. You find that when Aaron died, the clouds of glory departed and all Israel assembled to mourn him. They said, 'Moses mourns, Eleazar mourns, so who should not mourn?' What is immediately recorded there? *And the Canaanite, the king of Arad, who dwelt in the South, heard*[1] . . . *and he fought against Israel, and took some of them captive* (Num. XXI, 1). The Rabbis interpret the verse as referring to the destruction of the Temple. You find that every place where Israel attempted to flee the inhabitants stopped them. They attempted to flee northwards but the people would not let them, as it is written, *For three transgressions of Gaza, yea, for four, I will not reverse it: because they carried away captive a whole captivity, to deliver them up to Edom* (Amos I, 6). They attempted to flee eastward but the people would not let them, as it is written, *For three transgressions of Tyre, yea, for four, I will not reverse it; because they delivered up a whole captivity to Edom, and remembered not the brotherly covenant* (*ib.* 9). They attempted to flee westward but the people would not let them, as it is written, *The burden upon Arabia. In the thickets in Arabia shall ye lodge, O ye caravans of Dedanites* (Isa. XXI, 13).[2]

FOR THOU HAST DONE IT. It may be likened to a king who married a lady to whom he said, 'Have no intercourse with your [former] companions; borrow nothing from them and lend them nothing.' Subsequently the king became angry with her and drove her out of the palace. She went about to all her neighbours, but none

[1] Of the mourning for Aaron, and he used the occasion to launch an attack. Thus, THEY HAVE HEARD THAT I SIGH—and took advantage thereof. [2] Referring to Israel caught in the Arabian thickets.

would receive her. So she returned to the palace, and the king said to her, 'You have acted impudently [by coming back]!' She replied to the king, 'My lord, if I had lent them an article and borrowed one from them, and if some of my stuff was in their possession or their stuff in my possession, would they not have received me?'[1] Similarly, the Holy One, blessed be He, said to Israel, 'You have acted impudently [in appealing to Me].' They spake before Him, 'Lord of the Universe, didst Thou not write in Thy Torah, *Neither shalt thou make marriage with them: thy daughter thou shalt not give unto his son, nor his daughter shalt thou take unto thy son* (Deut. VII, 3)? If we had had relations with them and intermarried with them, would they not have received us? Hence, FOR THOU HAST DONE IT.'[2]

THOU WILT BRING THE DAY THAT THOU HAST PROCLAIMED, AND THEY SHALL BE LIKE UNTO ME. LIKE UNTO ME in trouble,[3] but not LIKE UNTO ME in relief.

57. LET ALL THEIR WICKEDNESS COME BEFORE THEE; AND DO UNTO THEM, AS THOU HAST DONE UNTO ME (I, 22). Bring upon them what Thou hast brought upon me; be as strict with them as Thou hast been strict with me. AND DO UNTO THEM, i.e. cut off their gleanings[4] as Thou hast cut off mine.

FOR MY SIGHS ARE MANY, AND MY HEART IS FAINT. You find that with the thing through which Israel sinned they were punished, and with the same thing they were comforted. They sinned with 'head', were punished with it and comforted with it. They sinned with 'head', as it is written, *Let us make a head, and return into Egypt* (Num. XIV, 4); were punished with 'head', as it is written, *The whole head is sick* (Isa. I, 5); and are comforted with 'head', as it is written, *And their king is passed on before*

[1] She was homeless because she obeyed her husband's command.
[2] Obedience to God's command is the cause of Israel's isolation.
[3] As mentioned in the next verse, *Do unto them, as Thou hast done unto me*. But whereas Israel's time of distress is limited theirs is without limit.
[4] Cf. § 40, p. 118, n. 1.

them, and the Lord at the head of them (Micah II, 13). They sinned with 'ear', as it is written, *They stopped their ears, that they might not hear* (Zech. VII, 11); were punished with 'ear', as it is written, *Behold, I will do a thing in Israel, at which both the ears of every one that heareth it shall tingle* (I Sam. III, 11); and are comforted with 'ear', as it is written, *And thine ears shall hear a word behind thee, saying: This is the way, walk ye in it* (Isa. XXX, 21). They sinned with 'eye', as it is written, *Because the daughters of Zion are haughty, and walk with stretched-forth necks and wanton eyes* (*ib.* III, 16); were punished with 'eye', as it is written, *Mine eye, mine eye runneth down with water* (Lam. I, 16); and are comforted with 'eye', as it is written, *For they shall see, eye to eye, the Lord returning to Zion* (Isa. LII, 8). They sinned with 'nose' (*af*), as it is written, *And, lo, they put the branch to their nose* (Ezek. VIII, 17); were punished with '*af*', as it is written, *I also* (af) *will walk contrary unto them* (Lev. XXVI, 41); and are comforted with '*af*', as it is written, *And yet* (af) *for all that, when they are in the land of their enemies, I will not reject them* (*ib.* 44). They sinned with 'mouth', as it is written, *And every mouth speaketh wantonness* (Isa. IX, 16); were punished with 'mouth', as it is written, *And they devour Israel with open mouth* (*ib.* 11); and are comforted with 'mouth', as it is written, *Then was our mouth filled with laughter* (Ps. CXXVI, 2). They sinned with 'tongue', as it is written, *And they bend their tongue, their bow of falsehood* (Jer. IX, 2); were punished with 'tongue', as it is written, *The tongue of the sucking child cleaveth to the roof of his mouth for thirst* (Lam. IV, 4); and are comforted with 'tongue', as it is written, *And our tongue with singing* (Ps. *loc. cit.*). They sinned with 'heart', as it is written, *Yea, they made their hearts as an adamant stone* (Zech. VII, 12); were punished with 'heart', as it is written, *And the whole heart faint* (Isa. I, 5); and are comforted with 'heart', as it is written, *Bid Jerusalem take heart* (*ib.* XL, 2). They sinned with 'hand', as it is written, *Your hands are full of blood* (*ib.* I, 15); were punished with 'hand', as it is written, *The hands of women full of compassion have sodden their own children*

(Lam. IV, 10); and are comforted with 'hand', as it is written, *The Lord will set His hand again the second time* (Isa. XI, 11). They sinned with 'foot', as it is written, *For their feet run to evil* (Prov. I, 16); were punished with 'foot', as it is written, *Before your feet stumble upon the mountains of twilight* (Jer. XIII, 16); and are comforted with 'foot', as it is written, *How beautiful upon the mountains are the feet of the messenger of good tidings* (Isa. LII, 7). They sinned with '*hu*' ('He'), as it is written, *They have belied the Lord, and said: It is not He* (Jer. V, 12); were punished with '*hu*', as it is written, *Therefore He was turned to be their enemy, Himself* (hu) *fought against them* (Isa. LXIII, 10); and are comforted with '*hu*', as it is written, *I, even I, am He that comforteth you* (*ib.* LI, 12). They sinned with 'this', as it is written, *For as for this Moses, the man that brought us up out of the land of Egypt* (Ex. XXXII, 1)[1]; were punished with 'this', as it is written, *For this our heart is faint* (Lam. V, 17); and are comforted with 'this', as it is written, *Lo, this is our God, for Whom we waited* (Isa. XXV, 9). They sinned with 'fire', as it is written, *The children gather wood, and the fathers kindle the fire* (Jer. VII, 18)[2]; were punished with 'fire', as it is written, *From on high hath He sent fire into my bones* (Lam. I, 13); and are comforted with 'fire', as it is written, *For I, saith the Lord, will be unto her a wall of fire round about* (Zech. II, 9). They sinned with '*yesh*' ('is there?'), as it is written, *Is* (ha-yesh) *the Lord among us, or not?* (Ex. XVII, 7); were punished with '*yesh*', as it is written, *If there be* (yesh) *any pain like unto my pain* (Lam. I, 12); and are comforted with '*yesh*', as it is written, *That I may cause those that love Me to inherit substance* (yesh), *and that I may fill their treasuries* (Prov. VIII, 21). They sinned doubly, as it is written, *Jerusalem hath grievously sinned* (Lam. I, 8)[3]; were punished doubly, as it is written, *She hath received of the Lord's hand double for all her sins* (Isa. XL, 2); and are comforted doubly, as it is written, *Comfort ye, comfort ye My people, saith your God* (*ib.* 1).

[1] Relating to the sin of the golden calf.
[2] To make cakes for *the queen of heaven*.
[3] Lit. 'sinned a sin', which is equal to sinning 'doubly'.

CHAPTER II

1. *Terrors are turned upon me* (Job XXX, 15): R. Ḥanina said: The Community of Israel spake before the Holy One, blessed be He: 'In the past I terrorised others, as it is stated, *They hastened*[1] *to bring Haman* (Est. VI, 14); another text has, *I will make thee a terror, and thou shalt be no more* (Ezek. XXVI, 21),[2] and it is likewise stated, *Then were the chiefs of Edom affrighted* (Ex. XV, 15). But now [terror] is turned upon me.' R. Aḥa said: It is like the segment of a column which rolls along in an open space until it knocks against[3] a stone and stops by it[4]; thus [it is written], *Thy wrath lieth hard upon me* (Ps. LXXXVIII, 8).

Thou chasest mine honour as the wind (Job *loc. cit.*): Thou dost chase as the wind the men who are noble-hearted and who should be the instruments of my deliverance. *And my salvation is passed away as a cloud* (*ib.*): Thou dost scatter and make to pass as clouds the men who are noble-hearted and through whom salvation should come to me; as it is said, HOW HATH THE LORD COVERED WITH A CLOUD THE DAUGHTER OF ZION IN HIS ANGER (II, 1).

It is likewise written, *As the nations that the Lord maketh to perish before you, so shall ye perish* (Deut. VIII, 20). Infer that as these[5] [perished] through priest and prophet,[6] so will Israel [be exiled together] through priest and prophet.[7] As they [were overthrown] with the blast of the ram's horn and shouting, so will Israel [be exiled] with

[1] The verb for 'hasten' and 'affrighted', *bahal*, is identified with *balahoth*, terrors.
[2] The reference is to Tyre. Apparently the Midrash translates: I will make thee (filled with) terror (inspired by Israel).
[3] Reading, with Buber, *we-hiṭṭiḥah* instead of *we-hiṭṭisah*, which is a misprint.
[4] So terrors rolled through the world, and, having struck Israel, stopped by him. [5] The heathen nations.
[6] At the overthrow of Jericho where Joshua (the prophet) ordered the priests to march round the wall and blow the ram's horn (Josh. VI).
[7] Through the denunciations of Jeremiah who was both priest and prophet.

the blast of the ram's horn and shouting.[1] And as [the Assyrian Empire was left] with fourteen nations, as it is said, *The Dinites, and the Apharesattechites, the Tarpelites, the Apharesites, the Archevites, the Babylonians, the Shushanchites, the Dehites, the Elamites, and the rest of the nations whom the great and noble Asenappar brought over* (Ezra IV, 9 f.)[2]; so was [Irael after the invasion left] with fourteen [towns], as it is stated, *In that day shall his strong cities be as the forsaken places . . . after the manner of woods and lofty forests*—amir (Isa. XVII, 9). What means '*amir*'? R. Phinehas said: As I [i.e. Isaiah] have said (*amri*).[3] R. Judah b. R. Simon said: As is stated (*amur*) in the Torah, '*As the nations that the Lord maketh to perish before you, so shall ye perish.*' Infer that as these [perished] through the collapse of the wall, as it is stated, *The wall fell down flat* (Josh. VI, 20), so will Israel [be exiled] through the collapse of the wall.[4] As they [were punished] through clouds, as it is stated, *They go into the clouds,*[5] *and climb up upon the rocks* (Jer. IV, 29), so shall Israel [be punished] with clouds, [as it is said,] HOW HATH THE LORD COVERED WITH A CLOUD THE DAUGHTER OF ZION IN HIS ANGER.

2. HOW HATH THE LORD COVERED WITH A CLOUD (YA'IB) THE DAUGHTER OF ZION IN HIS ANGER (II, 1). R. Ḥama b. R. Ḥanina said: It signifies, 'How hath the Lord condemned the daughter of Zion in His anger,' since there are places where the word for 'guilty', viz. *ḥayaba*, is pronounced '*ayaba*. R. Samuel b. R. Naḥmani said: It signifies, 'How hath the Lord smitten

[1] V. Jer. IV, 19.
[2] Nine nations are actually enumerated; but *the rest of the nations* indicates another two, and to these must be added *the rest that are in the country beyond the River* which represents two, and כענת (rendered 'and now') is taken as a name. Or possibly the others are those enumerated in II Kings XVII, 24 (q.v.), regarded as different peoples ('E.J.).
[3] This is the apparent meaning, Isaiah referring to what he has just said in v. 6, which is interpreted (as in Proem XXX) as meaning that only fourteen would be left. [4] V. Lam. II, 9, *Her gates are sunk in the ground.*
[5] E.V. '*thickets*'. Y.'A. remarks that since this verse speaks of Israel's punishment, it is inappropriate here. He suggests as a text, *Behold, the Lord rideth upon a swift cloud* (Isa. XIX, 1).

with pain in His anger,' since there are places where the word for 'pain', viz. *keba*, is pronounced *'ayba*. The Rabbis assert that it signifies, 'How hath the Lord penalised[1] the daughter of Zion in His anger.'

HE HATH CAST DOWN FROM HEAVEN UNTO THE EARTH THE BEAUTY OF ISRAEL. R. Huna and R. Aḥa said in the name of R. Ḥanina b. R. Abbahu: It may be likened to a king who had a son. The child wept and he placed him upon his knees. He continued to weep and he took him in his arms. He still wept and he set him upon his shoulder. The child then made a mess upon him, so the father immediately threw him to the ground. Nor was he thrown down in the same manner as he was lifted up. The raising up was gradual but the throwing down was in one movement. Similarly it is stated, *And I, I taught Ephraim to walk*,[2] *taking them by their arms* (Hos. XI, 3); after that, *I will make Ephraim to ride, Judah shall plow, Jacob shall break his clods* (*ib.* X, 11); but subsequently, HE HATH CAST DOWN FROM HEAVEN UNTO THE EARTH THE BEAUTY OF ISRAEL.

Another interpretation of HE HATH CAST DOWN FROM HEAVEN UNTO THE EARTH THE BEAUTY OF ISRAEL: R. Joshua b. R. Naḥman said: It may be likened to the inhabitants of a province who made a crown for the king. They then provoked him, but he bore with them. Again they provoked him and he bore with them. Finally the king said to them, 'Do you not provoke me simply because you take advantage of the crown with which you crowned me? Here, have it, it is thrown in your face!' Similarly spake the Holy One, blessed be He, to Israel: 'Do you not provoke Me because you take advantage of the likeness of Jacob[3] which is engraven upon My throne? Here, have it, it is thrown in your face!' Hence, HE HATH CAST DOWN FROM HEAVEN UNTO THE EARTH THE BEAUTY OF ISRAEL.

[1] Following Jast. who explains the word to mean 'impose a fine'. M.K. 'made desolate'. [2] This is understood as 'I placed him upon my legs'; and in the next quotation *ride* is taken to mean 'placed upon the shoulder'. [3] Cf. Gen. R. LXVIII, 12.

3. AND HATH NOT REMEMBERED HIS FOOTSTOOL (HADOM). R. Ḥanina b. Isaac said: The Holy One, blessed be He, does not remember the [circumcisional] blood (*ha-dam*) which was between the feet of the aged patriarch, as it is stated, *And Abraham was ninety years old and nine, when he was circumcised in the flesh of his foreskin* (Gen. XVII, 24). R. Judan said: It may be likened to a king who having captured his enemies, slew them, and his subjects wallowed in their blood.[1] On one occasion they provoked him and he drove them out of the palace. They exclaimed, 'The king does not remember how we wallowed in the blood of his enemies!' Similarly spake Israel before the Holy One, blessed be He: 'Thou rememberest not for us the incident of the blood in Egypt!' as it is stated, *And they shall take of the blood, and put it on the two side-posts and on the lintel* (Ex. XII, 7).

Another interpretation of AND HATH NOT REMEMBERED HIS FOOTSTOOL: FOOTSTOOL denotes nothing else than the Sanctuary, as it is stated, *Exalt ye the Lord our God, and prostrate yourself at His footstool; holy is He* (Ps. XCIX, 5).[2]

IN THE DAY OF HIS ANGER. R. Aḥa said: One day did the anger of the Holy One, blessed be He, last, and had Israel repented, He would have cooled it.[3]

Then He called in mine ears with a loud voice, saying: Cause the visitations of the city to draw near, every man with his destroying weapon in his hand (Ezek. IX, 1).[4] Until when did [the consequences of] the sin of the golden calf last? R. Berekiah—another version is R. Nehemiah b. Eleazar—said: Up to the time the calves of Jeroboam, the son of Nebat, were made[5]; as it is stated, *When I would heal Israel, then is the iniquity of Ephraim uncovered, and the wickedness of Samaria* (Hos. VII, 1). The Holy One, blessed be He, said: 'I have come to heal Israel of the sin of the golden calf, and now is the wickedness of Samaria [in

[1] To prove their loyalty, though it may have been distasteful ('E.J.).
[2] Explained as 'holy is *it*', viz. 'the footstool'.
[3] Repeated from the Midrash to I, 12.
[4] What follows is really a Proem to Lam. II, 2.
[5] Cf. 1 Kings XII, 28.

making the two calves] revealed.' R. Ishmael b. Naḥmani said in the name of R. Joḥanan: They lasted until the destruction of the Temple; as it is stated, '*Cause the visitations of the city to draw near, every man with his destroying weapon in his hand*'; and it is also written, *Nevertheless in the day when I visit*,[1] *I will visit their sin upon them* (Ex. XXXII, 34).

It is written, *And, behold, six men came forth from the way of the upper gate, which lieth toward the north, every man with his weapon of destruction in his hand; and one man in the midst of them clothed in linen, with a writer's ink-horn on his side. And they went in, and stood beside the brazen altar* (Ezek. IX, 2). The number 'six' is mentioned here; but there were five decrees, as it is written, *And to the others He said in my hearing: Go ye through the city after him, and smite; let not your eye spare, neither have ye pity* (*ib.* 5); and it is written, *Slay utterly the old man, the young man and the maiden, and little children and women* (*ib.* 6)![2] R. Joḥanan said: He spoke thus to the sternest of the angels, viz. Gabriel[3]; as it is stated, '*And one man in the midst of them clothed in linen, with a writer's ink-horn on his side.*' That angel served in three capacities: as scribe, executioner, and High Priest. 'Scribe,' as it is written, '*With a writer's ink-horn on his side*'; 'executioner,' as it is said, *He hath utterly destroyed them, He hath delivered them to the slaughter* (Isa. XXXIV, 2); and 'High Priest', as it is said, '*And one man in the midst of them clothed in linen,*' while of the High Priest it is written, *He shall put on the holy linen tunic* (Lev. XVI, 4).

'*Every man with his weapon of destruction in his hand*': viz. his weapon for fighting, his implement for rasing, and his instrument to cause the exile. 'His weapon for

[1] The final punishment of the sin, and this took place at the destruction of the Temple. The use of 'visitations' in Ezek. (E.V. '*them that have charge over*') suggests that this was the carrying out of the penalty threatened in Exodus. [2] Each angel was to destroy one section of the population, and five are enumerated here.

[3] He is the sixth and his duty was to give instructions to the other five. In Rabbinic exegesis an angel is never given two missions to perform at one time. For Gabriel's severity, v. on Lam. I, 13 (*supra*, I, 41).

fighting,' [as it is said,] '*Every man with his weapon of destruction in his hand.*' 'His implement for rasing,' [as it is said,] *When he maketh all the stones of the altar as chalkstones that are beaten in pieces* (Isa. XXVII, 9). 'His instrument to cause the exile,' as it is written, *Thou art My maul and weapons of war* (Jer. LI, 20).[1]

It is likewise written, '*And they went in, and stood beside the brazen altar.*' R. Judah b. R. Simon said: [They penetrated] to the end of their permitted area.[2] The Rabbis declare: [It signifies] that he stood there and recounted the sins of Ahaz, of whom it was written, *And king Ahaz commanded Urijah the priest, saying . . . but the brazen altar shall be for me to look to* (II Kings XVI, 15). What means '*for me to look to*'? R. Phinehas said: He rendered it unfit and made [the sacrificial animals] blemished, as the word is used in, *The priest shall not look to*[3] *the yellow hair; he is unclean* (Lev. XIII, 36).

And the Lord said unto him (elaw): *Go through the midst of the city, through the midst of Jerusalem* (Ezek. IX, 4). The word for '*unto him*' is written *elo*[4]; hence R. Simeon b. Lakish said: [God spoke] to the sternest of the angels, viz. Gabriel. *And set a mark*—taw (*ib.*): R. Nahman said: It alludes to the men who fulfilled the Torah from *aleph* to *taw* (A to Z).[5] The Rabbis say: It was the word of condemnation.[6] Rab said: Since He used the *taw* in every case, it might stand for 'be thou dismayed' or 'do thou

[1] In all these verses a word connected with the same root as 'destruction' in the first verse (*mappaz*) is used, thus suggesting identity of meaning. The last verse—*Thou art my maul,* refers to Nebuchadnezzar, who was the instrument of Israel's exile.

[2] Beyond the place where the altar stood they were not allowed to go. Cur. edd. '*his* permitted area'. With the singular the explanation may be slightly different, but the general sense is the same.

[3] E.V. '*seek*'. The verb is here used in connection with a leper being declared unclean. Therefore the word is given a similar meaning in II Kings XVI, 15. He declared that altar, built by Solomon, unfit, as though every animal offered upon it were blemished (Y.'A., 'E.J.).

[4] אלו instead of אליו. The word is consequently interpreted 'His strong one'.

[5] The men so marked had fulfilled the whole Torah.

[6] Reading with Levy התיבה פסיפס. The Heb. *taw* corresponds to the Greek *theta,* the initial of θάνατος 'death'.

live'.[1] R. Ḥanina b. Isaac said: [It indicates,] 'Ended (*tamah*) is the merit of their ancestors.'[2]

R. Hoshaiah sent this message to R. Simon: Since you reside in the house of the exilarch, why do you not rebuke the people [for their sins]? He answered: Would that we were of those concerning whom it is written, *That sigh and that cry for all the abominations that are done in the midst thereof* (*ib.*).[3] He retorted: Will not the punishment begin with them, as it is written, *And concerning these*[4] *He said in my hearing: Go ye through the city after him, and smite* (*ib.* 5)!

R. Eleazar said: The Holy One, blessed be He, never associates His name with what is bad, but only with what is good. Hence it is not written here, 'And concerning these *God* said in my hearing,' but, '*And concerning these* He *said in my hearing: Go ye through the city after him, and smite*'; *let not your eye spare, neither have ye pity; slay utterly the old man, the young man and the maiden, and little children and women; but come not near any man upon whom is the mark; and begin at My sanctuary* (*ib.* 5 f.). How can this be?[5] At that time the prosecution sprang before the Throne of Glory and spake before Him: 'Lord of the universe, which of them was slain for Thy name? Which of them had his head split open for Thy name? Which of them gave his life for Thy name?'[6] God replied, 'There is not in them [such wickedness] as to merit a document [of

[1] Probably a word for 'thou shalt die' is required, and the translation 'be thou dismayed' is uncertain. The initial letter would be the same for life and for death; but in the former case it was written in ink and in the latter in blood.

[2] Which protected them from punishment and now they will suffer for their misdeeds. The initial of 'ended' is *taw.*

[3] He implied that they were all confirmed in their wickedness and deserved punishment.

[4] E.V. '*and to the others*'. R. Hoshaiah applied the verse to the righteous who refrained from rebuking sinners.

[5] There is an apparent contradiction in the verse. The angel is told not to approach any person who has the mark on his forehead, and then it proceeds '*begin at My sanctuary*' where the righteous are presumably to be found!

[6] He argued that no one of them was righteous because none suffered to sanctify God's name.

extermination].' R. Aibu declared: The Holy One, blessed be He, replied to him, 'Let the Temple be destroyed, but let not a hand touch the righteous.'[1] R. Judah b. R. Simon said: [God said:] 'Both the Sanctuary and the people have merited a document [of extermination].'

R. Tanḥuma b. Abba[2] said in the name of R. Abba: The Holy One, blessed be He, never issued a good promise and then retracted, but in this instance He did retract[3]; as it is written, '*And begin at My sanctuary*'—read not *mimiḳdashi* ('at My sanctuary') but *mimeḳuddashai*, i.e. 'begin with My sanctified ones', which is immediately followed by, *Then they began at the elders that were before the house*. It is then written, *And He said unto them: Defile the house, and fill the courts with the slain; go ye forth. And they went forth, and smote in the city* (*ib.* 7). Then it is written, *And it came to pass, while they were smiting, and I was left, that I fell upon my face, and cried, and said: Ah lord God! wilt Thou destroy all the residue of Israel?* (*ib.* 8). '*Residue*' signifies nothing else than the righteous; therefore [Jeremiah] came and said, THE LORD HATH SWALLOWED UP UNSPARINGLY.

4. THE LORD HATH SWALLOWED UP UNSPARINGLY ALL THE HABITATIONS OF JACOB (II, 2). R. Phinehas said in the name of R. Hoshaiah: There were four hundred and eighty synagogues in Jerusalem. Whence is this known? From the word '*full*' in *She that was full of justice* (Isa. I, 21), which is spelt without the *aleph*.[4] In each there was an elementary school and an advanced school: an elementary school for Scripture and an advanced school for Mishnah.[5]

Another interpretation of THE LORD HATH

[1] That is the meaning of '*begin at My sanctuary*', viz. destroy the sanctuary, but spare the righteous. [2] So emend. The text has: R. Tanḥuma and R. Abba said in the name of R. Abba.
[3] At first He ordered the righteous to be spared; but in the sequel the massacre began with them when the Temple was destroyed.
[4] The numerical value of its letters gives that total. V. Proem XII.
[5] These schools were '*the habitations of Jacob*' which were swallowed up.

SWALLOWED UP UNSPARINGLY ALL THE HABITATIONS (NE'OTH) OF JACOB: i.e. all the celebrities (*ne'oth*) of Jacob, as e.g., R. Ishmael, R. Gamaliel, R. Yeshebab, R. Judah b. Baba, R. Ḥuẓapith the interpreter, R. Judah the baker, R. Ḥananiah b. Teradion, R. Akiba, Ben 'Azzai, and R. Ṭarfon. There are some who exclude R. Ṭarfon from the list and include R. Eleazar b. Ḥarsum.[1]

R. Joḥanan adduced sixty episodes to illustrate THE LORD HATH SWALLOWED UP UNSPARINGLY, and Rabbi [Judah ha-Nasi] twenty-four. But is not the number ascribed to R. Joḥanan greater than that of Rabbi![2] The reason is that as Rabbi was nearer in time to the destruction of the Temple, his recollection was so vivid that when he recounted the episodes he wept and had to be comforted.[3]

R. Joḥanan said: Rabbi used to expound *There shall step forth a star* (kokab) *out of Jacob* (Num. XXIV, 17), thus: read not '*kokab*' but *kozab* (lie). When R. Akiba beheld Bar Koziba[4] he exclaimed, 'This is the king Messiah!' R. Joḥanan b. Tortha retorted: 'Akiba, grass will grow in your cheeks[5] and he will still not have come!' R. Joḥanan said: *The voice*[6] *is the voice of Jacob* (Gen. XXVII, 22)—the voice [of distress caused by] the Emperor Hadrian, who slew eighty thousand myriads of human beings at Bethar. Eighty thousand trumpeters besieged Bethar where Bar Koziba was located who had with him two hundred thousand men with an amputated finger.[7] The Sages sent him the message, 'How long will you continue to make the men of Israel blemished?' He asked them, 'How else

[1] *Sic leg.* The printed edition has: Eleazar Ḥarsanah. We are given the list of the ten Rabbis who suffered martyrdom in the Hadrianic persecution. [2] The episodes referred to are in connection with the Roman oppression. Rabbi who lived closer to that period should have had a greater number of recollections.

[3] Consequently, although he remembered as many incidents as R. Joḥanan, he was unable to relate them to his disciples.

[4] Better known as Bar Kochba, the leader of the revolt against Rome. He was defeated and killed at Bethar in 135 C.E.

[5] You will be a long time in your grave.

[6] Here interpreted as the cry of distress.

[7] As a test of fortitude he ordered each recruit to cut off a finger.

shall they be tested?' They answered, 'Let anyone who cannot uproot a cedar from Lebanon be refused enrolment in your army.' He thereupon had two hundred thousand men of each class[1]; and when they went forth to battle they cried, '[O God,] neither help us nor discourage us!' That is what is written, *Hast not Thou, O God, cast us off? And go not forth,*[2] *O God, with our hosts* (Ps. LX, 12). And what used Bar Koziba to do? He would catch the missiles from the enemy's catapaults on one of his knees and hurl them back, killing many of the foe. On that account R. Akiba made his remark.[3]

For three and a half years the Emperor Hadrian surrounded Bethar.[4] In the city was R. Eleazar of Modim[5] who continually wore sackcloth and fasted,[6] and he used to pray daily, 'Lord of the Universe, sit not in judgment to-day!' so that [Hadrian] thought of returning home.[7] A Cuthean went and found him and said, 'My lord, so long as that old cock wallows in ashes you will not conquer the city. But wait for me, because I will do something which will enable you to subdue it to-day.' He immediately entered the gate of the city, where he found R. Eleazar standing and praying. He pretended to whisper in the ear of R. Eleazar of Modim. People went and informed Bar Koziba, 'Your friend, R. Eleazar, wishes to surrender the city to Hadrian.' He sent and had the Cuthean brought to him and asked, 'What did you say to him?' He replied, 'If I tell you, the king will kill me; and if I do not tell you, you will kill me. It is better that I should kill myself and the secrets of the government be not divulged.' Bar

[1] Viz. who had amputated a finger or uprooted a cedar.
[2] I.e. we do not want God to go with us. E.V. '*And Thou goest not forth*'.
[3] Thought he was the Messiah.
[4] This is not historically correct and is a reminiscence of Vespasian's siege of Jerusalem. The siege lasted about a year and the whole campaign three and a half years. It is probable, however, that the Midrash includes in this period the battles preceding the actual siege. V. Halevi, *Doroth*, I, 5, p. 614 (the whole course of the war is discussed at great length there, pp. 587 *et seq.*).
[5] A small town near Jerusalem, famous as the home of the Maccabees.
[6] As an act of asceticism to avert the fate which was threatening the people
[7] Abandoning the siege in despair. R. Eleazar's piety thwarted his plan.

Koziba was convinced that R. Eleazar wanted to surrender the city, so when the latter finished his praying he had him brought into his presence and asked him, 'What did the Cuthean tell you?' He answered, 'I do not know what he whispered in my ear, nor did I hear anything, because I was standing in prayer and am unaware what he said.' Bar Koziba flew into a rage, kicked him with his foot and killed him. A *Bath Ḳol* issued forth and proclaimed, '*Woe to the worthless shepherd that leaveth the flock! The sword shall be upon his arm, and upon his right eye*' (Zech. XI, 17). It intimated to him, 'Thou hast paralysed the arm of Israel and blinded their right eye; therefore shall thy arm wither and thy right eye grow dim!' Forthwith the sins [of the people] caused Bethar to be captured. Bar Koziba was slain and his head taken to Hadrian. 'Who killed him?' asked Hadrian. A Goth[1] said to him, 'I killed him.' 'Bring his body to me,' he ordered. He went and found a snake encircling its neck; so [Hadrian when told of this] exclaimed, 'If his God had not slain him who could have overcome him?' And there was applied to him the verse, *Except their Rock had given them over* (Deut. XXXII, 30).

They slew the inhabitants until the horses waded in blood up to the nostrils, and the blood rolled along stones of the size of forty *se'ah* and flowed into the sea [staining it for] a distance of four miles. Should you say that [Bethar] is close to the sea; was it not in fact four miles[2] distant from it? Now Hadrian possessed a large vineyard eighteen miles square, as far as from Tiberias to Sepphoris, and they surrounded it with a fence consisting of the slain at Bethar. Nor was it decreed that they should be buried until a certain king arose and ordered their interment. R. Huna said: On the day when the slain of Bethar were allowed burial, the benediction 'Who art kind and dealest kindly'[3] was instituted—'Who art kind' because the bodies did

[1] J. Tal. reads: A Cuthean, which is preferable.
[2] J. Ta'an. 69*a* reads 'forty miles'. The exact location of Bethar is uncertain.
[3] A benediction in the Grace after meals. Cf. A.P.B., pp. 283 f.

not putrefy, 'and dealest kindly' because they were allowed burial.[1]

Fifty-two years [of peace] did Bethar enjoy after the destruction of the Temple[2]; and why was it destroyed? Because the inhabitants kindled lamps [to manifest their joy] over the destruction of the Sanctuary. And why did they light them? It is said that the councillors in Jerusalem used to sit in the centre of the city; and when one of the inhabitants of Bethar went up there to pray, he would be asked by them, 'Do you wish to become a councillor?' When he answered 'No', the next question would be 'Do you wish to become a city magistrate?'[3] and he answered 'No'. Somebody would then say to him, 'Inasmuch as I have heard that you possess an estate, will you sell it to me?' On his replying that he had no such intention, the Jerusalemite would write out and send a [false] deed of possession to the steward of the man of Bethar [with the message], 'If So-and-so[4] comes, do not allow him to enter the estate because he has sold it to me.' [On discovering the fraud] the man would exclaim, 'Would that my leg had been broken so that I should not have gone up to that corner!'[5] That is what is written, *They hunt* (ẓadu) *our steps* (Lam. IV, 18)—[the men of Bethar said,] 'May the road [to Jerusalem] become desolate (*ẓedi'ah*) so that nobody will walk in these broad places!' '*Our end is near*' (*ib.*)—[they said,] 'May the end of this Temple [be near]!' '*Our days are fulfilled*' (*ib.*)—[they said,] 'May the days of this Temple [be fulfilled]!' Neither with them[6] did it fare well, as it is written, *He that is glad at calamity shall not be unpunished* (Prov. XVII, 5).

R. Joḥanan said: The brains of three hundred children

[1] Quoted from Ber. 48*b*, where the author is R. Mathna.

[2] This must be the meaning. It does not imply that it endured only that period (in fact, it lasted longer), but that the wars which led to its ultimate destruction started then; v. Halevi, *Doroth*, I, 5, pp. 587 *et seqq.*

[3] The questions were asked in a mocking spirit. They implied that he had not come to Jerusalem to pray but to acquire knowledge of affairs from the citizens of the metropolis.

[4] The owner of the estate. [5] A contemptuous reference to Jerusalem.

[6] The men of Bethar who wished Jerusalem ill.

[were dashed] upon one stone, and three hundred baskets of capsules[1] of phylacteries were found in Bethar, each basket being of the capacity of three *se'ah*, so that there was a total of three hundred[2] *se'ah*. R. Gamaliel[3] said: There were five hundred schools in Bethar, and the smallest of them had not less than three hundred children. They used to say, 'If the enemy comes against us, with these styluses we will go out and stab them!' When, however, [the people's] sins did cause the enemy to come, they enwrapped each pupil in his book and burnt him, so that I alone was left. He applied to himself the verse, *Mine eye affected my soul, because of all the daughters* [i.e. inhabitants] *of my city* (Lam. III, 51).

There were two brothers in Kefar Ḥaruba[4] who did not allow any Roman to pass there but they killed him. They said, 'The conclusion of the whole matter is that we must take Hadrian's crown and set it upon our own head.'[5] They heard that the Romans were coming towards them; and when they set out against them an old man met them and said, 'May the Creator be your help against them!' They retorted, 'Let Him neither help us nor discourage us!' Their sins[6] immediately caused them to be slain [in the battle]. Their heads were brought to Hadrian, who asked, 'Who killed them?' A Goth[7] replied, 'I slew them'; and the king ordered him to fetch their bodies. He went and found a snake encircling their necks; so [Hadrian, when told of this,] exclaimed, 'If their God had not slain them who could have overcome them!' And there was applied to them the verse, '*Except their Rock had given them over*' (Deut. XXXII, 30).

[1] Each phylactery consists of a capsule and thong, the former containing Biblical passages written on parchment. Every capsule mentioned here represented a slain person from whom it had been taken. Phylacteries used to be worn then during the day, not only at morning prayers.
[2] Correct, with Buber's text, to 'nine hundred'.
[3] Rashash emends: R. Simeon b. Gamaliel.
[4] By the lake of Gennesareth. It may be identical with Gabara, mentioned by Josephus (*Vita*, § 25) as a large city in Galilee.
[5] They must rebel against Roman dominion and restore the ruling power to the Jews. [6] In making the defiant exclamation.
[7] V. p. 159, n. 1.

There were two cedars on the Mount of Olives[1], beneath one of which were four[2] stalls of sellers of birds for ritual purification[3]; and from one of them they produced forty *se'ah* of pigeons every month from which the Israelites used to obtain the pairs of birds [which had to be brought to the Temple]. Mount Simeon[4] used to distribute three hundred *garab*[5] [of thin cakes among the poor every Friday]. Why were these places destroyed? If you answer that it was on account of the harlots, is it not a fact that there was only one girl there [who was a harlot] and they expelled her? R. Huna said: The reason was because they used to play a game with ball on the sabbath.[6]

There were ten thousand cities on the King's Mount. R. Eleazar b. Ḥarsum owned one thousand of them, and corresponding to them he owned a thousand ships on the sea. The taxes of three of these cities, viz. Kabul, Shiḥin and Magdala,[7] [were so heavy] that they had to be carried to Jerusalem [in a wagon].[8] Why was Kabul destroyed? Because of the dissension which was rife there. Shiḥin [was destroyed] because of witchcraft which prevailed in it, and Magdala because of its licentiousness.

There were three cities in the South which had a population double the number of the Israelites who left Egypt, viz. Kefar Bish, Kefar Shiḥlayim, and Kefar Dikrin.[9]

[1] Overlooking Jerusalem. Büchler suggests the possibility that the correct reading is 'the King's Mount' (mentioned in the next paragraph), the name of a district in Judea (*J.Q.R.*, *O.S.*, XVI, 189). The accounts which follow, hyperbolical in form, have the purpose of contrasting the former wonderful abundance in the country with its present desolation.

[2] Buber's text reads 'forty'. [3] Cf. Lev. XII, 8; XIV, 30.

[4] The place cannot be identified. The name implies that it was a stronghold in Judea.

[5] A measure. More probably here: three hundred barrels.

[6] They desecrated the holy day by indulging in sport. 'E.J. observes that there were certainly weightier sins than this, but the remark is homiletical and didactic in purpose.

[7] Kabul was a town south-east of Acco, Shiḥin near Sepphoris, and Magdala near Tiberias.

[8] The word for 'in a wagon' has fallen out of the text.

[9] Kefar Bish has been identified with Kafarabis in Upper Idumea mentioned in Josephus, *Wars*, IV, 9, 9; Kefar Shiḥlayim with Sachlin near Ascalon; and Kefar Dikrin was located north of Beth Gubrin, i.e. Eleutheropolis (v. Giṭ., Sonc. ed., p. 262, nn. 4 ff.).

Why was Kefar Bish called by that name?[1] Because it did not give hospitality to strangers. Why was Kefar Shiḥlayim[2] called by that name? Because the inhabitants reared their children like cress.[3] Why was Kefar Dikrin[4] called by that name? Because every woman in it gave birth to sons. Any woman who wished for a daughter went out of the city and gave birth to a girl, whereas any woman who wanted to bear a son came there and gave birth to a boy. But now, if you were to try to stick sixty myriads of reeds there, the site would not be able to contain them. R. Joḥanan said: [The reason is that] the land of Israel became contracted [after the destruction of the Temple].

R. Huna said: There were three hundred stalls of sellers of birds for ritual purification in Magdala of the Dyers,[5] and there were three hundred stalls of curtain-weavers[6] in Kefar Nimrah.[7] R. Jeremiah said in the name of R. Ḥiyya b. Abba: Eighty brothers[8] who were priests were married to eighty sisters who belonged to priestly families. They were married[9] on the same night in Gofnit[10]; and this was besides [the marriages of] brothers without sisters, of sisters without brothers, and of Levites and lay-Israelites.

Eighty thousand priestly novitiates were slain on account of the blood of Zechariah.[11] R. Judah asked R. Aḥa, Where did they slay Zechariah, in the Court of Israel or in the Court of the Women? He replied, In neither of these, but it was in the Court of the Priests. Nor did they treat

[1] It means 'bad town'. [2] Meaning 'cress'.

[3] This probably means, prolifically. The parallel passage in Giṭ. 57*a* has, 'because they made their living from *shiḥlayim* (watercress),' the text there being slightly different.

[4] Meaning 'males'. [5] A town near Tiberias.

[6] Emend to פינולס, i.e. '[weavers of] travelling cloaks'.

[7] N. of Samaria.

[8] In Ber. 44*a* the reading is: There was a city in the land of Israel named Gofnit in which were eighty pairs of brothers of a priestly family married to eighty pairs of sisters of a priestly family. I.e. in each case two brothers married two sisters.

[9] The text is corrupt. The reading of Y.'A., viz. כלליננהן has been adopted. Since so many marriages occurred in one night, the population must have been very large.

[10] The modern Jifna, and perhaps the Ophni of Josh. XVIII, 24.

[11] In expiation of his murder. Cf. Proem. XXIII.

his blood as was done with the blood of the hind or ram. There it is written, *And whatsoever man there be of the children of Israel . . . that taketh in hunting any beast or fowl that may be eaten, he shall pour out the blood thereof, and cover it with dust* (Lev. XVII, 13); but here it is written, *For her blood is in the midst of her; she set it upon the bare rock; she poured it not upon the ground, to cover it with dust* (Ezek. XXIV, 7). And for what purpose was all this? *That it might cause fury to come up, that vengeance might be taken, I have set her blood upon the bare rock, that it should not be covered* (*ib.* 8). Seven transgressions were committed by Israel on that day: they killed a priest, a prophet, and a judge, they shed innocent blood, they profaned the Divine Name, they defiled the Temple Court, and it happened on the sabbath which was also the Day of Atonement. When Nebuzaradan came up against Israel, he saw the blood of Zechariāh seething; so he asked them, 'What kind of blood is this?' They replied, 'The blood of bulls and lambs.' He had bulls and lambs brought, [and when they were slaughtered the blood] did not behave similarly. He had the blood of all kinds of animals brought, but it did not behave similarly. He said to them, 'If you tell me, well and good; otherwise I will comb your flesh with iron combs'; but they did not tell him.[1] Since, however, he spoke to them in this manner, they said to him, 'What can we hide from you? We had a prophet-priest who reproved us in the name of Heaven, [saying,] "Receive [my words]," but we did not receive them. We rose against him and killed him.' Nebuzaradan said, 'I will appease the blood.' He had the men of the Great Sanhedrin brought and slew them by it, but it did not stop. He slew the men of the Minor Sanhedrin by it, but it did not stop. He had the priestly novitiates brought and slew them by it, but it did not stop. He slew school-children by it, but it did not stop. He exclaimed, 'Zechariah! The choicest of your peōple have I slain; is it your wish that they all perish?' Immediately it stopped seething. The wicked Nebuzaradan

[1] I.e. at first, but his threat finally compelled them to reveal the truth.

contemplated repenting, and said, 'If in connection with one who destroys a single life from Israel it is written, *Whoso sheddeth man's blood, by man shall his blood be shed* (Gen. IX, 6), how much more will this apply to me who have slain many!' Forthwith the Holy One, blessed be He, was filled with mercy, and gave a hint to the blood, which was then and there absorbed in the ground.

Eighty thousand priestly novitiates, bearing golden shields, broke through the ranks of Nebuchadnezzar's army.[1] They went to the Ishmaelites [Arabs] who brought out for them salted foods[2] and blown-up skin-bottles.[3] [The young men] said to them, 'We will first drink'; but they replied, 'Eat first and then drink.' After they had eaten, each one of them took his bottle and placed it to his mouth; and the air penetrated his stomach and [distended it so that the wind] split it open. That is what is written, *The burden upon Arabia. In the thickets in Arabia shall ye lodge, O ye caravans of Dedanites. Unto him that is thirsty bring ye water! The inhabitants of the land of Tema did meet the fugitive with his bread* (Isa. XXI, 13 f.). [This passage is explained thus:] Who allowed you [Arabs] to lodge in the evening in the forest of Lebanon?[4] '*O ye caravans of Dedanites*,' i.e. should caravans consisting of children of Dedanites[5] act in this manner? Did the father [of Israel] behave so to your ancestor? What is written in connection with your ancestor? *And God opened her eyes, and she saw a well of water; and she went, and filled the bottle with water, and gave the lad to drink* (Gen. XXI, 19). You, however, have not fulfilled the exhortation, '*Unto*

[1] And escaped. [2] To increase their thirst.

[3] Filled with air, not water.

[4] To trap any Israelites who tried to escape. V. *infra*, p. 145. Possibly 'Lebanon' has been inserted in error, and the translation should be, 'to lodge in the Arabian forest.' The word for 'evening' has the same consonants as that for 'Arabia'.

[5] 'Dedanites' is connected with *dod*, a Heb. word denoting blood relationship. The passage might also be rendered, Who arranged it that you should lodge . . . in the forest of Lebanon? Surely the caravans of Dedanites (your blood relations)! I.e. it was providentially arranged that you should be there, so as to be able to afford relief to the refugees. But you did not act as Dedanites—relations.

him that is thirsty bring ye water.' Was it voluntarily that they came to you? [No,] *They fled away from the swords* (Isa. XXI, 15)—from before the sword of Nebuchadnezzar they fled. *From the drawn* (neṭushah) *sword* (*ib.*)—[this happened to them] because they did not observe the sabbatical years properly, as it is stated, *But the seventh year thou shalt let it rest and lie fallow*—neṭashtah (Ex. XXIII, 11). *And from the bent bow* (Isa. *loc. cit.*)—[this happened to them] because they did not observe the sabbath properly, as it is stated, *In those days saw I in Judah some treading*[1] *winepresses on the sabbath* (Neh. XIII, 15). *And from the grievousness of war* (Isa. *loc. cit.*)—[this happened to them] because they did not thrust and parry in the warfare of Torah, of which is written, *Wherefore it is said in the books of the Wars of the Lord* (Num. XXI, 14).[2]

R. Joḥanan said: Between Gibbethon and Antipatris[3] there were sixty myriads of towns, the smallest of which was Beth-shemesh, of which it is written, *And He smote of the men of Beth-shemesh . . . seventy men, and fifty thousand men* (I Sam. VI, 19); and now [after the destruction of the Temple] there is not [room for] even a hundred reeds there. R. Joḥanan said: Its watch[4] was the smallest of all the watches, and yet it produced eighty thousand novitiates.

How many battles did Hadrian fight? Two teachers give an answer. One said it was fifty-two and the other fifty-four.

R. Joḥanan said: Happy is he who beheld the downfall of Palmyra.[5] Why? Because it took part in the destruction of both Temples. R. Judah said: At the destruction of the first Temple it supplied eighty thousand archers and at the second forty thousand. R. Huna said: The number at the second was the same as at the first.

[1] The bow had to be trodden with the foot to bend it for shooting, and this was the penalty for treading the grapes with the foot on the sabbath.
[2] Understood in this sense, The Book of the contests about (the meaning and interpretation of) the Torah. [3] V. S.S. R. to I, 16, § 3.
[4] The priests and Levites it supplied for the service of the Temple
[5] An oasis in the Syrian desert.

5. HE HATH THROWN DOWN IN HIS WRATH THE STRONGHOLDS OF THE DAUGHTER OF JUDAH. R. Judah said: Every fortress in Jerusalem [was so strong] that it should not have been subdued in less than forty days (R. Phinehas said: In less than fifty days); but when the sins [of the people] caused [them to fall], HE HATH THROWN DOWN[1] IN HIS WRATH THE STRONGHOLDS OF THE DAUGHTER OF JUDAH; HE HATH BROUGHT THEM DOWN TO THE GROUND.

HE HATH PROFANED THE KINGDOM AND THE PRINCES THEREOF. HE HATH PROFANED THE KINGDOM, i.e. Israel, as it is stated, *And ye shall be unto Me a kingdom of priests, and a holy nation* (Ex. XIX, 6). AND THE PRINCES THEREOF, i.e. the celestial princes. You find that before the enemy came, Jeremiah kept saying to them, 'Repent so that you will not go into exile.' They retorted, 'If the enemy comes, what can they do to us?' One said, '[By invoking the aid of the celestial prince] I will surround the city with a wall of water.' Another said, '[By the same means] I will surround it with a wall of fire.' Still another said, 'I will surround it with a wall of iron.' The Holy One, blessed be He, said to them, 'Of My [angelic host] ye would avail yourselves!' The Holy One, blessed be He, arose and changed the names of the angels, setting the angel who had dominion over water to have dominion over fire, and the one who had dominion over fire to have dominion over iron, so that when they invoked their names below, they did not respond. That is what is written, *Therefore I have profaned the princes of the sanctuary* (Isa. XLIII, 28). Consequently when in consequence of their sins the enemy came, the people began invoking a particular angel, 'Come and do so-and-so for us'; but he replied, 'It is not within my power since I have been removed from [the control] of that element.' Another interpretation of HE HATH PROFANED THE KINGDOM AND THE PRINCES THEREOF: HE HATH PROFANED THE

[1] I.e. they fell without attack by the enemy, 'He' being referred to God.

KINGDOM, i.e. Zedekiah, king of Judah; AND THE PRINCES THEREOF, i.e. the celestial princes.[1]

6. HE HATH CUT OFF IN FIERCE ANGER ALL THE HORN OF ISRAEL (II, 3). There are ten horns: of Abraham, of Isaac, of Joseph, of Moses, of the Torah, of the priesthood, of the Levites, of prophecy, of the Temple, and of Israel. There are some who add: the horn of the Messiah. 'The horn of Abraham,' as it is said, *My well-beloved had a vineyard in a very fruitful hill* (Isa. V, 1).[2] 'The horn of Isaac,' as it is said, *Caught in the thicket by his horns* (Gen. XXII, 13).[3] 'The horn of Joseph,' as it is said, *And his horns are the horns of the wild-ox* (Deut. XXXIII, 17). 'The horn of Moses,' as it is written, *The skin of his face sent forth beams* (Ex. XXXIV, 29).[4] 'The horn of the Torah,' as it is written, *Horns hath He from His hands* (Hab. III, 4).[5] 'The horn of the priesthood,' as it is written, *His horn shall be exalted in honour* (Ps. CXII, 9).[6] 'The horn of the Levites,' as it is written, *All these were the sons of Heman the king's seer in the things pertaining to God, to lift up the horn* (I Chron. XXV, 5).[7] 'The horn of prophecy,' as it is written, *My horn is exalted in the Lord* (I Sam. II, 1).[8] 'The horn of the Temple,' as it is written, *From the horns of the wild-oxen do Thou answer me* (Ps. XXII, 22).[9] 'The horn of Israel,' as it is said, *And He hath lifted up a horn for His people* (*ib.* CXLVIII, 14). 'There are some

[1] 'E.J. emends: AND THE PRINCES THEREOF refers to his (Zedekiah's) princes. [2] Lit. 'in the horn of the son of oil'. Abraham is often referred to as God's 'beloved'. Cf., e.g., p. 44.

[3] Alluding to the ram which was sacrificed in place of Isaac.

[4] Lit. 'horns', i.e. rays of light. The Vulgate renders *cornuata facies* which gave rise to early representations of Moses with horns protruding from his head. [5] E.V. '*Rays hath He at His side*', and the context describes God as revealing Himself. [6] The word *honour* is also applied to the High Priest's garments (Ex. XXVIII, 2). [7] From the preceding chapter it is seen that the sons of Heman were Levites.

[8] Spoken by Hannah on the birth of Samuel, who became a prophet.

[9] Midrash Tehillim *ad loc.* narrates a legend that when David was a shepherd he found a wild ox asleep and sat on its horns. The animal awoke and stood up. It was very tall, and in his terror David prayed to be rescued, and promised to erect a temple which would be a hundred cubits high, the same height as the horns of the wild-ox.

who add the horn of the Messiah,' as it is written, *And He will give strength unto His king, and exalt the horn of His anointed* (I Sam. II, 10).

All of these horns were set on the head of Israel[1]; and when they sinned these were taken from them—as it is said, HE HATH CUT OFF IN FIERCE ANGER ALL THE HORN OF ISRAEL—and given to the other nations, as it is said, *And concerning the ten horns that were on its head, and the other horn which came up, and before which three fell* (Dan. VII, 20), after which it is written, *And so for the ten horns, out of this kingdom shall ten kings arise; and another shall arise after them; and he shall be diverse from the former, and he shall put down three kings* (*ib.* 24). When Israel repents, the Holy One, blessed be He, will restore the horns to their place, as it is stated, *All the horns of the wicked also will I cut off; but the horns of the righteous shall be lifted up* (Ps. LXXV, 11), i.e. the horns which the Righteous One of the Universe had cut off. When will He restore them to their place? When the Holy One, blessed be He, raises aloft the horn of His Messiah, as it is written, '*And He will give strength unto His king, and exalt the horn of His anointed.*'

HE HATH DRAWN BACK HIS RIGHT HAND FROM BEFORE THE ENEMY. R. 'Azariah said in the name of R. Judah b. R. Simon: When the sins of the people produced their effect and the enemy entered Jerusalem, they took the mighty men of Israel and bound their hands behind them. The Holy One, blessed be He, said, 'I wrote in the Torah, *I will be with him in trouble* (Ps. XCI, 15). Now that My children are plunged in distress while I am at ease'—if it is possible to say so, *He drew His hand behind His back*.[2] Subsequently He revealed it[3] to Daniel, as it is stated, *But go thou thy way till the end be* (Dan. XII, 13).

[1] The 'horn' is understood as a symbol of glory: glory was conferred upon Israel on account of all these.

[2] This is the translation given by the Midrash of the words rendered, '*He hath drawn back His right hand.*'—This symbolises God's endurance of the many indignities heaped by the heathens on His people and His Sanctuary, as though His hand were behind His back, powerless to avenge ('E.J.).

[3] Sc. that His right hand is drawn behind His back (M.K.).

[Daniel asked, 'Till what end be?'][1] He answered him, 'To give judgment and reckoning [for the sins Israel had committed].' The Holy One, blessed be He, told him, '*And thou shalt rest*' (*ib.*). Daniel asked, 'Is the rest [in death] to be for ever?' He replied to him, '*And thou shalt stand up*' (*ib.*). Daniel asked, 'With whom? With the righteous or the wicked?' He replied to him, '*To thy lot*' (*ib.*), which indicates with the righteous. Daniel asked, 'Will this be in the end of days or the end of the right hand?'[2] He answered him, '*At the end of the right hand* (*ib.*),[3]—that right hand which has become enslaved [while Israel is in captivity]. I have set a term for My right hand; when I have redeemed My children I shall have redeemed My right hand.' That is what David said, *That Thy beloved ones may be delivered, save Thy right hand*,[4] *and answer me* (Ps. LX, 7).

7. AND HE HATH BURNED IN JACOB LIKE A FLAMING FIRE, WHICH DEVOURETH ROUND ABOUT. R. Simeon b. Laḳish said: When punishment comes [into the world], Jacob alone experiences it.[5] What is the proof? AND HE HATH BURNED IN JACOB LIKE A FLAMING FIRE. And when good comes [into the world], Jacob alone experiences it, as it is stated, *Let Jacob rejoice, let Israel be glad* (*ib.* XIV, 7).

8. HE HATH BENT HIS BOW LIKE AN ENEMY (II, 4). R. Aibu said[6]: They [the Israelites] did not go to the extreme of rebellion against the Attribute of Justice,[7] and the Attribute of Justice did not go to the extreme in

[1] This sentence is added from Buber's text and has fallen out of the printed edition. [2] The word for 'days' is *yamim*; but in Dan. it is spelt *yamin*, which also denotes 'right hand'. The answer makes the distinction clear. [3] E.V. '*At the end of the days*'.

[4] E.V. '*Save with Thy right hand*'.—The exact text, as well as the meaning of the whole passage, is not quite clear, the interpretation of some commentators being quite different from that adopted in the text.

[5] The commentator Y.'A. interprets the text differently, viz. when punishment comes upon the people of Israel, only the patriarch Jacob (and not Abraham or Isaac) experiences the pain of it.

[6] Cf. I, 1 (§ 3), where the Rabbi's name is R. Abba b. Kahana.

[7] 'E.J., they did not sin so greatly as to deserve absolute condemnation.

punishing them. They did not go to the extreme of rebellion against the Attribute of Justice, as it is said, *And the people were as murmurers* (Num. XI, 1)—'murmurers' is not written here but '*as murmurers*'. *The princes of Judah are like them that remove the landmark* (Hos. V, 10)—'remove' is not written here but '*like them that remove*'. *For Israel is like a stubborn heifer* (*ib.* IV, 16)—'is a stubborn heifer' is not written here but '*is like a stubborn heifer*'. Similarly the Attribute of Justice did not go to the extreme in punishing them. 'He an enemy hath bent His bow' is not written here, but LIKE AN ENEMY.

Another interpretation of HE HATH BENT HIS BOW LIKE AN ENEMY: this alludes to Pharaoh, as it is stated, *The enemy said* (Ex. XV, 9). STANDING WITH HIS RIGHT HAND AS AN ADVERSARY (II, 4): this alludes to Haman, as it is said, *An adversary and an enemy, even this wicked Haman* (Est. VII, 6). Another interpretation of HE HATH BENT HIS BOW LIKE AN ENEMY: this alludes to Esau, as it is written, *Because the enemy hath said against you: Aha!* (Ezek. XXXVI, 2).[1]

AND HATH SLAIN ALL THAT WERE PLEASANT TO THE EYE. R. Tanḥum b. Jeremiah said: This refers to the children who were dear to their parents as the apple of their eye. The Rabbis said: This refers to the members of the Sanhedrin who were dear to Israel as the apple of their eye.

IN THE TENT OF THE DAUGHTER OF ZION HE HATH POURED OUT HIS FURY LIKE FIRE. There are four pourings [recorded] for good and four for evil. 'There are four pourings [recorded] for good,' as it is said, *And I will pour upon the house of David, and upon the inhabitants of Jerusalem, the spirit of grace and of supplication* (Zech. XII, 10); *And it shall come to pass afterward, that I will pour out My spirit upon all flesh* (Joel III, 1); *And also upon the servants and upon the handmaids in those days will I pour out My spirit* (*ib.* 2); *Nor will I hide My face any more from*

[1] The word *Aha* can also mean 'the brother', i.e. the brother of Jacob, Esau; hence 'the enemy Esau hath said'.

them; for I have poured out My spirit upon the house of Israel, saith the Lord God (Ezek. XXXIX, 29). 'And four pourings for evil,' as it is said, *Therefore He poured upon him the fury of His anger* (Isa. XLII, 25); in Ezekiel it is written, *In Thy pouring out of Thy fury upon Jerusalem* (IX, 8); and it is written, *The Lord hath accomplished His fury, He hath poured out His fierce anger* (Lam. IV, 11); and also the present instance, HE HATH POURED OUT HIS FURY LIKE FIRE.

9. THE LORD IS BECOME AS AN ENEMY (II, 5). R. Aibu said: They [the Israelites] did not go to the extreme of rebellion against the Attribute of Justice, and the Attribute of Justice did not go to the extreme in punishing them. They did not go to the extreme of rebellion against the Attribute of Justice, as it is written, '*And the people were as murmurers*' (Num. XI, 1)—'murmurers' is not written here but '*as murmurers*'. '*The princes of Judah are like them that remove the landmark*' (Hos. V, 10)—'remove' is not written here but '*like them that remove*'. '*For Israel is like a stubborn heifer*' (*ib.* IV, 16)—'is a stubborn heifer' is not written here but '*is like a stubborn heifer*'. Similarly the Attribute of Justice did not go to the extreme in punishing them, for it is written, THE LORD IS BECOME AS AN ENEMY—'the Lord is become an enemy' is not written here but AS AN ENEMY.

HE HATH SWALLOWED UP ISRAEL; HE HATH SWALLOWED UP ALL HER PALACES. R. Berekiah reported that R. Ḥelbo said[1] in the name of R. Samuel b. Naḥman: Three exiles were experienced by Israel: one to this side of the River Sambatyon,[2] one to Daphne of Antioch,[3] and one when the cloud descended upon them and covered them. When they return, they will return from the three captivities. What is the reason? *Saying to the prisoners: Go forth* (Isa. XLIX, 9), this alludes to those who were exiled to this side of the River Sambatyon; *To them*

[1] The correct reading is: R. Berekiah and R. Ḥelbo said.
[2] The legendary river which ceases flowing on the sabbath. The allusion is to the exile of the ten tribes to Assyria. [3] V. p. 56, n. 3.

that are in darkness: Show yourselves (*ib.*), this alludes to those upon whom the cloud descended to cover them; *They shall feed in the ways, and in all high hills shall be their pasture* (*ib.*), this alludes to those who were exiled to Daphne of Antioch.[1]

AND HE HATH MULTIPLIED IN THE DAUGHTER OF JUDAH MOURNING AND MOANING: i.e. the most intense afflictions.[2]

10. AND HE HATH STRIPPED HIS TABERNACLE, AS IF IT WERE A GARDEN (II, 6). R. Ḥama b. R. Ḥanina said: [Jerusalem] became like a garden which had been deprived of its water-supply so that its vegetation lost its greenness.[3] R. Simeon b. Naḥmani said: It became like Adam of whom it is stated, *So He drove out the man* (Gen. III, 24). R. Abbahu said: The word for 'tabernacle' (*sukko*) is written so that it can be read as *shukko*, i.e. when Israel was exiled the wrath of the Holy One, blessed be He, was appeased (*shakekah*).[4]

THE LORD HATH CAUSED TO BE FORGOTTEN IN ZION APPOINTED SEASON AND SABBATH. Is it possible that the Holy One, blessed be He, made the festivals and sabbaths of Israel to be forgotten? It refers in fact to the festivals and sabbaths of Jeroboam, the son of Nebat, which he invented for them; for is it not written, *Even in the month which he had devised of his own heart* (I Kings XII, 33)? Instead of *milibbo* ('of his own heart') the consonantal text reads *milebad* ('besides'), alluding to *Beside the sabbaths of the Lord* (Lev. XXIII, 38).

AND HE HATH REJECTED IN THE INDIGNATION OF HIS ANGER THE KING AND THE PRIEST: KING

[1] The translation has been made from the version in J. Sanh. 29*c*. The printed text is corrupt: To three places were Israel exiled: one within the River S., as it is written, *Saying to the prisoners*, etc., one outside the River S. *They shall feed*, etc., alludes to those upon whom a cloud descended and surrounded them; *And in all high*, etc., alludes to those who were exiled to Daphne of Antioch. Cf. Num. R. XVI, 25.

[2] Quoted in Proem XXVI.

[3] Lit. 'its verdure became white'.

[4] The text is thus interpreted: When He stripped [Jerusalem] like a garden, there was appeasement to Him.

refers to Zedekiah, AND THE PRIEST to Seraiah, son of Mahseiah.[1]

11. THE LORD HATH CAST OFF HIS ALTAR (II, 7). R. Haggai said in the name of R. Isaac: It may be likened to the inhabitants of a province who set tables[2] for the king. They provoked him to anger, but he bore with them. [When they had done this several times] he said to them: 'Do you not provoke me because you rely on the tables which you set before me? Here, have them, they are thrown in your face!' Similarly spake the Holy One, blessed be He: 'Do you not provoke Me because you rely on the sacrifices which you offer to Me? Here, have them, they are thrown in your face!'[3] That is what is written, THE LORD HATH CAST OFF HIS ALTAR, HE HATH ABHORRED HIS SANCTUARY.

R. Berekiah, R. Ḥelbo, and R. Aibu said in the name of R. Samuel b. Naḥmani: You find that when the heathens entered the Temple, they placed their hands behind their necks,[4] turned their faces upwards, blasphemed and reviled, and the nails of their boots made scratches upon the floor.[5] That is what is written, HE HATH GIVEN UP INTO THE HAND OF THE ENEMY THE WALLS OF HER PALACES; THEY HAVE MADE A NOISE IN THE HOUSE OF THE LORD, AS IN THE DAY OF A SOLEMN ASSEMBLY. R. Ḥanina, R. Aḥa, and R. Meiashah said in the name of R. Jannai: By the might of that noise Babylon fell,[6] as it is written, *Fallen, fallen is Babylon; and all the graven images of her gods are broken unto the ground* (Isa. XXI, 9).[7] R. Berekiah, R. Ḥelbo, and R. Aibu

[1] Jer. LI, 59, describes Seraiah as the son of Neriah and grandson of Mahseiah, who was *quartermaster* and not a priest. *Ib.* LII, 24, mentions *Seraiah the chief priest*. The two persons are therefore different, and it is probable that 'son of Mahseiah' has been inserted here in error.
[2] Arranged banquets for him. [3] Cf. on II, 1 (§ 2).
[4] To support the head as they looked upward.
[5] This is the probable meaning. The text is corrupt.
[6] As a punishment for their blasphemy.
[7] It is not clear how this verse proves it. Perhaps it is rendered: Fallen (is Israel, and because of the blasphemous revilings of its conqueror), fallen is Babylon ('E.J.).

said in the name of R. Samuel b. Naḥmani: This kingdom[1] has acted similarly; that is what is written, THEY HAVE MADE A NOISE IN THE HOUSE OF THE LORD, AS IN THE DAY OF A SOLEMN ASSEMBLY.[2] R. Ḥanina,[3] R. Aḥa, and R. Meiashah said in the name of R. Jannai: It is not necessary for this one either to fall, except as a consequence of the might of that noise.[4] That is what is written, *Because of the noise was Babylon taken* (Jer. L, 46).[5] R. Joshua b. Levi said: The noise of woeful disturbance and darkness ascends to the great city of Tyre[6]; and why? Because the noise of the Temple[7] condemns them; as it is written, *Hark! an uproar from the city, hark! it cometh from the temple, hark! the Lord rendereth recompense to His enemies* (Isa. LXVI, 6).

12. THE LORD HATH PURPOSED TO DESTROY THE WALL OF THE DAUGHTER OF ZION (II, 8). R. Joḥanan said: Not from now[8] [but from long ago hath He purposed to do this]; as it is written, *For this city hath been to Me a provocation of Mine anger and of My fury from the day that they built it* (Jer. XXXII, 31). R. Ilas[9] said: It is like a man who passes a filthy place and stops up his nose.[10]

HE HATH STRETCHED OUT THE LINE. There is a

[1] Possibly an allusion to Rome.
[2] Interpreting: They have made a noise in the house of the Lord, as on the day first appointed (for disaster)—i.e. as on the occasion of the destruction of the first Temple. Thus both conquerors, Babylon and Rome, acted alike. [3] The text has 'R. Huna'.
[4] The text is in the present tense, and presumably alludes to Rome Rome need not fall, but that she must be punished for her blasphemy. In that case the verse that is quoted, referring to Babylon, is hardly relevant, although it can be explained as indicating that since Babylon fell for this reason, Rome will likewise. M.K., however, substitutes for it, *The earth quaketh because of* (*E.V.* '*at*') *the noise of their fall* (Jer. XLIX, 21). This refers to Edom and Teman (v. verses 7 *seq*.), Edom in Rabbinic literature generally being made to apply to Rome.
[5] E.V. '*At the noise of the taking of Babylon*'. [6] Substitute for Rome.
[7] This is the reading adopted by Y.'A. The text has 'of Esau'.
[8] Reading *kedun* and not *keruz* 'announcement', though perhaps a similar idea can be read into the present text. [9] The text reads 'Ilam'.
[10] He interprets *appi* in the verse just quoted (E.V. '*Mine anger*') as My nose—possibly meaning—thus: For this city hath been as something offensive to My nose.

favourable and unfavourable *'line'*: favourable as in, *My house shall be built in it, saith the Lord of hosts, and a line shall be stretched forth over Jerusalem* (Zech. I, 16); and unfavourable as in the present instance, HE HATH STRETCHED OUT THE LINE.

HE HATH NOT WITHDRAWN HIS HAND FROM DESTROYING; BUT HE HATH MADE THE RAMPART AND WALL TO MOURN, THEY LANGUISH TOGETHER. This is as interpreted by R. Huna b. R. Aḥa, [RAMPART means] the large wall and [WALL] the smaller wall [which is within the other].

13. HER GATES ARE SUNK INTO THE GROUND (II, 9). R. Huna said in the name of R. Jose: The gates paid honour to the Ark of the Covenant, and for that reason the enemy had no power over them; that is what is written, *Lift up your heads, O ye gates* (Ps. XXIV, 7).[1] On that account, HER GATES ARE SUNK INTO THE GROUND,[2] HE HATH DESTROYED AND BROKEN HER BARS.

HER KING AND HER PRINCES ARE AMONG THE NATIONS, TORAH[3] IS NO MORE. Should a person tell you there is wisdom among the nations, believe it; as it is written, *Shall I not in that day, saith the Lord, destroy the wise men out of Edom, and discernment out of the mount of Esau?* (Obad. 8). But if he tells you that there is Torah among the nations, do not believe it; because it is written, HER KING AND HER PRINCES ARE AMONG THE NATIONS [WHERE] TORAH IS NO MORE.

HER PROPHETS, i.e. the false prophets; YEA [HER PROPHETS] includes the true prophets. Both classes FIND NO VISION FROM THE LORD.

14. THEY SIT UPON THE GROUND, AND KEEP SILENCE, THE ELDERS OF THE DAUGHTER OF ZION (II, 10). R. Eleazar said: Let not the chapter on vows[4]

[1] They opened to allow the Ark to enter; v. Shab. 30*a*.
[2] They escaped the fate of the bars, which were broken, by sinking into the ground. [3] E.V. '*instruction*'.
[4] I.e. Num. XXX. The meaning is: The power to absolve a vow must be exercised very carefully, or the consequences may be serious.

be lightly esteemed in your eyes, because on account of that chapter were the members of the Great Sanhedrin of Zedekiah slain. When Jeconiah was exiled, king Nebuchadnezzar appointed Zedekiah over five kings; [they are enumerated in] what is written, *And send them to the king of Edom, and to the king of Moab, and to the king of the children of Ammon, and to the king of Tyre, and to the king of Zidon, by the hand of the messengers that came to Jerusalem unto Zedekiah king of Judah* (Jer. XXVII, 3). Zedekiah used to enter and leave [the king's presence] without permission.[1] One day he entered his presence and found him tearing the flesh of a hare and eating it while it was yet alive. The king said to him, 'Swear to me that you will not disclose this about me,' and he swore. (By what did he make him swear? R. Jose b. R. Ḥanina said: By the inner altar.)[2] [Subsequently] the five kings were sitting and sneering at Nebuchadnezzar in the presence of Zedekiah, and they said to him, 'The kingship does not become Nebuchadnezzar, but it becomes you seeing that you are of the seed of David.' He too sneered at Nebuchadnezzar and said, 'I once saw him tear the flesh of a [live] hare and eat it.' They immediately sent and told the king, 'That Jew who enters and leaves your presence without permission has informed us, "I saw Nebuchadnezzar tear the flesh of a [live] hare and eat it."' That is what is stated, *And Zedekiah rebelled*[3] *against the king of Babylon* (II Kings XXIV, 20).

The latter forthwith came and took up his residence in Daphne of Antioch. The members of the Great Sanhedrin went out to meet him. When he saw that they were all men of imposing appearance, he ordered that seats of honour should be brought for them upon which he seated them. He said to them, 'Expound the Torah to me.' They immediately began to read it chapter by chapter and translate it before him. When they reached the chapter of vows, *When a man voweth a vow* (Num. XXX, 3), he said to them, 'If a person desires to retract a vow, can he do so

[1] This right indicated that he stood high in the favour of the king.
[2] Which was inside the Temple, in contrast to 'the outer altar' which was located in the court. [3] He violated the oath he had sworn.

or not?' They replied, 'He must go to a Sage who absolves him of his vow.' He said to them, 'It seems to me that you must have absolved Zedekiah of the oath which he swore to me.' He immediately ordered them [to be removed from their seats of honour] and placed them on the ground; that is what is written, THEY SIT UPON THE GROUND, AND KEEP SILENCE, THE ELDERS OF THE DAUGHTER OF ZION. THEY HAVE CAST UP DUST UPON THEIR HEADS, i.e. they began to recount the merit of Abraham[1] of whom it is written, *I am but dust and ashes* (Gen. XVIII, 27). THEY HAVE GIRDED THEMSELVES WITH SACKCLOTH, i.e. they began to recount the merit of Jacob of whom it is written, *He put sackcloth upon his loins* (*ib.* XXXVII, 34). What was done to them? Their hair was bound to the tails of their horses and they were made to run from Jerusalem to Lydda. That is what is written, THE VIRGINS OF JERUSALEM HANG DOWN THEIR HEADS TO THE GROUND.

15. MINE EYES DO FAIL WITH TEARS (II, 11). R. Eleazar said: A limit has been set for [the tears of] the eye.[2] [There are three kinds of tears which are beneficial;][3] tears caused by a drug,[4] mustard and *collyrium*, but the tears caused by laughter are best of all. There are three kinds of tears which are harmful: tears caused by smoke, weeping [through grief, and straining in] a privy, but [tears which result from the death] of a grown-up child are worst of all. It is related of a woman that she had a grown-up[5] son who died, and she wept over him at night until her eyelashes fell out. She went to a physician who told her, 'Paint your eyes with this *stibium* which I give you and you will recover.'

MY LIVER IS POURED UPON THE EARTH. It is related of a man that he had a grown-up son who died,

[1] That it might avail them in their peril. [2] If that limit is exceeded, the sight is damaged. [3] To be added from Shab. 151*b et seq.*
[4] Or chemical. Perhaps, however, *shum* (garlic) should be substituted for *sam*, though in Shab. 152*a* also the text has *sam*.
[5] Levi translates, *Herrscher*. Perhaps one should render, 'an eminent son,' throughout in this passage.

and he wept over him at night until his liver dropped. He said, 'My liver has dropped from weeping over him, but it has done no good.'[1]

16. THEY SAY TO THEIR MOTHERS: WHERE IS CORN AND WINE? (II, 12). R. Ḥanina said: [They asked for] white bread[2] and spiced wine. R. Simon said: [They asked for] white bread and old wine.

WHEN THEY SWOON AS THE WOUNDED IN THE BROAD PLACES OF THE CITY. A woman said to her husband: 'Take a bracelet or an earring, and go to the market; if you find anything there [to exchange for the article of jewellery] we shall have something to eat.' He went to the market and searched, but found nothing there; and he writhed in agony and died. She then said to her son, 'Go and see what has become of your father.' He went to the market and saw his father dead; so he writhed in agony and died by him. That is what is written, WHEN THEY SWOON AS THE WOUNDED IN THE BROAD PLACES OF THE CITY, which alludes to her husband and grown son. WHEN THEIR SOUL IS POURED OUT INTO THEIR MOTHER'S BOSOM refers to her young son who wished to suck but found no milk, and he writhed in agony and died.

17. WHAT SHALL I TAKE TO WITNESS FOR THEE? WHAT SHALL I LIKEN TO THEE? (II, 13). [The meaning of the first question is:] How many prophets did I [God] send to warn[3] you? Rabbi [Judah ha-Nasi] and R. Nathan suggest answers. Rabbi said: One prophet each morning and one at twilight; that is what is written, *Yet the Lord forewarned Israel, and Judah, by the hand of every prophet, and of every seer* (II Kings XVII, 13).[4] R. Nathan

[1] In like manner Israel's weeping brought them no relief, because God had taken no notice of it.

[2] The best kind of bread. '*Corn*' is so explained because corn is not a food in itself. They asked for luxurious food and drink, to which they were accustomed, when even the cheapest kind was unobtainable.

[3] The Heb. verb means both 'to witness' and 'to warn'.

[4] *Prophet* and *seer* are two; that these were sent every morning and evening is deduced from the verse quoted by R. Nathan ('E.J.).

said: Two prophets in the morning and two in the evening as it is stated, *And though I have sent unto you all My servants*[1] *the prophets, sending them betimes and often* (Jer. VII, 25)—'*betimes*' means in the morning and '*sending often*' refers to the evening.

Another interpretation of A'IDEK (WHAT SHALL I TAKE TO WITNESS FOR THEE?) R. Jonathan said: [It means,] How many spoils have I provided for you! The spoil of Egypt, the spoil at the Red Sea, the spoil of Sihon and Og, and the spoil of the thirty-one kings.[2] R. Levi said: In Arabia they call 'spoil' *'aditha.*

Another interpretation of A'IDEK: How many appointments I made (*ya'ad*) with you! In the Tent of Meeting, Gilgal, Shiloh, Nob, Gibeon, and the two Temples.

Another interpretation of A'IDEK: Rabbi [Judah ha-Nasi] said: With how many ornaments[3] have I adorned you! R. Joḥanan said: Sixty myriads of ministering angels descended with the Holy One, blessed be He, at Sinai with a crown in the hand of each wherewith to crown every individual of Israel. R. Abba b. Kahana said in the name of R. Joḥanan: A hundred and twenty myriads descended, one to adorn [each Israelite] and another to crown him.[4] R. Huna of Sepphoris said: [The angels put on them] girdles, as it is stated, *He looseth the bonds of kings,*[5] *and bindeth their loins with a girdle* (Job XII, 18).

WHAT SHALL I LIKEN UNTO THEE? To which nation have I likened you?[6] Which other nation have I redeemed with a mighty hand, bringing ten plagues upon its enemies? For which other nation did I rend the sea, cause manna to descend, make quails to swarm, and raise a well of water? Which other nation have I enveloped in clouds of glory brought before Mount Sinai and given My Torah?

[1] The plural indicates two. [2] V. Josh. XII, 7 ff.
[3] A word for 'ornament' is *'adi.*—Yet in spite of all this (whether it is translated spoil, appointments, or ornaments), ye were faithless and sinned against Me. [4] Cf. Shab. 88*a*.
[5] Applied to the release of Israel from Egypt.
[6] In the miracles I performed on your behalf (M.K.).

O DAUGHTER OF JERUSALEM: O daughter who fears and makes peace[1] with Me.

WHAT SHALL I EQUAL TO THEE, THAT I MAY COMFORT THEE? R. Jacob of Kefar Ḥanan said: When I [God] shall become equal to you—as it is written, *And I will walk among you and be your God, and ye shall be My people* (Lev. XXVI, 12)—at that time will I comfort you. I, in My glory, will come and comfort you.[2]

O VIRGIN DAUGHTER OF ZION: i.e. sons distinguished (*meẓuyyanim*)[3] by circumcision, [the prohibition against] beard-cutting[4] and *ẓiẓith.*

FOR THY BREACH IS GREAT LIKE THE SEA. R. Ḥilfai said: He who will heal the breach of the sea will heal you.[5] R. Abin said: He to whom you uttered a song at the Red Sea—viz. *This is my God, and I will glorify Him* (Ex. XV, 2)[6]—He will heal you. R. Joshua b. Levi said: He will heal your prophets for you.[7]

18. THY PROPHETS HAVE SEEN VISIONS FOR THEE OF VANITY AND DELUSION—TAFEL (II, 14). R. Eleazar said: In connection with the prophets of Samaria is unseemliness (*tiflah*) mentioned, as it is said, *And I have seen unseemliness in the prophets of Samaria* (Jer. XXIII, 13);

[1] יראה ומשלמת. The dotted letters form the Heb. name of Jerusalem. The point of the rebuke is that only after Jerusalem was brought to disaster and thus made to fear God did she make peace with Him by repentance (‘E.J.).

[2] The text is faulty and the explanations of the commentators are forced. The literal translation is: ‘When I become equal to you, I will comfort you, viz. when the day arrives of which it is written, *And the Lord alone shall be exalted in that day* (Isa. II, 11), at that time will I comfort you.’ For this has been substituted the version found in Pesiḳ. R. (ed. Buber), p. 156*b* as suggested by Radal.

[3] A play on the word ‘Zion’. [4] Lev. XIX, 27. [5] V. Ex. R. XV, 22.

[6] M.K. points out that the text adduced for proof should have been, *Who* (mi) *is like unto Thee, O Lord, among the mighty?* (Ex. XV, 11), the initial word being the same as in WHO (MI) CAN HEAL THEE? It is doubtful, however, whether such emendation is necessary.

[7] Y.‘A. I.e. When He again pours His spirit on the prophets, that will be the time of Israel's healing. ‘E.J. offers a very plausible reading which links this with the next section: Who is to heal thee, when THY PROPHETS HAVE SEEN FOR THEE VISIONS OF VANITY, etc.?—they who should have remonstrated with you.

and in connection with the prophets of Jerusalem is unseemliness mentioned, as it is said, VANITY AND TAFEL. R. Samuel b. Naḥmani said: In connection with the prophets of Jerusalem horror is mentioned, as it is stated, *But in the prophets of Jerusalem I have seen a horrible thing* (*ib.* 14); and similarly in connection with the house of Israel[1] is the same word mentioned, as it is stated, *The virgin of Israel hath done a very horrible thing* (*ib.* XVIII, 13).

AND THEY HAVE NOT UNCOVERED THINE INIQUITY, TO BRING BACK THY CAPTIVITY. [Your prophets] placed veils for your sake upon their faces.[2]

BUT HAVE PROPHESIED FOR THEE BURDENS OF VANITY AND SEDUCTION. The last word is written *madduḥam*.[3]

19. ALL THAT PASS BY CLAP THEIR HANDS AT THEE (II, 15). R. Joḥanan said in the name of R. Simeon b. Yoḥai: There was an Arcade of Reckonings[4] outside Jerusalem, and whoever wished to settle an account ran and paid it there, so that he should not leave Jerusalem with something on his mind; to fulfil what was said, THE JOY[5] OF THE WHOLE EARTH. But now, ALL THAT PASS BY CLAP THEIR HANDS AT THEE; THEY HISS AND WAG THEIR HEAD AT THE DAUGHTER OF JERUSALEM. The cities of the heathen peoples recount their praise with their own mouths, as it is written, *Thou, O Tyre, hast said: I am of perfect beauty* (Ezek. XXVII, 3); but as for Jerusalem, others recount her praise with their mouths, as it is written, IS THIS THE CITY THAT MEN CALLED THE PERFECTION OF BEAUTY, THE JOY OF THE WHOLE EARTH? R. Nathan said: A merchant went up [to Jerusalem] to sell wool. He fell asleep and did not sell it, so he exclaimed, 'Is this [city] what you call "the joy of the whole earth!"' He got up

[1] Y.'A. emends: the prophets of Israel.
[2] I.e. they pretended not to see your sins and did not reprove you.
[3] Meaning, 'the banishment [into exile]' is through their fault; cf. *supra*, I, 19, § 54.
[4] A kind of Exchange. V. Ex. R. LII *ad fin.*
[5] The effect of the city was to dispel anxiety and increase joy.

early and sold it, so he exclaimed, 'Rightly are you called THE JOY OF THE WHOLE EARTH!'

20. ALL THINE ENEMIES HAVE OPENED THEIR MOUTH WIDE AGAINST THEE (II, 16). Why does the verse beginning with the letter *peh* precede that beginning with the letter *'ain*?[1] Because they uttered with their mouth what they had not seen with their eye.[2]

21. THE LORD HATH DONE THAT WHICH HE DEVISED (II, 17). R. Ahaba b. R. Ze'ira said: Since the Holy One, blessed be He, declared, *And if ye will not yet for these things hearken unto Me, then I will chastise you seven times more for your sins* (Lev. XXVI, 18) . . . *then will I also walk contrary unto you* (*ib.* 24),[3] [you may think] that He has perhaps done so. Heaven forfend! but THE LORD HATH DONE THAT WHICH HE DEVISED; HE HATH PERFORMED HIS WORD. [The last clause indicates that] He made a compromise.[4] R. Jacob of Kefar Ḥanan said: [The clause means that] He rent His purple.[5]

AND HE HATH CAUSED THE ENEMY TO REJOICE OVER THEE. R. Aḥa said: When anything good [befalls Israel] He rejoices with them, as it is written, *For the Lord will again rejoice over thee for good, as He rejoiced over thy fathers* (Deut. XXX, 9); but when anything bad [befalls Israel] He causes others to do the rejoicing.[6] That is what is written, AND HE HATH CAUSED THE ENEMY TO REJOICE OVER THEE, HE HATH EXALTED THE HORN OF THINE ADVERSARIES.

On this account it is stated, THEIR HEART CRIED UNTO THE LORD: O WALL OF THE DAUGHTER OF ZION, LET TEARS RUN DOWN, etc. (II, 18).

22. ARISE, CRY OUT IN THE NIGHT, AT THE BE-

[1] The alphabetical order of these two verses is reversed. *Peh* means 'mouth' and *'ain* 'eye'. [2] Probably falsehoods.
[3] V.v. 19-23 enumerate the punishments they will receive.
[4] He did not exact the penalty in full. *'He hath performed'* is *bizza'*, which is explained in the sense of 'compromised' (from *baza*, to break off a part). [5] V. p. 68, n. 1. [6] Not He Himself.

GINNING OF THE WATCHES (II, 19). Rabbi [Judah ha-Nasi] said: There are four watches in the night and four in the day. An *'onah* is the twenty-fourth part of a *sha'ah*, an *'eth* is the twenty-fourth part of an *'onah*, and a *rega'* the twenty-fourth part of an *'eth.*[1] How long, then, is a *rega'*? R. Berekiah said in the name of R. Ḥelbo: The length of time it takes to pronounce the word. The Rabbis said: The twinkling of an eye. Samuel said: A *rega'* is one 56,548th part of a *sha'ah.*[2]

R. Nathan said: There are three watches in the night. R. Zeriḳa and R. Ammi said in the name of R. Simeon b. Laḳish: One verse states, *At midnight I will arise to give thanks unto Thee* (Ps. CXIX, 62), while another verse states, *Mine eyes forestalled the night-watches* (*ib.* 148). How can these two verses be reconciled? R. Hezekiah (another version: R. Zeriḳa) and R. Abba[3] discuss the question. One said that they can be explained on Rabbi's view [that there are four watches in the night], while the other said that they can be explained on R. Nathan's view [that there are three watches in the night]. There is no difficulty for one who accepts Rabbi's view[4]; he who accepts R. Nathan's view [bases it on the occurrence of the phrase] *The beginning of the middle watch* (Judg. VII, 19).[5] How, then, does R. Nathan explain the phrase 'at *midnight*'? Sometimes [David arose] '*at midnight*', and at other times '*Mine eyes forestalled the night-watches*'.[6]

But how did it happen [that David changed the time of his rising]? When David had his meal in private, he ate until the ninth hour, slept until the beginning of the middle

[1] Correct reading as in J. Ber. 2*d*. The text has: *'onah* is $\frac{1}{24}$ of *'eth*, *'eth* $\frac{1}{24}$ of *'onah*, and *rega'* $\frac{1}{24}$ of *'eth*. The *'onah* is defined by Jast. as a period of twelve astronomical hours, one half of the natural day and of the natural night, or at the solstice the natural day, or natural night.

[2] The number varies in the parallel passages. Mathematically the correct number is 82,080; v. S. Brodetsky in *Jewish Review*, II, p. 173; W. M. Feldman, *Rabbinical Mathematics and Astronomy*, p. 188.

[3] This is adopted from J. Ber. 2*d*. The printed ed. has 'R. Ammi'.

[4] If by rising *at midnight* David forestalled *night-watches* (the plural signifying two), there must be four watches in the night.

[5] A *middle* watch implies an odd number.

[6] These two verses do not denote the same point of time in his opinion.

watch, and then arose to engage in the study of the Torah; but when he had an official meal,[1] he ate until evening, slept until midnight, and then arose to engage in the study of the Torah from midnight onward. In any event, daybreak never found David asleep. That is what David said, *Awake, my glory; awake, psaltery and harp; I will awake the dawn* (Ps. LVII, 9), which means, Be awakened, my glory, before the glory of my Creator; my glory is nothing in comparison with the glory of my Creator. '*I will awake the dawn*', i.e. I will awaken the dawn and the dawn will not awaken me.

R. Phinehas said in the name of R. Eleazar b. Menaḥem: There was a harp placed beneath his pillow, and he used to rise and play on it in the night. R. Levi said: A harp was suspended above David's bed, and when the time of midnight arrived a north wind blew upon it so that it produced melody of its own accord. (That is what is stated *When the instrument*[2] *played* (II Kings III, 15)—it is not written here, 'when he played *on* the instrument' but '*when the instrument played*', i.e. the harp played of its own accord.) When David heard its sound, he rose and engaged in study of the Torah; and when the Israelites heard the sound of David engaged in study of the Torah, they used to say, 'If David, king of Israel, is engaged in study of the Torah, how much more should we be!' They forthwith rose and engaged in study of the Torah.

How does Rabbi explain the text ['*the middle watch*' upon which is based the view] of R. Nathan? R. Huna said: It indicates the end of the second watch and the beginning of the third, which divides the night.[3] R. Manni replied to him, If the text had used the phrase 'middle watches' that would have been correct[4]; but it says simply '*the middle watch*'! [The answer to this is that] the first watch

[1] Lit. 'a meal of kings', when he had guests. The meal was then more protracted. [2] E.V. '*minstrel*'.
[3] Y.'A. emends: From the beginning of the second watch until the end of the third which divides the night—i.e. a point in this period marks the middle of the night.
[4] And two watches would be implied.

is not reckoned because the time [for attacking the enemy] had not yet arrived.[1]

23. SEE, O LORD, AND CONSIDER (II, 20). It is related that Doeg b. Joseph died and left a young son to his mother, who used to measure him by handbreadths and give his weight in gold to the Temple every year. When, however, the besieging army surrounded Jerusalem, his mother slaughtered him with her own hand and ate him; and Jeremiah lamented before the Omnipresent, saying, SEE, O LORD, AND CONSIDER, TO WHOM THOU HAST DONE THUS! SHALL THE WOMEN EAT THEIR FRUIT, THE CHILDREN THAT ARE DANDLED IN THE HANDS? But the Holy Spirit retorted, SHALL THE PRIEST AND THE PROPHET BE SLAIN IN THE SANCTUARY OF THE LORD? referring to Zechariah the son of Jehoiada.[2]

24. THE YOUTH AND THE OLD MAN LIE ON THE GROUND IN THE STREETS (II, 21). It is written, *Therefore I am full of the fury of the Lord, I am weary with holding in: Pour it out upon the babes in the street, and upon the assembly of young men together; for even the husband with the wife shall be taken, the aged with him that is full of days* (Jer. VI, 11). On that account,[3] THE YOUTH AND THE OLD MAN LIE ON THE GROUND IN THE STREETS.

25. THOU HAST CALLED, AS IN THE DAY OF A SOLEMN ASSEMBLY, MY TERRORS (MEGURAI) ON EVERY SIDE (II, 22). What means MEGURAI? [Those who reside] within my house.[4] R. Eleazar b. R. Marinus said: [It signifies], men that were parasites at my table didst Thou lead against me.[5]

[1] Gideon (to whom the verse refers) had planned a night attack. He did not count the first watch because the enemy would be awake. What he called '*the middle watch*' therefore corresponded to the third of the four watches.
[2] Repeated from I, 16, § 51.
[3] Because *the fury of the Lord* is poured out upon them.
[4] The root *gur* also means 'to dwell'.
[5] The text is corrupt. V. Jast., p. 1337, s.v. קוסיטרפיזין.

AND THERE WAS NONE IN THE DAY OF THE LORD'S ANGER THAT ESCAPED OR REMAINED. R. Ḥiyya taught: This refers to the sons and daughters who will yet be born to you; your sin will cause them to perish.[1] 'Those that I have dandled and brought up' is not written here, but THOSE THAT I HAVE DANDLED AND BROUGHT UP HATH MINE ENEMY CONSUMED.[2]

[1] M.K. and Mah. Cf. the threat in Deut. XXVIII, 41.

[2] The meaning is obscure and Buber regards the sentence as wrongly inserted. The most probable explanation is: if the words '*hath mine enemy consumed*' had not been added, it would have been possible to join '*those that I have dandled*', etc., to what precedes and apply the destruction only to those children already born. But the addition of '*hath mine enemy consumed*' makes it clear that a different circumstance is intended in the latter part of the verse. If the preceding clause alludes to the destruction of children already born, the last clause must allude to the fate of those yet to be born. Y.'A. and 'E.J. render the passage quite differently: R. Ḥiyya taught: Sin will destroy (of your children) proportionately to the sons and daughters that you will have (i.e. a man with less children will not lose so many for the same sin as would another with more children), for I HAVE BROUGHT UP is not written *rabothi* but *ribbithi*. I.e. it is spelt רביתי, with a *yod* (י), which is suggestive of הרביתי 'I multiplied'; hence the verse is translated: Those that I have dandled, and in proportion to the number which I multiplied, hath the enemy consumed. This, though apparently very forced, may yet perhaps be the correct rendering.

CHAPTER III

1. I AM THE MAN (III, 1). R. Ḥama b. Ḥanina opened his discourse with the text, *Then took Jeremiah another roll, and gave it to Baruch the scribe, the son of Neriah; who wrote therein from the mouth of Jeremiah all the words of the book which Jehoiakim king of Judah had burned in the fire; and there were added besides unto them many like words* (Jer. XXXVI, 32). There was no necessity for the word '*like*'; so what is the purpose of its addition? R. Kahana said: '*And there were added besides unto them many like words*': '*words*' refers to the first, second, and fourth chapters of Lamentations, '*many*' to the fifth chapter, '*like*' to the third chapter which consists of a series of three verses [each commencing with the same letter of the alphabet].[1] That is what is stated, *Have not I written unto thee excellent things*—shalishim? (Prov. XXII, 20). i.e. words thrice repeated (*meshullashim*).[2] R. Samuel b. Naḥmani said: What means '*shalishim*'? 'Mighty warriors,' as it is stated, *And captains* (shalishim) *over all of them* (Ex. XIV, 7), which we render,[3] 'And mighty warriors appointed he over all of them.' Another interpretation of '*shalishim*': it refers to the third chapter of Lamentations, which consists of a series of three verses [each commencing with the same letter of the alphabet].

R. Joshua of Siknin said in the name of R. Levi: I AM THE MAN: [The Community of Israel said:] I am indeed experienced in sufferings; what pleaseth Thee is beneficial to me![4] It may be likened to a king who was

[1] Cf. Proem XXVIII. [2] Teachings stated in the Torah and repeated in the Prophets and the Writings (Mah. and 'E.J.).

[3] The reference is to the Aramaic version (Targum) of Onḳelos.

[4] The passage is rather doubtful. The rendering adopted is that of M.K., meaning, I recognise that when it pleases God to make me suffer, it is for my own benefit. The illustration which follows, however, seems to be entirely irrelevant on this interpretation. Y.'A. and 'E.J. explain thus: What gave pleasure to Thee (viz. my acceptance of the Torah) has indeed been of benefit to me! (Spoken in a mood of bitter sarcasm.) For had I not accepted the Torah I would not have been called to account for my sins any more than the heathens have been called to account. But because I pleased Thee by accepting it when no other nation would do so, I am now so grievously punished.

enraged against his consort and drove her out of the palace. She went and pressed her face against the pillar. It happened that the king passed and saw her, and said to her, 'You are acting impudently!'[1] She replied, 'My lord king, so it is seemly and right and proper for me to do, seeing that no other woman except me has accepted you.' He retorted, 'It was I who disqualified all other women [from marriage with me] for your sake.' She said to him, 'If that is so, why did you enter such-and-such a side street, such-and-such a court and place; was it not on account of a certain woman who rejected you?' Similarly spake the Holy One, blessed be He, to Israel: 'You are acting impudently.'[2] They replied: 'Lord of the Universe, so is it seemly and right and proper for us to do, seeing that no other nation except us accepted Thy Torah.'[3] He retorted, 'It was I who disqualified all other nations [from accepting it] for your sake.' They said to Him, 'If that is so, why didst Thou carry Thy Torah round to the nations for them to reject it?' For it has been taught: At first He revealed Himself to the sons of Esau; that is what is written, *And He said: The Lord came from Sinai, and rose from Seir unto them* (Deut. XXXIII, 2), but they rejected it. Then He offered it to the sons of Ishmael who rejected it, as it is written, *He shined forth from Mount Paran* (*ib.*). Finally He offered it to Israel who accepted it, as it is written, *And He came forth from the myriads holy, at His right hand was a fiery law unto them* (*ib.*)[4]; and it is also written, *All that the Lord hath spoken will we do, and obey* (Ex. XXIV, 7).[5]

[1] By clinging to the palace after having been expelled.
[2] By praying to Me after being driven into exile.
[3] According to the rendering of Y.'A. and 'E.J. (v. p. 109, n. 3), the meaning here is: God said to Israel, 'Ye have acted impudently, by your disobedience' (hence you are punished). To which Israel replied: 'Yes, I know that I have merited this punishment, seeing that no other nation but myself accepted the Torah.' The reading of the Yalkuṭ, which differs slightly from our version in cur. edd., supports this interpretation.
[4] V. 'A.Z. 2*b* (Sonc. ed.), p. 4 ff.
[5] Yalkuṭ adds: how many noble acts did I do before Thee! I sanctified Thy name at the Red Sea, I uttered song to Thee, I joyfully accepted Thy Torah which the other nations rejected; yet after all these praiseworthy deeds, I AM THE MAN THAT HATH SEEN AFFLICTION.

R. Joshua b. Levi said: I AM THE MAN, i.e. I am Job,[1] as it is said, *What man is like Job, who drinketh up scorning like water?* (Job XXXIV, 7). THAT HATH SEEN AFFLICTION ('ONI). R. Samuel b. Naḥman said: The Community of Israel declared: Because He beheld me poor (*'aniyah*) in the performance of the precepts and in good deeds, He brought upon me THE ROD OF HIS WRATH.[2]

R. Berekiah said: He strengthened me[3] to withstand all [afflictions]. You find that after the ninety-eight reproofs in Deuteronomy,[4] what is written? *Ye are standing this day all of you* (XXIX, 9), which we render [according to Onḳelos], 'Ye endure this day all of you,' i.e. you are strong men to withstand all these [reproofs].

HE HATH LED ME (III, 2): In this world which is called DARKNESS AND NOT LIGHT.

SURELY AGAINST ME HE TURNETH HIS HAND AGAIN AND AGAIN ALL THE DAY (III, 3). R. Simeon b. Laḳish said: This teaches that the Holy One, blessed be He, despairs of[5] the righteous in this world, but relents and has compassion upon them [in the World to Come]. That is what is written, SURELY AGAINST ME HE TURNETH [from anger to mercy].

2. MY FLESH HATH HE WORN OUT (III, 4): this alludes to the Community; AND MY SKIN: this alludes to the Sanhedrin. As the skin covers the flesh [for protection], so do the Sanhedrin cover Israel.

HE HATH BROKEN MY BONES (*'AẒMOTHAI*): i.e. my strength (*'iẓumi*), referring to men who were of the mightiest.[6]

[1] I have experienced all the sufferings of Job (so in Yalḳuṭ).
[2] He translates: I am the man (of suffering): He (God) saw my poverty (in precepts and good deeds, and so punished me) with the rod of His wrath. [3] *Geber* 'man' is understood as 'strong man' (*gibbor*).
[4] Ch. XXVIII. They are really curses rather than reproofs.
[5] And leaves them in their suffering—'despairs' is used in the sense of abandoning.
[6] כבני (*like* the sons of the mighty) is probably a misprint for בבני; the latter is given in two Warsaw edd. and has been adopted in the translation.

HE HATH BUILDED AGAINST ME, AND ENCOMPASSED ME WITH GALL—ROSH (III, 5): this is Nebuchadnezzar of whom it is written, *Thou art the head* (reshah)[1] *of gold* (Dan. II, 38). AND TRAVAIL: this is Nebuzaradan. Another interpretation: GALL alludes to Vespasian and TRAVAIL to Trajan.

HE HATH MADE ME TO DWELL IN DARK PLACES, AS THOSE THAT HAVE BEEN LONG DEAD (III, 6). R. Samuel said: Four [kinds of persons] may be regarded as dead, viz. the blind, for it is written, HE HATH MADE ME TO DWELL IN DARK PLACES AS THOSE THAT HAVE BEEN LONG DEAD; the leprous, as it is said, *Let her*[2] *not, I pray, be as one dead* (Num. XII, 12); the childless, as it is written in connection with Rachel, *Give me children, or else I die* (Gen. XXX, 1); and one who has become reduced in circumstances, as it is said, *For all the men are dead that sought thy life* (Ex. IV, 19). [Now these '*men*' were Dathan and Abiram,][3] so were they dead? It means they had become reduced in circumstances.

3. HE HATH HEDGED ME ABOUT, THAT I CANNOT GO FORTH (III, 7). R. Aibu said: This alludes to the Arab gaol. R. Berekiah said: It alludes to the stronghold of the Persians.[4] The Rabbis say: It refers to the mines of the Samaritans.[5]

HE HATH MADE MY CHAIN HEAVY: He made heavy upon me the tax on land produce, state-tax, and poll-tax.

YEA, WHEN I CRY AND CALL FOR HELP (III, 8). R. Aḥa said: To what is he like who prays together with the congregation? If men make a crown for a king, and a poor person comes and contributes his share towards it, what does the king say? 'Shall I refuse to[6] accept it because of

[1] This is the Aramaic form of the word. In Heb. *rosh* signifies both 'head' and 'gall'. [2] Miriam, who had become a leper.
[3] Added in 'A.Z. 5*a* (Sonc. ed., p. 21). These men were prominent later in Korah's rebellion.
[4] Probably a substitution for 'Romans', to satisfy the censor.
[5] The translation of the whole passage follows Levi. The fugitives were thrown into gaols, Roman (v. n. 4) strongholds, or condemned to work in the mines. [6] Reading with Radal איני instead of אני 'Shall I accept?'

this poor man [participating in it]!' The king immediately accepts it and sets it on his head. Similarly if there are ten righteous men standing in prayer and a wicked person joins them, what does the Holy One, blessed be He, say? 'Shall I refuse to accept their prayer because of this wicked person!' The Rabbis say: If a person comes after the congregation [has finished its prayer], his actions are scrutinised in detail.[1] It is as if a king's tenants and household entered his presence to pay him honour, but one person came late, so the king ordered, 'Let the wine bottle be stoppered for him.'[2] What caused this to happen to him? Because he came late. Similarly, whoever prays after the congregation [has finished its prayer], his actions are scrutinised in detail.[3] For that reason it is said, YEA WHEN I CRY AND CALL FOR HELP, HE SHUTTETH OUT (*SATHAM*) MY PRAYER. The word is written so that it can be read as *she-tam*, i.e. 'because' the congregation 'had finished' (*she-tammu*) their prayer.

HE HATH ENCLOSED MY WAYS WITH HEWN STONE (III, 9). The women of Lydda used to knead their dough and go up [to Jerusalem] to pray and return before it leavened.[4] The women of Sepphoris used to go and worship[5] in the Temple, and yet nobody came in the morning to gather figs earlier than they. The schoolmaster in Magdala[6] used to arrange the candles every Friday [in the Synagogue], go up [to the Temple] to worship, and return and kindle them [before the advent of the sabbath]. There are some who say that this schoolmaster used every Friday to go up and expound the Scriptural lection in the Temple and return to observe the sabbath at home. It once

[1] By God who punishes him for every misdeed.
[2] So that the late-comer should receive none. Or perhaps: let his wine cask (which he has brought as a gift) be shut up, as it gives me no pleasure now ('E.J.).
[3] The Attribute of Mercy is stopped up against him.
[4] All these facts are narrated to demonstrate how easy the journey to Jerusalem used to be because of the excellent roads.
[5] *Var. lec.* And spend the sabbath—yet after the termination of the sabbath they were able to get home so quickly as to be the first to gather figs the following morning.
[6] There may have been several towns of that name (Levi); v. *J.E.* s.v.

happened[1] that a man was standing and ploughing, when his cow ran away. He went and told the people what had occurred. They asked, 'Which way did it go?' He began to show it to them but could not find the way, and they applied to him this verse, HE HATH ENCLOSED MY WAYS WITH HEWN STONE, HE HATH MADE MY PATHS CROOKED. The last word, *'iwwah*, signifies 'He hath made desolate', as it is stated, *A ruin* ('awwah), *a ruin, a ruin, will I make it* (Ezek. XXI, 32).

4. HE IS UNTO ME AS A BEAR LYING IN WAIT (III, 10): this refers to Nebuchadnezzar, AS A LION IN SECRET PLACES: this refers to Nebuzaradan. Another explanation: A BEAR LYING IN WAIT refers to Vespasian; A LION IN SECRET PLACES refers to Trajan.

HE HATH TURNED ASIDE MY WAYS, AND PULLED ME IN PIECES (III, 11). [The verb signifies] split in pieces, as in the statement, 'If a tree is split[2] it may be tied up in the sabbatical year.'[3]

HE HATH BENT HIS BOW, AND SET ME (WAYYAẒẒIBENI) AS A MARK FOR THE ARROW (III, 12). Two teachers offer explanations. One said: As a wedge for the log[4]; while the other said: Like the post for arrows at which all shoot but it remains standing. R. Judah said: He strengthened me to withstand [all afflictions].[5] You find that after the ninety-eight reproofs in Deuteronomy what is written? *Ye are standing* (niẓabim) *this day all of you* (XXIX, 9), which we render [according to Onḳelos] 'Ye endure this day all of you', i.e. you are strong men to withstand all these [reproofs].[6]

5. HE HATH CAUSED THE ARROWS OF HIS QUIVER TO ENTER INTO MY REINS (III, 13). Rab and Samuel

[1] This is related in contrast to the preceding. It happened after the destruction, when the roads became desolate.
[2] The same root (*pashaḥ*). [3] Sheb. IV, 6.
[4] I.e. the wedge [Israel] is struck but the log [the enemy] is split (Jast.). Levi renders: like a shield before a spear.
[5] He translates *wayyaẓẓibeni*, 'He has made me stand firm.'
[6] The same comment occurs above on v. I in the name of R. Berekiah.

comment. Rab said: [THE ARROWS OF HIS QUIVER, lit. 'the sons of His quiver'] means the children of those He laid in ruins,[1] the children of those who raised a revolt against Him. Samuel said: [It means] men who eat a great deal and evacuate much fæces[2] He brought against me.

I AM BECOME A DERISION TO ALL MY PEOPLE (III, 14). It is written, *They that sit in the gate talk of me* (Ps. LXIX, 13). This refers to the nations of the world who sit in theatres and circuses. *'And I am the song of the drunkards'*: after they sit eating and drinking and become intoxicated they sit and talk of me, scoffing at me and saying, 'We have no need to eat carobs like the Jews!' They ask one another, 'How long do you wish to live?' To which they reply, 'As long as the shirt of a Jew which is worn on the sabbath!' They then take a camel into their theatres, put their shirts upon it, and ask one another, 'Why is it in mourning?' To which they reply, 'The Jews observe the law of the sabbatical year and they have no vegetables, so they eat this camel's thorns, and that is why it is mourning!' Next they bring a clown[3] with his head shaven into the theatre and ask one another, 'Why is his head shaven?' To which he replies, 'The Jews observe the sabbath, and whatever they earn during the week they eat on the sabbath. Since they have no wood to cook with, they break up their bedsteads and use them as fuel; consequently they sleep on the ground and get covered with dust, and anoint themselves with oil, which is very expensive for that reason!' Another interpretation of *'They that sit in the gate talk of me'*: It alludes to the Israelites who sit in the Synagogues and Houses of Study. *'And I am the song of the drunkards'*: after they sit eating and drinking and become intoxicated[4] at the meal which is preparatory to [the fast of] the ninth of Ab, they sit reading dirges and lament with *'Ekah*.

[1] So Jast. Levy explains it as 'the scourge hitherto withheld', lit. 'the sons of His confinement'. [2] The same word in Heb. as for '*quiver*'. [3] The whole of this passage is repeated from Proem XVII. There 'corpse' is substituted for 'clown'. [4] Through grief, not through drink (Mah.).

HE HATH FILLED ME WITH BITTERNESS (III, 15): On the first nights of the Passover Festival in connection with which it is written, *They shall eat it with unleavened bread and bitter herbs* (Num. IX, 11). HE HATH SATED ME WITH WORMWOOD: with what He filled me on the first nights of Passover He sated me on the night of the ninth of Ab, viz. wormwood. The night of the week on which the first day of Passover occurs is always the same as that on which the night of the ninth of Ab falls.[1]

6. HE HATH ALSO BROKEN MY TEETH WITH GRAVEL STONES (III, 16). It is related of the son of R. Ḥananiah b. Teradion that he became associated with a band of robbers whose secret he disclosed, so they killed him and filled his mouth with dust and pebbles. After three days they[2] placed him in a coffin and wished to pronounce a eulogy over him out of respect for his father, but the latter would not permit it. He said to them, 'Allow me and I will speak concerning my son.' He opened his discourse with the text, *Neither have I hearkened to the voice of my teachers, nor inclined mine ear to them that instructed me! I was well nigh in all evil in the midst of the congregation and assembly* (Prov. V, 13 f.). His mother quoted over him, *A foolish son is vexation to his father, and bitterness to her that bore him* (*ib.* XVII, 25); while his sister quoted over him, *Bread of falsehood is sweet to a man; but afterwards his mouth shall be filled with gravel stones* (*ib.* XX, 17).[3]

We have learnt[4]: At any meal which is preparatory to [the fast of] the ninth of Ab it is forbidden to eat meat, drink wine, or partake of two cooked dishes; nor is it allowed to bathe and anoint [the body after this meal before the commencement of the fast]. But at a meal which is not preparatory to [the fast of] the ninth of Ab it is permitted

[1] Repeated from Proem XVIII.
[2] Presumably in an indefinite sense (not the robbers).
[3] E.V. '*gravel*'. The occurrence of this word is the reason for the incident being cited as a comment on the verse. His family would not have a eulogy uttered over him when they knew that he did not deserve it.
[4] This term introduces a quotation from the Mishnah, but the passage occurs in the Gemara, Ta'an. 30*a*, where the text is slightly different.

to eat meat, drink wine, and partake of two cooked dishes.[1]

Whenever Rab had a meal [before the fast of Ab], he took a small piece of bread, sprinkled some ashes upon it, and said [when eating it], 'This is the meal before the ninth of Ab, to fulfil what is stated, HE HATH ALSO BROKEN MY TEETH WITH GRAVEL STONES, HE HATH MADE ME TO WALLOW IN ASHES.'

AND MY SOUL IS REMOVED FAR OFF FROM PEACE, I FORGOT PROSPERITY (III, 17). R. Eleazar b. R. Jose said in the name of R. Ḥananiah b. R. Abbahu[2]: A woman of Cæsarea once took her son to a baker and said to him, 'Teach my son the trade.' He replied to her, 'Let him stay with me five years and I will teach him five hundred confections with wheat.'[3] How many confections are possible with wheat? R. Aḥa said: With wheat of *Minnith*[4] they are numberless; but the Rabbis said: Five hundred confections can be made with wheat, according to the numerical value of the letters of the word *Minnith*. R. Ḥanina and R. Jonathan were sitting and reckoning [how many ways there were of baking wheat], and got to sixty when they stopped.[5]

R. Eleazar b. R. Jose also said: It happened that a woman took her son to a cook[6] and said to him, 'Teach my son the trade.' He replied to her, 'Let him stay with me five years and I will teach him a hundred dishes made from eggs.' Rabbi [Judah ha-Nasi] heard this and exclaimed, 'Such luxury we have never seen!'[7] R. Simeon b. Ḥalafta

[1] It is, of course, unnecessary to state this about a meal on an ordinary occasion. It refers either to a meal on the eve of the fast of Ab, but not the last one of the day which is preparatory thereto, or to the last meal preparatory to any other public fast, save that of the ninth of Ab ('E.J.).
[2] Mah. emends: R. Ḥananiah b. R. Abbahu said in the name of R. Eleazar b. R. Jose, the latter having been an earlier teacher than the former.
[3] This indicates the prosperity and luxury of Judea before the destruction.
[4] V. Ezek. XXVII, 17. [5] They could not think of any others. This was after the destruction. [6] Reading מגירום with Buber. The text has פרכוטם, which Jast. translates 'tavern-keeper'. Levi retains the present reading and gives the same rendering as adopted here.
[7] Living after the destruction he admitted that he had not seen such luxuries. This is a comment on I FORGOT PROSPERITY.

heard this and exclaimed, 'Such luxury we have never heard of!'[1]

R. Judah b. Bethyra went to Nisibis[2] on the eve of the great Fast [of the day of Atonement]. After he had taken the last meal before fasting, the exilarch heard of [his arrival], paid him a visit and said, 'Let my master favour me [by coming to my house for the meal].' He replied, 'I have already partaken of the concluding meal before the fast.' The exilarch urged, 'Let my master favour me [with his presence] that people should not say that he took no notice of me.' He pressed him until he went with him. Thereupon, the exilarch instructed his young servant, saying, 'Any course which you once serve to us must not be repeated.' As they sat at the meal, eighty courses were served to them and he partook of a small portion of each and drank one goblet from each jar of wine. His host said to him, 'My teacher, after having had your concluding meal [before the fast], you were served with eighty courses and from each you partook of a small portion and from every jar of wine you drank one goblet!'[3] He replied, 'Why is the appetite called *nefesh*? The more given to it the more it expands (*nefishah*).'

R. Abbahu went to Bozrah[4] and was given hospitality by Jose Resha. There were served to him eighty kinds of birds' brains; and the host said to him, 'Let not my master be angry,[5] but the catch [of birds to-day] has been insufficient!' People called him 'Jose Resha'[6] because his food was nothing else than birds' brains.

R. Ḥiyya Rabba[7] went to Darom[8] and was entertained

[1] He lived later than Rabbi, and he confesses that he had never heard of the luxuries, much less seen them.

[2] N.E. of Mesopotamia.

[3] He made the remark to boast of his lavish hospitality and insinuate that his guest had previously had an insufficient meal.

[4] A town in Idumea.

[5] He apologised for what he considered a poor course to be served to so distinguished a guest. [6] 'Resha' means 'head'.

[7] This generally refers to R. Ḥiyya the Elder. But as he was a second century Tanna, whereas R. Joshua b. Levi, whom he visited, was a third century amora, this must be an error for R. Ḥiyya b. Abba.

[8] A district in S. Palestine.

by R. Joshua b. Levi. Twenty-four cooked dishes were set before him. He asked, 'What do you do on the sabbath?'[1] He replied, 'We double the number of courses.' Some time afterwards R. Joshua b. Levi went to Tiberias and was entertained by R. Ḥiyya Rabba. The host gave the disciples of R. Joshua some drachmas and said to them, 'Go, provide for your master as he is accustomed.'[2]

R. Isaac b. R. Eliezer knew how to arrange meals according to the number of the days of the solar year.[3] When he had the means he did so; but when he did not have them, he took fruit-kernels[4] and counted them in order not to forget them.

I FORGOT PROSPERITY. R. Simeon b. Gamaliel said: This refers to [the comfort of] washing the hands and feet after a bath.[5]

AND I SAID: MY STRENGTH IS PERISHED, AND MINE EXPECTATION FROM THE LORD (III, 18). R. Simeon b. Laḳish said: When the Holy One, blessed be He, despairs of the righteous in this world, He relents and has compassion upon them [in the World to Come].[6] That is what is stated, AND I SAID: MY STRENGTH IS PERISHED.[7]

7. REMEMBER MINE AFFLICTION AND MINE ANGUISH—MERUDI (III, 19). The Community of Israel speaks before the Holy One, blessed be He: 'Lord of the Universe, remember the exactions which I inflicted [upon others][8] and my rebelliousness (*merodi*) against Thee, but also the sufferings [I endured] in that Thou hast sated me with WORMWOOD AND GALL; and let the latter be an expiation for the former.'

[1] Which had to be honoured by more substantial meals than on a weekday. [2] He did not know how to provide for his guest adequately.
[3] A different meal for each day.
[4] Each kernel representing a different meal.
[5] The text is corrupt as may be seen from Shab. 25*b*, where it is stated: '*I forgot prosperity*': R. Jeremiah said: This refers to a bath-house; R. Jonathan said: It refers to washing the hands and feet in hot water.
[6] Repeated from III, 3. [7] '*My strength is perished*' in this world, but '*mine expectation is from the Lord*' in the world to come.
[8] Mah., 'E.J., and Rashash translate differently.

MY SOUL HATH THEM STILL IN REMEMBRANCE (III, 20). R. Ḥiyya taught: It may be likened to a king who went forth to battle accompanied by his sons, but they provoked him. The following day the king went forth alone, without his sons, and he exclaimed, 'Would that my sons were with me even though they provoke me.'[1] Thus the king is the Holy One, blessed be He, and his sons are Israel. When the Israelites went forth to battle, the Holy One, blessed be He, used to go with them; but when they provoked Him to anger He did not accompany them.[2] When, however, Israel was no longer in the land, He said, 'Would that Israel were with Me even though they provoke Me.' We have three verses [to confirm this thought]: *Oh that I were in the wilderness, in a lodging-place of wayfaring men!* (Jer. IX, 1), i.e. would that My people were with Me as in the olden time when they were in the wilderness. It is also written, *Son of man, when the house of Israel dwelt in their own land, they defiled it* (Ezek. XXXVI, 17)[3]; and there is the present passage, MY SOUL HATH THEM STILL IN REMEMBRANCE,[4] AND IS BOWED DOWN WITH ME.

R. Judan said: MY SOUL HATH THEM STILL IN REMEMBRANCE: [Israel spake before Him:] 'I know that Thou rememberest[5] the nations of the world,[6] but what am I to do seeing that MY SOUL IS BOWED DOWN WITHIN ME?[7] A proverb declares: 'While the fat one grows lean, the lean one expires.'[8]

THIS I RECALL TO MY MIND, THEREFORE HAVE I HOPE (III, 21). R. Abba b. Kahana said in the name of R. Joḥanan: To what may this be likened? To a king who

[1] The text here erroneously inserts the words 'we have three verses . . . men', which occur again in their proper place below.
[2] Which caused their overthrow and exile.
[3] This is understood as: Would that Israel dwelt in their own land though they defiled it.
[4] Interpreted as: God has Israel still in remembrance.
[5] The verse is to be rendered: Do Thou remember, but my soul is bowed down, etc.
[6] Who have oppressed me, and in due course Thou wilt avenge me.
[7] Waiting for vengeance to be taken on them.
[8] The 'fat one' is the oppressor, 'the lean' the oppressed.

married a lady and made a large settlement upon her, saying to her, 'So many state-apartments[1] am I preparing for you, so many fine purple garments am I giving you.' The king left her, departed to a distant country and tarried there. Her neighbours visited her and vexed her by telling her, 'The king has left you, gone away to a distant country, and will never return to you.' She wept and sighed; but whenever she entered her room, she opened [the chest where it was deposited], took out her settlement and read it. On seeing therein, 'So many state-apartments am I preparing for you, so many fine purple garments am I giving you,' she was at once comforted. Eventually the king returned and said to her, 'My daughter, I wonder how you waited for me all these years.' She answered, 'My lord king, had it not been for the generous settlement which you wrote and gave me, my neighbours would long ago have caused me to perish.' In like manner the heathens vex Israel by saying to them, 'Your God has hidden His face from you and removed His *Shechinah* from your midst; He will return to you no more.' They weep and sigh; but when they enter their Synagogues and Houses of Study, read in the Torah and find written therein, *And I will have respect unto you, and make you fruitful, and multiply you . . . and I will set My tabernacle among you . . . and I will walk among you* (Lev. XXVI, 9 ff.), they are comforted. In the time to come when the era of the redemption arrives, the Holy One, blessed be He, will say to Israel: 'My sons, I wonder how you waited for Me all these years'; and they will speak before Him: 'Lord of the universe, had it not been for Thy Torah which Thou hast given us, the heathen peoples would long ago have caused us to perish.' Therefore it is stated, THIS I RECALL TO MY MIND and THIS indicates nothing else than the Torah, as it is said, *And this is the Torah* (Deut. IV, 44). Similarly did David declare, *Unless Thy Torah had been my delight, I should then have perished in mine affliction* (Ps. CXIX, 92).

[1] Levi renders: four posters (*Himmelbetten*), but it hardly seems appropriate. Perhaps one should render: boudoirs.

THEREFORE HAVE I HOPE in Him and proclaim the unity of His name twice daily and say, *'Hear, O Israel, the Lord our God, the Lord is one'* (Deut. VI, 4).

8. SURELY THE LORD'S MERCIES ARE NOT CONSUMED, SURELY HIS COMPASSIONS FAIL NOT (III, 22). R. Simeon b. Laḳish said: When the Holy One, blessed be He, despairs of the righteous in this world, He relents and has compassion upon them.[1] That is what is written, SURELY THE LORD'S MERCIES ARE NOT CONSUMED.

THEY ARE NEW EVERY MORNING; GREAT IS THY FAITHFULNESS (III, 23). R. Alexandri said: Because Thou renewest us [in life] every morning, we know that great is Thy faithfulness for the resurrection of the dead. R. Simeon b. Abba said: Because Thou renewest us in the morning[2] of the kingdoms of the world, we know that great is Thy faithfulness to redeem us.

R. Ḥelbo said: Every day the Holy One, blessed be He, creates a band of new angels who utter a new song before Him and then pass away. R. Berekiah said: I replied to R. Ḥelbo by quoting, *And he said: Let me go, for the day breaketh* (Gen. XXXII, 27) (and my time has arrived to utter a song before Him)[3]! But he answered me, 'You strangler, do you think to strangle me [with such a specious argument]? The angels [concerned in the incident with Jacob] were Gabriel and Michael who were celestial princes, and while the others pass away [daily], they do not pass away!'

Hadrian the accursed asked R. Joshua b. Ḥananiah: 'You declare that every day the Holy One, blessed be He, creates a band of new angels who utter a new song before Him and then pass away?' 'Yes,' he answered. 'Where, then, do they go?' he inquired. 'To where they

[1] V. *supra*, III, 18.

[2] I.e. the rise of a kingdom to power which is always followed by its decline; or, the rise of one kingdom which is always effected through the downfall of a previous one (Y.'A., 'E.J.).

[3] The words in brackets must be added from Gen. R. LXXVIII, 1. This proves that angels are not created every day for the purpose.

were created.' 'And whence were they created?' 'From the river of fire.'[1] 'And what is the nature of the river of fire?' 'It is like the Jordan which does not cease flowing night or day.' 'But,' he retorted, 'the Jordan flows by day and stops by night!' He replied, 'I kept watch at Beth Peor[2] and observed how the Jordan flowed at night the same as by day.' Hadrian asked, 'Whence does the river of fire originate?' He answered, 'From the sweat of the *Ḥayyoth*[3] caused by their carrying the divine throne.'

THE LORD IS MY PORTION, SAITH MY SOUL (III, 24). R. Abbahu said in the name of R. Joḥanan: It may be likened to a king who entered a province, and had with him generals, captains, and military commanders, and the notables of the province were sitting in its midst. One of them said, 'I will take a general to my house.'[4] Another said, 'I will take a captain to my house'; while still another said, 'I will take one of the commanders to my house.' But a shrewd man there said, 'I will take the king, because while the others may pass away the king will not do so.' Similarly there are idolaters who worship the sun, others the moon, and still others wood and stone; but Israel worship the Holy One, blessed be He, alone. That is what is written, THE LORD IS MY PORTION, SAITH MY SOUL, because I proclaim His unity twice daily, saying, '*Hear, O Israel, the Lord our God, the Lord is one*'.

9. THE LORD IS GOOD UNTO THEM THAT WAIT FOR HIM (III, 25). This might be taken to mean that [He is good] to all, therefore it is stated, TO THE SOUL THAT SEEKETH HIM. Similar to it is, *Surely God is good to Israel* (Ps. LXXIII, 1)—this might be taken to imply that [He is good] to all; therefore it is stated, *Even to such as are pure in heart* (*ib.*), i.e. they whose heart is pure and in whose hand is no iniquity. Still another passage like it is, *Happy is the man whose strength is in Thee* (*ib.* LXXXIV,

[1] V. Dan. VII, 10. [2] V. Deut. III, 29. A town on one of the hills overlooking the lower valley of the Jordan.
[3] The celestial creatures mentioned in Ezek. I, 13. [4] As his guest, hoping to secure his protection in return for the hospitality.

6)—this might be taken to imply that this refers to all; therefore it is stated, *In whose heart are the highways* (*ib.*), i.e. they in whose heart the paths of the Torah are preserved. Another parallel is, *Do good, O Lord, unto the good* (*ib.* CXXV, 4)—this might be taken to imply that this refers to all; therefore it is stated, *And to them that are upright in their hearts* (*ib.*).[1] Still another parallel is, *The Lord is nigh unto all them that call upon Him* (*ib.* CXLV, 18)—this might be thought to refer to all; therefore it is stated, *To all that call upon Him in truth* (*ib.*). Yet another parallel is, *Who is a God like unto Thee, that pardoneth iniquity, and passeth by transgression* (Micah VII, 18)—this might be thought to refer to all, therefore it is stated, *Of the remnant of His heritage* (*ib.*).

IT IS GOOD THAT A MAN SHOULD QUIETLY WAIT FOR THE SALVATION OF THE LORD (III, 26). R. Simeon b. Laḳish said: When the Holy One, blessed be He, despairs of the righteous in this world, He relents and has compassion upon them.[2] That is what is stated, IT IS GOOD THAT A MAN SHOULD QUIETLY WAIT FOR THE SALVATION OF THE LORD.[3]

IT IS GOOD FOR A MAN THAT HE BEAR THE YOKE OF HIS YOUTH (III, 27). I.e. the yoke of the Torah, of matrimony, and of an occupation.[4]

LET HIM SIT ALONE AND KEEP SILENCE (III, 28). R. Samuel b. Naḥman said: The Holy One, blessed be He, summoned the Ministering Angels and spake to them: 'If a human king [is in mourning], what does he do?' They replied, 'He dons black garments and covers his head with sackcloth.' He said to them, 'I will do likewise.' That is what is written, *I clothe the heavens with blackness, and I make sackcloth their covering* (Isa. L, 3). He further inquired

[1] 'E.J. '*The good*' may mean simply those who carry out their civic obligations, not from an inner sense of duty, but because they recognise that the strength of the community is their protection too. Therefore the Midrash states that this is not enough: they must be '*upright in their hearts*' too—their motives must be pure and disinterested.
[2] V. *supra*, III, 18.
[3] In the world to come. If it is not manifested here.
[4] These obligations should be assumed at an early age and not deferred

of them, 'What else does he do?' They replied, 'He extinguishes the lamps.' He said to them, 'I will do likewise.' That is what is stated, *The sun and the moon become black, and the stars withdraw their shining* (Joel IV, 15). He again inquired, 'What else does he do?' They replied, 'He walks barefooted.' He said to them, 'I will do likewise.' That is what is written, *The Lord, in the whirlwind and in the storm is His way, and the clouds are the dust of His feet* (Nahum I, 3). He again inquired, 'What else does he do?' They replied, 'He sits in silence.' He said to them, 'I will do likewise.' That is what is written, LET HIM SIT ALONE AND KEEP SILENCE, BECAUSE HE HATH LAID IT UPON HIM.[1]

LET HIM PUT HIS MOUTH IN THE DUST, IF SO BE THERE MAY BE HOPE. LET HIM GIVE HIS CHEEK TO HIM THAT SMITETH HIM, LET HIM BE FILLED FULL WITH REPROACH (III, 29 f.). Rabbi [Judah ha-Nasi] was expounding his portion of Scripture, and when he reached the following verse he wept: *And Samuel said to Saul: Why hast thou disquieted me, to bring me up?* (I Sam. XXVIII, 15).[2] And it is written, *For lo, He that formeth the mountains, and createth the wind, and declareth unto man what is his thought* (Amos IV, 13)—which implies that even actions of no consequence are inscribed against a man in his record; and who inscribes them? *That maketh the morning darkness* (*ib.*). *Seek ye the Lord, all ye humble of the earth*, etc. (Zeph. II, 3). Further, *Hate the evil, and love the good*, etc. (Amos V, 15). Why? *For God shall bring every work into the judgment concerning every hidden thing, whether it be good or whether it be evil* (Eccl. XII, 14). And also the present passage, LET HIM PUT HIS MOUTH IN THE DUST . . . LET HIM GIVE HIS CHEEK TO HIM THAT SMITETH HIM, LET HIM BE FILLED FULL WITH REPROACH.[3]

[1] Cf. *supra*, I, I. The verse is now made to refer to God.
[2] In Ḥag. 4*b* it is explained that Samuel was disquieted because he feared that he had been called to the Judgment; and if a man like Samuel felt like that, how much more must an ordinary person weep at the thought of what awaits him in the hereafter!
[3] All these verses made him weep.

FOR THE LORD WILL NOT CAST OFF FOR EVER (III, 31). If it is possible so to express oneself, He has not abandoned us and will not do so.

FOR THOUGH HE CAUSE GRIEF, YET WILL HE HAVE COMPASSION ACCORDING TO THE MULTITUDE OF HIS MERCIES (III, 32). R. Simeon b. Laḳish said: When the Holy One, blessed be He, despairs of the righteous in this world, He relents and has compassion upon them.[1] That is what is stated, FOR THOUGH HE CAUSE GRIEF, YET WILL HE HAVE COMPASSION.

FOR HE DOTH NOT AFFLICT WILLINGLY (III, 33). R. Berekiah said in the name of R. Levi: In two places Israel practised double-dealing: in one they did right with their mouth but not with their heart, and in the other they did right with their heart but not with their mouth, viz. at Sinai and in Babylon. At Sinai they did right with their mouth but not with their heart,[2] as it is written, *But they beguiled Him with their mouth, and lied unto Him with their tongue* (Ps. LXXVIII, 36). In Babylon they did right with their heart but not with their mouth, as it is written, FOR HE DOTH NOT AFFLICT WILLINGLY.[3] The Holy One, blessed be He, said: 'Let the mouth [which professed obedience] at Sinai come and atone for the mouth [which professed idolatry] in Babylon, and let the heart [which was loyal to God] in Babylon come and atone for the heart [which was disloyal] at Sinai.' For all that HE GRIEVED THE CHILDREN OF MEN,[4] i.e. He brought against them *An adversary and an enemy* (Est. VII, 6), viz. Haman who exposed[5] their degradation.

TO CRUSH UNDER FOOT ALL THE PRISONERS OF THE EARTH (III, 34). This alludes to Nebuchadnezzar of whom it is written, *And wheresoever the children*

[1] V. *supra*, III, 18.
[2] They promised obedience to the Torah, but their heart was not in what they said.
[3] Lit. 'of His heart'. God did not afflict them 'of His heart'—i.e. to the fullest extent—because they had not sinned to the fullest extent in those days; v. S.S. R. VII, 8.
[4] The continuation of Lam. III, 33. E.V. '*Nor grieve the children of men*'.
[5] The same verb as '*grieve*'. 'Degradation' is lit. 'wound'.

of men, the beasts of the field, and the fowls of the heaven dwell, hath He given them into thy hand, and hath made thee to rule over them all; thou art the head of gold (Dan. II, 38).

WHO IS HE THAT SAITH, AND IT COMETH TO PASS, WHEN THE LORD COMMANDETH IT NOT? (III, 37). Who commanded? Haman commanded, but the Holy One, blessed be He, did not command. Haman commanded, *To destroy, to slay, and to cause to perish, all the Jews* (Est. III, 13); whereas the Holy One, blessed be He, did not so command, but *That his wicked device, which he had devised against the Jews, should return upon his own head* (*ib.* IX, 25).

OUT OF THE MOUTH OF THE MOST HIGH PROCEEDETH NOT EVIL AND GOOD (III, 38)?[1] R. Eleazar said: From the time that the Holy One, blessed be He, declared, *See, I have set before thee this day life and good, and death and evil* (Deut. XXX, 15), good has not happened to the doer of evil and evil to the doer of good; but good has befallen the doer of good and evil the doer of evil; as it is stated, *The Lord reward the evil-doer according to his wickedness* (II Sam. III, 39).

WHEREFORE DOTH A LIVING MAN COMPLAIN? (III, 39). It is sufficient for him that he lives. R. Levi said: The Holy One, blessed be He, declared: 'Your existence is in My hand, and being alive you complain!' R. Huna said: Let him stand up like a brave man, acknowledge his sins, and not complain. R. Berekiah said: [The verse is to be interpreted thus:] Wherefore doth a man complain against Him who lives eternally? If a man wishes to complain, let it be about his sins. Rabbi [Judah ha-Nasi] says: [Israel] are the children of murmurers. [God said:] 'After all the favour I showed to Adam he complained before Me and said, *The woman whom Thou gavest to be with me, she gave me of the tree, and I did eat* (Gen. III, 12). Jacob acted similarly. I exerted Myself to make his son king in Egypt, and he complained and said, *My way is hid from the Lord*

[1] According as man merits one or the other; v. Deut. R. IV, 3.

(Isa. XL, 27).[1] His descendants behaved likewise. I exerted Myself to arrange a light diet for them so that none of them should be troubled with indigestion and diarrhœa, but they complained before Me and said, *Our soul loatheth this light bread* (Num. XXI, 5). Zion also behaved thus, viz. *But Zion said: 'The Lord hath forsaken me, and the Lord hath forgotten me'* (Isa. XLIX, 14).

LET US SEARCH AND TRY OUR WAYS, AND RETURN TO THE LORD. LET US LIFT UP OUR HEART WITH OUR HANDS UNTO GOD IN THE HEAVENS (III, 40 f.). R. Abba[2] b. Zabdi, R. Tanḥum b. Ḥanilai, and R. Joshaiah went out [into the public square to hold a service of prayer during] a fast. R. Abba b. Zabdi discoursed: Is it possible for a man to take his heart out[3] and restore it? But the meaning is, Let us make our heart [clean] like our hands [which must be clean], and then will it be UNTO GOD IN THE HEAVENS. If an unclean insect is in a man's hand, though he immerse himself in all the waters of the world he can never become ritually clean; but if he throw the defiling creature from his hand, immersion in forty *se'ahs* avails him [to regain his purity].

R. Tanḥum discoursed: *Then the princes of Israel and the king humbled themselves; and they said: The Lord is righteous* (II Chron. XII, 6); and it continues, *And when the Lord saw that they had humbled themselves, the word of the Lord came to Shemaiah, saying: They have humbled themselves; I will not destroy them; but I will grant them some deliverance, and My wrath shall not be poured out upon Jerusalem by the hand of Shishak* (*ib.* 7). It is not written here, 'And when the Lord saw that they had fasted' but '*That they had humbled themselves*'. R. Joshaiah discoursed, *Gather yourselves together, yea, gather together*—ḳoshu (Zeph. II, 1)—i.e. men should first correct (*ḳasheṭ*) themselves and then correct others. Since there is a person here who slandered me to R. Joḥanan, let him [stand up before] all

[1] He was perplexed by the trouble that had befallen him in the loss of Joseph. [2] The printed ed. has 'Beba' for Abba.
[3] Since the verse declares, LET US LIFT UP OUR HEART WITH OUR HANDS.

the people for judgment.[1] It is said that R. Ḥiyya, R. Ammi, and R. Jose were present, and they arose and departed.[2]

WE HAVE TRANSGRESSED AND HAVE REBELLED (III, 42). The Babylonian Rabbis said: When the endive is bitter the fermenting wine turns sour.[3] The Palestinian Rabbis[4] said: When acts are evil they are serious to the perpetrators.[5]

R. Huna said in the name of R. Joseph: WE HAVE TRANSGRESSED AND HAVE REBELLED, which is in accord with our nature: THOU HAST NOT PARDONED, is that in accord with Thy nature?[6] R. Levi said: WE HAVE TRANSGRESSED AND HAVE REBELLED, and Thou hast destroyed Thy Sanctuary.

THOU HAST COVERED WITH ANGER AND PURSUED US; THOU HAST SLAIN UNSPARINGLY. THOU HAST COVERED THYSELF WITH A CLOUD, SO THAT NO PRAYER CAN PASS THROUGH (III, 43 f.). R. Ḥelbo asked R. Samuel b. Naḥman: 'Since I have heard of you that you are a master of *Haggadah*, what means that which is written, THOU HAST COVERED THYSELF WITH A CLOUD, SO THAT NO PRAYER CAN PASS THROUGH?' He replied: 'Prayer is likened to a *miḳweh* and repentance to the sea. Just as a *miḳweh* is sometimes open and sometimes locked,[7] so the gates of prayer are sometimes locked and sometimes opened; but the sea is always open, and similarly the gates of repentance are always open.' R. 'Anan said: The gates of prayer are likewise never locked; that

[1] Or perhaps: therefore let all people stand in judgment before God—let every man search his heart. He preceded this by saying 'men should first correct themselves', etc., i.e. I admit that I have done wrong too ('E.J.).

[2] They were annoyed that he should have introduced a personal grievance into his address, especially as they had been concerned in the incident.

[3] I.e. sin leads on to sin. First Israel '*transgressed*' and then '*rebelled*'.

[4] Lit. 'the Rabbis of there . . . the Rabbis of here'—the translation follows the view that Lam. R. is a Palestinian work; v. Introduction.

[5] So here, the effect of rebellion is THOU HAST NOT PARDONED.

[6] It is natural for man to sin, but it is expected that the divine Attribute of Mercy would secure pardon.

[7] And therefore inaccessible to a person who wishes to immerse in its water for purification.

is what is written, *As the Lord our God is* [nigh] *whensoever we call upon Him* (Deut. IV, 7), and *'call'* signifies nothing else than prayer, as it is said, *And it shall come to pass that, before they call, I will answer* (Isa. LXV, 24).

R. Jose b. Ḥalafta said: There are times for prayer; for thus spake David before the Holy One, blessed be He: 'Lord of the universe, when I pray before Thee may my prayer be in an acceptable time'; that is what is stated, *Let my prayer be unto Thee, O Lord, in an acceptable time* (Ps. LXIX, 14).[1]

R. Akiba was standing on trial before Tineius Rufus,[2] and Joshua the grits-dealer was standing in prayer with him. A cloud descended and enveloped them, so the latter said, 'It seems to me that the cloud has descended and enveloped us only that the Rabbi's prayer should not be heard, as it is written, THOU HAST COVERED THYSELF WITH A CLOUD, SO THAT NO PRAYER CAN PASS THROUGH.'

THOU HAST MADE US AS THE OFFSCOURING AND REFUSE IN THE MIDST OF THE PEOPLES (III, 45). [Thou hast made us] loathsome outcasts.

ALL OUR ENEMIES HAVE OPENED THEIR MOUTH (III, 46). Why do the verses beginning with the letter *peh* precede those beginning with the letter *'ain?* Because they uttered with their mouth what they had not seen with their eye.[3]

MINE EYE IS POURED OUT, AND CEASETH NOT, WITHOUT ANY INTERMISSION, TILL THE LORD LOOK FORTH, AND BEHOLD FROM HEAVEN (III, 49 f.). R. Aḥa said in the name of R. Samuel b. Naḥman: In three places we find the Holy Spirit mentioned in connection with the redemption. They are[4]: *A joy of wild asses, a pasture of flocks* (Isa. XXXII, 14); and what is written after that? *Until the spirit be poured upon us from on high, and the wilderness become a fruitful field, and the fruitful*

[1] This implies that there are unacceptable times of prayer.
[2] V. p. 121, n. 2. He had ordered that the Torah should not be taught. and R. Akiba had ignored the edict. [3] V. II, 20 (on ch. II, 16).
[4] The printed text has 'what is the reason?'

field be counted for a forest (*ib.* 15).[1] Similarly, *The smallest shall become a thousand, and the least a mighty nation* (*ib.* LX, 22), and after that is written, *The spirit of the Lord God is upon me; because the Lord hath anointed me* (*ib.* LXI, 1). There is also the present passage, MINE EYE IS POURED OUT, after which is written, TILL THE LORD LOOK FORTH, AND BEHOLD FROM HEAVEN.

MINE EYE AFFECTED MY SOUL, BECAUSE OF ALL THE DAUGHTERS OF MY CITY (III, 51). R. Simeon b. Gamaliel said: There were five hundred schools in Bethar, and the smallest of them had not less than three hundred children. They used to say, 'If the enemy comes against us, with these styluses we will go out and stab them!' When, however, in consequence of the people's sins the enemy did come, they enwrapped each pupil in his book and burnt him so that I alone was left; and I applied to myself the verse, MINE EYE AFFECTED MY SOUL, BECAUSE OF ALL THE DAUGHTERS [i.e. the inhabitants] OF MY CITY.[2]

THEY HAVE CHASED ME SORE LIKE A BIRD, THAT ARE MINE ENEMIES WITHOUT CAUSE. THEY HAVE CUT OFF MY LIFE IN THE DUNGEON (III, 52 f.). This refers to [such as] Joseph, Jeremiah, and Daniel.[3]

WATERS FLOWED OVER MY HEAD; I SAID: I AM CUT OFF (III, 54). This alludes to the peoples of whom it is written, *Ah, the uproar of many peoples, that roar like the roaring of the seas; and the rushing of nations, that rush like the rushing of mighty waters!* (Isa. XVII, 12).

I CALLED UPON THY NAME, O LORD, OUT OF THE LOWEST DUNGEON (III, 55). This refers to [such as] Joseph, Jeremiah, and Daniel. THOU HEARDEST MY VOICE . . . THOU DREWEST NEAR IN THE DAY THAT I CALLED UPON THEE (III, 56 f.).[4]

[1] The first verse describes the desolation, and the second describes the rehabitation of the country through the Holy Spirit.
[2] Repeated from II, 4 (on ch. II, 2). [3] They were all cast into prison on false charges. V. Gen. XXXIX, 20; Jer. XXXVIII, 6; Dan. VI, 17.
[4] No comment is offered on this, which is itself probably to be taken as a comment on the preceding verse. I CALLED UPON THY NAME and THOU HEARDEST MY VOICE—i.e. God always hearkens to those who call upon Him.

O LORD, THOU HAST PLEADED THE CAUSES OF MY SOUL; THOU HAST REDEEMED MY LIFE. O LORD, THOU HAST SEEN MY WRONG; JUDGE THOU MY CAUSE (III, 58 f.). A Jew passed in front of Hadrian and greeted him. The king asked, 'Who are you?' He answered, 'I am a Jew.' He exclaimed, 'Dare a Jew pass in front of Hadrian and greet him!' He ordered, 'Take him and cut off his head.' Another Jew passed, and seeing what had happened to the first man, did not greet him. The king asked, 'Who are you?' He answered, 'A Jew.' He exclaimed, 'Dare a Jew pass in front of Hadrian without giving greeting!' He ordered, 'Take him and cut off his head.' His senators said to him, 'We cannot understand your actions. He who greeted you was killed and he who did not greet you was killed!' He replied to them, 'Do you seek to advise me how I wish to kill those I hate!' And the Holy Spirit cried out and said, THOU HAST SEEN ALL THEIR VENGEANCE AND ALL THEIR DEVICES AGAINST ME (III, 60).

THOU HAST HEARD THEIR TAUNT, O LORD . . . THE LIPS OF THOSE THAT ROSE UP AGAINST ME, AND THEIR MUTTERING AGAINST ME ALL THE DAY. BEHOLD THOU THEIR SITTING DOWN, AND THEIR STANDING UP; I AM THEIR SONG (III, 61 ff.). I am the subject of their [taunting] songs.

THOU WILT RENDER UNTO THEM A RECOMPENSE (III, 64). Jeremiah said, THOU WILT RENDER UNTO THEM A RECOMPENSE; and Asaph said, *And render unto our neighbours sevenfold into their bosom* (Ps. LXXIX, 12). What means '*into their bosom*'? R. Judah b. Gadya said: Render unto them a recompense for what they did to the Temple which was located in the bosom of the world[1]; as it is stated, *And from the bosom of the earth to the court* (Ezek. XLIII, 14).[2] The Rabbis said: [Render unto them a recompense] for what they did with the circumcision which is set in the bosom [i.e. the centre] of a man. For R.

[1] The tradition was that the Temple area was the centre of the universe.
[2] So lit. E.V. '*And from the bottom upon the ground to the settle*'.

Joshua of Siknin and R. Levi said in the name of R. Johanan: [The Amalekites] took the circumcised members of the Israelites, threw them upward and exclaimed, 'This is what Thou hast chosen; so take what Thou hast chosen,' until Samuel arose and exacted punishment of them. That is what is written, *Then said Samuel: Bring ye hither to me Agag the king of the Amalekites . . . And Samuel hewed Agag in pieces* (I Sam. XV, 32 f.). R. Abba b. Kahana said: Samuel began to cut pieces out of his flesh and feed ostriches with them; that is what is written, *It shall devour the members of his body* (Job XVIII, 13). R. Isaac said: He took four poles and stretched him upon them. *And Agag said: Surely the bitterness of death is at hand*—sar (I Sam. *loc. cit.*), i.e. are princes (*sarim*) executed with such a bitter form of death! R. Isaac said: Samuel castrated him, because he had taken the circumcised members [of the Israelites] and thrown them upward, and for that reason he exacted this punishment of him, as it is stated, *As thy sword hath made women childless,*[1] *so shall thy mother be childless among women* (*ib.* 33). '*And Samuel hewed*': this teaches that he cut him in four pieces.[2]

THOU WILT GIVE THEM HARDNESS (MEGINATH) OF HEART (III, 65). Two teachers [differ about the meaning of the word]. One said that it signifies breaking of heart,[3] the other that it signifies hardness of heart. He who said that it means 'breaking of heart' does so because it is stated, *Who hath delivered* (miggen)[4] *thine enemies into thy hand* (Gen. XIV, 20); and he who said that it means 'hardness of heart' does so because it is stated, *The shield* (magen)[5] *of thy help* (Deut. XXXIII, 29).

THY CURSE (TA'ALATHKA) UNTO THEM: torture (*teli*)[6] them with afflictions, and bring upon them all the curses (*aloth*) which are written in the Torah; as it is stated, *And the Lord thy God will put these curses upon thine*

[1] By castrating the men.
[2] Since the text does not mention whether he hewed him lengthwise or crosswise, it is assumed that he did both. Hence there were four pieces.
[3] I.e. grief. [4] As a result of breaking their courage and strength.
[5] *Shield* being a symbol of strength. [6] Lit. 'hang up'.

enemies, and on them that hate thee, that persecuted thee (*ib.* XXX, 7).

THOU WILT PURSUE THEM IN ANGER AND DESTROY THEM (III, 66). Jeremiah said, THOU WILT PURSUE THEM IN ANGER AND DESTROY THEM, and Moses said, *I will utterly blot out*[1] *the remembrance of Amalek from under heaven* (Ex. XVII, 14). Samuel said: '*Amalek*' is to be understood literally; '*remembrance*' alludes to Haman; '*blotting out*' refers to this world, '*I will blot out*' to the world to come; '*from under heaven*', i.e. him and the whole of that generation to the end of all generations. R. Joshua said: [It signifies] that Amalek shall have no descendants; '*from under heaven*' indicates that nobody will be able to say, 'This tree, or camel, or lamb belongs to Amalek.'[2]

R. Eliezer says: Because Amalek sought to destroy Israel from beneath the wings of heaven,[3] Moses spake before the Holy One, blessed be He: 'This wicked one has come to destroy Israel from beneath Thy wings, so who will read in Thy Torah which Thou hast given them?' Another interpretation: Because he sought to destroy the Israelites who are destined to be dispersed from one end of the world to the other, as it is stated, *And the Lord shall scatter thee among all the peoples, from the one end of the earth even unto the other end of the earth* (Deut. XXVIII, 64) [therefore his fate will be to be destroyed FROM UNDER THE HEAVENS].

R. Eliezer said: When will the name of these [persecutors of Israel] perish from the world, idolatry and its worshippers be uprooted from the earth, and the Holy One, blessed be He, be [acknowledged] as the one God in the world, according as it is said, *And the Lord shall be King over all the earth; in that day shall the Lord be one, and His name one* (Zech. XIV, 9)? At the time when THOU WILT PURSUE THEM IN ANGER, AND

[1] Lit. 'blotting out I will blot out'.
[2] There will be no trace left.
[3] This may mean simply, 'from the world,' or perhaps it is metaphorical: they tried to drive Israel from their allegiance to God.

DESTROY THEM FROM UNDER THE HEAVENS OF THE LORD.

R. Nathan said: Haman only came to provide a memorial for Israel. That is what is written, *That these days of Purim shall not fail from among the Jews, nor the memorial of them perish from their seed* (Est. IX, 28).

CHAPTER IV

1. HOW IS THE GOLD BECOME DIM! (IV, 1). R. Samuel said: The meaning is, how has the gold become covered over,[1] as the word is used in *There is no secret that they can hide*[2] *from thee!* (Ezek. XXVIII, 3). The Rabbis say: The meaning is, how has the gold become changed![3] R. Ḥama b. Ḥanina said: The meaning is, how has the gold become dim,[4] as it is said, HOW IS THE GOLD BECOME DIM! [The word having the same signification as in the following passage:] R. Ḥiyya learnt: When the text mentions *coals*,[5] one might think that dully burning[6] coals are intended; therefore it is stated, [*coals*] *of fire*. If the text had only mentioned '*fire*', it would have been possible to interpret it as denoting the flame; therefore it is stated, '*coals.*' How was it, then? He was to take of the glowing coals.

THE HALLOWED STONES ARE POURED OUT. When the scholars had to go out to seek their livelihood, the text THE HALLOWED STONES ARE POURED OUT was applied to them.[7]

Another interpretation is to understand the verse as an allusion to [the death of king] Josiah: HOW IS THE GOLD BECOME DIM! Because he was [to his people] like a golden ornament. HOW IS THE MOST FINE GOLD CHANGED! Because his body was like a precious stone and pearls. THE HALLOWED STONES

[1] So that it is not recognisable as gold while it yet remains gold. Similarly, in spite of their sins, occasioned to some extent by misery and exile, the nation in its heart of hearts remained faithful to God (Radal).
[2] The same verb as '*become dim*'.
[3] As the verse continues, HOW IS THE MOST FINE GOLD CHANGED! They maintain that the people's sins occasioned more than a superficial alteration.
[4] Lost its lustre; or, how feebly burns the flame of Judaism.
[5] This refers to Lev. XVI, 12, *And he shall take a censer full of coals of fire*.
[6] The same verb as '*become dim*', and that is why the extract is quoted from Pes. 75*b*.
[7] The times were so stringent that scholars took longer to earn sufficient to maintain themselves and had to reduce their study. Their '*hallowed*' occupation was thus '*poured out*', i.e. adversely affected.

ARE POURED OUT: this alludes to the fourth-parts[1] of his blood which Jeremiah collected [on the battlefield where he was slain] and buried; as it is written, *And he was buried in the sepulchres of his fathers* (II Chron. XXXV, 24). In how many graves, then, was he buried, since it states, '*In the sepulchres of his fathers*'! But it refers to the two fourth-parts of his blood which Jeremiah collected and buried.[2]

Another interpretation is to understand it as an allusion to the men of Jerusalem who were like a golden ornament, and their bodies like a precious stone and pearls. Should anybody tell you that the verse does not allude to the men of Jerusalem, answer that the next verse mentions THE PRECIOUS SONS OF ZION.

2. THE PRECIOUS SONS OF ZION (IV, 2). In what did their precious character consist? When a man of one of the other Palestinian towns married a woman of Jerusalem he gave her her weight in gold; and when a Jerusalemite married a woman from another town he received his weight in gold. Another explanation of their precious character: When a man [of Jerusalem] married a woman of superior status to his own, he made the tables [arranged for the wedding feast] more costly than his expenditure [on his domestic furnishings],[3] and when she was of inferior status he made his expenditure [on his domestic furnishings] more costly than the tables [arranged for the wedding feast].[4] Another explanation of their precious character: None of them would attend a banquet unless he was invited twice.[5]

3. It happened that a Jerusalemite once gave a dinner and instructed one of his household, 'Go and bring me my

[1] Of a *log*; v. Glos. [2] One-fourth of a *log* was considered the minimum quantity of blood in the body essential to life. V. Soṭ. 5*a* (Sonc. ed., p. 20). He gathered twice this amount, and buried half in separate graves. [3] As an indication of the honour conferred upon him by such a marriage. [4] Because in such circumstances he was bestowing honour upon the bride by accepting her. [5] To make sure that the first invitation had not been sent to him in mistake. As the next paragraph illustrates, such an error may have a tragic sequel.

friend Ḳamẓa'; but he went and invited Bar Ḳamẓa who was his enemy. The latter entered and sat among the invited. When the host came in and found him among the guests, he said to him, 'You are my enemy, and yet you sit in my house! Get up and leave my house!' He answered, 'Do not put me to shame, and I will pay you the cost of what I eat.' He said to him, 'You will not recline at the meal!' He said to him, 'Do not put me to shame, and I will sit without eating or drinking anything'; but he replied, 'You will not recline at the meal!' He pleaded, 'I will pay the cost of the whole meal'; but the host said, 'Go away!' R. Zechariah b. Eucolus, who was present, could have prevented [the host from treating the man in this manner] but did not intervene. Bar Ḳamẓa at once left the house, and said to himself, 'They feast and sit in luxury; I will go and inform against them.' What did he do? He went to the governor and said, 'The sacrifices which you send to the Jews to offer in the Temple they eat themselves and substitute [inferior animals] on the altar.' He reprimanded him[1]; but he went to him a second time and said, 'All the sacrifices which you send to the Jews to offer they eat themselves and substitute [inferior animals] on the altar; if you do not believe me, send an officer and some sacrificial animals with me, and you will immediately know that I am not a liar.' While they were on the journey the officer fell asleep, and in the night Bar Ḳamẓa secretly made all the animals blemished. When the priest saw [that they were blemished], he substituted others for them. The king's messenger asked him, 'Why do you not offer these animals which I brought?' He replied, 'I will do so to-morrow.'[2] He came on the third day but the priest had not offered them. He sent a message to the king, 'What the Jew told you is true.' The king forthwith came up against the Temple and destroyed it. Hence the popular saying: 'Because of the difference between [the names] Ḳamẓa and Bar Ḳamẓa was the

[1] The governor would not believe the charge.
[2] He prevaricated because he felt it would be an insult to the ruler that his animals were disqualified as a sacrifice.

Temple destroyed.' R. Jose said: The meekness of Zechariah b. Eucolus[1] burnt the Temple.

Another explanation of their precious character: Not one of them begat a child who was defective in limb or blemished in body.

4. R. Joshua b. Ḥananiah once went to the great city of Rome. He was informed that there was a [Hebrew] boy in the prison, kept there for an immoral purpose. He went and saw the boy who had beautiful eyes, a comely face, and curly locks and was used for a perverted practice. He stood at the doorway to test him, and cited this verse over him, *Who gave Jacob for a spoil, and Israel to the robbers?* (Isa. XLII, 24), to which the boy responded, *Did not the Lord? He against Whom we have sinned, and in whose ways they would not walk, neither were they obedient unto His law?* (*ib.*). When R. Joshua heard this he quoted over him, THE PRECIOUS SONS OF ZION, COMPARABLE TO FINE GOLD, and his eyes flowed with tears. He exclaimed, 'I call heaven and earth to witness that I am confident he will be a teacher in Israel. I swear by the Temple that I will not move from here without ransoming him at whatever price they set upon him!' It is said that he did not move from there until he had ransomed him at a high price; nor did many days pass before he became a teacher in Israel. Who was this boy? He was R. Ishmael b. Elisha.[2]

Another explanation of their precious character: None of them would attend a dinner without knowing who his fellow-diners were to be, nor sign a deed without knowing with whom he was signing[3]; to fulfil that which is said, *Put not thy hand with the wicked to be an unrighteous witness* (Ex. XXIII, 1).

Another explanation of their precious character: None of them would attend a dinner without changing his buckle.[4] For what purpose? That another should not extend to him a wasted invitation.

[1] In not intervening to prevent Bar Ḳamẓa from being insulted.
[2] V. Giṭ. 58*a* (Sonc. ed., p. 270). [3] Cf. Sanh. 23*a* (Sonc. ed., p. 131).
[4] From the right to the left shoulder (v. J. 'A.Z. 39*c*) to shew that he had accepted to dine.

Another explanation of their precious character: None of them ever made a claim which he could not justify. R. Simeon b. Gamaliel said: There was a fine custom in Jerusalem whereby [at the commencement of a meal] a cloth was spread over the door,[1] and so long as this was spread guests entered; but when it was removed, guests were only permitted to take three paces into the house.[2]

Another explanation of their precious character: They used to entrust the dinner to a caterer, and if he spoilt anything connected with the meal, they fined him in accordance with the status of the hosts and his guests.

Another explanation of their precious character: Whenever one of them gave a dinner, he indicated all the courses on a menu.[3] For what purpose? Because of those who were fastidious with their food, so that nobody should have to eat what was distasteful to him.

R. Ḥiyya the Bible-teacher said in the name of R. Samuel b. Naḥman: From the day that the Temple was destroyed, wine formed into a jelly and white glass ceased to be used [at a dinner]. What is[4] 'white glass'? Such as can be folded up.[5]

5. It happened that one of the eminent men of Jerusalem said to his servant, 'Go and fetch me some water,' and he watched him on top of the roof. The servant returned and said, 'I did not find any water.' The master said to him, 'Throw down your pitcher in front of me,' and he did so. He then threw himself from the top of the roof and fell and died, and his limbs were mingled with the pieces of earthenware. Concerning him it states, HOW ARE THEY ESTEEMED AS EARTHEN PITCHERS! (IV, 2).

[1] As an intimation that a meal was in progress within.
[2] In B.B. 93*b* (Sonc. ed., p. 388) the reading is 'no wayfarers entered'. Tosef. B.B. IV, 8, states, 'After three introductory courses have been served a guest may not enter,' and this has been distorted into the reading of the text. [3] This is the probable explanation given by one of the commentators, reading צייר for צר. Another translation is: 'he wrapped all the foodstuffs in a napkin,' but it is difficult to explain.
[4] This is Buber's reading. The text has 'why was it called?'
[5] Or, rolled together (Levi)—i.e. of a very fine texture.

6. EVEN THE JACKALS DRAW OUT THE BREAST THEY GIVE SUCK TO THEIR YOUNG ONES (IV, 3). The opossum[1] spreads a kind of veil over its face when it suckles its young so as not to see them, since it might have its ferocity aroused and devour them.

7. THE TONGUE OF THE SUCKLING CHILD CLEAVETH TO THE ROOF OF HIS MOUTH FOR THIRST (IV, 4). R. Abba b. Kahana said: A conduit ran from Eṭam,[2] but the besiegers destroyed it and poured its water away. When a man took his child to the conduit and found no water, his tongue clave to his palate for thirst.

THE YOUNG CHILDREN ASK BREAD, AND NONE BREAKETH (PORES) IT UNTO THEM. R. Judah, R. Nehemiah, and the Rabbis [comment on the word PORES]. R. Judah said: If there is nobody to give them bread who can comfort them? As it is stated, *Neither shall men break bread for them in mourning* (Jer. XVI, 7). R. Nehemiah said: There is nobody to give them a piece (*perusah*) of bread; as it is stated, *Is it not to deal* (paros) *thy bread to the hungry?* (Isa. LVIII, 7). The Rabbis said: There was nobody to stand in the row[3]; as the root is used in, *Whatsoever parteth the hoof*—parsah (Lev. XI, 3).

8. THEY THAT DID FEED ON DAINTIES ARE DESOLATE IN THE STREETS (IV, 5). R. Ḥanina b. Papa said: [By DAINTIES is to be understood] white bread and old wine.[4]

THEY THAT WERE BROUGHT UP IN SCARLET EMBRACE DUNGHILLS: they lie on dunghills.

9. FOR THE INIQUITY OF THE DAUGHTER OF MY PEOPLE IS GREATER THAN THE SIN OF SODOM (IV, 6). R. Joshua b. R. Nehemiah said in the name of R. Aḥa:

[1] The exact meaning is uncertain. 'Opossum' is suggested by Lewysohn, *Zoologie des Talmuds*, p. 371. [2] The name is corrupt in the text. Zeb. 54*b* mentions 'the well of Eṭam', in the territory of Benjamin.
[3] At a funeral the mourner passed through two rows of friends who comforted him. The root *paras* is explained in the sense of treading the ground (M.K.). [4] Cf. II, 16 (on ch. II, 12).

Scripture speaks of the tribes of Judah and Benjamin as it does not speak even of the Sodomites. In connection with Sodom it is written, *Their sin is exceedingly grievous* (Gen. XVIII, 20); but in connection with the tribes of Judah and Benjamin it is said, *Then said He unto me: The iniquity of the house of Israel and Judah is most exceedingly great* (Ezek. IX, 9).[1] R. Tanḥuma said: There is another, FOR THE INIQUITY OF THE DAUGHTER OF MY PEOPLE IS GREATER THAN THE SIN OF SODOM, THAT WAS OVERTHROWN AS IN A MOMENT, AND NO HANDS FELL UPON HER.[2] [The Sodomites] did not extend their hands to perform the precepts whereas [the men of Judah and Benjamin] did. That is what is written, THE HANDS OF WOMEN FULL OF COMPASSION HAVE SODDEN THEIR OWN CHILDREN (IV, 10). For what purpose? THEY WERE THEIR FOOD (*ib.*).[3]

10. HER PRINCES WERE PURER THAN SNOW (IV, 7). They used to drink snow.[4]

THEY WERE WHITER THAN MILK. They used to drink milk.[5]

THEY WERE MORE RUDDY IN BODY THAN RUBIES, THEIR POLISHING WAS AS OF SAPPHIRE. [Think you that] the sapphire is a fragile[6] thing? R. Phinehas said: A man once went to sell a sapphire in Rome. The would-be purchaser said to him, 'I will take it to test it.' He placed it upon the anvil and began to strike it with a hammer. The anvil was split, the hammer broke, but the sapphire

[1] In Gen. מאד 'exceeding' occurs once, in Ezek. twice.

[2] In Gen. R. XXVIII, 5, the question is inserted, 'Why, then, was a remnant of Judah and Benjamin spared and not of Sodom,' if the former sinned more grievously?

[3] Probably translated: To provide the mourner's meal; v. *infra*, § 13, and Gen. R. *loc. cit.* In their own plight the women had consideration for the distress of their neighbours.

[4] Which made their complexion clear. Radal emends 'drink' to 'wash in'.

[5] Cf. Keth. 59*b*, 'He who wishes his daughter to have a bright complexion let him, on the approach of her maturity, feed her with young fowls and give her milk to drink' (Sonc. ed., p. 354).—'E.J.: Her princes were pure *through* snow, and white *through* milk.

[6] Lit. 'light, insignificant'. The story proves that the sapphire is very hard, and that is why the princes were likened to it.

remained intact. (*Var. lec.* THEIR POLISHING (GIZRATHAM) WAS AS OF SAPPHIRE: every decree (*gezerah*) which befel Jerusalem was hard as a sapphire[1]; and should you call it fragile, R. Phinehas said, etc.)[2]

11. THEIR VISAGE IS BLACKER THAN COAL (IV, 8). R. Abba b. Kahana said: It was like the colour of shoe-blacking. R. Levi said: it was like the colour of soot.[3]

THEY ARE NOT KNOWN IN THE STREETS. R. Eliezer b. R. Ẓadoḳ said: May I not behold consolation [if this is not true]; although my father lived so many years after the destruction, his body never became normal again[4]; to fulfil what is said, THEIR SKIN IS SHRIVELLED UPON THE BONES; IT IS WITHERED, IT IS BECOME LIKE A STICK. (*Var. lec.* THEY ARE NOT KNOWN IN THE STREETS: R. Eliezer b. Ẓadoḳ said: A beggar once came and stood at the door of my father's house, and my father told me, 'Go and see whether he is a Jerusalemite.' I went and found there a woman whose hair had fallen out [through hunger] so that nobody could tell whether it was a man or woman. She only begged for a preserved fig; to fulfil what is said, THEY ARE NOT KNOWN IN THE STREETS; THEIR SKIN IS SHRIVELLED UPON THE BONES.)[5]

12. THEY THAT ARE SLAIN WITH THE SWORD ARE BETTER THAN THEY THAT ARE SLAIN WITH HUNGER (IV, 9). At the destruction of the first Temple people died from the smell caused by the thistles [which they were compelled to eat during the siege]; but at the destruction of the second Temple, there were not even thistles to eat. What did the enemy do to them? They brought kids which they roasted in the west of the city[6] and

[1] Rendering: Their (sc. the enemies') decrees were as (hard as) sapphire.
[2] The sentence in brackets (which occurs in the text) is an interpolation.
[3] The word is doubtful. Y.'A. suggests that it is lit. 'brightness', a euphemism for 'blackness'.
[4] From the privations it had suffered during the period of the destruction.
[5] The brackets occur also in the text.
[6] Whence the wind carried the smell to the starving besieged.

the smell aroused their appetite so that they died. This was to fulfil what is said, FOR THESE PINE AWAY, STRICKEN THROUGH, FOR WANT OF THE FRUITS OF THE FIELD.

13. THE HANDS OF WOMEN FULL OF COMPASSION HAVE SODDEN THEIR OWN CHILDREN (IV, 10). R. Huna said in the name of R. Jose: The Holy One, Blessed be He, declared: '[The women] did not allow Me to stretch forth My hand against My world.'[1] How was that? If one of them had a loaf of bread sufficient for the needs of herself and her husband for one day, and the son of her neighbour died, she would take it and comfort her therewith.[2] Scripture counts it to them as if they had sodden their own children for the fulfilment of a commandment.[3] That is what is stated, THE HANDS OF WOMEN OF COMPASSION HAVE SODDEN THEIR OWN CHILDREN. For what purpose? So that THEY WERE THEIR FOOD.[4]

14. THE LORD HATH ACCOMPLISHED HIS FURY, HE HATH POURED OUT HIS FIERCE ANGER (IV, 11). Rabbi [Judah ha-Nasi] said: There are four pourings [recorded] for good and four for evil. There are four pourings [recorded] for good, as it is said, *And I will pour upon the house of David, and upon the inhabitants of Jerusalem, the spirit of grace and supplication* (Zech. XII, 10); *And it shall come to pass afterward, that I will pour out My spirit upon all flesh*, etc. (Joel III, 1); *And also upon the servants and upon the handmaids in those days will I pour out My spirit* (*ib.* 2); *Neither will I hide My face any more from them; for I have poured out My spirit upon the house of Israel, saith the Lord God* (Ezek. XXXIX, 29). And four for evil, as it is said, *Therefore He poured upon him the fury of His anger* (Isa. XLII, 25); in Ezekiel it is written, *In Thy pouring out of Thy fury upon Jerusalem* (IX, 8); and

[1] To punish Israel fully for their sins. [2] According to Jewish law, the food eaten after a funeral is supplied to the mourners by friends. This act of charity caused God to withhold punishment. [3] Thus the verse of Lam. is not to be taken literally. [4] V. *supra*, p. 221, n. 3.

it is written, *He hath poured out His fury like fire* (Lam. II, 4); and there is the present passage, THE LORD HATH ACCOMPLISHED HIS FURY, HE HATH POURED OUT HIS FIERCE ANGER.[1]

AND HE HATH KINDLED A FIRE IN ZION. It is written, *A psalm of Asaph. O God, the heathen are come into Thine inheritance* (Ps. LXXIX, 1). The text should have used a phrase like, 'Weeping of Asaph,' 'Lament of Asaph,' 'Dirge of Asaph'; why does it say, '*A psalm*[2] *of Asaph*'? It may be likened to a king who erected a bridal-chamber for his son which he plastered, cemented, and decorated; but his son entered upon an evil course of living. The king forthwith ascended to the chamber, tore the curtains and broke the rods; but [the son's] tutor took a piece of rod which he used as a flute and played upon it. People said to him, 'The king has overthrown his son's chamber and you sit playing a tune!' He replied to them, 'I play a tune because the king overturned his son's chamber but did not pour out his anger upon his son.' Similarly people said to Asaph, 'The Holy One, blessed be He, has caused Temple and Sanctuary to be destroyed, and you sit singing a Psalm!' He replied to them, 'I sing a Psalm because the Holy One, blessed be He, poured out His wrath upon wood and stone and not upon Israel.' That is what is written, AND HE HATH KINDLED A FIRE IN ZION, WHICH HATH DEVOURED THE FOUNDATIONS[3] THEREOF.

15. THE KINGS OF THE EARTH BELIEVED NOT, NEITHER ALL THE INHABITANTS OF THE WORLD (IV, 12). There were four kings who made requests in an ascending scale, viz. David, Asa, Jehoshaphat, and Hezekiah. David said, '*Let me pursue mine enemies, and overtake them*' (Ps. XVIII, 38). The Holy One, blessed be He, said, 'I will do so.' That is what is written, *And David smote them from the twilight even unto the evening of the next day* (I Sam. XXX, 17). What means '*the next day*'? R. Joshua b. Levi said: [It indicates that he smote them] for two nights and one day. The Holy One,

[1] Repeated from II, 4, § 8. [2] Lit. 'a song'. [3] But not the people.

blessed be He, illumined the nights with meteors and lightning-flashes; as we have learnt in the Mishnah: 'For meteors, earthquakes, and lightnings.' That is what is written, *For Thou dost light my lamp*, etc. (Ps. XVIII, 29).

Asa stood up and said, 'I have not the strength to slay them, but I will pursue them and do Thou [the slaying].' He replied to him, 'I will do so'; as it is said, *And Asa . . . pursued them . . . for they were shattered before the Lord, and before His host; and they carried away very much booty* (II Chron. XIV, 12), and it is not written here 'before Asa' but '*Before the Lord, and before His host*'.

Jehoshaphat stood up and said, 'I have the strength neither to slay nor to pursue; but I will utter a song and do Thou [the slaying and pursuing].' The Holy One, blessed be He, replied, 'I will do so'; as it says, *And when they began to sing and to praise, the Lord set liers-in-wait* (*ib.* XX, 22).

Hezekiah stood up and said, 'I have the strength neither to slay nor to pursue nor to utter a song, but I will sleep upon my bed and do Thou [all these things].' The Holy One, blessed be He, replied, 'I will do so'; as it is said, *And it came to pass that night, that the angel of the Lord went forth, and smote in the camp of the Assyrians* (II Kings XIX, 35). How many of them survived? Rab said: Ten, as it is stated, *And the remnant . . . shall be few, that a child may write them down* (Isa. X, 19), and it is customary for a child to write the letter *yod*. R. Eliezer said: Six survived, because it is customary for a child to scratch a stroke. R. Joshua said: Five survived, as it is said, *Two* [and] *three berries in the top of the uppermost bough* (*ib.* XVII, 6). R. Judah b. R. Simon said: Nine survived; that is what is written, *Four* [and] *five in the branches of the fruitful tree* (*ib.*). R. Tanḥum b. Ḥanilai said: Fourteen survived; that is what is written, '*Two* [and] *three berries in the top of the uppermost bough, four* [and] *five in the branches of the fruitful tree.*' According to all opinions Nebuchadnezzar was one of the survivors; but when the Holy One, blessed be He, said to him, 'Go up and destroy the Temple,' he said, 'He only wants to entrap me in order to do me as He did to my ancestor.' So what did he do? He went and resided at Daphne in Antioch, and sent Nebuzaradan, the captain of the guard, to destroy Jerusalem. Three years and a half he was engaged upon the task. He daily compassed Jerusalem but was unable to subdue it. Being unable to subdue it, he wished to return; but the Holy One, blessed be He, placed an idea in his mind. He began to measure the wall, and it daily sank two and a half handbreadths until the whole of it was sunk in the ground. When it was wholly sunk, the enemy entered Jerusalem. With reference to that time it states, THE KINGS OF THE EARTH BELIEVED NOT, NEITHER ALL THE INHABITANTS OF THE WORLD, THAT THE ADVERSARY AND THE ENEMY WOULD ENTER INTO THE GATES OF JERUSALEM.[1]

16. IT IS BECAUSE OF THE SINS OF HER PROPHETS (IV, 13). R. Judan asked R. Aḥa: Where did the Israelites slay Zechariah, in the Court of Israel or the Court of Women? He replied: In neither of them, but it was in the Court of the Priests. Nor did they treat his blood as was done with the blood of a hind or ram; for in connection with the blood of these animals it is written, *And whatsoever man there be of the children of Israel . . . that taketh in hunting any beast or fowl that may be eaten, he shall pour out the blood thereof, and cover it with dust* (Lev. XVII, 13), but in this instance it is written, *For her blood is in the midst of her; she set it upon the bare rock; she poured it not upon the ground, to cover it with dust* (Ezek. XXIV, 7). And for what purpose was all this? *That it might cause fury to come up, that vengeance might be taken, I have set her blood upon the bare rock, that it should not be covered.*

Seven transgressions were committed by Israel on that day: they killed a priest, a prophet, and a judge, they shed innocent blood, they profaned the Divine Name, they defiled the Temple Court, and it happened on the sabbath which was also the Day of Atonement. When Nebuzaradan came up against Israel, he saw the blood

[1] Repeated from Proem XXX (q.v. for notes).

of Zechariah seething; so he asked them, 'What kind of blood is this?' They replied, 'The blood of bulls and lambs.' He had bulls and lambs brought, but the blood did not act similarly. He had all kinds of blood brought, but they did not act similarly. He said to them, 'If you tell me, well and good; otherwise I will comb your flesh with iron combs,' but they did not tell him [at first]. Since, however, he spoke to them in this manner, they said to him, 'What can we conceal from you? We had a prophet-priest who reproved us in the name of Heaven, saying, "Accept my words," but we did not accept it from him, and we rose against him and killed him.' He said to them, 'I will appease it.' He had the men of the Great Sanhedrin brought and slew them by it, but it did not stop. He slew the men of the Minor Sanhedrin by it, but it did not stop. He had the priestly novitiates brought and slew them by it, but it did not stop. He slew the schoolchildren by it, but it did not stop. Bending over it he exclaimed, 'Zechariah! the choicest of your people have I destroyed. Is it your pleasure that I exterminate them all?' It immediately stopped. The wicked Nebuzaradan contemplated repenting and said, 'If of one who destroys a single life from Israel it is written, *Whoso sheddeth man's blood, by man shall his blood be shed* (Gen. IX, 6), how much more will it be so with me who have slain many!' Forthwith the Holy One, blessed be He, was filled with mercy, and gave a hint to the blood, which was swallowed up in the same spot.[1] Of that time it states, IT IS BECAUSE OF THE SINS OF[2] HER PROPHETS, AND THE INIQUITIES OF HER PRIESTS, THAT HAVE SHED THE BLOOD OF THE JUST IN THE MIDST OF HER.

17. THEY WANDER AS BLIND MEN IN THE STREETS (IV, 14). The blind among the Israelites exclaimed, 'Who will show us the place where they killed Zechariah that we may go and embrace and kiss it?' To fulfil what is said, THEY WANDER AS BLIND MEN IN THE

[1] V. Proem XXIII and II, 4 (on ch. II, 2). [2] I.e. against the prophets.

STREETS, THEY ARE POLLUTED WITH BLOOD.[1] What did the lame among them say? 'Who will show us the blood of Zechariah that we may go and tread therein?' To fulfil what is said, SO THAT MEN CANNOT TOUCH THEIR GARMENTS.[2]

18. DEPART YE! UNCLEAN! MEN CRIED UNTO THEM (IV, 15). R. Ḥanina interpreted the verse in connection with the daughters of Zion. That is what is written, *Moreover the Lord said: Because the daughters of Zion are haughty and walk with stretched-forth necks* (Isa. III, 16), i.e. they were conspicuous in their height and walked in a haughty manner. '*And walk with stretched-forth necks*'—when one of them put on her ornaments, she used to turn her neck this way and that in order to display them. *And wanton* (mesaḳeroth) *eyes* (*ib.*)—R. Assi of Cæsarea said: They used to daub (*mesaḳeroth*) their eyes with red paint; while R. Simeon b. Laḳish said: With a red eye-salve. *Walking and mincing* (ṭafof) *as they go* (*ib.*)—if one of them was tall she used to make two short girls walk with her, one on each side, so that she should appear floating (*ṭafah*) above them; and when one of them was short, she would wear thick slippers in order to appear tall. *And making a tinkling* (te'akasnah) *with their feet* (*ib.*). R. Jose says: She used to have a picture of a serpent[3] on her shoes; while the Rabbis say: She took a hen's gullet, filled it with balsam and placed it between her heel and her shoe; and when she saw a band of young men, she pressed upon it so that the perfume went through them like the poison of a snake.

Jeremiah kept saying to them, 'Repent so that the enemy shall not come'; but they answered him, 'If the enemy should come against us, what can they do to us?' (That is what is written, *That say: Let Him make speed, let Him hasten His work, that we may see it; and let the counsel of*

[1] Viz. the blood of Zechariah.
[2] The text is explained: the men that cannot walk seek to touch the blood with their garments. The point is: even the blind and lame wished to touch his blood, though it required great expenditure of effort, and how much more people enjoying all their faculties (commentaries).
[3] A word for 'serpent' is *'ekes*.

the Holy One of Israel draw nigh and come, that we may know it! (*ib.* v, 19).) 'If a general sees me, he will take and seat me with him in his carriage.' They said to Jeremiah, 'We will know whose word will be fulfilled, ours or His.' When their sins took effect and their enemies came, they decked themselves and came out to them like harlots. A general saw a maiden and took her; a captain saw one and took her; a military chief saw one and seated her with him in his carriage. The Holy One, blessed be He, said, 'Shall My word not be fulfilled and theirs shall!' What did He do? *Therefore the Lord smote*[1] *with a scab* (sippaḥ) *the crown of the head of the daughters of Zion* (*ib.* III, 17). R. Eleazar and R. Jose b. R. Ḥanina comment. R. Eleazar said: He smote them with leprosy, as it is stated, *And for a rising, and for a scab* (sappaḥath), *and for a bright spot* (Lev. XIV, 56).[2] R. Jose b. R. Ḥanina said: He brought upon their heads swarms[3] of lice. R. Ḥiyya b. Abba said: [The enemy] made them handmaids (*shefaḥoth*), forced to hard labour. What does this phrase mean? Enslaved servants. R. Berekiah and Ḥilfai b. Zebid in the name of R. Isi ask: What means '*sippaḥ*'? He caused them to discharge blood (*shippa'*) in order to preserve the holy seed[4] from becoming mingled with Gentiles. The Holy One, blessed be He, said: 'I know that the idolaters will not keep aloof from [the daughters of Zion] because of their leprosy'; so what did He do? *The Lord laid bare*[5] *their secret parts* (Isa. *loc. cit.*). The Holy One, blessed be He, hinted to their source which discharged blood until it filled the whole of the carriage; and the commander stabbed the woman with his spear and placed her in front of the carriage, which passed over her and cut her in pieces. That is what Jeremiah says, DEPART YE (SURU)! UNCLEAN! MEN CRIED UNTO THEM: DEPART DEPART, TOUCH NOT. R. Abba said: It is a Greek word, viz. 'Sweep (*siron*), sweep'.[6]

[1] E.V. '*will smite*'. [2] All symptoms of leprosy.
[3] Lit. 'families' (*mishpaḥoth*). [4] The purity of the Hebrew race should not be contaminated by intercourse with heathens.
[5] E.V. '*will lay bare*'. The verb can also mean 'pour out'.
[6] Viz. σῆρον 'sweep', i.e. remove the bloodstains (so Jast.). Krauss identifies it with σάρον 'filth'.

YEA, THEY FLED AWAY (NAẒU) AND WANDERED. R. Ḥanina said: The Israelites were not exiled until they blasphemed (*ni'aẓu*) the Holy One, blessed be He. R. Simon said: The Israelites were not exiled until they became quarrelsome (*maẓẓoth*) towards the Holy One, blessed be He.

19. THE ANGER OF THE LORD HATH DIVIDED THEM (IV, 16). He scattered them in bands of a hundred or two hundred, for there[1] they call towns *mathan*.[2]

20. AS FOR US, OUR EYES DO YET FAIL (IV, 17). What did the ten tribes do? They exported oil to Egypt and brought back foodstuffs which they sent to Babylon,[3] so that if their enemies should advance, these[4] should come to their assistance. That is what is written, *And they make a covenant with Assyria, and oil is carried into Egypt* (Hos. XII, 2). Once the enemy came, and they sent to Pharaoh Neco [for help] when he was on a sea-voyage. The Holy One, blessed be He, hinted to the skeletons[5] which [ascended from the bottom and] floated on the surface of the water. [The Egyptians] asked one another, 'What is the nature of these skeletons?' He told them, 'The ancestors of this people rebelled against your ancestors, and arose and drowned them in the water.' They exclaimed, 'Thus they acted towards our ancestors and we shall go and assist them!' They at once turned back; that is what is written, *Behold, Pharaoh's army, which is come forth to help you, shall return to Egypt into their own land* (Jer. XXXVII, 7). For that reason it is said, IN OUR WATCHING WE HAVE WATCHED FOR A NATION THAT DOES NOT[6] SAVE.

21. THEY HUNT OUR STEPS, THAT WE CANNOT

[1] In Babylon (v. Introduction).
[2] The word means both 'towns' and 'two hundred'. Whereas the Israelites had lived in cities with large populations, after the destruction a settlement of a hundred or two was called a town.
[3] Emend: to Assyria, as *infra*, v. 6.
[4] The Egyptians and Assyrians, to preserve their trade with Israel.
[5] Of the Egyptians who had been drowned in the Red Sea. For 'skeletons' Buber reads 'bladders' blown up to resemble men.
[6] E.V. '*could not*'.

GO IN OUR BROAD PLACES (IV, 18). Fifty-two years did Bethar survive the destruction of the Temple; and why was it destroyed? Because the inhabitants kindled lamps [to manifest their joy] over the destruction of the Sanctuary. And why did they light them? It is related that the councillors in Jerusalem used to sit in the centre of the city; and when one of [the inhabitants of Bethar] went up there to pray, he would be asked, 'Do you wish to become a councillor?' When he answered, 'No,' [the next question would be,] 'Do you wish to become a city-magistrate?' and he answered, 'No.' Somebody would then say to him, 'Inasmuch as I have heard that you possess an estate, will you sell it to me?' On his replying that he had no such intention, the Jerusalemite would write out a [false] deed of possession and send it to the steward of the man of Bethar [with the message], 'If So-and-so comes, do not allow him to enter the estate because he has sold it to me.' Then the man would exclaim, 'Would that my leg had been broken before I should go up to that corner!' That is what is written, THEY HUNT OUR STEPS—[the men of Bethar said,] 'May the road become desolate so that nobody may walk in these broad places!' OUR END IS NEAR—[they said,] 'May the end of this Temple [be near]!' OUR DAYS ARE FULFILLED—[they said,] 'May the days of this Temple [be fulfilled]!' Neither with them did it fare well, as it is written, *He that is glad at calamity shall not be unpunished* (Prov. XVII, 5).

22. OUR PURSUERS WERE SWIFTER THAN THE EAGLES OF THE HEAVEN (IV, 19). The wife of Trajan the accursed gave birth to a child on the night of the ninth of Ab while all the Israelites were mourning [the destruction of the Temple]. The child died on Ḥanukkah. The Israelites said, 'Shall we kindle the lights or not?' They decided to light them and risk the consequences. They lit the candles, and some persons slandered them to Trajan's wife, saying, 'When your child was born the Jews mourned, and when it died they kindled lights!' She sent a letter to her husband: 'Instead of subduing the

barbarians, come and subdue the Jews who have revolted against you.' He boarded a ship and planned to do the voyage in ten days, but the winds brought him in five. On his arrival he found the Jews occupied with this verse, *The Lord will bring a nation against thee from far, from the end of the earth, as the vulture swoopeth down* (Deut. XXVIII, 49). He said to them, 'I am the vulture who planned to come in ten days, but the wind brought me in five.' He surrounded them with his legions and slaughtered them. He said to the women, 'Yield yourselves to my troops, or I will do to you what I did to the men.' They replied to him, 'Do to the inferiors what you did to the superiors.' He forthwith surrounded them with his legions and slaughtered them, so that their blood mingled with that of the men, and streamed [to the coast and stained the sea] as far as Cyprus.[1]

THEY CHASED US UPON THE MOUNTAINS. R. Aibu said: [The Romans] sent fire after them from their engines.[2] R. Jacob of Kefar-Ḥanin said: It alludes to Israel's pursuers, and therefore it is stated, THEY CHASED US UPON THE MOUNTAINS.

23. THE BREATH OF OUR NOSTRILS, THE ANOINTED OF THE LORD, WAS TAKEN IN THEIR PITS (IV, 20). Rabbi [Judah ha-Nasi] and R. Ishmael b. R. Jose were sitting and studying the Book of Lamentations on the eve of the ninth of Ab which occurred on sabbath at dusk. They left over one chapter[3] and said, 'We will go out and finish it to-morrow'; but when Rabbi went to his house he met with an accident to his finger. He applied to himself the verse, *Many are the sorrows of the wicked* (Ps. XXXII, 10). R. Ishmael b. R. Jose said to him, 'Even had we [not][4] been engaged in this subject and such an

[1] Repeated from I, 45 (on ch. I, 16).

[2] The text is uncertain. The translation is that suggested by Jast. Levi renders: They pursued them through the mountain passes. The verb '*chase*' also means 'kindle'. [3] Lit. 'one alphabet', the chapters being composed in the form of alphabetical acrostics.

[4] The word 'not' is printed in the Warsaw ed. and occurs in the parallel passages, J. Shab. 15*c*, Lev. R. XV, 4.

accident befell you, I would have said what I am about to say; now how much the more [must I say], THE BREATH OF OUR NOSTRILS, etc.'[1] When Rabbi arrived home he placed a dry sponge over the wound and tied it outside with reed-grass. R. Ishmael b. R. Jose said: We learnt three things from him: that a sponge[2] has no healing properties but protects the wound; that reed-grass which is inside a house is a prepared object[3]; and that we may not read the Scriptures [on the sabbath] except from *minḥah* onwards,[4] but it is permissible to study and expound them,[5] and when there is necessity to search for a text and read it, one may fetch a copy and read.[6]

Samuel said: A minute piece of earthenware [may be carried from the courtyard into the house on the sabbath]. R. Ze'ira said in the name of R. Samuel: The clay stopper of a cask and burned clay may be handled on the sabbath; but if they have been thrown on the ash-heap they may not be handled on the sabbath.[7]

But he that trusteth in the Lord, mercy compasseth him

[1] He interprets THE BREATH OF OUR NOSTRILS as symbolising the leaders, while WAS TAKEN IN THEIR PITS means that these are punished on account of the sins of the masses (it might also be rendered: was taken on account of their corruption). Hence he observed: Even if we had not been engaged on this verse, I still would have maintained that the accident befell you on account of some misdeed of the people, and not through your own wickedness; how much the more when we were actually engaged on this verse. [2] Since it was dry and without any lotion.

[3] And may be used on the sabbath to bind up a wound. It would have been prohibited if he had had to gather it outside the house.

[4] Otherwise Rabbi would have begun his exposition earlier and finished the chapter before the fast began at the termination of the sabbath. The reason for this prohibition was that during the afternoon public lectures were given, and it was thought preferable that the people should attend these rather than stay at home reading the Scriptures privately. But these lectures were generally not given after *minḥah*, hence there was no prohibition then. (These two Rabbis were expounding Lamentations privately, as appears from Lev. R. XVI, 4.) V. Shab. 115*a* and 116*b* for a fuller discussion and another reason.

[5] 'To study' verbally (M.K.): 'to expound' probably means publicly.

[6] I.e. though such study or expounding must be verbal, yet a text may be verified from a copy.

[7] Because they are no longer considered a vessel, and only a vessel may be carried from outside into a house on the sabbath. These laws are quoted because a statement has just been made about the handling of reed-grass.

about (*ib.*). R. Eleazar of Bozrah and R. Tanḥum in the name of R. Aḥa said: Even a wicked person who recants[1] is accepted by the Holy One, blessed be He; as it is stated, '*But he that trusteth in the Lord, mercy compasseth him about.*'

24. REJOICE AND BE GLAD, O DAUGHTER OF EDOM (IV, 21): i.e. Cæsarea.[2] THAT DWELLETH IN THE LAND OF UZ: i.e. Persia.[3] THE CUP SHALL PASS OVER UNTO THEE ALSO[4]; THOU SHALT BE DRUNKEN, AND SHALT MAKE THYSELF NAKED.

25. THE PUNISHMENT OF THINE INIQUITY IS ACCOMPLISHED, O DAUGHTER OF ZION (IV, 22). R. Ḥelbo said in the name of R. Joḥanan: Better was the granting of authority[5] by Pharaoh for persecuting Israel in Egypt than the forty years during which Moses[6] inveighed[7] against them, because the redemption came through the former but not through the latter. R. Simeon b. Laḳish said: Better was the granting of authority by Ahasuerus to persecute Israel in Media than the sixty myriads of prophets[8] who prophesied in the days of Elijah. Why? Because through the former there was redemption but not through the latter. The Rabbis said:

[1] The commentator Y.'A. remarks that it is obvious that a repentant sinner is accepted, and the proof-text has no bearing on this truth. He therefore reads: 'Even a wicked person who trusts in the Lord is accepted.' [2] In Meg. 6*a* Cæsarea is called 'the daughter of Edom', i.e. an outpost of the Roman Empire.

[3] Possibly a substitution for Rome, if the verse is understood as an allusion to Israel under Roman dominion. M.K. suggests that the verse refers to several oppressions by foreign powers, Uz signifying Persia and the phrase 'the cup', etc., indicating Media. [4] M.K. remarks that possibly 'i.e. Persia and Media' has fallen out of the text here.

[5] Lit. 'the removal of the ring' (cf. Gen. XLI, 42), often for the purpose of sealing a decree (cf. Est. III, 10). The meaning is: the cruel decrees which Pharaoh enacted through his taskmasters effected the release of Israel, which Moses' protestations during forty years failed to accomplish.

[6] Y.'A. proposes the emendation: eighty years during which Aaron prophesied to make Israel turn to God. But the taskmasters did effect this, and as a result God redeemed them. [7] Lit. 'prophesied'.

[8] For this number v. S.S. R. to IV, 11. In Meg. 14*a* it is explained that whereas the prophets were unable to turn Israel to God, the decree of Haman induced them to fast and weep.

Better was the Book of Lamentations[1] for Israel than the forty years during which Jeremiah inveighed against them. Why? Because in it Israel received full settlement for their iniquities on the day the Temple was destroyed. That is what is written, THE PUNISHMENT OF THINE INIQUITY IS ACCOMPLISHED, O DAUGHTER OF ZION.

HE WILL PUNISH THINE INIQUITY, O DAUGHTER OF EDOM. R. Phinehas said in the name of R. Hoshaiah: On what condition were the Divine visitations created? To fall upon the house where they ought to go.[2] That is what is stated, THE PUNISHMENT OF THINE INIQUITY IS ACCOMPLISHED, O DAUGHTER OF ZION, HE WILL PUNISH THINE INIQUITY, O DAUGHTER OF EDOM, HE WILL UNCOVER THY SINS.[3] It similarly fulfils what is said, *And the Lord will take away from thee all sickness . . . them that hate thee*, etc. (Deut. VII, 15); there, too, R. Phinehas said in the name of R. Hoshaiah: On what condition were Divine visitations created? To fall upon the house where they ought to go, thus it is written, '*But will lay them upon all them that hate thee.*' It is similarly stated, *The vision of Obadiah. Thus saith the Lord God concerning Edom: We have heard a message from the Lord, and an ambassador is sent among the nations: Arise ye, and let us rise up against her in battle* (Obad. I).[4] Our present verse [too implies this]: THE PUNISHMENT OF THINE INIQUITY IS ACCOMPLISHED, O DAUGHTER OF ZION, HE WILL NO MORE CARRY THEE AWAY INTO CAPTIVITY; HE WILL PUNISH THINE INIQUITY, O DAUGHTER OF EDOM, HE WILL UNCOVER THY SINS.

[1] I.e. all the miseries and calamities recorded therein ('E.J.).

[2] The translation follows M.K. and 'E.J. and possibly requires a slight emendation of the text. Mah. renders: On what . . . created? To be kept in suspense for the house, etc. I.e. if they do not fall on one person because he repents, there are unrepentant sinners to be punished with them.

[3] This explains the connection between Zion and Edom: now that Zion's punishment is completed, the sufferings decreed by God will not be wasted but are ready to fall upon Edom.

[4] This, too, is understood in the same sense: When Israel's sins are expiated, punishment will visit Edom.

CHAPTER V

1. REMEMBER, O LORD, WHAT IS COME UPON US (v, 1). R. Isaac opened his discourse with the text: *The greyhound* (zarzir); *the he-goat also* (Prov. xxx, 31). Naturally if a man trains two gladiators (*zarzar*)[1] within his house, one stronger than the other, he puts down the stronger rather than the other, in order to protect his property.[2]

R. Berekiah said: Israel spake before the Holy One, blessed be He: 'Lord of the Universe, didst Thou write for us in Thy Torah, *Remember what Amalek did unto thee by the way* (Deut. xxv, 17)—did he do it to me and not to Thee? Did he not destroy Thy Sanctuary?'[3] The Rabbis said: Israel spake before the Holy One, blessed be He: 'We are Thine and the heathen peoples are Thine; why hast Thou no pity upon Thy people [Israel in punishing only them]?' *And the king, against whom there is no rising up* (Prov. *loc. cit.*).[4] R. Isaac said: Israel spake before the Holy One, blessed be He: 'We are subject to forgetfulness, but Thou art not; seeing that there is no forgetfulness before Thee, therefore do Thou remember,' [as it is written], *Remember, O Lord, against the children of Edom the day of Jerusalem; who said: Rase it* ('aru), *rase it, even to the foundation thereof* (Ps. cxxxvii, 7). R. Abba b. Kahana said: ['*Rase*' means] 'destroy ye, destroy ye', while R. Levi said: It means 'clear it out, clear it out'. The one who says that it means 'destroy ye, destroy ye',

[1] Levi: war-horses, chargers.

[2] Buber's text adds: 'Thou, however, dost not protect Thy people but leavest them among the nations.' God's punishment had fallen upon the weaker [Israel] and not on the strong nations which had devastated them.

[3] Esau was the father of Edom (Gen. xxxvi, 9) and grandfather of Amalek (*ib.* 12). Therefore Amalek is connected with the children of Edom who were concerned in the destruction of the Temple (Ps. cxxxvii, 7).

[4] This is perhaps best explained by rendering the verse with Radal: (And why art Thou) a King who dost not rise up (to protect Thy people Israel)?

can cite in support, *The broad walls of Babylon shall be utterly overthrown*—'ar'er (Jer. LI, 58); while the one who says that it means 'clear it out, clear it out' can cite, '*Even to the foundation thereof*', i.e. reach down even to its foundations.

BEHOLD, AND SEE OUR REPROACH. R. Judan said: BEHOLD (HABIṬAH) means from near, SEE from afar. BEHOLD means from near, as it is said, *And he beheld, and, lo, there was at his head a cake baked on the hot stones* (I Kings XIX, 6); and SEE means from afar, as it is said, *He saw the place afar off* (Gen. XXII, 4). R. Phinehas said: BEHOLD means from afar, as it is said, *Behold* (habiṭah) *from heaven, and look* (Ps. LXXX, 15), and SEE means from near, as it is said, *And when he saw that he prevailed not against him, he touched the hollow of his thigh* (Gen. XXXII, 26).

OUR INHERITANCE IS TURNED UNTO STRANGERS (V, 2): with what kind of 'turning'? Like the overturning of Sodom. Jeremiah calls [the Temple] OUR INHERITANCE; Isaiah calls it *Our holy and our beautiful house* (LXIV, 10). Asaph came and said: It is not *our* inheritance, it is not *our* holy and *our* beautiful house; but the enemy entered into what is *Thine*. That is what is written, *O God, the heathen are come into* Thine *inheritance; they have defiled* Thy *holy Temple; they have made Jerusalem into heaps* (Ps. LXXIX, 1).

WE ARE BECOME ORPHANS AND FATHERLESS (V, 3). R. Berekiah said in the name of R. Levi: The Holy One, blessed be He, said to Israel: 'You weep and say before Me, WE ARE BECOME ORPHANS AND FATHERLESS; I swear by your lives, the deliverer whom I will raise up from among you in Media will likewise be fatherless and motherless.' That is what is written, *And he brought up Hadassah, that is, Esther, his uncle's daughter; for she had neither father nor mother* (Est. II, 7).

WE HAVE DRUNK OUR WATER FOR MONEY (V, 4). On one occasion the besiegers went up and seized their bread, wine, oil, and water. They then sold these to them, and the people cried, 'Woe to us that the verse has been fulfilled in us, WE HAVE DRUNK *OUR* WATER[1] FOR MONEY; *OUR* WOOD COMETH TO US FOR PRICE.'

TO OUR VERY NECKS WE ARE PURSUED (V, 5). Hadrian the accursed issued an order: 'If I come and find a hair upon [the head of] a Jew, I will cut off his head.'[2] That is what is stated, TO OUR VERY NECKS WE ARE PURSUED. Another interpretation of TO OUR VERY NECKS WE ARE PURSUED: because we acted treacherously with our necks[3] in the day of trouble.

WE LABOUR, AND HAVE NO REST. Nebuchadnezzar the accursed commanded Nebuzaradan, saying: 'The God of this people accepts the penitent and His hand is stretched forth to receive those who repent. When, therefore, you conquer them, do not allow them to pray, lest they should do penance and their God have mercy upon them, and I will have to go down [to Babylon] with blackened face.[4] So do not be lenient[5] with them.' When he conquered them, if one of them stood up [to pray], he seized him and tore him limb from limb. He cast [the dismembered body] before the people, and they went perforce [on the journey into exile] and much against their will.

R. Joshua b. Levi said: Nebuzaradan is identical with Arioch.[6] Why was his name called 'Arioch'? Because he roared at the captives like a lion (*ari*) until they reached the Euphrates. When they reached the Euphrates, he ordered his soldiers: 'Let them rest, because from here[7] their God will not turn [to have mercy] upon them.' That is what is written, *By the rivers of Babylon, there we sat down,*

[1] I.e. our own water.
[2] They all had to shave their heads as a mark of degradation.
[3] M.K. explains: against the Temple or against God. Radal suggests: because they broke the yoke of the Torah from off their necks, therefore they had no rest in the day of trouble. Y.'A. reads into the words the meaning: when Hadrian ordered them to shave off all their hair, which is contrary to the Torah (Lev. XIX, 27), they acted treacherously to him in the day of trouble by refusing to carry out his commandment. No certain interpretation can be offered. [4] Downcast by defeat.
[5] Reading מרפי for מפלי. With the present reading 'E.J. renders: do not consider them of no account—do not think that once you have conquered them they have no power at all. [6] Cf. Dan. II, 14.
[7] Having passed beyond the region dominated by Israel's God.

yea, we wept (Ps. CXXXVII, 1)—up to there we had not sat down.

WE HAVE GIVEN THE HAND TO EGYPT, AND TO ASSYRIA, TO HAVE BREAD ENOUGH (V, 6). What did the ten tribes do? They exported oil to Egypt and brought back foodstuffs which they sent to Assyria, so that if the [Babylonian] enemy should advance against them, the others would come to their assistance. That is what is written, *And they make a covenant with Assyria, and oil is carried into Egypt* (Hos. XII, 2).[1]

OUR FATHERS HAVE SINNED, AND ARE NOT; AND WE HAVE BORNE THEIR INIQUITIES (V, 7). The Holy One, blessed be He, said to them, 'Your own [iniquities and not your fathers'] are you enduring.' Another interpretation: [The ancestors] said to them, 'You are enduring for our sakes.'[2]

SERVANTS RULE OVER US (V, 8): viz. the Egyptians.[3]

THERE IS NONE TO DELIVER US OUT OF THEIR HAND: had it not been for Moses.

Another interpretation: SERVANTS RULE OVER US: viz. the four kingdoms[4]; THERE IS NONE TO DELIVER US OUT OF THEIR HAND: had it not been for the Holy One, blessed be He.

WE GET OUR BREAD WITH THE PERIL OF OUR LIVES (V, 9). R. Simeon b. Gamaliel said: Although the former generations experienced only part of what is inflicted [on us] by the [foreign] kingdoms they became impatient. In connection with our forefathers it is written, *And the soul of the people became impatient because of the way* (Num. XXI, 4). Daniel said, *As for me Daniel, my spirit was pained* (VII, 15). Isaiah said, *Therefore are my loins*

[1] Repeated from IV, 20 (on ch. IV, 17).

[2] The meaning is doubtful. Radal: Their ancestors said to them, 'On the contrary, you are preserved only for *our* sakes—otherwise your sins would have destroyed you entirely.' E.J.: Their ancestors said to them: '*We* endure the punishment for our sins—hence you are now being punished for your *own* sins, not for ours.'

[3] Who, as descendants of Ham, were declared to be slaves (cf. Gen. IX, 25, and X, 6).

[4] Babylon, Persia, Greece, and Rome.

filled with convulsion (XXI, 3). Jeremiah said, WE GET OUR BREAD WITH THE PERIL OF OUR LIVES. But we, who are set in the midst of the four kingdoms, how much more [should we complain]!

OUR SKIN IS HOT LIKE AN OVEN (V, 10). Two teachers comment. One said: Like a heated mass of grapes. The other said: Like an oven insufficiently heated.[1]

THEY HAVE RAVISHED THE WOMEN IN ZION (V, 11). Nebuzaradan commanded his troops saying: 'The God of this people hates lewdness; so take care not to touch any married woman.' When the [unmarried] women heard this, they went and said to a man, 'We will eat our own food and clothe ourselves at our own expense, only let your name be attached to us'; that is what is written, *And seven women shall take hold of one man in that day, saying: We will eat our own bread, and wear our own apparel; only let us be called by thy name* (Isa. IV, 1). [They all did this] except three women who were indifferent and were ravished. Therefore it is written, THEY HAVE RAVISHED THE WOMEN IN ZION, THE MAIDENS IN THE CITIES OF JUDAH—the word for MAIDENS is spelt so that it can be read 'maiden'.[2]

PRINCES ARE HANGED UP BY THEIR HAND (V, 12). When a governor entered a city, he took its best men and hanged them. The elders would go to him and try to dissuade him from doing this to them, but he refused to listen to them. Therefore it is said, PRINCES ARE HANGED UP BY THEIR HAND; THE FACES OF ELDERS ARE NOT HONOURED.

THE YOUNG MEN HAVE BORNE THE MILL (V, 13). You find that there were no mills in Babylon[3]; and when Nebuchadnezzar came up [against the land of Israel] he made the inhabitants carry mills and bring them down [to Babylon]. That is what is written, *For your sake I have sent to Babylon, and I will bring down all of them as fugitives*

[1] An oven which is adequately heated has a glowing appearance, otherwise its appearance is dull. [2] 'Women,' i.e. married women, in the plural denotes two, and 'maiden' makes the total of three. [3] Because there were no large stones in the country which could be used for grinding.

(Isa. XLIII, 14)—the word for '*fugitives*' (bariḥim) is spelt like *bereḥayim* 'with mills'. Another interpretation of THE YOUNG MEN HAVE BORNE THE MILL (ṬEḤON) is to regard it as a euphemistic expression, as in the phrase *And he did grind* (ṭoḥen) *in the prison-house* (Judg. XVI, 21).[1]

AND THE CHILDREN HAVE STUMBLED UNDER THE WOOD. R. Joshua b. Levi said: Three hundred children were found strung up [by the enemy] on one branch.

THE ELDERS HAVE CEASED FROM THE GATE, THE YOUNG MEN FROM THEIR MUSIC (V, 14). R. Abba b. R. Jeremiah said: They ceased from their music.[2]

THE JOY OF OUR HEART IS CEASED (V, 15). R. Ḥisda said: At first, when the fear of the Sanhedrin was upon Israel, lewd words were never inserted in songs, but when the Sanhedrin was abolished lewd words were inserted in songs. R. Jose b. R. Abin said in the name of R. Ḥisda: At first, when adversity came upon Israel, they put a stop to rejoicing in the face of it. When the Sanhedrin ceased to function, song ceased from the places of feasting; as it is said, *They drink not wine with a song* (Isa. XXIV, 9)[3]; but now that both[4] have ceased THE JOY OF OUR HEART IS CEASED, OUR DANCE IS TURNED INTO MOURNING.

THE CROWN IS FALLEN FROM OUR HEAD (V, 16). R. Jeremiah of the branch[5] used to take a crown formed of olive [branches] and bind it round his head [at a wedding]. Samuel heard about it and said, 'It were better that his head should be cut off, rather than that he should do this.'[6] [His words were] *Like an error which proceedeth from a ruler* (Eccl. X, 5); and so it happened to him.[7] Therefore it

[1] In Soṭ. 10*a* (Sonc. ed., p. 45), it is explained: '*grind*' means nothing else than sexual intercourse.

[2] The point of the comment is that the verb '*ceased*' governs both clauses.

[3] Cf. Soṭ. 48*a* (Sonc. ed., p. 256).

[4] The singing and the places of feasting, in consequence of the destruction of the Temple.

[5] He was given the name because of the way he danced before bridal couples with a crown of olive branches.

[6] This is explained by the statement, 'During the War with Vespasian the Rabbis decreed against the use of crowns worn by bridegrooms.' Soṭ. 49*a* (Sonc. ed., p. 265).

[7] R. Jeremiah's fate was to be beheaded, or perhaps he was accidentally decapitated.

is said, THE CROWN IS FALLEN FROM OUR HEAD; WOE UNTO US! FOR WE HAVE SINNED.

FOR THIS OUR HEART IS FAINT—DAWEH (V, 17). R. Simlai said: A great trouble did the Holy One, blessed be He, impose upon woman, that after guarding herself [against intercourse] during the days of her menstruation she has also to guard herself during the days of her blood-issue.[1] R. Eleazar b. R. Jose of Galilee said: Because a woman separates herself from her husband a few[2] days, the Torah calls her '*dawah*', as it is written, *And of her that is sick* (dawah) *with her impurity* (Lev. xv, 33); how much more should *we* be called 'faint' who are separated from the house of our life, namely the Temple, many days and many years! Therefore it is said, FOR THIS OUR HEART IS FAINT, FOR THESE THINGS OUR EYES ARE DIM.

FOR THE MOUNTAIN OF ZION WHICH IS DESOLATE (V, 18). Long ago, as R. Gamaliel, R. Eleazar b. 'Azariah, R. Joshua, and R. Akiba were on the way to Rome, they heard the noise of the crowds at Rome from Puteoli[3] a hundred and twenty miles away. They all fell a-weeping, but R. Akiba laughed. They said to him, 'Akiba, we weep and you are merry!' He replied to them, 'Wherefore are you weeping?' They answered, 'These heathen peoples who worship idols and bow down to images live in safety, ease, and prosperity, whereas the "Footstool" of our God[4] is burnt down by fire and has become a dwelling-place for the beasts of the field, so should we not weep?' He said to them, 'For that reason am I merry. If they that offend Him fare thus, how much better shall they fare that obey Him!' On another occasion they were coming up to Jerusalem, and when they reached Mount Scopus they rent their garments [in mourning]. When they arrived at the Temple Mount, they saw a fox emerging from the Holy of Holies. They fell a-weeping, but R.

[1] V. Lev. xv, 25 ff. The word for '*faint*' is analogous to the term for a woman in this condition.
[2] Lit. 'two or three'; in fact, the separation was longer.
[3] An Italian seaport. [4] Cf. Lam. II, 1.

Akiba laughed. They said to him, 'Akiba, you always surprise us. We weep and you are merry!' He replied to them, 'Wherefore are you weeping?' They answered, 'Shall we not weep that from a place of which it was written, *And the common man that draweth nigh shall be put to death* (Num. I, 51), a fox emerges, and concerning it the verse is fulfilled, FOR THE MOUNTAIN OF ZION, WHICH IS DESOLATE, THE FOXES WALK UPON IT?' He said to them: 'For that reason am I merry. Behold it states, *And I will take unto Me faithful witnesses to record, Uriah the priest, and Zechariah the son of Jeberechiah* (Isa. VIII, 2). Now what connection has Uriah with Zechariah? Uriah lived in the time of the first Temple while Zechariah lived in the time of the second Temple! But what did Uriah say? *Thus saith the Lord of hosts: Zion shall be plowed as a field, and Jerusalem shall become heaps* (Jer. XXVI, 18). And what did Zechariah say? *There shall yet old men and old women sit in the broad places of Jerusalem, every man with his staff in his hand for very age* (Zech. VIII, 4); and it continues, *And the broad places of the city shall be full of boys and girls playing in the broad places thereof* (*ib.* 5). The Holy One, blessed be He, said, "Behold I have these two witnesses, and if the words of Uriah are fulfilled, the words of Zechariah will be fulfilled; and if the words of Uriah prove vain the words of Zechariah will prove vain." I rejoiced because the words of Uriah have been fulfilled and in the future the words of Zechariah will be fulfilled.' Thereupon in these terms did they address him: 'Akiba, you have consoled us; may you be comforted by the coming of the herald [of the redemption]!'[1]

THOU, O LORD, ART ENTHRONED FOR EVER, THY THRONE IS FROM GENERATION TO GENERATION (V, 19). Is there enthronement without a throne or a king without a consort?[2]

WHEREFORE DOST THOU FORGET US FOR EVER? (V, 20). R. Joshua b. Abin said: Four expressions were used

[1] Cf. Mak. 24*a et seq.* (Sonc. ed., pp. 174 f.).

[2] The Temple is God's throne and Israel His consort; so there must be a restoration since the enthronement is for ever.

by Jeremiah, viz. 'rejection, loathing, forgetting, and forsaking'. 'Rejection and loathing,' as it is written, *Hast Thou utterly rejected Judah? Hath Thy soul loathed Zion?* (Jer. XIV, 19); and this was replied to through Moses, as it is written, *I will not reject them, neither will I abhor them* (Lev. XXVI, 44). 'Forgetting and forsaking,' as it is written, WHEREFORE DOST THOU FORGET US FOR EVER, AND FORSAKE US SO LONG TIME? and this was replied to through Isaiah, as it is written, *Yea, these may forget, yet will not I forget thee* (Isa. XLIX, 15). R. Joshua b. Levi said: Four expressions were used by Jeremiah, viz. 'Rejection, anger, forsaking, and forgetting.' 'Rejection' was replied to by himself, as it is written, *Thus saith the Lord: If heaven above can be measured, and the foundation of the earth searched out beneath, then will I also cast off all the seed of Israel for all that they have done, saith the Lord* (Jer. XXXI, 37). 'Anger' was replied to through Isaiah, as it is written, *I will not contend for ever, neither will I be always wroth* (Isa. LVII, 16).[1]

TURN THOU US UNTO THEE, O LORD, AND WE SHALL BE TURNED (V, 21). The Community of Israel spake before the Holy One, blessed be He: 'Lord of the Universe, it depends upon Thee, so TURN THOU US UNTO THEE.' He said to them, 'It depends upon you, as it is said, *Return unto Me, and I will return unto you, saith the Lord of hosts*' (Mal. III, 7). The Community spake before Him: 'Lord of the Universe, it depends upon Thee, as it is said, *Restore us, O God of our salvation* (Ps. LXXXV, 5), and therefore it is said, TURN THOU US UNTO THEE, O LORD, AND WE SHALL BE TURNED.'

RENEW OUR DAYS AS OF OLD (KE-ḲEDEM) like [the days of] Adam, as it is stated, *So He drove out the man; and He placed at the east* (mi-ḳedem) *of the garden of Eden the cherubim* (Gen. III, 24).[2] Another interpretation of

[1] The other two are disregarded, having already been dealt with in the preceding statement.

[2] And after being driven out, Adam repented of his sin. The comment is based on the use of *ḳedem* in both places, and the verse is interpreted: Renew our days like those of him in connection with whom *ḳedem* is stated.

RENEW OUR DAYS AS OF OLD: as it is stated, *Then shall the offering of Judah and Jerusalem be pleasant unto the Lord as in the days of old, and as in ancient years* (Mal. III, 4)—'*as in the days of old*' refers to Moses, for it is written, *Then His people remembered the days of old, the days of Moses* (Isa. LXIII, 11), '*and as in ancient years*' refers to the years of Solomon.[1] Rabbi [Judah ha-Nasi] said: '*As in the days of old*' refers to the days of Noah,[2] as it is said, *For this is as the waters*[3] *of Noah unto Me* (*ib.* LIV, 9), '*and as in ancient years*' refers to the years of Abel[4] up to whose time there was not yet idolatry in the world.

THOU CANST NOT HAVE UTTERLY REJECTED US, AND BE EXCEEDING WROTH AGAINST US (V, 22). R. Simeon b. Laḳish said: If there is rejection there is no hope; but if there is anger there is hope, because whoever is angry may in the end be appeased.[5]

[1] In whose reign the Temple was erected.
[2] When God renewed the world after the Flood.
[3] Read as one word the translation would be 'as the days of' (Radal on Lev. R. VII, 4).
[4] Of whom it was said that *The Lord had respect to Abel and to his offering* (Gen. IV, 4). [5] Quoted *supra*, I, 23 (on ch. I, 2).